EDMUND GESTE
AND HIS BOOKS

EDMUND GESTE AND HIS BOOKS

*Reconstructing the library
of a Cambridge don and
Elizabethan bishop*

David G. Selwyn

LONDON
THE BIBLIOGRAPHICAL SOCIETY
MMXVII

CONTENTS

*Those sections titled in italics are not included in the printed volume, but are available via www.bibsoc.org/publications/Geste. See page xvii.

FOREWORD AND ACKNOWLEDGEMENTS

THE ORIGINS of this reconstruction of Geste's library go back a very long time to work I was doing in the early 1960s on the English Reformation and the doctrinal ferment occasioned by the influx of various continental Protestant theologies since the 1520s. The first changes in the liturgy took place in the final years of Henry VIII's reign and the first years of his son, Edward VI, as the Latin mass was replaced in stages by the abolition of its traditional ceremonies, the introduction of vernacular devotions (1548) and its wholesale replacement by a new form of service – Cranmer's first Prayer Book (1549) – albeit with many cautiously conservative features, following much discussion among theologians and liturgists on both sides of the divide, which culminated in a full-scale debate in the House of Lords in December 1548. Edmund Geste was one of those who had taken part in the general debate with his *Treatise Against the Preuee Masse* published early in 1548, to be followed by others from Richard Bonner (November 1548), dedicated to Cranmer himself, and another from the Italian exile, Peter Martyr Vermigli, who had been invited by Cranmer to take part in the reform of the English Church, succeeding Richard Smith as Regius Professor of Divinity at Oxford in the Spring of 1548, and contributing his own treatise, 'Of the Sacrament of Thanksgiving', addressed to the Lord Protector Somerset only weeks before the House of Lords' Debate.

Geste's work, dedicated to John Cheke, tutor to the young Edward VI as well as Provost of his Cambridge college, King's, was intended, like those of Bonner and Vermigli, to influence those close to the religious changes being introduced. While welcoming what had already taken place (such as the abolition of chantries) Geste was clearly concerned that other desirable reforms (as he judged them to be) had not followed. He was also fearful that those in authority might still be swayed not only by 'our English Catholiques' but by the arguments of continental catholics such as the Cathedral Chapter at Cologne which had produced, in the *Antididagma* (1544), a counterblast to earlier liturgical reform proposals at Cologne put forward by Martin Bucer in 1543 under the patronage of Hermann von Wied, its archbishop. The writings of these continentals – on both side of the doctrinal divide – were well represented in Geste's library, as I was to discover.

It was not until a few years later that I first became acquainted with what remains of Geste's collection at Salisbury Cathedral. On this occasion (in 1967), my search was not so much for books which might have come from Geste's library, but for *any* copy of a particular work: the first edition of Vermigli's commentary on *First Corinthians* – an expanded version of his controversial lectures given in Oxford in 1548/49 (published at Zürich in 1551). No copy of this first edition was listed in Adams' *Catalogue of Books Printed on the Continent of Europe, 1501–1600 in Cambridge Libraries*, none was held by the Bodleian Library at Oxford, or the British Museum Library in London (as it was then), and in the days before online library catalogues the only copy in the UK at the time appeared to be the one at Salisbury Cathedral. In those days it was not that easy to gain access to the libraries of many English Cathedrals. Salisbury was no exception. The Cathedral Librarian, Dr Elsie Smith, with no one but herself to staff the library, quite properly took the view that priority should be given to scholars researching its unique medieval manuscript collection: its early printed books could be read in copies readily available elsewhere. It was only when she had been convinced that Salisbury held the only accessible copy of the commentary and also possessed a unique collection of sixteenth-century continental theology that she conceded my case and graciously admitted me. It was on that visit that it became clear that my particular book might have belonged to Geste, and that there were potentially many of his other books to be identified – a possibility which had been recognised in the printed catalogue by S. M. Lakin in 1880, though no one had ever attempted to list them. In the event, the Salisbury copy of Vermigli's commentary (as I was to discover) carried some of the 'fingerprints' associated with Geste's books: in this instance, a distinctive fore-edge title and an early press mark among them. Although still in a contemporary binding, it did not have one especially characteristic of Geste's other books, but it did carry the inscription of an earlier owner: 'Jo Winton 1553', i.e. John Ponet, who briefly replaced Stephen Gardiner as Bishop of Winchester (1551–1553). It proved to be one of Geste's many 'second-hand' acquisitions and carried some of Ponet's manuscript notes.

It was not until 1977 that the opportunity of future study leave made it possible to plan a more systematic search for Geste's books at Salisbury. Meanwhile, provenance research on another collection – that of Thomas Cranmer – had alerted me to the potential value of such projects, greatly encouraged by discussion and correspondence with Neil Ker, who at the time had been working on the medieval manuscripts in the library of my own institution for inclusion in the third volume of his *Medieval Manuscripts in British Libraries* (III, *Lampeter–Oxford*, 1983). Ker had worked on the Salisbury material in the course of writing on the origins of the medieval library at Salisbury, the medieval scribes and the later history of the manuscript collection, but he was also acquainted with the early printed books in connexion with his interest in pastedowns in Oxford and Cambridge bindings. In the 1940s he had identified a number of printed books with rolls and tools which he thought could be associated with Geste as a collector in Cambridge during the 1540s and early 1550s, and these he had listed in a letter to the Canon Librarian at the time, Canon Quirk, in 1948. His list remains a valuable starting point for identifying Geste's bindings and has greatly informed my own research in this area.

Meanwhile, in the summer of 1977 – when I was still drawing up my plans for this study leave – Neil Ker made a further visit to Salisbury searching for books with evidence of Geste's ownership and noted a number of 'fingerprints' which have since proved valuable in identifying his books. He also reported that Suzanne Eward, at the time working for the Cathedral Libraries Union Catalogue project supported by the Bibliographical Society, had begun to notice the same distinctive 'fingerprints' of Geste ownership that had struck him, and was now drawing up a provenance list of his books and other important former owners at Salisbury with a view to a wider project on book ownership during the sixteenth and seventeenth centuries in Cathedral libraries. Although her invaluable provenance information could not be incorporated into the final published form of volume two of the *Cathedral Libraries Catalogue* (1998), she generously made her own findings available, and much exchanging of information has enhanced both projects. This has greatly lightened my task by confirming and complementing my own findings. After completing her work for the Cathedral Libraries Catalogue, Suzanne Eward remained at Salisbury, when the Chapter replaced the interim arrangements set up for the care of the library following the retirement of Dr Elsie Smith in 1973 by appointing her Cathedral Librarian and Keeper of the Muniments. Although by rights she should have become joint author of this present work, her wider responsibilities for the reorganization of the library and muniments (following reconstruction work to the building in the 1980s), detailed re-cataloguing of the collection and work towards a comprehensive history of this remarkable library, have prevented her doing this. But she has remained an honorary 'co-author', and this work could not have reached its present stage without her interest, constant encouragement, and constructive criticism.

The work begun in 1978 established the outlines of Geste's library as he left it to Salisbury on his death in 1577, but there was still much work to be done on the contemporary bindings (many of them very worn and difficult to identify), the pastedowns and other fragments surviving in his bindings, and identifying the many pre-Geste owners of his earliest books. There also remained an 'uncertain area' of books in the library at Salisbury which contained neither positive or negative evidence of his ownership, leaving this researcher with the strong feeling that the whole story had not fully emerged. Reconstruction work in the Cathedral Library prevented further working on the collection for a number of years, and increasing academic, administrative and library responsibilities at my own institution made further delay inevitable.

In fact, it was only after retirement in 2003 that it became possible to resume work towards the completion of this project for publication. Although the long delay in publication has been regrettable (sorely testing the patience of the Society and its long-suffering Honorary Editors of Monographs since the early 1980s) at least five developments during this period have contributed towards forwarding this project.

The first was the publication in 1986 of Elisabeth Leedham-Green's *Books in Cambridge Inventories* [BiCI] which has made it possible to place Geste's books in the wider context of other Cambridge collections of his day, particularly that of Andrew Perne whose much larger library has only survived in part at Peterhouse. These inventories from the University Archives give a much clearer picture of what was commonly owned or unusual and rare in Cambridge at the time. Adams' *Catalogue*, valuable as it is, does not distinguish between books actually owned by Cambridge college libraries in the 1540s and 1550s and early printed books of the period not acquired until much later by donation or purchase. The distinction is an important one, because many college libraries (King's among them) had suffered huge losses during the period when Geste was in Cambridge and earlier, only recovering in the centuries that followed, up to and including the modern period, as a result of donated collections. A book owned by Geste which is recorded in Adams may not have been present in Cambridge in his day but only acquired by the institution concerned much later.

The second was the completion of the *Cathedral Libraries Catalogue* [CLC], a monumental project begun by Miss Hands in the 1940s, revived in the 1970s and brought to publication under the general editorship of David Shaw at the University of Kent at Canterbury in 1998. This has brought great benefits to the catalogue of Geste's library presented here, not least in helping to clear up a number of problematic items, and it has also made it possible for the first time to set Geste's collection at Salisbury in the context of other Cathedral Libraries in England and Wales. It has confirmed the rarity of a great many titles in Geste's collection, particularly in the area of contemporary continental theology. In fact, considerably more than sixty per cent of the items in his library proved to be the only copies recorded in CLC.

The third beneficial development during this period has been access to an increasing number of online catalogue databases and digitised copies of the books themselves. Although still greatly varying in uniformity of factual information, bibliographical detail and copy-specific notes relating to such matters as provenance, bindings and evidence of use in the form of MS annotation, these databases have often provided information which was not readily available before, even in the best printed catalogues. For this project, the online catalogue of the Herzog August Bibliothek at Wolfenbüttel [HAB] and the bibliographical database of sixteenth-century

German imprints (*Verzeichnis der im deutschen Sprachbereich erschienenen Drucke des 16. Jahrhunderts* [VD16]) have proved especially useful in suggesting printers and places of publication where this information was lacking in Geste's copies. The collections at Wolfenbüttel and Munich (the Bayerische Staatsbibliothek [BSB]) are particularly rich in titles printed in German-speaking countries including Switzerland, in which Geste's library abounds, and many of these are not found (or are inadequately described) in UK library catalogues, including the online catalogue of the British Library. In addition, online access to digitised copies, especially at the Bayerische Staatsbibliothek, has made it possible to clear up a number of bibliographical problems, particularly relating to collations. Another online database which has proved especially relevant is the much enhanced catalogue of the Parker Library at Corpus Christi College, Cambridge. This has provided copy-specific detail relating to Parker's ownership, contemporary bindings and MS annotations, which has made it possible to identify titles in his library of which Geste also owned copies, and thus provide an additional standard of comparison, along with holdings in Perne's library (where these survive at Peterhouse, Cambridge) as well as in contemporary Cambridge inventories (BiCI).

Fourthly, this period has also seen an enhanced interest in the value of provenance history as a discipline in its own right within book history. This is a discipline which now has its own textbook in David Pearson's *Provenance Research in Book History: A Handbook* (1994), and this interest in provenance history is reflected, for example, in contributions to recent collections such as the multi-volume *Cambridge History of the Book in Britain* and *The Cambridge History of Libraries in Britain and Ireland*. This increased attention to who may have owned a particular book and, in the case of second-hand books, from whom it may have been obtained, how that book might relate to other books in the collection, how it may have been regarded and used (if annotated) and how widely it may have been owned and used by others, are all matters which have been my concern in this present reconstruction of Geste's library. Online catalogue databases and comprehensive bibliographies may record what was *theoretically* available to a scholar in a particular subject discipline at a given time, but they do not necessarily reflect accurately what a Cambridge don such as Geste in the 1540s and 1550s might actually have been reading and acquiring. The surviving books of an individual, especially at a time when institutional libraries were often small and far from comprehensive can be a more valuable guide, a point which I had made in my earlier reconstruction of Cranmer's library in 1996 (*LTC*, p. lxviii). Even more than Cranmer, Geste was an inveterate annotator of his books, and a library such as his can suggest lines of enquiry as to how these books may have been used, and perhaps in what context and for what purpose.

Attempting to identify some of the former owners of Geste's books from inscriptions in his books has highlighted the desirability of developing a sixteenth-century provenance database for use by future researchers. There are two areas where an online database of names, with related images of ownership inscriptions, would be of potential value to provenance historians working on this kind of material. First, where ownership inscriptions have been damaged (often in re-binding) or erased, leaving them almost impossible to read. A complete example of the same ownership inscription preserved in another book could well provide the answer. Secondly, there are often problems identifying the owner, and in such instances pooling biographical information where the identity of an ownership inscription has been successfully established could be crucial for another provenance historian.

Fifthly, there have been significant developments in the study of English book-binding, particularly relating to Cambridge bindings during the sixteenth century and the study of bindings at the 'lower end' of the range. In the case of new work on Cambridge bindings, I must acknowledge here much help from David Pearson's published writings and personal communications over a number of years, some of it making use of unpublished research left behind by the late Neil Ker. This has shed new light on the likely place of binding in the case of certain rolls which had been left unassigned or attributed to London binders (by Oldham) for which there is now good reason to attribute to Cambridge binders. A number of these rolls were to be found on Geste's books during his Cambridge period, and the occurrence of these has further strengthened Pearson's case for attributing these books to Cambridge as the place of binding. Again, as with the future development of provenance-study, there would seem to be a strong case for developing an online bindings-database for panel and roll-bindings which would provide locations for all the surviving examples of the bindings covered in the two volumes of Oldham, supplemented by those bindings which have come to light since Oldham (of which the Parker library at Corpus Christi College as well as Geste's at Salisbury would provide a number of examples). This would greatly enhance the value of the pioneering work undertaken by Oldham in the 1950s and provide an essential tool for future binding-historians which could be extended as more examples are identified by researchers in the field.

Nearly two-thirds of Geste's books are still in contemporary bindings, and although these include just over one hundred and twenty of the more decorated bindings (such as panel or roll bindings, some of them signed by known Cambridge or London binders), the great majority belong to the 'lower end' of the range from limp parchment covers to simple calf bindings decorated only with small-tools or centrepieces or even without decoration altogether.

So much attention has been focussed in the past on identifying and classifying the more 'decorative' bindings (roll and panel) that the 'lower end' of the range has by comparison been under-researched. Yet large numbers of these simpler calf-bindings can be found in the libraries of scholarly collectors such as Geste, Perne and Matthew Parker, especially on smaller-format books (quartos, octavos and smaller) often of continental printing. David Pearson, in published work since 1994, has identified one particular category of these which he has designated 'centrepiece bindings' associated with the period 1560–1640, of which Geste had a dozen examples on books acquired towards the end of his life.

But far more numerous in his collection are examples of other simple calf-bindings which use small tools to form a centre-ornament (here designated 'centre-tool' bindings and listed in Appendix IV D), sometimes surrounded by a rectangular frame of fillets, which in some instances may include the same or another ornament at each angle of the frame. Over 180 of his books come into the category of these 'centre-tool' bindings [CT], using forty-seven different ornaments, and while in the majority of cases there are only single examples of each in his collection, there are significant numbers in the case of three of these 'centre-tool' bindings: twenty-five examples of the first [CT c.1] from his Cambridge period (a few combined with one of three rolls), twenty-two of the second [CT a] and no less than fifty-one of the third [CT b], these last two from his London and Salisbury periods. There seems to me to be a strong case here for further research to determine how far these types occur in other collections of the period, particularly if these can be associated with identifiable owners, with a view to the creation of a database to which images of the examples in Geste's collection could be contributed. The value of Geste's collection for this purpose is that his books are known to have been accumulated over a discrete period of some forty years (1536–1576), subdivided into two not quite equal segments (1536–1554 and 1554–1576), the former with acquisitions mainly in Cambridge (though with some from London), the latter almost entirely from London outlets with the possibility of some Salisbury bindings during his final years.

A further beneficial, and very practical, development during this period has been the result of advances in digital technology which have made available good quality digital cameras capable of taking images of bindings, pastedowns and annotations of acceptable quality under far from ideal conditions, hand-held without additional lighting and without the need for a copying stand. This has made it possible to make photographic images of a large number of books in the limited time the Cathedral Library has been open – enabling me to work on the material at other times to identify bindings in Oldham, compare pastedowns and study annotations. It is fair to say that this project could not have been completed without the good will and farsightedness of the Cathedral Librarian and the Chapter in allowing this digital photography to take place, and copies of the images taken during this period (over 2,700 of them) have been deposited in the Cathedral Library and with the Bibliographical Society in London.

No undertaking of this kind is ever complete. There remain a number of unresolved problems in this reconstruction. But it is time to hand over to others working in the field of provenance and binding history, and it is hoped that the development of online databases, such as those suggested above, will assist towards resolving some of these.

One such area left incomplete concerned the many pastedowns and fragments of MS and printer's waste that occur in the bindings – in over two-hundred and eighty of his books. Before Neil Ker's death in 1982, the question of whether he might be able to contribute a study of 'Paste-downs in Cambridge bindings in the library of Salisbury Cathedral' was discussed, and a list of those which had been noted by the Librarian, Suzanne Eward, and myself was passed on to him with this in mind. Understandably, his main concern at the time was to complete his *Medieval Manuscripts in British Libraries*, and his untimely death took place before further progress could be made.

The present work would not have filled that gap but for the timely intervention at a very late stage of Dr Christopher de Hamel, Donnelley Fellow Librarian at Corpus Christi, College, Cambridge, who generously offered to examine over a thousand images of these fragments which, it is intended, are to be mounted on the Bibliographical Society's web-pages. As a result of his contribution it has been possible to add identifications of nearly 240 manuscript fragments to the catalogue records and to Appendix IX, which lists these under the various binding types found on Geste's books. It is hoped that these may be of interest to others working in the field in the expectation that further identifications may be forth-coming, and fragments of printed books and MSS found in other books reported to the author for inclusion on the Society's web-pages.

Secondly, much more work is needed on the many bindings in limp parchment covers (over 120 of them), particularly on the origin of these bindings, than has been possible in the course of this reconstruction. Most of Geste's books, including those in parchment, were almost certainly imported unbound in sheets or in sewn book-blocks, in conformity with the legislation of 1534 intended to protect the binding arm of the English book-trade. But a small number in parchment covers of German or Flemish origin have been identified, and it is clearly possible that others of continental origin await discovery. Here I must acknowledge much help from Professor Nicholas Pickwood who has quite independently examined a number of Geste's books at Salisbury as well as viewing some of my images of others. It is to be hoped that more light will be shed on these questions when the detailed analysis of binding structure he has developed is extended to more of Geste's books still in parchment covers at Salisbury.

Over the thirty or more years during which this project has occupied my attention, I have accumulated a mounting debt to many kind people who have given generously of their time and support, and I am deeply grateful to them: the late Neil Ker and David Pearson, already mentioned; the former Librarian and Keeper of the Muniments at Salisbury Cathedral, Suzanne Eward, who in addition to sharing her own findings on Geste's library, has carried literally hundreds of his books, including heavy folios, for me to inspect; Dr Elisabeth Leedham-Green for her constant encouragement over many years, for reading earlier drafts of the book and for much expert help in transcribing difficult ownership inscriptions; the late Anthony Hobson for supporting this project when it was first being considered by the Bibliographical Society in 1980; Professor Mirjam Foot, for her support over many years and more recently, as the Society's Honorary Editor of Monographs, not only making many helpful comments on the catalogue, but spending two days at Salisbury with me examining Geste's continental bindings and some very worn examples of English bindings which had escaped Oldham's scheme of classification. I must also record my thanks to Canon Paul Welsby, at the time Librarian of Rochester Cathedral Library, for assisting me in my search for Geste's books on my visit there in 1981; to Mr Peter Jones, Fellow Librarian, and Dr Patricia McGuire, Archivist, at King's College, Cambridge, for guiding me to material there in the College archives on Geste and his time there as a Fellow and vice-Provost; similarly, to Pamela Stewart, Assistant Diocesan Archivist at Salisbury, for steering me through the material there relating to Geste's episcopate and the later history of the Cathedral library after his death; to Mr Malcolm Underwood, Archivist of St John's College, Cambridge, for information about the Brandisbys, Geste's relations, at the College; to Dr Anne Overell for her helpful comments and suggestions on the section 'Other Protestants and religious radicals'; to Dr Scott Mandelbrote, Fellow and Perne Librarian, for answering queries about Perne's books at Peterhouse, Cambridge; and to Dr Nicholas Thompson for identifying a fragment by Johann Eck which had eluded me. None of these kind people is in any way responsible for the use made of their suggestions, and any errors are entirely my own.

My thanks are also due to the University of Wales, Lampeter (now Trinity, St David's) for allowing me two periods of study leave, and to its Pantyfedwen Fund for a grant towards the cost of printing photographs taken in 1978.

A number of papers on aspects of Geste's library, deriving from earlier drafts of the Introduction have been given at conferences and symposia in recent years, and I am grateful to the organisers of these as well as to those who took part in questions and discussions at the time: the Society for Reformation Studies for arranging for two of these to be given at their annual conferences held at Westminster College, Cambridge (on 'Geste and liturgical reform in England' in 1999, and on 'Bullinger's works in Tudor Cambridge and in Edmund Geste's library' in 2004); to the Aberystwyth Bibliographical Group for inviting me to give a paper to their symposium at St Deiniol's Library, Hawarden in 2006 ('"Sum liber Edmundi Gest': reconstructing the library of an Elizabethan bishop') and to the Revd. Ben Elliott for inviting me to address the Guides of Salisbury Cathedral in 2011 (on 'Bishop Edmund Geste and his books: a notable benefaction').

I must also thank the Chapter of Salisbury Cathedral, custodians of Geste's benefaction, for their support for this project, and especially the present Chancellor, Edward Probert, for his personal interest and for permission to reproduce the images that appear in this book. Particular thanks is due to a former Dean, the late Sydney Evans, who not only gave much encouragement in the early stages of my work on Geste's books, but intervened decisively on my behalf when it looked as if work would grind to a halt because of building operations in the Cathedral Library in the autumn of 1978. I have been further indebted to Canon Probert and also to Emily Naish, the Archivist, for enabling me to consult some of Geste's books on recent visits to the Library since the retirement of the Librarian, Suzanne Eward, and I must also record my thanks to Peter Hoare, former Librarian of the University of Nottingham, who in retirement as a volunteer in the Cathedral Library kindly dealt with a number of my recent enquiries

I am also very grateful to the Honorary Editors of Monographs for the Bibliographical Society, Professor Mirjam Foot, and her successor, Dr David Shaw, and to Dr Paul Nash, designer and copy editor, for their scrupulous attention to detail in seeing this work through the press. I am particularly indebted to Dr Shaw, editor of the *Cathedral Libraries Catalogue*, who has been untiring in his search of continental databases for printers and places of publication where these had been missing in Geste's copies, determined that as few as possible should remain in the catalogue without these details. In addition, when the Society's Publication Sub-committee recommended the inclusion of references to online databases for all catalogue entries, Dr Shaw came to the rescue by contributing over a third of these, as well as checking over 1300 references and inserting these into the catalogue. I must also record my thanks to the four Readers who took time to work through parts of this book, noting matters for correction and making constructive suggestions for its improvement.

I would also like to thank my sister and her husband, Canon Roger Sharpe, for their generous hospitality during my many visits to work on Geste's books at Salisbury since retirement.

Finally, my wife, Pamela, has helped in the making of this book, not only enduring the 'presence' of a 'third person' in our household for thirty years and more, but bringing her own bibliographical expertise and critical eye in the field of provenance research to the task. In addition, she has dutifully acted as my research assistant on recent visits to Salisbury, keeping an accurate record of the hundreds of items examined and thereby saving me from much muddle and confusion. For her constant encouragement and support I am deeply grateful.

PUBLISHER'S NOTE

This work is being issued by the Society in two versions: an online version of the whole text supplemented by images of the pastedowns, manuscripts fragments and printer's waste listed in Appendix IX; and a hybrid version consisting of the catalogue (with an introduction) and Appendices I, VI, XII–XIII, available online on the Society's web-pages, with the rest of the text published in book form. Those sections only available online are indicated in the table contents in italic type.

LIST OF ABBREVIATIONS

Adams   H. M. Adams, *Catalogue of Books Printed on the Continent of Europe, 1501–1600 in Cambridge Libraries*. 2 vols. Cambridge: University Press, 1967.

Bailey   Harry Bailey, *Short notes on the bookbindings of Salisbury Cathedral Library*. Salisbury: Jay, [1950?].

Bancroft   London, Lambeth Palace Library, Lambeth Record MS F1. Catalogue of Richard Bancroft's 1610 bequest to Lambeth (compiled 1612).

Baudrier   H. L. and Julien Baudrier. *Bibliographie lyonnaise: recherches sur les imprimeurs, libraires, relieurs et fondeurs de lettres de Lyon au XVIe siècle*. 12 vols. Lyon: Brun, 1895–1921.

BiCI   E. S. Leedham-Green, *Books in Cambridge Inventories*. 2 vols. Cambridge: University Press, 1986. (*Vol. I: The Inventories. Vol. II: The Catalogue*).

BLJ   *The British Library Journal* (London).

BLR   *The Bodleian Library Record* (Oxford).

BMC   *Catalogue of Books Printed in the XVth Century now in the British Museum*. 13 vols. London: British Museum etc., 1908–2004.

BMDB   *Short-title Catalogue of Books Printed in the Netherlands and Belgium ... from 1470 to 1600 now in the British Museum*. London: British Museum, 1965.

BMFB   *Short-title Catalogue of Books Printed in France ... from 1470 to 1600 in the British Museum*. London: Printed by order of the Trustees, 1924. *Supplement*. London: British Library, 1987.

BMGB   *Short-title Catalogue of Books Printed in the German-speaking Countries ... from 1455 to 1600 now in the British Museum*. London: British Museum, 1962. *Supplement*. London: British Library, 1990.

BMIB   *Short-title Catalogue of Books Printed in Italy ... from 1465 to 1600 now in the British Museum*. London: British Museum, 1958.

BNF   Bibliothèque nationale de France.

BP16   *Bibliographie des éditions parisiennes du 16e siècle*. <http://bp16.bnf.fr/>.

BSB   Bayerische Staatsbibliothek (Munich) or its 'OpacPlus' catalogue. <https://opacplus.bsb-muenchen.de/>.

CCCC   Corpus Christi College, Cambridge.

CCEd   *CCEd: Clergy of the Church of England Database* [1540–1835]. <http://theclergydatabase.org.uk/>.

CHBB III — *The Cambridge History of the Book in Britain*. Vol. III: *1400–1557*, ed. by Lotte Hellinga and J. B. Trapp. Cambridge: University Press, 1999.

CHBB IV — *The Cambridge History of the Book in Britain*. Vol. IV: *1557–1695*, ed. by John Barnard and D. F. McKenzie. Cambridge: University Press, 2002.

CHLB I — *The Cambridge History of Libraries in Britain and Ireland*. Vol. I: *To 1640*, ed. by Elisabeth Leedham-Green and Teresa Webber. Cambridge: University Press, 2006.

CLC — *The Cathedral Libraries Catalogue, Volume Two: Books Printed on the Continent of Europe before 1701 in the Libraries of the Anglican Cathedrals of England and Wales*, ed. by D. J. Shaw. 2 vols. London: Bibliographical Society, 1998.

Col. — Colophon.

Coll. — Collation.

Cooper — C. H. and Thompson Cooper, *Athenae Cantabrigienses*. 2 vols. Cambridge: Deighton, Bell, 1858–1861. 'Republished' in facsimile: Farnborough: Gregg, 1967.

CP — Centrepiece (with tool reference, e.g. CP 1)

CS — Corner stamp (with tool reference, e.g. CS 1)

CT — Centre-tool (with tool reference, e.g. CT a)

CUL — Cambridge University Library, or its 'iDiscover' (formerly 'Newton') catalogue. <http://idiscover.lib.cam.ac.uk/>.

CUL 1583 — Elisabeth Leedham-Green and David McKitterick, 'A Catalogue of Cambridge University Library in 1583', in *Books and Collectors 1200–1700: Essays Presented to Andrew Watson*, ed. by James P. Carley and Colin G. C.Tite. London: British Library, 1997, pp. 153–235. Unless otherwise noted, references are to pages in this edition with the editors' serial number, followed by the current CUL class-mark.

DNB — *Dictionary of National Biography*. 21 vols, plus *Supplements*. London: Oxford University Press, 1921–1993.

Duff — E. Gordon Duff, *A Century of the English Book Trade*. London: Bibliographical Society, 1948.

Dugdale — Henry Geast Dugdale, *The Life and Character of Edmunde Geste, S.T.P.* London: William Pickering, 1840.

Edit16 — *Censimento nazionale della edizione italiane del XVI secolo (EDIT16)*. <http://edit16.iccu.sbn.it/web_iccu/>.

EEBO — *Early English Books Online*. <http://eebo.chadwyck.com/home>.

ESTC — *English Short Title Catalogue*. <http://estc.bl.uk/>.

Eward — Suzanne Eward, *Salisbury Cathedral Library*. [Revised edn]. [Salisbury: For the Library], 2004.

FB	*French Books III & IV: Books Published in France before 1601 in Latin and Languages other than French*, ed. by Andrew Pettegree and Malcolm Walsby. 2 vols. Leiden: Brill, 2011.
Foster	Joseph Foster, *Alumni Oxonienses: the Members of the University of Oxford, 1500–1714*. 4 vols. Oxford: J. Parker, 1891–92. Incorporated in *Oxford University Alumni, 1500–1886*, available via <http://www.ancestry.co.uk/>.
Foxe	John Foxe, *The Acts and Monuments*, ed. by Joseph Pratt. 4th edn. 8 vols. London: Religious Tract Society, 1877.
Frere, III	*Visitation Articles and Injunctions of the period of the Reformation. Volume III 1559–1575*, ed. by W. H. Frere. London: Longmans, Green & Co., 1910.
Geste, Treatise	Edmund Geste, *A Treatise Againste the Prevee Masse in the Behalfe and Furtheraunce of the Mooste Holye Communyon*. London: By [William Hill and] Thomas Raynald, 1548. STC 11802.
GGA 1527–33	Elisabeth Leedham-Green, D. E. Rhodes and F. H. Stubbings, *Garrett Godfrey's Accounts, c. 1527–1533*, Cambridge Bibliographical Society Monograph 12. Cambridge: Cambridge Bibliographical Society, 1992.
Gibson	Strickland Gibson, *Early Oxford bindings*. Oxford: Printed for the Bibliographical Society, 1903.
Gid	Denise Gid, *Catalogue des reliures françaises estampées à froid, XVe–XVIe siècle de la Bibliothèque Mazarine*. 2 vols. Paris: Editions du Centre national de la recherche scientifique, 1984.
GLN	Jean-François Gilmont, *GLN 15–16 (Bibliography of Books Printed in the 15th and 16th Centuries in Geneva, Lausanne and Neuchâtel)*. <http://www.ville-ge.ch/musinfo/bd/bge/gln/>.
Goff	Frederick R. Goff, *Incunabula in American Libraries: A Third Census*. New York: Bibliographical Society of America, 1964. Reprinted: Millwood, NY: Kraus, 1973.
Grace Book B	*Grace Book B. Part II. Containing the Accounts of the Proctors 1511–1544*, ed. by Mary Bateson. Cambridge: University Press, 1905.
Grace Book Δ	*Grace Book Δ: Containing the Records of the University of Cambridge for the Years 1542–1589*, ed. by John Venn. Cambridge: University Press, 1910.
Gray	George J. Gray, *The Earlier Cambridge Stationers & Bookbinders and the First Cambridge Printer*, Bibliographical Society Illustrated Monographs 13. Oxford: Printed for the Bibliographical Society at the Oxford University Press, 1904.

Gültlingen	Sybille von Gültlingen, *Bibliographie des livres imprimés à Lyon au seizième siècle,* Bibliotheca Bibliographica Aureliana. 12 vols. Baden-Baden: Bouxwiller/Valentin Koerner, 1992–2009.
GW	*Gesamtkatalog der Wiegendrucke.* Vol. 1– . Leipzig: Hiersemann, 1925– .
HAB	Herzog August Bibliothek, Wolfenbüttel, or its online catalogue <http://opac.lbs-braunschweig.gbv.de/>.
Harwood	Thomas Harwood, *Alumni Etonenses.* Birmingham: Printed by T. Pearson, for Messrs. Cadell, jun. and Davies...London; J. Deighton, Cambridge; and M. Pote, Eton, 1797. ESTC T146314.
HCUP	David McKitterick, *A History of Cambridge University Press: Volume I, Printing and the Book Trade in Cambridge, 1534–1698.* Cambridge: Cambridge University Press, 1992.
IB 16	*Iberian Books/Libros ibéricos: Books Published in Spanish or Portuguese or on the Iberian Peninsula before 1601,* ed. by Alexander S. Wilkinson. Leiden: Brill, 2010. Online edition <http://iberian.ucd.ie/>.
impf.	An imperfect copy.
ISTC	British Library, *Incunabula Short Title Catalogue.* <http://istc.bl.uk/>.
Jayne, *LCER*	Sears Jayne, *Library Catalogues of the English Renaissance.* Berkeley: University of California Press, 1956. Reissue with new preface and notes: Godalming: St Paul's Bibliographies, 1983.
JTS	*Journal of Theological Studies* (Oxford).
Ker, *BCL*	N. R. Ker, *Books, Collectors and Libraries: Studies in the Medieval Heritage,* ed. by A. G. Watson. London: Hambledon, 1985.
Ker, *Fragments*	N. R. Ker, *Fragments of Medieval Manuscripts used as Pastedowns in Oxford Bindings, with a Survey of Oxford Binding c. 1515–1620.* Oxford: Oxford Bibliographical Society, 1954. Reprinted (with corrigenda and addenda by the editors, David Rundle and Scott Mandelbrote) 2004.
Ker, *MLGB*	*Medieval Libraries of Great Britain: A List of Surviving Books,* ed. by N. R. Ker. 2nd edn. London: Offices of the Royal Historical Society, 1964.
Ker-Watson, *MLGB Suppl.*	*Medieval Libraries of Great Britain: A List of Surviving Books,* ed. by N. R. Ker. *Supplement to the Second Edition,* ed. by A. G. Watson, Royal Historical Society Guides and Handbooks 15. London: Offices of the Royal Historical Society, 1987.

Klaiber	Wilbirgis Klaiber, *Katholische Kontroverstheologen und Reformer des 16. Jahrhunderts.* Münster: Aschendorffsche Verlagsbuchhandlung, 1978.
Knowles, MRH	David Knowles and R. N. Hadcock, *Medieval Religious Houses: England and Wales.* London: Longman, 1953.
L. & P.	*Letters and Papers, Foreign and Domestic, of the Reign of Henry VIII ...,* ed. by J. S. Brewer, James Gairdner and R. H. Brodie. 21 vols. London: H.M.S.O., 1862–1932.
LTC	David G. Selwyn, *The Library of Thomas Cranmer.* Oxford: Oxford Bibliographical Society, 1996.
McKitterick (1991)	David McKitterick, 'Andrew Perne and his Books', in Perne (1991).
Moreau	Brigitte Moreau, *Inventaire chronologique des éditions parisiennes du XVIe siècle ... d'après les manuscrits de Philippe Renouard.* 5 vols. Paris: Service des Travaux Historiques de la Ville de Paris, 1972–2004.
NB	*Netherlandish Books: Books Published in the Low Countries and Dutch Books Printed Abroad Before 1601,* ed. by Andrew Pettegree and Malcolm Walsby. 2 vols. Leiden: Brill, 2010.
n.d.	no date.
NKCL	W. D. J. Cargill Thompson, 'Notes on King's College Library, 1500–1570', *Transactions of the Cambridge Bibliographical Society,* II, pt. 1 (1954), 38–54.
n. pl.	no place of publication / printing.
n. pr.	no printer.
ODNB	*Oxford Dictionary of National Biography: From the Earliest Times to the Year 2000,* ed. by H. G. C. Matthew and B. Harrison. 60 vols. Oxford: Oxford University Press, 2004. Online edition <http://www.oxforddnb.com/>.
Oldham, BPEB	J. Basil Oldham, *Blind Panels of English Binders.* Cambridge: At the University Press, 1958. Reprinted: New York, Garland, 1990.
Oldham, EBSB	J. Basil Oldham, *English Blind-Stamped Bindings.* Cambridge: At the University Press, 1952. Reprinted: New York, Garland, 1990.
Oldham, SSLB	J. Basil Oldham, *Shrewsbury School Library Bindings: Catalogue Raisonné.* Oxford: Printed for the Librarian of Shrewsbury School at the University Press 1943.
Ollard & Crosse	S. L. Ollard and Gordon Crosse, *A Dictionary of English Church History.* London: Mowbray, 1912.
Overell	Anne Overell, *Italian Reform and English Reformations, c. 1535–c. 1585.* Aldershot: Ashgate, 2008.

Pearson, BC	David Pearson, 'Bookbinding in Cambridge in the Second Half of the Sixteenth Century' in *'For the Love of the Binding': Studies in Bookbinding History Presented to Mirjam Foot*, ed. David Pearson. London: British Library; New Castle, DE: Oak Knoll, 2000, pp. 169–96.
Pearson, EBS	David Pearson, *English Bookbinding Styles 1450–1800: A Handbook*. London: British Library; New Castle, DE: Oak Knoll, 2005.
Pearson, OB	David Pearson, *Oxford Bookbinding 1500–1640*. Oxford: Oxford Bibliographical Society, 2000.
Perne (1991)	*Andrew Perne: Quartercentenary Studies*, ed. by D. McKitterick, Cambridge Bibliographical Society Monograph 11. Cambridge: Cambridge University Press, 1991.
Raine	Angelo Raine, *History of St. Peter's School, York, A.D. 627 to the Present Day*. London: G. Bell, 1926.
Sal. Cat.	*A Catalogue of the Library of the Cathedral Church of Salisbury* [compiled by S. M. Lakin]. London: Spotiswoode & Co., 1880. References are to page numbers, e.g. 'Sal. Cat. 105'.
Saltmarsh	John Saltmarsh, *King's College: A Short History*. Cambridge: [Water Lane Press and Cambridge University Press], 1958.
Sterry	Wasey Sterry, *Eton College Register 1441–1698*. Eton: Spottiswoode, Ballantyne & Co., 1943.
STC	A. W. Pollard and G. W. Redgrave, *A short-title catalogue of books printed in England, Scotland & Ireland ... 1475–1640*. 2nd edn. completed by K. F. Pantzer. 3 vols. London: Bibliographical Society, 1976–1991.
STCN	*Short Title Catalogue Netherlands, 1540–1800*. Koninklijke Bibliotheek, The Hague. <https://www.kb.nl/organis[-]atie/onderzoek-expertise/informatie-infrastructuur-diensten-voor-bibliotheken/short-title-catalogue-nether[-]lands-stcn>.
tp	title page.
Treptow	Otto Treptow, *John Siberch: Johann Lair von Siegburg*, translated by Trevor Jones. Cambridge: University Press, 1970.
USTC	Universal Short-Title Catalogue (a database of European books to 1600). <http://www.ustc.ac.uk/>.
VD16	*Verzeichnis der im deutschen Sprachbereich erschienenen Drucke des 16. Jahrhunderts*. <http://www.gateway-bayern.de/index_vd16.html >.
Venn	John and J. A. Venn, *Alumni Cantabrigienses: A Biographical List of all Known Students, Graduates and Holders of Office at*

the University of Cambridge ... Part I: From the Earliest Times to 1751. 4 vols. Cambridge: At the University Press, 1922–27. Incorporated in *A Cambridge Alumni Database* <http://venn.lib.cam.ac.uk/Documents/acad/>.

Williams   G. H. Williams, *The Radical Reformation*. Philadelphia: Westminster Press, 1962.

SYMBOLS USED IN COLLATION FORMULAE

[π]   indicates unsigned preliminary gatherings (avoiding the use of plain π as there are frequently books signed partly or entirely in greek).

$^{\pi}$A   indicates a signed preliminary gathering which has a signature letter which is also used in the main sequence of signatures.

χ   indicates unsigned leaves or quires inserted in the main sequence of signatures.

A, a, aa, etc.   the use of italics indicates an unsigned gathering at the start of an alphabetical sequence, e.g. A^6 B–K^8.

&   is used for the gothic form of 'et' which is often found following 'z' in collations.

[*con*], [*rum*]   are used to represent the contractions frequently found extending alphabetic sequences, e.g. a–z & [*con*] [*rum*].

For non-alphanumeric signatures an attempt has been made to produce an equivalent typographical symbol.

ILLUSTRATIONS

The images have been taken by the author, Julia Craig-McFeely and Ash Mills, and are reproduced by kind permission of the Chapter of Salisbury Cathedral and in the case of the memorial brass and portrait of Geste from Dugdale's *Life and Character of Edmund Geste* (1840) by kind permission of the publishers Pickering & Chatto.

IA (left). Memorial brass to Edmund Geste, now in the north-transept, placed in Salisbury Cathedral by his executor, Giles Eastcourt. The only known contemporary representation of the bishop (artist unknown). From Dugdale. IB (right). Modern rubbing of the same memorial brass.

INTRODUCTION

Geste's career as a book collector

I. FELLOW OF KING'S COLLEGE, CAMBRIDGE, AND ELIZABETHAN BISHOP

A little-known collection

A CONTEMPORARY monumental brass to Edmund Geste, bishop of Salisbury (now in the north-transept and originally placed in Salisbury Cathedral by his executor Giles Eastcourt, but perhaps not much noticed by visitors today)[1] records the bequest of his library following his death in 1577, describing it as 'a vast collection of choice books, almost beyond the confines of a single library'.[2] How far can that collection be traced today and how does it compare in size and content to others surviving from the same period? How far do its contents reflect the tastes and interests of its owner as a Cambridge don for some fifteen years (1539–1554) and then as an Elizabethan bishop from 1560 to 1577? What do the books themselves suggest of Geste as a bibliophile and as the owner of a working collection? Where might he have acquired his books? What was the importance of the bequest of his library for the Cathedral itself? And what is its significance for the study of the Reformation in England? These are some of the questions addressed in this study of what is one of the largest personal collections of Reformation writings to have survived from the Elizabethan period.

The existence of Geste's library has not however been that widely known among historians and historical bibliographers,[3] and even at Salisbury itself

---

1. The brass (fig.1) receives no mention in the Wiltshire volume of Nikolaus Pevsner's *The Buildings of England* (revised edition by Bridget Cherry) in the section describing the monuments in the Cathedral (2nd ed. Harmondsworth: Penguin Books, 1975, pp. 410–18) and presumably fell short of the criterion of 'outstanding quality' (Pevsner, p. 410). The brass also provides the only known contemporary representation of the bishop (artist unknown), showing him full length, wearing a skull cap with a trimmed beard, holding a closed book in the left hand, his pastoral staff in the right (see brass rubbing, fig. 1B). Dugdale included an engraving of the brass as a frontispiece to his biography in 1840. A portrait based on this, with his arms, inscribed 'Edmundus Geste | Aetat LXIII | Anno Domini | 1576' was made in the 19th century (fig. 2), and now hangs in the Cathedral Library (formerly in the Cathedral School); John Ingamells, *The English Episcopal Portrait 1559–1835: A Catalogue* ([London]: Published privately by The Paul Mellon Centre for Studies in British Art, 1981), p. 195. There is also a wooden head of Geste in the Choir Stalls (north side at the east end) based on the brass and/or the portrait, part of the upper stalls by Scott, c. 1870 (Pevsner, p. 409).
2. 'Et ingentem optimorum librorum vim quantam vix una capere Bibliotheca | Potest'. The text is reproduced in full in Dugdale, p. 58.
3. Only very briefly mentioned in Sal. Cat., p. vi.

2. Early nineteenth-century portrait of Geste (now in the
Cathedral Library) as reproduced in Dugdale.

it has, perhaps understandably, been overshadowed in the past by its unique
medieval manuscripts and by the better known printed-book collections of
Seth Ward and Izaak Walton.[4]

Although a few individual items had been identified as Geste's by former
librarians and visiting scholars, particularly the late Neil Ker,[5] it is only in

4. Eward, p. 6f.
5. E.g. Neil Ker in a letter to the Librarian, Canon Quirk, dated 17 September 1948,
identifying some thirty-four vols. which seemed to be Geste's on the evidence of
three roll-bindings.

the last thirty years that there has been any systematic attempt to record the contents of his library as it has survived today.[6] The absence of any contemporary catalogue or inventory attached to his will put it outside the range of Sears Jayne's *Library Catalogues of the English Renaissance* (1956), though its existence was briefly noted in the revised second edition.[7] At first, Geste's books were almost certainly kept together as a discrete collection in accordance with the terms of his will — a possibility supported by the survival of a sequence of early press marks on the books themselves[8] – but later reorganisation in the second half of the eighteenth century, brought about the dispersal of his books among those of the Cathedral Library as a whole, so that identification of his books and reconstruction of the original collection is now far from straightforward.

Edmund Geste lived through one of the most turbulent periods in the religious history of these islands. He had gone up to Cambridge in 1536 a few years after Henry VIII and Thomas Cromwell had brought about the severing of traditional links between the English Church and Rome, and at a time when its leaders were beginning to define the Church's doctrinal position in relation to the 'old faith' and the confessional formularies of continental Protestantism (1536–1544). Early in the reign of Edward VI, Geste made public his own position on the doctrinal issues being debated and on the liturgical reforms about to be implemented by issuing his first and only published work: *A Treatise Againste the Prevee Masse in the Behalfe and Furtheraunce of the Mooste Holye Communyon* (1548),[9] and this was followed up a year later when he took part in the second day of the Cambridge Disputation on the sacrament of the Eucharist held before the Visitors to the University (24 June 1549), briefly defending the Protestant position (along with Andrew Perne, Edmund Grindal and James Pilkington) against the Catholic, Dr William Glyn.[10] Less than five years later, with the accession of Mary, Geste (now Vice-Provost of his college) found himself on the wrong side of the doctrinal divide when he refused to attend the recently re-introduced Catholic services in King's chapel and was expelled by his College as a consequence (January 1554), an event which effectively signalled the end of his university career and connexions with Cambridge. During the

6. Suzanne Eward, the former Librarian and Keeper of the Muniments, compiled a card catalogue of his books recording evidence for his ownership and other provenance information in the course of re-cataloguing the whole Cathedral Library; the present author briefly summarized the scope and contents of Geste's library in C. B. L. Barr and David Selwyn, 'Major Ecclesiastical Libraries: From Reformation to Civil War' in CHLB I, pp. 379–82.
7. Reissued with new preface and notes, Godalming: St Paul's Bibliographies, 1983, p. xi.
8. See further on this in Introduction II, pp. 54–57, and Appendix V.
9. STC 11802.
10. Text in Foxe, vol. VI, pp. 324–25.

rest of Mary's reign he remained *incognito* in England, like others (Matthew Parker, Master of Corpus Christi College, among them) who preferred not to join the English Protestants in exile on the continent, until he emerged early in Elizabeth's reign as Parker's domestic chaplain and as one listed for preferment in the church. A favourite of the Queen (his bachelor status probably counting in his favour), recognition came rapidly to Geste. He was chosen as one of nine disputants on the Protestant side in the debate at Westminster with the Marian bishops in the critical spring of 1559 when the new Religious Settlement was being worked out; he was granted the archdeaconry of Canterbury in October of the same year and the see of Rochester in the following January. While at Rochester, he was the Queen's Lord High Almoner until 1572 following his translation to Salisbury as John Jewel's successor in December 1571 where he died after a short episcopate in 1577.

The outlines of Geste's career are clear, but with little surviving correspondence and other source material much detail is lacking. There has only been one biography, published as long ago as 1840: really no more than a memoir of less than seventy pages of text by an admiring though scholarly descendant, Henry Geast Dugdale, but valuable for the many documents supplementing the narrative which are included in the appendices.[11] Otherwise, Geste's life and career are only summarised in dictionary articles.[12] Geste actually wrote very little. The S T C (first and revised editions) credits him only with the single published work, the *Treatise,* already mentioned (1548); and John Bale in his *Catalogue of British Authors* (1557–59) gives him only a seven-line entry listing two further items up to the end of Edward VI's reign, neither of which has been identified.[13]

Geste and his Yorkshire connexions

Geste was a Yorkshireman by birth, from Allerton in the North Riding, more specifically the town of North Alverton, or Northallerton as it is known today.[14] Even the date of his birth is uncertain, ranging from 1514 (deduced

11. Dugdale, pp. 67–211.
12. For example by Cooper, pp. 361–62; F. O. White, *Lives of the Elizabethan Bishops of the Anglican Church* (London: Skeffington, 1898), pp. 127–34; Christopher Wordsworth in Ollard & Crosse, pp. 256–57; entries in *DNB* and *ODNB* (by Jane Freeman). All the above will be found under the modern spelling of his name 'Guest'.
13. *Scriptorum Illustrium Maioris Brytanniae* (Basileae: Apud Ioannem Oporinum, 1557–59), pt. ii, p. 107 (s.v. Gest). In addition to what must be the *Treatise* ('Contra missam papisticam, Lib.1.'), Bale mentions *'De Christi praesentia in coena, Lib.1.'* and *'De libero hominis arbitrio, Lib.1.'*.
14. John Speed's map of Yorkshire (1610) shows 'Allerton' as an area of the North Riding with the spelling 'Nth Alverton' for the town of Northallerton; Harwood, p. 155 (s.v. 1536), gives 'Allerton' in his entry for Geste; the entry for Geste's admission to King's in the college archives 'Liber Protocoll: 1500–1578', f. 81 has 'natus in villa de Afferton'.

from his reputed age of 63 at the time of his death in 1577)[15] to 1518/19 (based on his age of 18 at the time he was admitted to King's College, Cambridge, in August 1536).[16] King's College owned land in Allerton, and this may have been a factor in considering Geste's case for a scholarship either to the College or to its sister institution at Eton,[17] provided that other considerations of competence and suitability were fulfilled.[18] Geste began his formal grammar school education at St Peter's, York (sometime between 1520 and 1530) before going on to King's sister college of Eton in about 1532. Nothing further about his time at Eton survives as College records for the period before 1560 are scanty.[19]

The greater part of Geste's career was spent in the south of England, first at Eton, then Cambridge, and after the accession of Elizabeth I in the Canterbury and Rochester dioceses, at Court, and finally at Salisbury. Although Gestes are recorded in Yorkshire, the family on his father's side, it seems, came from the West Midlands: Row (or Rough) Heath in King's Norton parish, Worcestershire, with a branch in the adjoining county of Staffordshire in the parish of Halesowen. Quite why or when his family came to Yorkshire is not clear, but it seems possible that this branch to some extent lost contact with the Gestes of the Midlands after the move to Yorkshire. For the Heraldic Visitation of Worcestershire undertaken by Robert Cooke, Clarenceux King of Arms, in 1569 – presumably attended by one or more of the Midland Gestes but evidently not by Edmund (at that time bishop of

15. 1514 is the date adopted by Jane Freeman in the *ODNB,* following Dugdale. The monumental brass, which erroneously records the date of his death as 1578, gives his age as 63 which, with the correct date of 1577, would support this.
16. 'Liber Protocoll: 1500–1578', f. 81, admitted on 17 August 1536, aged 18. *DNB* adopted 1517–1518 as the date of Geste's birth, as does Ollard & Crosse.
17. King's had owned the manor of Allerton Mauleverer, near Knaresborough in the West Riding since its foundation until it was sold in 1544 to Thomas Mauleverer (cf. Saltmarsh, pp. 10, 12). It is not clear, however, whether Geste's birth at Northallerton, in the North Riding, counted in his favour in considering his eligibility for a scholarship to King's.
18. The relevant statute states that the necessary qualities of scholars are to be 'poor, indigent, most notable for their good behaviour and circumstances, adapted to study, of honest conversation, instructed in reading, plain song and Donatus', of appropriate age and free of any other disqualifications that would render them incapable of taking orders. I am grateful to Michael Meredith, College Librarian, and Mrs Penelope Hatfield, College Archivist, at Eton, and Peter Jones, Fellow and Librarian, at King's College, for information on these matters.
19. No early records survive either at St Peter's, York, or at Eton to confirm the dates of Geste's admission, but the dates for the former are suggested by Raine, p. 63. Wasey Sterry confidently gives 1532–1536 as the dates for Geste's time at Eton, but cites no evidence. I am grateful to John V. Mitchell, Archivist at St Peter's, York, for the former information and to Michael Meredith and Mrs Penelope Hatfield, at Eton, for the latter.

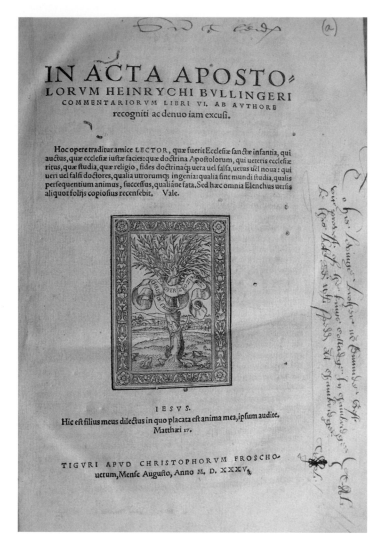

3. Inscription in one of three books presented to Geste after he had become Vice-Provost of King's College by his brother-in-law Christopher Leedes, February 1550/51. Cat. no. B122.

Rochester) – did not record the identity of Geste's mother or her family,[20] and neither does Geste's biographer, Dugdale, who had consulted a number of genealogical sources and prepared a pedigree of the family included in his book.[21] The matter is not unimportant, because the identification might shed light on Geste's family circle and potential influences on his intellectual

20. From BL Harleian MS 1586, f. 188v, ed. W. P. W. Phillimore for the Harleian Society (1888).
21. Dugdale, p. 13f. and the folding genealogical table following p. vii.

4. Inscription on a book donated to Geste early in his Cambridge career by his uncle, John Brandisby, D.D. Cat. no. E48. See Appendix X.

and theological development. Fortunately, some answer is provided by information in his will, the will of one of his relatives on his mother's side, and provenance evidence in a number of his books.

Geste's will (dated 28 February 1576/77) made no legacies to any relatives on his father's side, but only to one 'Christopher Leedes' who is described as his 'brother' [i.e. in-law].[22] However, among Geste's surviving books at Salisbury are three folios of continental printing (dated between 1531 and 1546), two of which retain their original blind-tooled 'roll' bindings, all three distinguished by the fact that they carry an almost identical inscription written *down* the outside margin of the title page: 'To my loving brother Mr Edmund Geste vice-provost of the king's college in Cambridge be this boke ... delyvered' and the date (in two instances) '10th February 1550 [1551 n.s.]'. Imbedded in all three inscriptions is a florid monogram including the initials 'C L' which would seem to stand for this same 'Christopher Leedes'.[23] A further clue is provided by the provenance of five other books of Geste's, all acquired second-hand during his time in Cambridge. All five carry the ownership inscription of John Brandisby (Brandesby, Brandisbie or Bransbei in various spellings), one of them explicitly acknowledging that the book was a gift to Geste from 'Dr Brandesby'.[24] A final clue comes in Brandisby's will, proved in February 1550, now in the Borthwick Institute at the University of York.[25] Among a large number of legacies, many of them to members of his family,

22. Text from PROB 11/59 (Prerogative Court of Canterbury) now at the National Archives, Kew, and transcribed in Dugdale, p. 56.
23. Catalogue items B122, E55 and J12 for further details. Two of these are still in their original (identical roll) bindings, but of uncertain origin. Oldham suggests an unidentified London binder, Pearson an Oxford origin. The third (B122) has been rebound. See Appendix IV B, under Oldham FP.a(8). One of these inscriptions is illustrated in fig. 3.
24. Cat. item E48 (see fig. 4). The other items are B6, F5, L72 and R17, for further details. On Brandisby, see Appendix X. He had taken his DD in 1532.
25. Will of John Brandisbye, clerk, Feb. 1550, Abp. Reg. 29, f. 154.

brothers, sisters, nephews and nieces, John Brandisby made bequests of money to Edmund Geste and to Christopher Leedes, both of whom are described as nephews. Clearly, Geste's father had married one of Brandisby's sisters, perhaps no longer alive at the time of John's death in December 1549. This was presumably not John's sister, Millicent Leedes, unless she was widowed and had married again, this time to one of the Leedes. Geste's father is not mentioned and had presumably died by this time.

John Brandisby, another northerner, had graduated in Cambridge (his college is not certain, though Michaelhouse seems likely) in 1513/14 (BA, MA 1517). Not long after that, he was evidently studying in Paris, for an undated letter of his from Lombards College survives in the archives at St John's College, Cambridge,[26] addressed to Nicholas Metcalfe (Master, 1518–1537) recalling a meeting 'with my lord of Rochester as I came to Paris' during which John Fisher gave him twenty shillings, 'and of his own mind (afore I spoke to his lordship) did remember my brethren [James and Richard], and said that he did not forget them, but that they should be the first that should be preferred into St John's college'. Brandisby's letter to Metcalfe, in which he went on to commend his younger brothers as 'very apt and studious', achieved its purpose, for they were admitted soon after, both graduating BA in 1522 (MA four years later), Richard becoming a classical scholar and a Fisher Fellow of his college in 1523, the same year as John was Preacher to the University and took his BD. Although nothing further has come to light on James, both of Geste's other uncles on his mother's side, therefore, had careers at Cambridge, and Richard was still at St John's when Edmund was admitted to King's in 1536. More significantly, both also illustrate divergent responses to the religious changes taking place at the time. Richard, who owed his place at St John's directly to Fisher, remained loyal to the bishop's stand on papal authority and was one of the college deputation which visited him in prison in 1534. It was presumably for the same ideological reasons that Richard left St John's in 1538 for the European continent, studying at Louvain, a place of exile for other Henrician Catholics such as Richard Smith, formerly Regius Professor at Oxford (after 1547), and was still there at the time of Edward VI's death in 1553.

By contrast, John Brandisby, although probably still fairly traditional in religious outlook,[27] clearly accepted the ecclesiastical changes under

26. Quoted in Maria Dowling, *Fisher of Men: A Life of John Fisher, 1469–1535* (Basingstoke: Palgrave Macmillan, 1999), p. 24, from St John's College Archives (D105.245). A date for the letter of about 1518 (inferred from the year of their degrees) is suggested by Malcolm Underwood, Archivist at St John's (personal communication), cf. his 'John Fisher and the promotion of learning' in *Humanism, Reform and the Reformation: The Career of Bishop John Fisher*, ed. by B. Bradshaw and E. Duffy (Cambridge: University Press, 1989), p. 39 and n. 63. I am grateful to Mr Underwood for this and much other information about the Brandisbys.
27. He bequeathed his soul to God, the Virgin Mary and the Saints. Cooper, I, p. 550.

Henry VIII. After Cambridge he went on to hold a number of livings in the Midlands and the North from 1517 (including Kirby Wiske not far from Northallerton, Edmund Geste's birthplace), until his death in 1549. He also held prebendal stalls at Lincoln (1529), Southwell (1534) and York (1539) where he died. It is not clear how much he may have furthered his nephew's education, but it is possible that he was to some extent his academic mentor, since one of the five surviving books that came to Edmund was Reuchlin's celebrated Hebrew grammar (1506). Hebrew was one of the three 'sacred languages' strongly represented in Geste's library but one which, at the time, was not that commonly taught or widely studied in Cambridge, as Gareth Lloyd Jones has shown.[28] How much Brandisby may have been an influence in an ideological direction as well can only be a conjecture from a mere five surviving books. But all were to some extent representative of the 'new learning' of the Renaissance humanists which had gained some footing in Cambridge since Colet, Fisher, More and the visit of Erasmus himself. Beside the Erasmus and Reuchlin books, Brandisby had passed on to Geste the *Epistolae* (F5) of the Italian humanist, Marsilio Ficino (Venice, 1495); one of the new editions of the Church Fathers, the works of the Cappadocian, Basil of Caesarea (B6), especially popular with the humanists, albeit in Latin translation (Basle, 1520); and, as some indication of interest in the new Protestant ideas which had been gaining ground at Cambridge since the early 1520s, a work of the German Reformer, Martin Luther himself: the *Propositiones* (L72), published at Wittenberg in 1538.[29]

Whatever other more direct influences the two Brandisby uncles may have had in the formation of his outlook, Geste can hardly have been unaware of this ideological diversity within his own family. And it may be that his concern to acquaint himself thoroughly with the writings and arguments of proponents on both sides of the Reformation debates, so evident from the extensive holdings in his library of contemporary Catholic as well as Protestant authors, owes something to this experience.

Geste at King's College, Cambridge

Geste entered King's College from Eton as the last named of six scholars admitted on 17 August 1536, in the final years of Edward Fox's time as Provost (1528–38) – at that time much involved in the matter of the King's divorce as well as holding the bishopric of Hereford (1535–38). Two of that year's entry rapidly disappear from the records, neither apparently

28. Gareth Lloyd Jones, *The Discovery of Hebrew in Tudor England: A Third Language* (Manchester: University Press, 1983).
29. The *Propositions* for the Amsdorf disputations of 1522 and 1535 on grace, good works and free will – issues central to Geste's interests as shown by many other annotated books in his library.

graduating,[30] but the other three, like Geste, became Fellows in 1539, graduating BA in 1540/41,[31] and MA in 1544.[32] Geste and two of the other three, William Wynke (or Whyncke) and Edward Aglionby, then proceeded to the study of theology, Geste taking his BD in 1551,[33] Wynke in 1555.[34] But while Geste was to support the Reformation changes, Wynke was to remain at heart an adherent of the 'old faith'. Although he apparently took orders in 1551 under the Ordinal issued that year, he was the Fellow chosen in 1553 early in Mary's reign to replace Geste as vice-Provost, holding the living of Fordingbridge in Hampshire from 1556, and after the accession of Elizabeth living as a Catholic recusant.[35]

The other two scholars of the 1536 entry followed very different careers. The first, Clement Adams (c. 1519–1587), a pupil at Cambridge of John Cheke, joined the circle of Sebastian Cabot in London from 1548, becoming distinguished in the field of map-engraving, navigation and discovery, as well as being appointed for life in 1552 'schoolmaster to the king's henchmen'.[36] The other, Edward Aglionby, left Cambridge (apparently without taking his BD) to enter public life as MP first for Carlisle (1547), and later, after a period of absence from public affairs during Mary's reign, MP for Warwick and from 1572 the town's Recorder until 1587.[37] His religious preferences during the Reformation period were less immediately obvious than those of Wynke or Geste. But in 1550 he issued an English translation of the anti-Nicodemist work of the Italian Protestant Matteo Gribaldi, Professor of Law at Padua, acquainting English readers with the sad fate of his colleague Francesco Spiera who in 1548 had recanted his faith before a local inquisition only to fall into depression at this betrayal and die in despair, convinced of his damnation.[38] Spiera's case became a *cause célèbre* among Protestant anti-Nicodemist propagandists, notably the Italian Pier Paulo Vergerio, and was even alluded to in a court sermon of Hugh Latimer delivered in 1552.[39]

---

30. Robert Columbell, from Marston, Derbyshire, and John Rookes, from Datchett, Buckinghamshire. Venn. Neither appears in *Grace Book B*.
31. *Grace Book B*, pp. 225, 230–31.
32. *Grace Book Δ*, p. 14.
33. *Grace Book Δ*, p. 73.
34. *Grace Book Δ*, p. 106.
35. See Provenance Index, Appendix X, under 'W, W', from Venn (who, however, gives the date as '1555'). CCEd, Clergy ID 65991, '1556'.
36. *ODNB* 'Clement Adams' (R. C. D. Baldwin).
37. *ODNB* 'Edward Aglionby' (Stephen Wright).
38. *Historia de Quodam (F. Spera) quem Hostes Evangelii in Italia Coergerunt Abiicere Cognitam Veritatem*, translated as *A Notable and Maruailous Epistle of the Famous Doctor, Mathewe Gribalde ... with a Preface of Doctor Caluine, Translated by E. A.* (1550), STC 12365. The work included Calvin's *Praefatio in Libellum de Francisco Spiera*. On this, see M. A. Overell, 'Vergerio's Anti-Nicodemite Propaganda and England, 1547–1558' in *JEH* 51 (2000), 296–318, and the literature cited there.
39. Cited in Overell, p. 303.

5. MS note in Geste's copy of a book by the Catholic, Georg Witzel: 'How we may with a good conscience use & suffer ye Romyshe masse'. Cat. no. W50.

Geste, like many others, may have already had to face the same dilemma of religious conformity and personal issues of conscience during the last years of the reign of Henry VIII, and was soon to do so under Mary, a conflict perhaps reflected in an annotation in one of his surviving books.[40]

Aglionby's translation of Gribaldi was reissued in 1570 in an expanded edition which may have appeared without the translator's knowledge (the initials 'E.A' in the first edition disappear from the title page),[41] but the issue was still a live one, and as MP for Carlisle he spoke in the 1571 parliamentary debate in favour of the Bill for Church Attendance, arguing that its provisions should not include the requirement to receive the sacrament which was a matter for a man's conscience.[42]

40. A note in his hand on a flyleaf in a volume of items by Catholic authors (1534–1542), including Eck and Witzel, reads 'Howe we may with a good Conscience use & suffer ye Romyshe masse' (W50), see fig. 5. It is not certain to what phase in Geste's career this alludes or its exact context. If not written in Mary's reign, it could just as well belong to the mid-1540s when he was beginning the formal study of theology and moving to a Protestant understanding of the mass which was to reach full expression in his *Treatise* of 1548.

41. '*Now newly imprinted with a preseruative against desperation*' (STC 12366). His name continues to appear in an acrostic, however, on another leaf, as in the first edition. By this time, Gribaldi had achieved notoriety as an anti-Trinitarian who had condemned Calvin for his part in the Servetus affair.

42. *ODNB*. 'Edward Aglionby' (Stephen Wright).

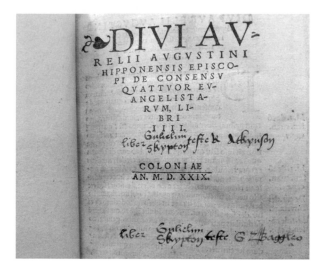

6. Inscription on a book (one of four) acquired by Geste from an older Fellow at King's College, William Skypton. Cat. no. A62. Both William Bagley and Richard Atkinson were also Fellows of King's, the latter as Provost when Geste was expelled in 1554. See Appendix X.

By contrast Geste had settled into a relatively uneventful academic career at King's, in the course of which he accumulated a large collection of printed books which he had studied closely, to judge by the high proportion which he annotated.[43] Although Geste had access to a substantial collection of books in the two College libraries (which might according to one estimate have numbered as many as five-hundred on the eve of the Reformation) this was a period of decline for the library at King's as for other institutions. The Royal Injunctions for the reform of the University and its studies at the time Geste began his Cambridge career resulted in the official purging of college libraries of much scholastic writing, particularly relating to the study of scripture and canon law, and probably inspired further losses and damage to books, compounded by unreturned loans, theft and general neglect. By the time the Marian Commissioners visited the College in January 1556/57 the collection at King's had been reduced to a little more than a hundred volumes. These included standard sets of the early Fathers, scholastic commentaries on scripture and even some humanist texts such as Erasmus' Annotations on the New Testament, but no Protestant authors (unless these had already been removed early in Mary's reign).[44] Like other Fellows, Geste

43. See Appendices III (listing the books with imprints during his time at King's) and XI (listing his books with annotations).
44. For the fortunes of King's College library during the period, evidence for the depredations especially as a result of the activities of such as Robert Commander, and for the text of the Marian Inventory, see *NKCL*.

had no alternative to building up his own collection by purchase and gift. A number of his books were acquired from older contemporaries at King's.

Among the more senior fellows from whom Geste obtained books was another Yorkshireman, William Skypton (admitted in 1522 and a fellow from 1525 to about 1543, the most senior at the time after the Vice-Provost, Robert Brassie), four of whose books were acquired by Geste.[45] Four other books in Geste's collection can almost certainly be traced to contemporaries at King's, and a fifth is a possibility. Among the four is a work by the Reformed Protestant, Oecolampadius,[46] formerly owned by Thomas Bulward, who had been admitted as a scholar from Eton in 1525, and a Fellow from 1528–1541; two others by Lutherans (a Brentz and a Sarcerius),[47] one with the inscription 'ex kervyle', the latter with the initials 'N K' stamped in blind on the covers, appear to have come from Nicholas Kervyle, a much younger contemporary, admitted in 1545, who went into exile for his Protestant convictions during Mary's reign (first at Zürich and then at Frankfurt), returning to England early in Elizabeth's reign to become chaplain to Edmund Grindal and subsequently a leading opponent of the prescribed clerical vesture to the annoyance of archbishop Matthew Parker. Another book was an Erasmus that had belonged to 'Pykering', perhaps the Robert Pykering MD, admitted in 1531 and a fellow from 1539–1549 who 'died in Dr Hatcher's house' that year, leaving a substantial collection of printed books listed in an inventory of his goods which survives in the University Archives.[48] The fifth item – a Cicero of 1541 (C74), with the initials 'W W' on the covers – may (just possibly) have belonged to the William Wyncke already mentioned, an exact contemporary, who was to follow Geste as Vice-Provost after the latter's removal in 1553, or even to William Whitelock, who had entered King's from Eton the year after Geste and Wynke (1537), succeeding the latter as Vice-Provost in 1556.[49]

The King's *Commons Books*[50] (not, unfortunately, complete for the whole period) record Geste's residence in College over three periods (1540–41, 1549–50 and 1553–54) as he worked his way up by seniority from a position as the most junior of the forty fellows in 1540 (when his name first appears in the surviving records, below his other three contemporaries, Edward

45. See Catalogue nos. A62 (illustrated in fig. 6) and E56 (bound in one volume), B35, H84 and T20.
46. See Catalogue no. O10.
47. See Catalogue nos. B72 and S17. Both carry the inscription 'ex kervyle', but the Sarcerius book (S17) also carries the initials 'N K' blind-stamped on the covers which strengthens the case for Nicholas Kervyle's ownership.
48. For the Pykering item see Catalogue no. E31. For the inventory of his library, containing at least 224 volumes, wide-ranging in content, see BiCI, I, 52, pp. 121–25.
49. For these possibilities see Appendix X 'Provenances', s.v. 'W, W'.
50. King's College Archives, *Libri Communarum*, vols. 14–16. Vol. 14 covers the period 1534–35, 1539–40, vol. 15 1549–50, and vol.16 1553–54, 1559–62.

Aglionby, Clement Adams and William Wynke, who had all been admitted in the same year (1536) and elected to fellowships in 1539, to a position as thirty-fourth in seniority (out of forty-three taking Commons) in the final entries (for August 1541) in the first of the three extant volumes (vol. 14).[51] The Vice-Provost at the time was Robert Brassie (admitted in 1526), who was to adhere to the 'old faith', becoming Provost during Mary's reign in 1556, after Geste's departure, and Vice-Chancellor of the University (1557) until his death in 1558. His successor as Vice-Provost (1542–48) was Richard Atkynson, from Ripley in Yorkshire (admitted in 1527), another of the 'old faith' who was to prosper during the reign of Mary and whose career was to impinge more directly on Geste's fortunes. A student of divinity like Geste, who held the degrees of BD (1542) and DD (1545) as well as being Lady Margaret Preacher in the same year, his name appears at about this time on two of Geste's books as one who had witnessed Skypton's ownership of two items.[52]

By the time of the next extant volume of the *Commons Books,* covering the years 1549–50, the changes associated with the first years of the Reformation under Edward VI were well under way. The Provost during the period 1538–47 had been a non-King's man, George Day of St John's College, a former chaplain to John Fisher, at the time Vice-Chancellor of the University, and from 1543 bishop of Chichester. A conservative in his theological outlook, Day had opposed the abolition of private masses in King's Chapel in 1547, censuring the Vice-Provost and fellows for doing so, and forbidding them from any further innovations in religion,[53] an action which may have provided the pretext for Geste's *Treatise* on this subject in 1548 which was published under the provostship of his successor, John Cheke (1548–53) to whom the work was dedicated. Under Cheke (Provost from 1548), with whom he shared the same Protestant outlook, Geste made rapid progress. In June 1549, he was chosen to take part in the second day of the Cambridge Disputation on the sacrament of the Eucharist held before the royal visitors to the University, briefly putting forward arguments against transubstantiation with other Protestant disputants. He was also advancing in seniority within King's. In the first of the entries for 1549, with Henry Bisell as Vice-Provost (1548–50), and forty-four fellows resident, Geste was fourteenth in order of seniority, and by the time of the last recorded entry for 1550,

---

51. Vol. 14, ff. 179 to the end of the volume at f. 198.
52. Two of the Skypton books mentioned in n. 45 (A62 and E56): 'teste R. Atkynson'.
53. Although Day served on the commission for the reform of the liturgy which compiled the first English Prayer Book under Edward VI, he voted against the book in its final form as well as the new Ordinal (1550) and opposed the religious changes being introduced, for which he was deprived of his see in 1551, briefly imprisoned in the Fleet and committed to the custody of Richard Goodrich, bishop of Ely, for the rest of the reign, until his re-instatement to Chichester under Mary where he remained until his death in 1556.

he had progressed to seventh out of thirty-eight in residence.[54] Later that same year he succeeded Bissell as Vice-Provost and in the autumn of the following year he was again taking part in a university disputation at a commence-ment, this time on the topic of Christ's descent into hell, involving his Provost, Sir John Cheke, against the views of Christopher Carlile of Clare College.[55] In the same year, he was granted his BD after six years of theological study.[56]

The reign of Mary: an exile from Cambridge

The final volume of the King's College *Commons Books* covers the transitional period of Edward's last year and the accession of Mary which saw the removal of Cheke from the office of Provost (late in 1553) and Geste from that of Vice-Provost (evidently in September the same year). At the beginning of this final volume, Geste, as Vice-Provost, had headed the list of forty-two resident fellows during 1553 until 11 September after which the entries abruptly cease for the rest of Mary's reign, only resuming early in Elizabeth's reign in 1559 when William Whitlocke headed the list towards the end of his term as Vice-Provost (1556–59). There are no entries during the term of Geste's immediate successor, William Wynke (1553–56) or for most of Whitlocke's.[57]

In the first year of Mary's reign, Atkynson had returned to King's as Provost (1553–56), following Sir John Cheke's arrest and imprisonment, and his name appears in the King's *Liber Protocol* when Geste was deprived of his right of Commons as a fellow on 2 January 1553/54, following his refusal to attend chapel under the restored Catholic forms of worship.[58] Two other names appeared in that same entry, both admitted to King's as scholars from Eton in the year after Geste (23 August 1537) and both men accepted the religious settlement under Mary. The first was Ralph Holland from Prescot in Lancashire (a King's living) who drafted and signed the order in his capacity as College Registrar and Public Notary, treating the incident as essentially a disciplinary matter of 'disobedience'. The second name was that of William Whitlocke, fellow from 1540 to 1560 and another student of theology, who

---

54. Vol. 15, unfoliated.
55. Carlile denied the literal truth of Christ's descent into hell. His views were attacked by Richard Smith in 1562 by that time dean of St Peter's Church, Douai, in his *De Missae Sacrificio*, a copy of which (not certainly of Geste's ownership) survives at Salisbury (see Appendix I, *S7), to which Carlile replied in his *Discourse Concerning Two Diuine Positions* (1582, STC 4654), a defence of Carlile's views with reference to the 1552 Disputation. Geste's arguments (and those of Cheke) are briefly summarised by Carlile, very much from his perspective, in the Preface.
56. *Grace Book* Δ, p. 73.
57. Vol. 16, ff. 3–62v. Entries resume for 1559 at f. 66.
58. *Liber Protocol*, f. 154.

became Vice-Provost of King's after Robert Brassie from 1556 to 1559, yet accepted preferment in the Elizabethan church, being granted a dispensation for pluralism, enabling him to hold the King's living of Prescot (as an absentee incumbent for almost the whole period, 1558 to 1583)[59] as well as Greenford in Middlesex, and continuing his career as a canon of Lichfield Cathedral (from 1561), writing up its history, in his 'Chronicon Lichefeldensis ecclesiae'.

Geste's contemporaries at King's, therefore, reflected something of the diversity and religious tensions that must have characterised so many colleges during this period, its members including a number who resented the religious changes introduced in Edward's reign, welcoming the restoration of Catholicism under Mary, others who managed to accommodate themselves to the ideological twists and turns of four reigns, and some like Robert Glover (admitted in 1533 and burnt at the stake in 1555 for his Protestant opinions) and Geste himself, who suffered the consequences of adhering to their convictions.

Geste's whereabouts during Mary's reign are not known, though he remained in England.[60] As one who had openly and forcefully defended the religious changes during Edward's reign, and taken an uncompromisingly Protestant position on that most contentious of issues (at least so far as the English Reformation was concerned), the doctrine of transubstantiation, he was clearly vulnerable to arrest. It would have been difficult for him to remain in Cambridge, for there were ex-colleagues in his own college, now prospering under the Marian regime, who may have resented his support for the Reformation and his term as Vice-Provost under a Protestant regime. Whether or not his survival involved frequent changes of residence to avoid arrest, Geste had managed to rescue over 330 books from his collection built up while he was at King's,[61] though it is not known where these were kept

59. See Christopher Haigh, *Reformation and Resistance in Tudor Lancashire* (London: Cambridge University Press, 1975), p. 237, and the references cited in n. 2.
60. Like Matthew Parker whose movements were also unknown. Dugdale (p. 31) following Strype (cf. *ODNB*, s.v. Guest, by Jane Freeman) notes that Geste was closely associated at this time with Nicholas Bullingham ('Nicolaus Bullingham ... et Edmundus Geste ... Hi duo in anglia, regnante Maria, Pontificiis dominantibus latebras quaesiverunt, easque crebro Pontificorum exploratoribus vix tuto esse poterunt crebro mutaverunt'). Bullingham, a former chaplain of Cranmer, a canon and archdeacon of Lincoln and the bishop's vicar-general, was deprived of his preferments in May 1554 as a married priest. But it is not clear how much he could have assisted Geste and for how long, as he also had to escape detection by lying low and went into exile soon afterwards, being enrolled as a citizen at Emden by November 1555, presumably after the usual year's residence (*ODNB*, s.v. Bullingham, by Julian Lock) which would suggest that he had left England late in 1554.
61. See Appendix III (listing imprints between 1553 and 1557) and Appendix IV (a chronological list of contemporary bindings with imprints between 1553 and 1557). It cannot be assumed that the items listed were actually acquired by Geste in the same year as their imprints, but some may have been acquired during the Marian period.

or whether these moved with him. Nor is it known whether he continued to collect books during the Marian period. Whether or not he was in a position to purchase books in his difficult circumstances, there are just over ninety items in his collection with imprints from between 1553 and 1557, though many of these were bound with others from the next reign and probably acquired at the same time. Even so, it is just possible that up to forty books were added during Mary's reign, including a significant number by Catholic authors.[62]

Preferment under Elizabeth I

After the death of Mary, Geste emerged from the obscurity of his 'exile' in England to make a modest, though still significant, contribution to the English Reformation: particularly in the fields of liturgical reform, doctrinal definition and biblical translation. By this time, his links with King's and the University were effectively at an end, though he did attend the Queen on her visit to Cambridge in August 1564.[63] But without in any way abandoning his scholarly interests – he continued to add to his already extensive library, annotating his books as thoroughly as ever – his career now took a different, more ecclesiastical direction, as he became, first, domestic chaplain to Matthew Parker, and then accepted preferments to the living of Cliffe in Kent, the archdeaconry of Canterbury in November 1559, and in 1560 the See of Rochester. There was also an appointment for him at Court when he was chosen to be the Queen's Lord High Almoner, a post he held until shortly after his translation to Salisbury in 1571.

Geste and liturgical reform

Geste's interest in the liturgical changes integral to the English Reformation is clear from his early, and only published work, *A Treatise Against the Prevee*

62. Luther, Chytraeus, Culman, Kirchmeyer, Musculus and Bullinger among Protestant authors, Edmund Bonner, Stephen Gardiner, Cuthbert Tunstall and Thomas Watson among English Catholic writers, Helmes, Sasbout, Tavernarius, Titelman and Witzel among continentals.

63. The claim that he was awarded a DD there in 1571 (made in the article on 'Guest' in the *DNB*) appears to be based on a misreading of *Grace Book* Δ, s.v. 1571/72, p. 257 where the candidate Edmund 'Roffensis' is clearly Edmund Freake not Edmund Geste who by this time had been translated to Salisbury. If Geste had not been exiled from Cambridge after 1554, he might have been expected to take his DD in the late 1550s, i.e. six years or so after his BD, as his uncle, John Brandisby had done in 1531/32 (*Grace Book* Δ, pp. 434, 529). Geste was also mentioned as a possible successor to Philip Baker as Provost of King's by Henry Howard (1540–1614), then a fellow and later Earl of Northampton, in a letter to William Cecil (2 March 1569/70), now in the Cotton MSS at the British Library (Titus C.VI, ff. 11–12v), but nothing came of it, and Geste's attitude to this suggestion is not known. I am very grateful to Daniel C. Andersson for this reference.

Masse of 1548 supporting the changes to the liturgy then in process of imple-
mentation. Geste had dedicated his book to John Cheke, the new Provost
of King's who was tutor (or 'scolemaister') to the young King Edward
VI, and evidently one who was himself deeply interested in the eucharistic
contro-versy since he later took part in 'conversations' on the subject at
the house of William Cecil in 1551.[64] Geste was writing at the very time
the first *Book of Common Prayer* (issued in 1549) was in an advanced stage
of preparation and on the eve of the crucial debate on eucharistic doctrine
that was to take place in the House of Lords in December 1548 between
representatives from both sides of the Reformation 'divide'.[65] At the time
he wrote his attack on private masses, the legislation against chantries had
been passed, but private masses themselves were still common (and legal),
and the old Latin canon of the mass remained in use, as it continued to be
even when the *Order of Communion*, with its provision for the communion
of the laity and preparatory devotions, was issued in time for Easter 1548.
Geste's aim in the *Treatise* was to point out the inconsistency of both with
the intentions of the 'worthy' Act of Parliament dissolving chantries and
to show that their continuance was incompatible with the 'furtherance
of the true masse, otherwise named the communion' and the rejection of
papal authority on which, he claimed, the 'preuee masse' depended. While
welcoming what had been achieved, Geste was clearly dissatisfied with
the present interim arrangements (as he judged them to be) and apparently
uneasy about future developments. By addressing his plea to one close to
the young king himself, he was hoping to ensure that the views of those
uneasy about the present direction and progress of the Reformation would
be heard in the proper quarter.[66]

Geste's *Treatise* belonged therefore to the religious changes being introduced in 1548. But it also had a continental context in the liturgical reforms
proposed for Cologne earlier in the 1540s by its archbishop, Hermann von
Wied, with the assistance of Martin Bucer, the Strasbourg Reformer, soon
to be exiled to England and appointed Regius Professor of Divinity at
Cambridge until his death there in 1551. Hermann's proposed reforms had
been published in 1543, with a Latin translation in 1545, known to the English
Reformers, such as archbishop Cranmer (whose copy survives to this day),[67]

64. John Strype, *Life of … Sir John Cheke* (Oxford: Clarendon Press, 1821), pp. 70–86,
   from Corpus Christi College, Cambridge, MS 102, pp. 253–66.

65. Colin Buchanan, *Background Documents to Liturgical Revision 1547–1549* (Bramcote:
   Grove, 1983), from BL Royal MS 17B XXXIX. Strype (*Life of … Sir John Cheke*, p. 171)
   claims that Cheke collected the arguments of those who took part in the Debate.

66. On the wider context, see 'The "Book of Doctrine", the Lords' Debate and the
   First Prayer Book of Edward VI: An Abortive Attempt at Doctrinal Consensus?',
   JTS NS 40 (1989), 446–80.

67. *Einfältigs Bedencken* (Bon: Laurentium von der Müllen, 1543); Latin translation
   Simplex ac Pia Deliberatio (Bonnae: Ex officina Laurentii Mylii, 1545). Cranmer's
   copy is in Chichester Cathedral Library. See LTC no. 147.

and in an English version (*A Simple, and Religious Consultation*) issued in 1547 ('perused and amended' in 1548), a copy of which Geste owned and annotated.[68] But Hermann's proposals were not acceptable to the conservative element in the Cologne Cathedral Chapter which in 1544 issued its own counter-proposals, the *Antididagma*. This book was also known and taken note of in England, not only by those who were opposed to the liturgical changes but even by Cranmer himself who had made reference to it on a number of occasions in his *Commonplace Books* dating from the 1540s,[69] and who, it was feared, might be swayed by its arguments to accommodate the views of those Geste called 'our English Catholiques' and to compromise on some of the crucial issues at stake in the reform of the liturgy. Geste, in fact, alluded to the work at two places in his *Treatise* and possessed a copy of the later Paris edition (1549) which, like the *Deliberatio*, he had closely studied and annotated.[70]

A little over ten years later, Geste was again active in the cause of liturgical reform, this time in events associated with the making of the Elizabethan Settlement early in 1559. Almost nothing for certain is known, however, about the process of liturgical revision in 1559 – whether there was a formal or even ad hoc committee, or whether it was the work of one or two individuals and, if so, who were directly involved. Parliamentary records – with no verbatim transcripts or even brief minutes at this time – give only the names of bills introduced into the Commons, when these were read for a first or second time, and when they were sent up to the Lords, but they yield no information about the content of the bills (or even who initiated them) unless they passed into law. It is known that a number of bills relating to a new form of service to replace the mass were proposed in the Commons during February and March 1559 and that these were either rejected in the Lords or drastically amended, but the records give no information about the content of the proposed services until the Uniformity Bill with a slightly revised form of the 1552 Book of Common Prayer established as the new form of service passed through both houses in April of that year.

68. STC 13213–14. Geste owned a copy of the 1548 edition (H42) and annotated most of the section on the eucharistic liturgy.
69. A point noted in 1891 by the anonymous author of 'Capitulum Coloniense: an Episode in the Reformation', *Church Quarterly Review*, xxxi (1891), 419–37, who showed that the passages in the *Commonplace Books* which referred to 'Capitulum Coloniense' (listed on pp. 420f.) were actually taken from the Louvain 1544 edition of *Antididagma, seu Christianae et Catholicae religionis* (see LTC, no. 71).
70. Cat. no. C95, a copy of the Paris 1549 edition; *Treatise*, A7v and J3r; on both occasions the reference is simply to 'Antididagma'. No copy of the earlier edition (1544) survives in his library, but the work was certainly circulating in Cambridge before 1546, as the inventory of Oliver Ainsworth (1546), a Fellow of Jesus College, demonstrates (BiCI, I, no. 130, item 128). See Introduction, II, p. 98.

What part the Queen herself played in this process and what her preferences were for a reformed liturgy are further unknown components in the making of the religious settlement. It is possible that she favoured a step-by-step approach once her own position had been consolidated and the Royal Supremacy established, perhaps even following to some extent the stages of reform early in Edward's reign with a moratorium on all preaching, but with provision for certain parts of the existing service, such as the lections, to be read in English (December 1558). This was followed in March 1559 by a further proclamation ordering communion to be ministered to the laity in both kinds at Easter that year, thus reviving the Act of 1547 'against such persons as shall unreverently speak against the Sacrament ... and for the receiving thereof under both kinds', but without any further changes in the liturgy at this stage. How far, if at all, she intended to progress beyond these measures towards a complete form of liturgy in English at this juncture is much less clear and has, notoriously, been the subject of much speculation and controversy.

Here the different agendas of the returning exiles from Frankfurt, Geneva and other continental centres, many of them future leaders in Elizabethan Protestantism, were a crucial ingredient which could not be ignored in any liturgical settlement, particularly in the case of those who had experienced at first hand the reformed rites of Calvin's Geneva or adaptations of Edward VI's second Prayer Book which on some matters of ceremonial had introduced restrictions which had gone far beyond the known intentions of its original creators.

Last, but not least, there was the question of the Marian Catholics and their response to what had already happened and to any intended changes to the Roman liturgy. How far could all or any of them be accommodated in the religious settlement? The omens were not good. Already, in January 1559, the Lower House of the Canterbury Convocation had drawn up uncompromising articles upholding transubstantiation and the sacrifice in the mass, and these had been approved in the Upper House and duly presented to the Lord Keeper of the Great Seal.

In the early years of Edward's reign matters had been brought to a head in a Disputation staged in the House of Lords (December 1548) between Catholic and Protestant bishops and divines, and something similar was planned to take place at Westminster over Easter 1559 while parliament was adjourned. The three propositions chosen by the Privy Council for debate related to the language of the liturgy, the right of every church to determine its rites and ceremonies, and the sacrifice of the mass – issues that were central to securing agreement (or otherwise) for any liturgical settlement. Although Geste was among the disputants on the Protestant side (and the only one who had not been in exile on the continent during Mary's reign) the precise extent of his involvement in the two prepared statements in defence of the Protestant position is not clear. The first day which began with a Protestant statement in favour of a vernacular liturgy introduced by Robert Horne (with a list of signatories in which Geste's name occurs last), was the only one to be in any sense a debate, though, even then, the Catholic bishops had prepared no equivalent statement of their position, it being left to Dr Henry Cole, Dean of St Paul's, to reply at length in opposition. On the second day, the Catholic disputants refused to follow the prescribed order to initiate the debate with their own prepared statement, and the proceedings progressed no further than procedural arguments, with no actual debate on either the second or third propositions. It was only after this fiasco, with the Catholic bishops now discredited, heavily fined and two of them sent to the Tower, that the final form of the Uniformity Bill was introduced (with the amended 1552 Prayer Book as the designated form of worship). And after debate in both houses, it passed into law as the decisive instrument in the Elizabethan Settlement of religion.

That Geste had some, if not a major part in this process, as claimed by the older historians Strype and Burnet and his biographer, Dugdale, seems likely, though far from proven, and his inclusion among the Westminster disputants as the only one who had not been in exile may favour this possibility, as Haugaard has suggested.[71] More problematic however is the unsigned and undated letter, now among the Parker MSS at Corpus Christi College, Cambridge,[72] next to a letter from Cecil to Parker in December 1566 sending 'this' (presumably the unsigned letter) 'w[hi]ch was don by my lord of Rochester, before he was Bushop' that Cecil had come across while looking for another 'writing w[hi]ch yo[u]r] grace desired, but yet I can not find it'.[73] Was this in fact Geste's letter or was the juxtaposition of the two documents accidental? The letter preserved at Corpus is clearly not in Geste's hand, but a copy – without its ending and his signature. E. C. Ratcliff, in correspondence with J. E. Neale in the 1950s, questioned Geste's authorship, not so much because of this deficiency but on the ground of Geste's belief in a real presence of Christ in the eucharist (though without identifying at what point in the letter this doctrinal divergence occurred) and he tentatively suggested John Jewel as a possible

---

71. W. P. Haugaard, *Elizabeth and the English Reformation* (Cambridge: University Press, 1968), pp. 98, 109.
72. CCCC MS 106, pp. 413–16. The text has been printed a number of times, e.g. Dugdale, pp. 142–49; H. Gee, *The Elizabethan Prayer Book and Ornaments* (London: Church Association, 1902), pp. 215–24, who, however, places it in the reign of Edward VI at the time the first Prayer Book (1549) was being considered for revision (*c.* 1552) rather than 1559 (pp. 31–50), a view accepted by (among others) W. S. Hudson, *The Cambridge Connection and the Elizabethan Settlement of 1559* (Durham NC: Duke University Press, 1980), p. 96, but firmly rejected by Haugaard (1964) in the article cited in n. 75 below at pp. 178f.
73. CCCC MS 106, p. 411.

alternative.[74] Haugaard is probably correct in thinking that it was the final section 'Of receiving [communion] standing or kneeling' which the letter treats as a matter 'indifferent' that lay behind Ratcliff's doubts about Geste's authorship;[75] for Ratcliff may have seen here echoes of the earlier controversy about kneeling in 1552 involving John Knox and Cranmer and the last minute addition to the Second Prayer Book of the so-called 'Black rubric' with its strong denial of Christ's real presence. But the author of the letter does not seem to have seen it as a doctrinal issue. 'Standing' rather than kneeling had been the practice of the early church, but both were lawful, and the choice should be left to 'every man' to 'follow ye one waye, or ye other'.[76]

On balance, Geste still remains the most likely candidate for the authorship of the letter once Ratcliff's objections over its alleged doctrinal inconsistency are met. The tone of the letter to Cecil, which is not only deferential (as was customary) but somewhat self-deprecatory, defensive and at times convoluted, is not far removed from that of the letter he wrote to Parker about his Psalms translation when bishop of Rochester,[77] as well as that of his earlier *Treatise* of 1548. The letter clearly takes the first Prayer Book (1549) rather than the second (1552), which is nowhere mentioned, as its point of departure – a point not lost on Neale in his reconstruction of the Elizabethan Settlement[78] – and this choice may well have reflected the preference of the Queen. But the ten points discussed in the letter also indicate a definite divergence from it, some consistent with the 1552 Book and its 1559 successor, but others which were not adopted in the 1559 Book, a fact which suggested to Haugaard that Geste was proposing a

74. See J. E. Neale, *Elizabeth I and her Parliaments 1559–1581* (London: Cape, 1953), p. 77, n. 1 on the correspondence with Ratcliff and Norman Sykes. See also Ratcliff's, 'The English Usage of Eucharistic Consecration 1548–1662' (1957) reprinted in *Liturgical Studies*, ed. by A. H. Couratin and D. H. Tripp (London: S.P.C.K., 1976), pp. 203–21, especially p. 220 n. 39.
75. William P. Haugaard, 'The Proposed Liturgy of Edmund Guest', *Anglican Theological Review*, xlvi (1964), 177–89, especially pp. 177, 183–85.
76. Dugdale, Appendix IV, p. 149, from CCCC MS 106, p. 416.
77. CCCC MS 114, p. 465; Dugdale, p. 141.
78. J. E. Neale, 'The Elizabethan Acts of Supremacy and Uniformity', *English Historical Review*, lxv (1950), 304–32. Neale's reconstruction was questioned by N. L. Jones, *Faith by Statute* (Royal Historical Society Studies in History, London: Royal Historical Society, 1982), and the debate on this, the Queen's preferences and her religious position, is likely to continue: Patrick Collinson, 'Elizabeth I (1533–1603)' (*ODNB*); Christopher Haigh, *English Reformations: Religion, Politics, and Society under the Tudors* (Oxford: Clarendon Press, 1993), ch. 14; Diarmaid MacCulloch, *Tudor Church Militant: Edward VI and the Protestant Reformation* (London: Allen Lane, 1999), pp. 185–222; Roger Bowers, 'The Chapel Royal, the First Edwardian Prayer Book, and Elizabeth's Settlement of Religion, 1559', *Historical Journal*, 43 (2000), 317–44; Susan Doran, 'Elizabeth I's Religion: the Evidence of her Letters', *JEH* 51 (2000), 699–720.

somewhat different revision of the Prayer Book liturgy to that eventually adopted, in some particulars more 'conservative', in others 'taking a different direction'.[79] More than that, it is clear that some of the proposals were at variance with the Queen's wishes as was evident in the new Ornaments rubric included in the Act of Uniformity[80] as well as ceremonial practice in the Royal Chapel.[81] This may account to some extent for the defensive tone of the letter at the beginning and the end.

Four of the ten points defend changes to the 1549 rite which had been adopted in 1552, though the letter makes no reference to the revision itself, preferring to justify the changes from scripture and the practice of the early church. Thus, ceremonies in the 1549 Book 'taken awaie as evill vsed' [in 1552] should not be revived now, 'thoughe they be not evill of themselves but might be well vsed' (point 1). The 'ceremonies' he had in mind were not identified, though presumably included practices such as exorcism, the crisom and anointings in the 1549 baptism rite that had been dropped in 1552 and left out in 1559. Whether there was any implicit reference here to certain liturgical ceremonies in the Royal Chapel as well is not clear and perhaps unlikely, but the fourth point, on clerical vesture, does appear to run directly counter to the 1559 Ornaments rubric and the Queen's express wishes: the surplice (replacing the 'white albe plain, with a vestment or cope' ordered in 1549 and therefore required by the Ornaments rubric) is, it states, 'enough' for the celebrating of communion as for other services – a point which was to prove a matter of contention with the returning Marian exiles, who rejected even the surplice as acceptable vesture. The other two points simply endorsed changes made in 1552 which were carried over into the 1559 revision. Praying for the dead in the Communion (part of the 1549 prayer of intercession) 'is not now vsed' (i.e. in the 1552 rite) and by implication should not be revived (point 7); and the sacrament should be received 'in our handes' at Communion (point 9), another measure adopted in 1552 and incorporated in the 1559 Book.

Of the remaining points, two (2 and 3) appear to relate to practices which had been revived during the Marian period but which the letter now wished to see eliminated: the Cross (evidently images of, rather than the sign of the cross, which had been retained in the 1552 baptism rite and carried over into that of 1559) and processions[82] which had not featured in the

---

79. Haugaard (1964), 179–80, 185.
80. 'Prouided always ... that suche orname[n]ts of the Churche, and of the ministers thereof, shalbe retained and be in vse as was in this Churche of England, by aucthority of Parliament, in the second yere of the raygne of Kyng Edward the vi. vntil other order shalbe therein take[n] ...'.
81. E.g. the cross and candles on the altar in the Royal Chapel which she insisted should be returned after they had been removed while she was away in the country during the summer of 1559; Haugaard (1968), 185–200.
82. Points 2 and 3 in the letter.

1549 rite in any case and which in the form of a processional Litany had been prohibited as early as the 1547 Injunctions. Such an attack on the Cross was a remarkable act of temerity on Geste's part in the context of the Queen's known attachment to it and her insistence on retaining her own cross (and candles) on the altar of the Royal Chapel, and it was not surprising in the circumstances that he confined his defence of this point to citing the classic text from Epiphanius, who once destroyed a painted image of Christ he had discovered in a church, and a few other patristic precedents.

Of particular interest are the parallels between the remaining points and proposals in the two documents of the earlier Cologne Reformation of the 1540s, copies of which, as already indicated, Geste possessed and annotated.[83] The most contentious issue raised in the eighth and longest of the points concerned the form of consecration in the eucharist: whether reciting Christ's words of institution at the Last Supper were sufficient or whether the bread and wine were not properly 'consecrated' without prayer and invocation. The Cologne *Deliberatio* had fallen short of contemporary Catholic practice on precisely this point, as the authors of the *Antididagma* pointed out. For though the *Deliberatio* retained the ancient *Sursum Corda* with a Preface commemorating Creation, the Fall and Christ's redemption on the Cross, it contained no invocatory prayer before the words of Institution were sung. Moreover, the *Deliberatio* claimed, in common with the Lutheran tradition, that 'the whole substance of the sacrament is contained in these words', a passage which Geste marked in the margin of his own copy.[84] That this was also an issue when the first English Prayer Book (1549) was being drawn up is evident from the *Questions on the Mass* sent to the bishops and selected divines in the winter of 1547–48, predictably dividing those who followed the 'old religion' from their Protestant opponents.[85] And a similar concern is evident in writings like Geste's and one by Richard Bonner addressed to people in a position to influence the course of reform.[86]

83. For his copy of the *Deliberatio* see Cat. no. H42 (fig. 10.2–3) and for the *Antididagma,* C95 (fig. 10.4).

84. 1548 edition, f. 210v. Geste had also marked in the margins parts of the section in the copy of the *Antididagma* (Paris, 1549 edition) which related to the question, 'An sine prece canonica, Ecclesiae consecratur Sacramentum', ff. 100r, 101r.

85. The issue is implicitly raised in Q.4 of the set, 'Wherein consisteth the Mass by Christ's institution' (text in Gilbert Burnet, *The History of the Reformation of the Church of England,* ed. by Nicholas Pocock (Oxford: Clarendon Press, 1865), vol. V, pp. 197–217, especially pp. 203–5), to judge by the answers of some of those questioned; more explicitly in the set of thirteen *Questiones de Missa,* 'Whether the communion or the Supper of the Lord should not be ryghtly ministered by scripture, if there were no moo words spoken, nor any other thing done at the administration of the same then that saint Paul reherseth i.Cor.11' (Bodleian MS Add. C.197, f. 66v).

86. E.g. Richard Bonner, author of *A Treatyse of ye Ryght Honourynge and Wourshyppyng of our Saviour Iesus Christe in the Sacrame[n]t* (Imprinted at Londo[n]: [By Nicholas Hill] for Gawlter Lynne ..., [1548]; STC 3287) dedicated to archbishop

For Geste, no 'consecratory' prayer additional to Christ's words of institution was required: the words themselves were 'consecratory' as he indicates in his marginal note to the relevant rubric in his copy of the *Deliberatio* (f. 210). As he put it in his 1548 *Treatise,* before the words of institution were uttered, the bread and wine were 'prophane and unholy', but afterwards, 'they be consecrate and made of prophane the holy sacramentes exhibitiues, of Christes body and bloud'.[87] In the eighth point in his letter to Cecil, he made it clear that he objected to the prayer in the 1549 Prayer Book for much the same reasons as he had criticised the invocation in the Roman mass. First, because 'petitition is not part of consecration because Christ in ordaining the sacrament made no petition, but a thanksgiving', i.e. to 'bless' is to 'give thanks'. And secondly, because the words in the 1549 prayer that the 'bread and wyne may be Christis body and blude … maketh for [th]e popishe transubsta[n]tiatio[n]'.[88] Geste remained unconvinced by the arguments of the Cologne *Antididagma* and, although there is no indication here of his preferred alternative, the 1559 Settlement adopted the wording of the prayer in the 1552 Book which contained no invocatory component but was a prayer for the communicants.

The two remaining points discussed in the letter related to the division of the service into two parts, and again the Cologne precedent seems to have played a part in Geste's thinking even though he did not follow it in all details but, as was his practice, supported his arguments with patristic texts. Hermann's proposals for Cologne were distinctive in providing for a separate preparatory service on the Saturday evening for intending communicants with a rubric to the effect that no person was to be admitted to communion before confession, catechizing and absolution.[89] The Sunday service itself was divided into two parts, following the practice, it claimed, 'of the old Church', so that those not of the congregation (i.e. the unbaptised) and the unrepentant would be excluded 'before the ministration of the sacrament should begin' (f. 208). The communicants were then to assemble at some appointed place 'nigh the altar'.[90] Geste's annotations indicate an

Cranmer, which made extensive use of Martin Bucer's reply to the Cologne *Antididagma.* Bonner had earlier written to Bucer on this same question. His letter has not survived, only Bucer's reply (4 September 1548), CCCC MS 113, pp. 315–29. See Constantin Hope, 'An English Version of Parts of Bucer's Reply to the Cologne *Antididagma* of 1544', *JTS* ns, xi (1960), pp. 94–110; Gordon Jeannes, 'Is the Institution Narrative Necessary in the Eucharist? The Opinion of Martin Bucer, Corpus Christi, Cambridge, MS 113, pp. 315–324' in *The Serious Business of Worship: Essays in Honour of Bryan D. Spinks*, ed. by M. Ross and S. Jones (Edinburgh: T. & T. Clark, 2012), pp. 88–100; text and translation of Bucer's letter.

87. Dugdale ed., p. 79.
88. Dugdale ed., p. 148.
89. Ff. 195 ff. in the 1548 English edition which Geste owned.
90. He has underlined the phrase on f. 209 and marked the passage with a line in the margin. However, in none of his ten points does he touch on the issue of where

interest in all these features. In the Preparatory service, he notes the requirement for confession (f. 195) and the form of absolution provided (f. 202). And in the long rubric before the *Sursum corda* he notes the warnings against the unrepentant who presume nonetheless to present themselves for communion and those who neglect the benefit of communion: both offend God, provoke his judgment and 'hurt the congregation very sore' (ff. 208v–209). In the fifth of the points in his letter to Cecil, Geste provides some patristic and scholastic precedents for dividing the service into two parts so that those being instructed for baptism (the 'learners') and those undergoing penance were excluded before the second part (the sacrament) began. Similarly, in his sixth point, Geste proposed that only those taking part in both sections of the service would be permitted to recite the Creed, again citing patristic precedent for it being restricted to the 'faithful' (Dugdale ed., pp. 145–46). The first Prayer Book had recognised this division, at least to the extent that a rubric at the offertory required those not intending to receive Communion to leave at that point, but this restriction did not apply to the Creed which had already occurred at an earlier point in the liturgy, as it had in the Cologne reform proposals. The second Prayer Book (1552) omitted this instruction altogether, as did that of 1559, though both envisaged that there would be occasions when there would be no Communion after the offertory, for which eventuality a choice of collects was provided to follow the prayer for the church, and the service would conclude at that point. In both instances, therefore, Geste's preferences were not followed in the Elizabethan Prayer Book.

> the communion is to take place, how this related to the position of existing altars, or the type of bread to be used. The Royal Injunctions of 1559 established what has been termed the 'peripatetic principle', ruling that the Holy Table be 'set in the place where the altar stood ... saving when the Communion of the Sacrament is to be distributed; at which time the same shall be so placed in good sort within the chancel, as whereby the minister may be more conveniently heard of the communicants in his prayer and ministration, and the communicants also more conveniently and in more number communicate with the said minister, And after the Communion done, from time to time the same holy table to be placed where it stood before' (Frere, III, pp. 27–28). The Royal Injunctions also laid down the type of communion bread to be used: no longer the 'common fine bread' in use during the reign of Edward VI, but wafer bread (Frere, III, p. 28). Neither of the Injunctions, however, appeared in the visitation articles of the bishops except in those issued by Parker and Geste. Geste's Visitation Articles and Injunctions for Rochester Cathedral (1565) included items on wafer bread (items 30 and 20 respectively, Frere, III, pp. 151 and 154) and those for the diocese in the same year: item 18 of the Articles on wafer bread, while item 18 of the Injunctions stipulated that 'when there is no Communion then shall a desk be set in place where the communion table should stand at the time of the administration thereof, and the priest or curate at the same desk to read all the service of the Communion, his face being towards the people' (Frere, III, pp. 159 and 161). On this, see K. Fincham and N. Tyacke, *Altars Restored: The Changing Face of English Religious Worship, 1547 – c. 1700* (Oxford: University Press, 2007), especially p. 46.

What are we to make of these proposals, then, in the context of the revision process which resulted in the Prayer Book of 1559? Geste writes as if he is defending the 'new service' from criticism with arguments derived almost exclusively from scripture and early church practice, although he is clearly well aware of the Cologne reforms. The service appears to be in its final form only awaiting 'parliament with one voice to enacte it, & the realme with true harte to vse it'.[91] The first Prayer Book (1549) was evidently Geste's point of departure – perhaps at the Queen's instigation. But he was seriously at odds with it at a number of points, such as its ceremonies, the prescribed vestments, prayers for the dead and the prayer of consecration. Most of his proposals in the letter were in line with the form of service eventually adopted in 1559 (a slightly, but significantly, modified version of the 1552 book, including the omission of the 'Black rubric' on kneeling to receive communion), but some of them diverged in detail from it. It would be possible to argue, therefore, that his letter was in fact a defence of the choice of the 1552 book for the Settlement as against that of 1549 which had evidently been the preferred starting point – with Geste proposing some further ideas of his own which were not eventually adopted, such as the division of the service into two, limiting the Creed to communicants, arguing for the surplice as the appropriate clerical dress for all the services of the church and standing for communion as an acceptable alternative to kneeling. It may not therefore be necessary to go the whole way with Haugaard (1964) who suggested that Geste's letter amounted to a proposed liturgy of his own, in some details 'beyond the 1552 book', but otherwise leaving the 1549 book 'substantially as it was'. Whatever view is taken – and the obscurity of Geste's argument at times and the lack of clarity at crucial points does not make for a straightforward choice between the different solutions proposed since Neale wrote in 1950 – it seems likely that these proposals were drafted at a time when the Queen may still have been hoping to make the First Book the basis of the Settlement, but before she was persuaded that only some form of compromise involving a modified version of the Second Book was likely to command the support of those she most needed for the future leadership of her church. Geste played a part in that process and remained in her favour, even though some of his ideas appear to have diverged from hers.

91. Dugdale, p. 149. The defensive tone of the letter to Cecil is evident from the start: 'Right honourable that you might well vnderstande that I have neither vngodlye allowed any thinge against [th]e scripture neither vnstedfastlye doen any thinge contrary to my writynge, neither rashely without just causse put away [tha]t, wiche be well suffered, nor vndiscretelye for noveltie brought in that, wich might be better left out, I am so bold to write to youre honoure some causses of [th]e order taken in [th]e new service, wich enterprice thoughe you may iustlie reprove for [th]e simple handlynge, yet I trust you will take it well for my good meanynge' (pp. 142–43).

Geste and the Articles of Religion

Geste also played a significant part in doctrinal definition, contributing a crucial section in Article 28 of the Elizabethan *Thirty-nine Articles* on the eucharist in 1563 and supplying his own gloss on its interpretation in letters to Cecil[92] written in 1566 and 1571, once more demonstrating a certain independent turn of mind which had characterised his proposals for liturgical reform. His interest in the doctrinal issues as well as liturgical practice was evident in the 1548 *Treatise* and is further confirmed by the large number of books he acquired and annotated relating not only to the controversies with Catholic theologians, but also to the divisions within Protestantism, particularly between the later Lutherans and the Calvinists.[93] Geste was clearly ill at ease with some of the stark negativities (as it would have seen to him) of the *Forty-two Articles* of Edward VI (1553),[94] and his view of Christ's presence in the eucharist showed closer affinities to the 'middle way' of his Cambridge colleague, the exiled Martin Bucer from Strasbourg, whose writings figure prominently among the Protestant authors in his library.[95] Ironically it was the single word 'only' in the paragraph he contributed to Article 28, replacing the more negative statement in the 1553 equivalent (Article 29), that was to cause him the most embarrassment in dealing with the objections of Richard Cheyney, bishop of Gloucester, and which was the immediate occasion of his letter to Cecil in December 1566.

Cheyney, who was in difficulties with his superiors for more reasons than doctrinal ones, had objected to the wording of the article on the grounds that to say that 'The body of Christ is given, taken, and eaten in the Supper *only* after an heavenly and spiritual manner' 'did take away the presence of Christ's body in the Sacrament'.[96] In his letter to Cecil, Geste denied this

92. The text of the letters, not known to Dugdale when writing in 1840, was included in G. F. Hodges, *Bishop Guest: Articles Twenty-eight and Twenty-nine* (London: Rivington, Percival, 1894), pp. 22–23, 24–27. Quotations from the Articles are taken from Charles Hardwick, *A History of the Articles of Religion* (London: George Bell & Sons, 1895).

93. See Subject Index to his annotations, Appendix XI 2, s.v. 'Eucharist'.

94. Particularly the penultimate section of Article 28, which Geste's paragraph replaced, adducing as arguments against the 'reall and bodilie presence' of Christ, that a body (and therefore Christ's body) 'can not bee presente at one time in many, and diuerse places' and that since his Ascension 'Christe was taken vp into heauen, and there shall continue vnto thende of the worlde' (Hardwick, p. 330).

95. Fourteen items (Cat. nos. B98–110, P47) including four with annotations on eucharistic doctrine.

96. Geste's summary of Cheyney's objection, Hodges, p. 22. On Cheyney and his doctrinal position, particularly Jewel's assertion that he approved of 'Luther's opinion respecting the eucharist', see Caroline J. Litzenberger, 'Richard Cheyney, Bishop of Gloucester: An Infidel in Religion?', *Sixteenth-Century Journal*, 25 (1994), 567–84; John Jewel to Heinrich Bullinger, *The Works of John Jewel ... Fourth*

inference, claiming that 'this word "only" did not exclude the presence of Christ's body from the Sacrament, but only the grossness and sensibleness in the receiving thereof.' And he went on to cite others on both sides of the Reformation divide who recognised this distinction: 'even D. Harding' (the Catholic) as well as John Jewel, the Protestant bishop of Salisbury.[97] Five years later, he revisited the matter again in another letter to Cecil, again with Cheyney's objection in mind, and at a time when the *Thirty-nine Articles*, approved by Convocation, were awaiting the Queen's ratification. This time, after giving much the same explanation as he had given in his earlier letter, he was prepared to make further concessions: 'Yet for all this, to avoid offence and contention, the word "only" may well be left out as not needful.' And, after making reference to the threat of excommunication which hung over Cheyney's head, he added, 'I think if this word "only" were put out of the book for his sake, it were the best'.[98]

Similarly, Geste acknowledged the difficulties of the word 'faith' in the section of Article 28 that followed: 'And the meane whereby the body of Christ is receaued and eaten in the Supper, is fayth'. For this raised a related, and highly contentious issue which had divided Continental Protestantism ever since the eucharistic controversies between the Lutherans and the Zwinglians began in the mid-1520s: 'Whether the evil do receive Christ's body in the Sacrament' or not. The Lutherans affirming that they do, albeit to their condemnation; the Reformed tradition insisting that only those who have faith can receive Christ's body, the 'evil' or faithless receiving only the sacraments of bread and wine. Geste argued that if the word 'profitably' were inserted before 'receaued and eaten' in the article then this contentious issue (the so-called *manducatio indignorum*) would be 'quite taken away' and controversy avoided.[99] However, to his great concern, Geste had discovered that the copy of the Articles that was to be presented by Parker to the Queen for her ratification contained an article on precisely this issue ('Evil men receive not the body of Christ') – an article which, he claimed, was 'not in the printed books either Latin or English', and which if 'confirmed and authorised by the queen's grace … will cause much business' because (as he argued) 'it is quite contrary to the Scripture [especially I Corinthians 11.27–29] and to the doctrine of the fathers'.[100] Geste's preference was for the omission of any such article, which had not even been part of the original Articles of 1553 or the 1563

Portion, ed. for the Parker Society by J. Ayre (Cambridge: University Press, 1850), pp. 1271–72; *ODNB*, 'Richard Cheyney' by Jane Reedy Ladley.

97. Hodges, p. 23.
98. Hodges, p. 23.
99. The Article would therefore read: 'But the mean whereby the body of Christ is *profitably* received and eaten in the Supper is faith', Hodges, p. 25.
100. Hodges, p. 25.

revision. Characteristically, Geste did in the end subscribe to Article 29 and to the unchanged text of Article 28 (with 'only' remaining in the text and without the insertion of 'profitably' which he had suggested, in a vain attempt to accommodate Cheyney's concerns) perhaps as Darwell Stone implied because, like many later Anglicans, he found it possible to do so without actually compromising his position.[101] He had shown a similar flexibility in subscribing to the 1559 Prayer Book despite the reservations and alternative proposals contained in his letter to Cecil at the time.

The Bishops' Bible

That Geste had some part in the projected revision of the English Bible, which became known as the *Bishops' Bible* eventually published in 1568, is confirmed by his undated letter to Parker in which he writes of sending his 'booke again with such notes & advertisementes that for my busynes I could well gather' and requesting their return 'when you have redde them', 'ffor Mr Secretary [Cecil] wold see them'.[102] The extent of Geste's involvement in Parker's project however is not altogether clear. Neither his name or his initials appears among the revisers credited in the letter Parker sent to Cecil in October 1568 just before the book was presented to the Queen , and there is no 'E.R' among the admittedly incomplete list of revisers' initials printed at the end of each book in the published version of the *Bishops' Bible*.[103] Geste's letter suggests that it was the translation of the Psalms that Parker had sent him for annotation and comment, but Parker's own list sent to Cecil omits the Psalms altogether. It was only the published version that had initials at the end of the Psalms and these were 'T.B.' (not 'E.R.') which Strype (1711) suggested stood for 'Thomas Becon', while William Aldis Wright (1905), more plausibly, conjectured Thomas Bickley, a chaplain of Parker who later became bishop of Chichester.[104] Was Geste simply being asked to look over and comment on the version of the Psalms that had already been completed

---

101. Darwell Stone, *A History of the Doctrine of the Holy Eucharist* (London: Longmans, Green & Co., 1909), vol. II, p. 213.

102. CCCC MS 114, p. 465, transcribed in Dugdale, p. 141. For Parker's involvement in the project, see V. J .K. Brook, *A Life of Archbishop Parker* (Oxford: Clarendon Press, 1962, reprinted with corrections, 1965), pp. 179–80, 246–49; S. L. Greenslade in *The Cambridge History of the Bible,* 3 vols. Cambridge: University Press, 1963–1970), vol. III, pp. 159–61.

103. *Correspondence of Matthew Parker*, ed. for the Parker Society by J. Bruce and T. T. Perowne (Cambridge: University Press, 1853), no. 258, pp. 334–37.

104. John Strype, *The Life and Acts of Matthew Parker* (1711), 3 vols (Oxford: Clarendon Press, 1821), vol. I, p. 222; D. S. Bailey, *Thomas Becon and the Reformation of the Church in England* (Edinburgh: Oliver and Boyd, 1952), p. 147 rejects Strype's suggestion; B. F. Westcott, *A General View of the History of the English Bible* (1868), 3rd ed. revised by W. A. Wright (London: Macmillan, 1905), p. 32.

by 'T.B.' whoever he was? Or had Geste originally been asked to prepare a revision of the Psalms translation, like the other contributing bishops and divines who had been allotted different books of the Bible for the project, but had not completed his assignment for some reason? Does the omission of the Psalms from Parker's list of contributors suggest that there had been a change of plan, perhaps because Geste had declined or had failed to complete his assignment, and the work had been subsequently re-assigned to 'T.B.'? Geste's letter to Parker suggests some diffidence, even awkwardness on his part as he returns the text of the Psalms translation, which might just possibly support this last conjecture.[105]

Whatever the explanation, Geste was certainly well equipped to perform the task which Parker had laid down for the contributors. What survives of his library was well stocked with aids for the study of the Hebrew text, with at least 39 books specifically on the Psalms, including a wide range of commentaries from the patristic and medieval periods as well as contemporary authors, Catholic as well as Protestant, twelve of them annotated.[106] His copy of a work by Rastell (R6), published in 1565–66, was wrapped in a sewn-in paper leaf, the verso of which consists of a fragment written in English in Geste's hand, apparently relating to a translation of the Psalms, detailing changes to the text – evidence of some activity on the project.

Other events and activities associated with Geste's career are less easy to relate to books in his library at Salisbury, but further research might well yield results. In September 1565, for example, he provided Cecil with a theological justification for military intervention in Scotland in his 'Pro defensione Religionis', which survives in the Lansdowne manuscripts,[107]

---

105. In addition to the extract cited at n. 102 above, Geste writes, 'If your grace will have me to amende them I am at your com[m]andement I will be with your grace upon frydaye to know your mynde & to have the booke[.] I have not altered [th]e translation but where it gyveth occasion of an errour.'; and (at the end), 'Thus trustynge that your grace will take in good part my rude handly[n]g of the psalmes ...', Dugdale, p. 141.

106. From the patristic period, Arnobius, the younger (Cat. no. A54) and Theodoret of Cyrus (T5), from the medieval, Dionysius the Carthusian (D12), the Byzantine, Euthymius (E58) and Haymo (H9), the humanist, Johann Reuchlin (R16), and among Catholic commentators, Jansen (J3–4), Puteo (P58), Titelman (T11) and Wild (W29). Among Protestants, Lutheran and Reformed, Aepinus (A4–8), Brentz (B73–74), Bucer (B98–99), Bugenhagen (B114), Calvin (C4), Cruciger (C113), Draconites (D23, D25), Luther (L53–56, M37), Meier (M27), Melanchthon (M43, M46), Mollerus (M76–77), Oecolampadius (O4–5), Rhegius (R18–20), and Siber (S54).

107. Written in response to 'a Question demanded upon the matter of Scotland'; BL Lansdowne MS 8, item 19, on which see Stephen Alford, *The Early Elizabethan Polity: William Cecil and the British Succession Crisis, 1558–1569* (Cambridge: University Press, 1998), pp. 133ff, who suggests that Geste's arguments are 'reminiscent' of John Ponet's *A Shorte Treatise of Politike Power* ([Strasbourg:

and there is a full-length sermon 'upon Repentance and Faith' preached before the Queen and her court in Lent 1560–61 extant among Parker's papers which has been taken as evidence that Geste was at heart a 'free-will' man, far removed from the Calvinistic outlook of many returning exiles. The greater part of the sermon – the only example of Geste's preaching to be preserved in its entirety – was a call to the court for self-examination and amendment of life in the light of God's law, drawing on exempla from classical authors, St Augustine and recent writers such as Erasmus and Thomas More, as well as elaborating on the demands of the Ten Commandments and the dangers of delaying repentance, and it concluded with what McCullough has termed a 'decidedly un-Genevan' claim that Christ's call to repent and believe the gospel 'doth unfaynedlie belong to all men and shall turn to all mens salvation that kepe it', and the fact that 'all men be not saved' is 'not because god would not but because we will not'. That Geste felt strongly on this point is clear from annotations he made in copies of two works by Jean Veron in his library. Both were published in 1561, one on predestination (V20), dedicated to the Queen herself, the other on free will (V21), to Robert Dudley. At several places in both works Geste has indicated his dissent from Veron's opinions, with comments in the margins such as 'harde to ye peoples understanding'(V21, at E7v), and at one point in the former he has protested, 'ye principall cause of o[u]r damnatio[n] is not goddes p[re]destination but o[u]r synne' (V20, at D4r) – a sentiment very much in keeping with his sermon the year before.

Geste was also chosen by the Queen to deliver a sermon at court on Good Friday 1565, in which he is reported to have preached on the real presence of Christ in the eucharist, and again on the first Sunday of Lent in 1566 as one of a series of Lenten sermons, according to a list drawn up by Parker, but only a brief extract from the former survives and nothing of the latter, though there are leaves bound into one of his copies of a Latin New Testament containing an exegesis in English of Matthew 16 which may derive from one of his expository sermons.[108] His library, in fact, contains just over eighty books of sermons, many of them being 'postils' or homilies on the

---

Printed by the heirs of W. Köpfel], 1556; STC 20178). If he did have a copy of this work, it has unfortunately not survived in what remains of his library, though one other item of Ponet's (P42) does and he owned a book which had once belonged to him (V15).

108. Cat. no. E29. The sermon on 'Repentance and Faith' is preserved in CCCC MS 104, pp. 277–95, and transcribed in Dugdale, Appendix VIII, pp. 179–200, especially pp. 199–200, on which see P. E. McCullough, *Sermons at Court: Politics and Religion in Elizabethan and Jacobean Preaching* (Cambridge: University Press, 1998), pp. 95–97 and accompanying *Calendar* (on diskette), p. 10, where Lent 1561 is suggested as the date when it was delivered. For his 1565 Good Friday sermon, see below p. 86 and n. 181. For his 1566 Lenten sermon, see McCullough, *Calendar*, p. 17.

liturgical lections for the different Sundays and feast days of the Christian year, and forty-five of them are annotated, suggesting that some of these may have formed the starting point for some of his own sermons. As with his collection of Psalms commentaries, the choice of these is very wide-ranging, including examples from the patristic period, such as the homilies of Peter Chrysologus (C65), Cyprian's 'Sermon on the Lord's Prayer'(C128), and sermons by Bede (part of A14), Eusebius of Emessa (E57), Gregory the Great (G31) and Maximus of Tyre (M19), though, surprisingly, lacking in other examples from the patristic period, such as those of John Chrysostom (unless these were among books lost or damaged after his death). Among his earlier printed books, there are examples from the medieval period, such as Albertus Magnus (A14–15), Aquinas (A465), Herolt (H43), Hugh of St Cher (H82–84), Jacobus de Voragine (J2), William of Paris (G49), and the anonymous 'Sermo de Coena Domini' (C127) attributed in the Middle Ages to the third-century Cyprian of Carthage. And among contemporaries, Catholic authors figure prominently, such as Antonius Broeckwey (B94), Vincenzo Cicogna (C75), Eisengrein (E10), Helmes (H18–22, a five-volume set of liturgical homilies, three of them annotated), Hofmeister (H62, H65), Nausea (N8), Pelbárt (P15), Placentius (P37), Radulphus (R5), Royard (R39), Sasbout (S27), Schopper the younger (S39),[109] no less than five examples of Johann Wild (W31, W37–40), Thomas Watson's two sermons on the eucharist (W2), and Georg Witzel (W49), with, as was to be expected, even more Protestant examples, particularly Lutheran, as well as Reformed.[110]

As bishop first of Rochester, then of Salisbury, Geste played a part with Parker in upholding and enforcing the Elizabethan Settlement of religion, particularly on the increasingly divisive issue of clerical vesture on which he contributed a paper (preserved in the Lansdowne manuscripts) in support of the official position, and he acted as one of the ecclesiastical commissioners who sat regularly in London seeking to enforce conformity among the clergy. In 1565 he was one of the bishops who assisted Parker in drawing up the *Book of Advertisements* and was the only member of the commission to support Parker in refusing the appeal of some twenty influential reformers led by Laurence Humphrey, President of Magdalen, and Thomas Sampson, Dean of Christ Church, Oxford, for liberty to follow their consciences on

---

109. S39 (3 vols, all annotated).
110. Five books of Luther (L64, L66–67, L69, L76), six of Brentz (B80–81, B84–86, B91), and three of Georg Meier (M29, M38–39); and single examples by Artopoeus (A56), Bugenhagen (B116), Culman (C122), Caspar Huberinus (H81), Loss (L44), Simon Pauli, *the elder*, of Rostock (P10), Selneccer (S44) and Wigand (W19). Among Reformed and other non-Lutheran authors, four of Bullinger (B120, B124, B132–33), five of Gualtherus (G37–41), two each of Brandmueller (B63–64) and Lavater (L19, L21), and single examples by Bèze (B22), Conrad Clauser (C77), Maecardus (M4), Mainardo (M6) and Oecolampadius (O16).

the use of the surplice.[111] In the same year he was one of the commissioners who headed the drive for ritual conformity in the diocese of London, supporting the deprivation of one of his own chaplains, Edward Brocklesby, vicar of Hemel Hempstead, for refusing to use the surplice.[112]

Right at the end of his life, as bishop of Salisbury, Geste took a stand on another issue which was threatening the unity of the Elizabethan church: the voluntary gatherings, mainly of clergy, known as 'prophesyings' – for preaching, discussion, biblical study, pastoral care and mutual criticism – which were regarded with suspicion in some quarters for being outside the structures of the church and potentially disruptive. The growth of such gatherings was welcomed by some, Grindal among them, because of their potential for clerical training, and even Parker may have been convinced of their value, but the Queen was strongly opposed and demanded their suppression. One of Geste's last recorded acts was to express his total opposition to such exercises in a reply (dated 18 December 1576) to archbishop Grindal's inquiry into these 'prophesyings'.[113]

Geste died in Salisbury the following year at the end of February, leaving gold rings to Lord Burghley, Sir Christopher Hatton and Sir Nicholas Bacon, money to the city of Salisbury, other legacies to his chaplains, servants, executors, and his brother [in-law], Christopher Leedes, and bequeathing all his books to the Cathedral Library, entrusting to the Dean and Chapter responsibility for taking measures to ensure their 'preservation and good keeping'.[114]

---

111. Fairhurst papers, Lambeth MS 2019. Geste's reply is in Strype, *Life of... Parker* (1821), III, App. XXXI, pp. 98–107, from BL, Lansdowne MS 7 item 92; Dugdale, App. VIII, pp. 201–11. The names of two signatories to the petition, Kervile and John Philpott, occur on three of Geste's books (B72, L41 and S17) but whether these identifications are correct and whether the books were given at this time or were intended to influence the outcome, it is clear that his attitude on this issue remained resolute. See Appendix X, s.v. Kervyle and Philpot.

112. Brett Usher, 'Edward Brocklesby: "the first put out of his living for the surplice"', *From Cranmer to Davidson: a Church of England Miscellany*, ed. by S. Taylor, for the Church of England Record Society (Woodbridge: Boydell, 1999), pp. 47–68.

113. Fairhurst papers, Lambeth MS 2003, f. 33.

114. Dugdale, pp. 55–56.

II. RECONSTRUCTING GESTE'S LIBRARY

Geste's bequest of 1577 and its significance

Geste bequeathed his books in 1577 to Salisbury Cathedral library which he described in his will as 'now decayed',

> there to be kept for perpetual remembrance and token of my favor and good will, to advance and further the Estate and Dignity of the same my Church and See ...[1]

The bequest in itself was highly significant, amounting to a 're-founding' of the collection. It represented a new initiative in provision for cathedral libraries in the post-Reformation era, larger in scale than any comparable developments taking place in other ecclesiastical libraries at the time until the even larger bequests of Richard Bancroft (to Lambeth Palace Library) in 1610 and Tobie Matthew (to York Minster) in 1628.[2] The cathedral libraries of England had suffered devastating losses in the upheavals of the Reformation and the monastic dissolutions and, following the dispersal of much of their collections, had shown few signs of recovery in the years that followed. As a 'secular' foundation, Salisbury had perhaps not suffered such a major dispersal of its medieval library as some (especially those of the 'religious' foundations) and in fact had retained much of its manuscript collection as Neil Ker had shown.[3] But Ker had not been able to find a single *printed* book from its pre-Reformation library, and although many books now in the Cathedral Library carry early imprints none of these is believed to have been acquired from the period before Geste's bequest in 1577.

The early history of the post-medieval library at Salisbury has still to be written.[4] The picture is unclear, but, from the little evidence that has come to light, the condition of the library was very unsatisfactory and had been so for some time. There is no record of donations from this period, and no Register of donors survives, if there ever was one. The Chapter Acts Books and accounts record no money having been spent by the Dean and Chapter on the purchase of books other than the required service books. Yet the Royal

1. Dugdale, p. 55.
2. C. B. L. Barr and D. G. Selwyn, 'Major Ecclesiastical Libraries' in CHLB I, pp. 375–99.
3. 'Salisbury Cathedral Manuscripts and Patrick Young's Catalogue' in Ker, *BCL*; Ker, *MLGB*, pp. 171–76; Ker-Watson, *MLGB Suppl.*, pp. 60–61; N. R. Ker and A. J. Piper, *Medieval Manuscripts in British Libraries 4: Paisley–York* (Oxford: Clarendon Press, 1992), pp. 253–66, including a few dispersed MS items successfully reclaimed by Salisbury in 1985.
4. See, however, the brief sketch by Eward (first published 1983); Suzanne Eward is now working on a much fuller history based on years of research on the Cathedral archives and the library itself.

Injunctions, issued specifically to Salisbury Cathedral in 1559, had reiterated the requirement of the earlier set of 1547 under Edward VI, that the Chapter

> shall make a librarye in some convenient place within there [sic] churche within the space of one yeare next ensuinge the visitation, & shal lay in the same these books following: – Augustinus, Basill, Gregore Nazianzene, Hierome, Ambrose, Chrisostome, Cyprian, Theophilacte, Erasmus, Clemens Alexandrinus, Justinus Martyr, Paraphrases, annotationes ipsius, Novum Testamentum ac alios continentes theologiam and other good writers' works.[5]

Although a library building existed, there is little evidence that anything was done to stock the library with the required authors. Apart from copies of Erasmus's *Paraphrases of the New Testament*, none of the above, with the possible exception of a 1565 edition of Basil,[6] appears to have been acquired within the time specified or indeed by the time of Geste's bequest – unless we are to believe that all the library's copies of the others had been subsequently lost or destroyed. In his will, Geste had described the library as 'now decayed', and the impression of 'decay' to which Geste referred appears to be have been a long-standing problem, a judgment reinforced by the Chapter's reply to Bishop Jewel's interrogatory (no. 29) relating to the Cathedral muniments at his visitation of 1562, that all is in decay and it is their predecessors' fault.[7] In the midst of so many concerns, scandals and other failings that must have weighed heavily on the mind of Jewel at the next Visitation in 1568, the condition of the Cathedral's books and even the whereabouts of some of its muniments continued to feature,[8] and remained a concern when Geste conducted his visitation there in 1574.[9]

Although Jewel has often been credited with having 'built' the library or at least having had a major role in its re-founding, there is no evidence that any of his own books were left to Salisbury. The claim, made by earlier writers such as Daniel Featley (1609) and Francis Godwin (1616), appears to derive from a tradition that there had at one time been an 'inscription' which Dugdale (1840) stated 'was formerly fixed' 'on the said library', though no longer extant when he wrote. No such inscription has been found, if one ever existed. However, there is a statement about the respective roles of

---

5. Statute Book (H), f. 109; Frere, III, Injunction 8, noting the addition of Clement of Alexandria and Justin Martyr to the original list of recommended authors. The same injunction on libraries was also issued to Exeter and Hereford.
6. Edited by Musculus at shelf A.4.6. This has been rebound and the fore-edges trimmed, destroying in the process potentially valuable evidence of its provenance.
7. Frere, III, no. XXV, p. 124, n. 3.
8. Frere, III, no. XLVI, Injunctions 17 and 22, p. 203.
9   See Injunctions 1 and 5 (relating to the fabric of the building), Frere, III, no. LXX, p. 367.

7.1. Inscription in Geste's copy of Placidus (P38) relating to the 're-founding' of the Cathedral Library by bishops John Jewel and Edmund Geste.

Jewel and Geste (dated 1578) on a flyleaf in one of Geste's books at Salisbury (a commentary on the Psalms by Placidus (P38), published in 1559, at shelf E.5.8) which agrees (some minor variations apart) with the text of Dugdale's 'inscription', and it seems likely that this (or some version of it), rather than any tablet affixed to a wall of the library, was the source of the tradition.

Both versions make a distinction between Jewel's role ('Bibliotheca extructa est sumptibus ... Juellj') and Geste's ('[Bibliotheca] ... instructa vero libris a ... Gest').[10] Geste's bequest furnished the library with books, but what was implied by 'Bibliotheca extructa' in Jewel's case? Dugdale claimed that

10. Fig. 7.1. 'Hac [sic] bibliotheca [?e]xtructa est sumptibus Reuerendij in Chr[ist]o p[at]ris ac D.D. Jo: Juellj/ Sar[um] Epi[scopi] instructa vero libris a Re/uerendo in Chr[ist]o p[at]ri ac D.D. Ed. Gest eiusdem Eccl[es]iae Ep[iscop]o quor[um] memoria in benedicti[on]e erit. An[n]o D[o]m[in]i 1578'. The reading 'extructa' in E.5.8 is far from certain, and 'restructa' has been suggested in a correspondence between Neil Ker and the Cathedral Librarian Suzanne Eward in October 1977. A copy of Ker's letter is now preserved in E.5.8. The text in Dugdale reads 'extructa' and on balance this is to be preferred, despite its difficulties. The authorship of the text in E.5.8 is not known. It begins at the top of the page 'Hanc bibliothecam' with a false start (implying a different construction) both words being erased. It then resumes half way down the page (as reproduced above) but 'ac D.D' in both instances has been added in the same hand above the line. Is this version the original form of the text ('composed at the time of writing' [Stroud]) or is it a copy (not always accurate) of some (now lost) original? I am grateful to Daphne Stroud for allowing me to make use of her unpublished paper, 'Bishop Jewel and Salisbury Cathedral Library', which discusses these issues, and also to Suzanne Eward who first discovered this MS note in E.5.8, drew my attention to Stroud's paper and subsequently shared her views on these matters.

'Jewel before his death, had built a most beautiful library'. But the library had already been in existence by this time for over a century. More likely, Jewel had at some time during his episcopate provided new library fittings, such as bookcases, at his own expense with a view to a significant expansion of the library which would include the books which the Chapter was in any case required to purchase in accordance with the Injunctions of 1559. When it came to writing his will in 1571, Jewel made no mention of the Cathedral Library. But he did bequeath £20 for 'repairs' to the Cathedral, and this, with a further sum of nearly £15 was used a few years later by the Chapter on repairs to the fabric of the library.[11] Whether or not Jewel had ever intended making a bequest of books to Salisbury, in the event this did not happen, and the books that remained in the bishop's palace after his death were soon purchased by Magdalen College, Oxford.[12] Whatever contribution Jewel may have made, Geste must be regarded as the real founder of the present collection of printed books at Salisbury Cathedral.

Salisbury was apparently the first cathedral library to have been effectively re-founded after the Reformation by a single major benefaction. Others followed this pattern in the succeeding century, but it was still more usual for book collectors in his position to make life-time donations and bequests to academic, rather than ecclesiastical institutions. Matthew Parker was a case in point. As archbishop of Canterbury, Parker could not have been unaware of how far cathedral libraries were falling short of the require-ments of the Elizabethan Injunctions (1559) – including his own at Canter-bury. But instead, he chose to make donations to Cambridge University (1574) and Gonville and Caius College, and he bequeathed the rest, including his unique manuscript collection, to his old college, Corpus Christi. John Whitgift and others did the same. By contrast, Geste did not leave any books to his old Cambridge college (King's) – how much the memory of his expulsion from the college in 1554 may have been a factor in that decision can only be conjectured. He also had no heirs. But it was probably his concern at the decayed state of the library at Salisbury that was uppermost in his thinking.

Geste's library, at the time of his death in 1577, was evidently a very substantial one, as the memorial brass, erected by his executors, implies. Unfortunately, no early catalogues or donations register survive, and there is no inventory of his books attached to his will. Clearly there have been some losses to the collection over the years – probably substantial ones –

11. Eward, p. 5.
12. Eighty-four of Jewel's books have been traced by Ker, though the 220 chains bought may indicate more accurately the actual number that came from Salis-bury. See N. R. Ker, 'The Library of John Jewel', *BLR* 9 (1977), pp. 256–65; C. B. Dobson, 'The "Bel-Ami" Volumes in John Jewel's Library at Magdalen College, Oxford', *BLR* 16 (1998), pp. 225–32.

7.2. Inscription in Geste's copy of a book by John Jewel recording its
return to the Cathedral Library at the Restoration. Cat. no. J8.

as a result of 'borrowings' not returned and conditions in the library
building itself, for the Chapter Act books record repairs to the roof and
windows on various occasions after Geste's death. There were probably
further losses during the Civil War Period because at least one of his books
was apparently 'brought in' again after the Restoration in 1664, a book by
his predecessor, John Jewel, his reply to Harding.[13]

How far is a reconstruction of his library possible? Clearly, in the absence
of any contemporary catalogue or inventory, the primary evidence has to
be the books that survive on the shelves. In addition, there are indications
in the books themselves that may take us further than that and may make it
possible to conjecture the approximate size of the collection as it once
existed, even if it is now impossible to establish its exact content. But to
begin with what actually remains on the shelves: how is a 'Geste book' to
be recognised?

Ideally, the provenance of his books could be established by the presence
of an ownership inscription on the title page or flyleaf of each item or some
readily identifiable mark or 'fingerprint', such as an armorial binding or
bookplate, preferably with the date (and even the place) of acquisition. The
presence of manuscript annotations in his hand would be an added bonus,
because it would reinforce that evidence or provide alternative confirmation
of ownership where an inscription is lacking. However, inscriptions of
ownership are vulnerable to unscrupulous signature collectors or rebinding

13.   Cat. no. J8.

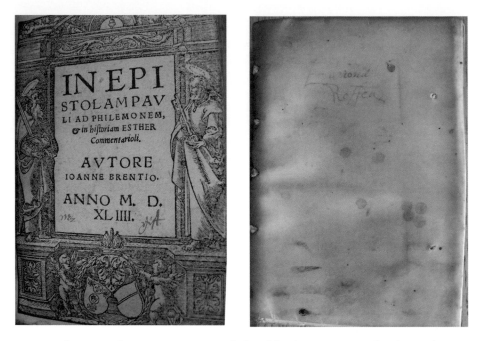

8. Geste's ownership inscriptions. 8.1 (left) Biblical commentary by the Lutheran, Johann Brentz (Cat. no. B89), one of only thirty- eight surviving such inscriptions in his books. 8.2 (right) An octavo of 1553 in parchment covers, with Geste's ownership inscription as bishop of Rochester. Cat. no. Z3.

when binders carelessly remove them by shearing off top or bottom edges where such signatures often occur. Geste's books fall far short of this ideal in almost every particular, with the exception of a few undated ownership inscriptions and the presence of his MS annotations. In his case, other 'fingerprints' have to be employed.

Geste's ownership inscriptions

In contrast with the surviving collections of his older contemporary, archbishop Thomas Cranmer (hundreds of whose books survive with his ownership inscription) or William Cecil (whose books often included dated ownership inscriptions), few of Geste's books carry his signature or name, and these occur mostly in books acquired during his period at Cambridge (1536–1554). Fifteen of these books carry imprint dates some years before his admission to Cambridge, though not more than seven of these carry any direct evidence of acquisition 'second-hand'.[14] Only two can be

14. E48 and F5, both given him by his uncle, John Brandisby. B102, B113, C82, E40 and V33 have annotations or traces of ownership inscriptions which pre-date his ownership. See fig. 8.1 for a 1544 item by Brentz (B89).

9. Geste's initials 'E G' stamped on the covers of an Erasmus volume (Cat. no. E33), one of twenty-five in this centre-tool binding (CT c.1) bound for him in Cambridge. See Appendix IV D.

dated with certainty after 1557, and soon after he became a bishop he appears to have stopped the practice of signing his books.[15] Some thirty-eight items (in twenty-nine of his books) occur with his name, almost all at the foot of the title page or in the form of his initials stamped on the covers.

In most cases these inscriptions are simply in the form 'gest', but others are signed in a manner, characteristic of the age, suggesting a more endearingly personal relationship with its owner, such as 'Sum liber Edmundi Gest teste Brandesbio' (E48), a book given him by his uncle, 'Geste me possidet teste scriptore' (C39, cf. S2) and another witnessed by two others, 'Geste me possidet teste Dixon et Hanson' (E28).

Two of the books carry his initials 'E G' stamped in blind on the calf binding,[16] and there is a single instance (Z3) where he has signed a book on the parchment covers 'Edmond Roffen', i.e. as Bishop of Rochester (fig. 8.2).

15. Z3 (as bishop of Rochester, i.e. after 1560), and one other which includes two items, B59–60 (both with 1557 imprints). See Appendix X for the Geste provenances.
16. E33, a quarto of 1532, and E38, an octavo, both Erasmus editions with imprints between 1525 and 1534. See fig. 9.

A further three carry presentation inscriptions from his brother-in-law, Christopher Leedes, sent to him in 1550/51 as vice-Provost.[17]

Twenty-nine books with Geste's ownership inscription represent only a very small proportion of his surviving library. What other 'fingerprints' make it possible to go further in reconstructing his library? Five of these are to be found in various combinations in a sizeable proportion of the books that contain his ownership inscription, and these and their occurrence elsewhere among the Salisbury books must now be explored and illustrated.

Books with annotations and manuscript notes

The first of these 'fingerprints' is the presence of his manuscript notes and other forms of annotation such as marginal lines and markings as well as underlined passages in the text.[18] Like Cranmer, Geste was an inveterate annotator of his books. These annotations range from lines and other markings in the margins, single words or very brief annotations (in which he is doing little more than note points or arguments that particularly strike him at the time to facilitate recall) to examples of intensive annotation where every available inch of margin on a page, flyleaf and even title pages (sides, top and bottom) has been covered with his handwriting.[19]

In addition, a number of his books have manuscript material in his hand as flyleaves,[20] apparently, in some instances unrelated to the book in which these are bound. These manuscript notes, whether in the text or bound in as flyleaves, are written in a cursive hand which can range from the relatively neat to the very rough and illegible. Of the thirty-eight items in which his name appears, ten are certainly annotated in his hand, with a further three where some doubt about the authorship of the annotations exists. Many of his second-hand books had already been annotated by their previous owners (these are excluded from the total) but even so, in the collection as a whole, an even higher proportion contain his annotations than in the thirty-four items with his ownership inscription already mentioned: a little over 500 separate items are certainly annotated in his hand, plus another ninety-eight items where some doubt about his authorship exists – striking testimony to his industry and his perseverance in a practice

17. B122 [shelf mark G.3.22; see fig. 3], E55 [E.4.1] and J12 [N.3.13].
18. These are listed in Appendix XI.1.
19. See his annotated copies of the Latin vulgate Bible published at Paris by Simon Colines (1526–32) which contain copious MS notes in his hand (B31–35).
20. See, for example, over a dozen closely written pages of MS bound in his copy of the *Novum Testamentum* of the Benedictine, Isidore Chiari, published at Antwerp in 1544 (C64), the text of which he had already annotated in great detail. See fig. 10.1 for the annotated title page.

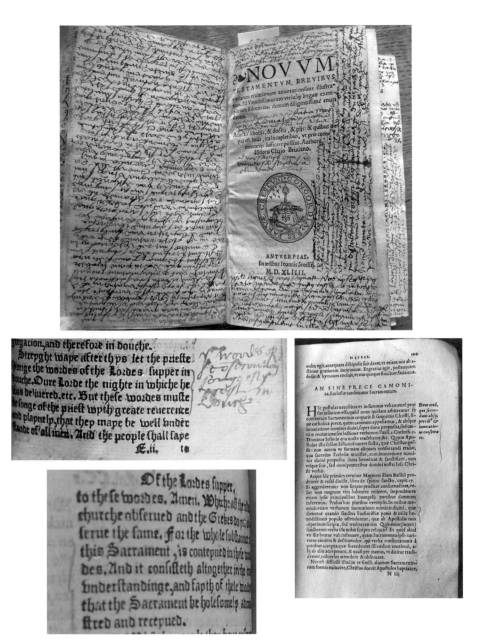

10. Fingerprints in Geste's books: annotations in his hand.
10.1 (top) Isidore Chiari. Title page with his annotations on the New Testament (1544) with Geste's annotations. Cat. no. C64. 10.2–3 (below left) The Reformation at Cologne. Hermann von Wied, *A simple, and Religious Consultation* (1548). Christ's words are sufficient in the eucharist. Cat. no. H42. 10.4 (below right) The *Antididagma* (1549) issued by the Cathedral Chapter at Cologne in response to Hermann. A prayer of invocation is necessary for the consecration of the eucharist. Cat. no. C95.

which he continued to the very end of his life, for he was still annotating pages in books published as late as 1576.[21]

Geste's manner of annotating also sheds some light on the form in which he acquired his books. To find a book with unopened leaves is often taken as an indication that the text has been little, if at all, read, much less studied, and therefore of little interest to its owner. With Geste, this was not necessarily the case. He *did* have books with unopened leaves, but there are also books of his with annotations on *inside* leaves, so that in their bound state both text and annotations are now inaccessible – evidence not only that he had acquired, read and annotated the books even before the sheets were folded, sewn and bound, but also (because those leaves remained unopened) that he did not find it necessary to return to those particular texts after binding had taken place. Five such books have been identified, with imprints between 1561 and 1573,[22] and there may have been others acquired and read in this unbound state, since many more of his books have unopened leaves as well as annotations:[23] it just happened that in these instances Geste found nothing to annotate on those particular leaves. This phenomenon, which may be less rare than has been generally recognised, suggests that Geste was sometimes acquiring items in this unbound state, not least because he wanted to have immediate access to new publications as these became available. This seems to have been the case particularly with octavos and smaller formats of continental printing, many of which were imported as unsewn sheets. After reading and, where appropriate, annotating them, he would then return them to his bookseller or stationer for binding, giving instructions as to what other items should be included in the volume and the type of binding – calf or simple parchment covers – he preferred. In the case of these five annotated, but unopened items, this is exactly what we find. All five are of small format: four octavos and one sextodecimo. All form part of composite volumes, ranging from between two to six items bound together. And two of the five retain their original binding instructions, one, an octavo, indicating on the title page of the first item and on the last leaf of the first quire, that the items were to be bound together 'in past', i.e. calf over pasteboard (in which they still are),[24] the other, a sextodecimo, numbering the four items in order, but with no surviving instructions indicating the

21. E.g. items by Augustine (A66), Boquinus (B56), Brentz (B68) and Wigand (W20).
22. These are listed in Appendix XI.1, Annexe 1.
23. To these five may be added the case of a volume of Horantius – H75 A.6.20(b) – in which quire B has been incorrectly folded and sewn, so that it now collates in the order B1, B6, B7, B4, B5, B2, B3, B8, with Geste's notes occurring in the order B4r, B5r, B2r–B3v. It seems likely that these annotations were made *before* the sheets were first folded, sewn and bound and that the error in the order of the leaves occurred at this stage rather than when the volume was later rebound.
24. F18 – shelf mark ZC2.2.4(a) – the first item of the volume containing W26 with the annotated, unopened leaves.

binding material to be used, which happens to be the original calf over pasteboard.[25] These binding instructions, still present in many Geste volumes, are in fact the second of the additional 'fingerprints' to be examined.

Geste's binding instructions and notes

These binding instructions generally occur at the foot of the title page, or, in a very few instances, on other leaves in the first gathering, In many cases, these instructions may have been sheared in the course of the original binding or in subsequent rebinding when the margins have been trimmed. Of the twenty-nine books that still carry Geste's name or initials, five retain these instructions (in one book, occurring in two of the items), and in the collection as a whole, 178 individual instances occur in 123 different volumes (some of them so badly cropped that they can no longer be fully deciphered).[26]

Most binding instructions which can be deciphered simply number the items in a volume in the preferred order: viz. 'first', 'second' (see fig. 11.1) and so on to 'last' [or a, b, c, or α, β γ, and so on]; or even, 'This with [th]e other fold in Last' (C41). Fortunately, this order of items has generally survived later rebinding, but not in one case, where a modern binder has carelessly ignored the original instruction, binding the items in the order (a), (c) and (b).[27] In some cases, Geste identifies the items to be bound together: e.g. 'This with the book against the anabaptists' (though the item requested is not included),[28] or 'This to be ioyned in the end/ to peter Martyr's book', which it still is (V13); or he requests his bookseller to look out for a particular item to be bound together with one he already has, 'Inquyre for Hessels' (H55). This was presumably an unsuccessful search, as in the event only the one item was included in this volume (unless it was a request for his bookseller to look out for other books by this same author, which may have been met subsequently by supplying three further Hessel items to order, all with imprints later than this one).[29]

But many of these binding instructions also indicate Geste's preferred binding materials: 'in p[ar]chme[n]t' (fig. 11.2), or 'C [presumably for 'Cover'

---

25. A50. The items are numbered at the foot of each title page, 'first' to 'third', the fourth being 'Last'. The binding is calf over pasteboard with centre-tool CT a. Not all Geste's binding instructions state the binding material to be used, and in some instances it is likely that these instructions were lost when the sheets were folded and cut for binding.
26. See Appendix VIII for a full listing and Appendix IV where these are listed under each type of binding.
27. Shelf mark E.6.26, now rebound in two volumes, the first volume in the order M21, C71 and S36.
28. Cat. no. O4.
29. E.g. items H52–54, with imprints between 1566 and 1568.

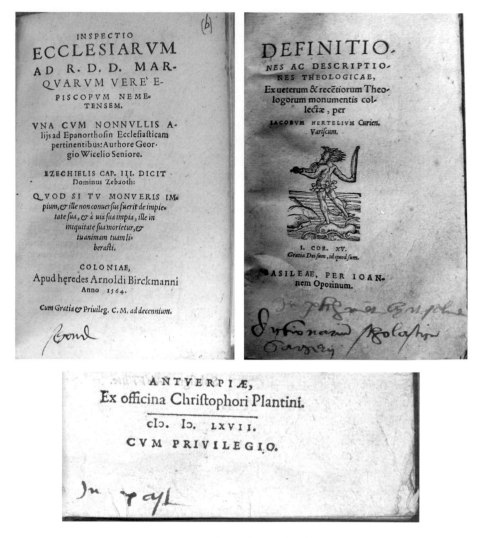

11. Fingerprints in Geste's books: his binding instructions.
11.1 (top left) Geste's instruction 'Second' at the foot of the title page,
indicating the order of items. Cat. no. W54. 11.2 (top right) 'In p[arch]ment
by it selue', with a further instruction to find a copy of, 'Dictionariu[m]
scholasticu[m] Sarcerij', of which no copy survives in his library. Cat. no. H45.
11.3 (bottom) 'In past', i.e. calf over pasteboard. Cat. no. S49.

or 'Case'] in p[ar]chme[n]t', i.e. parchment wrappers or covers.[30] The other
most frequently mentioned binding material is 'in past(e)' (fig. 11.3) or more
precisely, 'in pa[ste] bordes' (T9), i.e. boards made up of a laminate,
generally of paper, stuck together to form a board which would then be

30.   See items H4, M68 and W24. Other examples of 'in parchment' include C67, D22,
F3, G9, H15, M33 and M45.

covered with calf. The binder's waste used for this 'pasteboard' often included spoilt or surplus printed leaves or manuscript fragments which can sometimes be identified and dated when the pasteboard has come unstuck or frayed at the edges, exposing individual leaves. Geste's books provide many examples of these pasteboard bindings and of compacted leaves which have become exposed over time.

In a number of instances, however, Geste's binding notes evidently refer not to his preferred binding material but to the state of the book at acquisition *before* binding or, more precisely, 'rebinding'. One book printed in 1571, for example, now in a London roll binding signed 'R B', has the note 'Uncutt in parcheme[n]t' (L21), and presumably reflects the state of the book at the time of its acquisition from his bookseller – in parchment covers as imported from the continent – before being sent back to be covered in a more permanent calf roll-binding. Another, printed in 1565, still apparently in its original parchment covers, is described as 'in p[ar]chme[n]t not cutt but smothed' (L19), in all likelihood reflecting the condition in which it was imported and also his decision not to have it re-covered in a more permanent calf binding. Another seven books still retain such notes,[31] including one printed in 1565 (M35) now in a calf binding with a blank cartouche as centre-tool (CT b), which reads 'sewn ... not cut', evidently imported from the continent as a sewn book block without covers. In this particular instance, many of the leaves remain unopened, as is the case with another book of 1551 now in parchment covers (M67), but the other five (none with unopened leaves) contain his annotations. One of these (W19), now rebound, neatly illustrates the distinction by combining Geste's note about the present state of the book with an instruction about his preferred binding material (calf over pasteboard): 'This w[i]t[h] ye other in past. | Uncut in p[a]rchment'.

Whenever the books have survived in their original bindings it is clear that Geste's instructions in almost all cases have been carried out to the letter: the 'in parchment' items in limp parchment wrappers, and those 'in paste' in calf bindings over pasteboard, often decorated with simple tools to form a centre ornament, sometimes set within a rectangular frame defined by fillets, or bordered by one of the rolls in current use or placed at the centre of otherwise plain covers with a simple border of fillets at the outer edges.

As evidence of Geste's ownership of a book, most of these binding in-structions occur in books which already contain other evidence such as his manuscript annotations, but even so, this second 'fingerprint' points to a further forty or so volumes identified from his library.

Book titles on fore-edges or spines

The third 'fingerprint' that can distinguish a Geste book is a fairly distinctive fore-edge title or, in the case of books wrapped in parchment, a book title

31.   The seven books are F11, H63, L42, M35, M67, M79 and W19.

12. Fingerprints in Geste's books: book titles on fore-edges or spines.
12.1 (left) Fore-edge title and early press-mark on a calf binding. Cat. no.B50.
12.2 (right) Spine title and early press-mark on a book in
parchment covers. Cat. no.D30

on the spine. Of the twenty-nine books carrying Geste's initials on the
covers or his name on the title page, twenty have these fore-edge or spine
titles, two of the others probably having lost them in the course of later
rebinding – when the fore-edges were trimmed and coloured.

The practice of inscribing book titles in this way to facilitate searching for a book (in the absence of a catalogue or shelf-list) was of course common at the time, so there is nothing remarkable in itself to find this in the case of Geste's books. Books wrapped in parchment covers with a title written on the spine were shelved with the spine outwards and those bound in a more permanent material (such as calf) were shelved fore-edge outwards, so that the title could be easily read from the front. Many of the titles on Geste's books are now faded and unreadable, and some appear to have been inked over at a later date to make them more legible. The writing appears to be contemporary (if not necessarily by Geste himself, for some titles, in the case of second-hand items, were written by former owners) and, significantly, no book at Salisbury of post-Geste imprint appears to carry these fore-edge or spine titles.

Many of these book titles have probably been lost in the course of rebinding when the fore-edges have been trimmed and in some cases coloured. A few may never have had fore-edge or spine titles, even though early press marks on one or other remain clearly visible. Even so, 396 volumes retain their fore-edge titles (fig. 12.1), with another twenty where there is a possible trace surviving, and ninety-two carry spine titles (fig. 12.2) with an additional four where there is a possible trace – a total of over 512 in all.[32] This figure includes about a hundred or more instances where the book titles have survived rebinding. 184 of the volumes with book titles fall into the 'multi-item' category, containing between two and twelve separate titles apiece, a higher proportion of them in parchment covers,[33] and mostly in quartos and octavos.

The survival of so many book titles has been of considerable assistance in reconstructing Geste's library. For in many cases, the book titles make it possible to confirm the original *contents* of a volume (especially important in the few instances where a book has been rebound later and the items distributed over several volumes) and they may even help establish the original *order* of the separate items, especially when there are also binding instructions giving the order of items to corroborate this. It is clear from his binding instructions, where these survive, that Geste attached considerable importance to having particular items bound together within a single volume, and he was even interested in the *order* of the items, perhaps because of their associated subject matter or because they related to different stages in a particular controversy which interested him. This practice was to become, more often than not, the norm in the seventeenth and eighteenth centuries and will be familiar to anyone who has worked with pamphlet collections of that period, where thirty or more separate items on a particular

---

32. See Appendix VII for a complete listing.
33. Forty of those with spine titles (out of a total of 96) fall into the multi-item category, and 144 of those with fore-edge titles (out of a total of 416).

topic will be bound together in a single bulky pamphlet volume and perhaps listed in order on the inside covers or preliminary leaves. The early stages of that development can perhaps be glimpsed in Geste's practice here.

Geste's interest in binding together items of related subject matter in a single volume has some implications for presenting this reconstruction of his library and the form of the catalogue in particular. A conventional *author* catalogue by itself will not entirely do justice to this characteristic of his collection, and numerical cross-references to other numbered entries (e.g. 'bound with A31, T22 and V37') will still leave the user with the task of looking up each entry to establish the full contents of a volume. A catalogue by current *shelf order* (or even by the *original* shelf order, where this can be determined) giving entries for the contents of each volume would meet this point in the case of multi-itemed volumes. But it would be cumbersome to use and would still require an alphabetical author index, cross-referenced to the shelf-list catalogue, to make it usable. The compromise adopted here is to catalogue as the main entry the first item in each volume by author, with a concise list of the associated items bound with it at the end of the record. The associated items also appear under their respective authors, with a cross reference to the main entry by catalogue number to establish the association. This method is valid only when it can be established that the contents of each volume have remained together, and in the same order, as originally bound, and that neither has been disturbed by later rebinding. Fortunately, Geste's books have been little disturbed since the sixteenth century, and even when items have been separated in the course of rebinding it is often possible to establish the original relationships, sometimes with the use of fore-edge or spine titles, binding instructions (where these have remained intact), and occasionally from notes inserted at the time of rebinding which indicate that relationship. By presenting the catalogue in this way, it is intended that the user will gain a fuller picture of Geste's holdings of a particular author (e.g. Calvin) presented in alphabetical order, as well as an insight into how he may have associated other related items with a particular author or work.

Small-tool or centre-tool bindings

The full range of Geste's contemporary bindings are reviewed at a later stage,[34] but there are three binding types in particular which occur again and again in his collection – one from his time at Cambridge and two from the period after that, when he was purchasing most of his books in London – and these, it is suggested, constitute a fourth 'fingerprint' in his books, providing further evidence of his ownership, along with the various other 'fingerprints' already discussed. In fact, the three types of 'small-tool' or

34. See below, pp. 103–139.

'centre-tool' bindings considered here have a much larger representation in his collection than any of the other types of calf bindings which occur: over a hundred in all, and as many as fifty-two in the case of one of these (CT b). These are all examples of a fairly basic binding of calf-over-pasteboard covers, using one or more small tools in blind, to form a centre ornament, sometimes on otherwise plain covers, with a border of fillets at the outer edges, or within an otherwise plain rectangular frame defined by fillets. Some examples use the same or another tool at each angle of the rectangular frame, and there are also ten examples of one of these centre-tools (CT c) which have the rectangular frame surrounded by one of three rolls tooled in blind.[35]

As long ago as 1948, the late Neil Ker, in a memo to the librarian, Canon Quirk, had drawn attention to these three rolls, some of them combined with centre-tool CT c, or in a few cases one of three others, as evidence for Geste's ownership of these books. There are in fact twenty-eight examples of this centre-tool (CT c) in Geste's collection. In its most common form it consists of a simple fleuron forming a central ornament which in most cases recurs at each of the four angles of a plain rectangle frame, defined by fillets. But there are also three variations, with one example of each, in which the fleuron tool appears twice within the rectangular frame, either joined together (CT c.2) or placed at each end (CT c.3), or quadrupled to form a cruciform centre ornament (CT c.4).[36] In ten examples, the rectangular frame is itself surrounded by one of three rolls, which Ker at the time designated 'Rolls 1 to 3', but, since then, classified in Oldham's scheme for rolls as HM.h(28) – see fig.13.1 – HM.h(29) and FP.g(1).[37] In four instances the central fleuron is surrounded with the initials of former owners: 'E G' (Edmund Geste), 'N K' (Nicholas Kervyle) or 'T D' (probably another former Cambridge owner, perhaps Thomas Dickenson, also of King's College).[38]

All these examples of centre-tool CT c.1-4 at Salisbury occur on octavos and quartos printed between 1532 and 1548, and could therefore have been acquired during Geste's time in Cambridge. All but one of these books (an octavo copy of the Cologne *Consultation* (H42), printed in London in 1548 being the exception) were of continental printing, probably imported, unbound in sheets or sewn book blocks, the binding being done in England, almost certainly in Cambridge. In fact, the case for Cambridge as the place of binding is a strong one. All but two of the examples retain their original pastedowns, and these (some twenty-five of them) consist of full-size leaves

35. These are listed in Appendix IV D under CT c.1–3.
36. Examples of these are illustrated in figs. 9 (p. 41), 22.3 (p. 263), and (with rolls) 13.1 (p. 52) and 19.2 (p. 237). Centre-tool bindings CT c.1–4.
37. Listed in Appendix IV C, and for the examples combined with centre-tools, CT c.1–3 in Appendix IV D.
38. Two examples of 'E G' stamped on the covers (E33 – see fig. 9 – and E38), and one each of 'N K' (S17) and 'T D' (C64). On 'N K' and 'T D', see the Index of Provenances (Appendix X).

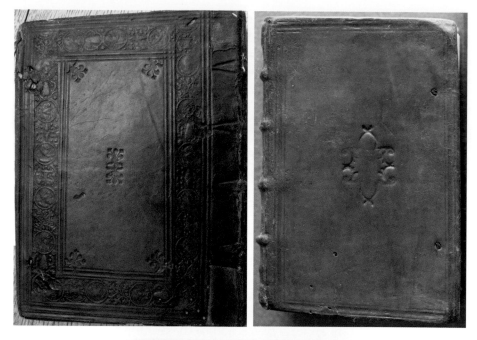

13. Fingerprints in Geste's books: three small-tool or centre-tool bindings.
13.1(top left) Centre-tool binding (CT c.2) with Oldham roll HM.h.(28) from
Geste's Cambridge period. Cat. no. M85. 13.2 (top right) Centre-tool binding
(CT a) from Geste's Rochester and Salisbury periods. Cat. no. H62. 13.3 (bottom)
Centre-tool binding (CT b) from Geste's Rochester period. Cat. no. H91.

from medieval MSS of the type found in books bound in Cambridge or Oxford where manuscript waste discarded by college libraries was plentiful.[39] Moreover, the three rolls which occur in ten of these centre-tool examples are now believed by David Pearson (following Neil Ker) to have been bound in Cambridge rather than London (as Oldham held), and Pearson has gone further by tentatively suggesting a possible link with Nicholas Spierinck from whom Geste obtained a number of his other roll bindings.[40]

The two other types of 'centre-tool' bindings also employed a single central ornament and, on the evidence of their imprints, belong to the time after Geste had left Cambridge and was making most of his purchases in London. The first of these (CT a) is perhaps easier to illustrate than describe.[41] It is also found in a Bullinger (1538), now in St Paul's Cathedral Library, in the centre of a rectangular frame surrounded by a roll originating with John Siberch who was active in Cambridge during the 1520s,[42] though Siberch's roll (Gray, Roll 2) in this instance had been used by a later binder (evidently not Nicholas Spierinck, though he had taken over some of Siberch's rolls) at a date not earlier than 1544.[43] None of the examples in Geste's collection are combined with a roll. In fact, the centre-tool ornament occurs most frequently on entirely plain covers or, less commonly, at the centre of a rectangular frame, with, more rarely, fleurons at each angle (C36).[44] Twenty-two examples have been identified of centre-tool CT a – all quartos and octavos. Sixteen of these preserve the original printed waste either with, or without, strips of parchment taken from medieval MSS, endleaf construction characteristic of London binding of the time where MS waste was less plentiful.[45] From the evidence of the imprints as well, which fall within the period 1564 to 1572, the binding of these books belongs to the period in which Geste was at Rochester, as its bishop, and from 1571 at Salisbury and, though not unique to Geste, it seems likely that he had been purchasing these books consistently from London booksellers (presumably the same one) during his visits there over a period of some years.[46]

The second of the two types (CT b.1–2), of which Geste had fifty-two examples, was a simple blank cartouche or shield (with no heraldic arms

39. On this, see Pearson, EBS, p. 38.
40. Pearson, BC, p. 171, and personal communication. An example of this centre-tool, CT c.1 binding, at Emmanuel College, Cambridge (c. 1545–1550) is illustrated in Pearson's, EBS, p. 54, fig. 3.32.
41. See fig. 13.2, Cat. no. C36.
42. Treptow, chapter two; Gray, pp. 54–61, and Plate XXII.
43. The Bullinger has endpapers of Jasper Laet's *Almanack & Prognostication* of 1544, so the binding cannot be earlier than 1544. Gray, p. 60; Treptow, p. 33.
44. For an example of this, see the first volume of his Canisius (C36), at shelf mark K.2.13, fig. 13.2.
45. Pearson, EBS, p. 38. Geste's examples are listed in Appendix D IV, under CT a.
46. For the question of whether Geste was purchasing from the same bookseller after his translation to Salisbury, see below, pp. 134f.

depicted) found in his books with imprints over the period 1547–1568 although, as there is only a single example from 1547 and all the other examples are from 1555 onwards, it seems likely that the actual binding of this one dates from a period early in Elizabeth's reign when he had emerged from hiding after Mary's death and was beginning to make his purchases from London booksellers. All are otherwise completely plain apart from the usual border of fillets at the outer edges.[47] Again, all the books are of continental printing and all are of small format (octavos mostly, but a few quartos among them). Like the centre-tool binding (CT a) already discussed, the end-leaf construction of those examples which retain their original manuscript and printed waste points to a London bookseller for Geste's purchases. For, twenty-seven of the fifty-one books retain strips of manuscript or blank parchment as strengtheners and three also use printed waste. There are no instances of full manuscript leaves being used as pastedowns in the Cambridge manner.

However 'plain' or 'basic' these three binding types may appear, they serve to make possible the identification of significant numbers of items from his collection which might otherwise have been overlooked. To this extent, these three centre-tool bindings (CT a–c) provide a further 'fingerprint' characteristic of Geste's ownership.

Early press marks

Most of the fore-edges or spines of Geste's books also carry an early press mark or shelf mark – the last of the 'fingerprints' to be considered. Of the twenty-nine volumes that carry Geste's initials on the covers or his ownership inscription on the title page, twenty-five also carry one of these early press marks, the other three having lost them in the course of rebinding. Taking his collection as a whole, 578 volumes retain these early press marks in some form, including 119 which have survived rebinding. Not all of these are fully legible: nine are little more than an illegible trace, and there are seventy-seven where the reading is in some doubt.[48]. These early press marks are of a very simple kind made up of two components: a letter to designate the book press or case (in a sequence, A–T), and a number to indicate the position of the book on the shelves (figs. 12.1–2). The individual shelves in a bookcase or 'press' are not given a separate number, so the individual books are simply numbered in a single sequence from one to twenty (in the case of press K, filled exclusively with folios) to over a hundred in the case of press F which was presumably made up of several shelves of small format books – octavos and smaller – far more, of course, than could ever have been accommodated on a single shelf.

47.   See fig. 13.3. The books with this binding are listed in Appendix IV D, under CT b.
48.   Listed in Appendix V. There are also thirteen books in contemporary bindings apparently without press marks, and these are also listed at the end of Appendix V.

When these early press marks were first noticed and recorded it seemed too good to hope that listing them in sequence would yield any information about the physical arrangement of the books or even the likely size of the collection at the time of Geste's death. There was, after all, nothing particularly distinctive about this fairly rudimentary system of book numbering adopted for his books. However, examination of other early printed books at Salisbury showed that this particular system of book numbering had not been adopted for other books with imprints within the period of Geste's lifetime, and only in one instance on a book printed after his death [shelf mark N.6.24]. This particular exception occurred in the case of a book printed in 1591 with the press mark 'C25' inscribed on the fore-edge, but it also carried a Seth Ward press mark on the title page, indicating that it had come to the Cathedral library with the rest of his books after his death in 1689. The 'C25' press mark, which duplicated an existing Geste item – a Sarcerius of 1543 (S12) – was evidently on the book before Seth Ward acquired it, having come from some collection which had followed the same system as that adopted for Geste's books. This exception presented therefore no insuperable difficulty to the possibility that the press marks did in some way define the limits of Geste's collection at the time of his death. Moreover, listing them in sequence revealed a fairly ordered arrangement of the books by subject matter, size and format. Books with press marks 'D' and 'H', for example, were all folios, while those with 'F' and 'R' contained octavos and smaller formats. And even in presses where the items were mixed in size, folios were grouped together, and so were the octavos and quartos. The arrangement of the presses also revealed a fairly logical sequence of subject matter, beginning with works relating to the study of the Bible, particularly commentaries (Cases A–D), then Theology, (from Case E onwards) with a particularly large collection relating to contemporary Reformation controversies, ending, admittedly, with something of a 'catch-all' case of miscellaneous subject matter (Case T).

However, it soon became clear that it could only have been at the very end of Geste's life that this numbering system was adopted. For books with imprints of the 1570s sit on shelves quite arbitrarily alongside books with imprints of the 1540s, 1550s, and earlier, so that the arrangement of the books on the shelves in no way related to their order of acquisition. Of course, the date of a book's *printing* should not be equated simply with the date of its *acquisition* – this particularly applies to older books acquired second-hand. But unless Geste was in the habit of filling gaps in his shelves, occasioned by lost or discarded items, with newly acquired books (admittedly a possibility, though difficult to prove or disprove), one might have expected, at the very least, to find that books with 1573–1575 imprints – which must have been acquired at the very end of his life – would be shelved at the *end* of a press sequence, not among books of earlier date. But this is not the case.

The first four books in Press N, for example, have imprint dates in the order 1572, 1533, 1570 and 1560; and those in Press S, 1567, 1550, 1535 and 1573.

If the press marks did not go back to Geste's own day, were they added *after* his books were removed from the bishop's palace to the Cathedral? In his will, Geste had required the Dean & Chapter to 'dispose all those my said books to places and Stalls as may be fit for the preservation and good keeping of the same', and it seems likely that the press marks were added in the course of this process. Furthermore, provision in his will was made for the continuing payment of his servants at the Palace from his Estate – perhaps for this very purpose.

It is unlikely that this task was undertaken much later than this, because there is no record in the Chapter Act Books of any decision relating to the re-organization of the library stock in the period after Geste's death, much less any expenditure for this purpose, and, in contrast to the late medieval period, the post-Reformation Chapter had a poor record for looking after its books. During the late medieval period the Chapter had recorded considerable donations to the library, laid down regulations for the repair of its books and the supervision of readers, appointed librarians from among the residentiary canons (1397) and actually built a new library and lecture room (in the 1450s). [49] By contrast, the post-Reformation picture was indeed one of neglect and indifference, and there was nothing to suggest that any radical improvement had taken place after Geste's death. There was no librarian until the eighteenth century, and apart from Patrick Young's visit to list the literary manuscripts in 1622, [50] and some cataloguing of the muniments in about 1600, there is scant evidence of any activity before the Restoration – certainly nothing to compare with the initiatives being taken in some other Cathedral or ecclesiastical libraries such as Hereford, York, Durham, Westminster Abbey, Ripon and even to some extent at Canterbury before the Civil War. It is improbable, then, that anything more was done than to shelve and number the books as they arrived from the bishop's Palace.

One further fact about the surviving press marks is worth noting. There are very considerable gaps in the sequences of press marks, so far as these can be reconstructed, suggesting that substantial losses have occurred. These losses show great variation from press to press, though allowance has to be made for the fact that books often lost their press marks (as well as their book titles) in the course of rebinding, as a result of trimming or colouring of the fore-edges. In Press A – a sequence of at least fifty-one quartos and octavos – forty-four books (over eighty-five per cent) retain their press mark, while (by contrast) in Case P only two out of at least twenty-eight (only seven per cent) can be identified today, and in Case I three or four at most (out

49. On this, see briefly Eward, pp. 3–5.
50. Neil Ker, 'Salisbury Cathedral Manuscripts and Patrick Young's Catalogue' (1950) in Ker, *BCL*, pp. 175–208, especially p. 184 on the damage done in the past to the manuscripts by damp and neglect.

of a potential twenty or at most twenty-two) remain. Some at least of these 'losses' are accounted for among those books which have lost their press marks in the course of rebinding (over a hundred volumes),[51] those which have only traces of press marks (nine volumes) and a further thirteen, still in their original bindings, which appear never to have had press marks. But even when some allowance is made for these, the number is still far short of the total suggested by the press mark sequences, even when the 569 books that still retain their press marks are included. For, if the highest surviving press mark number in each of the presses (A–T) is taken as a potential total for each press (for example, Case A (51), Case B (58), and so on), the total size of the collection as it might have been in Geste's day would have been at least 958 volumes,[52] far in excess of the present figure of 684 volumes, even when allowance is made for the contents of some multi-itemed volumes now being bound separately or re-distributed in the course of rebinding. On the face of it, then, it is possible that over a quarter of the collection may have been lost since Geste's death in 1577.

The exact circumstances of losses on this scale are unclear. It is likely, however, that these are not to be attributed to any single cause or event but occurred over a long period of neglect when conditions in the library were far from conducive to preserving the collection, and there are many examples among the surviving books of damp stains and decay to the binding structures. Disruption during the Civil War and the Commonwealth was likely to have been a further factor, though losses to the Cathedral archives during this period make it impossible to verify this in any detail. Certainly, the Cathedral Muniments had suffered major depredations and disruption at the time, as Bishop Henchman confirmed at the beginning of the Restoration in 1661, and it is unlikely that the library altogether escaped a similar fate.[53]

51. See the items marked 'R' in the third column of Appendix V and items marked '##' and '**' in the fourth column of Appendix IV H, listing rebound volumes.
52. Calculating the potential size of his collection on this basis may, of course, *underestimate* the original total number in each case, since the highest surviving press mark number may not have been that of the last book originally on the shelf.
53. On this see Suzanne Eward, '17th-Century Life and Strife at Salisbury Cathedral' (lecture given at 750th Anniversary Conference held at Salisbury, March 2008) in *Spire: Annual Report of the Friends of Salisbury Cathedral* (2009), pp. 22–31; 'Bishop Henchman in 1661 bemoaned the fact that many of the charters, volumes and registers "by the fraud and criminality of naughty men have perished in the late Troubles", and those which remained were in confusion' (p. 27). The huge task of re-ordering the muniments was entrusted to Richard Drake, Chancellor from 1663. That the recent 'troubles' were uppermost in the minds of the Chapter is evident from the answer given to bishop Seth Ward's 1672 Visitation: 'To the 24 they answer that the books of the Library were mostly embezzled in the times of the troubles except those which are left and of little value [*sic*]. Since the King's return some are given, some bought by them, and they duly take care to add more, and shall constantly [?]dispose them into certain classes' (Salisbury Cathedral Library, Cyril Everett, Notebook 'L', 5 recto). I am grateful to Suzanne Eward for this reference.

III. GESTE'S COLLECTION AS IT SURVIVES TODAY

Size and scope of the collection

Despite these losses and some uncertainties, 1,205 separate items remain from Geste's library and these now occupy, after some redistribution in the course of rebinding, 684 volumes. It is possible that further Geste items may have survived in the library, and the evidence for over a hundred of these is considered in Appendix I. None of these, however, contains conclusive evidence of his ownership, and the most that can be said of such books is that they lack sufficient positive indicators, such as the 'fingerprints' already considered, although it has to be said that they also lack negative evidence which would point to other owners or donors being involved. Moreover, in the case of these items listed in Appendix I, there is generally no surviving evidence at Salisbury either in the Cathedral archives or in the books themselves to suggest when they might have been acquired if they were not originally of Geste provenance. There are also a few possible candidates for inclusion among the books that have disappeared since the 1880 printed catalogue was published, but, in the absence of the books themselves, any attribution to Geste must remain only conjecture.

By contemporary standards, Geste's library, even in the truncated form in which it has survived today, was a very major collection, exceeding in size those held in Cambridge college libraries and that of the University Library itself, as well as by most individuals, which rarely exceeded a hundred volumes or so. In fact, its stands comparison, at least in the number of its printed books, with the libraries of Thomas Cranmer, Matthew Parker and the two medical collectors, John Hatcher and his son-in-law, Thomas Lorkyn, (all four containing between 600 and 800 printed volumes), and is surpassed only by the outstanding collections of John Dee (about 2,300 printed books), Andrew Perne and John, Lord Lumley[54] (both of about 3,000 volumes). In subject matter, however, its scope (at least as it has come down to us) was far more limited and specialised than any of these.

---

54. For the libraries of Hatcher, Lorkyn and Perne, see BiCI, I, nos. 154, 168 and 164 respectively, where their inventories are transcribed. On Perne, see also Perne (1991). For Parker, the estimate of 'over 600 printed books' at Corpus Christi College, Cambridge, to which should be added the 75 printed books given to the University Library in 1574 and a smaller donation to Gonville and Caius College in the same year, is given in *A Directory of Rare Books and Special Collections in the United Kingdom and the Republic of Ireland,* 2nd edn by B. C. Bloomfield (London: Library Association, 1997), pp. 25, 30, although the last named donation is not there mentioned. Records for Parker's printed books, with some copy-specific detail, now appear in the CUL online catalogue: some 1,075 separate bibliographical records for the books at Corpus, twenty-six (at the last count) for those in the University Library (retrospective re-cataloguing in progress) and currently

In fact, only about thirty or more items fell outside the area of theology, biblical studies (including works related to the study of Hebrew and Greek) and ecclesiastical history – less than three per cent of the surviving collection. The contrast with other collections of the period is striking. In the case of Thomas Cranmer's library (collected between *c.* 1503 and 1553), about 250 printed books (out of a total of a little under 600 survivals) were non-theological, about 130 of which fell into the category of 'Arts and Philosophy', many of them relevant to the Arts course at Cambridge when he was a Fellow at Jesus College. In Perne's case, the scope is even wider, with nearly half his collection being in fields other than theology.[55]

Geste's non-theological books

Geste's books give no indication of when or where they were acquired, apart from those that contain identifiable provenances or those that survive in contemporary bindings, where in some cases it may be possible to give an approximate date range when the binder can be identified.[56] But about a third of the surviving 'non-theological' books probably belong to the period when he was undertaking the Arts course at King's (1536–1544), and these include collections of wise sayings and exempla such as the *Disticha Catonis* (in the edition of Philip of Bergamo),[57] the *Polyanthea* of Mirabello,[58] and the *Sententiae* of Stobaeus,[59] literary and philosophical texts by classical authors such as Cicero,[60] Seneca (though his only copy could date from his time at Rochester, 1560–71),[61] and Suetonius (his *Lives of the Caesars*),[62] and two

fourteen at Gonville and Caius. For Dee's library see *John Dee's Library Catalogue,* ed. by Julian Roberts and Andrew Watson (London: Bibliographical Society, 1990) and the on-line supplement accessible on the Bibliographical Society's website. For Lumley's library, see *The Lumley Library: The Catalogue of 1609,* ed. by Sears Jayne and Francis R. Johnson (London: British Museum, 1956), and D. G. Selwyn, 'The Lumley Library: A Supplementary Checklist', *BLJ*, 7.2 (1981), pp. 136–48.

55. BiCI, I, no. 164. Of his 3,000 printed books, I have estimated just over 1,540 books in, or related to, theological studies.
56. See below, on 'Geste's contemporary bindings', pp. 103–107.
57. Lyon, 1497, Cat. no. P25.
58. Savona, 1503, Cat. no. N5.
59. Zürich, 1543, Cat. no. S89.
60. *De philosophica,* vol. 1. Strasbourg, 1541, Cat. no. C74.
61. *Lucubrationes omnes,* Basle, 1515, Cat. no. S45. With its Rochester provenance (see Appendix X), it would have seemed likely that he acquired this while bishop of Rochester, though books from religious houses were being disposed of before the Dissolutions, and some books 'on loan' to religious while studying in Cambridge may have been disposed of there rather than returned to the House. It is therefore possible that Geste acquired the book while in Cambridge, when (on the face of it) it would have been more relevant to his studies.
62. *Caesarum XII libri,* Basle, 1537, Cat. no. S96.

works by the humanist, Marsilio Ficino, the *Epistolae* in the first Venice edition of 1495 (given by his uncle, Dr John Brandisby) and the *Platonica theologica* in an edition of 1482.[63] Other items which may also have belonged to this early period, although imprint dates are far from being a reliable guide here, are his Foresti (the *Supplementum chronicarum* in an edition of 1503),[64] the *Officinae* of Ravisius Textor (a work Cranmer had also owned),[65] and Geste's only surviving medical work, the *Anatomice* of Alexander Benedictus, which, although carrying a 1528 imprint, may well have been acquired later, since it is in a parchment binding with an edition of Cicero by Conrad Clauser published in 1558.[66] The 'gaps' in these early holdings are too many to enumerate: texts on logic, many classical authors (notably, Aristotelian texts) and the 'non-theological' works of Erasmus, for example, such as the *Adagia*, the *De copia* and the *Colloquia* which figure so frequently in Cambridge inventories of the time.[67] Such items, especially in small-format copies, circulated among students, often passing from one generation to the next until they fell to pieces, and Geste may well have disposed of his copies, when he had no further use for them, after completing his Arts course and moving on to theology. Some may have been among the 'quarter' of his collection which, it is conjectured, may not have survived at Salisbury, and others may have had to be disposed of, or left behind at King's (though none has been identified there) when Geste was forced from his fellowship early in Mary's reign, in January 1554.

The remaining two-thirds of Geste's 'non-theological' books are a heterogeneous group carrying imprints, with few exceptions, from the early Elizabethan period between 1558 and 1569. The two books he acquired on logic and dialectic by Augustinus Hunnaeus (H91–92) were published at Antwerp by Christopher Plantin in 1566, his copy of Sextus Empiricus *Pyrrhonian Hypotyposes* (in the translation of Henri Estienne) at Geneva in 1562 (S53), and the two by Cornelius Valerius on moral and natural philosophy in 1566 and 1567 respectively (V1–2). Apart from Melanchthon's *Annotationes in officia* (M59) published at Wittenberg in 1562, the only other editions of Cicero, the two by Betuleius (B18) and Clauser (C76), already mentioned, date from the 1550s. The other items fall into the broad subject areas of history, law and politics (perhaps reflecting Geste's increased responsibilities at Court, as Elizabeth's Lord High Almoner and as one of her

63. Cat. nos. F5–6.
64. Venice, 1503. Cat. no. F30. Geste's copy of Josephus *Antiquities* (Basle, 1540, Cat. no. J16) may also have been acquired at this time.
65. Lyon, 1541, Cat. no. R12. Cranmer's copy was of the Paris, 1520 edition; *LTC* 518.
66. Strasbourg, 1528, Cat. no. B13, bound with Conrad Clauser, *De officijs, de amicitia, de senuctute, analysis,* Basle, 1558, Cat. no. C76.
67. On this and what follows, see E. Leedham-Green, 'University libraries and booksellers' and Kristian Jensen, 'Text books in the universities: the evidence from the books' in CHBB III, pp. 316–79.

bishops), and there is one book on astronomy by Bartholomaeus Schoen-born.[68] The historical items comprise two parts of Carion's *Chronicles* (1562 and 1566),[69] Josephus *Antiquities* (1540) – if not already acquired during his time at Cambridge (J16) – and a Suidas (1564).[70] The remaining books are a volume that includes Lawrence Humphrey's *Optimates, siue de nobilitate* (H90), bound with Machiavelli's *Il Principe* (in a Latin translation, published in 1560) and Widemann's *Politicus libellus* (1565),[71] another Machiavelli, his *Istorie Fiorentine* (1560),[72] Justinian's *Institutiones iuris civilis* (1555),[73] the *De hominis politici persona et officio* of Ernestus Regius (1568),[74] and a work on libel by Aurelio Vergerio (1564), the last in a volume of theological tracts on the ubiquitarian controversy.[75] Most of these later items, with the exception of the Clauser and Melanchthon editions of Cicero, the Regius, Schoenborn, Sextus Empiricus, Vergerio and Wide-mann, occur regularly in Cambridge inventories of the period (including many of them in Perne's library), but only the Carion *Chronicles* (C41–42) and the Justinian (J18) appear to have survived among the printed books of Matthew Parker at Corpus Christi College, Cambridge.

Like the personal collections of other scholars of his day, nearly all the books in Geste's library were in Latin, with a very few survivals in, or containing, Hebrew (some fourteen),[76] and even fewer in Greek (ten) – a surprising statistic, for this includes copies of the text of the New Testament and the Greek Fathers.[77] There are no books in French or German; in fact no vernacular language other than English was represented, and there are only twenty-one of these (with the possibility of a further five English items listed in Appendix I), and of the twenty-one which certainly belonged to

68. *Oratio de studiis astronomicis*, Wittenberg, 1564, Cat. no. S38.
69. Cat. nos. C41–42.
70. *Suidae historica*, Basle, 1564, Cat. no. S97.
71. Cat. nos. M3 and W17, respectively.
72. Cat. no. M2.
73. Cat. no. J18.
74. Cat. no. R14.
75. *Ad quaestionem de famosis libellis, tractatulus* (V9). Bound with three tracts by Jacob Andreae (A31, A33–34) and one by Jacob Schegk (S34), all published between 1564 and 1565.
76. *Alphabetum Hebraicum* (A22), Aurogallus (A68–69), Campensis (C29), Capito (C39), Clenardus (C81), Elias, *Levita* (E18), Estienne, R. (E54), Sebastian Münster (M83–85), Praetorius (P50), and Reuchlin (R16–17). There are three further items listed in Appendix I which may, just possibly, have belonged to him: Mercerus (*M3), Münster (*M4–M5).
77. Camerarius (C22), the 1522 edn of the Erasmus NT (E27), Germanus (G24), Gregory, *of Nazianzus* (G33), NT Lexicon (L28), Mark, *the Anchorite* (M11), Maximus, *of Tyre* (M19), Stobaeus (S89), Theodoret, *of Cyrus* (T7) which includes citations from other authors in Greek, and Theophylact (T9). Three other Latin items include annotations in Greek, but Geste's authorship of these notes is far from certain: Aretius (A51), Thomas More (M81) and Potho (P46).

Geste, fourteen were printed in London, the rest on the European continent.[78] In consequence, Geste's access to the output of continental theologians such as Luther, Zwingli or Calvin, for example, was restricted to those works published in or translated into Latin, a limitation (serious, in the case of Luther) shared with most contemporary English scholars.

Geste and the study of theology

Geste would have begun his theological studies in the mid-1540s, having graduated BA in 1540/41 and MA in 1544. The medieval curriculum had centred on the study of the Bible, interpreted according to the 'four senses' of scripture, and the *Sentences* of Peter Lombard, with a long tradition of commentaries on that textbook by many scholastic authors. But the Royal Injunctions to the University issued in the autumn of 1535 and the appointment of Thomas Cromwell as visitor, following the execution of John Fisher, brought about important changes to that curriculum in the direction of the 'new learning' as well as a new regime of direct control from the court.[79] Lectures on the *Sentences* were now forbidden, to be replaced by the study of Scripture 'according to the true sense thereof and not after the manner of Scotus, etc.' These restrictions, however, did not apply to the personal study of these texts, and Geste's library, like those of many other Cambridge contemporaries (as their *post mortem* inventories demonstrate),[80] contained numerous examples of the 'forbidden' texts and commentaries: editions of the *Sentences* themselves (P22–23) and commentaries on the text by Aquinas (A45), Gabriel Biel (B46–47), Bonaventura (B53), Duns Scotus (D33–35), Robert Holkot (H72) and Nicolaus de Orbellis (O19), representative of both the *via antiqua* and *via moderna* tendencies within scholasticism, and a collection comparable, albeit on a smaller scale, with that owned by one of an earlier generation, Thomas Cranmer.[81] Geste also owned copies of perhaps the most widely studied commentary on the Canon of the Mass by Gabriel Biel (B48) as well as the *Decretum* of Gratian (G30), precursor of the study of Canon Law, the teaching of which was now forbidden by the same Injunctions.

78. Edmund Bonner (B54–55), Council of Trent (C109), Hermann (H42), Horne (H77), Jewel (J7–8), Mainardo (M6), Martiall (M13), Nowell (N13–14), Ponet (P42), Rastell (R6–7), Richard Smith (S64), Stapleton (S85–86), Veron (V20–21), Watson (W2) and Whitgift (W16). A further five items listed in Appendix I may, just possibly, have belonged to him: Calfhill (*C1), Erasmus (*E1), Gardiner (*G1), Rastell (*R1) and Whitgift (*W1). The seven items of continental printing were M6 (at Strasbourg), M13 (Antwerp), P42 (?Strasbourg), R6–7 (Antwerp), S85 (Louvain) and S86 (Antwerp).
79. On this and what follows, see D. R. Leader, *A History of the University of Cambridge: Volume 1, the University to 1546* (Cambridge: University Press, 1988), p. 331f.
80. BiCI.   81. *LTC*, Introduction, pp. lxxiiif.

Geste and the study of Scripture

In the case of the Biblical text, no copy in his library of the folio edition of the vulgate Bible in six volumes with the Glossa ordinaria and postils of Nicholas of Lyra has been identified with certainty.[82] But Geste owned the postils of Hugh of St Cher (H82–84), and his copy of the Old Testament vulgate text (without either glossa or postilla) in the small format six-volume edition of Simon Colines (Paris, 1526–32) is copiously annotated throughout (B31–35), and this was probably the set he was using at Cambridge in the course of proceeding to the degree of BD in 1551. Although Geste had studied Hebrew, no copy of the Hebrew text (if he ever had one) survives, either in the editions published at Soncino (1488) or at Venice (the Rabbinic Bible of Daniel Bomberg, 1525–28), nor in the Complutensian polyglot Bible (1514–17, but not issued until after 1520). Similarly, he may not have had a text of the Old Testament in the Greek version. At least, no copy, such as that of the Aldine edition, has come down.[83]

For the New Testament, however, in addition to the Latin vulgate, there were now the editions of Erasmus with the Greek text and his new Latin translation. Geste had the third Erasmus edition of 1522 in folio (E27), but it was an octavo copy of the Latin version, published at Strasbourg in 1523, that contains his copious annotations (E28), and his collection also included copies of the fifth edition (1536) – again Latin only – interleaved with his annotations but now incomplete (E29), and two further small format copies, one incomplete from about 1550 (B36), the other published at Geneva in 1552 (B37).

For commentaries on the biblical text, as with his editions of the New Testament text itself, Geste's library increasingly reflected the new direction being taken by Cambridge theological scholarship, and this was even more evident in the period following his departure from King's College in 1554. His remarkable collection of over 360 commentaries and expositions for liturgical use, all but one published on the continent,[84] embraced authors on both sides of the ideological divide, including as many as sixty-three contemporary Catholic commentaries, in addition to twenty-seven from the patristic era, and twenty-three from the scholastic and late medieval periods. The medieval commentaries included a set by the Carthusian, Dionysius de Leuwis, that also features in the libraries of Cranmer, Parker, Perne and in some of the Cambridge inventories of the

---

82. The copy listed in Appendix I, *B6 lacks positive (and has some negative) evidence of Geste's ownership.
83. Cranmer had copies of all three, though not of the Aldine edition of the Greek Old Testament, *LTC* 29, 36–37.
84. The single exception being an anonymous commentary on II and III John published in London by John Byddell (B39).
85. Cat. nos. D10–19 and the references given there; for Cranmer, see *LTC* 193–205.

period.[85] Not surprisingly, Protestant authors contributed the greatest number to this total, with about 160 items of Lutheran origin, about half of which do not apparently occur in any of the Cambridge inventories or private collections of the period including those of Parker or Perne; six by Bucer or other Strasbourg reformers and just over forty by those in the Reformed tradition.[86] The commentaries are fairly evenly spread over both testaments, with significant collections on the Psalms, as was to be expected, because of their prominence in the liturgy and spirituality of the Christian tradition, but particularly because of Geste's known interest in their translation:[87] sixteen on the whole collection, and a further twenty-three on selected Psalms (nearly all by Lutheran writers); seventeen on the Epistle to the Romans (at least ten of them with his annotations), sixteen on Acts, and thirty-six commentaries or homilies on the liturgical Epistles and Gospels for the Christian year, again mostly by Lutherans and contemporary Catholics, many of them annotated.[88] In addition to these editions of the biblical text and commentaries, Geste possessed some of the new aids to biblical scholarship such as grammars,[89] lexicons[90] and concordances,[91] besides works concerned with its authority[92] and interpretation.[93]

The Church Fathers

From the patristic period, Geste had a substantial collection of 104 works by 68 authors. For Geste, as for John Jewel and Thomas Cranmer, the Church Fathers were an important resource, central to the debate with their Catholic opponents, playing a corroborative role (rather than as independent authorities in their own right) to confirm that their understanding of scripture was soundly based on that of its earliest interpreters ('the nearer the stream, the purer the source'), and references to these writers occur again

86. See Appendix XII.1, Index of Biblical Commentaries, Homilies, &c.
87. See above, Introduction I, pp. 30–31, on Geste's involvement in the revision of the English translation for the Bishops' Bible.
88. Especially in the two volumes by the Lutheran, Georg Meier (M28–29), and selected sermons by the Catholics, Heinrich Helmes (three, H18–20, of the five-volume set) and Johann Wild (W37–39).
89. E.g. the Hebrew and Chaldean grammar by Aurogallus (A69), Campensis (C29), Capito (C39) Clenardus (C81), Elias, *Levita* (E18), Sebastian Münster (M84–85), Abdias Praetorius (P50) and Johann Reuchlin (R17). There are no corresponding items for the study of Greek.
90. E.g. the *Lexicon Novi Testamenti* (L28).
91. Joannes Benedictus, *Concordantiae nouae vtriusque Testamenti* (B14).
92. By Bullinger (B127–128) and the Lutherans Hermannus Buschius (B137) and Georg Meier (M41).
93. By the Catholic, Johann Hofmeister (H66) and the Lutheran, Erasmus Sarcerius (S24).

and again in Geste's *Treatise* of 1548 and the unsigned 'letter' on liturgical revision among Parker's papers at Corpus Christi College, Cambridge.[94] As a patristic collection, Geste's is far surpassed by that of Perne who owned as many as 293 volumes by 93 authors,[95] but it greatly exceeds what has survived of those of Jewel[96] and Peter Martyr Vermigli[97] and compares not unfavourably with Cranmer's, in its range of authors (68, against the latter's 73) if not in sheer size (77 volumes of printed books, against Cranmer's 127 printed books and 23 manuscripts), and the printed books of his contemporary, Matthew Parker (over 70 authors in over 115 volumes).[98]

In Geste's case, the figure of seventy-three authors is inflated by some unusual items, fifteen of which are apparently not represented in surviving Cambridge inventories of the period, nor in the libraries of Parker or Perne,[99] but there are also some striking omissions which in all probability had at

---

94. CCCC MS. 106 (reproduced in Dugdale, Appendix IV). See above, Introduction I, p. 21f.
95. Figures based on the inventory in BiCI, vol. I, pp. 419–79, and in vol. II. Geste's patristic holdings are listed in Appendix XII.2.
96 On Jewel's library, see Neil Ker, 'The Library of John Jewel' in *BLR*, 9 (1977), 256–65. Ker traced eighty-four items, all but two at Magdalen College, Oxford. Only twenty volumes within the patristic and pre-scholastic period are extant, but as Ker pointed out, 'he must surely have had at the very least the *Opera* of Augustine, Ambrose and Gregory to set beside the *Opera* of Jerome' (p. 258) to which might be added those of Basil and John Chrysostom, among many others, a supposition supported by the numerous references in his published his works, indexed in the Parker Society edition of his *Works* (1850), vol. IV, pp. 1317–59.
97. What remains of Vermigli's library is a selection acquired by the city of Geneva, on which see J. P. Donnelly, *Calvinism and Scholasticism in Vermigli's Doctrine of Man and Grace* (Leiden: Brill, 1976), Appendix, pp. 208–17. This includes thirty-six volumes by eighteen authors within the patristic period.
98. No comprehensive reconstruction of Parker's collection of printed books has been published at the time this went to press. The figures given here derive from an examination of Adams in conjunction with the current on-line catalogues of Corpus Christi College, together with those of the University Library and Gonville and Caius College to both of which he made donations in 1574. All three now form part of the CUL online catalogue. The Corpus Christi catalogue includes provenance identifications, as well as much other copy-specific information, making it possible to identify books of Parker ownership, though it has not proved possible to examine the books themselves to confirm these details. For Cranmer's library see *LTC*. The figure of 73 authors and 127 printed books includes 11 authors and 25 printed books for which there is good evidence of Cranmer's ownership although his copies have not been traced. See *LTC*, Appendix D.
99. Works by John Cassian (C47), Cassiodorus (C48), Charlemagne (C57), Chrysologus (C65), Eusebius of Cremona (E56), Firmicus Maternus (F8), Florus (F26), Germanus (G24), Heracleides (H41), Isidore of Seville (I6–7), Palladius (P2), Rabanus Maurus (R1–2) and Zacharias (Z1). For a listing of his patristic books, see Appendix XII.2.

one time been in his library – though the text of some of these were in any case accessible to him in his own College library during his time in Cambridge – and some of them may have been among the losses which seem to have occurred at Salisbury after his day. Among the omissions were five 'required' authors listed in the 1559 Royal Injunctions, issued specifically for Salisbury Cathedral (which appears only to have acquired such copies as it had in the next century or later), all five of which, in any case, were of frequent occurrence in private collections: Ambrose, John Chrysostom (only the liturgy (L37) which bears his name is found in Geste's library), Eusebius of Caesarea, Jerome and Justin Martyr. In addition, although he possessed eight items of Augustine of Hippo[100] who was central to the Western theological tradition, there was no set of his *Opera*, unusual for a scholar in his position, and there are other significant editions missing, such as Boethius, collections of the Church Councils, and the works of Cyril of Alexandria (often discussed in connexion with the eucharistic controversies), Cyril of Jerusalem and Epiphanius.[101] Despite these deficiencies, it is clear that his was a large working collection, used as a resource in examining the arguments of contemporary theologians on the disputed issues of the day. Over thirty of the items contain annotations in his hand, among them such familiar writers as Augustine (A60, and possibly his copies of A61 and A66), Cyprian of Carthage (C127–28), Euthymius (E58–59), John of Damascus (J12–13), Prosper of Aquitaine (P55–56), and Theophylact (T8–9), and single volumes of Basil of Caesarea (B6), Bede (B10), pseudo-I Clement (C80), pseudo-Dionysius (D7), Eusebius of Emessa (E57), Haymo of Halberstadt (H9), Irenaeus (I5), Orosius (O22), Rabanus Maurus (R1), Tertullian (T3), and Theodoret of Cyrus (T4), among others.[102]

Scholastic and late-medieval books

Some items of Geste's scholastic and later medieval holdings have already been mentioned in connexion with his early years of study at Cambridge. Most of these carry early imprints, many of them incunabula, predating Geste's arrival in Cambridge (1536), some acquired 'second-hand' with evidence of use by former owners and readers in the form of marginalia and

100. Cat. nos. A60–67.
101. The inventory of King's College library (January 1556/57) drawn up for the Marian commissioners two years after Geste's departure lists sets of Augustine's works in six volumes (item 1), Jerome in five (2), Ambrose (3), and John Chrysostom in five (4), but not Eusebius of Caesarea or Justin Martyr. See *NKCL*.
102. See Appendix XII.2. Other annotated volumes are C57 (Charlemagne), O18 (Oecumenius), P53 (Primasius), S62 (Smaragdus), and Z1 (Zacharias). In the case of two further volumes it is not entirely certain that the annotations are by Geste: H41 (Heracleides) and O20 (Origen).

other annotations. Like Cranmer, his adoption of Protestant beliefs (quite apart from the controls already imposed on the University curriculum by the Henrician Injunctions) did not entail the exclusion of these scholastic writings from his library.[103] Not only were the older books retained, but among the eighty-five scholastic and late medieval items are eleven which on the evidence of their imprint dates must have been acquired towards the end of his time at Cambridge and afterwards, two of them towards the end of his life, as late as 1571. One of these was the *De officio episcopi* by Guibert of Tournai (G42), and the other a volume of sermons for Sundays and Festivals by St Thomas Aquinas (A46). His copy of Thomas à Kempis *The Imitation of Christ*, in the edition of Sebastien Castellio (K1), was published in 1563, Johann Tauler's *Exercitia* (T1) in 1565, and his annotated *Confessio* of the Waldensians, edited by Flacius Illyricus (W1), in 1568. He had copies of Anselm's commentaries on the Gospels and Pauline Epistles (A40–41) with imprints of 1549 and 1551, the latter (which Geste had annotated) also found in Perne's library,[104] but he had also acquired some items of more obviously scholastic outlook such as the *Paradisus animae* of Albertus Magnus printed at Antwerp in 1565 (A16), a *Flores operum* (1564) by St Bernard of Clairvaux (B16), and a work on the *Seven Sacraments* (1556) by Gulielmus Baufeti (G48). Most of Geste's scholastic books occur in some at least of the contemporary Cambridge inventories or in the libraries of Parker or Perne, but eleven appear to have been much less common, nine of them not even found in any of the Cathedral libraries, including the letters of Jan Hus (H93) and the *Confessio* of the Waldensians (W1) already mentioned (both with some of his annotations),[105] though other works of Hus and Thomas Netter's work against the Waldensians occur in these other collections. As with other sections of his library, a significant proportion of his medieval books contain some annotation in his hand, at least twenty-five items out of eighty-five, evidence that this was a working collection, even if the proportion annotated is not as high as it is for the biblical (about forty per cent) and patristic (thirty-four per cent) categories. There is evidence, for example, of considerable annotation in some of the books which probably belong to his early years of theological study at Cambridge, such as his copies of Biel on the Canon of the Mass (B46) – though nothing in his copy of William of Ockham *De sacramento altaris* (W41) – Bonaventura on the *Sentences* (B53), and two works of moral theology by the Dominican, Peraldus (P17) and Vincent of

---

103. *LTC*, Introduction, pp. lxxxv–lxxxvi.
104. Perne's inventory, no. 1333 in BiCI, I.
105. See Appendix XII.3 'Index of scholastic and late medieval works and authors'. In addition to the *Epistolae* of Jan Hus (H3) and the *Confessio* of the Waldensians (W1), he had works by Giles of Assisi (A3), Cagnazzo (C1), Castellensis (C49), Fidati (F7), Guibert (G42), Gulielmus, *Arvenus* (G46), Matthaei *de Utino* (M16) and Paulus *de Sancta Maria* (P13).

Beauvais (V27), as well as works on the biblical text, such as the Old Testament commentaries of Dionysius the Carthusian (D11–13), Hugh of St Cher, mainly on Proverbs (H82), and Pérez de Valentia on the Psalms (P18). His copy of Anselm (A41), however, in which some of the Pauline epistles have been annotated, must, on the evidence of its imprint (1551), date from at least the reign of Edward VI.

Contemporary scholarship and theology

But it was contemporary scholarship and theological writing that most engaged Geste's attention – on both sides of the Reformation divide – to judge by the sheer number of printed volumes he acquired and annotated right up to the year of his death.

Christian humanism

Like other collectors, his library reflected the impact of the 'new learning' of Christian humanism, with its emphasis on trilingual studies and the return to the sources as seen not only in the new editions of the scriptures (in the original languages) and the early Church Fathers, but also in its often radical approach to Christianity itself. Of the writings of the humanists themselves, Geste had inherited from his uncle, John Brandisby, books by Marsiglio Ficino (F5), Reuchlin (his Hebrew grammar, R17) and Erasmus (E48), and to these he added the *Platonica theologica* of Ficino (F6), Reuchlin's edition of the Hebrew text of the Penitential Psalms with his Latin translation (R18) and, over a long period, many more items of Erasmus, of which twenty-eight survive (E20–47], one with an imprint as late as 1555 (E43). Like his contemporary, Matthew Parker, who also had a substantial holding of Erasmus (though apparently smaller than that of Geste),[106] he did not own the 1540 edition of his collected works (at least it has not survived). It was evidently not common in Cambridge collections, though John Hatcher had a set, and Perne's is still extant at Peterhouse.[107] Other representatives of humanist scholarship in Geste's collection included Rodolphus Agricola (A12), Jodocus Badius (B2), Nicolaus Clenardus (C81), Sebastian Münster (M83–85), Robert Estienne (E53–54), Jacques Le Fèvre (L22–25), Thomas More (M81), Santes Pagninus (B30) and Vives (V38–39), as well as mainly theological and biblical works by Philip Melanchthon (M43–67) and Oecolampadius (O3–16). All these authors, though not necessarily all the individual items, as well as other humanist authors not represented in

---

106. Eighteen Erasmus items owned by Parker currently appear in the on-line catalogue of Corpus Christi College. For Geste's holdings of 'Humanist' authors, see Appendix XII.4.
107. BiCI, II, p. 305. Hatcher's 1587 Inventory no. 154, item 576; Perne's inventory no. 164, item 1339 (Peterhouse, I.11.13-20).

Geste's library (such as Guillaume Budé, Paul Fagius, Thomas Linacre and Polydore Vergil,[108] for example) occur in Cambridge inventories of the period as well as in the collections of Parker and Perne.

But it was biblical and theological works by contemporary Protestants as well as their Catholic counterparts that form the major ingredient of Geste's library as it survives today. Many of these were not common in Cambridge at the time on the evidence of contemporary inventories, some do not occur at all, even in the libraries of Parker and Perne, and the question of how these were obtained by Geste is one that will have to be addressed again at a later stage.[109]

Reformed Protestants

Of those in the Reformed Protestant tradition (as distinct from the Lutherans), 152 items by fifty authors remain in his library, nearly half of which carry annotations in his hand. To these should be added thirteen items of Martin Bucer, exiled from Strasbourg as Regius Professor of Divinity during Geste's time at Cambridge until his death in 1551, only three of which are without annotation, and a further three of Bucer's colleague in the Strasbourg reform, Wolfgang Capito (two with annotations).[110] In view of the Cambridge connexion, it is not surprising to find Bucer's works also well represented in the libraries of Parker (eleven), who was also a recipient of a number of Bucer's own copies after his death, and Perne (thirteen), while some seventeen of his works occur in Cambridge inventories of the period, though not with any frequency.[111] By contrast, Perne had no works by Capito, Parker only one, and over the period to 1561 only four Cambridge inventories record any of his works.[112]

Like other English collectors of the period, Geste had a substantial holding of Calvin's works: nineteen items (C2–20), a figure exceeded by Parker's collection of Calvin (at least twenty-three items), and only slightly lower than the number listed in Perne's inventory (twenty). Seven of Geste's copies have annotations in his hand, but, predictably, it was his copy of the *Institutes* (in the Latin edition of 1559, C16) that was the most heavily annotated of all because of his interest in current controversies within Protestantism, as well as with his Catholic opponents, on such matters as sacramental and

---

108. But see Appendix I, *V3 (Polydore Vergil) for one item which may just possibly have belonged to him.
109. See below pp. 90, 102, 138–39.
110. Cat. B98–112 and C37–39 respectively. His holdings of 'Reformed Protestants' and those of Bucer and the Strasbourg reformers are listed in Appendices XII.9 and XII.8 respectively.
111. BiCI, II, pp. 154–56, the most commonly occurring works being the commentaries on the Gospels and the Pauline epistles.
112. BiCI, II, p. 184.

eucharistic doctrine, justification, predestination and the Christian ministry. Much the same issues were attracting his attention in the other most annotated Calvin item, the *Interim adultero-Germanum* published at Geneva ten years earlier (C17) which, like copies of the *Institutes*, also featured in Parker's library.[113] Calvin's successor in the same theological tradition as well as a biblical scholar and textual critic, Theodore Beza, was also well represented, with ten items in Geste's library (B20–29, all but two annotated), as he was to a much larger extent in Perne's (some twenty-five), though only three apparently occur in Parker's. Among other Reformed Protestants, Geste had eight items each of the writings of Musculus (M88–95), François Lambert (L2–9) – more difficult to place, but one who had increasingly diverged from the Lutheran mainstream – and the Italian exile Pietro Martire Vermigli (Peter Martyr), Bucer's opposite number as Regius Professor at Oxford (V12–19, all but two annotated). In addition, Geste's collection included six items by the elder Rodolphus Gualtherus (G36–41), four of Joannes à Lasco, the Polish exile in London who became Superintendent of the Strangers' Church there during the reign of Edward VI (L10–13) and Theodore Bibliander (B40–43), as well as three each of Ludovic Lavater (L19–21), Nicolaus Gallasius (G4–6) and Pierre Viret (V34–36). Copies of their writings could also be found in the libraries of Perne and Parker in much the same numbers, as was to be expected, though Perne had notably larger collections of Gualtherus (over twenty; Parker nine), Vermigli (eleven; Parker twelve) and Lavater (both of them six), and Parker had no less than sixteen items of Musculus, while, remarkably, à Lasco did not occur in either collection (or in any of the Cambridge inventories) and Lambert was represented by only two items in Perne's and four in Parker's.

Over twenty other writers and church formularies in the Reformed tradition were also represented in his collection by one or more items,[114] and these included his much annotated *Unio dissidentium* (B51), a copy of which had been purchased from Garrett Godfrey's shop by his uncle, John Brandisby (perhaps this very one) and occurring in at least seventeen Cambridge inventories of the period, though apparently not in the libraries of either

---

113. *Institutes* (1561 edn), Corpus Christi, Cambridge, E.6.3; 1568 edn Cambridge University Library D*.2.9(B).

114. In addition to the *Unio dissidentium*, works by Rodolphus Agricola (A12), Aretius of Berne (A50–51, both annotated), Antoine de la Roche de Chandieu (C56), Johann Brandmueller (B63–64), Lambertus Danaeus (D2), Petrus Dathenus (D3), Thomas Erastus (E49–50), the *Confession de foy* of the Reformed Churches of France (F33), the Helvetic Confession (H23), Christian Hessiander (H56), François Hotman (H80), Wilhelm Klebitz (K6), Caspar Megander (M26), the Ministers of the Reformed Church of Metz (M74), Conrad Pellican (P16), Valérand Poullain (P47), Jean Ribit (R25), Josias Simler (S55–56), Johannes Sleidanus (S59), Bartholomaeus Sylvius (S98), Zanchius (Z2) and two works issued by the Ministers of the Reformed Church of Zürich (Z6–7).

Perne or Parker. Some of these authors were found frequently in Cambridge inventories, though not always the particular work owned by Geste. His copy of Agricola's *Oratio de natiuitate Christi* (A12), for example, occurs in none of these inventories, while the *De inventione dialectica* (listed in no fewer than thirty-six contemporary Cambridge inventories), is absent from Geste's collection, though it is difficult to believe that he never used or owned one. Again, works by Conrad Pellican (especially the biblical commentaries), Thomas Erastus, Josias Simler and Johannes Sleidan occur with some frequency in the inventories, including Perne's, but the particular works by these authors which Geste owned were actually quite rare. Both works of Erastus (E49–50), for example, occur in none of these collections; of the two items by Simler (both on the Trinity), only one (S55) is found in Cambridge (Perne's library); while Sleidan's *De statu religionis & reipublicae* (S59) and the Pellican commentary (P16) were only slightly more common in Cambridge, the former occurring in Perne's library and four inventories (though three of them date from after Geste's lifetime), and the latter found in one post-Geste inventory, Parker's and the 1583 University Library catalogue. Most of the works by Aretius of Berne, Lambertus Danaeus, La Roche de Chandieu and Zanchius, were not published during Geste's lifetime, but he owned the *Problemata theologica* (A51) of Aretius (found in Perne and eight inventories), while his *Examen theologicum* (A50), the *Refutatio* (C56) of La Roche and the *Miscellanea theologica* (Z2) of Zanchius were rarities in Cambridge at the time, and the *Elenchi haereticorum* (D2) of Danaeus occurred only in Perne and two of the inventories. The two volumes of wedding and funeral sermons (based on Lutheran models) which Johann Brandmueller published in 1572 and 1576 (B63–64) were also rare, occurring in only one Cambridge inventory, long after Geste,[115] and absent from the collections of Parker or Perne; and the items by Jean Ribit (R25) and Valerand Poullain (P47) were found only in a volume of Parker's devoted to Eucharistic doctrine comprising both Lutheran and Reformed writers, nine items of which are common to both collections.[116] Finally, four authors in the Reformed tradition – Hessiander (H53), Klebitz (K6), Megander (M26) and Sylvius (S98) – and a document issued by the Reformed Church of Metz (M74), were wholly absent from Cambridge collections of the time, Dathenus and François Hotman were represented in Cambridge only by other works, and two Reformed confessional formularies, one from France (F33), the other from Switzerland (H23), were found only in Perne's library and, in the case of the latter, possibly in one other inventory,[117] an indication of the rarity of so much of the material in Geste's collection.

115. An inventory dated 1592, BiCI, II, p. 141.
116. Parker's copy is CCCC, SP 42; the contents of Geste's volume are listed in W48.
117. One inventory of 1559 includes an item 'Helvetius', BiCI, II, p. 414.

From the Swiss-German tradition of Reformed Protestantism – on the face of it less amenable to Geste on account of its sacramental theology – only two Zwingli items occur in his library (Z6–7), far short of the twelve in Parker's and the four-volume collected *Opera* and the *Epistolarum libri quatuor* of Oecolampadius and Zwingli in Perne's (of which Cranmer had also owned copies).[118] But the writings of Zwingli's colleague at Berne, Oecolampadius, chiefly his biblical commentaries (much collected at least by English owners), number no fewer than fourteen in Geste's library (O3–16), with smaller, though still significant, collections in Perne (eight) and Parker (eleven), while at least thirteen of his works occur in one or more of the Cambridge inventories. The writings of Zwingli's successor at Zürich, Heinrich Bullinger, who had a wide circle of supporters and correspondents among English Reformers of the Swiss-German persuasion (which did not include, so far as is known, either Parker or Geste) were nonetheless well represented in their libraries, as well as that of Perne and other Cambridge libraries of the time. At least forty-four of his works occur in these libraries and inventories, sixteen of them being biblical commentaries, though only two of his works in English translation occur in these Cambridge collections, both in the stock of the stationer, John Denys, who died in 1578.[119] Geste owned at least seventeen of Bullinger's works (B118–34), with the possibility of a further five (listed in Appendix I, though the evidence for his ownership of these is not strong);[120] Parker had eighteen (four in Cambridge University Library, the others in the Parker Library at Corpus Christi College), and Perne fourteen.[121] Geste's holdings (at least as they survive today) show a greater preponderance of theological and polemical works over biblical commentaries. In fact, only three of the latter (on Jeremiah, Lamentations and the Acts) survive – a rather small number in comparison with those in the collections of Parker (ten) or Perne (six). Eight of Geste's copies contain some form of annotation. In all but two of these, this amounts to little

---

118. Cranmer in *LTC*, nos. 234 and 235.

119. *Questions of Religion* (STC 4054) and his *Common Places of Religion* (STC 4055); BiCI, II, pp. 160, 162; I, inventory no. 142, items 202 and 326.

120. See Appendix I, *B12–16.

121. Parker's Bullinger donations to the University Library were all biblical commentaries: Isaiah, D*.2.29(B); Daniel, D*3.17(B); the Epistles, D*.9.24(B); and the Apocalypse, D*.2.26(B). See CUL 1583, nos. 47.1, 50.3, 17 and 16, respectively. At Corpus Christi College, Parker's copy of *Historia evangelica* and the commentary on Mark were replaced by another in 1608 (now E.4.17), but his copies of those on Acts (SP.223), the Epistles (E.4.16), I Corinthians (SP.110), and I Peter (SP.253) remain, as well as works against the Anabaptists (Adams B3191, SP.228); his refutation of the Papal Bull against Elizabeth I (STC 4043), SP.344; his *De Coena Domini sermo* (Adams B3195), SP.42(5), *De origine erroris* (Adams B3201), SP.46, *De scripturae sanctae authoritate* (Adams B3206), SP.287, the *Decades* (Adams B3255–57), SP.163(1), SP.265(1) and SP.163(2), and his copy of Adams B3262B, SP.389(1). Perne's copies of Bullinger are listed in BiCI, II, pp. 160–62.

more than the occasional line in the margin or some underlining of the text, but the tract on justification was clearly of more interest to him,[122] and there are some notes relating to the sacraments in another of his works, Bullinger's *Fundamentum firmum* (B130). Geste's collection of Bullinger was probably one of the largest of the period, at least for a private library in England. As it survives today, it seems surprisingly short on Bullinger's biblical commentaries – perhaps there have been losses since Geste's death – and although nearly half of his copies are annotated in some way, his works do not seem to have attracted the detailed attention Geste gave to some other authors in the Reformed tradition.

Other Protestants and religious radicals

Like Perne and Parker, Geste had in his library writings by other non-Lutheran Protestants – less easy to classify, some strongly humanist in outlook, some associated with the Italian religious reform, some regarded by mainstream Protestant reformers as doctrinally heterodox on particular beliefs such as the Trinity or belonging to the 'Radical' wing of the Reformation as anabaptists or 'Spirituals'. Geste had, for example, copies of three of the Old Testament commentaries of Martin Borrhaus (Cellarius), all published at Basle (B59–61). Borrhaus (1499–1564) had been a friend of Melanchthon, his fellow student while at Tübingen, and briefly a follower of Luther before he was won over by Stübner to become a temporary adherent of the views of the radical Zwickau 'prophets' in 1526, publishing in the following year his *De operibus Dei* at Strasbourg, also owned by Geste (B62), a work which departed from Nicene terminology, leaving him doctrinally suspect in the eyes of mainstream Protestants, such as Calvin, for the rest of his life. In addition, Borrhaus was thought to be sympathetic towards the Anabaptists, though never himself becoming one.[123] Yet despite this background, his commentaries occur in a number of Cambridge inventories, including Perne's library, and there were four of them, presented to the University Library in 1574, as well as the *De operibus Dei*, still at Corpus Christi College, in Parker's.[124]

Another radical, and one-time Calvinist, the French-Italian humanist scholar, Sebastien Castellion, also found a place in Geste's library, not his

---

122. *De gratia Dei iustificante nos propter Christum, per solam fidem absq[ue] operibus bonis, fide interim exuberante in opera bona* (B125).
123. See in brief, Williams, pp. 47, 251, 628, who places him 'on the shifting boundaries between Spiritualism and Anabaptism'.
124. BiCI, II, p. 139; Parker's copy of *De operibus Dei* is in Corpus Christi College: Y.7.18(4); his copies of the biblical commentaries (Adams B2507–10) are in the University Library: D*.10.7(C), D*.3.18(B), D*.3.15(B) and D*.3.16(B) respectively. See Appendix XII.10 for a listing of his and the other writers discussed below.

work advocating 'liberal' views on the treatment of heretics under the pseudonym 'Martin Bellius' (which contributed to his final break with Calvin) or the *Dialogues*,[125] but the *Defensio*, advocating his translation of the Bible (C50). Castellion's entirely new Latin translation of the Bible, on the humanist principle of 'good Latinity' (1551), had been dedicated to the young Edward VI and included high praise for Cheke, Provost of Geste's college, King's; he was to be recommended by à Lasco as a possible successor to Bucer as Regius Professor at Cambridge.[126] Geste probably had a copy of one of the editions of Castellion's translation, as Parker did,[127] but none of the extant copies at Salisbury contains convincing evidence of his ownership (*B9–11), and only the *Defensio* is undoubtedly his, though without any annotation. Both Parker and Perne also had copies of the *Defensio*, and the *Dialogues* occur in several of the Cambridge inventories and in Perne's collection.[128]

A number of these writers found in Geste's library had earlier associations with the Italian religious reform, like the Reformed theologian, Pietro Martire Vermigli, taking an interest in the progress of Protestant reform in England, and some of them (like him) joining the growing number of foreigners who came to take part, in many different ways, often as religious exiles.

One of these, a colleague of Castellion at Basle, though never an exile in England, was the Italian 'Erasmian', Coelius Secundus Curio (Curione). Curio, like Vermigli, Ochino and the Hebrew scholar Tremellio, had fled from Italy in 1542 when it became clear that the teaching of these Italian 'reformers' was attracting unfavourable attention from the Church hierarchy. After crossing the Alps to Lausanne, Curio finally settled at Basle where he became a professor in 1547, remaining there for the rest of his life. Like Castellion, Curio never came to England, but, like other like-minded Italians who had come into contact with Englishmen travelling to Italy for study, he took an interest in its reform. When Ochino moved to England in 1547 at the invitation of Cranmer, Curio sent with him a letter of introduction, a message to Cheke and some of his own writings, clearly intending to be 'noticed' at Court,[129] and he followed this up in 1551 by dedicating his edition of Cicero's oration *Philippicae* to Edward VI himself.[130] Furthermore, in the reign of Elizabeth, Curio's anti-papal satyrical dialogue *Pasquillus Ecstaticus*, first published shortly after his flight from Italy, was translated into English (evidently by William Page) in 1566 and again in a new edition

125. *De haereticis* (1544, Adams C913); *Dialogi* (various items, Adams C914–18).
126. Overell, p. 86f.
127. Parker's copy of the 1573 edn (Adams B1083) was donated to Cambridge University Library in 1574 (CUL 1.23.39).
128. Parker's copy is CCCC SP.418, Perne's is item 514 in his inventory, BiCI, I, 164; BiCI, II, p. 190, lists four inventories earlier than Perne's of 1589.
129. Overell, especially p. 58.
130. Adams C1884; Overell, p. 86.

in 1580,[131] and the works of the classical humanist Olympia Fulvia Morata, which after her premature death in 1555 he had edited (as well as contributing some of his own letters and orations) at Basle in 1558 were issued again in three further editions all dedicated to the Queen between 1562 and 1580.[132] It is no surprise therefore to find a few of Curio's works cropping up in some of the Cambridge inventories and in the libraries of Parker (four items) and Perne (two), as well as one, and just possibly two items, in Geste's.[133] At least five of his works can be identified in one or more of the Cambridge inventories,[134] including the *Pasquillus ecstaticus,* the *De amplitudine beati regni Dei* (1554), expounding his own view of predestination and dedicated to the King of Poland, a copy of which was also owned by Perne,[135] and his *Pro uera & antiqua Ecclesiae Christi autoritate oratio* (1550) of which Parker and Geste as well as Perne had copies.[136] But although Parker possessed, in addition, copies of his *Thesaurus linguae Latinae* (though only two out of three volumes have survived) and an edition of Seneca,[137] none of the works Curio had dedicated specifically to Edward or Elizabeth occurs in the libraries of Geste, Perne or any of the Cambridge inventories.

The writings of probably the most renowned of these Italians exiled in England, the preacher and former Vicar-General of the Capuchin Franciscans, Bernardino Ochino, are actually rather less well represented in these Cambridge collections than Castellion or Curio. Ochino – a refugee from the occupation of Augsburg by imperial forces during the Schmalkaldic War – had been invited to England to assist in the reform of the church by Cranmer in 1547, and to this end he was appointed minister of the Italian congregation in Bonner's diocese of London with a royal pension and a prebendal stall at Canterbury until his return to the continent, again as an exile, during the reign of Mary. It is clear that his reputation as a preacher was particularly valued by his English patrons and this led to the publication of many of his sermons for a wider public in English translation over the years 1548–51,[138] as well as the translation by John Ponet, Cranmer's chaplain, of his play celebrating the overthrow of papal authority in England,

---

131. STC 6130–31, translated by 'W.P.'. The revised edition of STC, I, p. 275, notes that in one copy of STC 6130, the title page gives the name of the translator as 'William Page', further strengthening the case for Page put forward by Overell, p. 191f.

132. Overell, p. 168 n .6. Adams records only the 1572 and 1580 editions (M1741–42).

133. C124, and just possibly Appendix I, *C13.

134. BiCI, II, p. 252f.

135. Adams C3084: Perne (BiCI, I) no. 1282.

136. Adams C3091: Parker SP.209(1); Perne (BiCI, I) no. 513; Geste C124.

137. Adams C3094: Parker at CCCC L.7.18–19; Seneca (Adams S887), Parker copy at CCCC G.3.7(1).

138. STC 18764–67. Among the translators were the Princess Elizabeth, Anne Cooke and Richard Argentyne; Overell, pp. 47–49.

the *Tragoedie or Dialoge* in 1549.[139] However, apart from a Latin translation of his Romans commentary (1545) by his colleague Castellion in 1550,[140] it seems that little else was published during his time in England, and it was only after his return to the continent where he settled in Zürich that his theological writing resumed and became decidedly controversial, leading to his banishment from the city, following the publication of his *Dialogi XXX* in 1563. In this he was, in the eyes of his opponents, ambivalent on the Trinity, critical of those who practiced coercion in matters of faith (with particular reference to the treatment of Servetus and the anabaptists) and even seemed to condone polygamy.[141] It was perhaps this stain on his reputation – rather than accidents of survival – that accounts for his under-representation in the libraries of Geste's Cambridge contemporaries. Parker seems to have owned no Ochino at all – even from the pre-Zürich period – and no item of his appears among the Cambridge inventories, other than Perne who had a copy of his book on eucharistic doctrine against the Lutheran Westphal at the height of the ubiquitarian controversy.[142] It might have been thought that Geste would also have had a copy of this work, because of his interest in this controversy and eucharistic doctrine in general, but the Ochino item he owned was the *De Purgatorio dialogus* of 1555 (O2), and there is also a copy of the controversial *Dialogi XXX* at Salisbury which may just possibly have belonged to him.[143] All three Ochino items belong therefore to his Zürich period, but it is now impossible to ascertain what attitude Geste or Perne might have taken towards the ideas these contain. Perne's copy is no longer extant, Geste's copy of *De Purgatorio* is without annotation, and the notes in the copy of *Dialogi XXX* do not appear to be his, while his ownership in any case is far from certain.

Another of these Italians whose views on the Trinity were suspect in the eyes of mainstream Protestantism – though this time the clash took place in Geneva and involved Calvin – was Joannes Valentinus Gentilis. In 1558, Calvin had attempted to secure the assent of the Italian congregation in Geneva to an orthodox confession on the Trinity, but although some of his other opponents such as Gribaldi and John Alciati made their escape, Gentilis, after some resistance and imprisonment, eventually agreed to sign the confession and was obliged to make a very public and humiliating recantation of his opinions.[144] Although none of the writings relating to this

---

139. STC 18770–71. On this play, see Stephen Alford, *Kingship and Politics in the Reign of Edward VI* (Cambridge: University Press, 2003), pp. 105–16. I owe this reference to Dr Anne Overell.
140. Adams O27, from the Italian of 1545 (Adams O28–29).
141. Adams O23–24.
142. *Syncerae et verae doctrinae de Coena Domini defensio contra libros tres I. Westphali,* Zürich, 1556 (Adams O39); Perne (BiCI, I) inventory no. 164, item 538.
143. Appendix I, *O1.
144. On this, see Williams, especially pp. 635–38.

episode has been identified in contemporary Cambridge inventories, Geste (as well as Parker) had a copy of the *Impietas Valentini Gentilis detecta* with Calvin's Preface, published at Geneva in 1561 (G21), and a further volume at Salisbury relating to the affair (of which Perne also had a copy) may have belonged to him.[145]

Two other Italians who featured in Geste's library must be mentioned here, though. the first of them, Pier Paulo Vergerio, the former Catholic bishop of Capo d'Istria who converted to Lutheranism in the 1540s, never actually visited England, though taking a close interest in its reform, and later held a post at the court of the Lutheran Duke of Württemberg. In later years, Vergerio may have exaggerated his earlier acquaintance with Reginald Pole in the 'Italian reform', but when their ways parted, Pole remaining loyal to the Catholic Church and the papacy, Vergerio castigated him as a 'Nicodemite' for compromising his belief in justification by faith (he had earlier published his own version of the 'tragedy' of Francesco Spiera in 1551). And he attempted to embarrass Pole further by editing a re-issued text of the earlier *Pro ecclesiasticae unitatis defensione* in 1555, with additional anti-papal texts from Lutheran and Calvinist authors, at a time when Pole was now deeply involved in restoring the English Church to the Roman obedience.[146] Geste owned a copy of Vergerio's edition of Pole (P40) as well as the *Dialogi quatuor,* published in 1559 (V11), in which he defended himself and his fellow Lutheran, Brentz, against Stanislaus Hosius. Perne also had copies of both works, and both are still extant at Peterhouse.[147] But apart from possible references to the Pole item in two other Cambridge inventories,[148] no work by Vergerio occurs in any of the inventories or even in Parker's library.

The other Italian to be found in Geste's library, Jacob Acontius (Giacomo Aconcio), was almost as rare in Cambridge collections as Vergerio, perhaps because of his views on religious toleration and his support for some Anabaptist members of the Dutch Strangers' Church which had led to his excommunication by the bishop of London, Edmund Grindal. A native of

145. Parker's copy of the *Impietas Valentini Ge[n]tilis detecta* (Adams G429 / C373) is CCCC SP.406; the volume which may also have belonged to Geste consists of two items (Appendix I, *G2 and *A10) both published at Geneva in 1567, the first with a preface by Beza and Benedictus Aretius (Adams G428) and the second by Aretius (Adams A1625), and Perne's copy of the same editions, still extant at Peterhouse, Cambridge, N.11.38 (inventory no. 164 in BiCI, I, item 464), also combined both items.

146. On this, see Overell, especially chapter seven, 'Pier Paolo Vergerio and Cardinal Pole', pp. 145–66.

147. Perne's inventory in BiCI, I, no. 164, items 769 and 322, Peterhouse L.4.19 and L.5.37, respectively; BiCI, II, pp. 633 and 776.

148. BiCI, II, p.633: the reference in Buckley's inventory of 1559 ['The bishop of Canterburies boke'] may not even be to this work, and it is not certain whether the reference in Parkinson's inventory of 1569 is to Vergerio's edition or to Pole's original of 1536 (Adams P1742).

Trent and a former secretary to the governor of Milan, Cardinal Modruzzo, Acontius had fled from Italy in 1557, and in the course of his travels had spent nearly a year in Zürich, where Ochino, who held rather similar views on religious coercion, was pastor to the Italian community. He then moved on to Paris where he was recruited as a military engineer by Sir Nicholas Throckmorton. This brought Acontius to London in 1559 where besides furthering his engineering career and attempting to tidy up Ochino's English business affairs, he developed his ideas on religious toleration in his *Satanae Stratagemata* (religious persecution being one of 'Satan's Stratagems') which he had published at Basle in 1565.[149] It was this work of Acontius that features in Geste's library (A2), though unfortunately without any annotation. Perne also had a copy, apparently no longer extant,[150] and it occurs in one of the Cambridge inventories.[151] Once again, there is no known copy of this, or of any other work of his, in Parker's library.

Another theological writer in Geste's collection who shared similar views on religious toleration to Acontius was the Spaniard, Antonio del Corro, from Seville, who settled in London in 1567 after some years of exile in Lausanne and Flanders, having fled from Spain in 1558. Probably better known as the author of the first Spanish grammar to be published in England,[152] Corro attached himself to the Italian congregation in London, preaching to a group in Spanish, until his suspension by Grindal in 1569 after doubts were raised by the French pastors about his doctrinal orthodoxy. He then went on to hold teaching posts at the Middle Temple and at Oxford from 1578, as well as prebendal stalls at St Paul's and Lichfield cathedrals. But suspicions about his doctrinal soundness on predestination (as understood by the Calvinists) and the Trinity, as well as accusations of Pelagianism, continued to haunt him until his death in 1591, and although a number of his writings were published in England during his lifetime, no work of his appears in any of the Cambridge inventories or in the libraries of Perne or Parker. Geste appears therefore to have been unusual in possessing one of them, the commentary on Romans, *Dialogus theologicus* with his *Articuli fidei orthodoxae* (C101) published in London in 1574, a work judged to be potentially of interest to English readers since it was translated the following year and issued by the same printer, Thomas Purfoot.[153]

Other works by Protestant authors in Geste's collection who are not easy to classify theologically included three biblical items by the physician, botanist and teacher, the former Carthusian, Otto Brunfels, active in Strasbourg

---

149. Overell, pp. 176–78; Williams, p. 783f.
150. BiCI, II, p. 2; Perne inventory in BiCI, I, no. 164, item 473.
151. BiCI, II, p. 2. The Cambridge stationer, John Denys held a copy (BiCI, I, inventory no. 142, item 195) at his death in 1578. The only other work by Acontius that occurs is the *De methodo* (Adams A115–16), Perne inventory in BiCI, I, no. 164, item 268 and that of another Cambridge stationer, Reignold Bridges (inventory in BiCI, I, no. 167, item 177) in 1590/91.
152. STC 5790.   153. STC 5784; English translation STC 5786.

and Berne, who died in the latter in 1534.[154] Of these only the *Pandectae scripturarum veteris noui Testamenti* (B96) occurs with any frequency in contemporary Cambridge inventories[155] (though neither Perne or Parker appear to have had copies) while the other two, a commentary on the Gospels and Acts (B95), and his *Problemata* (B97) feature in none of these collections, though other works of his do appear, particularly in the fields of botany and medicine.[156] Other writers represented in Geste's collection whose theological outlook similarly eludes simple classification include the French jurist, Charles du Moulin (1500–1566), who in the course of his career had associations with both Calvinism (after his initial conversion to Protestantism in France), and later with Lutheranism, after moving to Germany in the 1540s to teach law before returning to France in 1557. Three of his works occur in Cambridge inventories of the period, two of these in Perne's library, but none in Parker's. Geste possessed one of the two books which Perne owned (D30), but the other in his collection, a Harmony of the Gospels (D29), is not otherwise found in Perne or any of the Cambridge inventories.[157]

Another writer of eclectic tendencies was the Flemish-born theologian, Andreas Gerhard Hyperius (1511–1564), Professor of theology at Marburg, author of a number of biblical commentaries, a catechism, works on the study of theology, homiletics, and the interpretation of scripture, as well as books on dialectic and rhetoric and a commentary on Aristotle's Nicomachean ethics.[158] At least eighteen of his works occur in the Cambridge inventories, twelve of them in Perne's library, though only one in Parker's.[159] His catechetical work, *Elementa Christianae religionis* (1563, H97), one of the four works of this author found in Geste's library (H95–98), does not occur in any of the extant Cambridge inventories, or in the libraries of Perne or Parker, though at Oxford it was actually listed as compulsory reading by Convocation (1578–79), alongside the catechisms of Nowell, Calvin and Heidelberg, in a new statute concerned with the instruction of its junior

154. Williams, p. 199f.
155. BiCI, II, p. 151. The work is listed in eleven inventories up to 1581/2.
156. BiCI, II, p. 151f., including one medical work owned by Perne (inventory no. 164, item 1020) and three items (including an edited work of Jan Hus [Adams H1201]) in Parker's library (Adams B2921 and B2928) at Corpus Christi College: SP.462(9); SP.462(4), bound together in a volume formerly owned by Martin Bucer, and EP.V.4, respectively.
157. BiCI, II, p. 287f.
158. In this connexion, C. M. Dent writes of 'a hybrid tradition in which elements drawn from both Calvin and Luther coexist', *Protestant Reformers in Elizabethan Oxford* (Oxford: University Press, 1983, p. 90), and draws attention to Calvin's praise for his 'exceptional godliness and erudition' as well as his admiration for Bucer's writings.
159. BiCI, II, pp. 445–47. The only work Parker owned was his *De honorandis magistratibus commentarius* (1542, Adams H1271): CCCC, SP.211.

members in religious piety.[160] Geste's copy is much annotated, and it may be that he was assessing its potential value as well as vetting its theology as part of his new diocesan responsibilities as bishop of Rochester.

Finally, three other non-Lutheran Protestant writers in Geste's library, all highly critical of contemporary Catholicism, must be mentioned. The first was the Dutch preacher and Latin teacher from Amsterdam, Sartorius (or Snijder, later publishing under the pseudonym Joannes Tosarrius), who was one of those, along with Cornelius Hoen and Wilhelm Gnapheus de Volder, who had been influenced by the former Dominican, Wouter, to adopt 'sacramentarian' views on the Lord's Supper and to write against transubstantiation, for which he was imprisoned at The Hague in 1525, subsequently recanting. Despite this confrontation with the ecclesiastical authorities, Sartorius continued his scholarly and teaching activities elsewhere in Holland and also in Basle where he published, under the pseudonym Tosarrius, his *Paraphrases on the Prophets and Wisdom of Solomon* in 1558.[161] It was this, rather than any of his polemical works, that Geste acquired, perhaps in the late 1560s, since his copy (T17) is bound with three other Old Testament commentaries by Lutheran and Reformed authors published in 1569–70. No copy of the *Paraphrases* occurs in any of the Cambridge inventories, Perne or Parker, but there was a copy in the University Library by 1583,[162] and another work attributed to him occurs in Perne's inventory, though apparently no longer at Peterhouse.[163]

The second of these writers was the German polemical dramatist and Protestant pastor, Thomas Kirchmeyer (Naogeorgus), whose best-known drama, the anti-papal *Tragoedia noua Pammachius* (1538), dedicated to Thomas Cranmer, had been performed at Christ's College, Cambridge in 1545 to the obvious fury of the University's then Chancellor, Stephen Gardiner, who detected in its critique of the papacy a more subversive attack on contemporary religious practice and ceremonies.[164] No copy of this survives among Geste's books (though Perne had a copy),[165] but he had Kirchmeyer's commentary on the First Epistle of John (K3), also found in one of the Cambridge inventories,[166] which had sealed the author's break with Lutheran

160. Dent, *Protestant Reformers* (1983), pp. 87–92.
161. Williams, p. 349f.
162. CUL 1583, p. 171, [31.2], now D*.7.32(B).
163. BiCI, II, p. 687, 'Disputatio de tribus generibus peccatorum', Perne inventory no. 164, item 791.
164. Diarmaid MacCulloch, *Thomas Cranmer: A Life* (New Haven and London: Yale University Press, 1996), p. 324, and references given there; Alec Ryrie, *The Gospel and Henry VIII: Evangelicals in the Early English Reformation* (Cambridge: University Press, 2003), pp. 179–82. I owe this second reference to Dr A. Overell.
165. Perne inventory in BiCI, I, no. 164, item 90 (though his copy is no longer extant at Peterhouse).
166. Inventory of Oliver Ainsworth, Fellow of Jesus College (1546), no. 30, item 91; BiCI, II, p. 566.

orthodoxy on account of his teaching on the state of the elect who sinned against their conscience. Geste also owned his later work, *De infantum ac parvulorum salute* (K4) published at Basle in 1556 which does not appear in any of the contemporary Cambridge inventories or collections.

The third of these writers represented in Geste's collection was the widely travelled German Protestant satirist, Johann Fischart (Donatus Gotvisus) who may have visited England in *c.* 1569/70 before publishing his polemic against the Jesuits, *Fides Iesu et Iesuitarum*, issued with a Preface by the Lutheran, Johann Marbach, in 1573 (F9). This was another work which did not figure in any of the contemporary Cambridge inventories (including the 1583 University Library catalogue), but Geste had clearly studied his copy closely, to judge by the frequent markings that occur in the margins, and both Perne and Parker also had copies.[167]

This relatively small group of twenty-four works by some fourteen authors of very varied outlook, six of them associated at some time with the Italian reform is not, therefore, strongly represented in contemporary Cambridge collections. No works by the Spaniard, Antonio del Corro (C101), for example, occur in any other collection than Geste's, despite the publication of his works, and even the translation of one of them, in England,[168] and it was only Perne (other than Geste) who possessed anything of Ochino – and that only a single work.[169] The University Library collection, then being built up from a very low base by donations, as a result of Perne's initiative, held copies of only four of the items which Geste owned – biblical commentaries by Borrhaus and Sartorius – and all four of these were gifts from Parker in 1574.[170]

Lutheran writers

By far the largest single component in Geste's collection of contemporary writers was Lutheran, far outnumbering – both in the authors represented and the number of their published works – those held by Perne, Parker or any of the inventories preserved in the Cambridge University archives.[171] In fact, the University Library's 1583 catalogue records works by only six Lutheran authors – Luther himself, Johann Brentz, Melanchthon, Georg Meier, the Magdeburg Centuriators, and Strigelius – many of them donated

---

167. Perne inventory (BiCI, I) no. 164, item 647 (though his copy is not extant at Peterhouse), BiCI, II, p. 389 (s.v. Gotvisus); Parker's copy is CCCC SP.260.
168. STC 5784–94.
169. BiCI, II, p. 576 (Perne inventory in BiCI, I, no. 164, item 538).
170. Sartorius [Tosarius], CUL 1583, p. 171 [31.2] C*7.32(B); Borrhaus, CUL 1583, pp. 171–74 [34.1] D*10.7(C); [38.2] D*3.18(B); [43.2] D*.3.15(B); and [48.1] D*.3.16(B) respectively.
171. See Appendix XII.7 for a listing of these Lutheran writers.

by Parker[172] in 1574. If the number of Lutheran items listed in the University Library's 1583 catalogue is taken at its face value – as a measure of interest in Lutheranism by the 1580s – then the most obvious inference to be drawn is that few Cambridge readers were expected to consult more than a few of their biblical commentaries – certainly none of their doctrinal or polemical writings.

Geste's was clearly a special case. It is not certain when he acquired his first Lutheran book, but there are three in his collection printed as early as 1521 – two of Luther's (L69, L74), one of Melanchthon's (M56) – presumably obtained fairly early on in his Cambridge career, and his uncle, John Brandisby, had given him Luther's *Propositiones* (L72), published at Wittenberg in 1538, one of five books from that source which, to judge from the wording of Geste's inscription on a leaf at the end of the text, 'good maister Brandes[by] | accept my wytt' – also belong to his early years at Cambridge.[173] From these beginnings Geste went on to add further Lutheran works to his collection throughout his career, and although he never purchased any of the collected editions of Luther or Melancthon – unlike Parker or Perne – he was acquiring single works by Lutheran authors right up to the end of his life, many of them annotated. Geste's purchases of Lutheran works in the last years of his life included a work of Luther's with an imprint as late as 1573 (L71), an edition of Melanchthon's letters (1570, M61), and even later items, such as a commentary on Numbers by Chytraeus (1572, C69), two books by Camerarius (1572, C24–25), the third and fourth parts of Chemnitz' work on the Council of Trent (1573, C61–62), biblical commentaries by Henricus Mollerus (1573–1574, M76–77), Tilemann Heshusius (1573, H47) and Johann Wigand, works on pastoralia, by Niels Hemmingsen (1574, H39), eucharistic doctrine by Flacius Illyricus (1574, F15) and Joachim Cureus (1575, C123), and the first volume of Brentz' collected works published as late as 1576 (B68) – only a year before Geste's death.

Geste's library (as it survives today) contains at least 373 works by 103 Lutheran authors, and this total includes 159 biblical commentaries or expositions of the liturgical lections, and a further four items on the

172. Luther: CUL 1583, p. 170 [23.1–2]: 'Lutherus in quosdam veteris test: Aliquot novi'; CUL 1583, p. 172 [35]: 'In Genes: Tom. 6'. No copies extant, so it is not now possible to know which commentaries and editions were involved. Melanchthon: CUL 1583, p. 170 [23.3–4]: 'Melancton in quosdam veteris test: Aliquot novi'. Similarly, no copies extant and editions unknown. Brentz: CUL 1583, pp. 168, 170, 172: commentaries in Matthew [8.1], John [9.2], Luke [10], Acts [13.1], Galatians – Philemon and Esther [21.2], in Leviticus [37.2], Exodus [37.3], Joshua [37.4], Judges and Ruth [38.3], and Samuel [39.1], all copies extant and all donations by Parker. Georg Meier [Major]: CUL 1583, p. 168: a commentary on the Pauline epistles [14], another Parker donation. Magdeburg Centuriators: CUL 1583, p. 228 [455], not located. Donated by George Gardiner, Dean of Norwich, 1583.
173. See Appendix X – Provenances, s.v. Geste and Brandisby.

authority of scripture or its interpretation. For comparison, Perne's much larger library held about 163 Lutheran items by forty-six authors, including two collected editions of Melanchthon and one of Luther,[174] and Parker's (about the same size as Geste's in the number of his printed books) about ninety items by twenty-six Lutheran authors, including the single volume 1520 edition of Luther's *Opera* and a four-volume edition of Melanchthon.[175] None of the contemporary inventories contains anything like a Lutheran collection of this size, but taking the inventories as a whole, nearly 260 items by forty-eight Lutheran authors are represented.

Geste's collection of Lutheran works includes some large holdings, many of them annotated (some 193 items, with a further nine not certainly in his hand), a practice he followed throughout his life. These included thirty-one items by Luther himself (twelve of them annotated); twenty-six of Johann Brentz (sixteen annotated); twenty-five of Melanchthon (thirteen annotated), and some slightly smaller, but still significant holdings of Hemmingsen and Georg Maier (both sixteen), Flacius Illyricus (fifteen) and Erasmus Sarcerius (fourteen). Comparisons with the holdings of Luther and Melanchthon are less easy to make in the cases of Parker and Perne because both owned collected editions of these authors, with much smaller numbers of individual items. But Perne, for example, had nineteen works of Brentz (Parker, sixteen) and nine each of Chytraeus and Hemmingsen, while by contrast, Parker had only three of Hemmingsen and none at all of Chytraeus. Although smaller by comparison with Geste's, Parker also had significant holdings of Bugenhagen (five items), and four each of François Lambert, Sarcerius and Westphal.[176]

Particularly interesting is the case of this last Lutheran author; for all Parker's known surviving copies of Westphal are to be found in a single multi-item volume on Eucharistic doctrine containing, beside Westphal's, works by Reformed writers, Calvin, Bullinger, Poullain, Ribittus and Sylvius,

174. Figures in Appendix XII.7. Perne had the seven-volume Wittenberg edition of Luther (1545–58), still extant at Peterhouse [E.9.4–10], and for this and his other holdings of Luther, see BiCI II, pp. 509–13 (with references to Adams). Parker's copy of the one-volume 1520 edition of Luther's works (Adams L1735) is Corpus Christi College, SP.116. His copy of the Melanchthon *Opera* (Adams M1068) is also at Corpus: E.3.9–12. Data for Parker is derived from Adams and the catalogues of Corpus Christi College and CUL, now the on-line Cambridge 'iDiscover' catalogue.

175. Thus Parker had, in addition to the one-volume Latin edition of 1520, only seventeen additional items of Luther, seven of them in common with Geste (L50, L52, L57, L61, L64, L75 and L78) and fourteen additional items of Melanchthon (beside the four-volume *Opera*), only three of them in common with Geste (M49, M62 and M63).

176. The figures for Perne are extracted from BiCI, II (under each author) and the 1589 inventory in BiCI, I, pp. 419–79; those for Parker are from Adams and the Corpus Christi College catalogue (as in n. 174, above).

nine of which occur in a similar volume owned by Geste.[177] Both are in contemporary bindings, and there is good reason, therefore, to suppose that the contents of both (and even the original order) are still intact. The Parker collection cannot be earlier than 1558 (the imprint date of the Westphal items), the Geste a little later (not earlier than 1562), if the edition of the first item (W48) – the text of the 1536 Lutheran Wittenberg Concord – is in fact a fragment extracted from a copy of Bucer's *Enarrationes perpetuae, in sacra quatuor Euangelia,* published at Leipzig in 1562.[178] It is not known to what extent the two owners influenced or even determined the content of these two volumes, or what role the bookseller (presumably in London) played in the selection of items, but the fact that nine of them are common to both can hardly be sheer coincidence. Nor is it clear what significance (if any) should be attached to the few items not common to each volume: in Geste's volume, a work by à Lasco and the text of the Wittenberg Concord, and in Parker's, the presence of a work by Micronius and the absence of à Lasco (not otherwise represented in his library) and one of the items by Westphal. But even with these minor divergences, both volumes still achieve an equal balance between Lutherans and writers in the Reformed tradition, five of each in Parker's, six of each in Geste's. While no more than speculation, a possible context for these two acquisitions might be the preparations early in Elizabeth's reign for the new Articles of Religion issued in 1563, and in particular the articles relating to eucharistic doctrine in which, as has already been suggested, there is evidence of some divergence between Geste and Parker.[179]

Whatever the context, Geste's copy of these works is of interest because of his practice of annotating works that particularly interested him, while leaving others without annotation and even unopened leaves. The item by Calvin (C20) which is directed specifically against Westphal's defence of the real presence is not annotated at all, though Geste had annotated other books of Calvin touching on these issues, notably his copy of the *Institutes* (C16). In fact, the only item containing annotations from the Reformed tradition is the Poullain (P47), but in this instance it is not the *Antidotus* of Poullain that has been annotated but the attached *Aphorisms* of Martin Bucer. In the case of the Lutheran items, Geste has annotated, often extensively, Westphal's *Apologia confessionis de Coena Domini* attacking Calvin (W10), and there are some annotations, mainly in the form of marginal lines, in the earlier *De Coena Domini confessio* (W12), though there are unopened leaves as well. The first of the ten items in Geste's copy, the Wittenberg *Concord* of 1536

177. Parker's copy is CCCC SP.42; Geste's copy is cat. no. W48.
178. Geste's copy (W48) is without title page or imprint. It appears to be, as the editors of the *Cathedral Libraries Catalogue* suggest (s.v. CLC B2567), a fragment extracted from a copy of the 1562 edition of Bucer's *Enarrationes perpetuae, in sacra quatuor Euangelia* no longer extant in Geste's library. There is a copy of the complete work in HAB.
179. See above, Introduction I, p. 29.

(W48), was also annotated, almost throughout. This *Concord*, which had brought agreement on the eucharist (albeit of only temporary duration) between the Lutherans and Reformed theologians through the instrumentality of Bucer and Melanchthon, had settled on a formula 'that with the bread and wine, the body and blood of Christ are truly and substantially present, offered and received', but without recourse to any defence of the 'real presence' along the lines of the ubiquity of Christ's human nature after his resurrection, employed by some Lutherans such as Brentz and Westphal. No copy of the Augsburg *Confession* (1530)[180] or the *Editio variata,* with its important changes to the wording of the Lutheran formula on eucharistic doctrine, published by Melanchthon in 1540, are among Geste's books (if he ever owned them), and his view on these issues – other than what is revealed in his correspondence on the Articles of Religion with Cecil in 1566 and 1571 – remains uncertain. But marginal comments in his copy of the Wittenberg *Concord* (W48) give some indication of how he understood the positions of Luther and Bucer on these matters. Of Bucer he notes, 'Bucerus nu[m]q[uam] negabit praesentia' of Christ in the Supper, and of Luther: 'Lutherus fatetur tantu[m] sacramentalem no[n] naturale[m] unione[m]', adding towards the end of his annotations on the *Concord,* 'Corpus Christi exhibetur substantialiter in cena' (W48).

Geste's collection of Lutheran writings is notable not only for its size, but for the comparative rarity – in an English library of the period – of so much of its content. Of the one hundred and three authors or item headings in his collection, fifty (or sixty-seven works) are not represented in any of the Cambridge inventories or the libraries of Parker and Perne, and a further fifteen (or twenty-four individual items) occur in only one of these. In addition, Geste's was clearly the working collection of a scholar concerned to acquaint himself with current continental thinking on issues which were not only of interest to him but which impinged on matters of debate in England at the time as the Queen and her government were seeking to find a durable 'Settlement of Religion' for the English Church. Evidence for his interest and close study of these Lutheran works – as in the case of his collections of Reformed and contemporary Catholic writings – is clear from the sheer number of those he had annotated, from lines and markings in the margins to his characteristic notes, sometimes spilling over from the margins to the bottom of a page. There are good reasons, therefore, for thinking that Geste's collection of Lutheran writings is probably the most extensive and significant to have survived in an English private library from this period.

How far this made Geste a 'Lutheran' as some of his contemporary opponents and modern historians have claimed remains a matter for debate, depending on how the label is understood and applied and whether it was

---

180. Parker however had copies of the 1530 edn (Adams A2132): CCCC. MS 435(7); and of the Wittenberg 1535 edn (Adams A2135): SP.133.

simply a term of opprobrium used by those of the 'Reformed' persuasion suspicious of any who deviated from their position. His denial of transubstantiation combined with a continuing belief in Christ's real presence inevitably invited comparison with Luther whose foremost concern had always been to affirm the real presence as essentially a miracle, defying rational analysis, to be accepted on the authority of Christ's words in scripture by simple faith in God's omnipotent power. In defending this belief in the face of his Zwinglian opponents, Luther and his followers had found it necessary to resort to theological argument, such as the appeal to the ubiquity of Christ's risen body, but such measures were essentially alien to his fundamental position, though they were to play a prominent part in the controversies between the later Lutherans and their Calvinist opponents. One of these, articulated in his anti-Zwinglian work of 1527, was the claim that Christ's real presence in the Sacrament, so far from detracting from the glory of God (as Zwingli supposed), was in fact another clear manifestation of the glorious condescension of God in the incarnation. This passage had evidently appealed to Cranmer at one stage – another labelled a Lutheran, at least until 1548 – who had it copied into his Commonplace Books along with other Lutheran extracts in the late 1530s, and it may be significant that by contrast Geste's copy of the same work in the published edition of 1556 (L70) was left entirely without annotation (unlike so many of his other Lutheran items), and it seems likely that it was not so much Lutheran theology but the authority of scripture, reinforced by the weight of patristic tradition, that lay behind his continuing belief in the real presence. This is the impression left in surviving reports of his Good Friday sermon at court in 1565 in which he chose to preach on the text, 'This is my body which is given for you'. This, it was claimed, 'he repeated many times and said, the same as was crucified for you, and as such you must accept it and believe it to be', eliciting from one listener the response, 'I do believe it, and he who doth not should be forthwith burnt'. The Spanish ambassador who made this report went on to observe that Geste 'did not enter into other questions or disputes on religious points' as the other bishops 'usually do' – a reticence on the mode of Christ's presence (other than its 'spiritual manner') which was evident in his later correspondence with Cecil concerning the views of Richard Cheyney. In another account of the same sermon, the Catholic Thomas Harding contrasted the 'more temperate nature' of Geste in confessing 'the real presence' with that of another preacher, Alexander Nowell, who had offended the Queen in an earlier sermon by attacking 'the reuerent vse of the cross' in her private chapel. Geste's continuing belief in the 'real presence' was evidence not so much of his supposed Lutheranism as for his innate 'conservatism' and moderation.[181]

181. On Geste's possible Lutheranism, see Patrick Collinson, *The Elizabethan Puritan Movement* (London: Cape, 1967), p. 61, 206; Kenneth Fincham and Nicholas

Contemporary Catholic works

No less remarkable was Geste's collection of contemporary Catholic writings, comprising some 316 separate works by 165 different authors and official bodies, not one of which, incidentally, was represented in the 1583 catalogue of the University Library at Cambridge.[182] Although many of these can be found in other collections in Cambridge of the period, forty-two of Geste's Catholic authors do not appear in any of these, and a further twenty-one are only represented by some of their other works. In fact, his collection greatly exceeded those of Matthew Parker (who had only thirty-one of the items in Geste's collection by twenty-five Catholic authors), and even Perne, with his much larger library, who had copies of only eighty of Geste's items by sixty-two Catholic authors. Even when other works by Catholic authors in Geste's collection are taken into account, the number of Catholic authors represented rises to only forty-one in Parker's case (not much more than a quarter of Geste's authors) and to 110 in the the case of Perne's (still only a little more than two-thirds of the authors represented in Geste's). In the case of the Cambridge inventories (BiCI) during the period, the position is much the same as it is in Perne's. Sixty-three of the authors in Geste's collection are represented in one or more of these inventories, while that figure rises to only eighty-one if other works by these authors are counted – still only half the number in Geste's. Perne's case is all the more striking when it is remembered that he remained in his post (unlike Geste and Parker) throughout the violent religious changes of the period, and it might have been expected that during those years he might have accumulated a much larger collection of Catholic works than he did.

On the face of it, the range of Geste's collection of contemporary Catholic writing far exceeded in scope and subject matter what might have been considered merely necessary to understand and, where thought necessary,

---

Tyacke, *Altars Restored: The Changing Face of English Religious Worship, 1547–c. 1700* (Oxford: University Press, 2007), pp. 31–32 on Elizabeth I and Lutheranism; P. E. McCullough, *Sermons at Court* (Cambridge: University Press, 1998), p. 96. The Lutheran work referred to is Luther's *Das diese Wort Christi 'Das ist mein Leib' noch fest stehen, wider die Schwärmgeister* (Nuremberg, Wittenberg, 1527 and other editions of that year) extracted in Cranmer's Commonplace Books, 'De Eucharistia', BL, MS Royal 7B.XI, ff. 113v–114r; Peter Brooks, *Thomas Cranmer's Doctrine of the Eucharist* (London: Macmillan, 1965), pp. 22–34. For Geste's 1565 Good Friday sermon, see *Calendar of Letters and State Papers Relating to English Affairs Preserved Principally in the Archives of Simancas: Vol. 1 Elizabeth, 1558–1567* (ed. by M. A. S. Hume. London: Eyre and Spottiswoode for HMSO, 1892), no. 295, and Thomas Harding, *A Confutation ... of An Apologie* (Antwerp, 1565, STC 12762), *2v.

182. These 'Contemporary Catholics' are listed in Appendix XII.6. Of these items 148 are annotated in his hand. There is less certainty about another eleven. For the Cambridge University Library figures, see CUL 1583.

confront the views of his ecclesiastical opponents. For his acquisitions in this area – in so far as imprint dates and bindings may provide some (if a very approximate) indication of when these may have been purchased – cover the whole of his career from his early days in Cambridge to the early 1570s when he accepted his final post as bishop of Salisbury. In fact he was still acquiring books by Catholic authors with imprints as late as 1573.[183]

His collection includes, as was to be expected, examples of the common stock of Catholic polemical writing from the early period of the Lutheran Reformation, such as works by Eck (E3, E6–8), Cajetan (V32), Clichtoveus (C82), Cochlaeus (C85, C87) and Latomus (L17)[184] – mostly well represented in other English collections of the period – as well as later works expounding and defending the doctrinal decrees of the Council of Trent and other controversialists such as the widely-read Portuguese Bishop of Silves, Jerónimo Osório (O24–27). But there is much else to suggest a wider, and less polemical, interest in the literature of contemporary Catholicism. For example, there are no less than forty-eight Biblical commentaries by twenty-five different Catholic authors, half of which contain his annotations. Many of these were widely represented in other contemporary collections in Cambridge and include works by writers such as Jacques Le Fèvre (L22–24), Cajetan (V29–31), Franz Titelman (T10–13) and Johann Wild [Ferus] (W27–30, 32–36), but there were others, like those by Cornelius Jansen (J3–5) and Sebastian Mayer (M20–22) which were much less commonly owned, and there were commentaries by five other authors which were represented only by other works in the collections surveyed, while a further ten authors were not found in any of these.[185]

Geste also acquired a number of Biblical homilies (some nineteen) on the lections for the liturgical year by nine Catholic writers, thirteen of these volumes annotated with his characteristic marginal lines often throughout selected sermons, though whether any of these provided starting points or ideas for his own liturgical preaching it would be difficult to establish in the absence of any published liturgical sermons by Geste. These include a set of

183. Some of his acquisitions carry imprints as late as 1571–73, e.g. Canisius (C32), Eisengrein (E10), the *Catholic Confession* of the Provincial Synod of Piotrków (P35), Serranus (S50–51) and Andreas Vega (V6).

184. Though not, it seems, anything by Alphonsus de Castro whose writings occur in the libraries of Parker, Perne and some of the Cambridge inventories, unless the copy in Appendix I (*C6) is his. It is also noteworthy that no work by John Fisher is represented either, the one item at Salisbury (at B.6.38) contains no evidence of Geste's ownership.

185. Folengius (F27), Fontaine (F28), Naclantius (N1–2), Pinto (P34) and Sasbout (S26) only occur as authors of other works in these Cambridge collections, while works by the authors Arias Montanus (A52), Campester (C31), Espence (E52), Forerius (F29), Francisco à Victoria (F34), Jean de Gagny (G1–2), Nannius (N3–4), Novicampianus (N12), Walterus Ruysius (R40) and Schatzger (S30), do not occur in these collections at all.

five volumes by Heinrich Helmes (H18–22), three of them annotated, four by Johann Hofmeister (H62–65, three with some annotation) and four of Johann Wild (W31, 37–39), all annotated.[186] The liturgical homilies of all three authors were also well represented in other collections, notably Perne's. In addition, Geste acquired four volumes of sermons, one by Johann Wild (W40) again, with his marginal lines in five of the sermons, a volume by Vincenzo Cicogna (C75) without annotation, and two by the Englishmen, Edmund Bonner (B55) and Thomas Watson (W2), this last extensively annotated. Only the Cicogna volume can be counted a rarity, appearing in no other contemporary Cambridge collection surveyed, while Bonner and Watson were better represented, though neither of the volumes Geste owned were in Parker's collection.

Perhaps of greatest interest to students of the English Reformation are Geste's copies of books relating to the Council of Trent, for its final sessions coincided with the early years of Elizabeth's Religious Settlement when the Anglican Church was defining its position in relation to the recent doctrinal decrees of that Council. The nine books in his collection directly related to the Council comprise editions of the *Canons and Decrees* (C108) published at Antwerp in 1564 and the *Catechism* (C110) in a Paris edition of 1567, four works by Catholic authors expounding and defending its doctrinal work, and three volumes from the Protestant side attacking the Council. All but one of the nine have been annotated, the exception being the *Catechismus scholasticus* (1571) of Lindanus (L31), although Geste had already annotated the Paris edition of the *Catechism* (C110) a year or two earlier. The other three have been annotated throughout: the first, the *Apologia Indictionis Concilij Tridentini* (1563) by Gaspar Cardillo de Villalpando (C40) has his notes on the issues of the papacy and church councils, scripture and tradition, and the interpretation of scripture. The second by Jean Porthaise (P44) was more narrowly focussed on the eucharist and Christ's words 'Hoc facite' and directed against the Lutheran, Matthias Flacius (1567). The third, providing the most comprehensive defence of the doctrinal decrees, was Ravesteyn's two-volume *Apologiae, seu defensionis* (R9) published in 1568 and 1570, attacking the *Examen decretorum Concilii Tridentini* of another Lutheran, Martin Chemnitz, whose work eventually appeared in four volumes over the years 1566 to 1573 – another work owned and annotated by Geste (C59–62). Geste's extensive annotations on this last item cover the whole range of issues raised by the Council and the response to them from Lutherans and other Protestant theologians, and would well repay further detailed study.

---

186. His copy of Johann Wild's *Postils on the Liturgical Epistles and Gospels* (W37) contains his marginal lines on a course of sermons during Lent on the Lord's Supper, and similarly on a number of sermons for the Sundays after Pentecost in another volume of Wild's *Homilies* (W38). For further details, see the relevant catalogue entries.

Two examples of this Protestant response come from the other two items relating directly to the Council of Trent. The first was Calvin's *Antidote* to the *Acta Synodi Tridentinae* (C107) covering the first sessions of the Council (1546–47) and interpolated with his critique. It was in the course of these sessions that the crucial issue of justification was debated and the Council's decree issued, and this doctrine and the Pauline texts relating to it were the focus of Geste's annotations in the form of his marginal lines. The second was the *Admonitio* concerning the decrees and canons of the Council variously attributed to the Lutherans, Matthias Flacius, or Jacob Andreae. Geste possessed copies of both the Latin original published in 1563 (C111) and the anonymous English translation printed by John Day in 1564 (C109), sometimes tentatively (but surely improbably) attributed (e.g. by the editors of STC) to Matthew Parker. Although both are annotated, it was the English version (C109) that received most attention, with Geste's marginal lines and notes (in English) almost throughout, touching on the same divisive issues that occupied him in his annotations on the *Canons and Decrees* (C108), the *Catechism* (C110) and Ravestyn's *Apologiae* (R9).

Quite how and why Geste should have accumulated such an extensive and significant collection of Catholic writing from the continent is not entirely clear. The large number of apparently rare items suggests that some at least of these were not regularly imported. Like Perne, Geste did not, so far as we know, travel to the continent which would have given him the opportunity to attend book fairs such as those held at Frankfurt or Antwerp, and in the absence of personal correspondence or notes in his books which might have alluded to such matters there is no surviving evidence to show that he made use of friends or agents travelling abroad who might have acquired books on his behalf in the way that William Cecil, first Lord Burghley, for example, clearly did. Whether his recusant uncle, Richard Brandisby, exiled in the Low Countries (possibly at Louvain) since leaving Cambridge in 1538,[187] played any part in this, directly or indirectly, is unclear, though possible. Many of Geste's Catholic books, as was to be expected, emanated from that important centre of printing.[188] In any case, as has already been noted,[189] Geste's experience of religious tensions within his own family and in his own College, both during the final years of the reign of Henry VIII and the first year of Mary's, may well, at the very least, have convinced him of the need to acquaint himself thoroughly with the continuing debate between proponents on both sides of the Reformation divide. His responsibilities at Court and as a bishop during Elizabeth's reign will have done nothing to reduce that necessity, and, as we have seen, this concern is reflected in the fact that he continued to make purchases of books

187. On Richard Brandisby, see Introduction I, pp. 8–9.
188. For these, see Appendix II, Index of Printers and Publishers, s.v. Louvain.
189. See above, Introduction, I, pp. 9, 11, 16.

by Catholic authors during the 1570s (some with imprints as late as 1573) right up to the last years of his life.

English writers

Twenty-two of these Catholic works by fourteen different authors form the largest component in Geste's small collection of English works, the remaining twelve coming from Protestants.[190] Three of the former date from the 1520s: the customary copy of Henry VIII's *Assertio septem sacramentorum* (H40),[191] bound with a work of Thomas More (M81) in one of the heraldic panel bindings by John Reynes; and a work of Edward Lee (L26) which may, as already suggested, have come to him through his uncle, John Brandisby. There are also two from the last year of Henry's reign: a work against Bucer by Gardiner (G13) and one of Richard Smith's books defending the Catholic doctrine of the eucharist (S64), dedicated, as Regius Professor at Oxford, to Henry VIII. No works with imprints from the reign of Edward VI are among these books, but there are seven from Mary's reign: the 'Protestant' reissue of Pole's *Pro ecclesiasticae unitatis defensione* by Pier Paulo Vergerio (P40), already mentioned;[192] two by Edmund Bonner – his *Profitable and Neccessarye Doctryne*, and *Homilies,* both issued in 1555 (B54–55); Gardiner against Bucer on the issue of clerical celibacy (G15); and three items on eucharistic doctrine: the same author's *Confutatio* (G14) directed against Cranmer's writings, Tunstall's *De ueritate corporis et sanguinis Domini nostri Iesu Christi in Eucharistia* (T26), and Watson's two Sermons (W2), only the last two items containing any of Geste's annotations.

The remaining ten Catholic books fall within Elizabeth's reign and reflect the growing polemic between the two sides of the doctrinal divide: two more from Richard Smyth, now an exile at Louvain, concerning the controversy with the continental Reformers, the first directed again the Lutheran Melanchthon (S65) and his *Loci communes*, the second (published anonymously) against Reformed Protestantism in the person of Calvin and Beza (S66), the other eight relating to England. These included works by two writers which had a direct bearing on the English Prayer Book of 1559: John Martiall's *Treatyse of the Crosse* (M13), which touched on the contentious issue of the invocation in the eucharistic prayer, and two by Nicholas Sander, one on images (S10) and the other on disputed matters relating to the Mass, such as the language to be used in the liturgy (S11). The last five

---

190. Figures in Index XII.11 'English writers and works in English'.
191. For example, copies were held by Parker, Perne, Cranmer (*LTC* 146) and William Cecil, First Lord Burghley (now at Christ Church, Oxford, e.6.4). The Geste, Parker and Cecil copies are all in John Reynes heraldic panel bindings. See Catalogue entry for H40.
192. See above, Introduction, II, p. 77.

items related to the controversies between Harding (H8), Rastell (R6–7) and Stapleton (S85–86), on the Catholic side, and their Anglican opponents, John Jewel, Geste's predecessor at Salisbury (J7–8), Robert Horne (H77) and Alexander Nowell (N13–14). Geste's annotations in Harding's *Rejoindre* to Jewel confirm that the work had been closely studied, as was the case with his copies of Rastell's *Replie* (R6) and Stapleton's *A Returne of Vntruthes Vpon M. Ievvelles Replie* (S86).

Geste's collection of English Catholic writers included no rarities, but there were some notable omissions, and subsequent losses at Salisbury may not account for all of these. It contained, for example, no work of John Fisher, not even his important treatise on the eucharist against Oecolampadius, while Parker's library, of comparable size, included that work and an additional three items by the author[193] and Cranmer had owned at least five.[194]

Perne's much larger collection included all but one of Geste's Catholic authors (the omission being Edward Lee) and a further fifteen, bringing the total number of works to forty-four, twice the size of Geste's. Perne, for example, had acquired two works each of William Allen, Thomas Dorman, and the Italian émigré Polydore Vergil, no less than five of Fisher, including the work against Oecolampadius, and single works of Edward Fox, Nicholas Harpsfield, Thomas Heskyns, Alban Langdale, Robert Pointz, John Redman, Richard Sampson, John Seton, John Taverner and John White, as well as a collection of Homilies.[195] While none of the individual Cambridge inventories preserved in the University archives for the period approaches these collections in size, the number of Catholic works represented in the inventories as a whole is even larger than that in Perne's. All of the fourteen authors in Geste's collection are found in one or other inventory (but with forty-six individual items against Geste's twenty-two), and there are twenty-one additional Catholic authors represented, nine of which are in neither Parker's or Perne's collections, increasing the total number of individual works by a further thirty.[196]

193. Parker's copy of Fisher's work against Oecolompadius (Adams F534) is CCCC F.7.2(2), and he had copies of *De unica Magdalena* (Adams F533), SP.193, and two other items: Adams F530 (SP.352) and his Sermon against Luther (1521, STC 10894), CCCC SP.335(1). While there were eight Catholic authors in Geste's collection not represented in Parker's (see Index XII.11 'English writers'), Parker had two works by the Italian émigré Polydore Vergil, and single works by Edward Fox, John Redman, John Seton, and John White, not found in Geste's.

194. *LTC* 173–175.2, which included *De unica Magdalena* (*LTC* 175) and two copies of his *Confutatio* (1523) against Luther (Adams F513), but not the work against Oecolampadius, though he quotes from it and almost certainly had a copy (*LTC* Appendix D, no. 43, p. 241).

195. For details of these see the relevant entries in BiCI, II.

196. James Brook, John Gwynneth, John Harpsfield, Miles Hogarde, Henry Joliffe and R. Johnson (against John Hooper), Thomas Lupset, William Peryn, Edward Powel, and John Standish. Details of the works involved are set out in BiCI, II.

Geste's collection of English Protestants, as it survives today, was even smaller, comprising only twelve individual items by eight different authors.[197] Parker's may not have been very much larger – including works by half of Geste's eight authors and an additional twenty-two items from eleven others[198] – but the contrast with Perne's holdings is striking.

Perne owned not only all but three of the items in Geste's collection,[199] but he also had copies of seventeen additional items by these same authors and a further thirty-two by twenty-two other authors not represented at all in Geste's,[200] making a total of fifty-eight individual works, nearly five times the size of Geste's collection, and over twice the size of Parker's. The position was much the same in the case of Geste's holdings and the Cambridge inventories. All of the authors in Geste's collection are represented in one or more of these inventories, though fewer of Geste's individual works are found in these than in Perne's library.[201] Of course, no two collectors' interests are alike, and it may not be possible to determine why

---

197. For these, see Index XII.11. Two other possible items are listed in Appendix I: one by James Calfhill (*C1) and the Latin translation of the *King's Book* (*P5), now missing.

198. These figures are provisional, based on a search of the Corpus Christi College catalogue as it appears in the CUL online catalogue. The search reveals that Parker owned two items each of Jewel, Nowell and John Foxe and one of John Whitgift among the authors in Geste's collection; and among the additional authors (not in Geste's), five items each of Sir John Cheke and Hugh Latimer, copies of the 1538 and 1547 Injunctions, two items of Walter Haddon and Richard Taverner, and single items of Roger Ascham, John Bale, James Calfhill, Robert Crowley, John Marbecke and James Pilkington – a total of twenty-eight items.

199. Ponet's *Short Catechism* (C52), Robert Horne's *Answeare* to Feckenham (H77) and Veron's *Treatise of Free Wil* (V21).

200. For these, see under the relevant authors in BiCI, II. The authors that have been identified (with the number of items in brackets) are George Acworth (1), Roger Ascham (1), John Aylmer (1), John Bale (3), William Barlow (1), Robert Barnes (1), Thomas Becon (2), John Bridges (1), James Calfhill (1), Thomas Cartwright (1), John Cheke (2), Miles Coverdale (1), Thomas Cranmer (3), William Fulke (3), Walter Haddon (3), Roger Hutchinson (1), John Knox (1), Hugh Latimer (1), John Marbecke (1), Alexander Neville (1), James Pilkington (1) and the Forty-two *Articles of Religion* (1).

201. Thus three works owned by Geste are not found in any of these inventories: single works by Robert Horne (H77), Lawrence Humphrey (H90) and John Ponet (P42). Copies of works by John Bradford, Sir Anthony Cope, Robert Crowley, John Frith, John Northbrooke, John Olde, John Philpot, Richard Taverner, Bartholomew Traheron, William Turner and William Tyndale, can be found in one or more of these inventories, but not in that of Perne (in BiCI, I). On the other hand, Perne had works by John Aylmer and William Barlow, neither of whom is represented in the Cambridge inventories. Works by John Hooper and Nicholas Ridley are absent from all these collections, including those of Parker and Perne.

Geste's collection of English Protestants appears so meagre, but apart from
the likelihood of later losses (which probably affected other sections of his
library), one possible factor, in any case, may have been the paucity of
biblical commentaries in English available during his lifetime (one of Geste's
major collecting interests), and he may not have been able to acquire (even
if he had wanted to) examples by William Tyndale, Lancelot Ridley, John
Hooper or James Pilkington. For apart from items by these authors, some
expositions of the Liturgical Gospels and Epistles, and translations of works
by continental writers such as Erasmus (the *Paraphrases on the New Testament*),
Bucer, Luther, Wolfgang Capito and Calvin (though most of Calvin's works
in translation did not appear during Geste's lifetime), there was little available
for English readers until later in the century.

Of the twelve English Protestant works held by Geste, four items (by
Horne, Jewel and Nowell) have already been mentioned in connexion with
the controversies concerning their Catholic opponents, Harding, Rastell and
Stapleton. His copy of Jewel's Reply to Harding (J8) contains some annotation in his hand, but the most extensive annotations occur in the writings of
their Catholic opponents, particularly Harding's *Reioindre* (H8). Of his other
items, four are without annotation: Lawrence Humphrey's *Optimates, siue
de nobilitate* (H90), John Foxe's *Commentarii rerum in Ecclesia gestarum*
(F32), Ponet's *Apologie* answering Gardiner on the marriage of priests (P42)
and Whitgift's work against Cartwright (W16). There are a few marginal
lines in his copy of the *Forty-two Articles* attached to Ponet's *Short Catechism*
which may be in his hand (C52), but the most interesting of those with
annotations are the two works by the French emigré Jean Véron, ordained
priest by Ridley in 1551: the first, *A Fruteful Treatise of Predestination* (V20),
and the second, *A Moste Necessary Treatise of Free Wil* (V21), both entered in
the Stationers' Register, in May 1561, the former dedicated to the Queen, the
second to Robert Dudley. Both were aimed at Anabaptists who in the second
of these works were accused of reviving the Pelagian heresy. Geste, to judge
by the extent of his annotations, had clearly studied both works closely,
but he was also critical of the 'hard' position being taken by the author: 'This
is harde for ye people', he observes at one point, and 'hardly spoken all this'
at another; and on the first treatise he comments at one point, 'ye principall
cause of o[u]r damnatio[n] is not goddess p[re]destination but o[u]r synne'.[202]
The issue of free will and predestination was one that recurs in other books
annotated by Geste and it persisted throughout the Elizabethan period.[203]

202. See entries for V19–20.
203. See Appendix XI.2 'Subject Index to MS Annotations', s.v. entries for 'Election',
 'Free will', and 'Predestination'. Some of the literature generated by these
 controversies is listed in Peter Milward, *Religious Controversies of the Elizabethan
 Age* (London: Scolar Press, 1977), pp. 157–63 (though Véron is not among them),
 and discussed in Peter White, *Predestination, Policy and Polemic* (Cambridge:
 University Press, 1992).

Liturgy

Geste's interest in liturgical reform, and the doctrinal issues bearing upon it, was a major preoccupation throughout his career, even from the time of the publication of his *Treatise Against the Preuee Masse* in 1548.

What of the liturgical resources in his library? Geste was clearly well acquainted with the available patristic accounts of worship and the celebration of the sacraments, and evidence of early church practice was important to him. In addition to the text of the Latin rite which would have been familiar to him (though no copy can certainly be attributed to his library among the editions at Salisbury), it is possible, for example, that he owned a copy of the Eastern liturgies of St James, St Basil & St John Chrysostom in the Latin edition of Claude de Sainctes published at Antwerp in 1562.[204] This was listed in the printed Catalogue of the Cathedral Library published in 1880, though without any provenance information. But it has since disappeared, and there is now no way of verifying Geste's ownership or determining the use he might have made of it. He certainly owned the 1541 Worms edition of the liturgy of St John Chrysostom (again in Latin), but unfortunately the Salisbury copy is without annotations (L37). This text also occurs in the libraries of Parker and Perne (as it had in Cranmer's) and one of the Cambridge inventories,[205] and a 'missa Iacobi' (edition unknown) is listed in Perne's inventory, though it is no longer extant.[206] Of the other Latin service books that he might have owned, such as the liturgical hours, breviaries, primers, antiphoners, hymnals and Processionals, there is no trace, though copies of these occur in some numbers in Cambridge inventories of the time. Similarly, the proposals for the reform of the breviary drawn up by Cardinal Quinones and published in two recensions in 1535–1536, on which Cranmer drew for his reform of the daily offices, are also absent.[207] A Pontifical at Salisbury, published at Venice in 1510, cannot with any certainty be attributed to his library,[208] although copies of other editions can be traced in those of Parker and Perne.[209]

204. See Appendix I, *L4 and the evidence for his ownership given there.
205. Parker had copies of the Greek text (Rome, 1526, Adams L837): SP.118(1); an edition with the Greek text and a Latin translation (Venice, 1528, Adams L838): SP.118(3); and two Latin-only editions (Colmar, 1540, Adams L840): SP.118(5) and (Worms, 1541, Adams L841): SP.118(4), all bound together in a single volume, this last being of the same edition as Geste's copy (L37). Perne's copies (inventory in BiCI, I, no. 164, items 714 and 1209), still extant at Peterhouse, are recorded, with one listed in an inventory of 1558, in BiCI, II, p. 498. Cranmer's copy of the Greek text with Erasmus' Latin translation (Paris, 1537) is now in Lambeth Palace Library (*LTC* 213).
206. 1589 inventory 1198 (not extant), BiCI, II, p. 500.
207. See *LTC*, p. 178f., MS 34 and the references given there. Parker, however, owned a copy of Quinones *Breuiarum Romanae Curiae* in the edition of 1537 (Adams L870): CCCC SP.201.
208. Listed in Appendix I, *P6.   209. Parker's copy of the 1561 Venice edition.

In addition to these liturgical texts, Geste owned a small collection of secondary works on the Mass and divine office, as Parker and Perne did. His copy of what had been from the late fifteenth century the standard text book on the Canon of the Latin Mass by Gabriel Biel, in the Basle 1510 edition, survives, with some annotations in his hand (B46). Parker and and Perne also owned copies, though by this time it does not appear to have been common in Cambridge.[210] He also had a copy of Helding's *Sacri canonis missae paraphrastica explicatio* (H17) published at Antwerp in 1559 which included prayers from non-Roman sources such as the liturgies of St. Ambrose and St. Basil. This was a work not found in surviving Cambridge inventories, though Perne had Helding's fifteen 'conciones' on the Sacrifice of the Mass which had appeared earlier, in 1549.[211] A third work in Geste's library – of more polemical intention and heavily annotated – was Georg Witzel's *Defensio ecclesiasticae liturgiae* (W52) published at Cologne in 1564, a work not found in any of the Cambridge inventories, or the libraries of Parker or Perne, and an author represented by only two works in Perne's and the inventories, and none at all in Parker's.[212] For the divine office, Geste had the thirteenth-century *Rationale* by William Durandus in the Paris edition of 1518, a work which occurs in at least six of the Cambridge inventories and in the libraries of Cranmer and Parker (both with two copies), though not, apparently, in that of Perne.[213] Unlike Geste's copies of Biel and Witzel, neither the Helding or Durandus have any of his annotations.

In the case of the Reformation period, none of the English liturgies or the Reformed rites of continental Protestantism are represented.[214] Of the Lutheran Church Orders, there is only one extant: the North German

(Adams L1241) is CCCC: D.3.18; Perne's (edition not known) is listed in the 1589 inventory (BiCI, I, no. 164, item 591), but is not extant at Peterhouse (BiCI, II, p. 500).

210. Parker's copy is of the later, 1555 Antwerp edition (Adams B2024): CCCC SP.271; Perne's (edition not known) is listed in the 1589 inventory (BiCI, I, no. 164, item 565) but is no longer extant at Peterhouse. No copy is listed in any of the contemporary Cambridge inventories (BiCI, II, p. 128).

211. 1589 inventory no. 164, item 521, BiCI, II, p. 413.

212. BiCI, II, p. 800 (s.v. Wicelius).

213. BiCI, II, p. 290. For Cranmer, who had earlier Lyons editions of 1506 and 1508, see *LTC* 93–94. Parker had copies of the Venice 1482 edition (ISTC id00426000): EP.G.14; and of the Lyons 1503 edition (Adams D1157): SP.51.

214. Among the missing items are the revised forms of service emanating from Strasbourg (Bucer), Geneva (Calvin), including the English version of the Genevan rite translated from the French by William Huycke and printed by Edward Whitchurche in 1550 (STC 16560), and any of the rites associated with the Marian exiles at Frankfurt-am-Main and Geneva, culminating in the Genevan Service Book (STC 16561), of which John Knox was one of the compilers, in 1556. Again, none of the service books drawn up for foreign congregations in London during the reign of Edward VI by the Frenchman, Valerand Poullain (STC 16566), or Joannes à Lasco [Jan Laski] (STC 16571) have been found, or Coverdale's translation of the order of service used by the church in Denmark, appended to

Kirchenordnung of Mecklenburg (M25), first published in 1552 and associated with the young David Chytraeus, at the time living at Rostock, whose later biblical commentaries abound in Geste's library (C66–72). Geste, in a MS note on the title page of his copy of the Latin translation by Johannes Freder, printed at Frankfurt in 1562, actually attributes the work, however, to Melanchthon and a few pages on the Lord's Supper have also been marked in the margins (though without any notes in his hand). The edition is too late, however, to have had any direct bearing on the preparations for the Elizabethan Prayer Book, though it confirms Geste's continuing interest in these matters.

In view of the large number of Lutheran works in his library, it might seem surprising that this was the only Church Order represented. But this dearth of Lutheran, Reformed and English texts is not unique to his collection, and in any case, it is not known how many items of his may have been lost in the centuries after his death. The liturgical section of Cranmer's library, a generation earlier, presents a similar problem, though in this instance we know that few of his Protestant books survived the confiscation of his library in 1553. In fact, none of the Lutheran Church Orders which Brightman and others conjectured as likely sources for Cranmer's liturgical reforms survive in what remains of his library.[215] Apart from vague entries such as 'Service books' in a few of the Cambridge inventories,[216] Reformation liturgical texts, Lutheran, Reformed and English are not generally, if at all, to be found in the collections of Geste's contemporaries, and this includes those of Parker and Perne. The one exception concerned the proposals for liturgical reform at Cologne.

The importance of the Cologne proposals for Geste (and before him, for Cranmer) has already been discussed in connexion with his liturgical interests.[217] His library preserves copies of the English version of Hermann's *Deliberatio* (first published in German in 1543), translated under the title *A Simple, and Religious Consultatio[n]* in the second, 'amended' edition, published by John Day and William Seres in 1548 (H42). And he also owned the 1549 Paris edition of the conservative counterblast to these proposals from the Cathedral Chapter at Cologne, the *Antididagma* (C75), first published in German early in 1544. Both works are extensively annotated;

Calvin's treatise on the sacrament (STC 4409.5). On these, see W. D. Maxwell, *The Liturgical Portions of the Genevan Service Book* (London: Oliver and Boyd, 1931; 2nd impression, London: Faith Press, 1963); B. D. Spinks, *From the Lord and "The Best Reformed Churches"; A Study of the Eucharistic Liturgy of the English Puritan and Separatist Traditions* (Rome: C.L.V. Edizioni Liturgiche, 1984).

215. F. E. Brightman, *The English Rite* (2 vols. London: Rivingtons, 1915), I, pp. xxx–xlix.

216. BiCI, II, p. 498. The entries are so imprecise that pre-Reformation service books could be intended.

217. See above, Introduction, I, pp. 18–27.

in the former, particularly on the form of service proposed for the Lord's Supper in which there are annotations on most pages; in the latter, especially on those points on which the *Antididagma* opposed the Bucer-Hermann proposals. In contrast to the absence of other Reformation liturgies in contemporary Cambridge collections, both works occur in significant numbers. Perne owned copies of both works, the Hermann in the 1545 Latin edition,[218] rather than the English version which Geste owned, and the *Antididagma,* in the Cologne 1544 edition,[219] bound together in a single volume, still extant at Peterhouse.[220] Both titles also occur in a number of the Cambridge inventories, one – that of Oliver Ainsworth of Jesus College – listing the *Antididagma,* as early as 1546,[221] establishing that copies of this work, at least, were circulating in Cambridge some time before Geste wrote his *Treatise*; for his copy (C95), in the Paris edition of 1549, actually postdates that publication, and he must therefore have had access to an earlier edition in writing his book. In fact, the *Antididagma* occurs in no less than ten of these Cambridge inventories, all but one of which are dated between Ainsworth's of 1546 and one of 1560, while Hermann's work occurs in possibly five others, dated between 1549 and 1567.[222] As was to be expected, Matthew Parker also had copies of both Cologne works: two Latin editions of the *Antididagma*[223] and one of Hermann's proposals, in his case, a copy of the original German edition published at Bonn in 1543, possibly the only one owned in Cambridge at the time.[224] The striking contrast in the incidence of ownership between these two books and the dearth of liturgical texts from other Protestant traditions is testimony to the importance accorded to the Cologne reform, and the controversy surrounding it, in Cambridge at the time.

Geste's legacy to Salisbury Cathedral

In bequeathing this new 'foundation collection' of printed books to his Cathedral, Geste was providing Salisbury with many of the resources of

218. Adams H342; 1589 inventory in BiCI, I, no. 164, item 1342.
219. Adams C2373; it shares the same inventory number.
220. Peterhouse N.1.17(1-2); BiCI, II, pp. 234, 418.
221. Item 128 in Oliver Ainsworth's inventory, BiCI, I, no. 30; BiCI, II, p. 234. Ainsworth, a Fellow of Jesus College, had a collection of over 200 books which included mainly Lutheran and Bucerian works from among the Protestant Reformers; BiCI, I, pp. 81–86.
222. BiCI, II, pp. 234, 418. The suggested figure of five in the case of the Hermann includes the vague entry, 'the bysshoppe of cullens book', in the inventory of Sir John Cheke's mother, Agnes, who died in 1549, but it could, of course, equally refer to one of his other English titles.
223. Cologne, 1544 edn (Adams C 2373): F.5.7(2); and Paris, 1545 edn (Adams C2376): SP.446.
224. Adams H343.

learning and scholarship appropriate for a cathedral in the second half of the sixteenth century – a balance of the best of the old and the new, as envisaged in the various sets of injunctions for cathedrals issued from the 1540s to those of Elizabeth I. In addition to his very large collection of contemporary theology and biblical study on both sides of the Reformation divide, he bequeathed over a hundred works by the early Church Fathers and Councils, mainly in the new editions of humanist scholars like Erasmus. Among the resources for biblical scholarship there were modern editions of the text in the three sacred languages of Hebrew, Greek and Latin (Erasmus, Pagninus and Sebastian Münster, for example), though not the whole of the Old Testament in Hebrew or Greek, as well as aids to study such as grammars, lexicons and concordances, and a wide range of the 'new' commentaries from brief annotations to longer expositions by leading Lutheran, Reformed Protestant and Catholic exegetes. Geste's collection also contained some resources for liturgical reform, dogmatics (including catechetical material from continental Protestantism as well as the Council of Trent), homiletics (with many sermons and 'postillae' from the medieval period as well as examples from both sides of the Reformation divide), works on moral and pastoral theology, ministry and church organization, clerical training and reform. Like Cranmer, Parker and Perne, Geste did not exclude medieval writers, including scholastics, or his Catholic contemporaries: over fifty authors of the former are represented (including commentators on Peter Lombard's *Sentences* and works of scholastic theology by Aquinas, William of Ockham and Gabriel Biel) and over three-hundred works by contemporary Catholics, predominantly continental, but some English as well. Such a resource potentially provided users of the library with a broad conspectus of the Christian tradition down the centuries which not many, if any, Cathedral libraries could rival until the seventeenth century or later.

Also remarkable was the high proportion of books that were not often, if ever, held in other Cambridge collections of the period, at least to judge by their total absence from contemporary inventories preserved in the University archives, or the libraries of Parker and Perne. In fact, taking Geste's collection as a whole, at least 477 titles – just under forty per cent of the titles (in any available edition) – are absent from these contemporary collections, and 243 titles – just over twenty per cent of his surviving collection – do not even figure in modern Cambridge libraries, including the University library. A more exact comparison might be with the figure for imprints with dates during his period at Cambridge (1536–54), which overlaps that of Parker and Perne, when the figure falls to just under thirty-four per cent. This slightly lower figure reflects, perhaps, the likelihood that during this period all three were presumably obtaining new titles stocked by mainly Cambridge booksellers and stationers[225] and therefore shared a larger

225. There are exceptions: for example, the three books sent to him in London bindings

proportion of the same titles, whereas in the case of Geste's pre-1536 imprints he could have been obtaining his books from a wide variety of sources, many of them second-hand, though including earlier owners in Cambridge.[226]

For the period after Geste left Cambridge in 1554, when he was no longer buying books in Cambridge, it is less possible to make meaningful comparisons. This is because there is, as yet, no readily accessible body of inventories and private libraries for London collectors and purchasers to cover the period (1554–1577) when Geste was making most, if not, all his purchases from London booksellers. No strictly London comparison, therefore, has been attempted here. Nevertheless – recognising the limitations of the comparison – it is worth noting that for the period from 1554 to the year of his death in 1577 (only two years after Parker's), no less than forty-seven per cent of Geste's books do not figure either in Parker's library or that of Perne (both of whom had also been making purchases in London) or in any of the Cambridge inventories. And even when the later, and much larger, library of Richard Bancroft (bequeathed to Lambeth Palace in 1610) is brought into the comparison, the number in the rarest category of some 243 titles is only reduced by fifteen to 228.[227]

Some idea of the rarity of so many titles in Geste's collection, particularly in the area of contemporary continental theology, can be gained from the fact that his copies are frequently found to be the only ones listed in the *Cathedral Libraries Catalogue* (1998) – in fact no fewer than 768 out of the 1205 items in his collection are the only ones listed there, about sixty-four per cent of what survives of his library. One probable reason for these rare acquisitions may have been Geste's particular concern (not apparently shared by other contemporaries on anything like the same scale) to engage with the increasing surge of continental writing that had arisen out of the doctrinal controversies between Catholic and Protestant theologians from

by his 'brother' [in-law] Christopher Leedes in February, 1550/51 (items B122, E55 and J12 in the catalogue).

226. The figure for these rises to forty-six per cent of the 181 pre-1536 items that survive in his collection, see Appendix III Chronological Index of imprints. Previous owners are listed in Appendix X.

227. For Bancroft, the 1612 inventory in Lambeth Records F1 has been used rather than the items of Bancroft provenance listed in the current on-line catalogue of Lambeth Palace Library which identifies a much smaller number of items, reflecting later losses, especially as a consequence of war damage in the 1940s. Sears Jayne estimated the number of Bancroft's printed books, some acquired from Whitgift and the old Royal Library, at 5,769 books. The 1612 inventory is a shelf-list, arranged by broad subject category and format, but without imprint dates, so exact matches are impossible to verify. There appear to be nine exact matches: A4 (Aepinus), A21 (Alesius), B65 (Bredenbach), C66–67 (Chytraeus), F34 (Francisco), M30 and M36 (Meier), and P30 (Phrygio). A further six items – Hemmingsen's commentaries on the Pauline Epistles in separate octavo editions (H25, H28–29, H31–32 and H34) are included in the single folio edition of his works owned by Bancroft.

the 1560s, following the Council of Trent, and within Protestantism itself between the later Lutherans and Calvinists, and even within Lutheranism.

Geste's continental acquisitions

Fewer than two per cent of Geste's surviving books were printed in England (all by London printers),[228] a figure which increases only to three per cent even if all the conjectural items in Appendix I are included. In an academic collection such as Geste's, such a low proportion of English imprints (and English-language books) was far from unusual – Perne's is another example – and it reflects the fact that with one or two possible exceptions there were no learned presses in England at the time comparable with some of those operating on the continent such as Froben and Oporinus at Basle or Froschauer at Zürich which issued so many of the scholarly books that abound in his library.[229] Of his books from the continent, the great majority – as might have been anticipated of a predominantly theological collection, heavily weighted towards contemporary Protestant and Catholic writing – were printed in German-speaking countries including what was to become Switzerland (sixty-six per cent) with significant numbers from Basle (176 items), Cologne (119), Wittenberg (ninety-five), Frankfurt-am-Main (ninety-two) and Strasbourg (seventy-three). Some forty different places of printing were involved, including some rarities at this period in English collections, such as Bautzen (Johann Wolrab, S41), Bonn (Laurent Mylius, L12), Christlingen (Gnadrich Gotwin, F9), Dortmund (Albertus Sartorius, S39), Neuburg on the Danube (Hans Kilian, B108), and Würzburg (an unidentified printer, M10). The printers most represented were Peter Braubach at Frankfurt-am-Main (50 items), Joannes Oporinus at Basle (39) and the Frobens (29), these last two both at Basle, and the Froschauers (38) at Zürich. The French-speaking countries accounted for some 224 items (just over eighteen per cent of the whole) from ten different centres, with significant numbers from Paris (119 items), Geneva (62) and Lyons (35), Paris represented by no fewer than 66 different printers and publishers, by far the highest figure from any of the centres. The Low Countries contributed a further 113 items (just over nine per cent of the whole), principally from Antwerp (71 items) and Louvain (38), and there was a much smaller number from Italy (28 items), principally Venice (18), only slightly fewer than the number printed in London. There were no books printed in Spain, but a single item from Portugal, a Lisbon imprint (O25), one of four items in Geste's collection by Osório da Fonseca (O24–27), and one from a printer in Denmark, a work by Hemmingsen (H37).

Where may Geste have obtained such a remarkable stock of continental printing, so many items of which do not figure in other collections of the

228. For these, see Appendix II 'Index of Printers and Publishers', s.v. 'London'.
229. As David McKitterick observes (McKitterick (1991), p. 47).

period? The question has already arisen in the case of suggesting sources for some of his less common Catholic books when attention was drawn to the possible role of his recusant uncle, Richard Brandisby, exiled in the Low Countries since 1538,[230] and it will arise again in connexion with his books in continental bindings. But it may be that his booksellers in Cambridge and later in London were perfectly capable of supplying most of his requests – even the rarer items – with the assistance of the Birckmanns and other importers of continental material, who in addition to their activities in London and the continent are known to have been suppliers of books to Cambridge booksellers.[231] There is some evidence, for example, from Geste's binding instructions that on occasion he requested his bookseller to search out copies of particular titles or authors as a 'special order' in cases where the title was not held in stock.[232] And it is not impossible that this was extended to requesting booksellers (and ultimately importers such as the Birckmanns) to look out for new titles by selected authors and in particular subject areas such as (in Geste's case) biblical commentaries – almost the equivalent of the modern 'standing order'. This possibility would go some way to account for the unusually large number of titles he acquired of certain authors, such as the Lutherans, Georg Meier (sixteen items, only one of which is found in other contemporary collections), Jacob Andreae (nine, only two otherwise found), Niels Hemmingsen (sixteen, only six of which occur elsewhere) and David Chytraeus (eight, only four held elsewhere), and, among subject areas, commentaries on the Psalms (forty titles, including those on selected Psalms, eighteen of which are not held in other collections). This practice might also help to explain the large number of 'rare' authors not otherwise recorded in contemporary English collections, such as the forty-four Lutheran authors,[233] including Joachim Camerarius, the elder (six items) and Johann Garcaeus (five), and the forty contemporary Catholics, including Conrad Kling (four items, all annotated by Geste).[234]

230. See above, pp. 69, 90, 138–39.
231. On the importing of books from the continent and the Birckmanns in particular, see Julian Roberts, 'The Latin Trade' in CHBB IV, pp. 141–73, especially pp. 153–56; Margaret Lane Ford, 'Importation of Printed Books into England and Scotland' in CHBB III, pp. 179–201; David McKitterick, HCUP, I, ch. 3: E. S. Leedham-Green, 'University Libraries and Book-sellers' in CHBB III, pp. 348, 353.
232. In his copy of the *Opuscula* of Ephraem, the Syrian (E19, 1563) he has written 'look for op[er]a' of Nicolai, a request which was met by supplying a copy of the works of Mark, the Anchorite (M11, also 1563) which included that author. In another book, this time by Joannes Hessels (H55, 1563), he has written 'Inquire for Hessels …', which, if intended to produce more works by the same author, was not immediately successful, as the book was supplied without any additional items, though it may have been achieved at a later stage, since Geste's collection did include three other items by the same author, all with imprints later than this one (H52–54).
233. See Appendix XII.7.   234. See Appendix XII.6.

IV GESTE AS BOOK OWNER

Geste's contemporary bindings

Salisbury Cathedral Library is fortunate in having so many of its early books still in their original bindings. This makes it a very important resource for the study of English book-binding history, as well as providing evidence for Geste's ownership of particular books (alongside the other 'fingerprints' already noted) and some clues as to where he may have obtained his books. In fact, the late Neil Ker (in a lecture on Cathedral Libraries published in 1967) remarked that 'Salisbury, thanks to Bishop Edmund Gheast, is as rich in Cambridge bindings as any Cambridge college, except perhaps Peterhouse' (to which Andrew Perne had bequeathed most of his vast collection of books in 1589).[235]

As might have been expected, many of the books at Salisbury containing evidence of Geste's ownership have been subsequently rebound – 239 volumes, including all but two of his fifteen incunabula and thirty of his forty-three post-incunabula (1500–20).[236] These rebound books are now covered mostly in boards, often lined with marbled paper of some kind, and some are in modern bindings by H. Bailey of Salisbury from the 1940s onwards. But by far the greatest number of Geste's surviving books are still in their original bindings. Of the 445 or so contemporary, or near contemporary, bindings that remain, a great variety of different types can be found, ranging from limp parchment covers for many of the smaller format items to examples of more decorated blind-stamped panel or tooled roll bindings. At the 'lower end' of the range, there are 121 of his books still in parchment covers or paper wrappers,[237] in six cases using discarded parchment leaves from medieval manuscripts as wrappers,[238] and in another three using paper wrappers, two of them consisting of MS in Geste's hand.[239] An additional thirteen, though rebound at a later date, retain Geste's original binding instructions, indicating that they had also been in parchment covers at some stage.[240] Such parchment bindings, numerous as they are, rarely provide clear evidence of where they may have been bound, though a number retain fragments from MSS or printed waste to form full leaves or narrower strips

---

235. 'Cathedral Libraries' first published in *Library History*, i (1967), pp. 38–45, reprinted in Ker, *BCL*, p. 295.
236. The rebound items are listed in Appendix IV H. The two incunabula still in their original bindings are B5, a Balbus *Catholicon* (1497) in a very worn calf binding (see fig. 16.1) and P23, Lombard's *Sentences* (1495) which incorporates what remains of the original French roll binding in a later rebinding (fig. 20.4). Appendix I lists other books which may have belonged to him, nearly all of which have been rebound.
237. Listed in Appendix IV G.
238. Cat. nos. C105, D1, F17, O21, S77 (see fig. 25.2), W43, all but one (D1) dating from his Cambridge period.
239. Cat. nos. L39, R6 and R16 (the last two with MS in Geste's hand).
240. Listed in Appendix IV G, Annexe 1.

for end-leaf guards which may point to a Cambridge, or London origin, respectively, while a number with exposed sewn book blocks, sewing-support slips or secondary tackets may have been imported from the continent in that state, even if there is much uncertainty about the origin of the attached wrappers.[241]

The remaining 325 or so contemporary bindings have calf covers over pasteboard or, in a very few instances, calf over wooden boards. Among the more decorated bindings in this category are twenty-two in calf with blind-stamped panels illustrating Gospel scenes, the lives of the Saints or purely secular subjects, such as the heraldic arms of King Henry VIII and his first wife, Katherine (H40), on his famous refutation of Luther (1521). All of these have imprints in the 1520s and 1530s and include signed panels by the Cambridge binder, Nicholas Spierinck (E28), and the London binders John Reynes (E31 and H40), Julian Notary (M23), Martin Dature (B72, I6 and L57) and 'T [or F] G' (E3 and L38) – possibly Thomas Godfray.[242]

Far more numerous, however, are the many blind-tooled roll bindings, just a hundred of them, again by a variety of London and Cambridge binders, including books signed by Garrett Godfrey, Nicholas Spierinck and the 'W G' and 'W G/I G' binders, of Cambridge, and ones signed by 'R B', 'F D' and 'I R' binders in London.[243] Most of his roll bindings, however, are unsigned and attributed by Oldham and others – with varying degrees of probability – to mainly unidentified binders in Cambridge, London and Oxford. There are also a few continental roll bindings – French and German – among his books, some of them second-hand, which are considered at a later stage.[244] These roll bindings can be found on books with a wide range of imprints from 1495 onwards, with fewer after Geste's time at Cambridge had come to an end, though there is one roll binding as late as 1574 when he was at Salisbury, a Whitgift (W16) in a binding showing four heads of the Reformers signed by the London binder 'F D' which had evidently been a donation. Although some books in London or Oxford roll bindings were reaching Geste even during his time at Cambridge, including a group of three (though one has since been rebound) sent up to him at King's by his 'brother'[-in-law], Christopher Leedes,[245] those he acquired after he left Cambridge, with a very few possible exceptions,[246] were all in London bindings.

241. Listed in Appendix IV G, Annexes 6–8.
242. Listed in Appendix IV A. The number of panel bindings would be increased to twenty-five, if Geste's ownership of three other items (listed in Appendix I) could be established. All three are London bindings: *P4 (1544) in MISC 8/9 by Martin Dature, but now missing; *C7 (1526) in HM 11/12 by the same binder; and *A2 in HM 2 by John Reynes, with a strip of MS as a strengthener.
243. Listed in Appendix IV B.
244. See below, pp. 137–39, and listed in Appendix IVB, pp. 244–50, Appendix D, pp. 280, 305, and Appendix G., p. 336.
245. Cat. nos. E55 and J12. The third (B122), sent at the same time, has been rebound.
246. See below, p. 125 and n. 318.

There remain about two-hundred books in contemporary calf bindings to be considered, and these fall into four types. The first and simplest type of these bindings (designated here PL a) are those in plain calf covers over pasteboard – some twenty-one occur altogether, with imprints from 1525 to 1561 – without any binder's tooling or decoration other than fillets in blind at the outer edges. In addition, there are nine examples of these plain calf bindings which incorporate one or more rectangular frames, again defined by fillets, linked together by straight or angled fillets (here designated PL b).[247] These nine carry imprints in the range c. 1524 to 1550, dates consistent with their acquisition by Geste during his Cambridge period. All nine also retain pastedowns incorporating leaves from medieval MSS – a fact which points towards their having been bound in Cambridge.

The second type, represented by only six examples among Geste's books, is here designated 'corner-ornament' bindings. These, like his plain calf bindings, contain no centre ornament or centrepiece of any kind, the only decoration on the covers being a small tool or corner ornament at each angle of a plain rectangular frame of fillets.[248] Of the six examples in this category, four different tools or corner ornaments can be distinguished and these occur on books with imprints from 1534 to 1554. The books provide few clues as to their likely place of binding All but one have imprints falling within the period of Geste's time in Cambridge, though the earliest, an Oecolampadius in quarto of 1534 (O8) has a strengthener in the form of a thin strip from a medieval MS, more characteristic of London binding practice than of Cambridge. Only two of the books have full pastedowns, both consisting of leaves from printed books rather than MSS, but both, two octavo commentaries on the liturgical lections (S75–76) by Johann Spangenberg (1547–48), fall within Geste's Cambridge period.

The third type falls into the category of what David Pearson has called 'centrepiece' bindings, having a single centrepiece on otherwise plain calf covers.[249] Geste had a dozen examples of this kind, with three different centrepieces involved (two of them oval in shape, but one of them, unusually, round), and there is a fourth at Salisbury on a book of which his ownership is by no means certain.[250] All but one of these types is represented by a single example, but one (here designated CP 2.1) has no fewer than nine examples with imprints in the range 1571–73, i.e. during Geste's Salisbury period. A further example (G39) of this particular centrepiece (CP 2.2) occurs within a rectangular frame surrounded by two very worn rolls (one, a

247. Listed in Appendix IV F and illustrated in figs. 24.1–2.
248. Listed in Appendix IV E and illustrated in figs. 23.1–5.
249. Listed in Appendix IV C and illustrated in figs. 18.1–4. D. Pearson, 'English centre-piece bookbindings, 1560–1640', *The Library*, 6th series vol. 16 (1994), 1–17 and *Eloquent Witnesses: Bookbindings and their history* (ed. M. M. Foot. London: Bibliographical Society, 2004), pp. 106–26.
250. Appendix I, *E3.

heads-in-medallions, the other a diaper, neither found in Oldham). In view of the date range of all Geste's centrepiece bindings (1558–73) a London origin for these seems most likely, though a Salisbury outlet for one of them (CP 2) cannot be ruled out.

However, by far the largest number of Geste's contemporary bindings (over 180 examples) fall into the fourth of these types, here termed 'small-tool' or 'centre-tool' bindings.[251] Three of these (CT a-c) have already been encountered among the five characteristic 'fingerprints' in his books which provide evidence of his ownership. Some forty-three of these 'centre-tool' bindings (with even more variants) have been identified in his library,[252] but in contrast to the three types CT a–c, already considered, which occur in larger numbers than any of the others (over a hundred in all), these are represented by only one to half a dozen examples each. These centre-tool bindings can be found on books acquired throughout the whole period of Geste's collecting, one with an imprint as early as 1532 (E33) on a book bound in centre-tool CT c.1, and another (W20) with an imprint as late as 1576, in centre-tool CT e, during his final year at Salisbury. Seven of these types (in addition to CT c) can be assigned with some confidence to the period of his collecting in Cambridge,[253] a rather larger number (twenty-two), in addition to the two large groups of centre-tool bindings CT a–b already mentioned, to his London period,[254] and three to the final years in Salisbury.[255] One (CT vv), of which there are two examples (both acquired second-hand, after Geste had left Cambridge), has been attributed to Oxford on the grounds of its occurrence in college libraries there.[256] There are eleven other types which are less easy to assign, six with imprints from his Cambridge period, the other five when he was collecting in London, and, although the necessary evidence is not forthcoming, it is quite possible that the former group of six were also bound in Cambridge and the other five in London.[257]

How frequently these centre-tool bindings occur in other collections of the period is not known. This area of binding history seems under-researched, probably because these particular bindings appear to be so common and, in consequence, are under-reported in comparison with the more decorative roll and panel bindings. But there are examples of them in

251. Listed in Appendix IV D and illustrated in figs. 22.1–49. The total of 180 includes twenty-three examples combined with rolls.
252. The total of forty-three includes one 'centre-tool' type bound in France (CT qq). Two others (CT xx and CT zz) occur on books of which Geste's ownership is uncertain, and these are listed in Appendix I.
253. CT m.2, CT q, CT r, CT z, CT ee, CT yy and CT aaa.
254. Appendix IV D, Annexe 1 'Place of binding', s.v. 'London'.
255. Appendix IV D, Annexe 1 'Place of binding', s.v. 'London or Salisbury'.
256. Pearson, OB, pp. 82–83. The two examples are M19 and S59 (both with 1557 imprints).
257. See Appendix IV D, Annexe I, s.v. 'Place of binding not known for certain'.

Matthew Parker's collection and in Andrew Perne's, to mention two obvious examples from among Geste's contemporaries at Cambridge.

It is not clear whether Geste had any say in the choice of these bindings: whether he was offered a choice from a variety of such types on offer or whether, having indicated his preference for a covering of 'calf over paste-board' he left the matter entirely in the hands of his bookseller to choose which tools would be used on the covers.[258] Many of the books, as already indicated, preserve Geste's binding instructions, but these do not go beyond a simple distinction between 'in paste' (i.e. pasteboard), 'in bordes', or 'in parchment' (i.e. limp parchment covers) and in the absence of evidence to the contrary it seems that Geste generally left the actual choice to the binder.

Geste's second-hand acquisitions

Like other collections of the period, Geste's library included a large number of books acquired from former owners, by gift, directly from colleagues or through the 'second-hand' book trade, which evidently stocked second-hand copies of standard texts that had passed through successive generations of students, to be discarded when they had no further use for them. Forty-two volumes carry former ownership inscriptions from thirty-nine different owners.[259] In the case of three former owners, more than one book was involved,[260] and five books had belonged to more than one owner.[261] Not all of these former owners have been identified. Some books have only the initials of former owners,[262] generally stamped on the covers, though some of these have been identified, and some signatures are now incomplete as a result of cropping in the course of rebinding and others have been deliberately erased. Most of these second-hand items had probably come into Geste's possession during his time at Cambridge, particularly during his early years – the subject matter of many of these points strongly in that direction – but because so many of their former owners have yet to be identified,[263] some uncertainty on this point is inevitable.

258. I have deliberately avoided using the terms 'trade bindings', 'bespoke' or 'off the peg' bindings in the light of David Pearson's wise observations on what has often become a misdirected debate. See Pearson, EBS, pp. 7–10.

259. Listed in Appendix X: Index of provenances and former owners.

260. John Brandisby, Geste's uncle (five books), William Skypton (four), and Nicholas Kervyle (two).

261. Cat. nos. B52 (three), L41, N14, P15, and S45 (two each).

262. Cat. nos. N14 ('H K'), C64 ('T D'), T2 ('W S'), and C74 ('W W').

263. In addition to those listed above (n. 262), a Duns Scotus *Questiones* (1481) on Peter Lombard's *Sentences* (D33) with a 'pertinet' inscription, apparently 'Swynne', in a fifteenth-century hand; a 1505 rebound Vivaldus (V37) with the inscription of a 'Thomas Smyth'; a *De vera philosophia* of Hadrianus Castellensis (C49) with the ownership inscription 'Bullore' or possibly 'Bulloke' written in ink at the top of the upper calf cover; a Haymo Psalms commentary of 1533 (H9) with the

The five books that came to Geste from his uncle, Dr John Brandisby, have already been mentioned.[264] These appear to have been received during Geste's early years as a student, and there may have been others without Brandisby's inscription which came to him after the former's death in 1549, though no books are actually mentioned in his will. Among these may have been two items which had probably belonged to former colleagues of his in the north of England: an edition of Gregory I (1523) with the inscription 'Langrigii liber' (G31), possibly that of Dr Richard Langrige, like Brandisby a former chaplain to Edward Lee, Archbishop of York, who like him had been involved in securing signatures for the Royal Supremacy in 1535; the other, the *Historia scholastica* of Peter Comestor (1503) with signatures of Lee himself (P20). Both, unfortunately, are no longer in their original bindings, as are all but two[265] of the five that carry Brandisby's name.

As might have been anticipated, some of Geste's books came from colleagues at King's, such as the four, already mentioned, from an older Fellow, William Skypton,[266] another like Geste from Yorkshire who had also entered the college as a scholar from Eton. Thomas Bulward (O10), Nicholas Kervyle (B72, S17), Robert Pykering (E31) and (if correctly identified) William Wynke or William Whitelocke (C74) were other former owners at King's, while a John Calvard (P33, *C7), may have been another Cambridge man (from Queens' College) if he has been correctly identified. Although in many cases rebinding has taken place, it is still possible to identify a number of Cambridge bindings, confirming their acquisition there, such as the Oecolampadius (1535) in a Garrett Godfrey roll, Oldham, D.1.h(3), that had belonged to Bulward, the Sarcerius (1541) in Oldham SW.b(4) from Nicholas Kervyle, and the Cicero (also 1541) that may have been Wynke's or Whitelock's, in Oldham HM.h(29). This last was one of thirteen examples of this roll among Geste's books, some combined with centre-tools such as this one (CT zz). But not all these books from former colleagues were in Cambridge bindings. Robert Pykering's copy of a 1522 Erasmus (E31) was in a London panel binding (Oldham, BPEB, BIB. 17 with ST 9), and the other book

inscription of a 'William Donwiche'; a commentary on Luke by Bonaventura (1539) with three inscriptions on the title page: 'D. gilpinnus', 'Johan[n]is [?]sedylli[us]' (both erased); and, 'Thomas Maxfeldus' (B52); and postils on the Epistles and Gospels by Antonius Broeckwey (1544) which had once belonged to a 'Joannes Mablistonus'. I am very grateful to Dr Elisabeth Leedham-Green for her assistance in transcribing many of these.

264. Introduction I, p. 7.
265. Cat. nos. L72 in parchment covers and E48 in a panel binding (Oldham, BPEB, TRIP. 9).
266. Skypton's signature occurs in five items (A62, B35, E56, H84 and T2), two of them parts of the same volume (A62 and E56, shelf mark A.6.32). Only one of them (B35), one of a six-volume set of small format Bibles printed in Paris by Simon Colines (1526–32), remains in a contemporary binding (Oldham, BPEB, panel TRIP. 9).

owned by Kervyle, by the Lutheran, Johann Brentz (B72), was in another
London panel binding (Oldham, BPEB, HM. 11/12) by Martin Dature, with
whom Geste also had dealings during his time in Cambridge.[267]

Like other collectors of the time, Geste acquired some of these second-
hand items from the dissolved religious houses or from former religious. One
of the earliest may have been a 1478 copy of the Postils of the Dominican,
Gulielmus of Paris (G49), albeit in a later rebinding, which had once belonged
to the House of Bonshommes at Edington, Wiltshire, in Geste's own diocese,
though exactly when it came into his collection is not known. An edition of
the works of John of Damascus (J13) has the signature of Chrysostom Kyrbe,
'canonicus' of Welbeck, possibly one of the Premonstratensian canons of the
Abbey of St James, Welbeck, in Nottinghamshire, though not among those
listed at the surrender in 1538. Both of these had lost their original bindings,
but a copy of *De Maria Magdalena* by Jacques Le Fèvre (L25), still in its
original Garrett Godfrey covers (though now re-mounted), had verses
on one of the flyleaves signed by a 'Joannes Lodyngton', third among
fourteen canons from Launde Augustinian priory of St John the Baptist in
Leicestershire who acknowledged the Royal Supremacy in 1534. Better
known (if the attribution is correct) was the owner of a *Decretum* of Gratian
(G30) published in 1519: William Blomfild, the Elizabethan alchemist and
author of *Blossoms* and *Quintaessens*, who had once been a Benedictine at
Bury St Edmunds, later converting to Protestantism, and briefly beneficed
at Norwich (1569). These four items had probably been acquired during
Geste's time at Cambridge, but a volume of sermons by Oswaldus Pelbárt
(P15), still in its contemporary 'Netherlandish' panel binding (fig. 14), had
evidently been purchased some time after 1565.

It had been once owned by Richard Brynckley, originally of the Cambridge
Franciscan Convent, who went on to become Provincial Minister of the
Order in 1518, incorporating his degrees at Oxford in 1524. Whether the book
remained with the Order from the time of his death, a year or two later, until
the Dissolutions is not clear, but the book had meanwhile acquired the name
of another owner, Thomas Potter, with a price and date (1565), before
joining the many other volumes of sermons, Catholic, Lutheran and Reformed, that adorned the shelves of Geste's library during Elizabeth's reign.

During the reign of Elizabeth, fewer second-hand acquisitions occurred.
But there were items from four former Catholic owners (if the identifications
have been correctly made), two of whom had played a prominent part in
the Marian proceedings against the Protestant Reformers. One was William
Chedsey, Canon of Christ Church, Oxford, who had opposed Peter Martyr
Vermigli at the Oxford Disputation (1549), taking part in the later Disputations

---

267. Geste had a volume from him with two items by Luther (1539) in the same binding
  (L57–58). This survives with his binding instructions, suggesting a direct relationship with the London binder concerned. See below, p. 124 .

14. A folio of 1521 in contemporary calf with a roll, possibly 'Netherlandish' or even German, formerly owned by Richard Brynckley, Provincial Minister of the Franciscans. Cat. no. P15.

15. A Lutheran book acquired by Geste from the library of Henry Fitzalan,
12th Earl of Arundel. Cat. no. A28. See Appendix X.

there against Cranmer, Ridley and Latimer (1554). After time in custody under
Edward VI, he was imprisoned in the Fleet from 1562 until his death, and it
was presumably during this time that his copy of Postel's Πανθενωσια
(P45), still in its parchment covers, came into Geste's possession. Hugh
Weston (if the 'Westonus' on two books is indeed this Weston) took part
in the same Disputation in 1554, but was deprived of his positions by Pole
himself, ending up in the Tower where he died shortly after Elizabeth's
accession in 1558. His copy of *De septem sacramentis* (1540) by Gulielmus
Baufeti, Bishop of Paris (G47) retains its parchment covers, but his other
book, a commentary on the Psalms and Canticles (T11) by the Catholic, Franz
Titelman (1531), was rebound for Geste in plain calf over pasteboard,
decorated only with simple corner ornaments (CS 4), for the latter's characteristic binding instructions are still visible at the foot of the title page.
Another Catholic in outlook – one of twelve Oxford and Cambridge theologians also present at the Oxford Disputations in 1554 – was Richard
Bruarne, a noted Hebrew scholar and Regius Professor at Oxford until 1559,
who was briefly Provost of Eton (1561), though elected by the Fellows
without the Queen's permission, before being forced to resign. His copy
of a work issued by the University of Wittenberg in 1559 (W45), now in a
later binding, was in parts extensively annotated by Geste who presumably
acquired it after Bruarne's death at Windsor in 1565.

The familiar 'Arundel' inscription identifies the third of these Catholic
owners: Henry Fitzalan, the 12th Earl, a notable collector in his own right
who acquired archbishop Cranmer's library after its confiscation by the
Crown in 1553. The book Geste acquired, a work by Nicolaus von Amsdorff
(1550) concerning the Lutheran Church at Magdeburg (A28), was evidently
a rarity in Cambridge at the time[268] and something of a surprise to find in
the collection of the Catholic Arundel. It may have been one of the books

268. It occurs in none of the contemporary Cambridge inventories (BiCI), the libraries
of Perne or Parker, or in Adams. The Arundel inscription is illustrated in fig. 15.

disposed of when Arundel's library was merged with that of his son-in-law, John, Lord Lumley, at Nonsuch Palace in 1557, or it may have been already removed, following the Marian purge of Protestant books earlier in her reign. The book, now without pastedowns and in a later binding, offers no clues as to its place of acquisition or binding.

Five other books with pre-Geste inscriptions can also be assigned to this period. Only three of these, however, have fully identified provenances.[269] The first of these, a Seneca of 1515 now in a later binding (S45), had been a donation from the vicar of Malling in Kent to the Benedictine Cathedral Priory of St Andrew, Rochester, presumably acquired by Geste during his time as its bishop (1561–77). The second of these, the first edition of the commentary on I Corinthians (1551) by Peter Martyr Vermigli (V15) and still in its original plain calf binding decorated only with corner ornaments of cornucopia (CS 2), had belonged to John Ponet, Stephen Gardiner's successor at Winchester (1551–1553), who had died in exile on the continent in 1556. It carries two dated inscriptions (1552 and 1553), the second as bishop of Winchester, and may have been left behind before he went into exile.[270] The third, also with Winchester associations, must have entered Geste's collection very late in his life. This was a copy of John Whitgift's *Defense of the Aunswere* (W16) against Thomas Cartwright (1574) with an 'ex dono' inscription from John Bridges, a prebend there until becoming Dean of Salisbury in 1578, a year after Geste's death. This is still in its original calf covers, signed by the London binder identified by the initials 'F D', with strap-work and heads-in-medallions rolls, Oldham SW.b(5) and HM.b(3), showing the heads of four 'Reformers', Melanchthon, Erasmus, Hus and Luther.

As might have been expected, few of these second-hand books were of any great rarity, occurring in at least some of the surviving Cambridge inventories and collections of the period. But six of these are not found in any of these inventories, nor in the libraries of Parker or Perne,[271] and

269. The owners of the other two have not been identified. The first, a copy of the first two parts of the *Annotations on the New Testament* (L41) by Lucas Loss (1554–59), now rebound, carries the inscriptions of 'Richard Lee and friends' and 'John Philpot and friends' on the title page, perhaps two groups of readers rather than owners. The second, a copy of *The Reproufe of M. Dorman* (1560) by Alexander Nowell (N14) has the ownership inscription of a John Appleby and the initials 'H K' stamped in gold on the front and back parchment covers.

270. Andrew Perne was another who acquired books formerly owned by Ponet, in his case three. McKitterick (1991), p. 41, suggests these may never have left Cambridge.

271. The Erasmus (E31) which had belonged to Robert Pykering; the Πανθενωσια by Guillaume Postel (P45), belonging to William Chedsey; a *De vera philosophia* (C49) by Hadrianus Castellensis (1507) with 'Bullore' or 'Bulloke' on the covers; and three others whose owners have not been traced – a Duns Scotus of 1509 (D32), a commentary on Romans by Oecolampadius (O12), and a work by Georg Witzel of 1537 (W53).

another five – including the Arundel item already mentioned (A28) – are even rarer, not occurring in the libraries of any Cambridge college at the time or since, or even the University Library, and therefore absent from Adams' *Catalogue* of these institutional collections (1967).[272]

In addition to these forty-two books with pre-Geste ownership inscriptions or initials, another sixty-seven volumes contain evidence of earlier ownership in the form of MS annotations in the text or on flyleaves, although in the absence of such inscriptions the owners can no longer be identified. Only three of these second-hand items can be assigned to the period after Geste left Cambridge.[273] Just over half of the others, presumably acquired between 1536 and 1554, have been rebound, including all but two of the ten incunabula and all but five of the nineteen post-incunabula, making it very difficult if not impossible to determine where these items may have been originally bound or obtained, particularly where no traces of the volume's original end-leaf construction has survived.

Of those still in contemporary bindings, one of the two incunabula may well be of Cambridge origin. This is a 1497 *Catholicon* by Joannes Balbus (B5), in calf over boards, its covers incorporating lozenge shaped and round stamps now too worn to be identified (fig. 16.1), with flyleaves and pastedowns (now unstuck), again in the Cambridge manner, in this instance, from Caxton's edition (1483) of John Gower's *Confessio amantis* (fig. 16.2) as well as MS leaves of twenty French basse dances in a fifteenth-century hand.

The *Catholicon* was another standard textbook which had apparently passed through a number of hands before Geste acquired it, for it contains MS annotations by previous owners as well as his, and the title (if not this edition) occurs in twelve Cambridge inventories of the period, as well as in Parker's library (in an edition of 1503). The other incunable, a Peter Lombard of 1495 (P23), retains parts of the original French roll binding re-mounted on later covers (fig. 20.4), and among the post-incunabula, two are from identifiable Cambridge binders, one each from Garrett Godfrey (P14) and Nicholas Spierinck (H83), and a third in parchment covers is probably also from Cambridge (R13), while it is clear that some of the books he was acquiring second-hand were in bindings from outside Cambridge: for in addition to the Peter Lombard (P23) in a French binding already noted,

272. Beside the Arundel item (A28), there are two items that had once belonged to William Skypton: Augustine on the Four Gospels (A62) and a volume of the Postills of Hugh of St Cher (H84); a commentary on Luke by Sarcerius (S17) formerly owned by Nicholas Kervyle; and Tavernarius (T2) on Eucharistic doctrine (1556) owned by an unidentified 'W S'.

273. Cat. nos. C76 (1558), in parchment covers, P9 (1560), rebound, and W27 (1565), in calf, with centre-tool CT b, one of a group of fifty-one with this tool, many of which, like this one, have strips of MS as strengtheners, and assignable with some certainty to London.

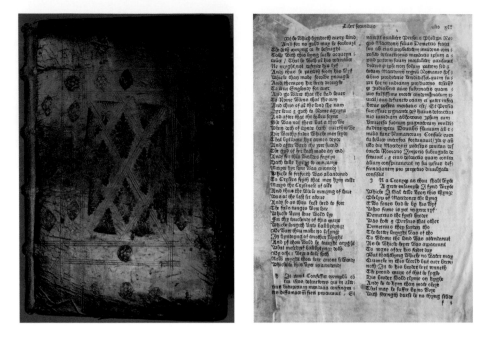

16. Geste's copy of Balbus *Catholicon* (1497). Cat. no. B5.

16.1 (left) The very worn unidentified contemporary calf binding.

16.2 (right) Fol. xl from John Gower's *Confessio amantis* printed by
William Caxton in 1483 used as a flyleaf.

the *Summa Summarum* (1517) by Cagnazzo (C1) has a London roll,[274] and
the *Vocabularius theologie* (1517) by Altensteig (A25), an Oxford one.[275]

Much the same pattern is evident in the case of his books with imprints
between 1521 and 1553. Of the twenty-three volumes still in contemporary
bindings, sixteen can be assigned to their place of binding with at least some
degree of confidence. Three are certainly in Cambridge bindings, one signed
by the 'W G' binder (C127)[276] and two more by Spierinck,[277] while another
nine in unsigned bindings also appear to be of Cambridge origin on the
grounds of their end-leaf construction.[278] Another is probably in a French

274. Oldham, EBSB, roll AN.g(1) with ornament B(3).
275. Oldham, EBSB, roll FL.a(3) (= Gibson roll I), with ornament 5; Ker, *Fragments*,
Appendix, no. xxxii.
276. His copy of Cyprian (1521) in Oldham, EBSB, roll AN.e(1).
277. His copies of a Clichtoveus (C82, 1524), in Oldham, EBSB, AN.f(2) (= Gray,
Roll I) with D1.a(2) (= Gray, Roll II), and a Lambert (L7, 1525), in Oldham,
EBSB, FL.a(1) (= Gray, Roll III).
278. His copies of a commentary by Bonaventura on the *Sentences* (1522), three out
of a four volume set (B53), in Oldham, EBSB, roll HM.d(4) with full MS
pastedowns, a roll which occurs on six of Geste's books; Valla's *Annotationes* on
the New Testament (V3) in the edition of Erasmus (1526), and the *Grammaticae
institutio* (G18) of Theodore of Gaza (1525), both in Oldham, BPEB, triple-panels

roll binding – a *Theosophia* by Arboreus (A49) printed in Paris in 1540 (fig. 20.3), though how it came into Geste's collection is not known; two more are certainly in London bindings, one, the *Aurea Rosa* on the gospels (1524) by Silvestro Mazzolini (M23) with two panels signed by Julian Notary,[279] and the other, a copy of *Ecclesiastae siue de ratione concionandi* (1535) by Erasmus (E36) in Oldham, BPEB, panels HM. 9/10, while a third, Reuchlin's commentary on the seven penitential Psalms (1529) in parchment covers (R16), with a thin strip of MS as a strengthener, may also be of London origin.

None of the other seven are assignable to a place of binding with any certainty, including an Oecolampadius (O7) of 1533 in a variant of the Marian triple panel [TRIP. 9], unusually surrounded by an unidentified narrow roll, the design of which Oldham had found in some Flemish rolls, though there is no reason to suppose that this is not an English binding.[280]

Three others are in parchment covers (O11, P36, and V7), the third of these (V7) in tacketed wrappers, probably of continental origin; one in plain calf over pasteboard (H13), is just possibly of Cambridge origin,[281] and another, an Oecolampadius of 1525 (O6), is in a heads-in-medallions roll, Oldham, EBSB, HM.f(1), which has been re-mounted on later calf covers, and in its present form can probably not be assigned with certainty to any place of binding, though it is certainly English.

The last of the seven items (B33), with annotations by a former, unknown owner, and without pastedowns, forms one of the set of six-volume Latin vulgate Bible published in Paris by Simon Colines (1526–32). Its calf binding incorporates a single panel of the 'Virgin of the Apocalypse' similar to the right-hand compartment of the Marian triple panel (Oldham, BPEB, TRIP. 9), of which Geste had several examples.[282] Its companion volume (B35) from the same set – once owned by Geste's former colleague at King's, William Skypton – was in the same binding and had leaves from an English s.xiii/xiv MS as pastedowns (PDN 8) in the Cambridge manner, a fact which, together with its provenance, would point to a Cambridge source for the book, and it is quite likely that the other volume (B33), though without the evidence of MS pastedowns, came from the same source. It

TRIP. 5/6, the former with a full MS pastedown; the *Summa caietana de peccatis* (1527) by Thomas de Vio (V33) and a commentary on Matthew and Luke (1531) by Melanchthon (M49), both in plain calf (PL b), also with full MS pastedowns; a 1528 Paschasius Radbertus (P6) in parchment covers using full MS leaves as flyleaves; and a copy of *Libellus de fide & operibus* (1530) by Latomus (L18) in a calf binding with centre-tool CT y and full MS pastedowns.

279. Oldham, BPEB, panels HE29 and RO14.
280. So Mirjam Foot (personal communication). Oldham's observation is made in a note, dated 9.1944, inserted in (O7). The binding is illustrated in fig. 17.
281. See Appendix IV F for other items in this binding, many of which retain full MS pastedowns of the Cambridge type, though no pastedown survives in this one.
282. O7 (with an unidentified panel), and H10, J2 and E48. All four appear to be English bindings.

17. One of Geste's twenty-two panel bindings: a Marian triple-panel (Oldham, BPEB, TRIP. 9), in this example combined with a roll. Cat. no. O7.

is fairly clear, however, that this six-volume vulgate had been 'made up', to judge by its varied bindings, two panel and one roll (the other three parts unfortunately rebound), and imprint dates ranging from 1526 to 1532. All but the last are extensively annotated in Geste's hand, indicative of his close study of the text during the 1540s. Some, perhaps all, were acquired second-hand, and the set most probably belonged to his student years as he turned to theological studies which involved the detailed study of the biblical text, preparatory to his BD taken in 1551.

Geste's second-hand items – amounting to slightly over fifteen per cent of his entire collection as it survives today[283] – account for a significant proportion of the books in more decorated bindings: twelve out of the twenty-two with panels, and at least twenty out of his hundred or so roll bindings. The great majority of these were probably acquired, as was to be expected, during his time in Cambridge, with imprints up to the 1540s. Although a high proportion of his books throughout his collecting career – 'new' as well as 'second-hand' – were in simple calf bindings or parchment covers, it is not to be thought that he had no interest in acquiring 'new' books in these more decorated bindings, either in Cambridge or later, when he would have been buying his books from London outlets. In fact, eighteen of his 'new' items acquired after leaving Cambridge (with imprints from 1553 to 1575) were in roll bindings, a number of them by the so-called 'R B' London binder.

Geste's new acquisitions

Where may Geste have obtained his 'new' books, particularly such a remarkable stock of continental printing, the great majority of which were bound in England? There is no simple answer to this. Little has come to light from the books themselves to provide more exact information about the identity of the 'outlets' from which he may have made his purchases: no dates or sources of acquisition, for example, with the exception of the three volumes in roll bindings presented to him in 1551 by his relative, Christopher Leedes, already mentioned.[284] No booksellers' marks of identification have been discovered, no booksellers' lists or accounts conveniently left among any of the flyleaves or pastedowns, and no references to Geste as a book purchaser in any surviving stationer's accounts. Geste himself left no correspondence that might shed light on this, and nothing has come to light in the Salisbury Cathedral archives.

Such information as there is to answer such questions has often to be teased out of some of the physical features of the books themselves such as the binding style or end-leaf construction, and even then such evidence (with the exception of the few books in signed bindings by Garrett Godfrey and others) only provides pointers at most to the *place* of binding, not to particular binders, stationers or booksellers. Moreover, even this limited information is only helpful in cases where the original bindings, pastedowns, flyleaves and other features indicative of Cambridge or London binding practice remain relatively intact. Where rebinding has taken place and such features lost there is very little if anything that can be said.

Exactly when Geste started to make his 'new' purchases in Cambridge is uncertain. Direct evidence of purchases from Garrett Godfrey has not

283. 109 volumes with evidence of pre-Geste ownership out of a total of 684.
284. See above, p. 42 n. 17.

survived, though his relatives, the Brandisbys, his uncle, John, and one or both of his two uncles at St John's College, Richard and James, bought books from Godfrey, as we know from the chance discovery of some years of his accounts, covering the period c. 1527 – c. 1533, in the pasteboard of a volume at Emmanuel College in 1988.[285] Of the few books of Geste's that can be traced to Garrett Godfrey, who had effectively retired soon after Geste entered King's College (1536), most, as we have seen, were evidently obtained second-hand,[286] though evidence of former ownership in these books does not by any means preclude their purchase from Godfrey's shop. For it is evident from Godfrey's *Accounts* that he dealt in the second-hand trade, as university book-sellers have done for centuries, stocking 'old' as well as 'new' books,[287] and it may be that some of Geste's second-hand books, especially those that have prices on the title page, come from this same source or from one of the other Cambridge stationers.

Of Geste's 'new' purchases from Godfrey there is evidence for four items. One, evidently purchased 'new', was the *Conciliationes locorum scripturae* by Andreas Althamer (Nuremberg, 1536) in one of his heraldic rolls (Oldham, EBSB, HE.b(2) = Gray, Roll III), for it carries at the foot of the title page a trace of what appears to be one of Geste's binding instructions (A27). But this may have been a book that was actually bound by Godfrey's partner, Nicholas Pilgrim (d. 1544/45), who succeeded him for about five years as one of the three University Stationers, inheriting some of his tools. This must have been the case with another of Geste's 'new' books (L5), also in a Godfrey roll binding, François Lambert's *Commentary on Revelation* (Basle, 1539), which had clearly appeared in print too late to have been bound by Godfrey himself.[288] Two other books without obvious evidence of former ownership – a volume of three Erasmus items bound with Cyprian *On the Lord's Prayer* (1524–1533)[289] in one of Godfrey's heraldic rolls (Oldham, EBSB, HE.b(2) = Gray Roll III), and a Bede of 1529 (B12) in the same roll combined with roll AN.f(1), both with full MS pastedowns – were almost certainly purchased new from Godfrey's shop.

These four books are the only 'new' purchases of Geste's that can certainly be linked with Godfrey, but the fragmentary *Accounts* covering the period approximately 1527–1533, confirm, as was suspected, that he was dealing in a far wider range of books than the fine, signed roll bindings

285. *GGA 1527–33*, nos. 1–3 ['Bromsby'], 248–51, 272–73, 418–30 ['Bronsby', this last group of purchases Godfrey lists under Bronsby of St John's College]. Elisabeth Leedham-Green suggests John, Richard and/or James as the purchasers involved.
286. This seems to be true of C49 (1507), P14 (1514), L25 (1518), T7 (1520) and O10 (1535).
287. See for example *GGA 1527–33*, p. 19, items 191–92, 194, copies of Erasmus, *Colloquia*. Some are described as 'old', some as 'new'.
288. Bound in Oldham, EBSB, roll Dl.h(3) = Gray, roll V.
289. Cat. nos. E30, E32, E39 and C128.

that have come to be associated with him, and it is quite possible – though at present impossible to demonstrate – that some at least of the many simpler binding styles, such as those designated here as 'centre-tool' and 'plain' bindings, may also have come from his shop and provided for customers like Geste, Perne and Parker, to cover the many continental octavos and books of even smaller format in their collections.

It is far from clear how far Godfrey would have been able to satisfy Geste's requirements as a customer in Cambridge since he had retired from book selling only three years after Geste first arrived in Cambridge, and no accounts have yet been found covering the final six years of his business which overlapped with Geste's time there. But fifty-one titles in Geste's collection were items which Godfrey stocked, according to his *Accounts* for the years 1527–33 (a small number, admittedly, out of over 1100 titles listed), and three of these survive in Godfrey's roll bindings – the Bede (B12) and Erasmus (E30) already mentioned, as well as the Theodoret (T7) among his second-hand acquisitions – with imprints between 1519 and 1533. It is tempting to suggest that one other book from Godfrey's shop listed in his *Accounts* may just possibly be one that survives in Geste's collection. This is a copy of 'Bodius' *Vnio dissidentium* (B51) published in Antwerp in about 1533 (*GGA 1527–33*, 3) which his uncle, John Brandisby ['Bromsby' in the *Accounts*] had purchased from Godfrey. If so, this would be an addition to the five books known to have been donated by Brandisby to Geste – perhaps coming to him after the death of his uncle in 1549, though the relevant provenance evidence to demonstrate this has not survived the book's drastic rebinding.[290]

The other Cambridge binder whose books appear in Geste's collection during his Cambridge period (1536–54) was Godfrey's contemporary, one of the other three designated University Stationers, Nicholas Spierinck – another who had his shop in the Parish of St Mary the Great, very conveniently placed for customers from King's College. Three of Geste's 'new' books can certainly be traced to Spierinck, one with blind panels, the other two with roll bindings,[291] but, if Pearson is correct, a further twenty-one 'new'

290. Nothing is known about the size of John Brandisby's collection at his death in 1549 (for which no *post-mortem* inventory survives) or whether he regularly signed his books as a mark of his ownership. It is quite possible, though impossible to prove in the absence of an inventory, that he only signed books he gave away during his lifetime, in which case there would be no insuperable objection to the Bodius having come to Geste (perhaps with other books) without Brandisby's signature after his death. His will, however, makes no mention of the disposal of his books, though Geste was a beneficiary (see above, Introduction I, pp. 7–9)

291. The 'new' book with panels is E28 (1523), an octavo in Oldham, BPEB, panels BIB. 2 and ST. 37 (Gray, p. 51 no. 36), the two with rolls are B111 (with a 1525 imprint), and M16 (1531), both octavos, in the same roll binding, Oldham, EBSB, FLa.1 (= Gray, roll III).

items with three different, unsigned rolls (which Oldham had attributed to London binders) may also have come from his workshop: four items in Oldham, EBSB, rolls FP.g(1), seven in HM.h(28), and ten in HM.h(29).[292]

It was probably in the early 1540s, when Geste had graduated, obtained his MA (1544) and was commencing the study of theology for his BD, that he was purchasing new books from this source. All were items in the field of theology and biblical studies: a polemical book by the Catholic, Joannes a Davantria (J9), a work on the New Testament by the Benedictine, Isidore Chiari, much annotated by Geste (C64), two works by humanists – a Latin New Testament by Erasmus (E28) and the Hebrew grammar of Sebastian Münster (M85) – and the rest by Protestant authors, mostly in the form of biblical commentaries, ranging from a number of Lutherans to those in the Reformed tradition, such as Zwingli, Oecolampadius and Bullinger.[293] Whether or not the Spierinck connexion can be sustained for all twenty-one of these items, the case at least for a Cambridge source for these books is strongly supported by the use of full leaves from medieval MSS in parchment in all the eighteen items that retain their pastedowns in tact,[294] and all twenty-one books fall within the period of Spierinck's known activity as a binder.

Seven other roll bindings in Geste's collection, totalling in all fifteen volumes, are also ones which have been assigned to Cambridge binders by Oldham or Pearson, and these must be considered here. Two books, without discernible evidence of earlier ownership, have imprints in the 1520s which pre-date Geste's arrival in Cambridge: a 1521 Cyprian (C127) with Oldham, EBSB, roll AN.e(1), signed 'W G', and a *Summa Angelica* of 1523 (A39) from the so-called 'W G/I G' workshop. The other five were contemporaneous with Geste's time at King's and were almost certainly

292. Pearson, BC, pp. 171, 182. The three rolls found in Geste's collection, now tentatively attributed to Spierinck by Pearson (personal communication), are Oldham, EBSB, FP.g(1): four items – Cat. nos. C64 (1544), S12 (two items, both 1543), both combined with centre-tool CT c.1 (see fig. 19.2), and C38 (1539), combined with CT c.3, all four in octavo; HM.h(28): seven items – Z6 (?1525), O13 (1534), S15 (1538), J14 (1535), L63 (1539), B127 (1538), all six in octavo, and M85 (1542), combined with CT c.2, in quarto (fig. 13.1); HM.h(29): ten items – S18 (1540), J9 (1533), L49 (1543), S25 (1539), all surrounding a plain rectangular frame, B83 (1542), S20 (1541), S21–22 (1544), B91 (1544), all five combined with CT c.1; and C37 (1536), combined with CT q, all ten in octavo. Two further items in HM.h(29) – C74 (1541) combined with CT zz, and L6 (1538) combined with CT q, appear to be second-hand copies, the former (if the owner 'W W' has been correctly identified) once owned by a colleague at King's.
293. Works by Luther (L49 and L63), and the Lutherans, Justus Jonas (J14), Johann Brentz (B83 and B91), and Erasmus Sarcerius (S12, S15, S17, S20–22 and S25), François Lambert (L6, second-hand), Wolfgang Capito (C37–38), and from those in the Reformed tradition, Zwingli (Z6), Oecolampadius (O13) and Bullinger (B127).
294. The three items without pastedowns are B91 – HM.h(29), C38 – FP.g(1) and Z6 – HM.h(28).

purchased new, though if he had ever indicated any choice of binding material (i.e. 'in paste[board]') the evidence, in the form of his binding instructions, no longer survives. The first (W50) was a volume containing five items by Catholic authors, Witzel and Eck among them, the latest item with a 1542 imprint (E8A), bound in a floral roll – Oldham, EBSB, FL.a(9) – with centre-tool CT z, which the late Neil Ker assigned to Cambridge rather than London.[295] The second and third bindings which Oldham had associated with London workshops have been re-assigned by Pearson to Cambridge, following earlier unpublished work by Neil Ker.[296] These are both 'strapwork' bindings, Oldham, EBSB, SW.b(3), of which Geste possessed three examples (L64, R34 and S13) with imprints between 1533 and 1540, and one (S17) dated 1541 of Oldham SW.b(4). All the works concerned were by Lutheran authors with imprints from Hagenau, Leipzig and Frankfurt-am-Main. The fourth of these rolls – Oldham, EBSB, HE.g(4) – had an earlier London history during the 1520s and 1530s, but it appears in Cambridge during the 1550s,[297] and Geste had a set of six volumes of the commentaries of Dionysius, the Carthusian, with imprints from 1542–52, all in bindings which combined this roll with two small-tool ornaments, and these were evidently acquired towards the end of his time at Cambridge.[298] The last of these rolls – another now assigned to Cambridge by Pearson – was Oldham, EBSB, FL.a(10), involving two items, an Erasmus New Testament (E29), in a different edition from the one bound for him by Spierinck (E28), and an exposition of Psalms 51 and 130 by Luther (L55).

One other binding, although not assigned to Cambridge by Oldham or Pearson, may, just possibly, be added to the list of Geste's Cambridge bindings. This is a heads-in-medallions roll, Oldham, EBSB, HM.d(4), of which Geste had six examples: two Biblical commentaries by the early-medieval author, Rabanus Maurus (R1–2) published in 1532, an incomplete set of Bonaventura's commentary on the *Sentences* of Peter Lombard in three volumes published in 1522 (B53), and a Suetonius *Caesars* of 1537 (S96). Although the two volumes of Rabanus Maurus are without pastedowns, the others with this roll all have pastedowns consisting of full leaves in parchment, trimmed down from medieval MSS in the Cambridge manner, and the Suetonius (S96) also carries Geste's ownership inscription on the title page in a form that suggests this was a textbook acquired early in his career as a student.[299]

---

295. The Cambridge attribution is made in Ker's annotated copy of Oldham, now in David Pearson's possession.

296. Pearson, BC, pp. 171, 184 n. 10, 189.   297. Pearson, BC, p. 171.

298. See entry in Cat. no, D10 for details. The other examples are D11–12, D14 and D17–18.

299. See entry in Cat. no. S96, with the inscription, 'Su[m] liber gest'. This was a book stocked by Garrett Godfrey, and it appears frequently in Cambridge inventories of the period.

These panel and roll bindings – amounting to some forty-nine volumes, with the possibility of a further eighteen without rolls from the same group of centre-tool CT c bindings[300] – account for only a very small proportion of the 'new' books Geste may have acquired during his time in Cambridge (1536–54).

How many more of the books with imprints from this period are also to be assigned to Cambridge shops it is less easy to say. Five books (printed between 1540 and c. 1552) in other centre-tool bindings have pastedowns of the Cambridge type which suggest that they may have been bound and acquired there.[301] To these may be added a larger number of plain calf bindings with full MS pastedowns, incorporating one or more rectangular frames linked to each other by straight and/or angled fillets, of which there are at least six examples with imprints between about 1524 and 1550,[302] and there are at least another twelve with imprints between 1525 and 1553 in completely plain calf apart from a border of fillets at the outer edges.[303] All eighteen of these have full MS pastedowns characteristic of Cambridge practice, and there are a further three, similarly in plain calf, though without pastedowns, where a Cambridge attribution, though possible, is much less certain.[304]

Similarly, a number of his 'new' books in parchment covers have full, page-size leaves from (in some cases, trimmed down) medieval MSS functioning as flyleaves or end-leaf guards – again pointing to a possible Cambridge outlet for these items: six with imprints ranging from 1528 to one as late as 1558 (after Geste had left Cambridge),[305] and five with parchment

300. See Appendix IV D, under CT c.1 – seventeen items, with continental imprints between 1532 and 1548, all but one (Z4) retaining full MS pastedowns: A5, A43, A55, B38, B88, C11, D6, E33, E38, G29, H42, L60, M20, R23, S14, and V39; and one example of CT.c.4: C102.

301. Another volume of Dionysius, the Carthusian (D21) and a commentary on the Pauline epistles by Oecumenius (O18), although whether this is of the 1552 edition is uncertain, both with centre-tool CT m.2; a biblical commentary by the Lutheran Caspar Cruciger (C114) with centre-tool CT r (1546); and two examples of centre-tool CT ee – one by the Lutheran Spangenberg (S80), bound with other works (1527–44), and the other by Oecolampadius (O4, 1544), both with Geste's binding instructions relating to associated items.

302. Listed in Appendix IV F under PL b. M49, O12 and V33, which appear to be second-hand items, have not been included in this figure.

303. Appendix IV F under PL a. H13, which appears to be a second-hand item, has not been included.

304. B89 (1544), H65 (1545) and R39 (1550).

305. Listed in Appendix IV G. Excluding P6 (Paschasius Radbertus) and P45 (the Πανθενωσια of Guillaume Postel) which were both acquired second-hand, the six items are: L15, the Catholic Latomus against Bucer (1546); C90, the Catholic Cochlaeus on the Confessio Augustana (1544); K2, a commentary on Philippians by Kinthisius (1544); B118, the Antiquissima fides et vera religio of Bullinger (1544); G15, Gardiner on celibacy against Bucer (1554); and S83, the Theologiae Lutheranae trimembris epitome of the Catholic Fridericus Staphylus (1558).

MS leaves sewn in as covers.[306] A further eleven books in parchment covers,[307] also with imprints during Geste's Cambridge period, but without MS flyleaves or end-leaf guards, cannot be assigned with any certainty to Cambridge binders, and may well include items imported from the continent with sewn book blocks, to which wrappers were attached in England before or at acquisition, and it is also quite possible that there are others of continental origin, in parchment covers, still to be identified. Two items in tacketed-parchment wrappers, for example, with German imprints of 1533 (B78) and 1535 (V7), and a third with a much earlier imprint from Milan in 1509 (D32), might, on the face of it, be exceptional cases of books imported already bound. But the third (D32) would appear to have been bound in England, having a strip from a MS of English origin as an end-leaf guard (Appendix IX, PDN 199), while the first (B78) has parchment covers which exhibit characteristics of English practice, only the second (V7) apparently without any evidence that would tell against it being an English binding.[308]

Understandably, very few of the later rebound volumes retain their original pastedowns or fly-leaves, but three with imprints between 1549 and 1550 retain pastedowns of the Cambridge type (though now unstuck).[309]

The remaining 'new' books with imprints during his Cambridge years lack the evidence necessary to determine their origin, though it seems probable – unless there is evidence in individual cases to the contrary – that Geste obtained most of these from Cambridge outlets. That he had been acquiring books from Godfrey and Spierinck, and in all likelihood the former's successor, Nicholas Pilgrim, is clear enough, but after their deaths nothing is known to link him directly with any of the other University's stationers between 1546 and his departure from King's College early in 1554.

---

306. O21, the rare Erasmus edition of Origen's commentary on Matthew 13–16 (*c.* 1527), but a work evidently available in Cambridge since it is recorded among the stock of Garrett Godfrey (GGA 1527–33, 113); W43, a very rare commentary on I & II Timothy by Jodocus Willich (1546); S77, a rare commentary on Acts by the Lutheran, Johann Spangenberg (1546); F17, *De vocabulo fidei* by the Lutheran Matthias Flacius Illyricus (1549); and C105, a collection of texts on the eucharist edited by the Catholic, Joannes Costerius (1551).

307. The eleven items are listed in Appendix IV G, Annexe 4, with an imprint date-range from 1526 to 1552.

308. The three items are listed in Appendix IV G, Annexe 8. The secondary tackets on the spine of B78 are illlustrated in fig. 25.1. Nicholas Pickwoad (in a personal communication) observes that 'the fore-edge flap on [B78] ZC2.6.9 ... extends from the left (front) cover in the English pattern as opposed to the German / Flemish pattern in which the fore-edge flap is typically an extension of the other (right) side of the wrapper'.

309. Listed in Appendix IV H. Cat. nos. G26, Conrad Gesner, *Partitiones theologicae* (1549); B36, an Erasmus New Testament in Latin (*c.* 1550); and M41, *De origine et autoritate verbi Dei, et quae Pontificum, Patrum & Conciliorum sit autoritas* by the Lutheran, Georg Meier (1550).

None of Geste's bindings have been identified among the few known examples of John Siberch's work, and no examples are known of the binding work of any of the other Cambridge stationers in this period, such as Segar Nicholson, Peter Bright, Peter Sheres (Pilgrim's successor), John Scarlet, Richard Noke or John Seth, to link any of them to Geste as a purchaser.

In addition to his purchases from Cambridge outlets, it is clear that Geste was also acquiring some 'new' books with London bindings during the period 1536 to 1554, but again it is only those in signed bindings that can be traced to any known London workshop. Of the ten 'new' items in panel bindings, two were by Thomas Godfray, in Oldham, BPEB, panels HM. 5/6: works by Johann von Eck (E3) and Gerhard Lorich (L38), both with 1536 imprints, and there were two panel bindings by Martin Dature: one (I6) – a volume of five items, the latest with a 1531 imprint[310] – in panels HE 6/ST 46, the other – a volume of two items by Luther (L57–58), the latest with an imprint of 1539 – in Oldham panels HM. 11/12, panels which had also been used on one of his second-hand acquisitions, a biblical commentary by Johann Brentz (B72). The Luther volume (L57–58) was the only one of these to retain Geste's characteristic binding instruction ('C in past'), which suggests a direct relationship with the London binder concerned. There were no 'new' books in bindings by John Reynes who had figured as the binder of two of his second-hand items (E31 and H40), and the other panel bindings among his new acquisitions were either bound in Cambridge by Spierinck (E28) or are unsigned and cannot be assigned to any particular binder or even to a known place of binding.[311]

There were also a small number of 'new' books in roll bindings from London outlets during his Cambridge period: eight with imprints between 1525 and 1550, though there is some uncertainty about the identification of two of them because of the worn state of the calf covers.[312] Two of them are in signed roll bindings, one by the 'I R' binder (M7), the other

310. The other items with imprints between 1514 and 1531 being Cat. nos. A12, A23, B38 and R29.
311. Three of these are without pastedowns or strengtheners: D34 in Oldham, BPEB, panels HE. 3/4; A18 in HM. 15/AN 14; and D26 in TRIP. 1, all unassigned by Oldham. The other two, H10 (1531 imprint) and J2 (1528), are in panel TRIP. 9, the former with a thin MS strip as a strengthener (pointing to a London outlet), the latter, however, with full MS pastedowns (which might suggest Cambridge or Oxford as the place of binding where waste MS in parchment was plentiful). Mirjam Foot (personal communication) points out, however, that 'panels were cast and not engraved and could in theory have been used anywhere at any time'. It is possible, therefore, that panel TRIP. 9 may have been used by binders in both London and Cambridge.
312. Two commentaries on the Pauline epistles, one by Primasius with a 1537 imprint (P53) in what may be an example of Oldham, EBSB, RP.a(1) with a MS strip as a binding strengthener, the other by Bugenhagen (1525, B117), with leaves from a printed book as pastedowns and flyleaves.

signed 'F I' (M86), and the other four, three Biblical commentaries[313] and a copy of the Hebrew grammar of Elijah ben Asher (E18),[314] all have London rolls according to Oldham. It is less possible to be certain about the London origin of his books in corner-ornament (CS), centre-tool bindings or parchment covers, but there is some reason for thinking this to be so in the case of at least one of the first type (CS),[315] two of the second, centre-tools CT j and CT pp,[316] and eight of those in parchment covers,[317] all of which have strips of MS as strengtheners, and a ninth, also in parchment covers, with an imprint of 1552 (B41), should also be included – provided that it had not been acquired after Geste left Cambridge in 1554.

After 1554 – until at least his translation to Salisbury in 1571 – Geste's 'new' purchases were made mostly from London outlets, and, with a few possible exceptions,[318] Cambridge bindings no longer figure in his collection. His whereabouts in England during Mary's reign are not known, and it is far from clear whether he was in a position to add to his collection during the years 1554 to 1558 or whether any of the books with imprints from this period were acquired then or after his re-appearance in 1558.

Although the majority of his books acquired after 1554 continued to be in simple calf bindings or parchment covers, Geste was still buying a significant number of his new books in more decorated roll bindings. Fourteen of these have been identified, five of which are signed by, or attributed to, the so-called 'R B' binder who was active in London from about 1550 to 1581 and therefore throughout the period when Geste was making his purchases there after leaving Cambridge. The imprints of these

313. Three commentaries: one on Kings by the Benedictine, Angelomus (A38) in Oldham, EBSB, roll CH.a(1); the second, on Ecclesiastes by the Lutheran Bugenhagen (B75) in FP.a(1); the third, on the NT Epistles by Conrad Pellican (P16) in HM.a(7), all three without extant pastedowns.
314. FP.f(6) with CT o, which had a strip from a MS as a strengthener.
315. See Appendix IV E for these. One book of 1534, a commentary on Ezekiel by Oecolampadius (O8), has a MS strip to strengthen the binding structure. Two are second-hand acquisitions (T11 and V15) without MS strips, and two octavos (S75–76) of 1547/48 have leaves from printed books as pastedowns, and a fifth item, a folio of 1554 (V36) is without pastedowns. None of these bindings have full MS pastedowns of the Cambridge type.
316. Listed in Appendix IV D. A work by Nicolas Gallasius (G5) in centre-tool CT j, and the *Officinae* of Ravisius Textor (R12) in two volumes, both with a lion rampant in gold as centre-tool (CT pp).
317. Appendix IV G, C39 (1525), R16 (1529), L67 (1538), M84 (1539), C29 (1539), H59 (1541), P29 (1543), and M10 (1545).
318. L50, vol. III of Luther's commentary on Genesis, with an imprint of March 1553 [1554] in plain calf (PL a) with a leaf of MS at the front folded over to leave a strip (stuck down); G15 (1554) a quarto in parchment covers with two leaves from a medieval MS, as flyleaves; D1 (1566), a quarto wrapped in a leaf of medieval MS; and S83 (1558), an octavo in parchment covers with leaves from two different medieval MSS as flyleaves.

'R B' bindings range from 1560 – a Gregory of Nyssa in Latin (G34), one of two books with two rows of Oldham, EBSB, roll 450, the other a Matthias Flacius Illyricus of 1567 (F13) – to 1570, an Irenaeus (I5) now in very worn calf covers which appears to combine two 'R B' rolls – Oldham, EBSB, HM.h(10) and HE.k(1) – though the date is later than the range (1556–68) suggested by Oldham for this particular combination. The other two signed 'R B' bindings were examples of Oldham, EBSB, HM.h(10), a work by Hermann Hamelmann on apostolic traditions (H2) and a copy of the Byzantine *Corpus vniuersae historiae* (B138), this last being the only one of these bindings to retain Geste's binding instructions, in this instance, 'In bord[?e]s', and one of the very few of bindings in his collection still in calf over boards (rather than pasteboard). Two examples of another London roll combination – HE.b(5) and MW.c(1) – also belong to this period: a commentary on Ezekiel by Ludwig Lavater (L21) and a volume of items by Georg Eder (E9) and Naclantius (N1), though not in this case attributed by Oldham to the 'R B' binder. The MW.c(1) roll can also be found alone in six of his other books with imprints between 1566 and 1569, all but one with strips of parchment MS as strengtheners and one of them retaining Geste's binding instruction.[319] The only other identified roll among the fourteen is an example of D1.e(2) – one with alternating ovals of fleur-de-lis and flowers – which Oldham attributed, evidently with some reservations, to an unidentified London binder.[320]

Three other examples bring the total of Geste's roll bindings from his London period to seventeen. All three of them are worn, making identification difficult in any case, but all three appear to be English bindings. The first, a commentary on Romans (1572) by Rodolphus Gualtherus (G39), includes a heads-in-medallions roll – bearing some resemblance to Oldham, EBSB, HM.h(9) – which borders an even more worn diaper roll, not found in Oldham; these two rolls surround a rectangular frame containing what Pearson designates a centrepiece (CP 2.2) with fleurons inside each angle. The second, in another very worn heads-in-medallions roll (not found in Oldham, EBSB) surrounding a plain rectangular frame, is an item by the Lutheran, Theodoricus Snepffius (S67), and the third, in yet another unidentified English roll, is a commentary on the Psalms by Placidus Parmensis (P38). These last two items have strips of parchment MS as strengtheners, pointing to their London origin, but the Gualtherus (G39) is without either pastedowns or strengtheners, and its London origin, though likely, is far from certain.

The great majority of Geste's acquisitions during this final period of his collecting were in simpler binding styles either in calf over pasteboard

319. Six items, in addition to the two combined with roll HE.b(5): Z2 and F23 (1566); N13 (1567); T16 and B29 (1568) and J4 (1569).
320. A polemical work by the Dominican, Joannes Slotanus (S61). The presence of a wide strip of parchment MS as a strengthener points to a London origin for this binding.

or parchment covers. Of the former, four different styles occur, three of which – centre-tool (CT), corner-ornaments (CS) and plain calf with fillets (PL) – were also in use during his Cambridge period, the fourth, now appearing for the first time, being the 'centrepiece' binding style, particularly associated with research undertaken by David Pearson.[321] Pearson notes the first appearance of centrepiece bindings in London about 1560 and their use in Oxford and Cambridge soon after, eventually spreading to other binding centres later in the century with hundreds of different variants. Three different types occur among Geste's books, all in blind with fillets at the outer edges.[322]

None of them exactly matches any of the common designs illustrated by Pearson, of which he admits there were many variants, but the first (CP 2.1), of which Geste had nine examples with imprints between 1571 and 1573 – during his Salisbury period – appears to be one of the many variants of Pearson's OL1 – an oval with a lozenge at the centre. Four of these books retain MS strips as binding strengtheners, pointing to a binder at least familiar with London practice. One item (S6) in a volume of six items (H37) contains leaves annotated on the inside of unopened leaves, indicating that Geste had annotated the book in an unbound state even before the sheets had been folded and sewn, and it is not unlikely that other books with this centrepiece had also been read before being bound.

A much less common variant of the same centrepiece (CP 2.2), already noted among his roll bindings, is to be found on the covers of another book (with an imprint of 1572) in which two rolls border a rectangular frame with four small-tool fleurons inside each angle of the frame (G39). The second type (CP 4) is another oval centrepiece which occurs on only one of Geste's books, the *Phrases Hebraicae* (1558) of Robertus Stephanus (E54). This has some slight points of similarity with Pearson's OL 13 and centrepiece xx(b) illustrated in his study of Oxford book binding (2000), but again there is no exact match.

The final type (CP 3), in a commentary on Matthew (1559) by Johann Wild (W32), is a round (rather than an oval) centrepiece of which there is no match in Pearson, and it is possible that this particular type, if not of continental origin, belongs to the early days of English centrepieces before oval centrepieces became dominant.[323] Neither of Geste's examples of the last two types have surviving MS strips or pastedowns, though a London source for the first (CP 4) is probable. The place of binding for the second (CP 3) cannot at present be determined.

The second of the four binding styles associated with Geste's London period was one which used one or more small tools to form a centre

---

321. See Pearson, EBS, pp. 55–57 and the examples illustrated there; Pearson, OB, pp. 75–86, 103–111,
322. Listed in Appendix IV C.   323. Pearson (personal communication).

18.1. An octavo of 1573, one of nine with an imprint date-range of 1571–73, acquired during Geste's Salisbury period. CP 2.1. Cat. no. C62.

18.2. A folio of 1572 with centrepiece CP 2.2 and two unidentified rolls (a heads-in-medallions and a diaper) also acquired during Geste's Salisbury period. Cat. no. G39.

18.3. An octavo of 1559 with a round centrepiece. CP 3. Cat. no. W32.

18.4. An octavo of 1558, *Phrases Hebraicae* by Robert Stephanus,
detail of the oval centrepiece. CP 4. Cat. no. E54.

ornament on calf over pasteboard covers.[324] 116 examples of these 'centre-
tool' bindings have imprints during this period. Of these, one with an imprint
of 1552 should probably be included,[325] as well as six items with imprints
between 1573 and 1576 which fall within his time at Salisbury.[326] Twenty-
seven different centre-tool bindings (including a few variants) can be identified, most with no more than one to five examples of each, but, as we have
already seen, there are two (CT a and CT b) which have as many as twenty-
two and fifty-one examples respectively.[327] Of these twenty-seven, twenty-
one have pastedowns or strengtheners of some kind: of these, fourteen
include examples with strips of MS as strengtheners,[328] three (CT h.1, CT
bb.1, CT ff.1) have leaves from printed books as pastedowns and flyleaves,

324. Listed in Appendix IV D and illustrated in fig. 22.
325. CT f, of which he had one example (B37). Although published in 1552, B37 has a
    MS strip as strengthener, characteristic of London binding practice, and this
    suggests that the book was not actually bound until later.
326. CT e: four examples with imprints of 1573–76; CT hh: two examples with
    imprints of 1573 and 1575.
327. See above at pp. 53–54.
328. Details in Appendix IV D, fourth column. CT b.1, CT d.1, CT e, CT h.2, CT k,
    CT n, CT t, CT v, CT bb.2, CT dd, CT hh, CT mm, CT nn, CT rr.

and the remaining four (CT a, CT b, CT ff.2 and CT kk) include examples with both leaves from printed books and MS strips. None of these contains full MS pastedowns of the Cambridge type, and a London origin for all twenty-one types seems probable. In addition to these, a further six centre-tool bindings from this period are without pastedowns, flyleaves or strengtheners of any kind,[329] and these cannot be assigned to any place of binding, though a London origin is possible.

There is some evidence that a number of books with these centre-tool bindings were originally acquired by Geste in an unbound state or limp parchment covers, subsequently sent (or returned) to his supplier with his binding instructions (generally at the foot of the title page) and even on occasion being annotated by him before binding. Nine books in centrepiece CT a, for example, retain binding instructions giving his preferred order for the four or five items to be included, and there are one or two examples in CT b and in three others (CT h.1, CT v and CT bb.1). Similarly, in the case of thirteen books in CT b bindings, the type of binding is indicated ('in paste', i.e. in pasteboard) as well as three examples in CT v bindings, and there are single instances in two others (CT bb.1 and CT ff.1), with a trace of his instruction in one other (CT a). In a few instances, Geste's binding note appears to indicate the state of the book *before* being sent for binding (in some cases, 'rebinding'): one has the binding note, 'sewn not [?cut]' (M35), and two (R35 of CT b type, and O22 of CT bb.1) have the note 'in parchment', which may have been the case at the time, but not in their final state which is calf over pasteboard. Moreover, the survival of a few books with Geste's annotations on the *inside* of unopened leaves provides further evidence that some books now in centre-tool bindings were in his possession for a time in an unbound state. One such instance has already been noted in a centrepiece binding (S6), and there are two other examples among his centre-tool bindings, one in a sextodecimo of 1570 containing four items (A50) now bound in CT a, and another, an octavo also containing four items all dated 1567 (W26), in centre-tool CT b. Both also include his binding instructions, the latter being one of a very few instances where Geste has written these instructions not only on the title page but on the final leaf of the first gathering as well. Although it is clear enough that these particular centre-tool bindings were of London origin, it is unfortunate that the identity of the binder is not known (and probably never will be), as Geste seems to have been a frequent customer and perhaps even on familiar terms with his supplier.

The third and fourth of the binding styles in calf associated with Geste's London period were even more basic in design. Both occur in books bound in calf over pasteboard. The third – the 'corner-ornament' binding style

---

329. CT d.2 (C16, 1559), CT W (L20, 1562), CT aa (N6, 1553), CT cc (V17, 1559), CT gg (F29, 1565) and CT jj (W37-38, 1555, 1558), these last both in gold, the others all in blind.

(CS) – is characterised by a plain rectangular frame defined by fillets in blind with a small-tool or corner ornament at each angle of the frame. Only one example – a folio of 1553–59 (V36) – has been found from Geste's London period, and this appears to be a variant of CS.1, but without either pastedown or MS strip as pointers to its place of binding. Most, if not all, of the other examples of this binding type are probably also London bindings though all have imprints dating from Geste's Cambridge period.[330]

The fourth of the binding 'styles' was entirely plain calf but for a border of fillets at the outer edges of the covers (here designated PL a).[331] Five examples with imprints between 1559 and 1563 occur, four of them with MS strips as strengtheners characteristic of London practice, the fifth, a folio of 1561 (A44), without either pastedown or strengthener. This last example retains Geste's binding instruction to include another named item (J17) within the same covers – which it does – and one other (C51) not only does the same but also designates the binding to be used – '[Th]is w[i]th Hemmyng in past' (H35).

Even more 'basic' were the numerous books from Geste's London period surviving in parchment covers.[332] Some eighty fall into this category and a further twelve (now in later bindings) retain his binding instructions, indicating that this had once been the case.[333] Of these eighty, thirty-one retain MS strips as strengtheners or flyleaves from printed books,[334] including six (and traces of a further three) with his binding instructions,[335] pointing to the likelihood of London binding. All but one of these (H77, a quarto by Robert Horne printed in London by Henry Wykes) had been printed on the continent, and it seems likely that these had been imported in sheets or, in some instances, in sewn book blocks, but without covers, as was to be the practice required by the legislation of 1534 intended to protect the binding sector of the English book trade. A further fifteen – all of continental printing – are without either MS strengtheners or flyleaves but retain Geste's binding instruction,[336] and although one item had evidently been imported 'in parchment uncutt' (M79) which Geste had subsequently rebound in parchment covers with the intention of including another item,[337] it is not unlikely that most if not all the others had been imported unbound, such as the one which is described in his binding notes as 'not cut but smothed' (L19).

330. See Appendix IV E, which includes other examples acquired during Geste's Cambridge period, discussed above at p. 105.

331. See Appendix IV F and fig. 24.1, which includes examples from his Cambridge period almost certainly from Cambridge outlets.

332. See Appendix IV G and figs. 25.1–3.   333. See Appendix IV G, Annexe 1.

334. See Appendix IV G, Annexe 5, listing post-1553 imprints.

335. See L81, M33, M45, N2, P35 and V25, and traces of these (H68, J5 and O2) listed in Appendix IV G, Annexe 4, final column.   336. See Appendix IV G, Annexe 3.

337. The binding instruction is only partly legible and it is far from clear that the associated item (G9) is actually what Geste had requested.

What of the other thirty or so books now in parchment covers *without* his binding instructions or strips from MSS or printed books as strengtheners or end-leaf guards? All but three of these were printed on the continent.[338] It is possible that some at least were imported already bound in parchment covers and acquired by Geste in this state from his London bookseller or through some other agency, and perhaps, because of their small format or for some other reason, not considered meriting a more permanent binding in calf. The quarto of 1535 in tacketed parchment wrappers (V7) already noted is a possible example,[339] and there may be others still to be identified. It may be that more light will be shed on this question when the detailed analysis of binding structure developed by Nicholas Pickwood is applied to those of Geste's books still in parchment covers at Salisbury.[340]

Geste's final years were spent as bishop of Salisbury (1571–77) and he continued to make book purchases right up to the end of his life, as four items survive with 1576 imprints.[341] Clearly he could have continued to purchase his books from London stationers. There are no details of Geste's travels and periods of residence during this final period. But as bishop of Salisbury, he had a London manor house in the parish of St Bride, Fleet Street,[342] as well as the palace in Salisbury, and could have continued to make some of his purchases on visits there, even though he had now relinquished the post of Lord High Almoner at Court following his translation to Salisbury.

At least seventy-five new items bound in forty books have survived from this period, all but one (C101) printed on the continent. Of the thirty-two books still in contemporary bindings, two of the folios have rolls, one by the London 'R B' binder (L21) which Geste had sent for binding 'Uncutt in parchement',[343] the other (G39), as we have seen, with two

338. See Appendix IV G, Annexe 6.
339. See above, pp. 115, 123. The tacketed parchment wrappers of V7 are illustrated in Appendix IV G, fig. 25.3.
340. See Nicholas Pickwood, 'The Interpretation of Bookbinding Structure' in *The Library*, 6th Series, 17 (1995), 209–49, and in *Eloquent Witnesses: Bookbindings and their History* (ed. by Mirjam M. Foot. London: Bibliograhical Society, 2004), pp. 127–70. In a personal communication, Professor Pickwood observes that 'the provenance of these parchment wrappers is unclear, as while they are most probably of German or Flemish in origin, it is possible that they were added to sewn bookblocks in England, a hypothesis supported by the fore-edge flap on [B78] ZC2.6.9 which extends from the left (front) cover in the English pattern as opposed to the German/Flemish pattern in which the fore-edge flap is typically an extension of the other (right) side of the wrapper'.
341. See Appendix III (Chronological Index) which lists his books with imprints from 1571 to 1576.
342. W. H. Jones, *Fasti Ecclesiae Sarisberiensis* (Salisbury: Brown & Co., 1879), p. 61.
343. Geste's binding note at the foot of the title page. One of two books with rolls HE.b(5) and MW.c(1), the other (E9) with an imprint of 1568 and presumably dating from his time at Rochester.

unassigned English rolls, both very worn, and an oval centrepiece with a lozenge at the centre. It is worth noting that the centrepiece concerned (CP 2.2) appears to have been a variant of one which occurs on nine of his other books, all with imprints during his Salisbury period (CP 2.1) but not found on any of his earlier acquisitions.[344]

As was to be expected, centre-tool bindings also occur on books he acquired while at Salisbury. Seven of these, all with MS strips as strengtheners or leaves from printers' waste as flyleaves or pastedowns, are examples of centre-tool CT a, which occurs on fifteen other books from his London period. But the other centre-tool bindings are not found before the move to Salisbury. One has a fleuron-type small tool in blind at the centre of a rectangular frame with fleurons at each angle (CT ff.1), of which Geste had two examples, both with leaves from printers' waste as pastedowns and flyleaves; one with a trace of his binding instruction 'in past by vt se[lf]' (W28), the other (C32), possibly a variant or a damaged version of the same tool (CT ff.2), with a strip of blank parchment as a strengthener. But of particular interest are two centre-tool bindings with 'silvered' ornaments, one (CT e) decorated inside with an eight-petal fleuron, all four examples in octavo (1573–76) with MS strips as strengtheners,[345] the other (CT hh) with a fleuron of four large petals at the centre of a rectangular frame, of which Geste had two examples, one with a MS strip as strengthener (A51).[346] How frequently these two particular centre-tool bindings occur in other collections of the period is not known, but as none of them are found on his books before the move to Salisbury it is not unreasonable to posit a connexion with whoever was responsible for binding his books during his time there.

Of the other binding types found on books dating from Geste's Cambridge and London periods, no examples of either corner-ornament (CS) or plain calf (PL) bindings occur on his books with imprints from the Salisbury period. But there are six in parchment covers, one printed in London (C101), the rest printed on the continent, one with a stub of paper between the first two and the last two quires, apparently intended as strengtheners (H56), and two others with the usual MS strip as strengtheners and his binding instruction in one of the two volumes (P35).

While most if not all of these could be London bindings, Geste could have also bought books in Salisbury. Almost nothing is known about the book trade and its members in Salisbury during this period. But a little is known about one of them – Henry Hammande (or Hamonde). Hammande,

---

344. Both appear to be variants of Pearson, EBS, OL1. For the nine items, see Appendix IV C. Four of the nine retain MS strips as strengtheners – characteristic of London binding.
345. M76–77, W20 and Z5.
346. The other example, without flyleaves, MS strip or pastedown, is B26.

an original member of the Stationers' Company (1556) and a stationer in London,[347] is also recorded as being active as a stationer in Salisbury (1571–76) during the years of Geste's episcopate, and his name occurs in the Subsidy Roll for the city, in the ward of New Street, in September 1571 and again in 1576. His son, Thomas, graduated at Oxford, proceeding Master of Arts in 1590, and stationers of this name are found at Salisbury well into the seventeenth century.[348] Although nothing is known about his work as a stationer either in London or Salisbury or whether he was even active as a binder, it is tempting – noting the coincidence of dates – to ask whether Geste had any dealings with Hammande as a purchaser during his years at Salisbury or even before that in London, and even to speculate as to whether Hammande's move to Salisbury had anything to do with Geste's translation from Rochester in the same year. From what survives of his purchases during the Salisbury period – some seventy-five items with imprints between 1571 and 1576 – Geste would have been a good customer. Many of these books could, of course, have been acquired in London, and it is true that one of the centre-tool bindings (CT a), for example, occurs with imprints (1564–1572) during both the London and Salisbury periods. On the other hand, if Hammande was responsible for using this particular centre-tool design in any case, then he could simply have continued to use that design on Geste's books for a year or two after the move to Salisbury.

Until the appropriate evidence is forthcoming, the case for Hammande or some other, at present unknown, Salisbury stationer – however tempting – is speculative and unverifiable. Geste's purchases during this period included many items not commonly available – twenty-six out of the seventy-five he acquired do not appear, for example, in contemporary Cambridge inventories and half of these are not even represented in modern Cambridge collections[349] – and these would have had to be obtained to 'special order' in any case from sources (such as the Birckmanns) with good contacts on the continent. But this would have been true even if Geste's suppliers during this period had been London-based, and presumably Hammande with his long experience as a stationer in London would have retained the necessary

347. References to him occur in the Register for the years 1558, 1562 and 1566. His address in London is not recorded. So Duff, p. 65.

348. *A Dictionary of Printers and Booksellers ... 1557–1640* (ed. by R. B. McKerrow. London: Bibliographical Society, 1910, reprinted 1968), p. 122. STC, III, p. 211 mentions another Henry Hammond, active as a printer, 1633–1637.

349. These are marked in Appendix III – the Chronological index of imprints – with $ following the catalogue number for items not recorded in contemporary Cambridge inventories (BiCI) or the collections of Perne or Parker, and $$ for those not in Adams (which covers later acquisitions in the modern period, in Cambridge Colleges as well as the University Library). Even if Bancroft's much larger collection of over 5700 items covering the period to the early seventeenth century is taken into account the number of these rarer items is only reduced by a further three (B68, C101 and H47) to twenty-three.

contacts with importers from the continent enabling him to supply Geste with these less common items during his time in Salisbury.

Geste's continental bindings

There remain the few continental bindings in his collection. How and where were these acquired? Since the legislation of 1534,[350] books from the continent were to be imported unbound in sheets to protect the binding arm of the English book-trade, though how far this was (or could be) enforced in practice is less certain, especially in the case of items issued on the continent in less permanent covers of limp parchment or vellum. In Geste's case, it seems that the majority of his continental books had been imported in unbound sheets or sewn book blocks, but there were evidently some in continental bindings. Most of these carried pre-1534 imprints and therefore fell outside the scope of that legislation. Nine or possibly ten books still in continental bindings have so far been identified, but there is some evidence from Geste's binding notes that there may have been others, originally imported in parchment, which he later had bound in more permanent covers of calf or which he simply retained in their original covers as imported.[351] Of the nine or ten, at least four in roll bindings (two in French, one possibly 'Netherlandish' and one of uncertain origin, but perhaps bound at its place of printing, Basle) were obtained second-hand, three probably during his time in Cambridge, the fourth sometime after 1565 when he was at Rochester.[352] Of the others, two early items without clear evidence of previous ownership are also in French roll bindings, one, a work by Richard of St Victor (R26) published in 1510 (Appendix IV B, fig. 20.1), and the other (fig. 20.2), one of a six-volume edition of Geste's Latin Bible in sextodecimo (1526, B34), both printed in Paris and perhaps originally bound there, but again, because of their early date, these were outside the scope of the 1534

---

350. The Act 'Concerning printers and binders of books' (25 Henry VIII cap. 15) which applied to printed books, 'ready bound in boards leather or parchment'. On this see Julian Roberts, 'The Latin Trade' in CHBB IV, pp. 141–73, at p. 144.
351. These are the books printed on the continent which in his binding notes at the foot of the title page he describes as 'in parchment' but which are now in English calf bindings: M14 (1540), O22 (1564) and R38 (1567). There is also one book described as 'Uncutt in parcheme[n]t' which he had bound in calf over boards (L21), one described as 'by itselue uncut' (M67) which is in parchment, still with its leaves mostly unopened, and three now in later bindings which were 'uncutt in parchment; (F11 and H63 – both with 1562 imprints) and another (M58, 1563) in parchment which was to be bound with another item 'in past'[board] (M59, 1562). It is possible that some (or all of these) may have been imported from the continent in parchment covers.
352. P23 (1495) is French, and A49 (1540) probably so; P15 (1521) which carries a date and price (1565) on the title page is possibly 'Netherlandish', and A56 (1538) may have been bound in Basle, its place of printing.

Act. The only other French binding so far identified is one with a double-crown ornament in gold at the centre of a rectangular frame (Appendix IV D, CT qq; fig. 22.42) on a book that was acquired during his time at Rochester with a Paris imprint of 1562 (B14). Both tools used were common on French bindings of the period,[353] and the book could have been bound in Paris, its place of printing, or elsewhere in France.

In addition to these French bindings, there are two (possibly three) others of continental origin. The first, a copy of the *Sententiae* of Joannes Stobaeus, printed at Zürich in 1543 (S89), is in contemporary German calf, with a roll depicting the Lifting up of the Brazen Serpent, the Crucifixion, and the Resurrection (Appendix IV B, fig.20.5). The second, an octavo containing two items by Joannes Rivius (R31–32), has an unidentified floral roll and a lozenge-shaped ornament in the centre and may just possibly have been bound in Basle, its place of printing (Appendix IV D; fig. 22.17). The third possibility, already considered in another connexion,[354] is a quarto of Michael Vehe printed at Leipzig in 1535 (V7), in parchment covers with two rectangular secondary tackets of tanned-leather on each side of an early spine title (Appendix IV G, fig. 25.3) It is one of three examples of such parchment covers with secondary tackets, but the other two (B78 and D32) exhibit features of English provenance,[355] and its continental origin, though likely, is far from certain.

It is doubtful if it will ever be known exactly how these books in continental bindings came into Geste's collection. One possibility is that some came from his uncle, John Brandisby, who had spent some time in France in about 1518 and who, as we have seen, had given Geste a number of books during his early years in Cambridge. But without evidence of any further visits to the continent, it would seem that only the one pre-1518 book in a French roll binding, could have been involved (R26).

Another possibility, however, is that some might have come to Geste through the agency of his other uncle, Richard Brandisby, a classical scholar and a former Fisher Fellow at St John's College, Cambridge. Unfortunately, nothing has come to light concerning Geste's relationship with this uncle. Richard Brandisby had left Cambridge for the continent as a religious exile in 1538, a few years after John Fisher's execution, and it is known that he was in Paris that year, later studied at Louvain, and was still living in the Low Countries corresponding with Roger Ascham from Brussels and Malines in 1553. Is it possible that he may have facilitated the importing of some books to his nephew including some already bound, even if he was not himself directly involved? There is some evidence of Richard as a collector and book-owner himself. It has already been noted that during

353. I am indebted to Mirjam Foot for this information.
354. See above, at pp. 115, 123.
355. See above, at pp. 115 and 123 n. 308.

his time in Cambridge his name appears as a purchaser of books from Garrett Godfrey,[356] and much later he is known to have been one who provided a manuscript for Johannes Vlimmerius, prior of St Martin, Louvain, who was preparing an edition of the Eucharistic treatises of Paschasius Radbertus and others, published there in 1561.[357] Clearly, it is possible that he might have played a part in Geste acquiring some of his many continental books, particularly those by contemporary Catholic authors which abound in his collection, and it is worth noting that about nine per cent of what remains of Geste's library had its origins in the printing houses of Louvain and Antwerp. But Richard's role is no more than a conjecture, difficult to test when the books themselves yield no evidence of a direct link, certainly not as explicit as those given him by John Brandisby or the three sent to him at King's by his brother-in-law, Christopher Leedes, in 1551.

V. THE IMPORTANCE OF GESTE'S COLLECTION

The most remarkable feature of Geste's library is the size of its collection of contemporary theology (over 900 works) which includes a collection of nearly 600 Protestant works – over half of them Lutheran (over 370 works) – as well as over three hundred works by contemporary Catholic authors. All but two per cent of these books were of continental printing, two-thirds of them from German-speaking countries, including Switzerland. With the possible exception of Andrew Perne's at Peterhouse, his library is almost certainly the largest collection of Reformation writings in any library – private or institutional – to have survived in England from the Tudor period.

Its uniqueness and importance for the student of the Reformation is further enhanced by the number of books Geste annotated, often in great detail, and on occasion undertaken even before his latest acquisition had been bound. In fact, over five hundred works (out of a total of over 1,200) are annotated in his hand – a practice he continued to the last year of his life, confirming the thoroughness of his reading and his desire to engage in depth with the diversity of continental opinion on both sides of the Reformation debate

For the provenance historian and for students of book history and book collecting, his library – even in the somewhat truncated form in which it has come down – is a remarkable survival and an important resource for the study of contemporary Cambridge and London binding practice over a period of more than forty years. In fact, almost two-thirds of his surviving

356. *GGA 1527–33*, p. 106 with references to items in the Accounts given there.
357. Adams P372. Prior Vlimmerius described Richard Brandisby as 'vir dum viveret, cum humanitatis tum antiquitatis amantissimus ac studiossimus'; N. R. Ker, 'English Manuscripts Owned by John Vlimmerius and Cornelius Duyn', *The Library*, 4th series, vol. 23 (1942), 205–07.

books are in contemporary bindings, exhibiting a great variety of styles, from decorated panels and rolls to very basic limp parchment covers, often with fragments from manuscript and printed waste as pastedowns and flyleaves still intact and, except in a very few instances when modern rebinding has intervened, even preserving the original order and arrangement of the individual items in the case of composite volumes. Of particular interest is the survival in 185 instances of Geste's binding notes and instructions, indicating in many cases his preferred binding material (pasteboard or parchment), the order in which the items were to be bound, and even on occasion requesting his book-seller to search for additional items for inclusion in a particular volume. Furthermore, despite the lack of any contemporary inventory or catalogue, the survival of early press marks on over five-hundred and fifty of his books makes it possible to make some estimate of the original size of his collection and how the books were arranged in the library before its reorganisation in the middle of the eighteenth century.

Some of these individual features may be found in other surviving collections from the period (some of William Cecil's books, for example, preserve his binding instructions), but there must be very few, if any, that exhibit so many of these and on such a scale, and taken together they provide a unique insight into the collecting practice and habits of a significant sixteenth-century English collector.

APPENDIX II

Index of Publishers and Printers

The information in each entry is given in the following order: imprint date, format, author, abbreviated imprint, catalogue no. and class-mark. Entries shown within square brackets are for books listed in Appendix I, 'Other books which may have belonged to Geste'.

Angers

Alexandre, Jean
[c. 1495–1500] 8°. Orbellis, N. de. expensis vero. (in domo J. richardi mercatoris) [col. studio et opera Magistri M. morin] O19 L.6.3.

Antwerp

Bellère, Jean [Iohannis]
1555 12°. Novicampianus, A. apud. N12 ZC2.8.3(a).
1556 12°. Helding, M. S. apud [col. Typis I. Vvithagij] H15 ZC2.8.5(d).
1558 12°. Jansen, C. apud. [col. typis Amati Calcographi] J5 E.6.19.
1559 12°. Helding, M. S. apud [col. typis I. VVithagii] H17 ZC2.8.5(e).
1560 8°. Charlemagne. apud. C57 M.2.21(a).
1562 12°. Canisius, P. apud. [col. Typis I. Vvithagij.] C34 ZC2.8.3(b).
1562 12°. Canisius, P. apud. C33 ZC2.8.3(c).

Birckmann, Arnold, heirs of
1559 8°. Wild, J. apud. [pt. 2 apud I. Steelsium] [col. typis I. Latij.] W32 D.2.11.

Bonte [Bontius] , Gregorius de
1539 (July) 8°. Bonaventura. apud.[col. excud. I. Crinitus, expensis G. Bontii] B52 C.4.1.

Cock [Cocus], Symon, & Nicolaus, Gerardus
1525 [col. Mar. 21] 8°. Ruysius, G. [col. excudebant.] R41 C2.1.1(c).

Coppens van Diest, Gillis [Aegidius]
1565 (X. Martij) 8°. Rastell, J. by. R6 O.2.41.

Crinitus, Joannes
1539 (July) 8°. Bonaventura. [col. excud. I. Crinitus, expensis G. Bontii.] B52 C.4.1.

Diest, Aegidius see Coppens van Diest, Gillis

Dumaeus, Antonius see Haeghen, Anthonis van der

Fowler [Fouler], John [Joannes]
1566 8°. Rastell, J. ex off. R7 O.2.45.
[1566 8°. Rastell, J. ex off. *R1 O.2.37.]

Graphaeus, Joannes
1533 8°. Erasmus, D. ex off. E39 N.6.3(b).
1533 8°. Erasmus, D. ex off. E32 N.6.3(c).
1534 8°. Isidore. [col. excudebat] (per I. Steelsium) I7 A.6.28(b).
1551 8°. Anselm. excudebat. A40 N.6.11(c).
1562 8°. Wild, J. in aedibus I. Stelsij [col. typis I. Graphei.] W39 G.5.12(a–b).

Haeghen, Anthonis van der.
1541 8°. Alardus excudebat. A13 ZC2.6.19(b).

Hillen[ius] van Hoochstraten, Michiel
1520 4°. Erasmus, D. [col. in aedibus.] E25 L.5.35(f).

Antwerp, Hillen[ius] van Hoochstraten, *continued*

>1520 (Apr.–Maio) 4°. Erasmus, D. in aedibus. E44 L.5.35(g–h).
>[*c.* 1525] 4°. Latomus, J. L17 ZC2.3.14(a).
>[*c.* 1526] 4°. George, *D. of Saxony.* impressum per. G22 ZC2.3.14(e).
>1530 [col. Mens. Nou.] 8°. Latomus, J. apud. L18 H.2.12(a).
>1536 8°. Eck, J. excudebat (Ioannis Stelsij expensis) E3 G.5.18.

Hoochstratus, Michael *see* Hillen van Hoochstraten, Michiel

Keyser [Caesar], Martin de

>1530 8°. Erasmus, D. apud. E38 ZC1.4.6(a).
>[*c.* 1533] 8°. Bodius, H. B51 H.2.5.
>1535 8°. Erasmus, D. excudebat. E36 D.3.7.
>1548 (mense Apr.) 8°. Aegidius, *of Assisi.* apud. A3 ZC2.6.19(a).

Laet [Latius], Jan [John]

>1558 8°. Eusebius, *of Emessa.* [col. Ioan. Latij.] (apud I. Steelsium) E57 E.6.20.
>1559 8°. Gagny, J. de. in aedibus. G1 C.3.10.
>1559 8°. Wild, J. apud haeredes A. Birckmanni [pt.2 apud I. Steelsium] [col. typis I. Latij.] W32 D.2.11.
>1564 8°. Martiall, J. Imprinted ... by. M13 O.2.39.
>1565 8°. Sander(s), N. excudebat. S11 ZC2.1.10(b).
>1566 4°. Stapleton, T. by. S86 O.1.4.

Malcotius, Libertus

>1564 12°. Clement I. excudebat. C80 B.6.35(a).

Nuyts [Nutius], Martin

>1555 4°. Soto, P. de. apud. S71 L.5.28(a–b).
>1565 8°. Tauler, J. apud. T1 ZC2.6.8.

Nuyts, Martin, Widow of

>1563 8°. Garetius, J. apud. G17 K.1.26.

Nuyts [Nutius], Philippe

>1562 8°. Tauler, J. apud. T1 ZC2.6.8.
>1565 8°. Forerius, F. apud [col. excudebat C. Plantinus] F29 D.2.9.
>1566 8°. Soto, P. de. apud. S73 H.1.3.

Plantin, Christopher

>1562 8°. Bernard. ex off. B17 M.2.21(c).
>1563 8°. Cassiodorus. ex off. C48 A.6.20(c).
>1564 16°. Canisius, P. ex off. C35 ZC2.8.5(b).
>1564 8°. Villavicentio, L. ex off. V25 ZC2.4.10(a).
>1565 16°. Albertus M. ex off. A16 K.3.13(b).
>1565 8°. Forerius, F. [col. excudebat.] apud P. Nutium. F29 D.2.9.
>1566 8°. Hessels, J. ex off. H53 I.1.5(e).
>1566 [col. xii. Calend. Martias] 8°. Hunnaeus, A. ex off. [col. excudebat.] H91 Z.4.23(a).
>1566 [col. xv. Calend. Nov.] 8°. Hunnaeus, A. ex off. [col. excudebat.] H92 Z.4.23(b).
>1567 8°. Valerius, C. ex off. V2 Z.5.108(a).
>1567 [col. Aug.] 8°. Seripando, G. ex off. S49 ZC1.4.2.
>1568–1570 4°. Lindanus, W. ex off. [pt.2 excudebat.] L30 I.8.3.
>1571 fol. Arias Montanus ex off. A52 E.3.5(b).
>1572 fol. Serranus, P. ex off. S50 G.2.4(a).
>1572 fol. Serranus, P. ex off. S51 G.2.4(b).

Silvius, Guillaume

>1564 8°. Councils – Trent. Canones. ex off. C108 B.6.41(c).
>1566 4°. Dalmada, E. ex off. D1 ZC2.3.4.
>[1567 8°. Petit, G. ex off. *P2 B.5.39.]

Steels, Joannes
>1534 8°. Isidore. per [col. excudebat I. Graph.] I7 A.6.28(b).
>1536 8°. Eck, J. expensis (excudebat M. Hillenius.) E3 G.5.18.
>1544 8°. Chiari, I. in aedibus. C64 C.3.12.
>1544 8°. Nausea, F. in aedibus. N7 N.6.6.
>1552 16°. Soto, P. de. in aedibus. [device] S72 ZC2.8.7.
>1558 8°. Eusebius, *of Emessa*. apud. [col. Ioan. Latij.] E57 E.6.20.
>1558 8°. Wild, J. in aedibus. W38 G.5.11.
>1559 8°. Wild, J. apud haeredes A. Birckmanni [pt.2 apud I. Steelsium.] [col. typis I. Latij.] W32 D.2.11.
>1561 8°. Sasbout, A. in aedibus. [col. typis I. Withagij.] S26 E.6.39.
>1562 16°. Gropper, J. in aedibus [col. typis I. Vvithagij.] G35 ZC2.8.6.
>1562 8°. Wild, J. in aedibus [col. typis I. Graphei.] W39 G.5.12(a–b).
>[1562 8°. Liturgies. Greek Rite. in aedibus. *L4 ZC2.8.15.]

Steels, Joannes, Widow & heirs of
>1564 8°. Gagny, J. de. in aedibus. G2 C.3.11.
>1570 4°. Pinto, H. in aedibus. P34 E.5.1.

Trognèse [Tronaesius], Emmanuel Philippus
>1567 8°. Porthaise, J. apud. P44 I.1.6(c).

Withagius, Joannes
>1555 12°. Fabri, J. apud. F1 ZC2.8.4(b).
>1555 8°. Lindanus, W. apud. L35 B.6.37(a).
>1556 12°. Helding, M. S. [col. Typis.] (apud I. Bellerum.) H15 ZC2.8.5(d).
>1558 8°. Staphylus, F. excudebat. S84 B.6.37(b).
>1559 12°. Helding, M. S. [col. typis] (apud.) H17 ZC2.8.5(e).

>1561 8°. Sasbout, A. in aedibus I. Steelsij [col. typis I. Withagij.] S26 E.6.39.
>1562 12°. Canisius, P. apud I. Bellerum [col. Typis] C34 ZC2.8.3(b).
>1562 16°. Gropper, J. [col. typis.] (in aedibus I. Stelsij.) G35 ZC2.8.6.
>1569 8°. Bunderius, J. [apud.] B135 ZC2.1.11.

Printer unknown
>*c.* 1520/1521 4°. Gocchius, J. G28 ZC2.3.5(g).

Augsburg

Grimm, Sigmund, & Wirsung, Marx
>[?1520 4°. Schatzger, C. *S2 L.5.30. CLC (*but see under* Cologne: apud I. Soterem, impensis G. Hittorpij.]

Miller, [Johann], *Officina*
>1514 (pridie nonas Apriles) 4°. Ricius, P. [col. E noua Augustae vindelicae officina]. R29 I.4.10(e). Printer from HAB and OCLC.
>1516 (quinto Idus Iun.) 4°. Ricius, P. [col. in off.] R30 ZC2.3.14(f).

Ruff, Simprecht
>1526 8°. Eck, J. E6 L.6.6(b). Printer suggested by VD16.

Steiner, Heinrich
>1541 8°. Luther, M. L79 H.1.8(d).

Ulhard, Philipp
>1544 4°. Musculus, W. [col. procusit.] M88 I.4.4(c).

Basle

Amerbach, Johann
>1489 fol. Holkot, R. [& J.Petri?] H71 L.2.18.
>1497 4°. Peraldus, G. per. P17 L.5.31.
>1498–1502 fol. Hugo. [for A. Koberger.] (Nuremberg.)] H82 L.2.1.

Basel, Amerbach, *continued*

[1502 [col. idibus Maii] fol. Bible.
Lat.Vulgate. [col. Pt.6: cura &
impensis. J. petri d'Langendorff
et J. froben ... Arte & industrria J.
froben.] *B6 E.2.13–17.]

Bebel, Johannes
1526 (Aug.) [col. Jul.] fol. Le Fèvre,
J. [col. et Bebelium] (apud A.
Cratandum.) L24 G.4.7(b).
1530 4°. Oecolampadius, J. apud.
O9 C.1.2(b).
1531 [Pref. Aug.] 8°. Alcuin. ex
officina Bebeliana. A18 D.2.7(a).
[1534–1535 fol. Münster, S. [col. ex
off. ... impendiis M. Isingrini et
H. Petri.] *M5 E.3.11.]
1535 (Aug.) 4°. Bugenhagen, J.
impensis. [excudebat P. Henricus.]
B114 C.2.11.

Berlaer, Theoderic, of Cologne
[printing at Basle], *see under*
Cologne
1515 fol. Bercheur, P. [col. aere &
impensis ... in off. libraria A.P.de
Langendorff.] B15 L.2.15(c).

Brylinger, Nicolaus
1539 8°. Lambert, F. per. L5 C.5.7.
1555 fol. Pantaleon, H. apud. P3
B.3.19(a).

Cratander, Andreas
[1521 (mense Iun.) 4°. Oecolampadius, J. apud. *O3 C.1.1(a).]
[1525 col.] 8°. Latomus, J. per. L16
ZC2.7.10.
1525 (Mar.) 4°. Oecolampadius, J.
[col. apud & device.] O6 C.1.10.
1526 [col. Jan.] 8°. Oecolampadius,
J. [col. per. & device.] O13 C.1.6(a).
1526 8°. Valla, L. [col. apud – with
device.] V3 C.4.6.
1526 (Aug.) [col. Jul.] fol. Le Fèvre,
J. apud. [col. et I. Bebelium.] L24
G.4.7(b).
[1527 col. (Jan.)] 4°. Oecolampadius, J. [col. apud.] O11 E.5.31.
[1533 [col. Sep.] 8°. Venatorius, T.
apud. *V1 C.6.6.]

1535 8°. Oecolampadius, J. [device.]
O10 C.1.5(a).

Cratander, Andreas and Bebel,
Johannes
1526 (Aug.) [July] fol. Le Fèvre, J.
apud. [A. Cratandrum et I.B.] L24
G.4.7(b).

Episcopius, Nikolaus, II, & Birckmann, Arnold, Heirs of
1562 fol. Gregory, *of Nyssa.*
excudebat. G34 A.4.20(a).

Ex off. Episcopiana, per Nicolaum
et Eusebium Episcopios fratres
[1564 fol. Athanasius. *A12 A.4.5.]

Franco, Bartholomaeus
1567 8°. Flacius, M. per. F18
ZC2.2.4(a).
[*c.* 1567] 8°. Heshusius, T. per. H50
K.2.16(b).

Ex officina Frobeniana
1521 (mense Nov.) fol. Cyprian ex
off. [col. apud I. Frobenium.]
C127 A.4.21.
1526 (mense Iul.) 8°. Erasmus, D.
apud. E40 L.6.4.
1526 [col. mense Mar.] 8°. Erasmus,
D. [device] [col. ex off.] E20
ZC1.4.6(f).
1528 (Mar.) fol. Tertullian. [col. in
off.] T3 A.4.22.
1529 (Mar.) 4°. Erasmus, D. [col. ex
off.] E45 I.3.8(b).
1531 8°. Erasmus, D. in off. E24
ZC1.4.6(c).
1531 (mense Sep.) fol. Eucherius. in
off. [col. per H. Frobenium &
N.Episcopium.] E55 E.4.1(a).
1532 8°. Erasmus, D. [device] [col.
in off.] E35 ZC1.4.6(d).
1532 8°. Erasmus, D. ex off. [col.
apud H. Frobenium & N.
Episcopium.] E41 ZC2.2.3.
1532 (mense Sept.) 4°. Erasmus, D.
in off. [in off. apud H. Frobenium
& N.Episcopium.] E33 I.3.8(a).
1534 [col. mense Apr.] 8°. Erasmus,
D. in off. [col. per H. Frobenium
& N. Episcopium.] E42
ZC1.4.6(e).

1539 fol. Josephus, F. in off. [col. in off. ... per H. Froben & N. Episcopium.] J16 L.2.23.

Froben, Hieronymus & Episcopium, Nicolaus

1531 8°. Erasmus, D. in off. Frobeniana [col. per.] E24 ZC1.4.6(c).

1531 (mense Sep.) fol. Eucherius. in off. Frobeniana [col. per.] E55 E.4.1(a).

1532 8°. Erasmus, D. [col. apud .] ex off. Frobeniana E41 ZC2.2.3.

1532 (mense Sept.) 4°. Erasmus, D. [col. in off. Frobeniana apud.] E33 I.3.8(a).

1534 [col. mense Apr.] 8°. Erasmus, D. [col. per.] in off. Frobeniana. E42 ZC1.4.6(e).

1537 (March) 8°. Elias. (device) [col. apud.] E18 F.2.19.

1540 fol. Josephus, F. [in off. F. per.] J16 L.2.23.

[1549 [col. cal. Sep.] 8°. Symmachus, Q. A. [with device] *S10 ZC2.6.20].

1550 fol. Hilary. (device) [col. apud.] H58 A.4.20(b).

1551 4°. Nannius, P. apud. (device) N3 C.2.9(b).

1560 8°. Arnobius. apud. (device) A54 A.6.17.

Froben, Hieronymus & Herwagen, Johann, & Episcopius, Nicolaus

1529 8°. Erasmus, D. [col. per.] E23 L.6.5(c).

Froben, Johann

[1502 [col. idibus Maii] fol. Bible. Lat.Vulgate. [col. Pt.6: cura & impensis I. de Amerbach. J. petri d'Langendorff et J. froben. Arte & industria J. froben.] *B6 E.2.13–17.]

1515 [col. Aug.] fol. Seneca. [col. Io. Frob.] S45 Y.2.16.

1516 [Ded.iii.id.Aug.] 4°. Schatzger, C. S30 I.3.10(b).

1521 (mense Nov.) fol. Cyprian [col. apud.] ex off. Frobeniana.] C127 A.4.21.

1522 fol. Erasmus, D. typis excudebat. E27 G.2.6.

1522 (8 idus Aug.) 8°. Erasmus, D. in aedibus. E31 N.6.1.

1523 (mense Oct.) 8°. Erasmus, D. per. E47 L.6.5(b).

1524 [col.Oct.] 8°. Erasmus, D. apud. E30 N.6.3(a).

1525 [col. Aug.] 8°. Erasmus, D. apud. E21 ZC1.4.6(b).

1526 (June) 8°. Erasmus, D. apud. E34 L.6.5(a).

1526 (mense Iul.) 8°. Erasmus, D. apud. E40 L.6.4.

[1526 [col. Aug.] 8°. Erasmus, D. [col. apud.] *E2 ZC2.6.5.]

1527 8°. Erasmus, D. [col. pt.1: apud] E48 H.1.2.

[1527 4°. Münster, S. apud. *M4 F.2.30(a).]

c. 1527 8°. Origen. [device] O21 ZC2.4.16.

Gemusaeus, Polycarp

1566 8°. Stein, J. per. S88 K.3.41(c).

Guarinus [Guerinus], Thomas

1555 8°. Hyperius, A. G. per. H97 ZC2.5.6(b).

1563 8°. Hyperius, A. G. per. H95 ZC2.5.6(a).

1566 fol. Clement, of Alexandria. per. C78 A.5.4(a).

1570 8°. Sonnius, F. S70 B.5.33.

Gymnicus, Arnold

1561 8°. Hertelius, J. [col. in off. ... sumptibus I. Oporini.] H44 E.6.36(b).

Henricpetri, Officina

1566 (Mar.) 8°. Fulgentius. ex off. F39 A.6.26(b).

Herwagen, Officina

[1557 (Mar.) fol. Musculus, W. ex off. [col. ex off. ... per I. Heruagium & B. Brand.] *M6 G.3.13.]

1560 fol. Musculus, W. ex off. M95 L.3.20.

Basle, Herwagen, *continued*

1561 fol. Musculus, W. ex off. M93
G.4.19(b).

1565 [col. Mar.] fol. Musculus, W.
[col. apud haeredes I. Heruagii]
M94 G.4.19(c).

Herwagen [Hervagius], Johann

1542 fol. Augustine. per. A60
A.4.23–24.

1542 fol. Augustine. per. A61 A.5.2
[vol.2 only].

1553 (Aug.) 8°. Musculus, W. per.
M90 ZC2.4.11(a).

1554 (Aug.) fol. Musculus, W. per.
M92 G.3.10.

1554 (mense Augusto) [col. Sep.]
fol. Musculus, W. per. M89
G.3.11.

1554 [col. mense Septembri] fol.
Theophylact. apud [col. per.] T8
G.2.18.

1556 fol. Musculus, W. per. M91
G.3.12.

[1557 (March) fol. Musculus, W. ex
off. [ex off. Heruagiana, per I.
Heruagiana & B. Brand.] *M6
G.3.13.]

1561 4°. Westhemerus, B. per [col.
ex off.] W8 C.1.13.

Herwagen, Johann, haeredes

1565 [col. Mar.] fol. Musculus, W.
[col. apud.] (ex off. Heruagiana.)
M94 G.4.19(c).

Herwagen [Hervagius], Johann, &
Brand, Bernard

[1557 (Mar.) fol. Musculus, W. ex
off. [ex off. Heruagiana, per I
Heruagiana & B. Brand.] *M6
G.3.13.]

Hornken, Ludwig

1513 (28 Iul.) fol. Petrus, *Lombardus*.
aere & impensis proprijs per A.
Petri. P22 L.3.7.

Isengrin [Isingrinius], Michael

1546 8°. Sarcerius E. [device] S24
ZC2.2.5.

1552 8°. Oecumenius. [device] O17
D.5.8.

[1552 or 1555] 8°. Oecumenius. O18
C.4.12.

[1557 fol. Vergil, P. apud. *V3
B.3.20.]

Isengrin, Michael, & Petri, Heinrich

[1534–35 fol. Münster, S. [col. ex off
Bebeliana, impendiis M. Isingrini
et H. Petri.] *M5 E.3.11.]

Kuendig [Parcus], Jakob [Jacobus]

1553 8°. Nardus, J. L. [col. pt. 1:
excudebat.] N6 N.6.9.

1558 [col. Aug.] fol. Bibliander, T.
[col. apud I.Parcum, expens. I.
Oporini.] B43 B.3.19(c).

1559 8°. Richter, M. [col. ex off.]
R28 L.6.13(b).

1560 8°. Flacius, M. F24 ZC2.1.8(c).

Lasius, Balthasar, and Platter,
Thomas, *see* Platter, Thomas,
and Lasius, Balthasar

Lucius, Ludovicus [Ludwig]

[1553 (Sep.) col.] 8°. Lübeck. [col.
excudebat.] L46 ZC2.4.11(e).

1555 [col.Mar.] fol. Borrhaus, M.
[per … sumptibus I. Oporini] B59
G.4.10(a).

1562 8°. Praetorius, A. ex off. P49
ZC2.7.6(b).

Lucius, Ludovicus, & Stella,
Michael Martinus, *see* Oporinus,
Joannes [Johann], Lucius,
Ludovicus, & Stella, Michael
Martinus

Oporinus [Oporiniana]

[c. 1555] 8°. Culman, L. C119
ZC2.4.11(d).

1570 (col. mense Aug.) 8°.
Hyperius, A. G. ex off. H98
ZC2.1.6(a).

Oporinus, Joannes [Johann]

1544 (Iun.) 8°. Vives, J. L. [col. ex off.] V39 N.6.5.

[c. 1545] 8°. Postel, G. P45 ZC2.6.4. Date and place of printing suggested by VD16 P 4483, USTC 682489. But FB 83762 and USTC 160468 suggest [?Paris, c. 1540].

[1546 col. Mar.] 8°. Rivius, J. R33 L.6.16(a). Printer suggested by OCLC.

1548 4°. Bucer, M. B110 L.5.16(a–b). Printer suggested by VD 16; or Basle: Johann Oporinus (Adams).

1548 8°. Rivius, J. R32 H.1.37(a). Printer suggested by COPAC.

1550 [col. mense Mart.] 8°. Bibliander, T. [col. ex off.] B42 H.1.29(a).

1550 [col. Mar.] 8°. Rivius, J. [col. per.] R31 H.1.37(b).

1550 [col. Sep.] 8°. Betuleius, X. per. B18 X.2.32.

[1550] 8°. Brentz, J. B74 H.1.29(b). Printer and date suggested by VD16.

[c. 1550] 8°. Curio, C. C124 L.6.16(b). Printer not certain.

[1550] 8°. Melanchthon, P. M65 B.5.34(a). Printer suggested by World Cat.

[1551 [col. Nov.] 4°. Perionius, J. [col. ex off.] *P1 Z.5.75(b).]

1552 (col. March) 8°. Bibliander, T. [col. ex off.] B41 E.6.23(a).

1553 8°. Massarius, H. M15 ZC2.5.1(b). Printer suggested by Adams.

1553 8°. Mazzolini, S. 'Romae: per iordanum typographum Pontificium'. M24 ZC2.5.1(c). Printer according to VD16 and EDIT16.

1553 (March) 8°. Alesius, A. per. A20 C.4.7.

[1554 (col. Mar.) fol. Bible. Lat. per. *B9 E.1.14.]

1555 (col. Jan.) 4°. Bibliander, T, ex off. B40 I.5.7(c).

1555 [col. Mar.] fol. Borrhaus, M. per [col. per L. Lucium, sumptibus I. Oporini.] B59 G.4.10(a).

[c. 1555] 8°. Ribittus, J. R25 ZC2.5.7(g). Printer suggested by HAB.

1556 8°. Artopoeus, P. A58 E.6.35(c).

[1556 fol. Bible. Lat. per [col. ex off. I. Oporini, I. Lucii et M. M. Stellae.] *B10 E.1.15.]

1556 (Mar.) 8°. Lasco, J. à. L13 ZC2.4.6(d).

1556 (Oct.) 8°. Kirchmeyer, T. per [col. ex off.] K4 ZC2.4.11(f)

[1556 (Dec.) 8°. Lasco, J. à. per. *L3 L.5.17(c).]

1557 [col. Sep.] fol. Borrhaus, M. per [col. ex off.] B60 G.4.10(b).

1557 [col. Sep.] fol. Bucer, M. per. B105 M.1.28(c).

1558 (Jul.) 8°. Clauser, C. per. C76 X.2.30(a).

1558 [col. Aug.] fol. Bibliander, T. per [col. apud I.Parcum, expens. I. Oporini.] B43 B.3.19(c).

1558 [col. pt. 1 Aug.] (pt.2 Sep.) fol. Tosarrius, J. [pt. 1 col. ex off. pt.2 per.] T17 G.4.1(a).

[1559 fol. Bullinger, H. per. *B13 G.3.24.]

1559 (Aug.) fol. Frycz, A. per [col. ex off.] F37 N.3.12(c).

1559 (Aug.) 8°. Hyperius, A. G. per [col. ex off.] H96 N.6.16(a).

1559 [col. Sep.] 8°. Humphrey, L. per. H89 L.6.12(b).

[1560 col.] 8°. Humphrey, L. per. H90 ZC2.5.2(a).

[1560 col. mense Feb.] fol. Magdeburg Centuriators. per. [col. opera et expensis partim … partim B. Brilingeri.] M5 M.4.9.

1561 8°. Hertelius, J. [col. sumptibus. (in off. A. Gymnici.)] H44 E.6.36(b).

[1561 col. (Jan.)] fol. Nicephorus. per. N9 B.3.19(b).

1561 [col. Jan.] 8°. Steckelius, L. per [col. ex off.] S87 L.5.19(b).

Petri, Adam, de Langendorff
  1510 [col. decimo Kal. Ianuarij.] 4°.
    Joannes, *de Colonia*. [col. ex off.]
    J11 L.5.40.
  1513 (28 Iul.) fol. Petrus, *Lom-bardus*. L. hornken aere &
    impensis proprijs per A. Petri.
    P22 L.3.7.
  1515 fol. Bercheur, P. in off. libraria.
    B15 L.2.15(c).
  1520 4°. Melanchthon, P. M56
    ZC2.3.6(b). Printer suggested by
    OCLC.
  [1522 [col.] 4°. Luther, M. [col.
    apud.] *L6 C.1.1(b).]
  [1522 4°. Luther, M. [?A. Petri.] *L9
    C.1.1(c).]
  1525 [col. Mar.] 8°. Jonas, J. apud.
    J14 D.2.6(a).
  1527 (Aug.) fol. Philippus, *the
    Presbyter*. per. P26 N.4.5(b).

Petri, Heinrich [Henricus]
  1528 (Mar.) fol. Sedulius. per. S40
    N.4.5(c).
  1529 (Mar.) fol. Bede. excudebat.
    B12 N.4.5(a).
  1532 (Mar.) 4°. Oecolampadius, J.
    excudebat. O3 C.1.2(a).
  1535 (Aug.) 4°. Bugenhagen, J.
    excudebat. impensis I. Bebelii.
    B114 C.2.11.
  1536 [col. Aug.] 8°. Münster, S.
    excudebat [col. apud.] M84
    F.2.3(a).
  [1537 col. Aug.] 8°. Suetonius. per.
    S96 Y.5.29.
  1539 8°. Aurogallus, M. apud. A69
    F.2.3(b).
  1542 [col. Mar.] 8°. Münster, S. [col.
    per.] M85 F.2.29.
  1543 (Mar.) 4°. Phrygio, P C. per
    [col. excud.] P29 E.5.32.
  1546 8°. Artopoeus, P. per. A55
    C.4.2.
  1546 [col. Mar.] 8°. Goeuschel, J.
    per. G29 F.2.10.
  1555 [col. Mar.] fol. Lactantius. per.
    L1 A.4.25(a).
  1555 [col. Aug.] 8°. Münster, S.
    apud. M83 F.2.8.

1559 (mense Sep.) fol. Cassian, J.
    per. C47 A.5.4(b).

Petri, Johann
  1489 fol. Holkot, R. [J. Amerbach &
    J. Petri?] H71 L.2.18.

Petri, Johann, & Froben, Johann
  [1502 [col. idibus Maii.] fol. Bible.
    Lat. Vulgate. [col. pt. 6: cura &
    impensis I. de Amerbach. J. petri
    d'Langendorff et J. froben …
    Arte & industrria J. froben.]
    *B6 E.2.13–17.]

Pfortzheim, Jacobus [Wolff] de
  [1508] fol. Biel, G. [pt. 3 per.] B47
    L.3.16.
  1510 (8 kal.mar.) fol. Biel, G. [col. a]
    B46 L.3.15.
  1512 [col.] fol. Biel, G. [col. a.] B48
    L.2.15(b).

Platter, Thomas & Lasius,
  Balthasar
  1535 [col. 1536 (Mar.)] 8°. Meg-
    ander, C. [col. per T. Platterum,
    & B. Lasium.] M26 D.2.6(c).
  [1536 [col. mense Martio] fol.
    Oecolampadius, J. & Zwingli, H.
    [col. per.] *O2 N.4.8.]
  [1537 (Mense Mar.) 4°. Calvin, J.
    [col. per B. Lasium et T. Plat-
    terum] *C4 L.5.41(b).]

Quecus [Queek], Paul
  1562 fol. Hamelmann, H. per …
    sumptibus H. Feirabent [Frank-
    furt-a-M]. H2 M.1.28(a).
  1565 [col. Mar.] 8°. Melanchthon, P.
    per. M60 K.1.28(a).
  1566 [col. Mar.] 8°. Vigne, P. della.
    per [col. pt. 1: ex off. P. Queci
    sumptibus I. Oporini; pt.2: ex
    off. I.Oporini.] V24 Z.5.109.
  1566 (Aug.) 8°. Wigand, J. per [col.
    per … sumptibus P. Brubachij.]
    W18 C.4.4(a).
  [1566 (Sept.)] 8°. Valerius, C. [col.
    per … sumptibus I. Oporini] per
    Ioannem Oporinum. V1
    Z.5.108(b).

Basle, Quecus, *continued*

Sylvius, Lambertus
    1552 8°. Honorius. prostant apud.
    H75 A.6.20(b).

Vilarmus, Gotthard ['Lutetiae
    Paris-iorum' = ?Basle (BMFB, p.
    8)]
        1573 4°. Albutius, P. per. A17
        L.5.32(b). Printer is actually
        Petrus Perna, Basle, according to
        HAB.

Westhemer[us], Bartholomaeus
    1538 8°. Artopoeus, P. ex off. A56
    E.6.5.
    1539 8°. Sarceriu s, E. ex off. S16
    D.5.4(b).
    1539 (Aug.) 8°. Sarcerius, E.
    [device] S19 D.2.4.
    [1540 col.] 8°. Sarcerius, E. [col.
    apud.] S18 D.2.5.
    1544 8°. Willich, J. [col. apud.] W42
    G.6.21(b).
    1545 8°. Brunfels, O. [col. apud.]
    B96 D.3.2.
    1545 [Pref. 4 June] 8°. Melanch-
    thon, P. [col. per.] M51 C.5.11(a).

Winter, Robert
    [1543 [col. Mar.] 8°. Eterianus, H.
    [col. apud.] *E4 L.6.22(a).]
    1544 8°. Oecolampadius, J. per. O5
    D.2.1.
    1544 8°. Oecolampadius, J. per. O4
    C.1.4.

Wolf[f], Thomas
    [c. 1523] 8°. Luther, M. L78
    ZC2.7.11.

No printer identified
    [1522 4°. Luther, M. *L8 C.2.5.]
    [1535 8°. Alexander, A. *A2
    ZC1.5.6.]
    1564 8°. Dick, L. D5 ZC2.8.13(b).
    1564 8°. Ulmer, J. C. U1 ZC2.3.13.
    1566 (Mar.) 8°. Flacius, M. F10
    ZC2.1.4(a).

Bautzen [Budissinae]

Wolrab, Joannes [Johann]
    1565 8°. Selneccer, N. per. S41
    ZC2.1.7(a).

Berne

Apiarius [Biener], Matthias [apud
    inclytam Auenticorum Bernam]
        1546 (Mar.) 8°. Mayer, S. per. M21
        E.6.26(a).
        1546 (Apr.) 8°. Oecolampadius, J.
        per. O14 E.6.26(d).

Bologna

Benedictis, Joannes Antonius de
    1507 4°. Castellensis, H. [col. per
    I. Nemantonium [sic].] C49
    H.1.21.

Hectoris, Benedictus
    1517 (19 id. Feb.) 4°. Cagnazzo, J. in
    edibus. C1 N.5.26.

Bonn

Mylius [Mülen, von der], Laurent
    [Laurenz]
        1542 (Jan.) 8°. Melanchthon, P. M48
        C.5.8(a). Printer from VD16.
        1545 8°. Lasco, J. à. ex off. L12
        ZC2.6.15.

Budissinae *see* **Bautzen**

Caen

Angier, Michael [Michel]
    1518 [col. 26 Mar.] 4°. Durandus, G.
    [col. Impressum Cadomi per L.
    hostingue pro.] (ab J. parvo.) D36
    L.5.13.

Hostingue, Laurent[ius]
    1518 [col. 26 Mar.] 4°. Durandus, G.
    [col. per ... pro M. angier.] (ab J.
    parvo.) D36 L.5.13.

Christlingen

Gotwin [Gotvisus], Gnadrich
[i.e. Strasbourg: Bernhard Jobin –
VD 16]
    1573 8°. Fischart, J. per. F9
    ZC2.7.5(f).

Cologne

Alopecius, Hero *see* Fuchs, Hero

Bathen[ius], Johann
    1558 8°. Slotanus, J. apud. S61
    ZC1.4.9.

Berlaer, Theoderic, of Cologne
[printing at Basle]
    1515 fol. Bercheur, P. [col. aere &
    impensis … in off. libraria A. Petri
    de Langendorff] B15 L.2.15(c).

Birckmann, Arnold
    1540 8°. Prosper. ex off. H. Alopecij
    (with device of A. Birckmann).
    P55 A.6.42.

Birckmann, Arnold, Heirs of
    1553 8°. Zegers, N. apud. Z3 E.6.30.
    1555 8°. Cassander, G. C45 B.6.41(a)
    [Adams] or G. Cervicornus
    [HAB].
    1555 12°. Erasmus, D. apud. E43
    ZC2.8.4(a).
    1555 8°. Wild, J. apud [col. pt. 2:
    typis I. Graphei.] W37 G.5.10.
    1560 24°. Vincent. apud. V28
    ZC1.4.13(d).
    1562 fol. Kling, C. apud. K7
    L.3.17(b).
    1563 fol. Kling, C. apud. K8
    L.3.17(a).
    [1563 8°. Johannes, *Arundinensis.*
    apud. *J1 ZC2.8.11.]
    1564 4°. Cassander, G. apud. C46
    K.2.26(d).
    1564 8°. Witzel, G. apud. W54
    B.6.42(b).
    1564 8°. Witzel, G. apud. W52
    B.6.42(c).
    1567 8°. Athenagoras. apud. A59
    A.6.20(a).

    1567 12°. Eck, J. apud. E8 ZC2.8.5(a).
    1567 fol. Hoffmeister, J. apud. H64
    G.3.9(c).
    1567 fol. Theophylact. apud. T9
    G.3.9(a).
    1567 fol. Wild, J. apud. W35
    G.3.9(b).

Birckmann, Arnold, Heirs of, &
  Bohemus, Franciscus
    1571 8°. Wild, J. sumptibus. W28
    D.2.10.

Birckmann, Johann
    1567 fol. Theodoret. apud. T4
    A.4.11–12.
    1570 fol. Gregory, *of Nazianzus.*
    apud. G32 A.4.8(b).
    1571 8°. Polygranus, F. apud. P41
    ZC1.4.5(a).

Birckmann, Johann, & Richwin,
  Werner
    1564 8°. Cucchus, M.A. apud. C117
    ZC2.8.13(a).

Calenius, Gervinus, & heirs of
  Quentel, Joannis *see also* Quentel,
  Joannes, Heirs of, & Calenius,
  Gervinus
    1562 fol. Eder, G. apud. E9 G.3.18(a–
    b).
    1568 4°. Bredenbach, T. apud. B67
    D.1.4(d).
    1569 (13 Cal. Feb.) fol. Du Préau, G.
    apud. D31 L.4.6(a).
    1569–70 4°. Canisius, P. apud. C36
    K.2.13–14.
    1572 fol. Vega, A. apud. V6 L.3.8.
    1573 8°. Eisengrein, M. apud. E10
    D.4.9.

Cervicornus, Eucharius
    1525 8°. Cyprian. in aedibus. C128
    N.6.3(d).
    [1526 fol. Herodotus. apud. *H2
    Y.3.19(a).]
    [1526 [col. Iun.] fol. Orosius, P.
    excudebat [col. Impensa & aere
    M. Godefridi Hydorpij]. *O5
    Y.3.19(b).]

Cologne, Cervicornus, Eucharius, *continued*

[1527 [col. 15 Cal. Maij] fol. Thucydides. excudebat [col. apud … aere & impensa M. G. Hittorpij]. *T3 Y.3.19(c).]

1530 fol. Angelomus. ex off. A38 N.3.18(a).

1532 8°. Sachs, H. apud. S2 ZC2.7.9(a). [VD16 ZV 1358].

1535 fol. Zacharias. excudebat. Z1 E.4.6(b).

1540 (Mar.) fol. Fidati, S. ex off. F7 L.4.1.

1532 8°. Sachs, H. apud. S2 ZC2.7.9(a). [CLC].

Cervicornus, Gottfried

1564 8°. Cassander, G. C45 B.6.41(a) [HAB] or Birckmann, A., heirs of [Adams].

Cholinus, Maternus

1557 8°. Bredenbach, M. apud. B65 M.2.40.

1557 8°. Cicogna, V. apud. C75 ZC2.1.3(c).

1557–60 8°. Billick, E. apud. B49 ZC2.5.8(b–c).

1558 8°. Staphylus, F. apud. S83 ZC2.4.12.

1558 8°. Treflerus, F. apud. T18 N.6.12(c).

1560 8°. Paulinus. apud. P9 A.6.21(a).

1561 8°. Orosius, P. apud. O22 B.6.16(a).

1562 8°. Via, J. à. apud. V22 ZC2.1.3(a).

1564 8°. Bebenburg, L. de apud. B9 B.6.19(b).

1564 8°. Burgundy. apud. B136 ZC2.4.10(d).

1564 8°. Hosius, S. apud. H79 B.6.41(b).

1564 8°. Kromer, M. apud. K12 ZC2.4.10(e).

1565 8°. Hosius, S. apud. H78 ZC2.4.10(b).

1571 8°. Borckensis, T. apud. B58 G.6.6(a).

1571 8°. Lindanus, W. apud. L33 ZC1.4.5(b).

1571 8°. Lindanus, W. apud. L31 ZC1.4.5(c).

1571 8°. Lindanus, W. apud. L32 ZC1.4.5(d).

1573 8°. Piotrków. Synod. apud. P35 ZC2.4.7–8.

Fuchs, Hero

1540 8°. Prosper. ex off. (with device of A. Birckmann.) P55 A.6.42.

Gennep[aeus], Jaspar [von]

1533 8°. Haymo. H9 D.5.13. Printer from VD16.

1536 8°. Sepúlveda, J. G. de. ex off. S48 ZC2.6.10(b).

1539 8°. Dionysius, C. [col. per.] D13 E.3.19(b).

1544 8°. Charles V. excudebat. C58 B.6.42(d).

1545 4°. Florebelli, A. excudebat. F25 ZC2.3.11(a).

1545 8°. Helmes, H. [excudebat.] H22 C.3.6.

1556 8°. Helmes, H. excudebat. H18 C.3.2.

1556 8°. Helmes, H. excudebat. H19 C.3.3.

1556 8°. Helmes, H. excudebat. H20 C.3.4.

1556 8°. Helmes, H. excudebat. H21 C.3.5.

1556 8°. Helmes, H. excudebat. H22 C.3.6.

1559 fol. Pontanus, R. apud. P43 L.4.6(b).

Graminaeus, Theodore

1569 8°. Eisengrein, M. apud. E13 B.6.42(a).

[1570 4°. Scaliger, P. ex off. typographica. *S1 H.1.24.]

Grapheus, Joannes

1555 8°. Wild, J. [col. pt. 2 typis.] W027 G.5.10.

Grapheus, Nicolaus *see* Schreiber, Nikolaus

Gymnicus, Johann

1526 (Aug.) 8°. Augustine. apud.
A63 A.6.32(d).

1527 (Sep.) 8°. Augustine. apud.
A67 A.6.32(c).

1529 8°. Augustine. A62 A.6.32(a)
[CLC].

1529 12°. Augustine. apud. A65
A.6.32(b).

[c. 1530 8°. Ambrose. *A4 A.6.30(b).
Printer from VD16 ZV484.]

[1532 (Mar.) 8°. Ambrose. excudebat. *A3 A.6.30(a).]

Hittorp[ius], M. Godefridus

1523 (Nou.) 8°. Lutzenburgo, B.
de. [col. impendio & ere.] L80
H.2.10.

[1526 [col.Iun.] fol. Orosius, P.
excudebat [col. Impensa & aere
M. Godefridi Hydorpij.] *O5
Y.3.19(b).]

1539 8°. Marulić, M. (I. Soter
excudebat.) [col. impensis.] M14
N.6.4.

Novesianus, Johann [von Neuss]

1555 4°. Slotanus, J. excudebat.
S60 L.5.8(a).

Novesianus, Melchior [von Neuss]

1533 8°. Joannes, a Davantria. J9
H.1.31. Printer from BSB.

1533 8°. Joannes, a Davantria. apud.
J10 H.2.12(b).

1534 8°. Tritheim, J. impensis. T21
ZC2.7.9(b).

1539 fol. Chrysologus, P. ex off. C65
E.4.1(b).

1540 fol. Dionysius. ex off. D21
N.4.2.

1540 4°. Eck, J. ex off. E5 I.7.6(d).

1542 (May) 4°. Eck, J. ex off. E4
D.1.4(c).

1542 (Aug.) fol. Pighius, A. ex off.
P33 N.4.6.

1545 4°. Carvialus, L. ex off. C44
K.2.26(a).

1545 4°. Latomus, B. ex off. L14
ZC2.3.12(e).

1546 4°. Latomus, B. ex off. L15
ZC2.4.1(a).

1550 fol. Royard, T. ex off. R39
E.4.2.

1552 8°. Lexicon Novi Testamenti.
excudebat. L28 E.6.23(b).

Praël, Johannes

[1531 8°. Didymus. excudebat. *D2
E.6.24(b).]

1531 (18 June) 8°. Haymo. apud.
H11 D.2.7(c).

[1531 [col. 14 Jul.] 8°. Angelomus.
excudebat. *A5 E.6.24(a).]

1531 (Aug.) 8°. Prosper. excudebat.
P56 ZC2.6.19(c).

1532 8°. Rabanus M. excudebat.
R2 C.5.2.

1532 (Mar.) 8°. Rabanus M. excudebat. R1 C.5.1.

Quentel, in officina [in aedibus]
(House of)

1531 [col. Jun.] fol. Ebser, J. [col.
ex aedibus.] E2 N.3.18(b).

1533 fol. Cologne. Canones. [col. ex
aedibus.] C97 B.3.21(a).

1536 fol. Cologne. Formula. in
off. C96 B.3.21(b).

1543 fol. Placus, A. [col. in aedibus.]
P39 N.3.13(b).

1546 fol. Dionysius, C. col. ex
aedibus. [expensis. P. Quentel.]
D19 E.3.21(b).

1549 fol. Dionysius. ex off. D15
E.3.18(b).

Quentel, Joannes [Johann]

1548 fol. Dionysius, C. ex off. D10
E.3.16.

1548 (Aug.) fol. Dionysius, C. ex
off. D14 E.3.18(a).

1549 fol. Dionysius, C. ex off. D15
E.3.18(b).

[1549 8°. Louis I. ex off. *L5
L.6.22(b).]

1549 8°. Witzel, G. ex off. W51
ZC2.2.8(b).

1551 fol. Dionysius, C. ex off.
'tametsi inter excudendum
defuncti'. D16 E.3.17(b).

1552 8°. Witzel, G. ex off. W55
ZC2.2.8(d).

Cologne, *continued*

Quentel, Joannes, Heirs of
1552 (Feb.) fol. Dionysius, C. ex off.
D11 E.3.17(a).
1553 fol. Witzel, G. ex off. W49
E.4.4.

Quentel, Joannes, Heirs of, &
Calenius, Gervinus *see also*
Calenius, Gervinus & Quentel,
Joannes
1558 8°. Bredenbach, T. apud. B67
D.1.4(d).
1562 8°. Bredenbach, M. apud. B66
M.2.40(d).
1562 fol. Helding, M. S. apud. H16
L.4.15.
[1564 8°. Fabri, J. *F1 L.6.28(c).]
[*c.* 1565] 8°. Czecanovius, S. C129
ZC2.8.12.

Quentel, Peter
1525 8°. Eck, J. E7 L.6.6(a). Imprint
from VD16.
1531 8°. Haymo. per. H10 C.4.9.
[1531 – col.] 4°. Tritheim, J. [col. per
me.] T20 B.5.44.
[1533 (Sep.) fol. Dionysius. suis
impensis excudebat. *D5 E.3.15.]
[*c.* 1534] 8°. Dionysius. [for] D20
ZC2.1.9.
[1534 (Mar.) fol. Dionysius. suis
impensis [col. in aedibus] …
excudebat. *D3 E.3.14.]
1540 (Aug.) fol. Nausea, F.
impensis. N8 N.3.16.
1543 (Jan.) fol. Dionysius, C.
excudebat. D17 E.3.20.
1545 4°. Hofmeister, J. ex off. H65
D.1.3.
1545 (Apr.) fol. Dionysius, C. apud.
D18 E.3.21(a).
1546. fol. Dionysius, C. expensis.
[col. ex aedibus Quentelianis,
1546.] D19 E.3.21(b).
1546 (Jan.) fol. John, *of Damascus.*
ex off. J12 N.3.13(a).

Richwin, Werner
1558 8°. Smith, R. apud. S66
ZC2.4.10(c).

Rost[ius], Adolf [Adolphus]
1571 12°. Guibert. excudebat. G42
K.3.31(b).

Schreiber [Graphaeus], Nikolaus
1567 8°. Lindanus, W. typis. L34
M.2.40(b).

Soter, Jakob
1558 fol. Sonnius, F. excudebat. S68
L.2.16(b).

Soter, Johannes
1525 8°. Gaza, T. opera & impensa.
G18 Y.5.14.

Copenhagen

Kaus, Baltzer
1571 8°. Hemmingsen, N. H37
ZC2.7.5(a). Printer from HAB and
COPAC, but [Leipzig: Ernst
Vögelin] according to VD 16
ZV 7660.

Cremona

Luere, Franciscus Ricardus de
[attrib. CLC]
[1519] 4°. Isolanis, I de. I8 I.3.10(c).
Date suggested by CLC and HAB.

Dillingen [Diling]

Mayer, Sebald
1559 4°. Staphylus, F. col. apud. S82
K.2.26(b).
1562 8°. Councils – Nicaea. Acta.
apud. C106 G.6.6(d).
[1563 post. Aug.] 8°. Ephraem.
apud. E19 A.6.41.
[1564] 8°. Holthusius, J. [excude-
bat.] H74 ZC2.8.13(c).
[*c.* 1565] 4°. Gail, C. excudebat. G3
E.5.28(b).
1567 4°. Torres, H. apud. T16A
A.6.5.
1569 8°. Osorio da Fonseca, J. ex
off. O26 M.2.40(a).
1571 4°. Canisius, P. excudebat. C32
C.2.4.
1571 12°. Holthusius, J. excudebat.
H73 K.3.31(a).

Dortmund [Tremoniae]

Sartor[ius], Albert[us]
1560–1561 8°. Schopper, J. excudebat. S39 D.3.9–11.

Douai

Boscard[us] [Bosschaert], Jacob[us]
1558 8°. Smith, R. typis. S65 I.1.5(c).

Emden

Erven, Gilles van der
[1554] 8°. Lasco, J. à. L11 ZC2.5.7(f).

Erfurt

Bauuman, Georg
1563 fol. Musculus, A. per. M87 L.2.7(a).

Stürmer, Gervasius
1544 8°. Melanchthon, P. excussit. M67 ZC2.6.16

Florence

Miscomini, Antonio
1482 (vii. idus Novembris) fol. & 4°. Ficino, M. per. F6 Y.3.25.

Frankfurt-am-Main

Bassaeus, Nicolaus
1569 8°. Chytraeus, D. [col. apud.] C71 E.6.26(c).

Brubach[ius] [Braubach], Peter
1539 8°. Hoffman, C. ex off. H59 E.6.33.
1540 8°. Brentz, J. B83 C.6.3. Printer from HAB.
1542 fol. Rhegius, U. ex off. R24 G.3.6(b).
1542 (Sep.) fol. Brentz, J. ex off. B71 G.3.6(a).
1543 8°. Rhegius, U. excudebat. R20 C.6.5(c).
1544 8°. Aepinus, J. excudebat. A6 C.6.5(b).
1544 8°. Aepinus, J. excudebat [col. ex officina.] A5 D.5.6(a).
1544 8°. Brentz, J. [col. excudebat – with Janus device.] B89 C.6.5(a).
1544 8°. Kirchmeyer, T. [Janus device.] K3 D.2.8(c).
1544 8°. Rhegius, U. excudebat. [col. ex off.] R21 ZC2.8.1(c).
1544 8°. Rhegius, U. ex off. R22 ZC2.8.1(b).
1544 (Ian.) fol. Luther, M. ex off. L75 L.2.7(d).
1545 8°. Aepinus, J. ex off. A7 D.5.6(b).
1545 8°. Hoffman, C. ex off. H60 D.5.6(c).
1545 8°. Hoffman, C. ex off. H61 D.5.6(d).
1545 8°. Rhegius, U. ex off. R23 H.1.8(a).
1546 [col. 1545] 8°. Mayer, S. excudebat. [col. ex off.] M20 D.2.8(a).
1546 4°. Aepinus, J. ex off. A10 ZC2.3.5(c).
1548 8°. Brentz, J. ex off. [with Janus device.] B88 C.6.4.
1549 (Nou.) fol. Brentz, J. ex off. B85 G.3.8(b).
1552 4°. Flacius, M. apud. F14 ZC2.3.8(e).
1553 8°. Aepinus, J. ex off. A8 ZC1.4.10(d).
1553 (Mar.) 8°. Luther, M. ex off. L50 C.4.3.
1555 8°. Luther, M. L51 E.6.37. Printer as tomus tertius (L50)?
1555–1556 8°. Aepinus, J. excudebat. A4 E.6.35(d–e).
1556 4°. Brentz, J. apud. B92 K.2.11(a).
1556 4°. Brentz, J. excudebat. B69 K.2.11(c).
1557 8°. Aepinus, J. excudebat. A9 K.2.15(c).
1557 4°. Brentz, J. excudebat. B70 L.5.7(a).
1558 4°. Andreae, J. [col. excudebat.] A37 K.2.11(b).
1558 8°. Brentz, J. apud. B80 G.5.16.
1558 [col. Jun.] 8°. Pfeffinger, J. ex off. P24 L.6.13(a).

Frankfurt-am-Main, Brubachius, *continued*

1559 8°. Wigand, J. ex off. W25 L.6.13(f).

1559 (June) 8°. Andreae, J. ex off. A36 L.6.13(e).

1560 4°. Monner, B. ex off. typographica. M80 I.3.9(b).

1560 (Mar.) 4°. Andreae, J. in off. A35 ZC2.3.5(a).

1561 8°. Hall, Suabian. excudebat. H1 ZC2.2.7(a).

1561 fol. Würtemberg Confession. apud. W60 L.2.20.

1562 8°. Mecklenberg. excudebat. M25 L.6.24(b) .

1562 8°. Melanchthon, P. excudebat. M45 K.1.7(a).

1562 8°. Wigand, J. apud. W24 L.6.26(a).

1562 (Mar.) fol. Brentz, J. B76 G.3.7(b).

1563 4°. Councils – Trent. apud. C111 ZC2.3.8(d).

1564 fol. Brentz, J. [col. ex off. typographica.] B87 G.3.7(c).

1565 4°. Schegk, J. ex off. typographica. S34 K.2.8(d).

1566 8°. Brentz, J. apud. B77 C.4.4(b).

1566 8°. Wigand, J. excudebat. W23 K.2.15(a).

1566 (Ian.) 8°. Wigand, J. excudebat. W21 K.2.15(b).

1567 8°. Flacius, M. typis & sumptu haec sunt elaborata. F22 K.2.17.

Corvinus, Georg[ius]

1572 8°. Heshusius, T. [col. apud.] H51 ZC1.4.3(c).

1573 8°. Chemnitz, M. [col. apud. impensis Sigismundi Feyerabend.] C61 C.7.3.

1573 8°. Chemnitz, M. [col. apud. impensis Sigismundi Feyerabend.] C62 C.7.4.

Egenolff, Christian

1537 [col. Mar.] Sarcerius, E. [col. apud.] S15 C.6.9.

[1538 Pref. Dec. 1] 4°. Sarcerius, E. apud. S23 ZC2.3.6(a).

[1539 col.] 8°. Sarcerius, E. apud. S13 D.2.3.

[1539 col. Sep.] 8°. Sarcerius, E. [col. per.] S25 ZC2.1.5.

[?1540] 8°. Sarcerius, E. excudebat. S14 G.5.14. Date suggested by CLC.

[1541 col.] 8°. Sarcerius, E. apud. [col. apud.] S17 C.6.10.

[1541 col. (Pref. 15 Jun.)] 8°. Sarcerius, E. apud. S20 C.6.11.

1541 (cal. Apr.) 8°. Lorich, G. [col. Vuetzflarij] L39 ZC2.8.1(a).

[1542 col.] 8°. Imler, C. apud. I2 C.5.10(b).

1542 [col. Mai.] 8°. Imler, C. excudebat [col. apud.] I3 D.6.7(d).

[1543 col. vol. 2] 8°. Sarcerius, E. apud. S12 C.6.7–8.

1544 8°. Kinthisius, I. apud. [col. apud.] K2 G.6.17.

[c. 1544] 8°. Imler, C. apud. I1 D.3.6.

[?1544] 8°. Spangenberg, J. apud. S78 ZC2.2.9(b). Date suggested by CLC.

1544 [col. Sep.] 4°. Dietrich, V. apud. D6 G.5.4.

1545 8°. Spangenberg, J. apud. S75 D.3.4.

[1546 col. Jun.] 8°. Spangenberg, J. apud. S77 G.6.23.

[1548 col. Feb.] 8°. Spangenberg, J. apud. S76 D.3.5.

[1552] 8°. Loss, L. apud. L43 D.3.3.

[1552 col.] 8°. Loss, L. apud. L45 ZC2.6.18(f).

[1553 col.] fol. Kling, M. apud. K10 L.2.7(b).

[1554] 8°. Germanus. apud. G24 N.6.16(c).

1554 (Jan.) 8°. Huberinus, C. apud. [col. apud.] H81 N.6.16(b).

1554 (Aug.) fol. Loss, L. apud.
[Tom. 2] L41 G.2.15.
1558 4°. Dathenus, P. D3 K.2.11(e).
Printer from HAB.

Egenolff, Christian, Heirs of
1559 (Mar.) fol. Loss, L. apud.
[Tom. 1] L41 G.2.15.
1562 fol. Loss, L. apud. L42 G.2.16.
1564 8°. Machiavelli, N. apud. M2
B.6.16(b).
1564 8°. Spangenberg, J. apud. S79
ZC2.5.10(a).
1570 fol. Loss, L. apud. L40
G.4.1(b).

Fabricius [Fabritius], Petrus *see*
Schmidt, Peter

Feyerabend [Feirabent], Hieronymus.
1536 fol. Hamelmann, H. sumptibus (per P. Quecum [Basle].)
H2 M.1.28(a).

Feyerabend [Feirabent], Sigismund, & Huder [Hüter], Simon.
1536 8°. Carion, J. per P. Fabricum,
impensis S. Feyrabend & S.
Huteri. C42 B.6.18(b).
1566 8°. Chemnitz, M. [device.] C59
C.7.1.
1566 8°. Chemnitz, M. [device.] C60
C.7.2.
1573 8°. Chemnitz, M. [col. apud G.
Corvinum, impensis.] C61 C.7.3.
1573 8°. Chemnitz, M. [col. apud G.
Corvinum, impensis.] C62 C.7.4.

Huder [Hüter], Simon.
1569 8°. Wigand, J. per M. Lechler
[col. per M. Lechler, impensis S.
Huteri.] W22 N.6.10(a).

Lechler, Martin
1569 8°. Wigand, J. per [col. per …
impensis S. Huteri.] W22
N.6.10(a).

Lucius, Ludovicus [Ludwig]
1562 8°. Praetorius, A. ex off. P49
ZC2.7.6(b).

Rhebartus, Thomas, & Feyerabend, Sigismund
1566 fol. Kirchener, T. per. K5 L.3.6.

Schmidt, Peter [Fabricius, Fabritius],
[Petrus]
1536 8°. Carion, J. per … impensis S.
Feyrabend & S. Huteri. C42
B.6.18(b).

No printer identified
1553 4°. Saxony – Lutheran
Church S29 L.5.7(e). [Leipzig or
Frankfurt-am-Main suggested by
OCLC.]

Frankfurt an der Oder

Eichorn, Johann
1551 8°. Gigas, J. [col. in off.] G27
B.5.34(d).

Sciurus, Johann
1549 8°. Artopoeus, P. in off. A57
E.6.35(b).

Freiburg im Breisgau

Delenus, Daniel
1561 4°. Klebitz, W. excudebat. K6
ZC2.3.9(e).

Geneva

Badius, Conrad
1558 8°. Bèze, T. excudebat. B21
ZC2.4.6(e).
1558 8°. Calvin, J. ex off. C12
ZC2.4.6(a).
1561 8°. Gentilis, J. V. G21 ZC2.1.8(d).

Barbirius, Nicolaus, & Courteau,
Thomas
1564 8°. Calvin, J. excudebat. C4
D.1.9.

Bourgeois, Jacques
[1543 4°. Calvin, J. [J. Girard suggested by Adams – J. Bourgeois
according to BMFB Suppl. 21]
*C5 L.5.41(a).]

Geneva, *continued*

Crispinus [Crespin], Joannes [Jean, II]

1552 16°. Bible. NT. ex off. B37
G.6.7.

1552 fol. ex off. Calvin, J. C9
G.4.4(b).

1552 8°. Hotman, F. apud. H80
ZC1.4.8(g).

1552 8°. Viret, P. ex off. V35
ZC2.1.6(f).

1554 fol. Calvin, J. ex off. C10
G.4.4(b).

1556 8°. Calvin, J. ex off. typographica. C14 ZC2.4.6(b).

1557 (20 Aug.) 8°. Calvin, J. apud
[col. excusum.] C20 ZC2.5.7(c).

1559 fol. Calvin, J. apud. C5
E.4.8(b).

1559 fol. Calvin, J. apud. C8
G.4.4(c).

1560 fol. Gallasius, N. apud. G4
E.4.8(a).

1561 8°. Calvin, J. [apud.] C19
K.3.31(c).

1563 [col. Iul.] fol. Calvin, J. apud.
[col. excudebat.] C6 E.4.8(c).

1565 fol. Bibliotheca. apud. B44
L.2.9–10.

1566 8°. Bèze, T. apud. B28
ZC2.1.6(d).

1566 8°. Erastus, T. apud. E49
ZC1.4.8(d).

1566 8°. France. F33 ZC2.1.6(e).

1566 fol. Lavater, L. apud. L21
E.3.5(a).

1566 8°. Simoni, S. [device]. S57
ZC1.4.8(f).

1566 4°. Zanchius, H. Z2 I.5.5(a).
Printing started in Basel by
Oporinus in 1563 and completed
by Crespin in 1566 (J.-F. Gilmont,
*Bibliographie des éditions de Jean
Crespin* Verviers: Librairie P. M.
Gason, 1981, pp. 191–92).

1567 8°. Bèze, T. apud. B23
ZC1.4.8(b).

1567 8°. Bèze, T. apud. B29
ZC2.1.8(a).

1567 8°. Chandieu, A. [device]. C56
ZC1.4.8(c).

1567 8°. Erastus, T. apud. E50
ZC1.4.8(e).

1568 8°. Palingenius, E. P1
ZC2.1.6(e). Printer from HAB
(Gilmont).

1570 8°. Serres, J. de. S52 ZC1.5.21.

[1570 8°. Serres, J. de. *S3 B.5.40.]

1571 8°. Bèze, T. apud. B20
K.1.33(a).

1571 8°. Hessiander, C. apud. H56
ZC2.3.1.

1572 8°. Bèze, T. apud. B27
K.1.33(b).

Durant, Jean [Joannes]

1570 16°. Aretius, B. apud. A50
ZC1.4.13(a).

Estienne [Stephanus], Henri, II

1557 8°. Maximus. ex off. M19
Y.5.19.

1562 8°. Sextus. excudebat ... H.
Fuggeri typographicus. S53
ZC1.5.19.

Estienne [Stephanus], Robert[us]

1553 fol. Bucer, M. Oliua. B100
G.2.20(a).

1553 (Idib. Ian.) fol. Estienne,
R. Oliua [col. excudebat in sua
officina.] E53 G.4.4(a).

1553 [col. 14 Cal. Iul.] fol. Viret, P.
Oliua [col. excudebat.] V36
N.3.12(a).

[1554 8°. Calvin, J. Oliua. *C3
L.5.17(b).]

1554 (8 Cal Feb.) fol. Viret, P. Oliua
[col. excudebat ... in sua off.] V34
N.3.12(b).

1554 [col. prid. id. Mai.] fol. Bucer,
M. Oliua. B99 G.2.20(b).

1555 8°. Calvin, J. Oliua. C13
ZC2.4.6(c).

1558 (cal. Feb.) 8°. Estienne,
R. Oliua [col. exc. ... in sua
officina.] E54 F.2.24.

[1559 8°. Bèze, T. de. Oliua. *B5
L.5.17(a).]

1559 (17. cal. Sep.) fol. Calvin, J.
oliua. C16 N.2.9.

Fugger, Huldrych *see* Estienne,
Henri, II

Girardus [Gerard], Joannes [Jean]
1543 4°. Calvin, J. per. C15 K.2.3.
[1543 4°. Calvin, J. [printer suggested by Adams – Jacques
Bourgeois according to BMFB
Suppl.21] *C5 L.5.41(a).]
1544 8°. Paris, Univ. of. [Pressa
ualentior.] P4 H.1.8(b).
1545 8°. Calvin, J. per. C18
ZC2.1.6(b).
1545 8°. Gallasius, N. [device.]
G5 ZC2.7.13(a).
1547 8°. Councils – Trent. Acta.
[device.] C107 ZC1.4.7(c).
1549 8°. Calvin, J. [Pressa Valentior,
with device.] C17 ZC2.7.13(c).
1549 8°. Gallasius, N. [Pressa
Valentior.] G6 ZC2.8.1(e).
1550 8°. Calvin, J. C2 ZC2.6.18(c).

Gueroult [Guerault], Guillaume
1555 8°. Justinian I. [col. excudebant G. Symon ... à Bosco &
Gueroult, Gulielmus.] J18 L.6.8.

Laonius [de Laon], Joannes [Jean]
[1561 fol. Calvin, J. excudebat. *C2
G.3.23(b).]

Le Preux, Jean [Ioannis], I
1570 fol. Irenaeus. apud ... & I.
Paruum. I5 A.4.8(a).

Perrin[us], François [Franciscus]
1564 8°. Calvin, J. ex off. C2
D.6.1(b).
1565 4°. Calvin, J. ex off. C7 G.5.5.
1566 8°. Metz. apud. M74 ZC1.4.8(a).
[1567 4°. Aretius, B. ex off. *A10
L.5.42(b).]
[1567 4°. Gentilis, J. V. ex off. *G2
L.5.42(a).]

Petit [Parvus], Jean [Ioannis], III
1570 fol. Irenaeus. apud I. le Preux
& I. Paruum. I5 A.4.8(a).

Pressa Valentior *see* Girardus
[Gerard], Joannes [Jean]

Symon, G. à Bosco, & Gueroult,
Gulielmus *see* Gueroult, Guillaume

Stephanus, Robertus *see* Estienne,
Robert

Stoer, Jacques
1574 8°. Bèze, T. B22 ZC1.4.4(c).

Vignon, Eustathius
1573 8°. Bèze, T. apud. B24
K.1.33(c).
1573 8°. Bèze, T. apud. B25
ZC2.7.5(c).
1573 8°. Bèze, T. excudebat. B26
M.2.20(a).
1573 8°. Danaeus, L. excudebat. D2
M.2.20(b).
1573 8°. Saillans, F. de. excudebat.
S6 ZC2.7.5(d).
1576 8°. Augustine. apud. A66
A.6.23.

Ghent [Gandavi]

Manilius, Cornelius
1556 8°. Bacherius, P. excudebat.
B1 ZC2.1.10(a).

Manilius, Gislenus
1570 8°. Garetius, J. excudebat. G16
G.6.6(f).

Hagenau

Anshelm, Thomas
1520 [col.] fol. Fulgentius. [col.] In
off. (impensis Kobergerorum
Norinbergensium.) F38 A.5.3(b).

Brubach, Peter [Petrus]
1535 (Jul.) 8°. Luther, M. ex off. L68
C.1.5(c).
1536 8°. Brentz, J. [Janus device.]
B72 C.6.1. Printer from BSB and
OCLC.
1536 8°. Brentz, J. in off. B86
G.3.22(b).

Hagenau, *continued*

Gran, Heinrich, impens. Joannis
Rynman de Oringaw
[1500 (11 Apr.) 4°. Councils.
Constance. expensis J. Rynman
[col. per industrium H. Gran …
expensis … I. Rynman.] *C12
B.5.43.]
1512 fol. Aquinas, T. per. A47
L.3.10.
1517 (13 Dec.) fol. Altensteig, J. [col.
excusus in off. industrij H. Gran
… impensis sumptibus … J.
Rynman.] A25 Y.3.32
1521 (col. pt.1: 5 Feb.; Pt. 2:
vigesimo Maii) fol. Pelbárt, O.
impressum ac revisum per …
expensis ac sumptibus … J.
Rynman [col. pt. 2: impressique
… expensis … J. Rynman … in
off. industrij H. Gran.] P15
M.1.27(a–b).

Rynman[n], Joannes [Johann] de
Oringaw, in off. Henrici Gran
1504 (Aug. kal. ix) fol. Albertus
Magnus. impensis, in off.
industrii H. Gran. A15 G.3.20.
1504 (7 Dec.) fol. Albertus Magnus.
expensis, industrii H. Gran in
offic. A14 G.3.19.
1517 (13 Dec.)] fol. Altensteig, J.
[col. excusus in off. industrij H.
Gran … impensis sumptibus …
J.Rynman.] A25 Y.3.32.
1521 (Pt. 1: 5 Feb.; Pt. 2: vigesimo
Maii) fol. Pelbárt, O. impressum
ac revisum per H. Gran. expensis
ac sumptibus … J. Rynman [col.
pt.2: impressique … expensis …
J. Rynman … in off. industrij H.
Gran.] P15 M.1.27(a–b).

Secer [Setzer], Johann
1525 8°. Bugenhagen, J. B116
C.5.11(b). Place of publication
and date from VD16 B9351; or
Strasbourg: J. Knobloch, 1524
from VD16 B 9349.

1525 8°. Hegendorff, C. per. H13
D.5.7.
1528 (Mense Ian.) 4°. Paschasius, R.
per. P6 ZC2.3.10.
1528 (Aug.) 8°. Melanchthon, P.
per. [col. excussit.] M46 C.5.4(e).
1529 [col. Feb.] 8°. Brentz, J. per
[col. excudebat.] B75 C.6.2.
1529 (mense Martio) 4°. Isidore.
per. I6 I.4.10(a).
[1530 (Sep.) col.] 8°. Luther, M.
[col. per.] L61 C.1.5(d).
1531 8°. Melanchthon, P. [col. per.]
M49 D.6.3(a).
1531 (Aug.) 4°. Alphabetum Theologicum. in off. A23 I.4.10(c).
1532 8°. Potho. per. P46 A.6.21(c).
1532 (Feb.) 8°. Patriarchs. per. P7
ZC2.6.19(d).
1532 (Feb.) 4°. Salonius. ex off. S9
C.2.9(a).

Seceriana, House of [in officina]
1533 [col. Mar.] 8°. Brentz, J. in off.
B78 ZC2.6.9.
1533 [col. Aug.] 4°. Luther, M. ex
off. L64 C.2.3.

Seltz, Guilelmus
1528 (7 Sep.) 8°. Wilramnus.
excusum. W44 D.2.7(b).

Setzer, Johann, *see* Secer [Setzer],
Johann

No printer identified
[*c.* 1525] 8°. Bugenhagen, J. B116
C.5.11(b). [Place of publication
and date from VD16 B9351.]
1536 8°. Smaragdus. S63 E.6.9(c).

Hall[e] [Halae Suevorum]

Brubach, Petrus
1536 (men. Aug.) 8°. Luther, M. ex
off. L57 D.5.5(c).
1538 (Mar.) 8°. Luther, M. ex off.
L67 E.6.29(a).
1539 (mense aug.) 8°. Corvinus, A.
C102 A.6.31.
1544 8°. Brentz, J. ex off. B91 H.2.7.

Frentz[ius], Petrus, & Brubacchius,
Petrus
>1545 fol. Brentz, J. excudebant. B84
>G.3.8(a).
>
>1545 8°. Melanchthon, P. ex off. P.
>Frentz, impensis P. Brub. M53
>C.5.10(a).

Hamburg

Rhodus, Franciscus [Franz]
>[1536 col.] 8°. Rhegius, U. [col. in
>off.] R19 C.6.5(e).
>
>1536 [col. cal. Sep.] 8°. Rhegius, U.
>[col. apud.] R18 C.6.5(d).

Printer not identified
>1561 8°. Eitzen, P. von. E15
>ZC2.2.7(b). HAB conjectures
>Hamburg as place of printing,
>though printer not identified.
>But printer may have been
>Nicolaus Henricus (at Ursel),
>as E17 – another item by this
>author in the same volume.
>
>1561 8°. Eitzen, P. von. E16
>B.5.34(c). As E15, above.

Heidelberg

Agricola, Martinus
>1567 8°. Jonathan, *ben Uzziel*.
>excudebat. J15 D.6.5(a).

Harnisch, Matthaeus
>1576 8°. Boquinus, P. impensis.
>B56 K.1.27(b).

Meyer, Johann, *aus Regensburg*
>1566 12°. Heidelberg. Catechesis.
>H14 K.3.31(d). Printer from VD16.
>
>1575 8°. Cureus, J. [col. excude-
>bat.] C123 K.1.27(a).
>
>1576 8°. Boquinus, P. excudebat …
>impensis M. Harnisch. B56
>K.1.27(b).

Schirat, Michael
>1566 4°. Maulbrunn Colloquy. [col.
>excudebat.] M18 I.4.5(a).

Ingolstadt

Ex officina Weissenhorniana
>1544 8°. Cochlaeus, J. [col. ex off.]
>C90 ZC2.6.17.
>
>1567 4°. Ingolstadt, *Univ. of.* ex off.
>I4 D.1.4(b).
>
>1568 4°. Torres, H. ex typographia.
>T16 D.1.4(a).

Weissenhorn, *Brothers*
>1565 4°. Sperling, A. excudebant
>VVeissenhornij fratres. S81
>ZC2.3.9(b).

Weissenhorn, Alexander (I)
>1540 4°. Cochlaeus, J. C89 L.4.30(a).
>Printer from HAB.
>
>1541 4°. Placentius, C. excudebat.
>P37 I.7.6(b).
>
>1543 4°. Eck, J. excudebat. E8A
>I.7.6(e).
>
>1544 4°. Cochlaeus, J. apud. C91
>L.4.30(b).
>
>1544 4°. Cochlaeus, J. excudebat.
>C92 L.4.30(c).
>
>[1544 4°. Cochlaeus, J. ex off. ★C11
>ZC1.2.15(a).]
>
>[1545 (Ian.) 4°. Cochlaeus, J.
>excudebat. ★C8 ZC1.2.15(b).]
>
>1546 8°. Hofmeister, J. excudebat.
>H67 ZC2.8.1(d). Printer from
>VD16.
>
>1546 4°. Rome. City of. ex off. R37
>ZC2.3.11(b).

Weissenhorn, Alexander (III)
>1570 4°. Macer, C. excudebat. M1
>L.5.8(c).

Weissenhorn, Alexander, &
Weissenhorn, Samuel
>1563 4°. Cardillo, G. per. C40
>B.5.5(a).
>
>1565 8°. Eisengrein, M. [col.
>excudebant.] E11 ZC2.6.11(c).
>
>1565 8°. Eisengrein, M. [col.
>excudebant.] E12 ZC2.6.11(d).
>
>1566 8°. Eisengrein, M. excude-
>bant. E14 ZC2.5.10(b).

Ingolstadt, Weissenhorn, Alexander, & Weissenhorn, Samuel, *continued*

    1566 4°. Gamaren, H. de. excudebant. G7 L.5.8(d).

Jena

Gera [Geranus], Ernst von [Ernestus]
    1573 8°. Heshusius, T. typis. H47 D.4.6(a).

Huttich, Günther, Widow of
    1572 4°. Heshusius, T. ex off. typographica. H46 ZC2.3.16.

Rebart[us], Thomas
    1567 8°. Selneccer, N. ex off. S43 D.4.7.
    1567 8°. Selneccer, N. excudebat. S44 G.6.2(a).
    [?1567] 8°. Wigand, J. W26 ZC2.2.4(d). Printer uncertain. A quarto edition was printed by Thomas Rebart at Jena in 1560 (HAB).

Richtzenhan, Donat[us]
    1567 8°. Chemnitz, M. ex off. C63 N.6.10(b).
    1570 4°. Altenburg, Colloquium of. A24 I.7.7(b).
    1572 8°. Heshusius, T. ex off. typographica. H49 ZC1.4.3(a).

Königsberg [Regiomontus]

Daubmann[us], Iohann [Hans], Heirs of
    1575 8°. Wigand, J. [col. typis … impensis C. Hoffmanni.] W20 C.4.5(a).

Hoffmann, Christoph
    1575 8°. Wigand, J. [col. typis haeredum I. Daubmanni, impensis C. Hoffmanni.] W20 C.4.5(a).

Lausanne

Le Preux, Franciscus [François]
    1575 8°. Aretius, B. excudebat. A51 ZC2.7.1.

Leipzig

Blum, Michael
    1534 4°. Haner, J. [col. excudebat.] H5 I.7.6(c).
    1535 4°. Vehe, M. [col. apud.] V7 ZC2.3.17.
    1544 8°. Spangenberg, J. excusit. S80 ZC2.2.9(a).
    1550 8°. Alesius, A. A21 G.6.22(b).

Faber, Nicolaus
    1533 4°. Witzel, G. excudebat. W50 I.7.6(a).
    [1534 (col. Jun.) 4°. Cochlaeus, J. [col. excudebat.] *C9 L.5.24.]
    1536 [MS 1546.] 8°. Witzel, G. W57 ZC2.2.8(c).

Hantzsch, Georg[ius]
    1554 [col. 1553] 8°. Brentz, J. in off. B79 G.6.4(b).

Lotter [Lotther], Melchior (I)
    1516 (prid. kal. Ian.) 4°. Basil. B8 I.4.10(b).
    1537 8°. Witzel, G. W53 ZC2.6.10(a).

Rhambau, Hans (I)
    1569 8°. Camerarius, J. [col. excudebat.] C27 L.6.27.
    1569 fol. Selneccer, N. [col. excudebat.] S42 G.4.5.

Schmidt, Nickel *see* Faber, Nicolaus

Schneider, Andreas, typis Voegelianis
    1571 (Ded. 25 June) 8°. Siber, A. imprimebat. S54 D.4.6(b).
    1572 8°. Camerarius, J. [col. imprimebat.] C24 ZC2.7.5(e).
    1572 4°. Camerarius, J. [col. exprimebatur per.] Edito Lips. procurante. C26 D.1.5(a).

Schumann, Valentin
  [1529 (10 Maias Cal.) 4°. Cochlaeus,
    J. impressit. *C10 L.5.23.]

Voegeliana [Vögelin]
  1562 8°. Novissima confessio –
    Wittenberg Concord [Bucer].
    W48 ZC2.5.7(a).
  1563 [col.] 8°. Catechesis. in off. C51
    ZC2.7.7(b).
  [?1567] 8°. Weller, H. in off. W5
    G.6.2(b).
  1568 8°. Camerarius, J. [typis.] C22
    D.6.1(c).
  1568 8°. Camerarius, J. [typis.] C23
    D.6.1(d).
  1572 (Ded. 25 June) 8°. Siber, A.
    imprimebat A. Schneider, typis.
    S54 D.4.6(b).
  1572 8°. Camerarius, J. typis. [col.
    imprimebat A. Schneider.] C24
    ZC2.7.5(e).
  1572 8°. Luther, M. characteribus.
    L71 ZC2.7.5(b).

Voegelin [Vögelin], Ernst
  [c. 1560] 8°. Hemmingsen, N. in off.
    H35 ZC2.7.7(a).
  1562 8°. Hemmingsen, N. in off.
    H37 ZC2.7.6(a).
  [c. 1562] 8°. Hemmingsen, N.
    (device.) H24 D.6.10(a).
  1564 8°. Theodoret. [col. in off.] T6
    ZC2.5.3(b).
  1564 (Jul. 14) 8°. Salmuth, H. S8
    M.2.35(c). Printer from VD16.
  [c. 1564] 8°. Hemmingsen, N.
    (device.) H25 C.4.10(a).
  1569 fol. Strigelius, V. [col. in off.]
    S92 G.4.1(c).
  1571 8°. Hemmingsen, N. H37
    ZC2.7.5(a). Printer from VD 16
    ZV 7660, but [Copenhagen:
    Baltzer Kaus] according to HAB
    and COPAC.
  1572 4°. Camerarius, J. Edito
    denuo, procurante. C25 D.1.5(b).
  1572 4°. Camerarius, J. Edito Lips.
    procurante. C26 D.1.5(a).

[1574] 8°. Hemmingsen, N. in off.
    H39 K.3.41(a).

Wolrab, Nicolaus
  1537 8°. Witzel, G. per. W56
    ZC2.6.10(c).
  1540 8°. Rivius, J. apud. R34
    D.6.7(a).
  1542 8°. Schenck, J. excudebat. S36
    E.6.26(b).

Lisbon [Olyssippone]

Corre[i]a, Franciscus [Francisco]
  [1572 col. Ian.22] 8°. Osorio da
    Fonseca, J. ex off. I. Hispani [col.
    excudebat F. Correa.] O25 I.2.10.

Despanha [Hispanus], João [Joannes]
  [1572 col. Ian.22] 8°. Osorio da
    Fonseca, J. ex off. [col. excude-
    bat F. Correa.] O25 I.2.10.

London

Berthelet, Thomas
  1534 4°. Fox, E. in aedibus. F31
    L.5.29.
  [1544 4°. Pia et catholica christiani
    hominis institution. *P5 [K.2.20].]

Byddell, John
  [1536] 4°. Bible. Com. II & III
    John. per me. B39 D.2.8(b).

Bynneman, Henry
  1567 [col. Nov.24] 4°. Nowell, A.
    imprinted ... by. N13 T.6.4(a).
  [1572 4°. Whitgift, J. [for H. Toy]
    *W1 O.1.5.]
  1574 fol. Whitgift, J. Imprinted ...
    by, for H. Toye. W16 T.3.8.

Cawood, John
  1554 (10 May) 8°. Watson, T.
    imprinted ... by. W2 O.2.46.
  [1555] 4°. Bonner, E. in aedibus.
    B54 O.1.10(a).
  1555 4°. Bonner, E. by. B55
    O.1.10(b).

London, *continued*

Day, John
1564 (19 Feb.) 4°. Councils – Trent.
Decrees. Imprinted by. C109
T.6.4(b).
[1571 4°. Bullinger, H. apud. *B14
L.5.21.]

Day, John, & Seres, William
[1548] 8°. Hermann. Imprinted ...
by. H42 O.1.25.

Denham, Henry
[1565 4°. Calfhill, J. for L. Harry-
son. *C1 O.1.17.]

Grafton, Richard
[?1548] 4°. Aepinus, J. A11 I.4.4(b).

Harrison, Luke [Lucas]
[1565 4°. Calfhill, J. H. Denham, for.
*C1 O.1.17.]

Her[t]ford, John
[1546 8°. Gardiner, S. [col. J.
Herforde, at the costes and
charges of R. Toye.] *G1 R.6.19.]
1545 8°. Smith, R. by ... at the
costes and charges of R. Toye.
S64 R.6.46.

Myerdmann[us], Stephen
1552 (Apr.) 8°. Lasco, J. à. per. L10
H.2.11.

Purfoot, Thomas
1574 (Pridie cal. Iun.) 8°. Corro, A.
de. excudebat. C101 E.6.34.

Pynson, House of
1521/1522 4°. Henry VIII. in
aedibus. H40 N.5.13(a–c).

Pynson, Richard
1523 4°. More, T. M81 N.5.13(d).

Tisdale, John
1561 (11 May) 8°. Veron, J. V20
O.2.47(b).
1561 (11 May) 8°. Veron, J. V21
O.2.47(a).

Toy[e], Humphrey [Humfrey]
1574 fol. Whitgift, J. Imprinted ...
by H. Binneman, for H. Toye
W16 T.3.8.

Toy[e], Robert
1546 8°. Smith, R. by J. Herforde at
the costes and charges of. S64
R.6.46.

Whitchurch, Edward
[1551 fol. Erasmus, D. printed ...
by. *E1 R.3.13.]

Wolf, Rayner [Reginald]
1553 8°. Catechism [Ponet]. apud.
C52 H.2.15.

Wykes [Wekes], Henry
1565 fol. Jewel, J. Imprinted at ...
by. J8 T.3.3(a).
1566 4°. Horne, R. Imprinted at ...
by. H77 O.2.2.
1566 4°. Nowell, A. Imprinted ...
by. N14 O.1.16.
1567 (27 Oct.) fol. Jewel, J.
Imprinted ... by. J7 T.3.3(b).

Louvain

Bathen, Iacobus
1551 (ipso die qui coenae Dominicae est sacer.) 8°. Costerius, J.
[col. typis.] C105 ZC2.6.2.

Berga[i]gne, Antonius Maria
[1554 (In die Cinerum) fol. Bononia,
J. à. ex off. *B11 L.4.32.]
1556 8°. Sasbout, A. prostant apud.
S27 E.6.22.

Birckmann, Arnold, Heirs of
1562 fol. Hof[f]meister, J. sumptibus (excudebat vidua S. Sasseni.)
H63 G.4.2.

Birckmann, Arnold, Heirs of,
& Bohemus, Franciscus, &
sociorum
1565 8°. Wild, J. excudebat S.
Sassenus, sumptibus haeredum
A. Birckmanni & F. Bohemi &
soc. W27 D.5.10.

Bogard, Jan [Ioannis]
[1562 8°. Hessels, J. apud [col. typis
S. Valerii.] *H3 ZC2.8.14(a).]
[1562 8°. Hessels, J. apud [col. typis
S. Valerii.] *H5 ZC2.8.14(b).]

[1562 8°. Smith, R. apud. [col. typis S. Valerij.] *S4 L.6.10(a).]

[1562 8°. Smith, R. apud. *S5 L.6.10(d).]

[1562 8°. Smith, R. apud. [col. typis S. Valerij.] *S7 L.6.10(c).]

[1562 8°. Smith, R. apud. *S8 L.6.10(b).]

1563 8°. Hessels, J. ex off. H55 L.6.15.

[1563 8°. Smith, R. ex off. *S6 L.6.28(a).]

1564 8°. Mermannius, A. ex off. M69 ZC2.4.14(a).

1564 8°. Mermannius, A. ex off. M70 ZC2.4.14(b).

1564 8°. Mermannius, A. ex off. M71 ZC2.4.14(e).

[1565 8°. Baius, M. ex off. *B1 L.6.28(b).]

1566 8°. Baius, M. apud. B4 I.1.5(d).

1566 8°. Mermannius, A. apud. M72 ZC2.6.11(a).

1566 8°. Mermannius, A. apud. M73 ZC2.6.11(b).

1567 8°. Hessels, J. apud. H54 I.1.6(b).

1567 8°. Sonnius, F. apud. S69 I.1.5(b).

1568 8°. Hessels, J. apud. H52 C.3.8(b).

[1571/1572 8°. Hessels, J. apud. [col. typis I. Heybergii, 1572] *H4 ZC2.6.1.]

Colonaeus [Colonia], Petrus [a]
1554 8°. Gardiner, S. apud [col. typis R. Velpij.] G14 K.1.31.

Fowler [Fouler], John [Joannes], *Anglus*
1567 4°. Harding, T. apud. H8 O.1.12.

1567 4°. Stapleton, T. apud. S85 O.1.13.

1569 8°. Sander(s), N. apud. S10 G.6.6(e).

Gravius, Bartholomaeus
1533 (quarto Idus Iun.) fol. Driedo, J. a [col. ex off. R. Rescij] D28 L.2.13.

1546 fol. Driedo, J. ex off. D27 L.3.19.

1555 8°. Petrus, *Diaconus.* ex off. P21 A.6.28(a).

Gravius, Bartholomaeus, with Zangrius, Petrus
1563 8°. Baius, M. excudebat … suis sumptibus. B3 ZC2.4.14(c).

Gualther[i]us, Stephanus, & Batenius [Bathen], Joannes [Johann]
1554 4°. Gardiner, S. [col. ex off. typographica] (prostant apud I. VVaen Scotum.) G15 ZC2.3.7.

1554 4°. Nannius, P. ex off. typographica. N4 C.2.9(c).

Heyberghs, Jacob
[1571/1572 8°. Hessels, J. apud I. Bobardum [col. typis I. Heybergii, 1572.] *H4 ZC2.6.1.]

Martens [Martinus], Thierry [Theodoricus]
[*c.* 1517] 4°. Erasmus, D. E22 L.5.35(a).

Phalèse [Phalesius], Pierre [Petrus]
1551 (ipso die qui coenae Dominicae est sacer.) 8°. Costerius, J. apud. C105 ZC2.6.2.

Rescius, Rutger
1533 (quarto Idus Iun.) fol. Driedo, J. [col. ex off.] a B. Gravio. D28 L.2.13.

1534 [col. quinto Idus Mart.] 4°. Driedo, J. ex off. D26 N.5.5(a).

Sassenus [Zassenus], Servatius (I)
1546 (Mar.) 4°. Gardiner, S. G13 ZC2.3.11(c).

Sassenus [Zassenus], Servatius (I), Widow of
1562 fol. Hofmeister, J. excudebat … sumptibus haeredum A. Byrckmanni. H63 G.4.2.

Sassenus, Servatius (II)
1565 8°. Wild, J. excudebat … sumptibus haeredum A. Birckmanni & F. Bohemi & soc. W27 D.5.10.

Louvain, *continued*

Valerius, Stephanus
[1562 8°. Hessels, J. apud I.
Bogardum [col. typis S. Valerii.]
*H3 ZC2.8.14(a).]
[1562 8°. Smith, R. apud I. Bogardum [col. typis S. Valerij.] *S4
L.6.10(a).]
1563 12°. Augustine [col. ex off.]
A64 B.6.35(b).

Velpius, Rutger
1554 8°. Gardiner, S. [col. typis.]
(apud P. Colonaeum.) G14 K.1.31.

Velpius, Reinerus [Reyner]
1558 (Mar.) 8°. Orosius, P. apud M.
Verhasselt. [col. typis Reyneri
Velpij.] O23 B.6.16(c).

Verhasselt, Martin
[1555 fol. Tapper, R. apud. *T1
L.4.2.]
1558 (Mar.) 8°. Orosius, P. apud.
[col. typis R. Velpij.] O23
B.6.16(c).

Waen, Johann [*Scotus*]
1554 4°. Gardiner, S. prostant apud
[col. ex off. typographica S.
Gualtheri & I. Bathenii.] G15
ZC2.3.7.

Wellaeus [Well], Hieronymus
1563 12°. Augustine. apud. A64
B.6.35(b).
1568 8°. Usuardus. apud. U2
B.6.19(a).

Zangrius, Petrus [Peter], *Tiletanus*
1567 8°. Ravestyn, J. apud. R11
I.1.5(a).
1568 8°. Ravestyn, J. apud. R10
I.1.6(a).
1568/1570 8°. Ravestyn, J. apud. R9
B.5.9–10.
1569 4°. Jansen, C. apud. J3 E.5.5.
1569 4°. Jansen, C. apud. J4 E.5.4.

**Zangrius, Petrus [Peter], *Tiletanus*,
with Gravius, Bartholomaeus**
1563 8°. Baius, M. [excudebat.] B3
ZC2.4.14(c).

Zassenus, Servatius *see* **Sassenus,
Servatius (II)**

Lucerne

No printer identified
1528 (uigesima quinta Augusti.) 4°.
Murner, T. M86 I.3.10(a).

Lyon

Ausultus [Ausoult], Joannes [Jean]
1554 12°. Titelman, F. apud G.
Rouillium [col. excudebat I.
Ausultus.] T10 G.6.16(a).

Boyer[ius], Jacob[us] [Jacques]
1557 8°. Francisco. apud. F34 H.1.4.

Clein [Cleyn], Johann
1510 (id. Aprilis) 4°. Holcot, R.
impressi a. H72 L.5.9.

**Durye [Du R[o]y], Antoine
[Antonius]**
1527 [col. idibus Apr.] 8°. Vio, T.
de. [col. in edibus … sumptibus
J. de Giunta.] V33 K.3.42.
1528 4°. Bible. per. (impensis F.
Turchi, & D. Berticinium, & I. de
Giuntis.) B30 E.5.18.

Faure, Jacobus [Jacques]
1554 16°. Titelman, F. [col. excu-
debat] (apud I. F. de Gabiano.)
T14 ZC2.8.2(b).
1556 8°. Euthymius. [col. excudebat.] (apud S. B. Honorati.) E59
A.6.25.

Frellon, Joannes [Jean] (II)
1555 8°. Vives, J. L. apud [col. M.
Sylvii typis.] V38 Z.5.121.
1556 8°. Lycosthenes, C. apud. [col.
excudebat M. Syluius.] L82
M.2.43.

**Frellon, Joannes [Jean], & Fran-
ciscus [François] fratres**
1544 8°. Campeggio, L. [Col.
excudebant.] C28 B.6.4(c).
1544 8°. Cologne. Canones. [col.
Excudebant.] C98 B.6.4(a).
1544 8°. Cologne. Enchiridion. [col.
Excudebant.] C99 B.6.4(b).

[1545 16°. Rome. Cancellaria
Apostolica. [col. excudebant.] *R3
Z.5.32.]

Gabiano, Joannis Franciscus [Jean-
François] de
1554 16°. Titelman, F. apud [col.
excudebat I. Faure.] T14
ZC2.8.2(b).
1559 8°. Wild, J. apud. W36
D.4.5(b).

Gaspar à Portonariis *see* Portonariis, Gaspard de

Giunta, Jacobus [Jacques] de
1527 [col. idibus Apr.] 8°. Vio, T.
de. sumptibus. [col. in edibus A.
du Roy.] V33 K.3.42 .

Giunta, Jacobus [Jacques], &
François] de, ac sociorum
1520 (kal. Apr.) 8°. Duns, J. sumptu
… (excusus in edibus
J. Myt.) D34 L.6.32.
1523 (15 Jan.) 8°. Mazzolini, S.
[col. impensisq[ue]] (opera J.
Houdouart & B. Bonnyn.) M23
D.3.14.

Gryphius, Sebastien (I)
1536 fol. Sadoleto, J. excudebat. S3
G.3.21.
1537 8°. Primasius. apud. P53 D.1.8.
1541 8°. Ravisius, J. apud. R12
X.2.17–18.
1544 8°. Bible. Com. Rom. & Gal.
apud. B38 C.4.14.
1555 8°. Folengius, J.B. apud. F27
C.3.8(a).

Honorat, Barthélemy
1556 8°. Euthymius. apud. [col.
excudebat I. Faure.] E59 A.6.25.

Houdouart, Joannes [Jean], &
Bonyn, Benedictus [Benoît]
1524 (15 Jan.) 8°. Mazzolini, S.
opera … impens. (J. q. f. de
Giunta ac soc.) M23 D.3.14.

Huguetan, Jean (I)
1515 (col. xvij mensis Augusti.) 4°.
Jerome. abs. [col. per J. Myt.] J6
L.4.31.

1523 4°. Angelus, de Clavasio. in
edibus. A39 L.5.33.

Moylin, Jean
1523 (20 Mar.) 4°. Angelus, de
Clavasio. [col. excusa in edibus.]
A39 L.5.33.

Myt, Jacques [Jacobus]
1515 [col. xvij mensis Augusti.] 4°.
Jerome. abs J. Huguetan. [col.
per.] J6 L.4.31.
1520 (kal. Apr.) 8°. Duns, J. excusus
in edibus … sumptu … I. & F.
de Giunta & soc. D34 L.6.32.

Payen [Paganus], Thibaud
[Theobaldus]
1557 8°. Resende, L. A. de. apud.
R15 ZC2.2.2(a–b).

Petit, Nicolas, & Penet, Hector
[1534 8°. Petrus, *Comestor*. [col.
apud.] *P3 L.6.2.]

Portonariis, Gaspard de [à]
1558 8°. Vio, T. de. apud. V30
D.5.11.
1558 8°. Vio, T. de. apud. V31
D.5.12.

Rollet[ius], Philibert[us], &
Fraenus [Frein], Bartholomaeus
[Barthélemy]
1548 8°. Titelman, F. apud. G.
Rouillium [col. pt. 2 excudebant
P. Rolletius et B. Fraenus.] T11
C.5.15.

Rouillé, Guillaume [Gulielmus] (I)
1548 8°. Titelman, F. apud. [col. pt.
2 excudebant P. Rolletius et B.
Fraenus.] T11 C.5.15.
1554 12°. Titelman, F. apud [col.
excudebat I. Ausultus.] T10
G.6.16(a).
1555 12°. Titelman, F. apud. T12
G.6.16(b).
1558 16°. Titelman, F. apud. T15
ZC2.8.2(a).
1564 16°. Bernard. apud. B16
A.6.37.
1564 4°. Rome, Church of, Index.
apud. R36 ZC2.3.3(b).

Lyon, Rouillé, Guillaume, *continued*

[1570 16°. Bernard. apud. *B4 A.6.36.]

Silvius [Sylvius], Michael
1555 8°. Vives, J. L. [col. M. Sylvii typis.] (apud I. Frellonium.) V38 Z.5.121.
1556 8°. Lycosthenes, C. [col. excudebat.] (apud I. Frellonium.) L82 M.2.43.
[1567 8°. Petit, G., *Neubrigensis*. ex officina. *P2 B.5.39.]

Tournes, Jean de (I), & Gazeau, Guillaume
1553 16°. Prudentius. apud. P57 A.6.35.
[1558 8°. Erasmus, D. apud. *E3 N.6.37.]

Trechsel, Melchior & Gaspard
[1532 8°. Bible. Lat. Vulg. ex off. *B7 C.3.13.]

Turchus [Turchi], Franciscus [François], & Bertus [Bertieinius], Dominicus [Dominique], & Giunta, Jacobus [Jacques] de
1528 4°. Bible. impensis (per A. du Ry.) B30 E.5.18.

Vincent, Antoine
1551 8°. Du Moulin, C. D30 ZC2.5.1(a). Printer suggested by HAB. CLC suggests Paris as place of printing (*see under* Printer not identified).

Vingle, Jean de
[1497 col. 28 Jan.] 4°. Philippus, J., *de Bergamo*. per. P25 L.5.1.

No printer identified
1540 8°. Gulielmus, *Baufeti*. G47 ZC2.6.12.

Magdeburg

Gisecke[n], Matthias
1569 8°. Saccus, S. excusum a. S1 M.2.26(b).

Lotter, Michael
1549 8°. Flacius, M. [col. excude- bat.] F12 ZC2.8.10(b).
[1550] 4°. Amsdorff, N von. per. A28 L.5.22.

Printer not identified
1561 8°. Heshusius, T. H48 ZC2.2.8(a).

Mainz

Behem, Franciscus [Franz]
1541 4°. Cochlaeus, J. excusum … apud S.Victorem, in officina typographica. C88 L.4.30(d).
1544 4°. Hofmeister, J. [col. ad Diuum Victorem excudebat.] H66 ZC2.3.12(c).
1544 4°. Hofmeister, J. [col. ad Diuum Victorem in off. typo- graphica.] H69 L.5.8(e).
1544 4°. Hofmeister, J. [col. ad Diuum Victorem in off. typo- graphica.] H70 ZC2.3.12(d).
1549 (5 Apr.) 8°. Cochlaeus, J. [col. Apud S. Victorem … excudebat.] C86 ZC2.7.13(b).
1550 4°. Wild, J. apud D. Victorem, excudebat. W30 D.1.12(a).
1550 4°. Wild, J. apud D.Victorem, excudebat. W31 D.1.12(b) .
1550 [col.Sep.] fol. Wild, J. apud Diuum Victorem, excudebat. W34 G.2.14.
1556 8°. Wild, J. [col. excudebat.] W29 G.6.6(c).
1556 8°. Wild, J. excudebat. W33 G.6.6(b).
1559 8°. Hofmeister, J. excudebat. H68 ZC2.5.8(a).
1561 fol. Wild, J. apud. W40 L.3.18.

Schoeffer, Ivo
1536 (mense sep.) 8°. Lorich, G. excusum expensis autoris. L38 M.2.11
1542 4°. Marius, A. M10 ZC2.3.12(a). Printer from VD 16.

Marburg

Cervicornus, Eucharius
1537 8°. Corvinus, A. apud. C104
D.6.7(e).

Egenolff, Christian
1540 (col. Mar.) 8°. Draconites, J.
[pt. 1.] D23 D.5.5(a).
1543 8°. Draconites, J. [col. pt. 2 in
off.] D23 D.5.5(a).

Kolb, Andreas
1544 (Aug.) 8°. Draconites, J. D24
C.5.8(c). Printer from HAB.

Kolb [Colb], Andreas, Heirs of
1569 8°. Hamelmann, H. apud. H3
N.6.11(b).

Rhode, Franz
1528 [col. 14 kal. Aug.] 8°. Buschius, H. B137 D.6.7(f). Printer
from CLC.
1531 8°. Luther, M. L76 ZC2.6.18(a).

Meldis [Meaux]

Colinaeus [Colines], Simon
[1522 col. (Jun.)] fol. Le Fèvre, J.
[col. impensis.] L22 G.4.6.

Milan

Ferrariis, Johannes Jacobus [de]
1509 (13 Sep.) 4°. Duns, J. per. D32
ZC2.3.15.

Mühlhausen

Hantsch, Georg
[1570 8°. Stigelius, J. excudebat. *S9
L.6.20.]

Neuburg ad Danubium [on the Danube]

Kilian[us], Johann [Hans]
1546 (6 Apr.) 4°. Bucer, M. [col.
apud.] B108 I.4.4(a).

Nuremberg

Aich, Leonardus de
1528 8°. Althamer, A. impensis
(excud. F.Peypus) A26 D.2.6(d).

**Berg [Montanus], Johann vom, &
Neuber, Ulrich**
[c. 1545] 8°. Luther, M. [col.
excudebant.] L54 E.6.27.
1550 8°. Culman, L. [col. in off.]
C122 M.2.36.
1550 8°. Culman, L. [col. in off.]
C122 M.2.37.
1550 8°. Culman, L. [col. in off.]
C122 M.2.38.
1556 8°. Luther, M. [col. apud.] L70
ZC1.4.10(a).
1560 fol. Weller, H. excudebant.
W3 G.3.15(b).
1561 8°. Weller, H. apud. W4
D.6.6(a).
1561 8°. Rabus, L. [col. apud.] R4
D.6.11.
1562 8°. Weller, H. in off. W6
K.1.7(b).

**Berg [Montanus], Johann vom,
Heirs of, & Neuber, Ulrich**
1562 8°. Nopper, H. apud. N11
M.2.35(d).

Daubman, Hans
1548 8°. Culman, L. apud. C120
M.2.29.

Guldenmundt, Joannes
1536 8°. Valliculus, G. apud. V4
D.6.7(c).

Koberger
1520 [col.] fol. Fulgentius. [col.]
impensis. In off. T. Anshelmi
[Hagenau.] F38 A.5.3(b).

Koberger, Anton (I)
1485 (8 id. Feb.) fol. Vincent.
impensis. V27 Z.1.62.
[1498–1502] fol. Hugo, de Sancto
Charo. [J. Amerbach (Basle) for.]
H82 L.2.1.

Nuremberg, *continued*

Koberger, Johann

1520 (7 Mar.) fol. Herolt, J. sumptibus ... J. Kobergers (in off. J. Stuchs.) H43 L.4.14.

Montanus, Joannes, & Neuber, Ulrich *see* Berg, Johann vom, &c.

Neuber, Ulrich, & Berg [Montanus], Johann vom, Heirs of *see* Berg, &c.

1564 8°. Nopper, H. apud. N11 M.2.35(d).

Neuber, Valentin

[*c.* 1550] 8°. Culman, L. apud. C118 H.1.29(d).
[1550] 8°. Culman, L. [col. apud.] C121 H.1.29(c).

Petreius, Johann

1523 8°. Melanchthon, P. M50 D.6.3(b).
1523 [col. Nov.] 8°. Lambert, F. apud. L4 C.5.6(a).
1524 8°. Lambert, F. apud. L2 C.1.5(b).
1524 8°. Oecolampadius, J. apud. O16 C.1.3(b).
1524 8°. Venatorius, T. V8 ZC2.6.18(h).
1524 [col. Oct.] 8°. Bugenhagen, J. [col. apud.] B111 D.3.1(a).
[*c.* 1524] 8°. Oecolampadius, J. [device.] O12 C.1.3(a).
1525 8°. Lambert, F. per. L3 C.5.6(b).
1525 [col.] 8°. Lambert, F. apud. L9 H.1.6(b).
1525 (Feb.) 8°. Lambert, F. L7 H.1.6(a).
1527 (Mense Ian.) 8°. Pirckheimer, B. P36 ZC2.6.6. Printer from HAB.
[1534 4°. Venatorius, T. apud. *V2 C.2.5.]
1536 8°. Althamer, A. apud. A27 D.6.12.

Peypus, Friedrich

1528 8°. Althamer, A. excud. (impensis L. de Aich.) A26 D.2.6(d).

Stuchs, Johann

1520 (7 Mar.) fol. Herolt, J. in off. ... sumptibus ... J. Kobergers. H43 L.4.14.

Oberursel *see* Ursel[lius]

Padua

Galassi [Gallassius], Marc'Antonio

1564 4°. Theodoret. apud. [col. apud L. Pasquatium.] T5 A.6.3.

Pasquato, Lorenzo

1564 4°. Theodoret. apud. M. A. Gallassium [col. apud L. Wetzler Pasquatium.] T5 A.6.3.

Paris

Ascensius, House of [in aedibus]

1514 fol. Cusa, N. de. in aedibus [col. ex off.] C125 L.4.7.
1514 fol. Cusa, N. de. in aedibus [col. ex off.] C125 L.4.8(a).
[1514] fol. Cusa, N. de. in aedibus. C126 L.4.8(b).
1520 [col. Aug.] fol. Philo. in aedibus. [col. sub prelo.] P27 A.5.3(c).

Badius, Jodocus [Josse], *Ascensius*

[1515 col. (ad sextum id. April)] fol. Pérez de Valentia, J. P18 G.3.16.
1520 (id.Feb.) fol. Badius, J. B2 A.5.3(d).
1520 (ad idus Nov.) fol. Basil. venund. eisdem Ascens. [col. impressa impens. & recogn.] B6 A.4.7(a).
1521 [col. kal.Iun.] fol. Bede. vaenundatur I. Badio Ascensio, & I. Paruo [col. in off. I. Badii.] B10 A.4.7(b).
[1526 fol. Beda, N. Vaenundantur Badio [col. in typographia I. Badii.] *B3 G.2.3.]
[1531 col. Jul.] fol. Paris, Univ. of. sub Prelo. P5 N.3.18(e).

Badius, Jodocus [Josse], & Petit [Parvus], Jean
  1519 [col. Tom. 4: id. Febr.] fol. Origen. venundantur ... in edibus (Tom. 1–3); in aedibus Ascensianis (Tom. 4). O20 A.4.1–2.
  1521 [col. kal. Iun.] fol. Bede. vaenundatur. [col. in off. I. Badii.] B10 A.4.7(b).
  1522 [col. ad Idus Feb.] fol. Bede. vaenundatur. [col. in chalcographia ... impensis communibus ipsius.] B11 A.4.19.
  [1526] fol. Hugo, *de Sancto Victore.* [Quae omnia vaenundantur.] H85 L.1.8.
  1526 [col. ad idus Oct.] fol. Hugo, *de Sancto Victore.* Quae omnia vaenundantur [col. typis I. Badii.] H86 L.1.9.

Badius, Jodocus [Josse], & Roigny, Jean [Ioannis de]
  [1534 fol. Castro, A. de. Vaenundantur. *C6 L.2.22.]

Bellovisiana, House of
  1504 (Idibus Iuliis) fol. Heracleides. [col. ex off. ... impensis I. Parui] [device of I. Petit.] H41 A.5.7.

Bene-natus, Joannes
  1569 8°. Génébrard, G. apud. G20 N.6.10(c).

Bogard[us], Jacob [Jacques]
  1542 8°. Nonnus. apud. N10 N.6.11(d).

Bonhomme, Yolande, Widow of Kerver, Thielman (I) *see* Kerver, Thielman (I), Widow of (Bonhomme, Yolande)

Bonnemère, Antoine
  [*c.* 1507] fol. Paulus. impressum me ... expensis ... I. frellon [with device of F. Regnault.] P13 L.4.34.

Cavellat, Gulielmus [Guillaume]
  1549 16°. Ceneau, R. apud. C55 ZC1.4.13(c).

Charron, Jean
  1567 8°. Patrizi, F. ex off. P8 ZC1.5.4.

Chaudière, Guillaume
  1567 fol. Byzantine History. apud. B138 Z.2.19.

Chesnau, Nicola[u]s
  1565 8°. Horantius, F. apud. H76 K.2.18

Chevallon, Claude
  1523 [col. decimosexto calendes martias.] fol. Gregory I. apud (with device of B. Rembolt) [col. apud ... ipsius impensis.] G31 A.1.15.

Chevallon, Claude, Widow of *see* Guillard, Carola, Chevallon, Claude, Widow of, & Des Bois, Guillaume

Colinaeus [Colines], Simon [de]
  1523 4°. Campester, L. in aedibus. C31 ZC2.3.14(b).
  1523 4°. Campester, L. in aedibus. C30 ZC2.3.14(c).
  1524 fol. Clichtoveus, J. ex off. C82 N.3.17.
  1524/1526 [pt. 2 ix. cal. Dec. 1526] 16°. Bible. ex off. [pt. 2 apud. col. Imprimebat.] B35 G.6.14.
  1526 [pt. 2 ix. cal. Dec.] 16°. Bible. ex off. [pt. 2 apud.] B34 G.6.12.
  [1526 [col. 9 Mar.] 4°. Clichtoveus, J. ex [col. in.] *C7 H.1.19.]
  1529 [pt. 2 July, 1528] 16°. Bible. ex off. [pt. 2 apud.] B33 G.6.13.
  1529 [xi. cal. Maii] 16°. Bible. ex off. B32 G.6.11.
  1529 (4 Sep.) fol. Sens, Council. ex off. S46 N.3.18(d).
  1532 16°. Bible. in off. B31 G.6.10.
  1532 (13 Mar.) fol. Sens, Council. ex off. S47 N.3.18(c).
  1534 [col. 1533 (Dec.)] 4°. Viexmontis, C. apud. V23 N.5.5(b).
  1540 [col. Jan.] fol. Arboreus, J. apud. A49 M.1.17.

David, Matthaeus [Mathieu]
1556 4°. Camerarius, J. ex typographia. C21 L.5.3.

De la Barre *see* La Barre, Nicolas
de

Desboys [Des Bois], Gulielmus
[Guillaume] *see* Guillard, Carola,
Chevallon, Claude, Widow of,
& Des Bois, Guillaume

Des Prez [Pratis], Nicolaus
[Nicolas de]
[1513 (21 Iun.) fol. Duns, J. a. [col.
pt.2: opera N. de pratis pro I.
Granion.]*D8 L.4.19–20(a).]
1516 (5 Julij) fol. Gulielmus, *Avernus.*
in off. G46 L.4.22. Title-page
compartment with the initials
NDP.

Du Pré, Galliot, à Prato, & Roigny,
Jean de [Ioannes]
1538 (14 cal. April) 16°. Clichtoveus
apud. [col. in off. Oliverij Mal-
lardi, impens.] C83 K.3.13(a).

Du Puys, Jacques (I)
1550 8°. Mainz. apud. M7 B.5.16.

Estienne [Stephanus], Henricus
[Henri] (I)
1510 [col. 19 Iulij.] 4°. Richard, *St
Victor.* [col. ex off.] R26 I.4.9(a).
1512 (Nonis Feb.) fol. John, *of
Damascus.* ex off. J13 L.4.5.
1513 [col.] 4°. Clichtoveus, J. in off.
C84 I.4.9(b).
1515 fol. Le Fèvre, J. ex off. L23
G.4.7(a).
1517 (Oct. decim. die) 4°. Hugo, *de
Sancto Victore.* in off. H87
L.5.36(b).
1518 4°. Le Fèvre, J. ex off. L25
L.5.36(a).
1519 (4 No. Maii) 4°. Erasmus, D.
apud ... expensis C. [Resch]. E26
L.5.35(b–c).
1519 [col. Jul.] fol. Theodoret. in
off. T7 A.5.3(a).

Estienne [Stephanus], Robert[us]
(I)
[1532 fol. Bible.Lat. ex off. *B8
E.1.18.]
[1549 4°. Giovio, P. ex off. *G5
ZC1.2.4.]

Foucher [Foucherius], Jean [Ioannes]
1555 8°. Hofmeister, J. apud. H62
G.5.15(a).

Frellon, Jean (I)
[c. 1507] fol. Paulus. impressum
me A. bonne mere expensis ...
I. frellon [with device of F.
Regnault.] P13 L.4.34.

Frémy, Claude
1556 8°. Tavernarius, J. apud. T2
ZC2.6.3.
1560 8°. Fontaine, S. apud. F28
D.6.1(a).
1564 8°. Radulphus, A. apud. R5
D.4.1.
1567 8°. Fabricius, G. apud. F2
N.6.12(b).
1567 8°. Sainctes, C. de. apud. S7
N.6.12(a).
[1569 8°. Optatus. apud. *O4
B.6.14.]

Gaudoul, Pierre [Petrus]
1531 fol. Hugo, *de Sancto Charo.*
Prostat apud I. paruum [col. typis
et characteribus ... P. Vidouei,
impensis I. Parui, A. Gormontii,
P. le Preux ac P. Gaudoul.] H84
G.2.5.

Gaultier [Galterus], Pierre
[1546 fol. Aquinas, T. ex off. *A8
G.2.10.]

Gering, Ulrich
1478 (30 Oct.) 4°. Gulielmus,
Parisiensis. per. G49 L.5.10.

Girault [Gyrault], Ambrose
[Ambroise], & Petit, Jean
1531 [col. ad primas kal. Junij.] 8°.
Matthei, L. [impens. J. Petit et A.
girault.] M16 D.3.8.

Gourmont, Gilles de [Aegidius]
　　[1520] 4°. Lee, E. in edibus. L26
　　　　L.5.35 (d–e).
　　1531 fol. Hugo, *de Sancto Charo*.
　　　　Prostat apud I. paruum [col. typis
　　　　et characteribus ... P. Vidouei,
　　　　impensis I. Parui, A. Gormontii,
　　　　P. le Preux ac P. Gaudoul.] H84
　　　　G.2.5.

Granjon, Jean
　　[1513 (21 Iun.) fol. Duns, J. a. [col.
　　　　pt. 2: opera N. de pratis pro I.
　　　　Granion.] *D8 L.4.19–20(a).]
　　1517–1518 fol. Duns, J. a J. G.
　　　　bibliopola. D35 L.4.18.

Gualtherot, Viventius
　　1543 8°. Pighius, A. apud. P31
　　　　I.1.6(d).

Guillard, Charlotte [Carola]
　　1542 fol. Dionysius, C. in aedibus
　　　　[col. excud. I. Lodoycus Tile-
　　　　tanus.] D12 E.3.19(a).
　　1545 8°. Billick, E. apud. B50
　　　　ZC2.7.2.
　　1549 8°. Pighius, A. apud. P32
　　　　M.2.6.

Guillard, Charlotte, Chevallon,
　　Claude, Widow of, & Des Bois,
　　Guillaume
　　1548 8°. Florus. apud C. Guillard
　　　　viduam C. Chevallonii ... & G.
　　　　desbois. F26 M.2.21(b).

Guillard, Guillaume [Gulielmus],
　　& Warrencore [Warancore],
　　Almaric [Amaury]
　　1560 8°. Abdias. apud. A1 A.6.22(b).
　　[c. 1560] 4°. Liberinus, A. L29
　　　　I.5.5(b). Printer from CLC. Date
　　　　from Adams.
　　1562 [col. Aug.] fol. Benedictus, J.
　　　　apud [col. excudebat G. Guillart.]
　　　　B14 E.3.4.

Jouvenel [Iuvenis], Martin
　　[1550 4°. Mercerus, J. apud. *M3
　　　　F.2.30(b).]
　　1555 4°. Palladius. apud. P2 B.5.3.

1567 [col. 3 Id. Iul.] fol. Génébrard,
　　G. apud [col. excudebat.] G19
　　L.4.6(c).

Julian[us], Michael
　　1562 16°. Cochlaeus, J. apud. C85
　　　　ZC1.4.13(b).
　　1565 8°. Kling, C. apud. K9 I.1.7.

Juvenis, Martin[us] *see* Jouvenel
　　[Iuvenis], Martin

Kerver, Jacques
　　1543 4°. Antiochus. vaenundatur.
　　　　A43 C.2.13.
　　[1563 or 1564] 4°. Lefèvre, J. L27
　　　　ZC2.3.3(a).
　　1567 8°. Council of Trent. Cate-
　　　　chism. in aedibus [col. ex
　　　　typographia I. Le Blanc.]
　　　　C110 ZC2.2.10(a).

Kerver, Thielman (I)
　　1515 (23 Dec.) 8°. Raymond. apud
　　　　[ex off. ... expensis suis atque C.
　　　　Leporis.] R13 K.3.46.

Kerver, Thielman (I), Widow of
　　(Bonhomme, Yolande)
　　1528 8°. Jacobus, de Voragine.
　　　　Venundantur ... apud. J2 D.4.10.
　　　　Printed by the widow of Thiel-
　　　　man Kerver (Moreau, III, 1528,
　　　　no. 1525/6/7).
　　1536 8°. Ludolf. apud. [col. excudit
　　　　J. bonhomme uidua T. kerver.]
　　　　L48 L.6.7.

La Barre, Nicholas [Nicolas] de
　　1513 8°. William, *of Ockham*. in
　　　　edibus [col. in edibus.] W41
　　　　ZC2.1.12.

Le Blanc, Jean [Joannes] (I)
　　1567 8°. Council of Trent. Cate-
　　　　chism. [col. ex typographici.]
　　　　in aedibus J. Kerver. C110
　　　　ZC2.2.10(a).

Le Lièvre [Leporis], Constantin
　　1516 (23 Dec.) 8°. Raymond. apud
　　　　[ex off. ... expens. suis atque C.
　　　　Leporis.] R13 K.3.46.

Paris, *continued*

Le Preux, Poncet
1531 fol. Hugo, *de Sancto Charo.*
Prostat apud I. paruum [col. typis
et characteribus … P. Vidouei,
impensis I. Parui, A. Gormontii,
P. le Preux ac P. Gaudoul.] H84
G.2.5.

Lepus [Leporis], Constantin *see* Le
Lièvre, Constantin

Loys [Lodoicus, Lodoycus], Jean
[Joannes], *Tiletanus*
1542 fol. Dionysius, C. [col. excud.]
in aedibus C. Guillardae. D12
E.3.19(a).

Mallard, Olivier
1538 (14 cal.April.) 16°. Clichtoveus, J. [in offic. libraria, impens.
G. Pratensis & I. Roigny.] C83
K.3.13(a).

Marchant, Jean
1504 (Idibus Iuliis) fol. Heracleides.
[device of Iehan Petit] [col. ex
off. Bellovisiane [Jean Marchant]
… impensis Ioannis Parui.] H41
A.5.7.

Marnef, Hieronymus [Jérôme,] de
& Dionysius [Denis] de, *fratres*
1549 fol. Anselm. apud. A41
G.4.12(b).

Menier, Maurice
1550 8°. Guilliaud, C. excudebat A.
Petit Mauricius Menier [col. apud
A. Paruum.] G44 C.3.1(a).

Morel [Morellus], Federicus
[Fédéric]
1562 [col. Mar.] fol. Guillard, C. [col.
excudebat.] (apud I. de Roigny.)
G43 G.4.13.
1562 [col. id. Aug.] 8°. Mark. [col.
excudebat A. Paruo F. Morellus.]
M12 ZC2.5.13.

Morel [Morelius], Gulielmus
[Guillaume]
1558 8°. Basil. apud. B7 A.6.22(a).

1561 fol. Apostolic Canons. apud.
A44 B.3.9(a).
1563 8°. Mark. apud [col. excudebat.] M11 A.6.24.

Nivelle, Sebastian [Sébastien]
1556 16°. Gulielmus, *Baufeti.* apud.
G48 ZC2.8.5(c).
1570 8°. Mouchy, A. de. apud. M82
ZC2.1.3(b).

Parvus [Petit], Audoënus [Oudin]
1532 8°. Titelman, F. apud. T13
C.5.14.
[1545 [col. Oct.] 8°. Rupert. apud
[col. G. Thibaut imprimebat.] *R4
H.1.30.]
1548 8°. Guilliaud, C. apud [excud.
I. Roigny & A. Petit & B. Prae-
uost.] G45 C.3.1(b).
1550 8°. Guilliaud, C. apud [col.
excudebat A. Petit M. Menier.]
G44 C.3.1(a).
1555 fol. Joverius, F. apud [col. Ex
chalc. I. Sauetier.] J17 B.3.9(b).
1563 [col. id. Aug.] 8°. Mark. apud.
[col. excudebat … F. Morellus.]
M12 ZC2.5.13.

Parvus [Petit], Joannes [Jean,
Iehan]
1504 (Idibus Iuliis) fol. Heracleides.
[device] [col. ex off. Bellovisiane
[Jean Marchant] … impensis.]
H41 A.5.7.
[1506] 4°. Hugo, *de Sancto Charo.*
[device.] H83 D.1.2.
[c. 1508] 8°. Eusebius, *of Cremona.*
[device.] E56 A.6.32(e).
[1513 (Id. Feb.) fol. Duns, J. mandato et expensis. *D9 L.4.20(b).]
1518 [col. 26 Mar.] 4°. Durandus, G.
ab. [col. Impressum Cadomi per
L. hostingue pro M. angier.] D36
L.5.13.
1528 8°. Jacobus, de Voragine.
Venundantur … apud. J2 D.4.10.
1531 fol. Hugo, *de Sancto Charo.*
Prostat apud. [col. typis et characteribus … P. Vidouei, impensis
I. Parui, A. Gormontii, P. le Preux
ac P. Gaudoul.] H84 G.2.5.

1531 (ad prim. kal. Jun.) 8°. Matthei,
L. [device.] [impens. J. petit et A.
girault.] M16 D.3.8.

1532 8°. Titelman, F. apud. T13
C.5.14.

1534 fol. Puteo, F. de. Vaeneunt in
aedibus. P58 E.3.12.

1539 fol. Vio, T. de. apud V29
G.2.17.

Praevost [Prévost], Benedictus
[Benoît] *see* Roigny, Jean, &
Petit [Parvus], Audoënus [Oudin],
& Praevost [Prévost], Bene-
dictus [Benoît]

Pratis, Nicolas de *see* Des Prez,
Nicolaus

Regnault [Reginaldus], François
[Franciscus]

1505 8°. Vivaldus, J. L. venundatur
a [col. impressum sumptibus.]
V37 L.6.1.

[*c*. 1507] fol. Paulus. impressum me
A. bonne mere … expensis …
I. frellon [with device of F.
Regnault.] P13 L.4.34.

[1514 col. 21 Aug.] 4°. Pavinis, J. F.
de. [col. impressus impensis.]
P14 L.5.37(a).

[1514 col. 2 Oct.] 4°. Suberti, P. de.
[col. impensis.] S95 L.5.37(b).

1516 (5 Julij) fol. Gulielmus,
Avernus. in off. G46 L.4.22.

[1518 [col. x. vero mensis Feb.] 8°.
Burgo, J. de. [col. impensis.] *B17
H.2.14.]

1519 [die vero sexto decimo mensis
Feb.] 8°. Gratian. in edibus
[impens. opera P. Oliuier
(Rouen).] G30 H.2.54.

1522 [pt. IV 12 kal. Jun.] 8°. Bonaventura. prostat venale in edibus.
B53 H.1.38–40.

Regnault, Petrus [Pierre]

1531 8°. Vio, T. de. vaenundatur …
in aedibus. V32 I.1.6(e).

Rembolt, Berthold

1522 [col. decimosexto calendas
martias] fol. Gregory I. [device]
apud C. cheuallon [col. apud C.
Cheuallon, ipsius impensis.] G31
A.1.15.

Resch, Conrad [Konrad]

1519 (4 No. Maii) 4°. Erasmus, D.
apud H. Stephanum … expensis.]
E26 L.5.35(b–c).

1522 [?col. Iulij] fol. Stunica, J. L.
apud [col. apud Vidouaeum,
sumptibus C. Resch.] S94 L.4.12.

Richard[us], Thomas

1549 8°. Perionius, J. apud [col.
excudebat.] P19 ZC2.7.3.

Roigny, Jean [Ioannis] de

1543 8°. Broeckwey, A. apud
[impressum per G. Thibout.] B94
D.4.8.

1549 8°. Cologne Antididagma.
apud. C95 ZC2.4.14(d).

1551 [col. Nonis Ian.] fol. Arboreus,
J. apud. A48 E.4.3.

[1558 16°. Arnoldus. apud. *A11
K.3.19.]

1560 8°. Euthymius. apud [col. ex
calc. I. Sauetier.] E58 C.4.13.

Roigny, Jean [de], & Petit [Parvus],
Audoënus [Oudin], & Praevost
[Prévost], Benedictus [Benoît]

1548 8°. Guilliaud, C. [col. excudebat]
(apud A. Paruum.) G45 C.3.1(b).

1562 [col. Mar.] fol. Guillard, C.
apud [col. excudebat I. de R. F.
Morellus.] G43 G.4.13.

Ruelle [Ruellius], Jean [Ioannes]

[1540 fol. Aquinas, T. in aedibus.
*A7 G.2.11.]

[1548 8°. Dionysius, *Carthusianus.*
apud. *D4 .D.3.13.]

Savetier, Joannes [Jean]

1555 fol. Joverius, F. apud A.
Paruum [col. Ex chalc. I.
Sauetier.] J17 B.3.9(b).

1560 8°. Euthymius. [col. ex calc.]
apud I. de Roigny. E58 C.4.13.

Paris, *continued*

Sonnius, Michael [Michel]
  1566 fol. Catharinus, A. apud. C53
    G.4.12(a).
  1567 (17 Jun.) 8°. Espence, C. d'.
    apud. E52 D.5.9 .
  1568 8°. Clement I. [apud.] C79 B.6.5.
  1568 8°. Lucifer. apud. L47
    A.6.26(a).

Thibou[s]t, Gulielmus [Guillaume]
  1544 8°. Broeckwey a Konigstein,
    A. [impressum per] (apud I.
    Roigny.) B94 D.4.8.
  [1543 [col. Oct.] 8°. Rupert. apud
    A. Paruum [col. G. Thibaut
    imprimebat.] *R4 H.1.30.]

Tiletanus, Lodoycus *see* Loys
  [Lodoicus, Lodoycus], Jean
  [Joannes], *Tiletanus*

Vascosan[us], Michael [Michel de]
  1554 4°. Tunstall, C. ex off. T26
    ZC2.3.2.

Vidoue [Vidouaeus], Pierre
  1522 [col. Iulij] fol. Stunica, J. L.
    apud C. Resch [col. apud
    Vidouaeum, sumptibus C.
    Resch.] S94 L.4.12.
  1529 (mense Iun.) 8°. Erasmus, D.
    [col. sub praelo.] E46 ZC2.8.1(f).
  1531 fol. Hugo, *de Sancto Charo*.
    Prostat apud I. paruum [col. typis
    et characteribus … P. Vidouei,
    impensis I. Parui, A. Gormontii,
    P. le Preux ac P. Gaudoul.] H84
    G.2.5.

Vilarmus, Gotthard
  1573 4°. Albutius, P. per. A17
    L.5.32(b). Printer is actually
    Petrus Perna, Basle, according
    to HAB.

Wechel, Christian [Chrétien]
  1534 8°. Alphabetum Hebraicum.
    excudebat. A22 F.2.5(c).
  1537 8°. Philo, *of Carpasia*. in off.
    P28 C.5.3.
  1539 8°. Campensis, J. apud. C29
    F.2.5(a).

1540 8°. Clenardus, N. excudebat.
  C81 F.2.5(b).

Printer not identified
  [c. 1540] 8°. Postel, G. [?Paris.] P45
    ZC2.6.4. Date and place of
    printing suggested by Adams,
    FB 83762 and USTC 160468. But
    VD16 P 4483, USTC 682489
    suggest [Basel: J. Oporinus, c.
    1545?].
  1565 (Aug.) 4°. Du Moulin, C. D29
    C.2.14. HAB suggests – Lyon:
    Vincent, Antoine.

Pavia

Burgofrancho, Jacob de
  [1510–1511 4°. Ricius, P. [col. pt. 2:
    per.] *R2 L.5.39.]

Pfortzheim

Anshelm, Thomas
  1505 (sexto. Kal. Apriles) fol. Reuch-
    lin, J. in aedibus. R17 E.4.13.

Ratisbon [Regensburg]

Geissler, Heinrich
  [c. 1561] 4°. Praetorius, Z. P52
    ZC2.3.8(b). Printer mentioned in
    HAB, but not in VD16 P 4687.
    CLC ?Wittenberg.

Regiomontus *see* Königsberg

Rome

Accoltus [Accolto], Iulius [Giulio]
  1571 8°. Aquinas, T. apud. A46
    G.5.15(b).

Blado, Antonio
  1557 4°. Turrianus, F. apud. T27
    L.5.8(b).

Jordanus (typographicus Ponti-
  ficius) [=Oporinus, Basle]
  1553 8°. Mazzolini, S. per. M24
    ZC2.5.1(c). Printer suggested by
    VD16 and EDIT16.

Rostock

Lucius, Jakob, Transylvanus (I)
1565 8°. Paulli, S. excudebat. P11
ZC2.1.7(b).
1567 8°. Paulli, S. excudebat. P10
G.6.5.
1567 8°. Rostock. – Academia.
excudebat. R38 H.1.9.
1569 8°. Paulli, S. in off. [Pt. 2
excudebat.] P12 M.2.26(a).

No printer identified
1566 8°. Richter, M. R27 K.2.16(d).

Rouen

Morin, Martin
[[c. 1495–1500] 8°. Orbellis, N. de in
domo J. richardi mercatoris [with
device.] [col. studio et opera
Magistri M. morin expensis vero
I. alexandri librarii.] O19 L.6.3.]

Olivier, Petrus [Pierre]
1519 [die vero sexto decimo mensis
Feb.] 8°. Gratian. C [col. impens.
opera] (in edibus F. Regnault.)
G30 H.2.54.
1522 [pt. IV col. (Rouen) apud
Olivier Pierre, apud François
Regnault (Paris). 12 kal. Jun.] 8°.
Bonaventura. B53 H.1.38–40.

Richard [Ricardus], Jean [Joannes]
[c. 1495–1500] 8°. Orbellis, N. de.
in domo J. richardi mercatoris
[with device.] [col. studio et opera
Magistri M. morin expensis vero
I. alexandri librarii.] O19 L.6.3.

Savona

Ecclesia, Bernardinus de
1503 (id. Feb.) fol. Nannus Mira-
bellius, D. per F. de Silua …
impensa B. de Ecclesia. N5
L.2.14.

Silva, Franciscus de
1503 (id. Feb.) fol. Nannus Mira-
bellius, D. per … impensa B. de
Ecclesia. N5 L.2.14.

Solingen [Salingiaci]

Soter, Johannes
1540 8°. Maruliæ, M. excudebat
[col. impensis … G. Hyttorpij.]
M14 N.6.4.

Speier

Drach, Peter
[1495 col.] 4°. Petrus, Lombardus.
P23 L.5.38. Printer from ISTC.

Strasbourg

Albertus [Albrecht], Ioannis
[Johann]
1536 8°. Luther, M. apud. L62
D.4.3(b).

Apiarius [Biener], Matthias
1533 [col. Sep.] 4°. Oecolampadius,
J. [col. in off.] O7 G.5.2.
1534 [col. Mar.] 4°. Oecolampadius,
J. apud. O8 C.1.9.
1534 (Aug.) 8°. Oecolampadius, J.
apud. [col. in off.] O15 C.1.6(b).
1534 [col. Sep.] 8°. Bucer, M. [col.
per.] B109 ZC2.2.9(c).

Apronianus, Johann see Schaefer,
Petrus, & Apronianus Johann,
socios

Beck, Balthasar, Heirs of
1552 8°. Rabus, L. in off. R3 B.6.10.

C[a]ephalius [Köpfel], Wolfgang
1525 [col. 1 Apr.] 8°. Capito, W.
apud. C39 F.2.4.
1538 [col.] 8°. Draconites, J. apud.
D25 C.5.4(c).

Emmel, Samuel
1565 8°. Spangenberg, C. excudebat. S74 K.1.28(b).
1567 8°. Praetorius, A. imprimebat.
P48 ZC2.2.4(b).
1567 8°. Regius, E. R14 K.2.16(c).

Fabricius, Blasius [Blase]
1556 8°. Westphal, J. excudebat.
W15 ZC2.2.7(e).
1557 8°. Westphal, J. excudebat.
W14 ZC2.2.7(d).

Strasbourg, *continued*

Flach, Martin

1494 (3 id. Aug.) fol. Gerson, J. C. de. G25 L.3.14.

[1494 (Id. Dec.) fol. Gerson, J. C. de. *G3 L.3.12–13.]

Frölich, Jakob

[1555]. 4°. Dialogus. D4 ZC2.3.8(c). Printer from HAB.

Grüninger [Grieninger], Johann

1524 (12 Mar.) 4°. Treger, C. per. T19 ZC2.3.12(b).

Herwagen [Hervagius], Johann [Iohannes]

1523 (17 kal. Apr.) 8°. Erasmus, D. apud. E28 G.5.20.

[1524 [col.18 Kal.Feb.] 8°. Melanchthon, P. [col. apud.] *M1 C.5.12.]

1525 8°. Luther, M. L77 D.6.7(b).

[?1525 8°. Lambert, F. *L2 C.5.5(b). Printer from OCLC.]

[1525 [col. Mar.] 8°. Lambert, F. apud. *L1 C.5.5(a).]

1526 8°. Lambert, F. [col. apud.] L6 C.5.4(a).

1526 (Mar.) 8°. Luther, M. [col. apud.] L65 D.5.2(b).

1527 8°. Borrhaus, M. B62 ZC2.2.9(d).

1527 8°. Bucer, M. B102 C.1.6(c). Printer from VD 16; or Zürich: Froschauer, Christoph (Adams).

1527 (Jan.) 8°. Luther, M. [col. apud.] L59 E.6.29(b).

1527 (mense Aug.) 8°. Strasbourg Church. S90 H.1.8(c). Printer from VD16 C833.

1528 8°. Capito, W. apud. C37 D.4.3(a).

1528 (Mar.) 8°. Benedictus, A. [col. apud.] B13 X.2.30(b).

Hug[o], Peter

1565 8°. Widemannus, J. excudebat. W17 ZC2.5.2(e).

Husner, Georg

1496 fol. Jacobus, *de Voragine*. J1 L.4.17.

1502 (In die ... Vitalis) fol. Dionysius. D9 A.5.8(b).). ?Printer as D7, from HAB.

1502 (In die ... Vita et Modesti) fol. Dionysius. D8 A.5.8(c). ?Printer as D7.

1503 (8 kal. feb.) fol. Dionysius. D7 A.5.8(a). Printer from HAB.

[1503 (col. 16 ka. dec.)] fol. Petrus, *Comestor*. P20 L.4.10.

Jobin, Bernhard

1573 8°. Fischart, J. per. F9 ZC2.7.5(f). Printer from VD16.

Knoblo[u]ch, *House of*

1525 8°. Knopken, A. excudebat. K11 D.2.6(b).

1525 (Jul.) 8°. Bugenhagen, J. excudebat. B117 C.4.8.

1545 (mense Aug.) 4°. Bucer, M. [col. ex off. ... per G. Machaeropoeum.] B104 L.5.15(b).

1548 4°. Bucer, M. [officina.] B110 L.5.16(a–b). Printer suggested by Adams; or, Basle: Johann Oporinus (VD16).

Knobloch, Joannes [Johann]

1512 fol. Aquinas, T. impens. A47 L.3.10.

1523 (Nov.) 8°. Bugenhagen, J. excudebat. B112 D.3.1(b).

1524 8°. Bugenhagen, J. B116 C.5.11(b). Place of publication and date from VD16 B 9349; or Hagenau: J. Setzer, 1525 from VD16 9351.

1526 8°. Bugenhagen, J. B113 C.5.4(f).

Köpfel, Wolfgang, *Heirs of*

1555 [col. Apr.] 8°. Ponet, J. [col. Zürich: by C. Froschauer (= ?Strasbourg: heirs of W. Köpfel, according to STC and CLC).] P42 R.6.21(b).

1556 8°. Mainardo, A. M6 R.6.21(a).

Messerschmidt [Machaeropoeus], Georg

1545 (mense Aug.) 4°. Bucer, M. [col. ex off. Knoblochiana per.] B104 L.5.15(b).

Messerschmidt [Machaeropoeus], Paul

1562 8°. Firmicus Maternus, J. apud … sumptibus I. Oporini. F8 A.6.20(d).

1562 (Mar.) fol. Flacius, M. apud … sumptibus I. Oporini [col. ex off. I. Oporini.] F11 L.4.4.

Müller [Mylius], Christian (I)

1564 4°. Vergerio, A. apud. V9 K.2.8(e).

[1565 col.] 8°. Maecardus, J. [col. exprimebat.] M4 K.3.41(d).

1566 8°. Erythraeus, V. apud. E51 ZC2.1.4(b).

Müller [Mylius], Kraft [Crato]

1538 8°. Phrygio, P. C. (device) [col. apud.] P30 C.5.4(d).

[1538 col.] 4°. Rome, Church of. [col. ex off.] R35 ZC2.3.5(b).

1539 (Non. Maij) 8°. Luther, M. apud. L55 D.5.2(a).

1539 (Sep.) 8°. Sadoleto, J. apud. S5 L.6.11(c).

1542 8°. Willich, J. [col. apud.] W43 G.6.21(a).

1546 8°. Cruciger, C. apud. C114 D.4.4.

Oporinus, Johann

1562 8°. Firmicus Maternus, J. apud P. Machaeropoeum, sumptibus. F8 A.6.20(d).

1562 (Mar.) fol. Flacius, M. apud P. Machaeropoeum … sumptibus [col. ex off. I. Oporini.] F11 L.4.4.

Prüss, Johann (II)

[1521] 4°. Luther, M. L69 L.5.34(b).

Rihel[ius], Josias (I)

1564 8°. Chytraeus, D. excudebat. C73 M.2.35(f).

[1570] 4°. Marbach, J. excudebat. M9 L.5.15(d).

Rihel[ius], Josias (I) & Theodosius

1556 8°. Chytraeus, D. C70 D.6.2(a). Printer from VD16.

Rihel, Wendelin

1539 (Sep.) 8°. Capito, W. per. C38 M.2.3.

1539 (Sep.) 8°. Sadoleto, J. per. S4 L.6.11(b).

[?1540] 4°. Bucer, M. [device.] B106 L.5.15(a).

1541 8°. Cicero, M. T. [col. apud.] C74 X.2.16.

1543 [?W. Rihel – Adams] 8°. Bucer, M. B107 H.1.5.

[1544 col. (Aug.)] 8°. Sarcerius E. [col. per.] S21 D.6.8.

[1544 col. (Aug.)] 8°. Sarcerius E. [col. per.] S22 D.6.9.

1546 8°. Calvin, J. per. C11 ZC1.4.7(a).

[1547 [col.] 8°. Dasypodius, P. apud. *D1 X.1.20.]

1554 8°. Foxe, J. excudebat. F32 B.6.11.

1555 fol. Pole, R. excudebat. P40 L.2.7(c).

Schaefer, Petrus, & Apronianus, Johann, socios

1530 (kal. Mar.) 8°. Alcuin apud. A19 A.6.21(b).

1530 8°. Strasbourg Church. [col. communibus expensis excudebant.] S91 ZC2.5.9(a).

Schott [Scottus], Johann

[1523] 4°. Brunfels, O. B97 K.2.11(d). Imprint from HAB.

[1524] 8°. Hutten, U. von. [excudit Scottus.] H94 ZC2.5.9(b). Printer and date from VD16.

1525 8°. Luther, M. L66 ZC2.6.18(d).

Ulricher, Georgius [Georg], *Andlanus*

1532 (Mar.) fol. Bucer, M. excudebat. B98 E.4.7.

1535 (Sep.) fol. Brunfels, O. impressore. B95 G.4.18.

1536 (Mar.) fol. Smaragdus. impressore. S62 E.4.6(a).

Wyriot, Nikolaus

1573 4°. Marbach, J. excudebat. M8 L.5.32(a).

Strasbourg, *continued*

Printer not identified.
[1543 4°. Aepinus, J. *A1 C.2.5.]
1557 8°. Sleidanus, J. S59 B.6.1.

Tremoniae, Dortmund *see* Dortmund

Tübingen

Gruppenbach[ius], Georg[ius]
1576 fol. Brentz, J. excudebat. B68 L.2.2.

Morhart, Ulrich
[1524 col.] 4°. Tuberinus, J. T25 ZC2.3.14(d). Printer from VD16 and HAB.
1525 8°. Cochlaeus, J. C87 ZC2.1.1(d).
[1525 col.] 8°. Schatzger, C. [col. per.] S32 ZC2.1.1(b).
[1525 col. Jan.] 8°. Schatzger, C. [col. per.] S31 ZC2.1.1(a).
1527 (Jan.8) 4°. Agricola, R. [col. per] A12 I.4.10(d).
1550 8°. Brentz, J. per. B73 ZC1.4.10(e).

Morhart, Ulrich, Heirs of
1556 4°. Melanchthon, P. M57 L.5.7(d). Printer from VD16.

Morhart, Ulrich, widow of [vidua]
1557 8°. Beurlin, J. ex off. typographica. B19 C.4.11(c).
1559 8°. Vergerio, L. V10 ZC2.2.7(c). Printer from HAB.
1559 (Mar.) 4°. Vergerius, P. P. V11 ZC2.2.1(b). Printer from HAB.
1563 (Jul.) 4°. Vannius, V. apud. V5 I.4.2.
1564 4°. Andreae, J. apud. A30 ZC2.3.9(a).
1564 4°. Andreae, J. apud. A31 K.2.8(b).
1564 4°. Andreae, J. apud. A32 L.5.27(a).
1564 4°. Brentz, J. apud. B93 L.5.27(b).

1564 4°. Maulbrunn Colloquy. M17 ZC2.3.9(d). Printer from OCLC.
1565 4°. Andreae, J. A29 ZC2.3.9(c). Printer from HAB.
1565 4° Andreae, J. A33 K.2.8(c). Printer from HAB.
1565 4° Andreae, J. A34 K.2.8(a). Printer from HAB.
1566 4°. Bidembach, W. [col. apud.] B45 I.4.6(b).
1566 fol. Brentz, J. apud. B82 G.3.7(a).
1566 4°. Schegk, J. apud. S33 I.3.9(c).
1566 4°. Schegk, J. apud. S35 I.4.5(b).
1567 4°. Heerbrand, J. H12 L.5.15(c).
1568 4°. Snepffius, T. S67 I.7.7(a).

Morhart, Ulrich, widow of [vidua], & Gruppenbach, Georg, & Brubach, Petrus
1566 fol. Brentz, J. [col. apud.] B82 G.3.7(a)

Ursel[lius] [Oberursel]

Henricus [Heinrich], Nikolaus
1557 8°. Eitzen, P. von. excudebat. E17 B.5.34(b).
1557 8°. Brentz, J. excudebat. B81 G.6.4(a).
1558 8°. Westphal, J. excudebat. W9 ZC2.5.7(k).
1558 8°. Westphal, J. excudebat. W10 ZC2.5.7(i).
1558 8°. Westphal, J. excudebat. W11 ZC2.5.7(j).
1558 8°. Westphal, J. excudebat. W12 ZC2.5.7(h).
[1558 8°. Westphal, J. [Quire E only = ?part of W11] W13 ZC2.5.7(l)].
1561 8°. Eitzen, P. von. E15 ZC2.2.7(b). HAB conjectures Hamburg as place of printing, though printer not identified. But printer may have been Nicolaus Henricus (at Ursel), as E17 – another item by this author in the same volume.

1561 8°. Eitzen, P. von. E16
B.5.34(c). Printer as E15 or
[Hamburg: n. pr.] (VD16).

1562 8°. Hamelmann, H. excudebat. H4 L.6.24(a).

[1562] 8°. Menzel, H. [col. excudebat.] M68 L.6.25.

1563 8°. Obenheim, C. excudebat.
O1 ZC2.5.6(d).

1564 8°. Flacius, M. excudebat. F20
ZC2.5.6(c).

1565–1566 8°. Wigand, J. ex off.
[col. pt. 2: extendebat.] W19
E.6.9(a–b).

1574 8°. Flacius, M. F15 ZC1.4.4(b).
Printer from VD16.

Venice

Academia Veneta [University of]
1559 4°. Placidus. P38 E.5.8.

Bernardinus, *de Tridino see*
Stagnino, Bernardino

Blondus, Hieronymus
1495 (Vigilia Diui Gregorii) fol.
Ficino, M. impensa p[ro]uidi [*sic*].
(opera ... M. Capcasae.) F5 Z.2.56.

Capcasa, Matteo
1495 (Vigilia Diui Gregorii) fol.
Ficino, M. impensa p[ro]uidi [*sic*]
H. Blondi ... opera. F5 Z.2.56.

Colonia, Johannis de
1481 (8 July) fol. Aquinas, T. [col.
impendio.] A45 L.3.9.

Colonia, Johannis de, & Jenson,
Nicolas, & Co.
1481 4°. Duns, J. [col. opera ac impensa. N. Jenson: sociorumque.
Curam ac diligentiam adhibuit I.
de Selgenstat.] D33 L.4.25.
[1481 (22 Nov.) 4°. Duns, J. opera ac
impensa: N. Ienson sociorumque.
Curam ac diligentiam adhibuit I.
de Selgenstat. *D6 L.4.26.]

Comin da Trino
1563 8°. Dominicis, D. de. D22
ZC2.5.5(a).

Fontana, Benedetto
1506 [col. 21 Oct.] fol. Hugo, *de
Sancto Victore*. [col. in mandato &
expensis ... per I. pentium
Leucensem.] H88 L.2.15(a).

Giunta [Giuntis], Giontini di
[Giunta de], *Florentini*
[1515 (7 mar.) fol. Aquinas, T. [col. a
P. Pincio Manutuana impressa.
Impensis d. Geontini de Gionta
Florentini.] *A9 G.2.9.]

Giunta [Iunta], Lucantonio [Lucas
Antonius] (I)
[1510 fol. Pontifical [Latin Rite.]
cura: arte: atque sumptibus. *P6
ZC1.1.2.]

Giunta [Iunta], Lucantonio [Lucas
Antonius] (II)
1567 fol. Naclantius, J. apud [col. in
off.] N1 G.3.18(c).

Gregoriis, Gregorius de
[1505 (Dec. tertio kal. Aug.) fol.
Duns, J. mandato ac impressa
Bernardini de Tridini ... per G.
de Gregoriis. *D7 L.2.12.]

Gryphius, Joannes
1564 4°. Osorio da Fonseca, J. [col.
excudebat.] (ex off. I. Zileti.) O24
B.5.5(b).

Hamman, Johannes [Hertzog,
Johannes]
1497 (pridie kal Martias) fol. Balbus,
J. arte. [col. Iussu & impensis P.
liechtenstein.] B5 Y.2.12.

Herbort, Joannes, de Seligenstadt
1481 fol. Duns, J. [col. Curam ac
diligentiam adhibuit I. de Seling-
stat.] (opere ac impensa I. de
Colonia: N. Jenson: sociorumque.) D33 L.4.25.
1481 (8 July) fol. Aquinas, T. [col.
Impendio J. de Colonia: N.
Jenson sociorumque.] A45 L.3.9.
[1481 (22 Nov.) fol. Duns, J. opera
ac impensa: N. Ienson sociorumque. Curam ac diligentiam
adhibuit I. de Selgenstat. *D6
L.4.26.]

Venice, *continued*

Hertzog, Johannes *see* Hamman, Johannes

Jenson, Nicolas *see also* Colonia, Johannis de, & Jenson, Nicolas, & Co.
1481 (8 July) fol. Aquinas, T. [col. impressum] A45 L.3.9.

Liechtenstein, Hermann
1494 (nonis sep.) fol. Vincent. impensis. V26 L.1.15.

Liechtenstein, Petrus
1497 (pridie kal Martias) fol. Balbus, J. Iussu & impensis. (Arte Joannis hertzog.) B5 Y.2.12.

Lorenzini, Francesco
1559 8°. Cauzio, C. [device.] C54 ZC2.5.5(b).

Manuzio, Aldo, heirs of, & Torresanus [Asulanus], Andreas, *de Asula*
[1534 [col. Mense Maio] fol. Themistius. in aedibus. *T2 Z.2.52.]

Manuzio, Paulo
1566 8°. Milan. M75 ZC2.2.10(b). Printed suggested by OCLC and CLC.

Pentius [Pencio], Jacobus [Jacopo], *Da Lecco* [Leucenses]
1505 [col. 21 Oct.] fol. Hugo, *de Sancto Victore*. per. [col. in mandato & expensis B. fontanae, per.] H88 L.2.15(a).

Pincio, Filippo
[1515 (7 mar.) fol. Aquinas, T. [col. a P. Pincio Mantuano impressa. Impensis d. Geontini de Gionta Florentini.] *A9 G.2.9.]

Seligenstadt [Selgenstat], Johannes de *see* Herbort, Joannes, de Seligenstadt

Stagnino, Bernardino
[1505 (Dec. tertio kal. Aug.) fol. Duns, J. mandato ac impressa … per G. de Gregoriis. *D7 L.2.12.]

Valgrisi, Vincenzo
[1559 8°. Antidotarium. *A6 ZC1.3.12. Printer suggested by OCLC.]

Vercellensis, Albertinus [De Lissona]
1503 (iiii Maii) fol. Foresti, J. P. per. F30 Z.2.25.

Vicentius [Vincenzo], Josephus [Giuseppe]
1557 4°. Naclantius, J. apud. N2 E.5.28(a).

Vitali, Bernardino dei
1525 (Sep.) fol. Georgius, F. in aedibus. G23 L.3.21.

Ziletti [Ziletus], Giordano [Iordanus]
1563 4°. Osorio da Fonseca, J. ex off. O27 B.5.5(c).
1563 fol. Sirenius, J. ex off. S58 L.2.16(a).
1564 4°. Osorio da Fonseca, J. ex off. [col. I. Gryphius excudebat.] O24 B.5.5(b).

No printer identified
[1559 8°. Antidotarium. *A6 ZC1.3.12.]

Vienna

Hoffhalter, Raphael
[c. 1560] 8°. Freiesleben, C. excudebat. F35 B.6.40.

Wes[s]el

No printer identified
1543 8°. Melanchthon, P. M55 L.6.11(a).

Wetzlar

1541 (cal. Apr.) 8°. Lorich, G. [col. Vuetzflarij]. L39 ZC2.8.1(a). Actually printed at Frankfurt-am-Main by Christian Egenolff (VD16 L2516)

Wittenberg

Klug [Clug], Josef

1527 (Sep.) 8°. Aurogallus, M. [col. in aedibus.] A68 ZC2.8.8.

1529 8°. Reuchlin, J. apud. R16 F.2.6.

1541 [col.] 8°. Melanchthon, P. [col. per.] M52 C.5.9.

1541 4°. Ratisbon – Colloquy. impressum per. R8 ZC2.3.5(d).

1542 4°. Melanchthon, P. per. M54 ZC2.3.5(e).

1546 8°. Cruciger, C. [col. per.] C113 E.6.28.

Krafft [Crato], Johann [Iohannes]

1552 8°. Brentz, J. [col. typis excudebat.] B90 M.2.25.

1557 8°. Chytraeus, D. excudebat. [col. impensis C. Ruelii.] C66 E.6.35(a).

1561 8°. Chytraeus, D. excudebat. C67 E.6.36(a).

1562 fol. Melanchthon, P. excudebat. M43 L.2.3.

1563 8°. Chytraeus, D. excudebat. C72 D.6.10(b).

1563 8°. Cogler, J. [device.] C94 C.5.13(b).

1564 8°. Cogler, J. excudebat. C93 C.5.13(c).

1564 8°. Hemmingsen, N. [device.] H26 C.5.13(a).

1564 8°. Hemmingsen, N. [device.] [col. excudebat.] H28 C.4.10(c).

1564 fol. Melanchthon, P. excudebat. M44 L.2.4.

1564 8°. Schoenborn, B. excudebat. S38 M.2.35(e).

1564 8°. Stummelius, C. S93 M.2.35(b). Printer from HAB.

1564 8°. Trotzendorf, V. F. [col. excudebat.] T23 M.2.35(g).

1565 8°. Garcaeus, J. [device.] G8 ZC2.1.7(d).

1565 8°. Garcaeus, J. excudebat. G11 ZC2.1.7(e).

1565 8°. Garcaeus, J. excudebat. G12 ZC2.1.7(c).

1565 8°. Hemmingsen, N. [device.] [col. excudebat.] H27 C.4.10(b).

1565 8°. Trotzendorf, V. F. excudebat. T22 K.3.45(b).

1565 8°. Trotzendorf, V. F. [col. excudebat.] T24 K.3.45(a).

1566 8°. Garcaeus, J. [device.] G9 ZC2.4.9(b).

1566 8°. Garcaeus, J. [device.] G10 K.3.41(e).

1566 8°. Hemmingsen, N. [col. excudebat.] H29 D.6.6(c).

1566 8°. Hemmingsen, N. [col. excudebat.] H30 C.4.11(a).

1566 8°. Hemmingsen, N. excudebat. H31 D.6.6(b).

1566 8°. Hemmingsen, N. excudebat. H33 D.6.6(d).

1566 8°. Hemmingsen, N. excudebat. H36 K.3.41(b).

1567 8°. Cruciger, C. excudebat [for Konrad Rühel, according to VD 16]. C115 D.4.5(a).

1569 8°. Chytraeus, D. [device.] C68 G.5.17(a).

1570 8°. Hemmingsen, N. [col. excudebant C. Schleich & A. Schöne] H34 C.4.11(b).

1572 8°. Chytraeus, D. excudebat. C69 G.5.17(b).

1573 8°. Mollerus, H. excudebat. M76 D.1.7.

1574 8°. Mollerus, H. excudebat. M77 G.5.6.

Kreutzer [Creutzer, Creucer], Veit [Vitus]

1542 8°. Melanchthon, P. [col. per.] M47 C.5.8(b).

1549 8°. Flacius, M. [col. apud.] F17 ZC2.4.15.

1555 8°. Meier, G. ex off. typographica. M42 ZC1.4.10(b).

1562 8°. Ebert, P. à. E1 K.1.7(c).

1562 8°. Melanchthon, P. [col. ex off. typographica.] M58 L.6.19(a).

Wittenberg, *continued*

Lotter, Melchior (II)
  [1521] 4°. Luther, M. L74 L.5.34(a).
  Printer and date from Adams and
  CLC.

Lufft, Hans [Joannes]
  1525 8°. Luther, M. [col. apud.] L52
  D.2.2.
  1537 8°. Hus, Jan. ex off. H93 L.6.23.
  1538 8°. Luther, M. [col. typis.] L63
  D.5.4(a).
  1538 [col. V. idus. Sep.] 8°. Luther,
  M. typis. L72 ZC2.6.14.
  1539 8°. Luther, M. typis. L58
  D.5.3(b).
  1543 8°. Luther, M. [col. apud.] L49
  L.6.30.
  1545 8°. Luther, M. excudebat. L60
  D.5.1.
  1548 8°. Cruciger, C. ex off. C116
  ZC1.4.7(b).
  1550 8°. Meier, G. ex off. M41
  ZC2.8.10(a).
  [1550 8°. Melanchthon, P. per. *M2
  L.6.20.]
  1557 8°. Meier, G. per. M30
  D.6.2(b).
  1557 8°. Meier, G. excudebat. M31
  D.6.2(c).
  1559 8°. Meier, G. ex off. M27
  E.6.25.
  1559 8°. Meier, G. excudebat. M32
  C.6.12.
  1560 8°. Melanchthon, P. excudebat. M62 K.3.38.
  1562 8°. Meier, G. ex off. M38
  G.5.21(a).
  1562 8°. Meier, G. ex off. M40
  G.6.20.
  1562 8°. Meier, G. excudebat. M33
  G.6.24(a).
  1563 8°. Meier, G. ex off. M34
  G.6.24(b).
  1563 8°. Meier, G. excudebat. M35
  D.6.4(a).
  1564 8°. Meier, G. ex off. M28
  G.6.19.
  1565 8°. Meier, G. ex off. M36
  D.6.4(b).

1566 8°. Meier, G. ex off. M29
  E.6.21.
  1571 8°. Meier, G. ex off. M37
  C.6.13.

Rhau, Georg
  1534 8°. Luther, M. [col. per.] L56
  D.5.5(c).

Rhau, Georg, Heirs of
  1558 4°. Wittenberg, Academia.
  [col. excudebant.] W47 K.2.26(c).
  1559 4°. Wittenberg, Academia.
  excudebant. W45 B.5.8.
  1559 [col. Aug.] 8°. Melanchthon, P.
  excudebant. M66 L.6.13(c).
  1560 [col.] 8°. Froeschel, S. [col.
  excusae ab.] F36 G.6.22(a).
  1561 8°. Loss, L. excudebant. L44
  G.6.18.
  1562 8°. Lybius, C. excudebant. L81
  E.6.31(a).
  1563 8°. Praetorius, A. [col. excudebant.] P51 M.2.35(a).

Ruhel[ius] [Rühel], Cunrad [Konrad]
  1557 8°. Chytraeus, D. excudebat
  I. Crato. [col. impensis.] C66
  E.6.35(a).
  1564 8°. Mollerus, H. excudebat
  I. Schvvertelius [col. excudebat
  I. Schvvertelius impensis
  C. Ruhelii.] M78 D.6.5(b).
  1567 8°. Cruciger, C. [For K. Rühel –
  VD16] [excudebat I. Crato]. C115
  D.4.5(a).

Schleich, Clemens (I), & Schöne,
Anton[ius]
  1569 8°. Hemmingsen, N. [col.
  excudebant.] H34 C.4.11(b).
  1570 8°. Melanchthon, P. excudebant. M61 L.6.21.
  1571 8°. Carolinus, P. [col. excudebant.] C43 H.1.7(a).
  1571 8°. Ferinarius, J. excudebant.
  F4 ZC1.4.3(d).
  1571 8°. Wittenberg, Academia.
  excudebant. W46 ZC2.7.8(a).

Schwenck, Lorenz [Laurentius]
  1563 8°. Praetorius, A. ex off. P50
  L.6.19(b).

Schwertel[ius], Johann

1567 8°. Mollerus, H. excudebat
[col. excudebat ... impensis
C. Ruhelii.] M78 D.6.5(b).

1567 8°. Sascerides, J. S28 N.6.11(a).
Printer uncertain. HAB records a
paginated edition of 1567 by this
printer.

1568 8°. Hemmingsen, N. [col.
excudebat.] H32 E.6.26(e).

1570 8°. Armenia, Church of. [col.
excudebat.] A53 H.1.7(b).

Seitz, Peter (I)

1546 4°. Bugenhagen, J. [col. in
off.] B115 C.2.10.

1561 8°. Corvinus, A. excudebat.
C103 E.6.9(d).

1562 8°. Carion, J. excudebat. C41
B.6.18(a).

1562 8°. Meier, G. ex off. M39
G.5.21(b).

1562 8°. Melanchthon, P. excudebat. M59 L.6.19(c).

Weiss, Hans [Johann]

1534 8°. Luther, M. [col. per.] L53
D.5.5(b).

No printer identified

[?1522 4°. Luther, M. *L10 C.2.5.
Now missing. BMGB records
Wittenberg and Basle edns of
1522.]

1558 8°. Luther, M. L73 L.6.12(a).
Printer not identified in VD16.

1571 8°. Crellius, P. C112 ZC2.7.8(b).
Printer not identified in HAB.

Worms

Köpfel [Cephalaeus], David

[c. 1573] 4°. Harchius, J. apud. H7
L.5.32(d).

Wagner, Sebastian

[1538 col.] 8°. Lambert, F. [col.
excudebat.] L8 C.5.4(b).

1541 4°. Liturgies. Greek rite.
excudebat. L37 ZC2.4.1(b).

Zürich

Froschauer, in officina [apud],
House of

[?1525] 8°. Zwingli, U. ex off. Z6
N.6.13.

1538 (mense Martio.) 4°. Bullinger,
H. in off. B127 H.1.20.

[?1539] fol. Mayer, S. in off. M22
E.3.6(b).

1539 (mense Aug.) fol. Pellicanus,
C. in off. P16 E.3.6(a).

1554 4°. Bullinger, H. ex off. B125
L.5.7(b).

1556 8°. Bullinger, H. apud. B134
ZC1.4.10(c).

Froschauer, Christoph (I)

1527 8°. Bucer, M. B102 C.1.6(c).
Printer from Adams; or Stras-
bourg: Johannes Herwagen
(VD 16).

1535 (mense Mar.) 8°. Zwingli, U.
Z7 L.6.14.

1535 (mense Aug.) fol. Bullinger, H.
apud. B122 G.3.22(a).

1543 fol. Stobaeus, J. excudebat.
S89 M.1.15.

1544 (Aug.) 8°. Bullinger, H. apud.
B118 ZC2.6.7.

1544 (Aug.) 4°. Bullinger, H. apud.
B123 I.4.11(b).

1545 8°. Gualtherus, R. apud. G36
ZC2.6.18(g).

1545 8°. Zurich, Confessio. apud.
Z4 M.2.16.

1551 4°. Vermigli, P. M. ex off. V15
C.2.2.

1551 (Mar.) 4°. Bullinger, H. apud.
B133 I.4.11(a).

[1555 fol. Gesner, C. apud. *G4
Y.3.28.]

[1555 [col. Apr.] 8°. Ponet, J. by.
P42 R.6.21(b). [= ?Strasbourg:
?heirs of W. Köpfel, according to
STC and CLC.]

1558 8°. Bullinger, H. B124
ZC2.5.7(b). Printer from VD16.

1558 fol. Bullinger, H. apud. B132
M.1.28(b).

Zurich, Froschauer, Christoph
(I), *continued*

1559 fol. Vermigli, P. M. V18 L.2.21.
1561 8°. Bullinger, H. excudebat. B120 G.6.3(a).
1561 8°. Bullinger, H. excudebat. B121 G.6.3(b).
[1561 (Aug.) 8°. Bullinger, H. excudebat. *B15 B.5.38(a).]
1562 (Calend. Maij) fol. Gualtherus, R. excudebat. G41 G.4.15(b).
[1562 (May) 8°. Bullinger, H. excudebat. *B16 B.5.38(b).]
1562 (mense Aug.) 4°. Lavater, L. excudebat. L20 G.5.1.
1563 8°. Bullinger, H. apud. B130 ZC2.7.6(d).

Froschauer, Christoph (II)

1563 8°. Simler, J. excudebat. S56 ZC2.7.6(c).
1565 fol. Gualtherus, R, excudebat. G38 G.4.15(a).
1565 (mense Aug.) 4°. Lavater, L. excudebat. L19 G.5.26.
[1565 (Aug.) fol. Bullinger, H. excudebat. *B12 G.3.23(a).]
1566 (Mar.) 4°. Helvetic Confession. excudebat. H23 I.3.9(a).
1566 (Mense Mar.) fol. Vermigli, P. M. excudebat. V13 G.3.15(a).
1568 fol. Bullinger, H. excudebat. B126 M.1.28(b).
1568 8°. Simler, J. apud. S55 ZC2.1.8(b).
1569 fol. Vermigli, P. M. excudebat. V12 G.3.14.
1570 fol. Gualtherus, R, excudebat. G37 G.4.14.
1570 fol. Wolf, J. excudebat. W59 G.4.1(d).
1571 8°. Bullinger, H. excudebat. B127 ZC1.4.3(b).
1572 fol. Gualtherus, R. excudebat. G39 G.3.17.
1572 fol. Gualtherus, R. excudebat. G40 G.4.16(a–b).
1574 8°. Zurich, Reformed Church. excudebat. Z5 ZC1.4.4(a).

Gesner [Gessner]

[1555] 8°. Ochino, B. apud. O2 L.6.13(d).

Gesner [Gessner], Andreas & Jacobus, *Brothers*

[1556] 8°. Bullinger, H. apud. B119 ZC2.4.11(g).
[c. 1560] fol. Procopius. apud Gesneros fratres [col. per.] P54 G.4.8(a).

Gesner, Andreas, & Weissenbach [Wissenbach], Rodolph [Rudolf]

1551 [col. Oct.] 8°. Bullinger, H. [col. excudebat.] B131 ZC2.4.11(b).
1552 8°. Bullinger, H. [col. ex off.] B129 ZC2.4.11(c).
1552 8°. Vermigli, P. M. apud. V16 N.6.8(a).
1552 8°. Vermigli, P. M. apud. V19 N.6.8(b).
1552 4°. Westhemerus, B. apud. W7 ZC2.2.1(a).

Weissenbach [Wissenbach], Rodolph.

[1551] 8°. Clauser, C. ex off. C77 ZC2.6.18(e).

No Printer identified

1550 8°. Sylvius, B. [?Zurich.] S98 ZC2.5.7(d). No printer suggested by HAB or COPAC.
1557 8°. Poullain, V. P47 ZC2.5.7(e). ?Zurich conjectured by Adams.
1563 8°. Fabricius, J. [?Zurich.] F3 ZC2.5.3(a).

Unidentified Place of Publication & Printer / Publisher

German-speaking countries

[1521 4°. Luther, M. *L8 C.2.5. Now missing. Edition unknown. CLC lists editions printed in Basle, Wittenberg and Zwolle.]
[?1522 4°. Luther, M. *L7 C.2.5. Now missing. Edition unknown. BMGB records editions from Basle, Strasbourg and Wittenberg.]

[*c.* 1525] 8°. Erasmus, D. E37 ZC2.6.18(i). CLC suggests no place of printing.

[1531 8°. Haymo. [device of BVM & Apostles] *H1 D.3.12. No place of publication suggested by Adams or CLC.]

1536 8°. Melanchthon, P. M63 L.6.18. Printer not identified in OCLC, HAB or COPAC records.

[?after] 1536 4°. Erasmus, D. E29 D.1.13–14. CLC suggests no place of printing.

[*c.* 1540] 4°. Schmalkalden. [Fragment.] S37 ZC2.3.5(f). Date from CLC.

[*c.* 1550] 16°. Bible. NT B36 G.6.8. Date from CLC.

1561 8°. Monhemius, J. M79 ZC2.4.9(a). Printer not identified in CLC, OCLC, HAB or COPAC.

Low Countries

1567 8°. Lindius, S. L36 ZC2.2. 4(c). Printer not identified in CERL or OCLC.

APPENDIX III

Chronological Index of Imprints

Imprint dates are not, of course, a sure guide to the year of acquisition, even after 1536 when Geste was in a position to purchase books as soon as these became available from Cambridge booksellers. It was not Geste's practice to record when a book was acquired, and in only a very few instances is there any indication in the item itself, e.g. in the case of three presentations in February 1551 (B122, E55 and J12) and second-hand copies in which a purchase price and date occurs (P15). As was to be expected, the earliest imprints often contain evidence of previous ownership. Of his sixteen incunabula, for example, all but three contain evidence of previous ownership. Over half of his post-incunabula (1500–1520) were clearly second-hand (thirty-four out of sixty-four), and of the remaining items with imprints which pre-date Geste's admission to King's College in August 1536 (a little over two hundred), forty-six carry clear evidence of earlier ownership and there are a further twenty-four where there is less certainty. Such second-hand items are indicated after the class-mark by † for a pre-Geste ownership inscription or ‡ for pre-Geste MS annotations, book-price or book-title(s) on fore-edge or spine. After 1536, most of his acquisitions were of new copies, with only fourteen of those with imprints between 1536 and 1554 of pre-Geste provenance (out of about three hundred), and of the remaining items obtained after Geste left Cambridge in 1554 (over six hundred) only eight have been identified with pre-Geste ownership inscriptions.

In the index which follows, the year of publication is given as this appears in the imprint or colophon, except where a date between January and March is given. In such instances the date is adjusted to include our modern reckoning and shown in the form, e.g. '1566/67'.

In the case of items in composite volumes containing publications of different dates, the year of the latest item is given in the second column after the imprint date. Although Geste may have purchased the item concerned at about the time of its publication or soon after, it is not always possible to tell, even from his binding instructions (where these survive), whether he had purchased all the items (of different dates) at the same time (perhaps already bound) or whether he had accumulated the items over a period time to have them all bound together at about the date of the latest item or sometime after that. Those books with his instructions giving the books to be included or the order of the items to be bound together are shown by '+' after the date in the second column.

Many of Geste's books were not commonly held in other Cambridge libraries or private collections of the period, including contemporary inventories (BiCI), and the libraries of Andrew Perne and Matthew Parker. These are shown by a $ after the catalogue-number and amount to nearly forty per cent of his collection. Some twenty per cent (shown by $$ after the catalogue number) do not even occur in Adams, which includes later Cambridge college acquisitions, or in the University Library.

The geographical origin of items still in contemporary bindings are shown by the following codes:

C	Cambridge	SW	'Swiss' [Basle]
L	London	U	Contemporary bindings
O	Oxford		(especially parchment
S	Salisbury		covers) that cannot be
F	French		assigned with any cer-
G	German		tainty to any one of these
N	Netherlandish		locations

Other binding codes (including binders' initials):

CP	Centre-piece	NP	Nicholas Pilgrim
CS	Corner ornament	NS	Nicholas Spierinck
CT	Centre-tool	P	Panel bindings
D	Dis-bound items	PL	Plain
GG	Garrett Godfrey	PT	Parchment
JN	Julian Notary	R	Items which have been
JR	John Reynes		rebound.
MD	Martin Dature	RL	Roll
MS	Items covered only by	TG	Thomas Godfray
	a leaf of manuscript		
	(generally parchment)		

Further binding details are given in the catalogue records.

Year of imprint	Earliest date	Author of first item	Imprint	for-mat	bind-ing	Cat. no.	Class-mark
Incunabula							
1478	–	Gulielmus, *Parisiensis*	Paris	4°	R	G49	L.5.10†
1481	–	Aquinas, T.	Venice	fol.	R	A45	L.3.9‡
1481	–	Duns, J.	Venice	fol.	R	D33	L.4.25†
1482	–	Ficino, M.	Florence	fol.	R	F6$	Y.3.25‡
1485/86	–	Vincent.	Nuremberg	fol.	R	V27	Z.1.62‡
1489	–	Holkot, R.	Basle	fol.	R	H71	L.2.18‡
1494	–	Gerson, J.	Strasbourg	fol.	R	G25	L.3.14‡
1494	–	Vincent, *of Beauvais*	Venice	fol.	R	V26	L.1.15
[1495]	–	Petrus, *Lombardus*	Speier	4°	RL F	P23	L.5.38 ?‡
1495/96	–	Ficino, M.	Venice	fol.	R	F5	Z.2.56†
1496	–	Jacobus, *de Voragine*	Strasbourg	fol.	R	J1	L.4.17‡
1497	–	Peraldus, G.	Basle	4°	R	P17	L.5.31‡
[c. 1497]	–	Orbellis, N. de.	Rouen	8°	R	O19	L.6.3
1497/98	–	Balbus, J.	Venice	fol.	RL?C	B5	Y.2.12‡
[1497/98]	–	Philippus, J.	Lyon	4°	R	P25	L.5.1‡
[1498–1502]	–	Hugo, *de Sancto Charo*	Basle	fol.	R	H82	L.2.1
Post-incunabula period (1501–1520)							
1502	1504	Dionysius [*pseud.*]	Strasbourg	fol.	R	D8	A.5.8(c)‡
1502	1504	Dionysius [*pseud.*]	Strasbourg	fol.	R	D9	A.5.8(b)‡
1503	–	Foresti, J. P.	Venice	fol.	R	F30	Z.2.25‡
[1503]	–	Petrus, *Comestor*	Strasbourg	fol.	R	P20	L.4.10†
1503/04	1504	Dionysius [*pseud.*]	Strasbourg	fol.	R	D7	A.5.8(a)‡
1503/04	–	Nannus Mirabel-lius, D.	Savona	fol.	R	N5	L.2.14
1504	–	Albertus M.	Hagenau	fol.	R	A14	G.3.19‡
1504	–	Albertus M.	Hagenau	fol.	R	A15	G.3.20‡

1504	–	Heracleides	Paris	fol.	R	H41$	A.5.7‡
1505	–	Vivaldus, J. L.	Paris	8°	R	V37	L.6.1†
1506	–	Reuchlin, J.	Pfortzheim	fol.	R	R17	E.4.13†
[1506]	–	Hugo, de Sancto Charo	Paris	4°	RL C NS	H83	D.1.2‡
1507	–	Castellensis, H.	Bologna	4°	RL C	C49$	H.1.21†
[c. 1507]	–	Paulus, de Sancta Maria	Paris	fol.	R	P13	L.4.34
[1508]	–	Biel, G.	Basle	fol.	R	B47	L.3.16‡
[c. 1508]	1529	Eusebius, of Cremona	Paris	8°	R	E56$	A.6.32(e)†
1509	–	Duns, J.	Milan	4°	PT	D32$	ZC2.3.15†
1510	–	Holcot, R.	Lyon	4°	R	H72	L.5.9
1510	1513	Richard, St Victor	Paris	4°	RL F	R26	I.4.9(a)
1510/11	–	Biel, G.	Basle	fol.	R	B46	L.3.15 ?‡
1510/11	–	Joannes, de Colonia	Basle	4°	R	J11	L.5.40
1512	–	Aquinas, T.	Hagenau	fol.	R	A47	L.3.10
1512	1515	Biel, G.	Basle	fol.	R	B48	L.2.15(b)‡
1512/13	–	John, of Damascus	Paris	fol.	R	J13	L.4.5†
1513	–	Clichtoveus, J.	Paris	4°	RL F	C84	I.4.9(b)
1513	–	Petrus, Lombardus	Basle	fol.	R	P22	L.3.7‡
1513	1569+	William, of Ockham	Paris	8°	R	W41	ZC2.1.12
1514	–	Cusa, N. de	Paris	fol.	R	C125	L.4.7‡
1514	–	Cusa, N. de	Paris	fol.	R	C125	L.4.8(a)‡
1514	1531	Ricius, P.	Augsburg	4°	P L	R29$$	I.4.10(e)
[1514]	–	Cusa, N. de	Paris	fol.	R	C126	L.4.8(b)‡
[1514]	–	Pavinis, J. F. de	Paris	4°	RL C GG	P14	L.5.37(a)‡
[1514]	–	Suberti, P. de	Paris	4°	RL C	S95	L.5.37(b)‡
1515	–	Bercheur, P.	Basle	fol.	R	B15	L.2.15(c)‡
1515	–	Jerome	Lyon	4°	R	J6	L.4.31
1515	1527	Le Fèvre, J.	Paris	fol.	R	L23	G.4.7(a)
1515	–	Seneca	Basle	fol.	R	S45	Y.2.16†
[1515]	–	Pérez de Valentia, J.	Paris	fol.	R	P18	G.3.16
1516	–	Gulielmus, Avernus	Paris	fol.	R	G46$	L.4.22‡

1516	–	Raymond	Paris	8°	PT ?C	R13	K.3.46‡
1516	1526	Ricius, P.	Augsburg	4°	PT U	R30$$	ZC2.3.14(f)
1516	1528	Schatzger, C.	Basle	4°	RL L	S30$$	I.3.10(b)
1516/17	1531	Basil	Leipzig	4°	P L	B8$	I.4.10(b)
1517	–	Altensteig, J.	Hagenau	fol.	RL O	A25$$	Y.3.32‡
1517	1518	Hugo, *de Sancto Victore*	Paris	4°	RL C	H87	L.5.36(b) ?†
[c. 1517]	1520	Erasmus, D.	Louvain	4°	R	E22$	L.5.35(a)
1517/18	–	Cagnazzo, J.	Bologna	4°	RL L	C1$$	N.5.26‡
1517/18	–	Duns, J.	Paris	fol.	R	D35	L.4.18
1518	–	Durandus, G.	Paris	4°	R	D36	L.5.13‡
1518	–	Le Fèvre, J.	Paris	4°	RL C GG	L25	L.5.36(a) ?†
1519	1520	Erasmus, D.	Paris	4°	R	E26	L.5.35(b–c)
1519	1521	Theodoret	Paris	fol.	RL C GG	T7	A.5.3(a)
1519/20	–	Gratian	Paris	8°	R	G30	H.2.54†
1519/20	–	Origen	Paris	fol.	R	O20	A.4.1–2‡
[c. 1519/20]	1528	Isolanis, I. de	Cremona	4°	RL L	I8$$	I.3.10(c)
1520	1521	Basil	Paris	fol.	R	B6	A.4.7(a)†
1520	–	Duns, J.	Lyon	8°	P ?L	D34	L.6.32
1520	–	Erasmus, D.	Antwerp	4°	R	E25	L.5.35(f)
1520	–	Erasmus, D.	Antwerp	4°	R	E44	L.5.35(g–h)
1520	1521	Philo	Paris	fol.	RL C	P27$$	A.5.3(c)
[1520]	1521	Fulgentius	Hagenau	fol.	RL C	F38	A.5.3(b)
[1520]	–	Lee, E.	Paris	4°	R	L26	L.5.35(d–e)
1520/21	–	Badius, J.	Paris	fol.	RL C	B2$	A.5.3(d)
1520/21	1560	Gocchius, J.	[?Antwerp]	4°	PT ?L	G28$	ZC2.3.5(g)
1520/21	–	Herolt, J.	Nuremberg	fol.	R	H43	L.4.14‡

Beginnings of the Reformation period

1521	–	Bede	Paris	fol.	R	B10	A.4.7(b)†
1521	–	Cyprian	Basle	fol.	RL C 'W G'	C127	A.4.21 ?‡
1521	1523	Henry VIII	London	4°	PLJR	H40	N.5.13 (a–c)†
1521	1538	Melanchthon, P.	[?Basle]	4°	PT U	M56$$	ZC2.3.6(b)
[1521]	–	Luther, M.	Strasbourg	4°	R	L69	L.5.34(b)‡
[1521]	–	Luther, M.	Wittenberg	4°	R	L74	L.5.34(a)‡
1521/22	1565	Pelbárt, O.	Hagenau	fol.	RL N	P15	M.1.27(a–b)†

1522	–	Bonaventura	Paris	8°	RL ?C	B53	H.1.38–40?‡
1522	–	Erasmus, D.	Basle	fol.	R	E27	G.2.6
1522	–	Erasmus, D.	Basle	8°	PL JR	E31$	N.6.1†
1522	–	Le Fèvre, J.	Meaux	fol.	R	L22	G.4.6‡
1522	–	Stunica, J. L.	Paris	fol.	R	S94$	L.4.12
1522/23	–	Bede	Paris	fol.	R	B11	A.4.19
1523	1526	Campester, L.	Paris	4°	PT U	C30$	ZC2.3.14(c)
1523	1526	Campester, L.	Paris	4°	PT U	C31$$	ZC2.3.14(b)
1523	–	Erasmus, D.	Strasbourg	8°	P C NS	E28$$	G.5.20†
1523	1529	Erasmus, D.	Basle	8°	R	E47	L.6.5(b)
1523	–	Lutzenburgo, B. de	Cologne	8°	R	L80	H.2.10
1523	1531	Melanchthon, P.	Nuremberg	8°	PL ?C	M50	D.6.3(b)‡
1523	–	More, T.	London	4°	P L	M81$	N.5.13(d)†
[?1523]	1558	Brunfels, O.	Strasbourg	4°	CT ?L	B97$$	K.2.11(d)
[?1523]	1530	Hutten, U. von	Wittenberg	8°	PT U	H94$$	ZC2.5.9(b)
[c. 1523]	–	Luther, M.	Basle	8°	R	L78	ZC2.7.11
1523/24	–	Angelus de Clavasio	Lyon	4°	RL C 'WG/IG'	A39	L.5.33
1523/24	–	Gregory I.	Paris	fol.	R	G31	A.1.15†
1524	1525	Bugenhagen, J.	Nuremberg	8°	RL C NS	B111	D.3.1(a)
1524	–	Clichtoveus, J.	Paris	fol.	RL C NS	C82	N.3.17?‡
1524	1533	Erasmus, D.	Basle	8°	RL C GG	E30	N.6.3(a)
1524	1535	Lambert, F.	Nuremberg	8°	RL C GG	L2	C.1.5(b)†
1524	–	Oecolampadius, J.	Nuremberg	8°	PL ?C	O16$$	C.1.3(b)?†
[1524]	1526	Tuberinus, J.	Basle	4°	PT U	T25$	ZC2.3.14(d)
[c. 1524]	–	Oecolampadius, J.	Nuremberg	8°	PL ?C	O12$$	C.1.3(a) ?†
1524/25	–	Mazzolini, S.	Lyon	8°	P JN	M23	D.3.14‡
1524/25	1545	Treger, C.	Strasbourg	4°	PT ?L	T19$	ZC2.3.12(b)
1525	–	Bugenhagen, J.	Strasbourg	8°	RL C	B112	D.3.1(b)
1525	–	Bugenhagen, J.	Strasbourg	8°	RL ?L	B117	C.4.8
1525	–	Capito, W.	Strasbourg	8°	PT U	C39	F.2.4
1525	–	Cochlaeus, J.	Tübingen	8°	PL ?C	C87$	ZC2.1.1(d)
1525	1533	Cyprian	Cologne	8°	RL C	C128	N.6.3(d)

1525	1526	Eck, J.	[n. pl.]	8°	R	E7	L.6.6(a)
1525	1534	Erasmus, D.	Basle	8°	CT C	E21$	ZC1.4.6(b)
1525	–	Gaza, T.	Cologne	8°	P ?C/U	G18$$	Y.5.14‡
1525	–	Georgius, F.	Venice	fol.	R	G23$	L.3.21
1525	–	Hegendorff, C.	Hagenau	8°	PL U	H13	D.5.7 ?‡
1525	1536+	Knopken, A.	Strasbourg	8°	RL C	K11$	D.2.6(b)
1525	–	Lambert, F.	Nuremberg	8°	PL ?C	L3	C.5.6(b)
1525	–	Lambert, F.	Nuremberg	8°	PL ?C	L4	C.5.6(a)
1525	–	Luther, M.	Wittenberg	8°	PL ?C	L52	D.2.2
1525	1553	Luther, M.	Strasbourg	8°	PT U	L66	ZC2.6.18(d)
1525	1542	Luther, M.	Strasbourg	8°	RL C	L77	D.6.7(b)
[1525]	1526	Lambert, F.	Nuremberg	8°	RL C	L9	H.1.6(b)‡
[1525]	–	Latomus, J.	Basle	8°	R	L16	ZC2.7.10
[1525]	1526	Schatzger, C.	Tübingen	8°	PL ?C	S32$$	ZC2.1.1(b)
[?1525]	–	Zwingli, U.	Zürich	8°	RL C	Z6	N.6.13
[c. 1525]	1545	Bugenhagen, J.	[n.pl.]	8°	R	B116$$	C.5.11(b)
[c. 1525]	1553	Erasmus, D.	[n.pl.]	8°	PT U	E37$$	ZC2.6.18(i)
[c. 1525]	1526	Latomus, J.	Antwerp	4°	PT U	L17	ZC2.3.14(a)
1525/26	1536+	Jonas, J.	Basle	8°	RL C	J14$	D.2.6(a)
1525/26	–	Lambert, F.	Nuremberg	8°	RL C NS	L7	H.1.6(a)‡
1525/26	–	Oecolampadius, J.	Basle	4°	RL U	O6	C.1.10 ?‡
1525/26	–	Ruysius, G.	Antwerp	8°	PL ?C	R40$$	ZC2.1.1(c)
[1525/26]	–	Schatzger, C.	Tübingen	8°	PL ?C	S31$$	ZC2.1.1(a)
1526	–	Bible	Paris	16°	RL F	B34	G.6.12
1526	–	Bible	Paris	16°	P ?C	B35	G.6.14†
1526	1538	Bugenhagen, J.	Strasbourg	8°	RL/CT C	B113	C.5.4(f)?†
1526	–	Eck, J.	[?Cologne]	8°	R	E6	L.6.6(b)
1526	1529	Erasmus, D.	Basle	8°	R	E34	L.6.5(a)
1526	–	Erasmus, D.	Basle	8°	R	E40	L.6.4 ?‡
1526	–	Hugo, de Sancto Victore	Paris	fol.	R	H86	L.1.9‡
1526	1538	Lambert, F.	Strasbourg	8°	RL/CT C	L6	C.5.4(a)?†
1526	–	Valla, L.	Basle	8°	P ?C	V3	C.4.6 ?‡
1526	1553	Venatorius, T.	Nuremberg	8°	PT U	V8$$	ZC2.6.18(h)

[1526]	–	Hugo, *de Sancto Victore*	Paris	fol.	R	H85	L.1.8
[c. 1526]	–	George, *D. of Saxony*	Antwerp	4°	PT U	G22$$	ZC2.3.14(e)
1526/27	1539	Luther, M.	Strasbourg	8°	RL C	L65	D.5.2(b)
1526/27	1534+	Oecolampadius, J.	Basle	8°	RL C	O13$	C.1.6(a)‡
1527	–	Aurogallus, M.	Wittenberg	8°	R	A68$	ZC2.8.8
1527	1544	Borrhaus, M.	Strasbourg	8°	CT ?C	B62	ZC2.2.9(d)
1527	1534+	Bucer, M.	Zürich	8°	RL C	B102	C.1.6(c)‡
1527	–	Erasmus, D.	Basle	8°	P ?C	E48	H.1.2†
1527	–	Le Fèvre, J.	Basle	fol.	R	L24	G.4.7(b)‡
1527	1529	Philippus	Basle	fol.	RL C	P26	N.4.5(b)
1527	1545	Strasbourg Church	Strasbourg	8°	CT C	S90$	H.1.8(c)
1527	–	Vio, T. de.	Lyon	8°	PL ?C	V33	K.3.42 ?‡
[c. 1527]	–	Origen	Basle	8°	MS U	O21	ZC2.4.16
1527/28	1531	Agricola, R.	Tübingen	4°	P L	A12$	I.4.10(d)
1527/28	1538	Luther, M.	Strasbourg	8°	PT ?L	L59	E.6.29(b)
1527/28	–	Oecolampadius, J.	Basle	4°	PT U	O11	E.5.31 ?‡
1527/28	–	Pirckheimer, B.	Nuremberg	8°	PT U	P36$$	ZC2.6.6?‡
1528	1536+	Althamer, A.	Nuremberg	8°	RL C	A26$$	D.2.6(d)
1528	–	Bible	Lyon	4°	R	B30	E.5.18
1528	1536	Capito, W.	Strasbourg	8°	RL/CT C	C37$	D.4.3(a)
1528	–	Jacobus, de Voragine	Paris	8°	P ?C	J2	D.4.10
1528	1538	Melanchthon, P.	Hagenau	8°	RL/CT C	M46	C.5.4(e)?†
1528	–	Murner, T.	Lucerne	4°	RL L	M86$$	I.3.10(a)
1528	1531	Wilramnus	Hagenau	8°	P U	W44$	D.2.7(b)
1528/29	1558	Benedictus, A.	Strasbourg	8°	PT U	B13	X.2.30(b)‡
1528/29	–	Paschasius Radbertus	Hagenau	4°	PT ?C	P6	ZC2.3.10‡
1528/29	1529	Sedulius	Basle	fol.	RL C	S40	N.4.5(c)
1528/29	–	Tertullian	Basle	fol.	R	T3	A.4.22
1529	–	Augustine	Cologne	8°	R	A62	A.6.32(a)†
1529	–	Augustine	Cologne	8°	R	A63	A.6.32(d)†
1529	–	Augustine	Cologne	8°	R	A65$$	A.6.32(b)†
1529	–	Augustine	Cologne	8°	R	A67$$	A.6.32(c)†
1529	–	Bible	Paris	16°	R	B32	G.6.11

1529	–	Bible	Paris	16°	P ?L	B33	G.6.13‡
1529	1542	Buschius, H.	Marburg	8°	RL C	B137	D.6.7(f)
1529	–	Erasmus, D.	Basle	8°	R	E23$	L.6.5(c)
1529	1549	Erasmus, D.	Paris	8°	PT U	E46$	ZC2.8.1(f)
1529	1531	Isidore	Hagenau	4°	P L MD	I6$	I.4.10(a)
1529	–	Reuchlin, J.	Wittenberg	8°	PT ?L	R16	F.2.6 ?‡
1529	1532	Sens, Council	Paris	fol.	RL L	S46$	N.3.18(d)
1529/30	–	Bede	Basle	fol.	RL C GG	B12	N.4.5(a)
1529/30	–	Brentz, J.	Hagenau	8° .	RL U	B75	C.6.2
1529/30	1534	Erasmus, D.	Basle	8°	CT C	E20$	ZC1.4.6(f)
1529/30	1532	Erasmus, D.	Basle	4°	CT C	E45$	I.3.8(b)
1530	1532	Angelomus	Cologne	fol.	RL L	A38	N.3.18(a)
1530	1534	Erasmus, D.	Antwerp	8°	CT C	E38	ZC1.4.6(a)
1530	1537	Latomus, J.	Antwerp	8°	CT ?C	L18	H.2.12(a)‡
1530	1532	Oecolampadius, J.	Basle	4°	PL ?C	O9	C.1.2(b)
1530	–	Strasbourg Church	Strasbourg	8°	PT U	S91$$	ZC2.5.9(a)
[1530]	1535	Luther, M.	Hagenau	8°	RL C	L61	C.1.5(d)†
1530/31	1560+	Alcuin	Strasbourg	8°	R	A19	A.6.21(b)
1531	–	Alcuin	Basle	8°	P U	A18$	D.2.7(a)
1531	–	Alphabetum	Hagenau	4°	P L	A23$$	I.4.10(c)
1531	1532	Ebser, J.	Cologne	fol.	RL L	E2	N.3.18(b)
1531	1534	Erasmus, D.	Basle	8°	CT C	E24$	ZC1.4.6(c)
1531	1551	Eucherius	Basle	fol	RL ?O/?L	E55	E.4.1(a)
1531	–	Haymo	Cologne	8°	P L	H10	C.4.9
1531	–	Haymo	Cologne	8°	P U	H11$	D.2.7(c)
1531	–	Hugo, de Sancto Charo	Paris	fol.	R	H84$	G.2.5†
1531	1553	Luther, M.	Marburg	8°	PT U	L76	ZC2.6.18(a)
1531	–	Matthei, L.	Paris	8°	RL C	M16$$	D.3.8
1531	–	Melanchthon, P.	Hagenau	8°	PL ?C	M49	D.6.3(a)‡
1531	1548	Prosper	Cologne	8°	R	P56	ZC2.6.19(c)
1531	–	Tritheim, J.	Cologne	4°	R	T20	B.5.44†
1531	1568+	Vio, T. de	Paris	8°	CT L	V32$$	I.1.6(e)
[1531]	1532	Paris, University of	Paris	fol.	RL L	P5	N.3.18(e)

1532	–	Bible	Paris	16°	R	B31	G.6.10‡
1532	–	Erasmus, D.	Basle	4°	CT C	E33	I.3.8(a)
1532	1534	Erasmus, D.	Basle	8°	CT C	E35	ZC1.4.6(d)
1532	–	Erasmus, D.	Basle	8°	R	E41	ZC2.2.3‡
1532	1560+	Potho	Hagenau	8°	R	P46$	A.6.21(c)‡
1532	–	Rabanus, M.	Cologne	8°	RL ?C	R2$$	C.5.2
1532	1534	Sachs, H.	Cologne	8°	R	S2	ZC2.7.9(a)
1532	–	Titelman, F.	Paris	8°	R	T13	C.5.14
1532/33	–	Bucer, M.	Strasbourg	fol.	R	B98	E.4.7
1532/33	–	Oecolampadius, J.	Basle	4°	PL ?C	O3	C.1.2(a)
1532/33	1548	Patriarchs	Hagenau	8°	R	P7	ZC2.6.19(d)
1532/33	–	Rabanus M.	Cologne	8°	RL ?C	R1	C.5.1
1532/33	1554	Salonius	Hagenau	4°	R	S9	C.2.9(a)
1532/33	–	Sens, Council	Paris	fol.	RL L	S47	N.3.18(c)
1533	–	Driedo, J.	Louvain	fol.	R	D28	L.2.13
1533	–	Erasmus, D.	Antwerp	8°	RL C	E32	N.6.3(c)
1533	–	Erasmus, D.	Antwerp	8°	RL C	E39	N.6.3(b)
1533	–	Haymo	Cologne	4°	P C	H9$	D.5.13†
1533	–	Joannes, a Davantria	Cologne	8°	RL C	J9	H.1.31?‡
1533	–	Luther, M.	Hagenau	4°	RL C	L64	C.2.3
1533	–	Oecolampadius, J.	Strasbourg	4°	P ?U	O7	G.5.2
1533	1543	Witzel, G.	Leipzig	4°	CT C	W50$	I.7.6(a)
[c. 1533]	–	Bodius, H. [pseud.]	Antwerp	8°	R	B51	H.2.5?†
1533/34	–	Brentz, J.	Hagenau	8°	PT ?G	B78	ZC2.6.9
1534	1540	Alphabetum	Paris	8°	PT U	A22	F.2.5(c)
1534	1544	Bucer, M.	Strasbourg	8°	CT ?C	B109	ZC2.2.9(c)
1534	–	Erasmus, D.	Basle	8°	CT C	E42$$	ZC1.4.6(e)
1534	–	Fox, E.	London	4°	R	F31	L.5.29 ?‡
1534	1543	Haner, J.	Leipzig	4°	CT C	H5	I.7.6(c)
1534	1555	Isidore	Antwerp	8°	R	I7$$	A.6.28(b)
1534	1543	Luther, M.	Wittenberg	8°	PL C	L53	D.5.5(b)
1534	1543	Luther, M.	Wittenberg	8°	PL C	L56	D.5.5(c)
1534	–	Oecolampadius, J.	Strasbourg	8°	RL C	O15	C.1.6(b)‡
1534	–	Puteo, F. de	Paris	fol.	R	P58	E.3.12
1534	–	Tritheim, J.	Cologne	8°	R	T21	ZC2.7.9(b)
1534	–	Viexmontis, C.	Paris	4°	P U	V23	N.5.5(b)

[c. 1534]	1569+	Dionysius, Carthusianus	[Cologne]	8°	CT L	D20	ZC2.1.9
1534/35	–	Driedo, J.	Louvain	4°	P U	D26	N.5.5(a)
1534/35	–	Oecolampadius, J.	Strasbourg	4°	CS ?L	O8	C.1.9
[1534/35]	1570+	Witzel, G.	Leipzig	8°	R	W58$	L.5.8(f)
1535	–	Brunfels, O.	Strasbourg	fol.	R	B95$	G.4.18
1535	–	Bugenhagen, J.	Basle	8°	R	B114	C.2.11
1535	?1551	Bullinger, H.	Zürich	fol.	R	B122	G.3.22(a)
1535	–	Erasmus, D.	Antwerp	8°	P L	E36	D.3.7‡
1535	–	Luther, M.	Hagenau	8°	RL C	L68	C.1.5(c)†
1535	–	Oecolampadius, J.	Basle	8°	RL C	O10	C.1.5(a)†
1535	–	Vehe, M.	Leipzig	4°	PT ?G	V7	ZC2.3.17?‡
1535	1536	Zacharias	Cologne	fol.	R	Z1$	E.4.6(b)
1535/36	–	Zwingli, U.	Zürich	8°	R	Z7	L.6.14 ?‡

Geste in Cambridge (1536–1554)

1536	–	Althamer, A.	Nuremberg	8°	RL C GG	A27	D.6.12
1536	–	Brentz, J.	Hagenau	8°	P L MD	B72	C.6.1†
1536	?1551	Brentz, J.	Hagenau	8°	R	B86	G.3.22(b)
1536	1538	Cologne. Formula	Cologne	fol.	R	C96$	B.3.21(b)
1536	–	Eck, J.	Cologne	8°	P L ?TG	E3	G.5.18
1536	–	Lorich, G.	Mainz	8°	PL TG	L38	M.2.11
1536	–	Ludolf	Paris	8°	R	L48	L.6.7
1536	1539	Luther, M.	Halle	8°	P L MD	L57	D.5.3(a)
1536	1543	Luther, M.	Halle	8°	PL C	L57	D.5.5(c)
1536	–	Luther, M.	Strasbourg	8°	RL/CT C	L62	D.4.3(b)
1536	–	Melanchthon, P.	[n. pl.]	8°	R	M63	L.6.18 ?‡
1536	1539	Münster, S.	Basle	8°	PT ?L	M84	F.2.3(a)
1536	1544	Rhegius, U.	Hamburg	8°	PL U	R18$$	C.6.5(d)
1536	–	Sadoleto, J.	Lyon	fol.	R	S3	G.3.21
1536	1537	Sepúlveda, J.G. de	Cologne	8°	PT U	S48$	ZC2.6.10(b)?†
1536	1566+	Smaragdus	?Hagenau	8°	R	S63	E.6.9(c)
1536	1542	Valliculus, G.	Nuremberg	8°	RL C	V4$	D.6.7(c)

1536	1561	Witzel, G.	Leipzig	8°	CT L	W57$	ZC2.2.8 (c)
[1536]	1546	Bible. Com. II & III John	London	4°	CT C	B39$	D.2.8(b)
[1536]	1544	Rhegius, U.	Hamburg	8°	PL U	R19$$	C.6.5(e)
[c. 1536]	–	Erasmus, D.	[n. pl.]	4°	RL C	E29$$	D.1.13–14
1536/37	–	Megander, C.	Basle	8°	RL C	M26$$	D.2.6(c)
1536/37	–	Smaragdus	Strasbourg	fol.	R	S62	E.4.6(a)
1537	1542	Corvinus, A.	Marburg	8°	RL C	C104$	D.6.7(e)
1537	–	Hus, Jan	Wittenberg	8°	R	H93$	L.6.23
1537	–	Joannes, a Davantria	Cologne	8°	CT ?C	J10	H.2.12(b)
1537	–	Philo, of Carpasia	Paris	8°	R	P28	C.5.3
1537	–	Primasius	Lyon	8°	RL ?L	P53	D.1.8
1537	–	Witzel, G.	Leipzig	8°	PT U	W53$	ZC2.6.10 (a)?†
1537	–	Witzel, G.	Leipzig	8°	PT U	W56$	ZC2.6.10 (c)?†
[1537]	–	Suetonius	Basle	8°	RL ?C	S96	Y.5.29
1537/38	–	Elias	Basle	8°	CT L	E18	F.2.19
1538	–	Artopoeus, P.	Basle	8°	RL ?SW	A56	E.6.5†
1538	1565	Clichtoveus, J.	Paris	16°	R	C83	K.3.13(a)
1538	–	Cologne. Canones	Cologne	fol.	R	C97	B.3.21(a)
1538	–	Draconites, J.	Strasbourg	8°	RL/ CT C	D25$$	C.5.4(c)?†
1538	–	Lambert, F.	Worms	8°	RL/ CT C	L8	C.5.4(b)?†
1538	1539	Luther, M.	Wittenberg	8°	RL C NS	L63	D.5.4(a)
1538	–	Luther, M.	Wittenberg	8°	PT U	L72	ZC2.6.14†
1538	–	Phrygio, P C.	Strasbourg	8°	RL/ CT C	P30$$	C.5.4(d)?†
[1538]	1560	Rome, Church of	Strasbourg	4°	PT ?L	R35	ZC2.3.5(b)
[1538]	–	Sarcerius, E.	Frankfurt-a-M.	4°	PT U	S23	ZC2.3.6(a)
1538/39	–	Bullinger, H.	Zürich	4°	RL C NS	B127	H.1.20
1538/39	–	Luther, M.	Halle	8°	PT ?L	L67	E.6.29(a)
1538/39	–	Sarcerius, E.	Frankfurt-a-M.	8°.	RL C NS	S15$	C.6.9
1539	–	Aurogallus, M.	Basle	8°	PT ?L	A69$	F.2.3(b)

1539	–	Bonaventura	Antwerp	8°	R	B52	C.4.1†
1539	1540	Campensis, J.	Paris	8°	PT U	C29	F.2.5(a)
1539	–	Capito, W.	Strasbourg	8°	RL C ?NS	C38	M.2.3
1539	–	Corvinus, A.	Halle	8°	CT ?C	C102$	A.6.31
1539	1542	Dionysius, Carthusianus	Cologne	fol.	RL/ CT C	D13	E.3.19(b)
1539	–	Lambert, F.	Basle	8°	RL C GG/ ?NP	L5	C.5.7?†
1539	–	Luther, M.	Strasbourg	8°	RL C	L55	D.5.2(a)
1539	–	Luther, M.	Wittenberg	8°	P L	L58	D.5.3(b)
1539	–	Mayer, S.	Zürich	fol.	RL L	M22	E.3.6(b)
1539	–	Pellicanus, C.	Zürich	fol.	RL L	P16	E.3.6(a)
1539	1543	Sadoleto, J.	Strasbourg	8°	R	S4	L.6.11(b)
1539	1543	Sadoleto, J.	Strasbourg	8°	R	S5	L.6.11(c)
1539	–	Sarcerius, E.	Basle	8°	RL C	S16$	D.5.4(b)
1539	–	Vio, T. de	Paris	fol.	R	V29$	G.2.17
[1539]	–	Sarcerius, E.	Frankfurt -a-M.	8°	RL C	S13	D.2.3
[1539]	–	Sarcerius, E.	Frankfurt -a-M.	8°	RL C ?NS	S25$	ZC2.1.5
1540	–	Clenardus, N.	Paris	8°	PT U	C81	F.2.5(b)
1540	1544	Cochlaeus, J.	Ingolstadt	4°	R	C89	L.4.30(a)
1540	–	Dionysius, Carthusianus	Cologne	fol.	RL/ CT ?C	D21	N.4.2
1540	–	Gulielmu, *Baufeti*	Lyon	8°	PT U	G47	ZC2.6.12†
1540	–	Josephus, F.	Basle	fol	R	J16	L.2.23
1540	–	Marulić, M.	Solingen	8°	PL ?C	M14	N.6.4
1540	–	Nausea, F.	Cologne	fol.	RL ?L/?O	N8	N.3.16
1540	–	Prosper	Cologne	8°	PT U	P55	A.6.42
1540	1542	Rivius, J.	Leipzig	8°	RL C	R34$$	D.6.7(a)
1540	–	Sarcerius, E.	Basle	8°	PL C	S19$$	D.2.4
[1540]	–	Sarcerius, E.	Basle	8°	RL C ?NS	S18	D.2.5
[?1540]	1570+	Bucer, M.	Strasbourg	4°	R	B106	L.5.15(a)
[?1540]	–	Sarcerius, E.	Frankfurt -a-M.	8°	CT C	S14	G.5.14

[c. 1540]	1560/61	Schmalkalden	[n. pl.]	4°	PT ?L	S37$$	ZC2.3.5(f)
1540/41	–	Arboreus, J.	Paris	fol.	PL ?F	A49	M.1.17
1540/41	1543	Draconites, J.	Marburg	8°	PL C	D23	D.5.5(a)
1540/41	–	Fidati, S.	Cologne	fol.	R	F7	L.4.1
1541	1548	Alardus	Antwerp	8°	R	A13$$	ZC2.6.19(b)
1541	1551	Chrysologus, P.	Cologne	fol.	RL ?O/?L	C65$$	E.4.1(b)
1541	–	Cicero, M. T.	Strasbourg	8°	RL/ CT C ?NS	C74	X.2.16
1541	1544	Cochlaeus, J.	Mainz	4°	R	C88$	L.4.30(d)
1541	–	Hoffman, C.	Frankfurt -a-M.	8°	PT ?L	H59	E.6.33
1541	1546	Liturgies. Greek Rite	Worms	4°	PT ?C	L37	ZC2.4.1(b)
1541	1549	Lorich, G.	Wetzlar	8°	[PT] U	L39	ZC2.8.1(a)
1541	1545	Luther, M.	Augsburg	8°	CT C	L79	H.1.8(d)
1541	1543	Placentius, C.	Ingolstadt	4°	CT C	P37$$	I.7.6(b)
1541	1560	Ratisbon – Colloquy	Wittenberg	4°	PT ?L	R8$	ZC2.3.5(d)
1541	–	Ravisius, J.	Lyon	8°	CT ?L	R12	X.2.17–18
[1541]	–	Melanchthon, P.	Wittenberg	8°	R	M52	C.5.9
[1541]	–	Sarcerius, E.	Frankfurt -a-M.	8°	RL C	S17$$	C.6.10†
[1541]	–	Sarcerius, E.	Frankfurt -a-M.	8°	RL/ CT C ?NS	S20$$	C.6.11
1542	–	Augustine	Basle	fol.	R	A60	A.4.23–24
1542	–	Augustine	Basle	fol.	R	A61	A.5.2
1542	–	Brentz, J.	Frankfurt -a-M.	fol.	R	B71	G.3.6(a)
1542	–	Brentz, J.	Frankfurt -a-M.	8°	RL/ CT C ?NS	B83	C.6.3
1542	–	Dionysius, Carthusianus	Paris	fol.	RL/ CT C	D12	E.3.19(a)
1542	1568	Eck, J.	Cologne	4°	RL L	E4	D.1.4(c)
1542	1543	Eck, J.	Cologne	4°	CT C	E5	I.7.6(d)
1542	–	Imler, C.	Frankfurt -a-M.	8°	RL C	I3$$	D.6.7(d)

1542	1545	Marius, A.	Würzburg	4°	PT ?L	M10	ZC2.3.12(a)
1542	1544	Melanchthon, P.	Wittenberg	8°	R	M47	C.5.8(b)
1542	1560	Melanchthon, P.	Wittenberg	4°	PT ?L	M54$	ZC2.3.5(e)
1542	1569+	Nonnus	Paris	8°	CT L	N10	N.6.11(d)
1542	–	Pighius, A.	Cologne	fol	CT U	P33	N.4.6†
1542	–	Rhegius, U.	Frankfurt -a-M.	fol.	R	R24	G.3.6(b)
1542	1569+	Schenck, J.	Leipzig	8°	R	S36$$	E.6.26(b)
1542	1546	Willich, J.	Strasbourg	8°	MS U	W43$$	G.6.21(a)
[1542]	1545	Imler, C.	Frankfurt -a-M.	8°	R	I2$$	C.5.10(b)
1542/43	–	Münster, S.	Basle	8°	RL/ CT C ?NS	M85	F.2.29
1543	–	Antiochus	Paris	4°	CT C	A43	C.2.13
1543	–	Bucer, M.	?Strasbourg	8°	PL C	B107	H.1.5
1543	–	Calvin, J.	Geneva	4°	PT U	C15$$	K.2.3
1543 [pt. 2]	–	Draconites, J.	Marburg	8°	PL C	D23	D.5.5(a)
1543	–	Eck, J.	Ingolstadt	4°	CT C	E8A$$	I.7.6(e)
1543	–	Luther, M.	Wittenberg	8°	RL C ?NS	L49	L.6.30
1543	–	Melanchthon, P.	Wesel	8°	R	M55$$	L.6.11(a)
1543	1568+	Pighius, A.	Paris	8°	CT L	P31	I.1.6(d)
1543	1551	Placus, A.	Cologne	fol.	RL ?O/?L	P39$	N.3.13(b)
1543	1544	Rhegius, U.	Frankfurt -a-M.	8°	PL U	R20$$	C.6.5(c)
1543	–	Stobaeus, J.	Zürich	fol.	RL G	S89	M.1.15
[1543]	–	Sarcerius, E.	Frankfurt -a-M.	8°	RL C	S12	C.6.7–8
1543/44	–	Dionysius, Carthusianus	Cologne	fol.	RL C	D17	E.3.20
1543/44	–	Melanchthon, P.	[n.pl.]	8°	R	M48	C.5.8(a)
1543/44	–	Phrygio, P. C.	Basle	4°	PT ?L	P29$$	E.5.32
1544	1545	Aepinus, J.	Frankfurt -a-M.	8°	CT C	A5	D.5.6(a)
1544	–	Aepinus, J.	Frankfurt -a-M.	8°	PL U	A6	C.6.5(b)
1544	–	Bible. Comm. Rom. & Gal.	Lyon	8°	CT C	B38$$	C.4.14

1544	–	Brentz, J.	Frankfurt-a-M.	8°	PL U	B89	C.6.5(a)
1544	–	Brentz, J.	Halle	8°	RL C ?NS	B91	H.2.7
1544	–	Broeckwey, A.	Paris	8°	RL/CT ?L	B94	D.4.8†
1544	–	Bullinger, H.	Zürich	8°	CT ?C	B118$$	ZC2.6.7
1544	1551	Bullinger, H.	Zürich	4°	PL ?C	B123	I.4.11(b)
1544	–	Campeggio, L.	Lyon	8°	CT U	C28$$	B.6.4(c)
1544	–	Chiari, I.	Jena	8°	RL/CT C ?NS	C64$$	C.3.12
1544	–	Cochlaeus, J.	Ingolstadt	8°	PT ?C	C90	ZC2.6.17
1544	–	Cochlaeus, J.	Ingolstadt	4°	R	C91$	L.4.30(b)
1544	–	Cochlaeus, J.	Ingolstadt	4°	R	C92$	L.4.30(c)
1544	–	Cologne.Canones	Lyon.	8°	CT U	C98	B.6.4(a)
1544	–	Cologne. Enchiridion	Lyon	8°	CT U	C99	B.6.4(b)
1544	–	Draconites, J.	Marburg	8°	R	D24	C.5.8(c)
1544	–	Kinthisius, I.	Frankfurt-a-M.	8°	PT ?C	K2$$	G.6.17
1544	1546	Kirchmeyer, T.	Frankfurt-a-M.	8°	CT C	K3$$	D.2.8(c)
1544	1549	Musculus, W.	Augsburg	4°	CT C	M88	I.4.4(c)
1544	–	Nausea, F.	Antwerp	8°	RL U 'R W'	N7$$	N.6.6
1544	–	Oecolampadius, J.	Basle	8°	CT ?C	O4	C.1.4
1544	–	Oecolampadius, J.	Basle	8°	PL ?C	O5	D.2.1
1544	1545	Paris, Univ. of	Geneva	8°	CT C	P4	H.1.8(b)
1544	1549	Rhegius, U.	Frankfurt-a-M.	8°	[PT] U	R21$$	ZC2.8.1(c)
1544	1549	Rhegius, U.	Frankfurt-a-M.	8°	[PT] U	R22	ZC2.8.1(b)
1544	–	Spangenberg, J.	Leipzig	8°	CT ?C	S80	ZC2.2.9(a)
1544	–	Vives, J. L.	Basle	8°	CT C	V39	N.6.5
[1544]	–	Sarcerius E.	Strasbourg	8°	RL/CT C ?NS	S21$	D.6.8
[1544]	–	Sarcerius E.	Strasbourg	8°	RL/CT C ?NS	S22$	D.6.9
[?1544]	–	Spangenberg, J.	Frankfurt-a-M.	8°	CT ?C	S78$$	ZC2.2.9(b)

[c. 1544]	–	Imler, C.	Frankfurt-a-M.	8°	RL ?L	I1$$	D.3.6
1544/45	1563	Luther, M.	Frankfurt-a-M.	fol.	R	L75	L.2.7(d)
1545	–	Aepinus, J.	Frankfurt-a-M.	8°	CT C	A7	D.5.6(b)
1545	–	Billick, E.	Paris	8°	PL ?C	B50	ZC2.7.2
1545	1549	Brentz, J.	Halle	fol.	R	B84	G.3.8(a)
1545	1570+	Bucer, M.	Strasbourg	4°	R	B104	L.5.15(b)
1545	1570+	Calvin, J.	Geneva	8°	CT L	C18$$	ZC2.1.6(b)
1545	1564	Carvialus, L.	Cologne	4°	CT L	C44	K.2.26(a)
1545	–	Dietrich, V.	Frankfurt-a-M.	4°	CT C	D6$	G.5.4
1545	1548	Dionysius, *Carthusianus*	Cologne	fol.	RL/CT C	D18	E.3.21(a)
1545	1546	Florebelli, A.	Cologne	4°	PT U	F25$	ZC2.3.11(a)
1545	1549	Gallasius, N.	Geneva	8°	CT?L	G5$$	ZC2.7.13(a)
1545	1553	Gualtherus, R.	Zürich	8°	PT U	G36	ZC2.6.18(g)
1545	–	Hoffman, C.	Frankfurt-a-M.	8°	CT C	H60$	D.5.6(c)
1545	–	Hoffman, C.	Frankfurt-a-M.	8°	CT C	H61$	D.5.6(d)
1545	–	Hofmeister, J.	Cologne	4°	PL U	H65$	D.1.3
1545	–	Hofmeister, J.	Mainz	4°	PT ?L	H66$	ZC2.3.12(c)
1545	1570+	Hofmeister, J.	Mainz	4°	R	H69	L.5.8(e)
1545	–	Hofmeister, J.	Mainz	4°	PT ?L	H70	ZC2.3.12 (d)
1545	–	Lasco, J. à	Bonn	8°	PT ?G	L12	ZC2.6.15
1545	–	Latomus, B.	Cologne	4°	PT ?L	L14	ZC2.3.12 (e)
1545	–	Luther, M.	Wittenberg	8°	CT C	L60	D.5.1
1545	–	Melanchthon, P.	Halle	8°	R	M53	C.5.10(a)
1545	–	Rhegius, U.	Frankfurt-a-M.	8°	CT C	R23	H.1.8(a)
1545	–	Zürich, *Confessio*	Zürich	8°	CT ?C	Z4	M.2.16
[c. 1545]	–	Luther, M.	Nuremberg	8°	R	L54	E.6.27
[c. 1545]	–	Melanchthon, P.	Basle	8°	R	M51	C.5.11(a)
[c. 1545]	–	Postel, G.	[Basle]	8°	PT ?O/?C	P45$	ZC2.6.4†
1546	1560	Aepinus, J.	Frankfurt-a-M.	4°	PT ?L	A10	ZC2.3.5(c)

1546	–	Artopoeus, P.	Basle	8°	CT C	A55	C.4.2
1546	1549	Bucer, M.	Neuburg	4°	CT C	B108	I.4.4(a)
1546	–	Bugenhagen, J.	Wittenberg	4°	R	B115	C.2.10
1546	1548	Calvin, J.	Strasbourg	8°	CT C	C11	ZC1.4.7(a)
1546	–	Cruciger, C.	Wittenberg	8°	R	C113$$	E.6.28
1546	–	Cruciger, C.	Strasbourg	8°	CT C	C114	D.4.4
1546	1548	Dionysius, Carthusianus	Cologne	fol.	RL/CT C	D19	E.3.21(b)
1546	1549	Hofmeister, J	?Freiburg	8°	[PT] U	H67	ZC2.8.1(d)
1546	–	Latomus, B.	Cologne	4°	PT ?C	L15	ZC2.4.1 (a)
1546	–	Mayer, S.	Frankfurt-a-M.	8°	CT C	M20$	D.2.8(a)
1546	1569+	Oecolampadius, J.	Berne	8°	R	O14$	E.6.26(d)
1546	–	Rome. City of	Lyon	4°	PT U	R37$$	ZC2.3.11(b)
1546	–	Sarcerius E.	Basle	4°	RL ?L	S24	ZC2.2.5
1546	–	Smith, R.	London	8°	CT L	S64	R.6.46†
1546	–	Willich, J.	Basle	8°	MS U	W42$$	G.6.21(b)
[1546]	–	Spangenberg, J.	Frankfurt-a-M.	8°	MS ?C	S77$	G.6.23
1546/47	–	Gardiner, S.	Louvain	4°	PT U	G13	ZC2.3.11(c)
1546/47	–	Goeuschel, J.	Basle	8°	CT C	G29$$	F.2.10
1546/47	1551	John, of Damascus	Cologne	fol.	RL ?O/?L	J12	N.3.13(a)
1546/47	1569+	Mayer, S.	Berne	8°	R	M21$	E.6.26(a)
[1546/47]	c. 1550	Rivius, J.	Basle	8°	R	R33	L.6.16(a)
1547	–	Brunfels, O.	Basle	8°	CT L	B96	D.3.2
1547	1548	Councils – Trent. Acta	Geneva	8°	CT C	C107	ZC1.4.7(c)
1547	–	Driedo, J.	Louvain	fol.	R	D27	L.3.19
1547	–	Spangenberg, J.	Frankfurt-a-M.	8°	CS U	S75	D.3.4
1548	–	Aegidius	Antwerp	4°	R	A3$	ZC2.6.19(a)
1548	–	Brentz, J.	Frankfurt-a-M.	8°	CT C	B88	C.6.4
1548	–	Bucer, M.	?Strasbourg	4°	R	B110	L.5.16(a–b)?†
1548	1569+	Charles V	Cologne	8°	D ?L	C58	B.6.42(d)
1548	–	Cruciger, C.	Wittenberg	8°	CT C	C116$$	ZC1.4.7(b)
1548	–	Culman, L.	Nuremberg	8°	CT L	C120$$	M.2.29

1548	–	Dionysius, *Carthusianus*	Cologne	fol.	RL/CT C	D10	E.3.16
1548	1549	Dionysius, *Carthusianus*	Cologne	fol.	RL/CT C	D15	E.3.18(a)
1548	1565	Florus	Paris	8°	CT L	F26$$	M.2.21(b)
1548	1550?+	Guilliaud, C.	Paris	8°	CT L	G45	C.3.1(b)
1548	–	Hermann	London	8°	CT C	H42	O.1.25
1548	1550	Rivius, J.	Basle	8°	RL ?SW	R32	H.1.37(a)
1548	–	Titelman, F.	Lyon	8°	CS U	T11	C.5.15†
[?1548]	1549	Aepinus, J.	London	4°	CT C	A11	I.4.4(b)
[1548/49]	–	Spangenberg, J.	Frankfurt-a-M.	8°	CS U	S76	D.3.5
1549	1566	Anselm	Paris	fol.	R	A41	G.4.12(b)
1549	1557	Artopoeus, P.	Frankfurt-an-der-Oder	8°	PT U	A57$$	E.6.35(b)
1549	–	Brentz, J.	Frankfurt-a-M.	fol.	R	B85	G.3.8(b)
1549	–	Calvin, J.	[Geneva]	8°	CT ?L	C17	ZC2.7.13(c)
1549	1570+	Ceneau, R.	Paris	16°	CT L	C55$$	ZC1.4.13(c)
1549	–	Cochlaeus, J.	Mainz	8°	CT ?L	C86$	ZC2.7.13(b)
1549	1564+	Cologne *Antididagma*	Paris	8°	PT U	C95	ZC2.4.14(d)
1549	–	Dionysius, *Carthusianus*	Cologne	fol.	RL/CT C	D15	E.3.18(b)
1549	1550	Flacius, M.	Magdeburg	8°	R	F12$$	ZC2.8.10(b)
1549	–	Flacius, M.	Wittenberg	8°	MS ?C	F17	ZC2.4.15
1549	–	Gallasius, N.	[Geneva]	8°	[PT] U	G6$	ZC2.8.1(e)
1549	–	Gesner, C.	Zürich	fol.	R ?C	G26$	L.4.16
1549	–	Perionius, J.	Paris	8°	PL ?C	P19	ZC2.7.3
1549	–	Pighius, A.	Paris	8°	CT U	P32	M.2.6
1549	1561	Witzel, G.	Cologne	8°	CT L	W51	ZC2.2.8(b)
1550	1560	Alesius, A.	Leipzig	8°	PT ?L	A21$$	G.6..22(b)
1550	–	Betuleius, X	Basle	8°	PT U	B18	X.2.32
1550	–	Brentz, J.	Basle	8°	PL ?C	B74$$	H.1.29(b)
1550	1553	Calvin, J.	Geneva	8°	PT U	C2	ZC2.6.18(c)
1550	–	Culman, L.	Nuremberg	8°	PL ?C	C122	M.2.36
1550	–	Culman, L.	Nuremberg	8°	PL ?C	C122	M.2.37

1550	–	Culman, L.	Nuremberg	8°	PL ?C	C122	M.2.38
1550	–	Guilliaud, C.	Paris	8°	CT L	G44	C.3.1(a)
1550	1562	Hilary	Basle	fol.	RL L	H58	A.4.20(b)
1550	–	Mainz	Paris	8°	RL ?L 'I R'	M7$	B.5.16
1550	–	Meier, G.	Wittenberg	8°	R	M41	ZC2.8.10(a)
1550	–	Royard, T.	Cologne	fol.	PL U	R39	E.4.2
1550	–	Wild, J.	Main	4°	PL ?C	W30	D.1.12(a)
1550	–	Wild, J.	Mainz	4°	PL ?C	W31	D.1.12(b)
1550	–	Wild, J.	Mainz	fol.	R	W34	G.2.14
[1550]	–	Amsdorff, N.	Magdeburg	4°	R	A28$$	L.5.22†
[1550]	–	Culman, L.	Nuremberg	8°	PL ?C	C121$$	H.1.29(c)
[1550]	1561	Melanchthon, P.	Basle	8°	R	M65$	B.5.34(a)
[c. 1550]	–	Bible. N.T.	[n.pl.]	16°	R	B36$$	G.6.8 ?‡
[c. 1550]	–	Culman, L.	Nuremberg	8°	PL ?C	C118$$	H.1.29(d)
[c. 1550]	–	Curio, C.	Basle	8°	R	C124	L.6.16(b)
1550/51	–	Bibliander, T.	Basle	8°	PL ?C	B42	H.1.29(a)
1550/51	–	Rivius, J.	Basle	8°	RL ?SW	R31	H.1.37(b)
1551	1569+	Anselm	Antwerp	8°	CT L	A40	N.6.11(c)
1551	1556	Bullinger, H.	Zürich	8°	PL ?L	B131$	ZC2.4.11(b)
1551	–	Costerius, J.	Louvain	8°	MS ?C	C105	ZC2.6.2
1551	1552	Dionysius, Carthusianus	Cologne	fol.	RL/CT C	D16	E.3.17(b)
1551	1561	Gigas, J.	Frankfurt-an-der-Oder	8°	R	G27$	B.5.34(d)
1551	–	Melanchthon, P.	Erfurt	8°	PT U	M67$$	ZC2.6.16
1551	1562	Sylvius, B.	?Zürich	8°	PT U	S98$	ZC2.5.7(d)
1551	–	Vermigli, P. M.	Zürich	4°	CS U	V15	C.2.2†
[1551]	1553	Clauser, C.	Zürich	8°	PT U	C77	ZC2.6.18(e)
1551/52	–	Arboreus, J.	Paris	fol.	R	A48	E.4.3
1551/52	–	Bullinger, H.	Zürich	4°.	PL ?C	B133	I.4.11(a)
1552	–	Bible. NT.	Geneva	16°.	CT ?L	B37$$	G.6.7 ?‡
1552	1556	Brentz, J.	Tübingen	8°	CT L	B73$$	ZC1.4.10(e)
1552	–	Brentz, J.	Wittenberg	8°	CT ?L	B90	M.2.25
1552	1556	Bullinger, H.	Zürich	8°	PL ?L	B129$$	ZC2.4.11(c)
1552	1562	Calvin, J.	Geneva	fol.	R	C9	G.4.4(b)
1552	1553	Du Moulin, C.	Paris	8°	PT ?L	D30	ZC2.5.1 (a)

1552	1565	Flacius, M.	Frankfurt-a-M.	4°	PT ?L	F14	ZC2.3.8(e)
1552	1567	Honorius	Cologne	8°	R	H75$	A.6.20(b)
1552	–	Lasco, J. à	London	8°	R	L10	H.2.11
1552	–	Lexicon Novi Testamenti	Cologne	8°	PT ?L	L28	E.6.23(b)
1552	1554	Nannius, P.	Basle	4°	R	N3$	C.2.9(b)
1552	–	Oecumenius	Basle	8°	CT ?L	O17	D.5.8
1552	–	Rabus, L.	Strasbourg	8°	R	R3$$	B.6.10
1552	–	Soto, P. de.	Antwerp	16°	PT U	S72$	ZC2.8.7
1552	–	Vermigli, P. M.	Zürich	8°	CT ?C	V16	N.6.8(a)
1552	–	Vermigli, P. M.	Zürich	8°	CT ?C	V19	N.6.8(b)
1552	1570+	Viret, P.	Geneva	8°	CT L	V35	ZC2.1.6(f)
1552	1559	Westhemerus, B.	Zürich	4°	PL ?L	W7	ZC2.2.1(a)
1552	1561	Witzel, G.	Cologne	8°	CT L	W55$	ZC2.2.8(d)
[1552]	–	Loss, L.	Frankfurt-a-M.	8°	CT ?L	L43	D.3.3
[1552]	1553	Loss, L.	Frankfurt-a-M.	8°	PT U	L45	ZC2.6.18(f)
1552/53	–	Bibliander, T.	Basle	8°	PT ?L	B41	E.6.23(a)
1552/53	–	Dionysius, Carthusianus	Cologne	fol.	RL/CT C	D11	E.3.17(a)
[1552 or 1555]	–	Oecumenius	Basle	8°	CT U	O18	C.4.12
1553	1556	Aepinus, J.	Frankfurt-a-M.	8°	CT L	A8$$	ZC1.4.10(d)
1553	1554	Bucer, M.	Geneva	fol.	R	B100	G.2.20(a)
1553	–	Catechism	London	8°	R	C52	H.2.15
1553	1567	Hotman, F.	Geneva	8°	CT L	H80$	ZC1.4.8(g)
1553	–	Mazzolini, S.	Rome	8°	PT ?L	M24$	ZC2.5.1(c)
1553	1556	Musculus, W.	Basle	8°	PL ?L	M90$$	ZC2.4.11(a)
1553	–	Nardus, J. L.	Basle	8°	CT ?L	N6$	N.6.9
1553	–	Nardus, J. L.	Basle	8°	PT U	N6$	ZC2.6.18(b)
1553	–	Prudentius	Lyon	16°	R	P57	A.6.35
1553	1557	Saxony – Lutheran Church	?Basle	4°	R	S29	L.5.7(e)
1553	–	Witzel, G.	Cologne	fol.	RL L	W49	E.4.4
1553	–	Zegers, N.	Cologne	8°	PT U	Z3$	E.6.30

[1553]	1563	Kling, M.	Frankfurt-a-M.	fol.	R	K10$$	L.2.7(b)
[1553]	1556	Lübeck	Basle	8°	PL ?L	L46$$	ZC2.4.11(e)
[1553]	–	Massarius, H.	Basle	8°	PT ?L	M15$	ZC2.5.1(b)
1553/54	–	Alesius, A.	Basle	8°	R	A20$	C.4.7
1553/54	1562	Estienne, R.	Geneva	fol.	R	E53$	G.4.4(a)
1553/54	–	Luther, M.	Frankfurt--a-M.	8°	PL?C	L50	C.4.3

The Marian period

1554	1558	Brentz, J.	Leipzig	8°	CT ?L	B79$$	G.6.4(b)
1554	–	Bucer, M.	Geneva	fol.	R	B99	G.2.20(b)
1554	1557	Bullinger, H.	Zürich	4°	R	B125$	L.5.7(b)
1554	1567	Calvin, J.	Geneva	fol.	R	C10	G.4.4(b)
1554	–	Foxe, J.	Strasbourg	8°	R	F32	B.6.11
1554	–	Gardiner, S.	Louvain	8°	PT U	G14	K.1.31
1554	–	Gardiner, S.	Louvain	4°	PT ?C	G15	ZC2.3.7
1554	–	Musculus, W.	Basle	fol.	R	M89	G.3.11
1554	–	Musculus, W.	Basle	fol.	R	M92	G.3.10
1554	–	Nannius, P.	Louvain	4°	R	N4$	C.2.9(c)
1554	–	Theophylact	Basle	fol.	R	T8	G.2.18
1554	1555	Titelman, F.	Lyon	12°	PT L	T10	G.6.16(a)
1554	1558	Titelman, F.	Lyon	16°	PT ?L	T14$$	ZC2.8.2(b)
1554	–	Tunstall, C.	Paris	4°	PT U	T26	ZC2.3.2
1554	1559	Viret, P.	Geneva	fol.	CS U	V36	N.3.12(a)
1554	–	Watson, T.	London	8°	PT ?L	W2	O.2.46
[1554]	1559	Germanus.	Frankfurt-a-M.	8°	CT L	G24$$	N.6.16(c)
[1554]	1562	Lasco, J. à.	Emden	8°	PT U	L11	ZC2.5.7(f)
1554/55	1559	Huberinus, C.	Frankfurt-a-M.	8°	CT L	H81$$	N.6.16(b)
1554/55	1559	Viret, P.	Geneva	fol.	CS U	V34$	N.3.12(b)
1555	–	Bonner, E.	London	4°	PT U	B55	O.1.10(b)
1555	1558	Calvin, J.	Geneva	8°	PT U	C13$$	ZC2.4.6(c)
1555	1559	Erasmus, D.	Cologne	12°	PT U	E43	ZC2.8.4(a)
1555	1568	Folengius, J.B.	Lyon	8°	R	F27$	C.3.8(a)
1555	1571	Hofmeister, J.	Paris	8°	CT L	H62	G.5.15(a)
1555	1561+	Joverius, F.	Paris	fol.	PL U	J17	B.3.9(b)

1555	–	Justinian I	Geneva	8°	R	J18	L.6.8
1555	–	Luther, M.	Frankfurt-a-M.	8°	PT ?L	L51	E.6.37
1555	1556	Meier, G.	Wittenberg	8°	CT L	M42	ZC1.4.10(b)
1555	1562	Novicampianus, A.	Antwerp	12°	PT ?L	N12$$	ZC2.8.3(a)
1555	–	Palladius	Paris	4°	CT L	P2	B.5.3
1555	–	Petrus, *Diaconus*	Louvain	8°	R	P21	A.6.28(a)
1555	1563	Pole, R.	Strasbourg	fol.	R	P40	L.2.7(c)
1555	1556	Ponet, J.	?Strasbourg	8°	R	P42	R.6.21(b)
1555	1570+	Slotanus, J.	Cologne	4°	R	S60	L.5.8(a)
1555	–	Titelman, F.	Lyon	12°	PT L	T12$$	G.6.16(b)
1555	–	Vives, J. L.	Lyon	8°	CT L	V38	Z.5.121
1555	–	Wild, J.	Cologne	fol.	CT U	W37	G.5.10
[1555]	–	Bonner, E.	London	4°	PT U	B54	O.1.10(a)
[1555]	1565	Dialogus	Strasbourg	4°	PT ?L	D4$	ZC2.3.8(c)
[1555]	1559	Ochino, B.	Zürich	8°	R	O2$	L.6.13(d)
[c. 1555]	1556	Culman, L.	Basle	8°	PL ?L	C119$	ZC2.4.11(d)
[c. 1555]	1562	Ribittus, J.	Basle	8°	PT U	R25	ZC2.5.7(g)
1555/56	1557	Aepinus, J.	Frankfurt-a-M.	8°	PT U	A4$$	E.6.35(d–e)
1555/56	1557	Bibliander	Basle	4°	R	B40	L.5.7(c)
1555/56	1557+	Borrhaus, M.	Basle	fol.	R	B59	G.4.10(a)
1556	1557	Artopoeus, P.	[Basle]	8°	PT U	A58$	E.6.35(c)
1556	1569+	Bacherius, P.	Ghent	8°	R	B1$	ZC2.1.10(a)
1556	1558	Brentz, J.	Frankfurt-a-M.	8°	CT L	B69$$	K.2.11(c)
1556	1558	Brentz, J.	Frankfurt-a-M.	8°	CT L	B92$$	K.2.11(a)
1556	–	Bullinger, H.	Zürich	8°	CT L	B134	ZC1.4.10(c)
1556	1558	Calvin, J.	Geneva	8°	PT U	C14$$	ZC2.4.6(b)
1556	–	Camerarius, J.	Paris	4°	R	C21	L.5.3
1556	1558	Chytraeus, D.	Wittenberg	8°	CT L	C70	D.6.2(a)
1556	–	Euthymius	Lyon	8°	CT ?L	E59	A.6.25†
1556	1567	Gulielmus, *Baufeti*	Paris	16°	R	G48	ZC2.8.5(c)
1556	1567	Helding, M.S.	Antwerp	12°	R	H15$$	ZC2.8.5(d)
1556	–	Helmes, H.	Antwerp	8°	CT L	H18	C.3.2
1556	–	Helmes, H.	Antwerp	8°	CT L	H19	C.3.3

1556	–	Helmes, H.	Antwerp	8°	CT L	H20	C.3.4
1556	–	Helmes, H.	Antwerp	8°	CT L	H21	C.3.5
1556	–	Helmes, H.	Antwerp	8°	CT L	H22	C.3.6
1556	–	Kirchmeyer, T.	Basle	8°	PT ?L	K4$$	ZC2.4.11(f)
1556	–	Luther, M.	Nuremberg	8°	CT L	L70	ZC1.4.10(a)
1556	–	Lycosthenes, C.	Lyon	8°	CT ?L	L82	M.2.43
1556	–	Mainardo, A.	Strasbourg	8°	R	M6	R.6.21(a)
1556	1557	Melanchthon, P.	Tübingen	4°	R	M57$$	L.5.7(d)
1556	–	Musculus, W.	Basle	fol.	R	M91	G.3.12
1556	–	Sasbout, A.	Louvain	8°	PT U	S27$$	E.6.22
1556	–	Tavernarius, J.	Paris	8°	PT ?L	T2$$	ZC2.6.3†
1556	1561	Westphal, J.	Strasbourg	8°	CT L	W15$$	ZC2.2.7(e)
1556	1572	Wild, J.	Mainz	8°	CT L	W29$	G.6.6(c)
1556	1572	Wild, J.	Mainz	8°	CT L	W33	G.6.6(b)
[1556]	–	Bullinger, H.	Zürich	8°	PT ?L	B119$	ZC2.4.11(g)
1556/57	1558	Lasco, J. à	Basle	8°	PT U	L13	ZC2.4.6(d)
1557	1566	Aepinus, J.	Frankfurt-a-M.	8°	CT L	A9	K.2.15(c)
1557	1569	Beurlin, J.	Tübingen	8°	CT L	B19$$	C.4.11(c)
1557	–	Borrhaus, M.	Basle	fol.	R	B60	G.4.10(b)
1557	1569+	Bredenbach, M.	Basle	8°	CT L	B65$$	M.2.40(c)
1557	–	Brentz, J.	Frankfurt-a.M.	4°	R	B70$$	L.5.7(a)
1557	1568	Bucer, M.	Basle	fol.	RL L	B105	M.1.28(c)
1557	1562	Calvin, J.	Geneva	8°	PT U	C20	ZC2.5.7(c)
1557	–	Chytraeus, D.	Wittenberg	8°	PT U	C66$$	E.6.35(a)
1557	1570+	Cicogna, V.	Cologne	8°	CT L	C75$$	ZC2.1.3(c)
1557	1561	Eitzen, P. Von	Ursel	8°	R	E17$	B.5.34(b)
1557	–	Francisco, à V.	Lyon	8°	CT L	F34$$	H.1.4
1557	–	Maximus, *of Tyre*	Geneva	8°	CT ?O	M19	Y.5.19
1557	1558	Meier, G.	Wittenberg	8°	CT L	M30$$	D.6.2(b)
1557	–	Münster, S.	Basle	8°	CT ?L	M83	F.2.8
1557	1565	Naclantius, J.	Venice	4°	PT ?L	N2$	E.5.28(a)
1557	1562	Poullain, V.	Zürich	8°	PT U	P47	ZC2.5.7(e)
1557	–	Resende, L. A. de	Lyon	8°	CT L	R15$	ZC2.2.2(a–b)
1557	–	Sleidanus, J.	Strasbourg	8°	CT?O	S59	B.6.1
1557	–	Soto, P. De	Antwerp	4°	R	S71	L.5.28(a–b)

| 1557 | 1570+ | Turrianus, F. | Rome | 4° | R | T27$ | L.5.8(b) |
| 1557 | 1561 | Westphal, J. | Strasbourg | 8° | CT L | W14$$ | ZC2.2.7(d) |

The Elizabethan years (1558–1577)

1558	–	Andreae, J.	Frankfurt a-M.	4°	CT L	A37$$	K.2.11(b)
1558	1560	Basil	Paris	8°	CT L	B7$	A.6.22(a)
1558	–	Bèze, T.	Geneva	8°	PT U	B21$	ZC2.4.6(e)
1558	1561	Bibliander, T.	Basle	fol.	PL ?L	B43	B.3.19(c)
1558	–	Brentz, J.	Frankfurt-a-M.	8°	CT ?L	B80	G.5.16
1558	–	Brentz, J.	Ursel	8°	CT ?L	B81	G.6.4(a)
1558	1562	Bullinger, H.	Zürich	8°	PT U	B124	ZC2.5.7(b)
1558	1568	Bullinger, H.	Zürich	fol.	RL L	B132$	M.1.28(b)
1558	–	Calvin, J.	Geneva	8°	PT U	C12$	ZC2.4.6(a)
1558	–	Clauser, C.	Basle	8°	PT U	C76$$	X.2.30(a)‡
1558	–	Dathenus, P.	Frankfurt-a-M.	4°	CT L	D3$$	K.2.11(e)
1558	–	Eusebius, *of Emessa*	Antwerp	8°	PT ?L	E57	E.6.20
1558	–	Jansen, C.	Antwerp	12°	PT ?L	J5	E.6.19
1558	1559	Luther, M.	Wittenberg	8°	R	L73	L.6.12(a)
1558	–	Meier, G.	Wittenberg	8°	CT L	M31$$	D.6.2(c)
1558	1559	Pfeffinger, J.	Frankfurt-a-m.	8°	R	P24$$	L.6.13(a)
1558	–	Slotanus, J.	Cologne	8°	RL ?L	S61$	ZC1.4.9
1558	1564	Staphylus, F.	Cologne	4°	CT L	S82	K.2.26(b)
1558	–	Staphylus, F.	Cologne	8°	PT U	S83	ZC2.4.12
1558	1559	Staphylus, F.	Antwerp	8°	PT ?L	S84	B.6.37(b)
1558	–	Titelman, F.	Lyon	16°	PT ?L	T15	ZC2.8.2(a)
1558	1570+	Tosarrius, J.	Basle	fol.	R	T17	G.4.1(a)
1558	–	Vermigli, P. M.	Basle	fol.	R	V14	G.3.1
1558	–	Vio, T.	Lyon	8°	CT L	V30	D.5.11
1558	–	Vio, T.	Lyon	8°	CT L	V31	D.5.12
1558	1562	Westphal, J.	Ursel	8°	PT U	W9	ZC2.5.7(k)
1558	1562	Westphal, J.	Ursel	8°	PT U	W10$$	ZC2.5.7(i)
1558	1562	Westphal, J.	Ursel	8°	PT U	W11	ZC2.5.7(j)
1558	–	Wild, J.	Antwerp	8°	CT U	W38	G.5.11

1558	1564	Wittenberg, Academia	Wittenberg	4°	CT L	W47$$	K.2.26(c)
1558/59	–	Estienne, R.	Geneva	8°	CP U	E54$	F.2.24
1558/59	1564+	Orosius, P.	Louvain	8°	CT ?L	O23$	B.6.16(c)
1559	–	Andreae, J.	Frankfurt-a-M.	8°	R	A36$$	L.6.13(e)
1559	1563	Calvin, J.	Geneva	fol.	R	C5	E.4.8(b)
1559	1562	Calvin, J.	Geneva	fol.	R	C8	G.4.4(c)
1559	–	Calvin, J.	Geneva	fol.	CT ?L	C16	N.2.9
1559	1563	Cauzio, C.	Venice	8°	PT U	C54$	ZC2.5.5(b)
1559	–	Fabri, J.	Antwerp	12°	PT U	F1	ZC2.8.4(b)
1559	–	Frycz, A.	Basle	fol.	CS U	F37$$	N.3.12(c)
1559	–	Gagny, J. de	Antwerp	8°	CT L	G1$$	C.3.10
1559	1567	Helding, M. S.	Antwerp	12°	R	H17	ZC2.8.5(e)
1559	1560	Hofmeister, J.	Mainz	8°	PT ?L	H68	ZC2.5.8(a)
1559	–	Humphrey, L.	Basle	8°	R	H89	L.6.12(b)
1559	–	Hyperius, A.G.	Basle	8°	CT L	H96	N.6.16(a)
1559	–	Lindanus, W.	Antwerp	8°	PT ?L	L35	B.6.37(a)
1559	–	Meier, G.	Wittenberg	8°	R	M27$$	E.6.25
1559	–	Melanchthon, P.	Wittenberg	8°	R	M66$$	L.6.13(c)
1559	1569	Pontanus, R.	Cologne	fol.	R	P4	L.4.6(b)
1559	–	Placidus	Venice	4°	RL ?L	P38$	E.5.8
1559	–	Richter, M.	Basle	8°	R	R28$$	L.6.13(b)
1559	1564	Staphylus, F.	Dillingen	4°	CT L	S82	K.2.26(b)
1559	1561	Vergerio, L.	Tübingen	8°	CT L	V10$	ZC2.2.7(c)
1559	–	Vermigli, P. M.	Basle	8°	CT U	V17	N.6.7
1559	–	Vermigli, P. M.	Zürich	fol.	R	V18	L.2.21
1559	–	Wigand, J.	Frankfurt-a-M.	8°	R	W25$$	L.6.13(f)
1559	–	Wild, J.	Antwerp	8°	CP U	W32	D.2.11
1559	1567+	Wild, J.	Lyon	8°	CT L	W36	D.4.5(b)
1559	–	Wittenberg, Academia	Wittenberg	4°	R	W45	B.5.8†
[1559]	1566	Cassian, J.	Basle	fol.	R	C47	A.5.4(b)
1559/60	–	Loss, L.	Frankfurt-a-M.	fol.	R	L41	G.2.15†
1559/60	–	Vergerius, P. P.	Tübingen	4°	PL ?L	V11	ZC2.2.1(b)
1560	–	Abdias	Paris	4°	CT L	A1	A.6.22(b)

1560	–	Arnobius	Basle	8°	CT U	A54	A.6.17
1560	–	Billick, E.	Cologne	8°	PT ?L	B49$	ZC2.5.8(b–c)
1560	1569+	Bredenbach, M.	Cologne	8°	CT L	B66$$	M.2.40(d)
1560	1565	Charlemagne	Antwerp	8°	CT L	C57$	M.2.21(a)
1560	1562	Conradus, A.	Basle	8°	PT ?L	C100$	E.6.31(b)
1560	–	Euthymius	Paris	8°	CT ?L	E58	C.4.13
1560	1568	Flacius, M.	Basle	8°	RL L	F24$$	ZC2.1.8(c)
1560	1568+	Fontaine, S.	Paris	8°	CT ?L	F28$$	D.6.1(a)
1560	1563	Gallasius, N.	Geneva	fol.	R	G4	E.4.8(a)
1560	1565+	Machiavelli, N.	Basle	8°	PT U	M3	ZC2.5.2(b)
1560	–	Meier, G.	Wittenberg	8°	CT ?L	M32$	C.6.12
1560	–	Melanchthon, P.	Wittenberg	8°	R	M62	K.3.38
1560	1566	Monner, B.	Wittenberg	4°	R	M80$$	I.3.9(b)
1560	–	Musculus, W.	Basle	fol.	R	M95	L.3.20
1560	–	Paulinus	Cologne	8°	R	P9	A.6.21(a)
1560	1570+	Vincent	Cologne	24°	CT L	V28	ZC1.4.13(d)
1560	1566+	Weller, H.	Nuremberg	fol.	R	W3$$	G.3.15(b)
[1560]	–	Froeschel, S.	Wittenberg	8°	PT ?L	F36$$	G.6.22(a)
[1560]	1565+	Humphrey, L.	Basle	8°	PT U	H90	ZC2.5.2(a)
[?1560]	–	Freiesleben, C.	Vienna	8°	PT ?L	F35$$	B.6.40
[c. 1560]	1563+	Hemmingsen, N.	Leipzig	8°	PL ?L	H35	ZC2.7.7(a)
[c. 1560]	1566	Liberinus, A.	Paris	4°	RL L	L29	I.5.5(b)
[c. 1560]	1565	Praetorius, Z.	?Ratisbon	4°	PT ?L	P52$$	ZC2.3.8(b)
[c. 1560]	1564+	Procopius	Zürich	fol.	R	P54	G.4.8(a)
1560/61	–	Andreae, J.	Frankfurt-a-M.	4°	PT ?L	A35	ZC2.3.5(a)
1560/61	–	Schopper, J.	Dortmund	8°	CT ?L	S39$$	D.3.9–11
[1560/61]	–	Magdeburg Centuriators	Basle	fol.	R	M5	M.4.9

Bishop of Rochester (1560–1571)

1561	–	Apostolic Canons	Paris	fol.	PL U	A44	B.3.9(a)
1561	–	Bullinger, H.	Zürich	8°	CT ?L	B120	G.6.3(a)
1561	–	Bullinger, H.	Zürich	8°	CT ?L	B121$	G.6.3(b)
1561	1571	Calvin, J.	Geneva	8°	R	C19$	K.3.31(c)
1561	–	Chytraeus, D.	Wittenberg	8°	PT U	C67$$	E.6.36(a)
1561	1566+	Corvinus, A.	Wittenberg	8°	R	C103	E.6.9(d)

1561	–	Eitzen, P. von	?Ursel	8°	CT L	E15$$	ZC2.2.7(b)
1561	–	Eitzen, P. von	?Ursel	8°	R	E16$$	B.5.34(c)
1561	1568	Gentilis, J. V.	[Geneva]	8°	[PT] L	G21	ZC2.1.8(d)
1561	–	Hall[e], Suabian	Frankfurt-a-M.	8°	CT L	H1$$	ZC2.2.7(a)
1561	1566+	Hamelmann, H.	[n.pl.]	8°	PT U	H2A$$	ZC2.4.9(a)
1561	–	Hertelius, J.	Basle	8°	PT U	H44$	E.6.36(b)
1561	–	Heshusius, T.	Magdeburg	8°	CT L	H48	ZC2.2.8(a)
1561	1565	Klebitz, W.	Freiburg	4°	PT U	K6$	ZC2.3.9(e)
1561	–	Loss, L.	Wittenberg	8°	PT U	L44	G.6.18
1561	1565	Musculus, W.	Basle	fol.	R	M93	G.4.19(b)
1561	1564+	Orosius, P.	Cologne	8°	CT ?L	O22	B.6.16(a)
1561	–	Pantaleon, H.	Basle	fol.	PL ?L	P3	B.3.19(a)
1561	–	Rabus, L.	Nuremberg	8°	CT L	R4	D.6.11
1561	–	Sasbout, A.	Antwerp	8°	PT U	S26$	E.6.39
1561	1567	Treflerus, F.	Cologne	8°	CT ?L	T18	N.6.12(c)
1561	–	Veron, J.	London	8°	R	V20	O.2.47(b)
1561	–	Veron, J.	London	8°	R	V21$	O.2.47(a)
1561	1566	Weller, H.	Nuremberg	8°	CT L	W4$$	D.6.6(a)
1561	–	Westhemerus, B.	Basle	4°	PL ?L	W8$	C.1.13
1561	–	Wild, J.	Mainz	fol.	R	W40	L.3.18
1561	–	Würtemberg Confession	Frankfurt-a-M.	fol.	R	W60	L.2.20
[c. 1561]	1565	Praetorius, Z.	?Ratisbon	4°	PT ?L	P52$$	ZC2.3.8(b)
1561/62	–	Boquinus, P.	Basle	8°	R	B57$$	L.5.19(c)
1561/62	–	Melanchthon, P.	Basle	8°	R	M64	L.5.19(a)
1561/62	–	Steckelius, L.	Basle	8°	R	S87$$	L.5.19(b)
[1561/62]	–	Nicephorus	Basle	fol.	PL ?L	N9	B.3.19(b)
1562	–	Benedictus, J.	Paris	fol.	CT F	B14	E.3.4
1562	1565	Bucer, M.	Basle	fol.	R	B101	G.4.19(a)
1562	–	Canisius, P.	Antwerp	12°	PT ?L	C33$$	ZC2.8.3(c)
1562	–	Canisius, P.	Antwerp	12°	PT ?L	C34	ZC2.8.3(b)
1562	1566+	Carion, J.	Wittenberg	8°	R	C41	B.6.18(a)
1562	1570+	Cochlaeus, J.	Paris	16°	CT L	C85$$	ZC1.4.13(b)
1562	–	Ebert, P.	Wittenberg	8°	PT ?L	E1	K.1.7(c)
1562	1567	Firmicus Maternus, J.	Strasbourg	8°	R	F8$	A.6.20(d)
1562	–	Gregory, *of Nyssa*	Basle	fol.	RL L 'R B'	G34	A.4.20(a)

1562	–	Gropper, J.	Antwerp	16°	PT U	G35	ZC2.8.6
1562	1565	Gualtherus, R.	Zürich	fol.	R	G41	G.4.15(b)
1562	–	Hamelmann, H.	Ursel	8°	R	H4$$	L.6.24(a)
1562	–	Helding, M. S.	Cologne	fol.	R	H16$	L.4.15
1562	1563+	Hemmingsen, N.	Leipzig	8°	CT ?L	H37	ZC2.7.6(a)
1562	–	Hofmeister, J.	Louvain	fol.	R	H63$	G.4.2
1562	1563	Kling, C.	Cologne	fol.	R	K7$	L.3.17(b)
1562	–	Lavater, L.	Zürich	4°	CT U	L20	G.5.1
1562	–	Loss, L.	Frankfurt-a-M.	fol.	R	L42	G.2.16
1562	–	Lybius, C.	Wittenberg	8°	PT ?L	L81	E.6.31(a)
1562	–	Mecklenberg	Frankfurt-a-M.	8°	R	M25$	L.6.24(b)
1562	–	Meier, G.	Wittenberg	8°	PT ?L	M38$$	G.5.21(a)
1562	–	Meier, G.	Wittenberg	8°	PT ?L	M39$$	G.5.21(b)
1562	–	Meier, G.	Wittenberg	8°	PT U	M40$$	G.6.20
1562	–	Melanchthon, P.	Wittenberg	fol.	R	M43	L.2.3
1562	–	Melanchthon, P.	Wittenberg	8°	PT ?L	M45$	K.1.7(a)
1562	1563+	Melanchthon, P.	Wittenberg	8°	R	M58$$	L.6.19(a)
1562	1563+	Melanchthon, P.	Wittenberg	8°	R	M59$$	L.6.19(c)
1562	1563+	Praetorius, A.	Frankfurt-a-M.	8°	CT ?L	P49$$	ZC2.7.6(b)
1562	–	Sextus	Geneva	8°	PT U	S53$	ZC1.5.19
1562	1565+	Smith, R.	Cologne	8°	PT ?L	S66$	ZC2.4.10(c)
1562	–	Weller, H.	Nuremberg	8°	PT ?L	W6$$	K.1.7(b)
1562	–	Wigand, J.	Frankfurt-a-M.	8°	R	W24$$	L.6.26(a)
1562	–	Wild, J.	Antwerp	8°	CT ?L	W39	G.5.12(a–b)
1562	–	Wittenberg Concord	Leipzig	8°	PT U	W48$$	ZC2.5.7(a)
[1562]	–	Bucer, M.	Basle	fol.	R	B103	G.4.20
[c. 1562]	1563+	Hemmingsen, N.	Leipzig	8°	R	H24	D.6.10(a)
[c. 1562]	–	Menzel, H.	Ursel	8°	R	M68$	L.6.25
1562/63	1566	Brentz, J.	Frankfurt-a-M.	fol.	R	B76	G.3.7(b)
1562/63	–	Castellion, S.	Basle	8°	R	C50	L.6.26(b)
1562/63	–	Flacius, M.	Strasbourg	fol.	R	F11	L.4.4
1562/63	–	Guillard, C.	Paris	fol.	R	G43	G.4.13

1563	1564	Augustine	Louvain	12°	PT U	A64	B.6.35(b)
1563	1564+	Baius, M.	Louvain	8°	PT U	B3$	ZC2.4.14(c)
1563	–	Bullinger, H.	Zürich	8°	CT ?L	B130$	ZC2.7.6(d)
1563	–	Calvin, J.	Geneva	fol.	R	C6	E.4.8(c)
1563	1564	Cardillo, G.	Ingolstadt	4°	R	C40$	B.5.5(a)
1563	–	Chytraeus, D.	Wittenberg	8°	R	C72	D.6.10(b)
1563	1564	Cogler, J.	Wittenberg	8°	R	C94$$	C.5.13(b)
1563	1565	Councils – Trent	Frankfurt-a-M.	4°	PT ?L	CIII	ZC2.3.8(d)
1563	–	Dominicis, D. de	Venice	8°	PT U	D22$	ZC2.5.5(a)
1563	1564	Fabricius, J.	?Zürich	8°	PT U	F3$	ZC2.5.3(a)
1563	–	Garetius, J.	Antwerp	8°	PT U	G17	K.1.26
1563	–	Hessels, J.	Louvain	8°	R	H55	L.6.15
1563	1564	Hyperius, A. G.	Basle	8°	PT?L	H95	ZC2.5.6(a)
1563	1564	Hyperius, A. G.	Basle	8°	PT?L	H97$	ZC2.5.6(b)
1563	–	Kempis, T. à	Basle	8°	R	K1$	K.3.44
1563	–	Kling, C.	Cologne	fol	R	K8$	L.3.17(a)
1563	–	Mark	Paris	8°	R	M11$	A.6.24
1563	–	Mark	Paris	8°	PT U	M12	ZC2.5.13
1563	–	Meier, G.	Wittenberg	8°	PT ?L	M33$$	G.6.24(a)
1563	–	Meier, G.	Wittenberg	8°	PT ?L	M34$$	G.6.24(b)
1563	–	Musculus, A.	Erfurt	fol.	R	M87	L.2.7(a)
1563	1564	Obenheim, C.	Ursel	8°	PT ?L	O1	ZC2.5.6(d)
1563	1564	Osorio da Fonseca, J.	Venice	4°	R	O27	B.5.5(c)
1563	–	Praetorius, A.	Wittenberg	8°	R	P50$$	L.6.19(b)
1563	1564	Praetorius, A.	Wittenberg	8°	R	P51$$	M.2.35(a)
1563	–	Simler, J.	Zürich	8°	CT ?L	S56$$	ZC2.7.6(c)
1563	–	Sirenius, J.	Venice	fol.	R	S58	L.2.16(a)
1563	1567	Smith, R.	Douai	8°	CT L	S65	I.1.5(c)
1563	–	Sonnius, F.	Cologne	fol.	R	S68	L.2.16(b)
1563	–	Vannius, V.	Tübingen	4°	CT ?L	V5$$	I.4.2
[1563]	–	Catechesis	Leipzig	8°	PL ?L	C51	ZC2.7.7(b)
[1563]	–	Ephraem	Dillingen	8°	R	E19	A.6.41
1563/64	–	Lactantius	Basle	fol.	R	L1	A.4.25(a)
[c. 1563/64]	–	Lefèvre, J.	Paris	4°	PT U	L27	ZC2.3.3(a)
1564	1565	Andreae, J.	Tübingen	4°	PT U	A30$$	ZC2.3.9(a)

1564	–	Andreae, J.	Tübingen	4°	PT U	A31$$	K.2.8(b)
1564	–	Andreae, J.	Tübingen	4°	R	A32$	L.5.27(a)
1564	1568	Bebenburg, L.	Cologne	8°	R	B9	B.6.19(b)
1564	–	Bernard.	Lyon	16°	R	B16	A.6.37
1564	–	Borrhaus, M.	Basle	fol.	R	B61	G.4.8(b)
1564	1566	Brentz, J.	Frankfurt-a-M.	fol.	R	B87	G.3.7(c)
1564	–	Brentz, J.	Tübingen	4°	R	B93	L.5.27(b)
1564	1565	Burgundy	Cologne	8°	PT ?L	B136$	ZC2.4.10(d)
1564	1568+	Calvin, J.	Geneva	8°	CT ?L	C2	D.6.1(b)
1564	–	Calvin, J.	Geneva	8°	CT L	C4	D.1.9
1564	–	Cassander, G.	Cologne	8°	PT ?L	C45	B.6.41(a)
1564	–	Cassander, G.	Cologne	4°	CT L	C46$	K.2.26(d)
1564	–	Chytraeus, D.	Strasbourg	8°	R	C73$$	M.2.35(f)
1564	–	Clement I	Strasbourg	12°	PT U	C80	B.6.35(a)
1564	–	Cogler, J.	Wittenberg	8°	R	C93$$	C.5.13(c)
1564	–	Councils – Trent. Canones	Antwerp	8°	PT ?L	C108	B.6.41(c)
1564	–	Cucchus, M. A.	Cologne	8°	R	C117	ZC2.8.13(a)
1564	–	Dick, L.	Basle	8°	R	D5$	ZC2.8.13(b)
1564	–	Flacius, M.	Ursel	8°	PT ?L	F20$$	ZC2.5.6(c)
1564	–	Gagny, J. de	Antwerp	8°	CT L	G2$	C.3.11
1564	–	Hemmingsen, N.	Wittenberg	8°	R	H26	C.5.13(a)
1564	1565	Hemmingsen, N.	Wittenberg	8°	CT U	H28$$	C.4.10(c)
1564	–	Hertelius, J.	Basle	8°	PT U	H45$	ZC2.4.13
1564	–	Hosius, S.	Cologne	8°	PT ?L	H79	B.6.41(b)
1564	1565+	Kromer, M.	Cologne	8°	PT ?L	K12$$	ZC2.4.10(e)
1564	–	Machiavelli, N.	Frankfurt-a-M.	8°	CT ?L	M2	B.6.16(b)
1564	–	Martiall, J.	Antwerp	8°	PT U	M13	O.2.39
1564	1565	Maulbrunn Colloquy	Tübingen	4°	PT U	M17	ZC2.3.9(d)
1564	1565	Meier, G.	Wittenberg	8°	CT L	M35$$	D.6.4(a)
1564	–	Melanchthon, P.	Wittenberg	fol.	R	M44	L.2.4
1564	–	Mermannius, A.	Louvain	8°	PT U	M69$	ZC2.4.14(a)
1564	–	Mermannius, A.	Louvain	8°	PT U	M70$	ZC2.4.14(b)
1564	–	Mermannius, A.	Louvain	8°	PT U	M71$	ZC2.4.14(e)
1564	–	Osorio da Fonseca, J	Venice	4°	R	O24	B.5.5(b)

1564	–	Radulphus, A.	Paris	8°	CT L	R5$$	D.4.1
1564	–	Rome, Church of	Lyon	4°	PT U	R36	ZC2.3.3(b)
1564	–	Salmuth, H.	?Leipzig	8°	R	S8$	M.2.35(c)
1564	–	Schoenborn, B.	Wittenberg	8°	R	S38$$	M.2.35(e)
1564	1566	Spangenberg, J.	Frankfurt-a-M.	8°	PT U	S79	ZC2.5.10(a)
1564	–	Stummelius, C.	Wittenberg	8°	R	S93$	M.2.35(b)
1564	–	Suidas	Basle	fol.	R	S97	A.4.25(b)
1564	–	Theodoret	Padua	fol.	CT U	T5$	A.6.3
1564	–	Theodoret	Leipzig	8°	PT U	T6	ZC2.5.3(b)
1564	–	Trotzendorf, V. F.	Wittenberg	8°	R	T23$$	M.2.35(g)
1564	–	Ulmer, J. C.	Basle	8°	PT ?L	U1$$	ZC2.3.13
1564	1565	Vergerio, A.	Strasbourg	4°	PT U	V9$$	K.2.8(e)
1564	1565+	Villavicentio, L.	Antwerp	8°	PT ?L	V25$	ZC2.4.10(a)
1564	1569+	Witzel, G.	Cologne	8°	D ?L	W52$	B.6.42(c)
1564	1569+	Witzel, G.	Cologne	8°	D ?L	W54$	B.6.42(b)
[1564]	–	Holthusius, J.	Dillingen	8°	R	H74$$	ZC2.8.13(c)
[c. 1564]	1565	Hemmingsen, N.	Leipzig	8°	CT U	H25$$	C.4.10(a)
1564/65	1567	Councils – Trent. Decrees	London	4°	RL L	C109	T.6.4(b)
1565	–	Acontius, J.	Basle	4°	PT?L	A2	ZC2.3.8(a)
1565	–	Albertus M.	Antwerp	16°	R	A16$$	K.3.13(b)
1565	–	Andreae, J.	Tübingen	4°	PT U	A29	ZC2.3.9(c)
1565	–	Andreae, J.	Tübingen	4°	PT U	A33$$	K.2.8(c)
1565	–	Andreae, J.	Tübingen	4°	PT U	A34$$	K.2.8(a)
1565	–	Bernard	Antwerp	8°	CT L	B17$	M.2.21(c)
1565	–	Bibliotheca	Geneva	fol.	R	B44	L.2.9–10
1565	–	Calvin, J.	Geneva	4°	CT U	C7	G.5.5
1565	–	Du Moulin, C.	Paris	4°	R	D29$	C.2.14
1565	1566	Eisengrein, M.	Ingolstadt	8°	PT U	E11	ZC2.6.11(c)
1565	1566	Eisengrein, M.	Ingolstadt	8°	PT U	E12$$	ZC2.6.11(d)
1565	–	Forerius, F.	Antwerp	8°	CT U	F29$	D.2.9
1565	–	Garcaeus, J.	Wittenberg	8°	CT L	G8$	ZC2.1.7(d)
1565	–	Garcaeus, J.	Wittenberg	8°	CT L	G11$$	ZC2.1.7(e)
1565	–	Garcaeus, J.	Wittenberg	8°	CT L	G12$$	ZC2.1.7(c)
1565	–	Gualtherus, R.	Zürich	fol.	R	G38	G.4.15(a)
1565	–	Hemmingsen, N.	Wittenberg	8°	CT U	H27	C.4.10(b)
1565	–	Horantius, F.	Paris	8°	R	H76	K.2.18

1565	–	Hosius, S.	Cologne	8°	PT ?L	H78$	ZC2.4.10(b)
1565	1567	Jewel, J.	London	fol.	R	J8	T.3.3(a)
1565	–	Kling, C.	Paris	8°	R	K9$	I.1.7
1565	–	Lavater, L.	Zürich	4°	PT U	L19	G.5.26
1565	–	Meier, G.	Wittenberg	8°	PT U	M2$$	G.6.19
1565	–	Meier, G.	Wittenberg	8°	CT L	M36$$	D.6.4(b)
1565	–	Paulli, S.	Rostock	8°	CT L	P11	ZC2.1.7(b)
1565	–	Schegk, J.	Frankfurt-a-M.	4°	PT U	S34$	K.2.8(d)
1565	–	Selneccer, N.	Bautzen	8°	CT L	S41$$	ZC2.1.7(a)
1565	–	Spangenberg, C.	Strasbourg	8°	R	S74$	K.1.28(b)
1565	–	Sperling, A.	Ingolstadt	4°	PT U	S81$	ZC2.3.9(b)
1565	–	Tauler, J.	Antwerp	8°	PT U	T1	ZC2.6.8
1565	–	Trotzendorf, V. F.	Wittenberg	8°	PT U	T22$$	K.3.45(b)
1565	–	Trotzendorf, V. F.	Wittenberg	8°	PT U	T24$	K.3.45(a)
1565	–	Widemannus, J.	Strasbourg	8°	PT U	W17$$	ZC2.5.2(e)
1565	–	Wild, J.	Louvain	8°	CT L	W27	D.5.10?‡
[1565]	1574	Maecardus, J.	Strasbourg	8°	R	M4	K.3.41(d)
[c. 1565]	1566+	Antichristus	Basle	4°	RL L	A42$	I.5.5(c)
[c. 1565]	–	Czecanovius, S.	[Cologne]	8°	R	C129$	ZC2.8.12
[c. 1565]	–	Gail, C.	Dillingen	4°	PT ?L	G3$	E.5.28(b)
1565/66	–	Melanchthon, P.	Basle	8°	R	M60	K.1.28(a)
1565/66	–	Musculus, W.	Basle	fol.	R	M94	G.4.19(c)
1565/66	–	Rastell, J.	Antwerp	8°	MS U	R6$	O.2.41
1565/66	–	Wigand, J.	Ursel	8°	R	W19	E.6.9(a–b)
1566	1567	Baius, M.	Louvain	8°	CT L	B4	I.1.5(d)
1566	–	Bidembach, W.	Tübingen	4°	RL L	B45$	I.4.6(b)
1566	–	Brentz, J.	Frankfurt-a-M.	8°	CT L	B77$$	C.4.4(b)
1566	–	Brentz, J.	Tübingen	fol.	R	B82	G.3.7(a)
1566	–	Carion, J.	Frankfurt-a-M.	8°	R	C42	B.6.18(b)
1566	1567	Cassiodorus	Antwerp	8°	R	C48$	A.6.20(c)
1566	–	Catharinus, A.	Paris	fol.	R	C53	G.4.12(a)
1566	–	Chemnitz, M.	Frankfurt-a-M.	8°	CT L	C59	C.7.1
1566	–	Chemnitz, M.	Frankfurt-a-M.	8°	CT L	C60	C.7.2

1566	–	Clement, of Alexandria	Basle	fol.	R	C78	A.5.4(a)
1566	–	Dalmada, E.	Antwerp	4°	MS U	D1	ZC2.3.4
1566	–	Eisengrein, M.	Ingolstadt	8°	PT U	E14$$	ZC2.5.10(b)
1566	1567	Erastus, T.	Geneva	8°	CT L	E49$	ZC1.4.8(d)
1566	–	Erythraeus, V.	Strasbourg	8°	CT L	E51	ZC2.1.4(b)
1566	1570+	France.	[Geneva]	8°	CT L	F33	ZC2.1.6(c)
1566	1570+	Gamaren, H. de	Ingolstadt	4°	R	G7	L.5.8(d)
1566	–	Garcaeus, J.	Wittenberg	8°	PT U	G9$	ZC2.4.9(b)
1566	1574	Garcaeus, J.	Wittenberg	8°	R	G10$	K.3.41(e)
1566	1571	Heidelberg Catechism	Heidelberg	12°	R	H14$	K.3.31(d)
1566	–	Hemmingsen, N.	Wittenberg	8°	CT L	H29$$	D.6.6(c)
1566	1569	Hemmingsen, N.	Wittenberg	8°	CT L	H30	C.4.11(a)
1566	–	Hemmingsen, N.	Wittenberg	8°	CT L	H31$$	D.6.6(b)
1566	–	Hemmingsen, N.	Wittenberg	8°	CT L	H33	D.6.6(d)
1566	1574	Hemmingsen, N.	Wittenberg	8°	R	H36	K.3.41(b)
1566	1567	Hessels, J.	Antwerp	8°	CT L	H53	I.1.5(e)
1566	–	Horne, R.	London	4°	PT ?L	H77	O.2.2
1566	–	Hunnaeus, A.	Antwerp	8°	CT L	H92	Z.4.23(b)
1566	–	Kirchener, T.	Frankfurt-a-M.	fol.	R	K5$	L.3.6
1566	–	Maulbrunn. Colloquy	Heidelberg	4°	CT L	M18	I.4.5(a)
1566	–	Meier, G.	Wittenberg	8°	PT U	M29$$	E.6.21
1566	–	Mermannius, A.	Louvain	8°	PT U	M72$	ZC2.6.11(a)
1566	–	Mermannius, A.	Louvain	8°	PT U	M73$	ZC2.6.11(b)
1566	1567	Metz	Geneva	8°	CT L	M74$$	ZC1.4.8(a)
1566	1567	Milan	Venice	8°	CT L	M75	ZC2.2.10(b)
1566	–	Nowell, A.	London	4°	PT U	N14	O.1.16†
1566	–	Rastell, J.	Antwerp	8°	R	R7$	O.2.45
1566	1568	Richter, M.	?Rostock	8°	CT L	R27$	K.2.16(d)
1566	1569+	Sander(s), N.	Antwerp	8°	R	S11$	ZC2.1.10(b)
1566	–	Schegk, J.	Tübingen	4°	R	S33	I.3.9(c)
1566	–	Schegk, J.	Tübingen	4°	CT L	S35	I.4.5(b)
1566	–	Soto, P. de	Antwerp	8°	CT ?L	S73	H.1.3
1566	–	Stapleton, T.	Antwerp	4°	PT U	S86	O.1.4
1566	1574	Stein, J,	Basle	8°	R	S88$$	K.3.41(c)

1566	–	Wigand, J.	Basle	8°	CT L	W18	C.4.4(a)
1566	–	Wigand, J.	Frankfurt-a-M.	8°	CT L	W23$$	K.2.15(a)
1566	–	Zanchius, H.	[n. pl.]	4°	RL L	Z2$$	I.5.5(a)
[1566]	–	Flacius, M.	Basle	8°	RL L	F23	I.4.6(a)
[?1566]	1567	Valerius, C.	Basle	8°	CT L	V1	Z.5.108 (b)
1566/67	–	Flacius, M.	[?Basle]	8°	CT L	F10$	ZC2.1.4 (a)
1566/67	1568	Fulgentius	Basle	8°	CT L	F39	A.6.26(b)
1566/67	–	Helvetic Confession	Zürich	4°	R	H23	I.3.9(a)
1566/67	–	Hunnaeus, A.	Antwerp	8°	CT L	H91	Z.4.23(a)
1566/67	–	Vermigli, P. M.	Zürich	fol.	R	V13	G.3.15(a)
1566/67	–	Vigne, P. della.	Basle	8°	CT L	V24$	Z.5.109
1566/67	–	Wigand, J.	Frankfurt-a-M.	8°	CT L	W21$	K.2.15(b)
1567	–	Athenagoras	Cologne	8°	R	A59	A.6.20(a)
1567	–	Bèze, T.	Geneva	8°	CT L	B23	ZC1.4.8(b)
1567	–	Byzantine History	Paris	fol.	RL L 'R B'	B138$	Z.2.19
1567	–	Canisius, P.	Antwerp	16°	R	C35	ZC2.8.5(b)
1567	–	Chandieu, A.	Geneva	8°	CT L	C56$$	ZC1.4.8(c)
1567	–	Councils – Trent. Catechism	Paris	8°	CT L	C110	ZC2.2.10(a)
1567	–	Cruciger, C.	Wittenberg	8°	CT L	C115$	D.4.5(a)
1567	–	Eck, J.	Cologne	12°	R	E8	ZC2.8.5(a)
1567	–	Erastus, T.	Geneva	8°	CT L	E50$$	ZC1.4.8(e)
1567	–	Espence, C. d'	Paris	8°	CT L	E52$	D.5.9
1567	–	Fabricius, G.	Paris	8°	CT ?L	F2$$	N.6.12(b)
1567	–	Flacius, M.	Basle	8°	CT L	F18$	ZC2.2.4(a)
1567	–	Flacius, M.	Frankfurt-a-M.	8°	CT L	F22	K.2.17
1567	1569	Génébrard, G.	Paris	fol.	R	G19	L.4.6(c)
1567	–	Harding, T.	Louvain	4°	PT U	H8	O.1.12
1567	1568+	Hessels, J.	Louvain	8°	CT L	H54$	I.1.6(b)
1567	–	Hoffmeister, J.	Cologne	fol.	R	H64$$	G.3.9(c)
1567	1568	Ingolstadt, Univ. of	Ingolstadt	4°	RL L	I4$$	D.1.4(b)
1567	–	Jewel, J.	London	fol.	R	J7	T.3.3(b)
1567	–	Jonathan, ben Uzziel	Heidelberg	8°	CT L	J15$$	D.6.5(a)

1567	1569+	Lindanus, W.	Cologne	8°	CT L	L34	M.2.40(b)
1567	–	Lindius, S.	[n. pl.]	8°	CT L	L36	C2.2.4(c)
1567	–	Mollerus, H.	Wittenberg	8°	CT L	M78$$	D.6.5(b)
1567	–	Naclantius, J.	Venice	fol.	RL L	N1$	G.3.18(c)
1567	–	Nowell, A.	London	4°	RL L	N13	T.6.4(a)
1567	–	Patrizi, F.	Paris	8°	CT L	P8	ZC1.5.4
1567	–	Paulli, S.	Rostock	8°	CT L	P10	G.6.5
1567	1568+	Porthaise, J.	Antwerp	8°	CT L	P44$	I.1.6(c)
1567	–	Praetorius, A.	Strasbourg	8°	CT L	P48$	ZC2.2.4(b)
1567	–	Ravestyn, J.	Louvain	8°	CT L	R11	I.1.5(a)
1567	–	Rostock – Academia	Rostock	8°	CT L	R38$$	H.1.9
1567	–	Sainctes, C. de	Paris	8°	CT ?L	S7$$	N.6.12(a)
1567	1569+	Sascerides, J.	Wittenberg	8°	CT L	S28$$	N.6.11(a)
1567	–	Selneccer, N.	Jena	8°	CT L	S43$	D.4.7
1567	–	Selneccer, N.	Jena	8°	CT L	S44	G.6.2(a)
1567	–	Seripando, G.	Antwerp	8°	CT L	S49	ZC1.4.2
1567	–	Simoni, S.	Geneva	8°	CT L	S57$	ZC1.4.8(f)
1567	–	Sonnius, F.	Louvain	8°	CT L	S69	I.1.5(b)
1567	–	Stapleton, T.	Louvain	4°	PT ?L	S85	O.1.13
1567	–	Theodoret	Cologne	fol.	R	T4	A.4.11–12
1567	–	Theophylact	Cologne	fol.	R	T9	G.3.9(a)
1567	–	Torres, H.	Dillingen	4°	R	T16A	A.6.5
1567	–	Valerius, C.	Antwerp	8°	CT L	V2	Z.5.108(a)
1567	–	Wigand, J.	[n. pl.]	8°	CT L	W26$	ZC2.2.4(d)
1567	–	Wild, J.	Cologne	fol.	R	W35	G.3.9(b)
[1567]	–	Gregory, of Nazianzus	Basle	8°	CT L	G33	A.6.11
[?1567]	–	Weller, H.	Leipzig	8°	CT L	W5	G.6.2(b)
[c. 1567]	1568	Heshusius, T.	Basle	8°	CT L	H50$	K.2.16(b)
1567/68	–	Flacius, M.	Basle	fol.	RL L 'R B'	F13	G.4.9
1568	–	Bèze, T.	Geneva	8°	RL L	B29	ZC2.1.8(a)
1568	–	Bredenbach, T.	Cologne	8°	RL L	B67$	D.1.4(d)
1568	–	Bullinger, H.	Tübingen	fol.	RL L	B126	M.1.28(b)
1568	–	Camerarius, J.	Leipzig	8°	CT ?L	C22	D.6.1(c)
1568	–	Camerarius, J.	Leipzig	8°	CT ?L	C23$	D.6.1(d)
1568	–	Clement I	Paris	8°	R	C79	B.6.5

1568	–	Eder, G.	Cologne	fol.	RL L	E9$	G.3.18(a–b)
1568	1570	Flacius, M.	Basle	8°	PT U	F21$	K.1.35(a)
1568	–	Hamelmann, H.	Basle	fol.	RL L ['RB']	H2	M.1.28(a)
1568	1569+	Hemmingsen, N.	Wittenberg	8°	R	H32$$	E.6.26(e)
1568	–	Hessels, J.	Lyon	8°	R	H52$$	C.3.8(b)
1568	–	Lucifer	Paris	8°	CT L	L47	A.6.26(a)
1568	–	Ravestyn, J.	Louvain	8°	CT ?L	R9	B.5.9
1568	–	Ravestyn, J.	Louvain	8°	CT L	R10	I.1.6(a)
1568	–	Regius, E.	Strasbourg	8°	CT L	R14$$	K.2.16(c)
1568	–	Simler, J.	Zürich	8°	RL L	S55	ZC2.1.8(b)
1568	–	Torres, H.	Ingolstadt	4°	RL L	T16$	D.1.4(a)
1568	–	Usuardus	Louvain	8°	R	U2	B.6.19(a)
1568	–	Confessio Waldensium	Basle	8°	CT L	W1$$	K.2.16(a)
1569	–	Bunderius, J.	Antwerp	8°	R	B13$$	ZC2.1.11
1569	–	Camerarius, J.	Leipzig	8°	R	C27$	L.6.27
1569	1572	Chytraeus, D.	Wittenberg	8°	CP U	C68	G.5.17(a)
1569	–	Chytraeus, D.	Frankfurt-a-M.	8°	R	C71$$	E.6.26(c)
1569	–	Eisengrein, M.	Cologne	8°	D ?L	E13	B.6.42(a)
1569	1570	Flacius, M.	Basle	8°	PT U	F16$	K.1.35(b)
1569	1570+	Génébrard, G.	Paris	8°	CT L	G20	N.6.10(c)
1569	–	Hamelmann, H.	Marburg	8°	CT L	H3$$	N.6.11(b)
1569	1570+	Heerbrand, J.	Tübingen	4°	R	H12$$	L.5.15(c)
1569	–	Hemmingsen, N.	Wittenberg	8°	CT L	H34$$	C.4.11(b)
1569	–	Jansen, C.	Louvain	4°	R	J3$	E.5.5
1569	–	Jansen, C.	Louvain	4°	RL U	J4$	E.5.4
1569	–	Osorio da Fonseca, J.	Dillingen	8°	CT L	O26	M.2.40(a)
1569	1570+	Palingenius, E.	Geneva	8°	CT L	P1	ZC2.1.6(e)
1569	–	Paulli, S.	Rostock	8°	CT ?L	P12	M.2.26(a)
1569	–	Saccus, S.	Magdeburg	8°	CT ?L	S1	M.2.26(b)
1569	1572	Sander(s), N.	Louvain	8°	CT L	S10$	G.6.6(e)
1569	–	Selneccer, N.	Leipzig	fol.	R	S42	G.4.5
1569	1570	Snepffius, T.	Tübingen	4°	RL ?L	S67$	I.7.7(a)
1569	1570	Strigelius, V.	Leipzig	fol.	R	S92	G.4.1(c)
1569	–	Vermigli, P. M.	Zürich	fol.	R	V12	G.3.14

1569	1570+	Wigand, J.	Frankfurt-a-M.	8°	CT L	W22$$	N.6.10(a)
1569/70	–	Du Préau, G.	Cologne	fol.	R	D31	L.4.6(a)
1570	–	Altenburg	Jena	4°	RL ?L	A24	I.7.7(b)
1570	–	Aretius, B.	Paris	16°	CT L	A50	ZC1.4.13(a)
1570	1571	Armenia	Paris	8°	CT L	A53$	H.1.7(b)
1570	–	Bèze, T.	Geneva	8°	CT L	B28	ZC2.1.6(d)
1570	–	Canisius, P.	Cologne	4°	CT L	C36	K.2.13–14
1570	–	Chemnitz, M.	Jena	8°	CT L	C63$$	N.6.10(b)
1570	–	Flacius, M.	Basle	8°	PT U	F1 $$	K.1.35(c)
1570	1572	Garetius, J.	Ghent	8°	CT L	G16$	G.6.6(f)
1570	–	Gregory, of Nazianzus	Cologne	fol.	RL ?L [?'R B']	G32	A.4.8(b)
1570	–	Gualtherus, R.	Zürich	fol.	R	G37	G.4.14
1570	–	Hyperius, A.	Basle	8°	CT L	H98	ZC2.1.6 (a)
1570	–	Irenaeus	Geneva	fol.	RL ?L	I5	A.4.8(a)
1570	–	Lindanus, W.	Antwerp	4°	CT L	L30	I.8.3
1570	–	Loss, L.	Frankfurt-a-M.	fol.	R	L40	G.4.1(b)
1570	–	Macer, C.	Ingolstadt	4°	R	M1$$	L.5.8(c)
1570	–	Melanchthon, P.	Wittenberg	8°	R	M61	L.6.21
1570	–	Mouchy, A. de	Paris	8°	CT L	M82$$	ZC2.1.3(b)
1570	–	Pinto, H.	Antwerp	4°	CT L	P34$	E.5.1
1570	–	Ravestyn, J.	Louvain	8°	CT ?L	R9	B.5.10
1570	–	Serres, J. de	Geneva	fol.	R	S52$	ZC1.5.21
1570	–	Sonnius, F.	Basle	8°	PT U	S70$	B.5.33†
1570	–	Via, J. à	Cologne	8°	CT L	V22	ZC2.1.3(a)
1570	–	Wolf, J.	Zürich	fol.	R	W59	G.4.1(d)
[1570]	–	Marbach, J.	Strasbourg	4°	R	M9$$	L.5.15(d)
1571	–	Aquinas, T.	Rome	8°	CT L	A46	G.5.15(b)
1571	–	Arias Montanus	Antwerp	fol.	RL L	A52$$	E.3.5(b)
1571	1573	Bèze, T.	Geneva	8°	PT U	B20	K.1.33(a)
1571	1572	Borckensis, T.	Cologne	8°	CT L	B58$	G.6.6(a)
1571	1572	Bullinger, H.	Zürich	8°	CT L	B128$	ZC1.4.3(b)
1571	–	Canisius, P.	Dillingen	4°	CT ?L	C32	C.2.4
1571	–	Carolinus, P.	Wittenberg	8°	CT L	C43	H.1.7(a)
1571	–	Crellius, P.	Wittenberg	8°	CT L	C112$	ZC2.7.8(b)
1571	1572	Ferinarius, J.	Wittenberg	8°	CT L	F4$$	ZC1.4.3(d)

1571	–	Guibert	Cologne	12°	R	G42	K.3.31(b)
1571	1573	Hemmingsen, N.	[Copen-hagen]	8°	CP ?L	H37	ZC2.7.5(a)
1571	–	Hessiander, C.	Geneva	8°	PT ?L	H56$	ZC2.3.1
1571	–	Holthusius, J.	Dillingen	12°	R	H73$$	K.3.31(a)
1571	–	Lavater, L.	Geneva	fol.	RL L	L21	E.3.5(a)
1571	–	Lindanus, W.	Cologne	8°	CT L	L31	ZC1.4.5(c)
1571	–	Lindanus, W.	Cologne	8°	CT L	L32	ZC1.4.5(d)
1571	–	Lindanus, W.	Cologne	8°	CT L	L33	ZC1.4.5(b)
1571	–	Meier, G.	Wittenberg	8°	CP ?L	M37	C.6.13
1571	–	Polygranus, F.	Cologne	8°	CT L	P41	ZC1.4.5(a)
1571	1573	Siber, A.	Leipzig	8°	CP ?L	S54	D.4.6(b)
1571	–	Wild, J.	Cologne	8°	CT ?L	W28	D.2.10
1571	–	Wittenberg, Academia	Wittenberg	8°	CT L	W46$$	ZC2.7.8(a)

Bishop of Salisbury (1571–1577)

1572	1573	Bèze, T.	Geneva	8°	PT U	B27$$	K.1.33(b)
1572	–	Brandmueller, J.	Basle	8°	CP ?L	B63	G.6.1
1572	1573	Camerarius, J.	Leipzig	8°	CP ?L	C24$$	ZC2.7.5(e)
1572	–	Camerarius, J.	Leipzig	4°	CP ?L	C25$	D.1.5(b)
1572	–	Camerarius, J.	Leipzig	4°.	CP ?L	C26$	D.1.5(a)
1572	–	Chytraeus, D.	Wittenberg	8°	CP U	C69	G.5.17(b)
1572	–	Councils – Nicaea. *Acta*	Dillingen	8°	CT L	C106	G.6.6(d)
1572	–	Gualtherus, R.	Zürich	fol.	RL/CP ?L	G39	G.3.17
1572	–	Gualtherus, R,	Zürich	fol.	R	G40	G.4.16(a–b)
1572	–	Heshusius, T.	Jena	4°	PT U	H46	ZC2.3.16
1572	–	Heshusius, T.	Jena	8°	CT L	H49$$	ZC1.4.3(a)
1572	–	Heshusius, T.	Frankfurt-a-M.	8°	CT L	H51	ZC1.4.3(c)
1572	–	Serranus, P.	Antwerp	fol.	R	S50	G.2.4(a)
1572	–	Serranus, P.	Antwerp	fol.	R	S51	G.2.4(b)
1572	–	Vega, A.	Cologne	fol.	R	V6$	L.3.8
[1572/73]	–	Osorio da Fonseca, J.	Lisbon	8°	CT L	O25	I.2.10
1573	–	Albutius, P.	Paris	4°	R	A17$	L.5.32(b)
1573	–	Bèze, T.	Geneva	8°	PT U	B24$$	K.1.33(c)

1573	–	Bèze, T.	Geneva	8°	CP ?L	B25$$	ZC2.7.5(c)
1573	–	Bèze, T.	Geneva	8°	CT ?L/?S	B26	M.2.20(a)
1573	–	Chemnitz, M.	Frankfurt-a-M.	8°	CP ?L	C61	C.7.3
1573	–	Chemnitz, M.	Frankfurt-a-M.	8°	CP ?L	C62	C.7.4
1573	–	Danaeus, L.	Geneva	8°	CT ?L/?S	D2	M.2.20(b)
1573	–	Eisengrein, M.	Cologne	8°	CP ?L	E10$$	D.4.9
1573	–	Fischart, J.	Christlingen	8°	CP ?L	F9	ZC2.7.5(f)
1573	–	Harchius, J.	Basle	4°	R	H6$	L.5.32(c)
1573	–	Heshusius, T.	Jena	8°	CP ?L	H47$$	D.4.6(a)
1573	–	Luther, M.	Leipzig	8°	CP ?L	L71	ZC2.7.5(b)
1573	–	Marbach, J.	Strasbourg	4°	R	M8 $	L.5.32(a)
1573	–	Mollerus, H.	Wittenberg	8°	CT ?L/?S	M76	D.1.7
1573	–	Piotrków. Synod	Cologne	8°	PT ?L	P35	ZC2.4.7–8
1573	–	Saillans, F. de	Geneva	8°	PT ?L	S6$$	ZC2.7.5(d)
[c. 1573]	–	Harchius, J.	Worms	4°	R	H7$	L.5.32(d)
1574	–	Bèze, T.	Geneva	8°	CT ?L/?S	B22	ZC1.4.4(c)
1574	–	Corro, A. de	London	8°	PT U	C101$	E.6.34
1574	–	Flacius, M.	Oberusel	8°	CT ?L/?S	F15$$	ZC1.4.4(b)
1574	–	Mollerus, H.	Wittenberg	8°	CT ?L/?S	M77	G.5.6
1574	–	Whitgift, J.	London	fol.	RL L	W16	T.3.8†
1575	–	Aretius, B.	Lausanne	8°	CT ?L/?S	A51	ZC2.7.1
1575	1576	Cureus, J.	Heidelberg	8°	PT U	C123	K.1.27(a)
1575	1576	Wigand, J.	Königsberg	8°	CT ?L/?S	W20$$	C.4.5(a)
1575	–	Zürich, Reformed Church	Zürich	8°	CT ?L/?S	Z5	ZC1.4.4(a)
1576	–	Augustine	Geneva	8°	R	A66	A.6.23
1576	–	Boquinus, P.	Heidelberg	8°	PT U	B56$$	K.1.27(b)
1576	–	Brandmueller, J.	Basle	8°	CT ?L/?S	B64	C.4.5(b)
1576	–	Brentz, J.	Tübingen	fol.	R	B68$	L.2.2

APPENDIX IV

Bindings

A: *Blind-stamped panel bindings*

Classification according to Oldham, BPEB.

Abbreviations

CP	Binding instruction: 'in past' (i.e. calf over pasteboard).
MS	Leaves or leaf from a MS.
MS+	MS strip only, to strengthen spine and/or binding structure.
Pb	Leaves or leaf from printed book.
PDN	Image number of pastedown, flyleaf or MS strip (see the database at www.bibsoc.org.uk/Geste).
$	Compacted leaves as pasteboard.
$$	Flyleaves.
**	Pastedown or flyleaves now kept separately.
†	Pre-Geste ownership inscription.
‡	Pre-Geste MS annotations, book-price or book-title(s) on fore-edge or spine, but no pre-Geste ownership inscription.

English Panels, in Oldham Classification Order

*The tabular information, printed in grey type below,
is laid out in the following columns*

Cat. no	Imprint date	Format	Shelf-mark	Pastedown &c.	Image number	Binding instruction

AN. 14 – Animal panel
    with HM. 15 – Heads-in-medallions panel
    See under HM. 15

BIB. 2 – Annunciation panel, signed 'N S' (= Nicholas Spierinck, Cambridge)
    with ST. 37 – Saint Nicholas panel, signed 'N S' (= Nicholas Spierinck) [Gray, p. 51, no. 36]

Cat. no	Imprint date	Format	Shelf-mark	Pastedown &c.	Image number	Binding instruction
E28	1523	8°	G.5.20	MS**	PDN 1	–

    Introduction, p. 119, n. 291.

BIB. 17 – Jesus's baptism by John the Baptist, on verso
    with ST. 9 – St George slaying the Dragon, signed 'I R' (= John Reynes, London)

Cat. no	Imprint date	Format	Shelf-mark	Pastedown &c.	Image number	Binding instruction
E31†	1522	8°	N.6.1	–	–	–

HE. 3 & 4 – Heraldic double panel depicting the arms of King Henry
   VIII and Queen Katherine of Aragon. Unassigned, ?London

| D34 | 1520 | 8° | L.6.32 | – | – | – |

   Introduction, p. 124, n. 311.

HE. 6 – Heraldic, signed 'M D' (=Martin Dature, London)
   with ST. 46 – St Paul and the Four Evangelists

| I6 | 1531 | 4° | I.4.10 | – | – | – |

   Introduction, p. 124.

HE. 21/22 – Heraldic double panel – showing the arms of Henry VIII
   and the Tudor Rose, signed 'J R' (= John Reynes, London)
   with REL. 5 – Arma Mundi Redemptoris panel

| H40† | 1521 | 4° | N.5.13 | MS+ | PDN 2 | – |

HE.29 – Heraldic panels (Julian Notary, London)
   with RO. 14 – Rose panel (Weale R.112)

| M23‡ | 1524 | 8° | D.3.14 | – | – | – |

   Introduction, p. 115, n. 279.

HM. 2 – Heads-in-medallions panel, signed with the monogram of the
   London stationer John Reynes

| *A2 | 1535 | 8° | ZC1.5.6 | MS+ | PDN 3 | – |

HM. 5 & 6 – Heads-in-medallions panels – ?Thomas Godfray, London

| E3 | 1536 | 8° | G.5.18 | – | – | – |
| L38 | 1536 | 8° | M.2.11 | MS+ & Pb $ | PDN 4 | – |

   Introduction, p. 104.

HM. 9 & 10 – Heads-in-medallions panels – Unassigned, ?London

| E36‡ | 1535 | 8° | D.3.7 | MS+ Pb $$ | PDN 5 | – |

   Introduction, p. 115.

HM. 11 & 12 – Heads-in-medallions panels (Weale R.218), both signed
   'M D' (= Martin Dature, London)

*C7	1526	4°	H.1.19	–	–	–
B72†	1536	8°	C.6.1	–	–	–
L57	1539	8°	D.5.3	MS+ Pb $$	PDN 6	CP

   Introduction, p. 124.

HM. 15 – Heads-in-medallions panel, Unassigned
   with AN. 14 – animal panel

| A18 | 1531 | 8° | D.2.7 | – | – | – |

   Introduction, p. 124, n. 311.

MISC. 8 & 9 – Miscellaneous panels, signed 'M D', presumably Martin
Dature, London

[*P5   1544   4°   K.2.20, now missing, not seen. Whether this
had belonged to Geste is not known.]

RO. 14 – Rose panels, signed 'I N' (= Julian Notary, London)
with HE. 29 – heraldic panel
See above under HE. 29

ST. 9 – St George slaying the Dragon, signed 'I R' (= John Reynes,
London)
with BIB. 17 – Jesus's baptism by John the Baptist
See above, under BIB. 17

ST. 21 – St John Baptist preaching (Oldham, BPEB), I.G.(A). Unassigned
with ST. 29 – St John Baptist with the Lamb, signed 'I G'

H9†   1533   8°   D.5.13   –   –   –

ST. 37 – Saint Nicholas panel
with BIB. 2 – Annunciation panel
See above, under BIB. 2

TRIP. 1 – Triple panels. Unassigned

D26   1534   4°   N.5.5   –   –   –

Introduction, p. 124, n. 311

TRIP. 5/6 – Triple panels. ?Cambridge

G18‡   1525   8°   Y.5.14   –   –   –

V3?‡   1526   8°   C.4.6   M S   PDN 7   –

Introduction, p. 114, n. 278

TRIP. 9 – Marian triple panels of the Annunciation (Weale R.412).
English, unassigned

H10   1531   8°   C.4.9   MS+   PDN 11 –

J2   1528   8°   D.4.10   MS   PDN 10 –

E48†   1527   8°   H.1.2   MS   PDN 9   –

Introduction, pp. 115, 124, n. 311

with a narrow unidentified roll

O7‡   1533   4°   G.5.2   MS+   PDN 12 –

According to a note by Oldham, dated 9.1944, inserted in the
book, the roll appears to be separate, not appearing on the
seven other examples known to him, 'though the design does
appear sometimes on Flemish heads-in-medallions panels'. See
fig. 17.

Single panel of the Virgin of the Apocalypse, similar to the right hand
   compartment of the Marian triple-panel (Oldham, BPEB, TRIP. 9)
   ?Cambridge

B33‡	1529	16°	G.6.13	–	–	–
B35†	1526	16°	G.6.14	M S	PDN 8	–

   Introduction, p. 115.

Total: 22*

B: *Blind-tooled rolls*

Abbreviations

MS	Leaves or leaf from a MS.
MS*	Blank leaf [leaves] of parchment.
MS**	Flyleaves from a MS in Geste's hand.
Pb	Leaves or leaf from printed book.
PDN	Image number of pastedown, flyleaf or MS strip (see the database at www.bibsoc.org.uk/Geste).
$	Compacted leaves as pasteboard.
$$	Flyleaves.
+	Strip only, to strengthen spine and/or binding structure.
£	Pastedown or MS+ now covered over by modern paper endleaf/flyleaf.
*	Pastedown or flyleaves now kept separately.
†	Pre-Geste ownership inscription.
‡	Pre-Geste MS annotations, book-price or book-title(s) on fore-edge or spine, but no pre-Geste ownership inscription.

Binding instructions

B	Instruction to bind other (named) items in the same book.
CB	'In bordes'.
CP^	Now calf covers, though instruction to binder reads, 'in parchment'.
F	Instruction to find other items to bind in the same book.
IP	'In paste', i.e. calf over pasteboard.
O	Order of items to be bound together.
UIP	'Uncutt in parchement'.
**	Trace only – instruction uncertain.

In the case of multiple items bound together, the imprint year given below
is the latest of the imprint years, and probably closer to the date of binding.

* Excluding *P4 (now missing) and *A2 and *C7 from Appendix I (Geste's ownership
   uncertain).

The tabular information, printed in grey type below,
is laid out in the following columns

Cat. no	Imprint date	Format	Shelf-mark	Pastedown &c.	Image number	Binding instruction

Oldham, EBSB, classifications

I R binder – Oldham, EBSB, 447 – signed with the initials 'I R', possibly a London binder active *c.* 1538–1561

| M7 | 1550 | 8° | B.5.16 | – | – | – |

'RB' London binding – Oldham, EBSB, 450 with the Falcon, Golden Fleece and Cherub. With two rows of Oldham, EBSB, roll 450

| G34 | 1560 | fol. | A.4.20 | | | |
| F13 | 1567 | fol. | G.4.9 | Pb & MS+ | PDN 13 | – |

Introduction, p. 126.

WG/IG workshop at Cambridge – Oldham, EBSB, tools 20–22, inside and outside a diaper frame

| A39 | 1523 | 4° | L.5.33 | – | – | – |

Classified Rolls

AN.e(1) 559 – Signed 'WG' – Cambridge
   with a rectangular lattice frame of 12 perforations with 4 whole and 8 half ornaments of Oldham, EBSB, type E.(1) 986

| C127‡ | 1521 | fol. | A.4.21 | MS£ | PDN 14 | – |

Introduction, p. 114, n. 276, p. 120.

AN.f(1) 561 – Signed 'GG'. By Garrett Godfrey, Cambridge (=Gray Roll I)
   with heraldic roll HE.b(2) 747 (=Gray, Roll III)

T7‡	1520	fol.	A.5.3	MS	PDN 16	–
P14‡	1514	4°	L.5.37	MS	PDN 17	–
B12	1529	fol.	N.4.5	Pb	PDN 18	– See fig. 19.1

with D1.a(1) 593, 1503–1530. By Garrett Godfrey, Cambridge (= Gray, Roll IV)

| L25?† | 1517/18 | 4° | L.5.36 | MS | PDN 15 | – |

AN.f(2) 562 – By Nicholas Spierinck, Cambridge. (= Gray, Roll I)
   with D1.a(2) 594 – Diaper roll by Nicholas Spierinck (= Gray, Roll II)

| C82?‡ | 1524 | fol. | N.3.17 | MS | PDN 19 | – |

Introduction, p. 114, n. 277.

19.1 – One of Geste's three volumes of Bede, printed at Basle, 1527–29,
with two rolls of Garrett Godfrey, Oldham, EBSB,
AN.f(1) and HE.b(2). Cat. no. B12.

AN.g(1) 563 – London binding – intersecting roll with a lattice of 4 full
and 8 half perforations of ornament B(3) 971

    C1‡   1517   4°   N.5.26   MS+   PDN 20   –

    Introduction, pp. 113–14, n. 274.

CH.a(1) 574 – London roll

    A38   1530   fol.   N.3.18   –   –   –

    Introduction, p. 125, n. 313.

D1.a(1) 593 – Wide diaper roll of quatrefoils in lozenges, Cambridge (Oldham, EBSB)

| C49† | 1507 | 4° | H.1.21 | MS | PDN 22 | – |

D1.a(2) 594
> with AN.f(2) 562
> See under AN.f(2) 562

D1.e(2) 611 – alternating ovals (?London – Oldham, EBSB)

| S61 | 1558 | 8° | ZC1.4.9 | MS+ | PDN 24 | – |

> *Introduction*, p. 126.

D1.h(3) 617 – Garrett Godfrey, Cambridge (= Gray Roll V)

| O10† | 1535 | 8° | C.1.5 | MS | PDN 25 | ** |
| L5 | 1539 | 8° | C.5.7 | Pb & MS | PDN 26 | – |

> *Introduction*, p. 118, n. 288

FC.h(2) 633 – Foliage type-roll, signed 'R W'. Unassigned

| N7 | 1544 | 8° | N.6.6 | M S | PDN 27 | – |

?FC.h(11) 642 – (London). Identification uncertain

| I1 | *c*. 1544 | 8° | D.3.6 | – | – | – |

FL.a(1) 704 – Floral Roll, Spierinck, Cambridge (=Gray Roll III, Pearson, BC, p. 182)

B111	1525	8°	D.3.1	–	–	–
M16	1531	8°	D.3.8	MS	PDN 29	–
L7‡	1525	8°	H.1.6	MS	PDN 28	–

> *Introduction*, p. 114, n. 277, p. 119, n. 291.

FL.a(3) 706 – Oxford intersecting floral roll (= Gibson Roll I)
> with ornament 5 (Ker, *Fragments*, Appendix no. xxxii)

| A25‡ | 1517 | fol. | Y.3.32 | MS+ | PDN 30 | – |

> *Introduction*, p. 114, n. 275.

FL.a(9) 712 – Floral Roll – Cambridge (according to N. R. Ker's annotated copy of Oldham, EBSB – personal communication from D. Pearson)
> with centre-tool CT z

| W50 | 1542 | 4° | I.7.6 | MS | PDN 180 | – |

> *Introduction*, p. 119.

FL.a(10) 713 – Floral Roll – Cambridge (Pearson)

| E29 | *c*. 1536 | 4° | D.1.13–14 | MS | PDN 31 | – |
| L55 | 1539 | 8° | D.5.2 | MS | PDN 32 | – |

FL.b(1) 720 – London (Oldham, EBSB)
> with FP.a(6) 648, signed 'F.I' or 'I R'.

| M86 | 1528 | 4° | I.3.10 | – | – | – |

Introduction, p. 124.

?FP.a(1) 643 – London (Oldham, EBSB)

| B75 | 1529 | 8° | C.6.2 | – | – | – |

> Blind-tooled, now very worn, with an unidentified roll, possibly Oldham, EBSB, FP.a(1) 643, with a date range of 1539–44 suggested by Oldham.
> *Introduction*, p. 125, n. 313.

?FP.a(2) 644 – London

| B117 | 1525 | 8° | C.4.8 | Pb & $$ | PDN 36 | – |

> A blind-tooled binding with a very worn, unidentified roll, just possibly Oldham, EBSB, FP.a(2) 644, though Oldham suggests a date range between 1537–40.

FP.a(6) 648
> with FL.b(1) 720
> See under FL.b(1) 720

FP.a(8) 650 – Foliage
> with HM.a(17) 786 – capstan roll. ?London (Oldham, EBSB) or ?Oxford (Pearson, BC)

| E55 | 1541 | fol. | E.4.1 | MS | PDN 33 | – |
| | [1551] | | | | | |

> Presentation note to Geste, 10 February 1551 at King's College, Cambridge.

| J12 | 1546 | fol. | N.3.13 | MS | PDN 34 | – |
| | [1551] | | | | | |

> As E55 E.4.1 (above).

FP.f(6) 679 – [London]
> with centre-tool CT o

| E18 | 1537 | 8° | F.2.19 | MS+ | PDN 35 | – |

> *Introduction*, p. 125, n. 314.

FP.g(1) 685 – [?London] (Oldham, EBSB); [Cambridge – Some possible association with Nicholas Spierinck (Pearson)]
> with centre-tool CT c.1.

| C64 | 1544 | 8° | C.3.12 | MS & MS** | PDN 38 | – |

| S12 | [1543] | 8° | C.6.7 | MS & Pb$ | PDN 37 | – |

19.2. Geste's second-hand copy of the New Testament annotations of
Isidore Chiari (Antwerp, 1544) in a Cambridge roll binding, Oldham,
EBSB, FP.g(1), with centre-tool CT c.1. Cat. no. C64.

S12	1543	8°	C.6.8	MS&Pb$	PDN 37	–

with CT c.3

C38	1539	8°	M.2.3	–	–	–

Introduction, p. 119.

HE.b(2) 747 – Heraldic roll – signed 'G G' (= Garrett Godfrey, Cambridge) – (Gray Roll III)

A27	1536	8°	D.6.12	MS&MS$	PDN 41	?**
E30	1533	8°	N.6.3	MS	PDN 40	–

Introduction, p. 118.
with AN.f(1) 561 – signed 'G G' (= Garrett Godfrey, Cambridge) – (Gray Roll I)
See under AN.f(1) 561
Introduction, p. 118.

HE.b(5) 751 – Heraldic roll – by 'RB' [London]
with MW.c(1) 862 – Bar in centre

E9	1568	fol.	G.3.18	–	–	–
L21	1571	fol.	E.3.5	Pb&MS+	PDN 76	UIP

Introduction, pp. 126, 134, n. 343.

HE.g(4) 761 – Heraldic roll – Cambridge
with centre-tool CT m.2

D10	1548	fol.	E.3.16	MS	PDN 44	–
D11	1552	fol.	E.3.17	Same MS	PDN 45	–
D12	1542	fol.	E.3.19	MS	PDN 42	–
D14	1548	fol.	E.3.18	–	–	–
D17	1543	fol.	E.3.20	–	–	–
D18	1545	fol.	E.3.21	MS(2) &Pb$$	PDN 43	–

with Oldham, EBSB, ornament C(4)

*H2	1531	fol.	Y.3.19	–	–	–

Introduction, p. 126.

HE.k(1) 766 – Heraldic roll
with HM.h(10) 835 – heads-in-medallions roll
See under HM.h(10) 835

HM.a(7) 776 – Heads-in-medallions – London capstan roll with a single row of slightly wavy hatching and an unidentified ornament

P16	1539	fol.	E.3.6	–	–	–

Introduction, p. 125, n. 313

HM.a(17) 786 – Heads-in-medallions capstan roll

N8	1540	fol.	N.3.16	–	–	–

with FP.a(8) 681 – [?London or Oxford]
See under FP.a(8) 681

HM.b(3) 795 – Heads-in-medallions roll – signed 'F.D'
See under SW.b(5) 948

HM.d(4) 808 – Heads-in-medallions roll. [?Cambridge]

R1	1532	$8°$	C.5.1	–	–	–
R2	1532	$8°$	C.5.2	–	–	–
B53?‡	1522	$8°$	H.1.38–40	MS(2)&$	PDN 46–48 (3 items)	–
S96	1537	$8°$	Y.5.29	MS	PDN 49	–

Introduction, p. 114 n. 278, p. 121.

HM.f(1) 815 – Flowers-in-medallions roll. Unassigned

O6	1525	$8°$	C.1.10	–	–	–

Remounted on later calf with imitation roll decoration at the outer
edges. Now unclear whether originally combined with one of
the other rolls suggested by Oldham, EBSB, e.g. RC.b(2).
Introduction, p. 115.

?HM.h(9) 834 – Heads-in-medallions roll. Unassigned
A worn heads-in-medallions roll in blind, possibly Oldham, EBSB,
HM.h(9) 834, bordering an even more worn unidentified diaper
roll not in Oldham, EBSB, surrounding a rectangular frame with
an oval centre-piece (tool CP 2.2) and a fleuron inside each
angle.

G39	1572	fol.	G.3.17	–	–	–

Introduction, pp. 126–27.

HM.h(10) 835 – Heads-in-medallions roll – signed 'R B' – London

H2	1568	fol.	M.1.28	MS+	PDN 52	–
B138	1567	fol.	Z.2.19	Pb	PDN 51	CB

with HE.k(1) 766 – Heraldic roll by 'R B' – London

I5	1570	fol.	A.4.8	Pb(2)&$$	PDN 50	–

Introduction, p. 126.

**HM.h(28) 853 – Heads-in-medallions roll – [London] (Oldham, EBSB);
[Cambridge] – some possible association with Nicholas Spierinck
(Pearson)**

Z6	?1525	$8°$	N.6.13	–	–	–
O13	1534	$8°$	C.1.6	MS	PDN 53	O

S15	1538	8°	C.6.9	MS	PDN 56	–
J14	1535	8°	D.2.6	MS(2)	PDN 54	O
L63	1539	8°	D.5.4	MS	PDN 57	–
B127	1538	8°	H.1.20	MS	PDN 55	–

with centre-tool CT c.2

M85	1542	4°	F.2.29	MS	PDN 58	–

    Introduction, p. 120 (illustrated in fig. 13.1).

HM.h(29) 854 – Heads-in-medallions roll – [London] (Oldham, EBSB); [Cambridge] tentatively attributed to Nicholas Spierinck but unsigned (D. Pearson – personal communication)

S18	1540	8°	D.2.5	MS	PDN 61	–
J9	1533	8°	H.1.31	MS&Pb$	PDN 59	–
L49	1543	8°	L.6.30	MS	PDN 62	–
S25	1539	8°	ZC2.1.5	MS&Pb$	PDN 60	–

with centre-tool CT c.1

S20	1541	8°	C.6.11	MS&Pb$	PDN 63	**
B83	1542	8°	C.6.3	MS & MS**	PDN 64	?O**
S21	1544	8°	D.6.8	MS&Pb$	PDN 65	–
S22	1544	8°	D.6.9	MS&Pb$	PDN 66	**
B91	1544	8°	H.2.7	–	–	–

with centre-tool CT q

L6?†	1538	8°	C.5.4	MS	PDN 67	–

    See fig. 22.18.

with centre-tool CT yy

C74†	1541	8°	X.2.16	MS	PDN 68	CP^

    See fig. 22.47.

with centre-tool CT aaa

C37	1536	8°	D.4.3	MS&Pb$	PDN 170	–

    Introduction, p. 120. See fig. 22.49.

MW.a(1) 857 (= Gibson roll XII) – signed 'G K'. Oxford

*D4	1548	8°	D.3.13	MS & Pb$$	PDN 70	–

MW.c(1) 862 – Bar in centre – London

Z2	1566	4°	I.5.5	Pb&MS+	PDN 75	–
F23	1566	8°	I.4.6	MS+	PDN 71	IP

N13	1567	4°	T.6.4	MS+ & Pb$$	PDN 72	–
T16	1568	4°	D.1.4	MS+ (or MS)£	PDN 74	–
B29	1568	8°	ZC2.1.8	MS+ & Pb$$	PDN 73	–
J4	1569	4°	E.5.4	Pb£	PDN 32A	–

Introduction, p. 126.
with HE.b(5) 751 – by 'R B', London
See under HE.b(5) 751

?RP.a(1) 892 – Capstan – London

P53	1537	8°	D.1.8	MS+	PDN 83	–

A wide roll of capstan type, just possibly Oldham, EBSB, RP.a(1) 892, but now too worn to be identified with any certainty.
Introduction, p. 124, n. 312.

SW.b(3) 946 – Strapwork roll – London (Oldham, EBSB); Cambridge (Pearson)

L64	1533	4°	C.2.3	MS, Pb$$ & MS**	PDN 78	–
S13	1539	8°	D.2.3	–	–	–
R34	1540	8°	D.6.7	MS	PDN 79	–

Introduction, p. 121.

SW.b(4) 947 – Strapwork roll – London (Oldham, EBSB); Cambridge (Pearson)

S17†	1541	8°	C.6.10	MS	PDN 80	–

Introduction, p. 121.

SW.b(5) 948 – Broad strapwork roll – by the London binder 'F.D.'

W16†	1574	fol.	T.3.8	–	–	–

With four rows of heads-in-medallions roll HM.b(3) 795, showing the heads of the reformers, Melanchthon (signed 'F D'), Erasmus, Hus and Luther, arranged lozenge-shaped.

Classified stamps

Diaper design incorporating four full and eight half stamps of Oldham, EBSB, ornament K.(4) 1017 (= Gray, Stamp 2) – Nicholas Spierinck, Cambridge

H83‡	1506	4°	D.1.2	MS	PDN 81	–

See fig. 19.3.

19.3. Geste's copy of the *Postilla* of Hugh of St Cher (Paris, 1506) in a binding of diaper design incorporating stamps of Oldham, EBSB, ornament K.(4) by Nicholas Spierinck. Cat. no. H83.

20.1. One of Geste's four French roll bindings. His copy of a Richard of St Victor (1510) in a roll binding possibly from Paris. Cat. no. R26.

Continental

French

A contemporary French calf binding (possibly Paris), blind-tooled with a wide roll surrounding a rectangular frame containing two perpendicular rows each of two rolls – one of flies and the other of a spiral stem with four-petal flowers.

Gid, pl. 181, RC c 4 and AN c 2, both on binding 342.

| R26 | 1510 | 4° | I.4.9 | – | – | – |

See fig. 20.1.

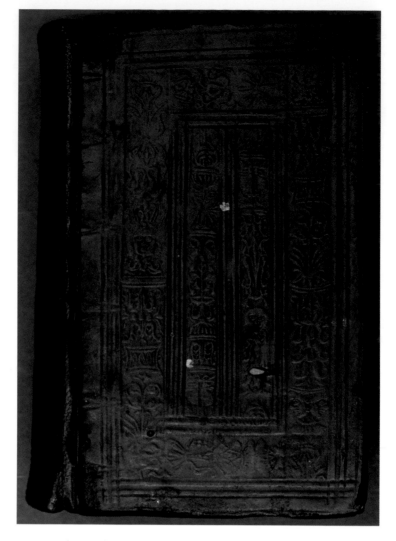

20.2. A volume from a sextodecimo set of the vulgate Bible in a contemporary French calf binding, printed in Paris (1526). Cat. no. B34.

French

    A contemporary French calf binding, blind-tooled with a wide roll surrounding a rectangular frame in which are two rows of another, narrow, roll, probably from Paris.

    Compare Gid, pl. 79, Fsj 1 or possibly Fsj 2, and cf. Gid FP a(12), and pl. 47 CH I 4, which occur on Gid, bindings 118 and 123 (Paris).

B34   1526   16°   G.6.12   –   –   –

    See fig. 20.2.

20.3. Geste's copy of the *Theosophia* by Joannes Arboreus (1540) in contemporary calf, with a floral roll, probably French. Cat. no. A49.

French

A contemporary calf binding probably French, blind-tooled with a floral roll though not found in Gid, surrounding a rectangular frame and repeated at the outer edges, with a floral tool comprising four fleurons placed cross-wise in the centre, and a single fleuron at each corner of the frame.

A49?‡   1540   fol.   M.1.17   MS+   PDN 21   –

See fig. 20.3.

20.4. A Peter Lombard of 1495 in a nineteenth-century re-binding
with parts of the original early sixteenth-century French calf-covers
overlaid, with three rolls in blind. Cat. no. P23.

French

A nineteenth-century re-binding with parts of the original early
sixteenth-century French calf covers overlaid, with three rolls
in blind: (1) a wide roll surrounding (2) a narrower roll, incorporating a diaper, fleur-de-lis, fleurons, and other tools, enclosing a rectangular frame with fillets, inside which is (3) a
single row of quatrefoils between two regular, undulating lines
(Gid, pl. 58 ENc 4 or Enc 2(?); RC 13).

P23?‡   1495   4°   L.5.38   MS   PDN 85   –

See fig. 20.4.

20.5. A Stobaeus of 1543 in a contemporary German calf-binding, blind-tooled with a roll divided into compartments depicting the Lifting up of the Brazen Serpent, the Crucifixion, and the Resurrection. Cat. no. S89.

German

A contemporary German calf binding, blind-tooled with a roll divided into compartments depicting the Lifting up of the Brazen Serpent, the Crucifixion, and the Resurrection, surrounded by fillets with a floral ornament outside each angle, enclosing a rectangular frame in which there is a single narrow row of a floral roll at each end and a lozenge-shape frame of fillets, with a diamond-shaped central-ornament made up of four strikes of a renaissance-type cross-shaped floral tool, with the same tool at each angle of the frame touching the four sides of the rectangular frame.

S89 1543 fol. M.I.15 MS+ PDN 84 –

See fig. 20.5.

Netherlandish

Contemporary calf over pasteboard, blind-tooled with a roll-binding of 'Netherlandish design (b)' (Oldham, EBSB, Pl. V and p. 10), repaired with new spine panels.

P15† 1521 fol. M.I.27 –   –   –

See fig. 14.

Unassigned

Contemporary calf over pasteboard, blind-tooled with an unidentified floral roll which among other motifs includes a seven-petal flower and what appears to be a heart (perhaps pierced by an arrow), both within double-circle roundels (probably not English and perhaps imported already bound from the continent), surrounding a rectangular frame with a lozenge-shaped ornament [CT p] at the centre (fig. 22.17).

R32 1548 8° H.I.37 –   –   –

See fig. 22.17.

Unassigned

Contemporary calf binding, blind-tooled with an unidentified roll (not English or French but perhaps imported already bound from its place of printing, Basle) surrounding a plain rectangular frame.

A56‡ 1538 8° E.6.5 –   –   –

See fig. 20.6.

20.6. An octavo of 1538 in contemporary calf with an unidentified
roll, possibly imported already bound from its place
of printing, Basle. Cat. no. A56.

Unidentified or unconfirmed English bindings and stamps

Unconfirmed stamps

> A contemporary early sixteenth-century English calf binding (now very worn) over original boards, blind-tooled with intersecting borders containing rose and pineapple tools (too worn to identify with any certainty) surrounding a rectangular frame with a lattice of four full and eight half perforations containing a worn lozenge-shaped tool (cf. Oldham, EBSB, stamp 206).

B5‡   1497   fol.   Y.2.12   MS &   PDN 82   –
                                                    Pb$$*

> See fig. 16.1.

Blind-tooled binding

> With an unidentified English roll not found in Oldham, EBSB.

P38   1559   4°   E.5.8   MS+   PDN 77   –

> See fig.21.1.

Blind-tooled binding

> With an unidentified roll of diaper design (not found in Oldham, EBSB), consisting of quatrefoils in lozenges, surrounding a plain rectangular frame, with fillets extending to the outside edges creating four square (two long and two shorter) plain rectangular frames.

S24   1546   8°   ZC2.2.5 MS+   PDN 23   –

> See fig. 21.2.

Blind-tooled English binding

> With a blank cartouche ornament (CT ss) surrounded by an unidentified roll, closest to, but not identical with, Oldham, EBSB, FP.a (1).

B94†   1544   8°   D.4.8   MS+   PDN 39   –

> See fig. 21.3.

Blind-tooled binding

> Now very worn; with an unidentified heads-in-medallions roll (not found in Oldham, EBSB) surrounding a plain rectangular frame.

S67   1567   4°   I.7.7   MS+   PDN 69   ?*

> See fig. 21.4.

21.1. A commentary on the Psalms by Placidus (1559) in very worn contemporary calf, with an unidentified English roll. Cat. no. P38.

21.2. One of Geste's unidentified English roll bindings. An
octavo printed at Basle in 1546. Cat. no. S24.

21.3. An octavo of 1544 in a single example of centre-tool CT ss,
surrounded by a worn unidentified roll. Cat. no. B94.

21.4. A quarto of 1569–1570 in very worn contemporary calf, with an unidentified heads-in-medallions roll. Cat. no. S67.

C: *Centrepiece bindings*

Pearson notes the first appearance of centrepieces in London about 1560 and their use in Oxford and Cambridge soon after, eventually spreading to other binding centres later in the century using hundreds of different centrepiece tools, many of them variants of a smaller number of common designs (Pearson, OB, pp. 75–86, 103–111; Pearson, BC, pp. 169–196; Pearson, EBS, p. 55 f.).

Abbreviations

MS+   Strip from a MS only, to strengthen spine and/or binding structure.

PDN   Image number of pastedown, flyleaf or MS strip (see the database at www.bibsoc.org.uk/Geste).

$$$ Some annotations on inside of unopened leaves, i.e. annotated *before* binding.

In the case of multiple items bound together, the imprint year given below is the latest of the imprint years – and probably closer to the date of binding. None of Geste's books in these bindings retains binding instructions (if there ever were any).

The tabular information, printed in grey type below,
is laid out in the following columns

Cat. no	Imprint date	Format	Shelf-mark	Pastedown &c.	Image number

CP 1

Oval centrepiece blind-stamped at the centre of otherwise plain covers with fillets at the outer edges (cf. Pearson 097; Pearson, EBS, fig. 5.12, the last of the bindings shown on p. 130)).

[*E3	1558	8°	N.6.37	–	–

Geste ownership uncertain]

CP 2.1

Oval centrepiece blind-stamped at the centre of otherwise plain covers with fillets at the outer edges. One of many variants of Pearson OL1; Pearson, BC, p. 193, C8 (an oval with a lozenge at the centre).

M37	1571	8°	C.6.13	–	–
H37	1571	8°	ZC2.7.5	MS+	PDN 86 $$$
B63	1572	8°	G.6.1	MS+	PDN 87
C26	1572	4°	D.1.5	–	–

C68	1572	8°	G.5.17	–	–
C61	1573	8°	C.7.3	–	–
C62	1573	8°	C.7.4	MS+	PDN 88
E10	1573	8°	D.4.9	MS+	PDN 89
H47	1573	8°	D.4.6	–	–

Introduction, p. 127. C62 is illustrated in fig. 18.1.

CP 2.2

Oval centrepiece in a rectangular frame surrounded by a heads-in-medallions roll which bears some resemblance to Oldham, EBSB, HM.h(9) 834 and an unidentified diaper roll.

| G39 | 1572 | fol. | G.3.17 | – | – |

Introduction, p. 127. G39 is illustrated in fig. 18.2.

CP 3

Round centrepiece on otherwise plain covers with fillets at the outer edges. No match in Pearson.

| W32 | 1559 | 8° | D.2.11 | – | – |

Introduction, p. 127. W32 is illustrated in fig. 18.3.

CP 4

Oval centrepiece on otherwise plain covers with fillets at the outer edges. No match with any Pearson OL centrepieces, though some slight points of resemblance to OL13.

| E54 | 1558 | 8° | F.2.24 | – | – |

Introduction, p. 127. E54 is illustrated in fig. 18.4.

D: *Centre-tools and ornaments*

Books bound in fairly basic calf-over-pasteboard covers, tooled, generally in blind, with one or more small tools to form a centre ornament, sometimes on otherwise plain covers with fillets at the outer edges or within an otherwise plain rectangular frame defined by fillets, some with the same small tool or another tool at each angle of the rectangular frame. Some of these small tools, e.g. that used in CT c.1, have been associated by Pearson, BC, with Cambridge bindings in conjunction with Cambridge rolls such as Oldham, EBSB, FP.g(1), HM.h(28) and HM.h(29). References to Pearson's classification are added where appropriate.

Abbreviations

MS	Leaf or leaves from a MS as pastedown.
MS+	MS strip to strengthen binding structure.
MS(G)	Leaf or leaves from a MS in Geste's hand.

Pb   Leaf or leaves from printed book as pastedown.
PDN   Image no. of pastedown, flyleaf or MS strip (see the
          database at www.bibsoc.org.uk/Geste).
†   Pre-Geste ownership inscription.
‡   Pre-Geste MS annotations, book-price or book-title(s)
          on fore-edge or spine, but no pre-Geste ownership
          inscription.
$ Compacted leaves as pasteboard.
$$ Flyleaves.
++   Stub/strip from fold-over of same MS/Pb.
£   Pastedown or MS+ now covered over by modern paper
          endleaf/flyleaf.

Binding instructions
B   Instruction to bind other (named) items in the same book.
CP^   Now in calf covers, though instruction to binder reads,
          'in parchment'.
F   Instruction to find other items to bind in the same book.
IP   'In paste', i.e. calf over pasteboard.
O   Order of items to be bound together.
U   'uncutt'.
★★   Trace only – instruction uncertain.

In the case of multiple items bound together, the imprint year given below
is the latest of the imprint years – and probably closer to the date of binding.

*The tabular information, printed in grey type below,
is laid out in the following columns*

Cat. no	Imprint date	Format	Shelf-mark	Pastedown &c.	Image number	Binding instruction

CT a
  Calf-over-pasteboard covers, blind-tooled with one ornament or
    tool forming a centrepiece, usually on plain covers with fillets at
    the outside edges or within an otherwise plain rectangular
    frame defined by fillets (fig. 22.1), some with fleurons at each
    angle of the rectangular frame, e.g. C36, K.2.13 .
  Early example in Gray, pl. XXII and p. 60, stamped at a later date
    on John Siberch's Roll II. The book is a Bullinger of 1538, but
    the binding must be at least post-1544 because of the endpapers
    from Jasper Laet's Almanack and Prognostication of 1544, and
    the CT could have been added much later.

G2	1564	8°	C.3.11	Pb MS+	PDN 91	–

22.1. A quarto, with the latest item dated 1570, in centre-tool CT a, one of twenty-two examples, with an imprint date-range 1564–1572 during Geste's London and Salisbury periods. Cat. no. C36 (K.2.14).

C44	1564	4°	K.2.26	Pb$ MS+	PDN 90	–
H30	1569	8°	C.4.11	Pb	PDN 92	–
F28	1569	8°	D.6.1	–	–	O
O26	1569	8°	M.2.40	–	–	O

S28	1569	8°	N.6.11	–	–	O/**
D20	1569	8°	ZC2.1.9	–	–	O
C36	1569	4°	K.2.13	Pb MS+	PDN 94	–
C36	1570	4°	K.2.14	MS+	PDN 95	–
P34	1570	4°	E.5.1	Pb	PDN 98	–
L30	1570	4°	I.8.3	Pb	PDN 97	O
W22	1570	8°	N.6.10	–	–	O
A50	1570	16°	ZC1.4.13	Pb MS+	PDN 93	O
V22	1570	8°	ZC2.1.3	–	–	O
H98	1570	8°	ZC2.1.6	MS+	PDN 96	O/?IP
H62	1571	8°	G.5.15	Pb MS+	PDN 101	–
B58	1571	8°	G.6.6	Pb&MS+	PDN 99	–
C43	1571	8°	H.1.7	Pb$$MS+	PDN 100	–
P41	1571	8°	ZC1.4.5	Pb MS+	PDN 102	–
W46	1571	8°	ZC2.7.8	Pb$$MS+	PDN 103	–
O25	1572	8°	I.2.10	Pb MS+	PDN 105	–
H49	1572	8°	ZC1.4.3	Pb MS+	PDN 104	–

Total: 22

CT b

Blank cartouche or shield in blind on otherwise plain covers with
one or more fillet(s) at the outer edges (figs.13.3 and 22.2).
Date range 1547–1568.

B96	1547	8°	D.3.2	MS+ MS(G)$$	PDN 106	–
G44	1550	8°	C.3.1	–	–	**
P2	1555	4°	B.5.3	–	–	**
H18	1556	8°	C.3.2	–	–	–
H19	1556	8°	C.3.3	MS+	PDN 118	–
H20	1556	8°	C.3.4	MS+	PDN 119	–
H21	1556	8°	C.3.5	–	–	–
H22	1556	8°	C.3.6	–	–	–
R15	1557	8°	ZC2.2.2	MS+	PDN 107	–

22.2. An octavo of 1567 in centre-tool CT b, one of fifty-one, with an imprint date-range 1547–1568, all probably bound during Geste's London period. Cat. no. S49.

V30	1558	8°	D.5.11	–	–	–
V31	1558	8°	D.5.12	MS+	PDN 108	–
G1	1559	8°	C.3.10	–	–	–
H96	1559	8°	N.6.16	MS+	PDN 109	–
B7	1560	8°	A.6.22	MS+	PDN 110	–
S64†	[1561]	8°	R.6.46	Pb+ MS letter [1561] $$	PDN 113	–
R4	1561	8°	D.6.11	–	–	–
H1	1561	8°	ZC2.2.7	MS+ (blank)	PDN 111	–
H48	1561	8°	ZC2.2.8	MS+ (blank)	PDN 112	–
C4	1564	8°	D.1.9	MS+ (blank)	PDN 114	–
R5	1564	8°	D.4.1	–	–	–
W27‡	1565	8°	D.5.10	MS+	PDN 116	–
M35	1565	8°	D.6.4	–	–	U
C57	1565	8°	M.2.21	–	–	–
S41	1565	8°	ZC2.1.7	MS+	PDN 115	IP
W18	1566	8°	C.4.4	MS+	PDN 122	IP
C59	1566	8°	C.7.1	–	–	–
C60	1566	8°	C.7.2	–	–	–
W4	1566	8°	D.6.6	–	–	–
M18	1566	4°	I.4.5	–	–	IP
W23	1566	8°	K.2.15	MS+	PDN 123	IP
H91	1566	8°	Z.4.23	MS+	PDN 120	–
V24	1566	8°	Z.5.109	MS+	PDN 121	–
F10	1566	8°	ZC2.1.4	MS+	PDN 117	IP
S44	1567	8°	G.6.2	MS+ (blank)	PDN 131	IP
P10	1567	8°	G.6.5	–	–	–
R38	1567	8°	H.1.9	MS+	PDN 130	CP^
R11	1567	8°	I.1.5	MS+ (wide)	PDN 129	IP

G33	1567	4°	A.6.11	–	–	IP
C115	1567	8°	D.4.5	–	–	IP**
S43	1567	8°	D.4.7	–	–	–
E52	1567	8°	D.5.9	[Pb]	–	–

(a pastedown reportedly kept separately is now mislaid)

J15	1567	8°	D.6.5	–	–	IP
F22	1567	8°	K.2.17	MS+	PDN 126	IP
V2	1567	8°	Z.5.108	–	–	–
S49	1567	8°	ZC1.4.2	MS+ (blank)	PDN 132	IP
M74	1567	8°	ZC1.4.8	Pb(2)$$ & MS+	PDN 127	–
P8	1567	8°	ZC1.5.4	MS+	PDN 128	–
F18	1567	8°	ZC2.2.4	–	–	IP
C110	1567	8°	ZC2.2.10	MS+ (wide)	PDN 125	–
L47	1568	8°	A.6.26	MS+	PDN 133	–
R10	1568	8°	I.1.6	Pb & $$ & MS+	PDN 134	O

Total: 51

CT b.1

Cartouche in blind within which are two asymmetrically crossed lines on otherwise plain covers with fillets at the outer edges. Variant of CT b or mis-strike.

W1	1568	8°	K.2.16	MS+	PDN 135	–

CT c.1

Small fleuron tool (?= Pearson, Small tools 1) in blind at the centre of a rectangular frame with the same tool at each angle (fig 22.3). Some examples have the panel surrounded by one of two rolls, both of which Pearson tentatively links with Nicholas Spierinck: Oldham, EBSB, HM.h(29) 854 or Oldham, EBSB, FP.g(1) 685.

E33	1532	4°	I.3.8	MS with 'E G' on covers	PDN 136	IP
E38	1534	8°	ZC1.4.6	MS with 'E G' on covers	PDN138A	**

22.3. An octavo, with the latest item dated 1546, in centre-tool CT c, one of twenty-five (some with rolls, see fig. 19.2), with an imprint date-range 1532–1548 during Geste's Cambridge period. Cat. no. M20.

S14	1539	8°	G.5.14	MS	PDN 137	–
S20	1541	8°	C.6.11	MS [Pb$] with HM.h(29)	PDN 63	**
B83	1542	8°	C.6.3	MS & MS(G) with HM.h(29)	PDN 64	O**
A43	1543	4°	C.2.13	MS	PDN 138	–
S12	1543	8°	C.6.7	MS & Pb$ with FP.g(1)	PDN 37	–
S12	1543	8°	C.6.8	MS,++ & Pb$ with FP.g(1)	PDN 37	–
C64	1544	8°	C.3.12	MS & MS(G) with FP.g(1) and 'T D' on covers	PDN 38	–
B38	1544	8°	C.4.1	MS	PDN 139	–
S21	1544	8°	D.6.8	MS with HM.h(29)	PDN 65	–
S22	1544	8°	D.6.9	MS (same MS as D.6.8) with HM.h(29)	PDN 66	**
B91	1544	8°	H.2.7	– with HM.h(29)	–	–
V39	1544	8°	N.6.5	MS(2)	PDN 140	–
L60	1545	8°	D.5.1	MS & Pb$	PDN 141	–
A5	1545	8°	D.5.6	MS(2)	PDN 142	–
D6	1545	4°	G.5.4	MS	PDN 143	?O**
R23	1545	8°	H.1.8	MS & Pb$	PDN 144	–
Z4	1545	8°	M.2.16	–	–	–
M20	1546	8°	D.2.8	MS & Pb$	PDN 147	–
G29	1546	8°	F.2.10	MS	PDN 146	–
A55	1546	8°	C.4.2	MS, Pb$ & MS(G)	PDN 145	–

B88	1548	8°	C.6.4	MS & MS(G)	PDN 148	–
H42	1548	8°	O.1.25	MS	PDN 150	–
CII	1548	8°	ZC1.4.7	MS & Pb$	PDN 149	O**

Total: 25

CT c.2
Double version of CT c.1 with two small fleurons joined together at the centre of a rectangular frame, with a single fleuron at each angle – surrounded by Oldham, EBSB, roll HM.h(28) 853 (fig. 13.1).

| M85 | 1542 | 4° | F.2.29 | MS | PDN 58 | – |

CT c.3
Two small fleurons at each end of a rectangular frame, surrounded by Oldham, EBSB, roll FP.g(1) 685 which Pearson tentatively links with Nicholas Spierinck, Cambridge – all in blind.

| C38 | 1539 | 8° | M.2.3 | – | – | – |

CT c.4
Quadruple version with four fleurons in blind in the form of a cross at the centre of a plain rectangular frame with the same fleuron at each angle.

| C102 | 1539 | 8° | A.6.31 | – | – | – |

CT d.1
Lozenge-shaped ornament in blind on otherwise plain covers with fillets at the outer edges (fig 22.4).
Date range: 1556–1558.

C70	1556	8°	D.6.2	MS+	PDN 153	–
L70	1556	8°	ZC1.4.10	MS+ (wide)	PDN 151	–
B80	1558	8°	G.5.16	–	–	–
B81	1558	8°	G.6.4	–	–	–
B92	1558	4°	K.2.11	MS+	PDN 152	–

CT d.2
Lozenge-shape ornament in blind with fleurons at each point at the centre of a rectangular frame defined by fillets with fleurons outside each angle with fillets at the outer edges (fig. 22.5).

| C16 | 1559 | fol. | N.2.9 | – | – | – |

22.4. A quarto, with the latest item dated 1558, in centre-tool CT d.1, one of five examples with an imprint date-range of 1556–1558. Cat. no. B92.

22.5. A folio of 1559 in a single example of centre-tool
CT d.2 (detail). Cat. no. C16.

CT e

Silvered lozenge-shaped ornament decorated inside with an eight-petal fleuron within a rectangular frame defined by fillets, with fleur-de-lis outside each angle (fig 22.6).

Date range: 1573–1576.

M76	1573	8°	D.1.7	MS+	PDN 154	**
M77	1574	8°	G.5.6	MS+ (wide)	PDN 155	–
Z5	1575	8°	ZC1.4.4	MS+ (wide)	PDN 156	–
W20	1576	8°	C.4.5	MS+ (2; 1 wide)	PDN 157	–

22.6. An octavo of 1573 in centre-tool CT e, one of four examples with an imprint date-range of 1573–1576 during Geste's Salisbury period. Cat. no. M76.

22.7. A sextodecimo of 1552 in a single example of
centre-tool CT f. Cat. no. B37.

CT f

> Formal renaissance design, lozenge-shaped overall, incorporating
> four overlapping ovals surrounded by arabesque decoration in
> gold on otherwise plain covers, with fillets in blind at the outer
> edges (fig. 22.7).

| B37 | 1552 | 16° | G.6.7 | MS+Pb$ | PDN 158 | – |
| | | | | & MS(G) | | |

22.8. An octavo of 1544 in a single example of
centre-tool CT g. Cat. no. C98.

CT g

Floral ornament of splayed sepals, stamped in gold, at the centre of
a rectangular frame defined by fillets with fleur-de-lis outside
each angle, also in gold, with fillets in blind at the outer edges
(fig. 22.8).

C98   1544   8°   B.6.4   –   –   –

22.9. A quarto of 1564, one of four examples, in centre-tool CT h.1
with an imprint date-range of 1560–1564. Cat. no. T5.

CT h.1

Floral ornament stamped in gold in the centre of plain covers with
fillets in blind at the outer edges (fig. 22.9).

Date-range: 1560–1565

A54	1560	8°	A.6.17	Pb	PDN 159	–
T5	1564	4°	A.6.3	–	–	–
H25	1565	8°	C.4.10	–	–	O
C7	1565	4°	G.5.5	–	–	–

22.10. An octavo of 1562 in a single example of
centre-tool CT h.2. Cat. no. W39.

CT h.2
> Floral ornament at the centre of a rectangular frame with large
> fleurons outside each angle, all in gold, and fillets in blind at the
> outer edges (fig. 22.10).

W39   1562   8°   G.5.12   MS+   PDN 160 –
                                                    (wide)

22.11. An octavo of 1549, in a single example
of centre-tool CT j. Cat. no. G5.

CT j

   Formal ornament stamped in gold at the centre of otherwise plain
   covers, with fillets in blind at the outer edges (fig. 22.11).

G5   1549   8°   ZC2.7.13 MS+   PDN 161 –
                             (blank)

22.12. An octavo of 1557 in centre-tool CT k, one of three
examples with a date-range of 1557–1567. Cat. no. F34.

CT k

> A floral ornament in blind at the centre of otherwise plain covers
> with fillets at the outer edges (fig. 22.12).

F34	1557	8°	H.1.4	MS+	PDN 162	–
S73	1566	8°	H.1.3	MS+	PDN 163	–
S7	1567	8°	N.6.12	–	–	–

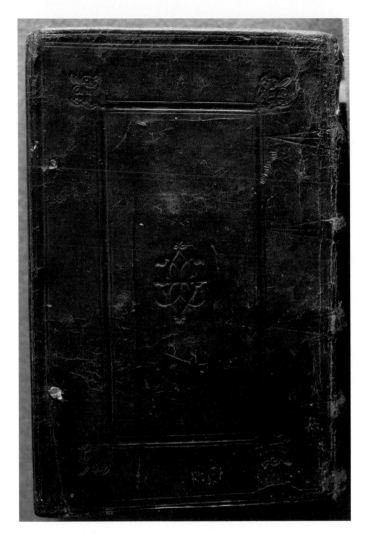

22.13. An octavo of 1552 in centre-tool CT m.1, one of three
examples with a date-range of 1548–1552. Cat. no. B90.

CT m.1

A formal renaissance ornament (= Pearson, small-tool 3), either at
the centre of a rectangular frame with large fleurons (= Pearson,
small-tool 7) outside each angle and fillets at the outer edges, or
on otherwise plain covers [¶] with fillets at the outer edges, all
in blind (fig. 22.13).

C120	1548	8°	M.2.29	Pb$$, Pb$	PDN 164	–
				& MS+		
L43¶	1552	8°	D.3.3	Pb & MS+	PDN 166	–
B90	1552	8°	M.2.25	MS+	PDN 165	–

CT m.2

A formal renaissance ornament (apparently the same ornament as
CT m.1) at the centre of a rectangular frame with a small fleuron
outside each angle and fillets at the outer edges, all in blind.
Date range: 1540–1555.

| D21 | 1540 | fol. | N.4.2 | MS & Pb$ £ | PDN 167 – |
| O18 | 1552 or 1555 | 8° | C.4.12 | – | – – |

The same surrounded by Oldham, EBSB, roll HE.g(4) 761, with
a fleuron (= Pearson, small-tool 7) outside each angle and with
fillets at the outer edges all in blind . This roll was evidently used
first in London (1523–1534), and later in Cambridge shortly after
1550 until at least 1565 (Pearson, BC, pp.171f., 183.) (fig.22.14).

D12	1542	fol.	E.3.19	MS	PDN 42 –
D17	1543	fol.	E.3.20	–	– –
D18	1545	fol.	E.3.21	MS(2) & Pb$$	PDN 43 –
D10	1548	fol.	E.3.16	MS	PDN 44 –
D14	1549	fol.	E.3.18	–	– –
D11	1552	fol.	E.3.17	MS	PDN 45 –

CT n

A Tudor rose ornament in the centre of a rectangular frame
defined by fillets with small sunbursts or daisies outside each
angle, all in gold (fig. 22.15).

| M32 | 1560 | 8° | C.6.12 | MS+ | PDN 168 – |

CT o

A floral ornament in the centre of a rectangular frame, surrounded
by Oldham, EBSB, roll FP.f(6) with fillets at the outer edges, all
in blind (fig. 22.16).

| E18 | 1537 | 8° | F.2.19 | MS+ | PDN 35 – |

CT p

A lozenge-shaped ornament stamped in blind at the centre of a
rectangular frame surrounded by an unidentified floral roll
(which among other motifs includes what appears to be a heart
pierced by an arrow – not English and probably imported
already bound from the continent) (fig. 22.17).

| R32 | 1550 | 8° | H.1.37 | – | – – |

22.14. A folio, with the latest item dated 1552, in centre-tool CT m.2 with Oldham, EBSB, roll HE.g(4), one of six examples (two without the roll) with a date range of 1542–1555. Cat. no. DII.

22.15. An octavo of 1560 in a single example of
centre-tool CT n. Cat. no. M32.

22.16. An octavo of 1537 in a single example of centre-tool CT o
with Oldham, EBSB, roll FP.f(6). Cat. no. E18.

22.17. An octavo, with the latest item dated 1550, in a single example of centre-tool CT p with an unidentified roll, probably imported already bound from the continent. Cat. no. R32.

22.18. An octavo, with the latest item dated 1538, in a single example of centre-tool CT q with Oldham, EBSB, roll HM.h(29). Cat. no. L6.

CT q

    A fleur-de-lis type ornament at the centre and each angle of a rectangular frame surrounded by Oldham, EBSB, roll HM.h(29) tentatively attributed by Pearson to Nicholas Spierinck, Cambridge, all in blind (cf. CT aaa) (fig. 22.18).

    L6   1538   8°   C.5.4   MS   PDN 67   –

22.19. An octavo of 1546 in a single example of
centre-tool CT r. Cat. no. C114.

CT r

A fleur-de-lis type ornament in blind at the centre and inside each
angle of a rectangular frame, defined by fillets at the outer
edges). Cf. Pearson, BC, p. 196, ST 6 (fig. 22.19).

C114   1546   8°   D.4.4   MS   PDN 171   −

22.20. A folio of 1542 in a single example of
centre-tool CT s. Cat. no. P33.

CT s

A renaissance ornament in blind (apparently made up of a double
strike of the same tool), at the centre of a large rectangular
frame defined by fillets with a small fleuron outside each angle
(fig.22.20).

P33†   1542   fol.   N.4.6   –   –   –

22.21. An octavo of 1561 in centre-tool CT t, one of two examples
with a date-range of 1555–1561. Cat. no. B120.

CT t

A formal renaissance ornament in blind (apparently made up of a
double strike of the same tool) at the centre of otherwise plain
covers, with fillets at the outer edges (fig. 22.21).

V38	1555	8°	Z.5.121	MS+	PDN 172 –
B120	1561	8°	G.6.3	MS+ & Pb$$	PDN 173 –

22.22. An octavo of 1560 in centre-tool CT v, one of five examples
with a date-range of 1552–1562. Cat. no. S39.

CT v

A formal (rather squat) ornament in blind at the centre of otherwise plain covers with fillets at the outer edges (fig. 22.22).

O17	1552	8°	D.5.8	MS+	PDN 174	–
S39	1560	8°	D.3.9	–	–	IP/O
S39	1560	8°	D.3.10	MS+&Pb	PDN 175	–
S39	1561	8°	D.3.11?	?Pb £	PDN 176	IP/O
H38	1562	8°	ZC2.7.6	–	–	IP

22.23. A quarto of 1562 in a single example of
centre-tool CT w. Cat. no. L20.

CT w

> A formal ornament in blind at the centre of a rectangular frame,
> with a fleur-de-lis ornament outside each angle and fillets at the
> outer edges (fig. 22.23).

L20   1562   4°   G.5.1   –   –   –

22.24. A quarto, with the latest item dated 1549, in centre-tool CT x, one of two examples with a date-range of 1544–1552. Cat. no. B108.

CT x

A formal renaissance ornament in blind at the centre of a plain rectangular frame defined by fillets with fleurons outside each angle and fillets at the outer edges (fig.22.24).

| B108 | 1549 | 4° | I.4.4 | MS | PDN 177 | – |
| V16 | 1552 | 8° | N.6.8 | MS&MS+ | PDN 178 | – |

22.25. An octavo, with the latest item dated 1537, in a single
example of centre-tool CT y. Cat. no. L18.

CT y

A small fleuron ornament in blind at the centre of a rectangular
frame defined by intersecting fillets extending to the outer edges
of the covers, with the same ornament inside each angle (fig.
22.25).

L18‡   1537   8°   H.2.12   MS(2) & PDN 179 –
                                  MS+

22.26. A quarto, with the latest item dated 1543, in a single example of centre-tool CT z with Oldham, EBSB, roll FL.a(9). Cat. no. W50.

CT z

A cross-shaped ornament of five fleurons in blind at the centre of a rectangular frame, with the same fleuron ornament inside each angle, surrounded by Oldham, EBSB, roll FL.a(9), with fillets at the outer edges (fig. 22.26).

W50   1542   4°   I.7.6   MS   PDN 180 –

22.27. An octavo of 1553 in a single example of
centre-tool CT aa. Cat. no. N6.

CT aa

    A cross-shaped fleuron ornament in blind at the centre of a rec-
tangular frame defined by fillets with a fleur-de-lis outside each
angle and fillets at the outer edges (fig. 22.27).

| N6 | 1553 | 8° | N.6.9 | – | – | – |

22.28. An octavo, with the latest item dated 1564, in centre-tool CT bb.1, one of two examples with a date-range of 1560–1564. Cat. no. O22.

CT bb.1

A small renaissance ornament in blind at the centre of otherwise plain covers with fillets at the outer edges (fig. 22.28).

| E58 | 1560 | 8° | C.4.13 | – | – | IP |
| O22 | 1564 | 8° | B.6.16 | Pb | PDN 181 | CP^/O** |

22.29. A quarto of 1563 in a single example of
centre-tool CT bb.2. Cat. no. V5.

CT bb.2

A small fleuron tooled in gold at the centre of otherwise plain
covers with fillets in blind at the outer edges (fig. 22.29).

V5   1563   4°   I.4.2   Pb&MS+ PDN 182 –

22.30. An octavo of 1559 in a single example of
centre-tool CT cc. Cat. no. V17.

CT cc

A small fleuron tooled in blind on otherwise plain covers with
fillets at the outer edges (fig. 22.30).

V17   1559   8°   N.6.7   –   –   –

22.31. An octavo of 1569 in a single example of
centre-tool CT dd. Cat. no. P12.

CT dd

A floral ornament tooled in blind at the centre of otherwise plain
covers with fillets at the outer edges (fig. 22.31).

P12   1569   8°   M.2.26   MS+   PDN 183 –

22.32. An octavo of 1544, one of two examples,
both of 1544, in centre-tool CT ee. Cat. no. O4.

CT ee

A fleuron ornament tooled in blind at the centre and inside each
angle of a large rectangular frame defined by fillets with fillets at
the outer edges (fig. 22.32).

S80	1544	8°	ZC2.2.9	MS(2) &	PDN 185	O**
				Pb$		
O4	1544	8°	C.1.4	MS	PDN 184	O

22.33. An octavo of 1571 in a single example of
centre-tool CT ff.1. Cat. no. W28.

CT ff.1

A fleuron-type ornament in blind at the centre of a rectangular
frame defined by fillets with a small fleur-de-lis ornament
outside each angle and fillets at the outer edges (fig. 22.33).

W28   1571   8°   D.2.10   Pb   PDN 186 IP**

22.34. An octavo of 1571 in a single example of
centre-tool CT ff.2. Cat. no. C32.

CT ff.2

A fleuron-type ornament in blind (possibly a variant or a worn/
damaged version of CT ff.1) at the centre of a rectangular frame
defined by fillets with a small fleur-de-lis ornament outside each
angle and fillets at the outer edges (fig. 22.34).

C32   1571   8°   C.2.4   Pb &   PDN 187 –
                                      MS+**

22.35. An octavo of 1565 in a single example of
centre-tool CT gg. Cat. no. F29.

CT gg

    A hexagonal ornament within a rectangular frame defined by fillets
with a fleuron outside each angle, all in gold, with fillets in
blind at the outer edges (fig. 22.35).

F29   1565   8°   D.2.9   –   –   –

22.36. An octavo of 1573 in centre-tool CT hh, one of two examples with a date-range of 1573–1575 during Geste's Salisbury period. Cat. no. B26.

CT hh

> A large four-petal fleuron in silver at the centre of a rectangular frame with another fleuron also in silver outside each angle with fillets in blind at the outer edges (fig. 22.36).

B26	1573	8°	M.2.20	–	–	–
A51	1575	8°	ZC2.7.1	MS+	PDN 188	–

22.37. An octavo of 1558, one of two examples with a date-range
of 1555–1558, in centre-tool CT jj. Cat. no. W38.

CT jj

A circular ornament at the centre of a rectangular frame with a
large fleur-de-lis outside each angle, all in gold, with fillets in
blind at the outer edges (fig. 22.37).

| W37 | 1555 | 8° | G.5.10 | – | – | – |
| W38 | 1558 | 8° | G.5.11 | – | – | – |

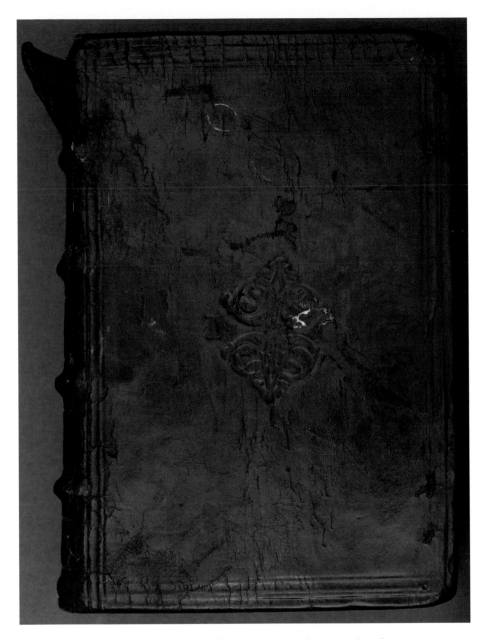

22.38. An octavo of 1556 in a single example of
centre-tool CT kk. Cat. no. E59.

CT kk

A large double floral ornament in blind stamped with the initials
'I' and 'G' on each side of the ornament at the centre of otherwise plain covers with fillets at the outer edges (fig. 22.38).

E59†   1556   8°   A.6.25   Pb &MS+ PDN 189 –

22.39. An octavo of 1568, in centre-tool CT mm, one of two examples
with a date-range of 1568–1570. Cat. no. R9 (B.5.9).

CT mm

A floral ornament (?acanthus leaves) in blind at the centre of
otherwise plain covers with fillets also in blind at the outer
edges (fig. 22.39).

| R9 | 1568 | 8° | B.5.9 | – | – | – |
| R9 | 1570 | 8° | B.5.10 | MS+ & MS(G)$$ | PDN 190 | – |

22.40. An octavo of 1556 in a single example of
centre-tool CT nn. Cat. no. L82.

CT nn

A star-shaped ornament in blind made up of a single tool repeated four times on otherwise plain covers with fillets at the outer edges (fig. 22.40).

L82   1556   8°   M.2.43   MS+   PDN 191   –

22.41. One of two octavos of 1541 in the only examples of
centre-tool CT pp. Cat. no. R12 (X.2.17).

CT pp
A lion rampant in gold at the centre of a rectangular frame defined
by fillets with fleur-de-lis outside each angle in gold and fillets
in blind at the outer edges (fig. 22.41).

R12	1541	8°	X.2.17	MS+	PDN 192	–
R12	1541	8°	X.2.18	MS+ & MS(G)$$	PDN 193	–

22.42. A folio of 1562 in a single example of a
French centre-tool CT qq. Cat. no. B14.

CT qq

A contemporary French calf binding with two hatched tools in
gold at the centre of a rectangular frame with a renaissance-style
fleuron tool, also in gold, outside each angle. Both tools very
common in French bindings of the period (fig. 22.42).

B14   1562   fol.   E.3.4   –   –   –

22.43. An octavo of 1557 in a single example of centre-tool CT rr. Cat. no. M83.

CT rr

A fleuron of four petals in faded silver or gold at the centre of a rectangular frame defined by fillets with fleur-de-lis in gold outside each angle and with fillets in blind at the outer edges (fig. 22.43).

M83   1557   8°   F.2.8   MS+   PDN 194 –

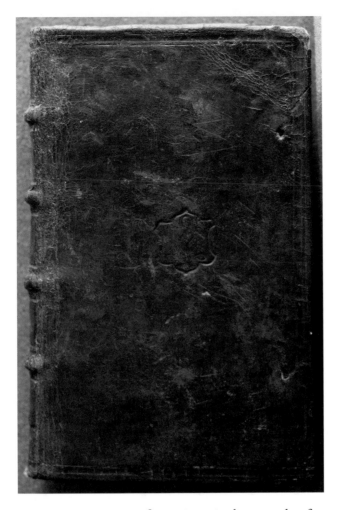

22.44. An octavo of 1549 in a single example of
centre-tool CT tt. Cat. no. P32.

CT ss

> A plain cartouche ornament in blind [different from CT b] at the
> centre of an otherwise plain rectangular frame defined by fillets
> and surrounded by a worn unidentified roll with some simi-
> larities to Oldham, EBSB, FP.a(1). See fig. 21.3 (p. 253).

B94†   1544   8°   D.4.8   MS+   PDN 39   ?**

CT tt

> A plain cartouche ornament in blind, within which is a feint line-
> decoration incorporating two small diamond and three oval
> shapes at the centre of otherwise plain covers with fillets at the
> outer edges (fig. 22.44).

P32   1549   8°   M.2.6   –   –   –

22.45. An octavo of 1557 in centre-tool CT vv,
one of two examples both dated 1557. Cat. no. M19.

CT vv

> A stag-in-flight in gold at the centre of a rectangular frame defined
> by fillets, with small sunbursts [††] or a fleur-de-lis [‡‡] outside
> each angle also in gold and fillets in blind at the outer edges.
> Pearson (OB, 82–83) assigns the former to Oxford as 'Centre-
> piece' xxix with tool 36a, though recognising that it should not
> be classified as a centrepiece, but as a small tool (fig. 22.45).

| S59 | 1557 | 8° | B.6.1[††] | – | – | – |
| M19 | 1557 | 8° | Y.5.19[‡‡] | MS+ | PDN 195 | – |

22.46. A sextodecimo of 1570 in a single example of
centre-tool CT xx. Cat. no. *B4.

CT xx

A very worn lozenge-shape ornament (now in blind, but perhaps
formerly in gold) at the centre of a rectangular frame defined by
fillets with fleur-de-lis in gold outside each angle and fillets in
blind at the outer edges (fig. 22.46).

*B4   1570   16°   A.6.36   –   –   –
Geste ownership doubtful.

22.47. An octavo of 1538 in a single example of centre-tool CT yy
with Oldham, EBSB, roll HM.h(29). Cat. no. C74.

CT yy

A floral-type ornament (possibly a leaf and stem) stamped apparently four times to make an ornament in blind at the centre of a
rectangular frame, the same floral-type ornament stamped inside
each angle – surrounded by Oldham, EBSB, roll HM.h(29), with
fillets in blind at the outer edges (fig. 22.47).

C74†   1541   8°   X.2.16   MS   PDN 68 CP^

22.48. A sextodecimo of 1558 in a single example of
centre-tool CT zz. Cat. no. *A11.

CT zz

A diamond-shaped floral ornament tooled in gold at the centre of a
rectangular frame defined by fillets in blind, with fleurons, also
in gold, at each angle and fillets in blind at the outer edges (fig.
22.48).

*A11   1558   16°   K.3.19   MS+   PDN 294 –
Geste ownership doubtful. With an inscription dated 1572.

22.49. An octavo, with the latest item dated 1536, in a single example of centre-tool CT aaa with two rectangles enclosing Oldham, EBSB, roll HM.h(29). Cat. no. C37.

CT aaa

A small circular ?floral tool at the centre of a rectangular frame defined by fillets with a fleur-de-lis type ornament at each angle (cf. CT q) surrounded by two rectangular frames enclosing Oldham, EBSB, roll HM.h(29), tentatively attributed to Nicholas Spierinck, Cambridge (by Pearson) (fig. 22.49).

C37   1536   8°   D.4.3   MS & Pb$ PDN 170 –

Totals: 157 items.[1]

43 different CT types.[2]

1. Excluding two items from Appendix I, and twenty-three items combined with rolls (already included in Appendix IV B).
2. Excluding eight variants and two CT types (CT xx and CT zz) of which the only examples are from Appendix I.

Annexe 1 – Suggested place of binding (often far from certain)

Tool	Date range	Number of examples	Tool	Date range	Number of examples
Cambridge			**London,** *continued*		
CT c.1	1532–1548	23	CT nn	1556	1
CT c.2	1542	1	CT pp	1541	2
CT c.3	1539	1	CT rr	1557	1
CT c.4	1539	1	CT ss	1544	1
CT m.2	1540–1552	8	Total: 113		
CT q	1536–1538	2	**London or possibly Salisbury**		
CT r	1546	1	CT e	1573–1576	4
CT z	1542	1	CT ff.1	1571	1
CT ee	1544	2	CT ff.2	1571	1
CT yy	1541	1	CT hh	1573–1575	2
CT aaa	1536	1	Total: 8		
Total: 42			**French**		
Oxford			CT qq	1562	1
?CT vv	1557	2	**Unassigned**		
London			CT g [?Cambridge]	1544	1
CT a	1564–1572	22	CT p [?Cambridge]	1550	1
CT b	1547–1568	51	CT s [?Cambridge]	1542	1
CT b.1	1568	1	CT x [?Cambridge]	1549–1552	2
CT d.1	1556–1558	5	CT y [?Cambridge]	1537	1
CT d.2	1559	1	CT tt [?Cambridge]	1549	1
CT f	1552	1	CT w [?London]	1562	1
CT h.1	1560–1565	4	CT aa [?London]	1553	1
CT h.2	1562	1	CT bb.1 [?London]	1560–1564	2
CT j	1549	1	CT gg [?London]	1565	1
CT k	1557–1567	3	CT jj [?London]	1555–1558	2
CT m.1	1548–1563	4	Total: 14		
CT n	1560	1			
CT o	1537	1			
CT t	1555–1561	2			
CT v	1552–1561	4			
CT bb.2	1563	1			
CT cc	1559	1			
CT dd	1569	1			
CT kk	1556	1			
CT mm	1568–1570	2			

E: *Corner-ornament bindings*

Blind-stamped bindings with a plain rectangular frame defined by fillets with a small tool or corner-ornament [CS] at each angle.

Abbreviations

MS+	MS strip to strengthen binding structure.
Pb	Leaf or leaves from printed book as pastedown.
PDN	Image number of pastedown, flyleaf or MS strip (see the database at www.bibsoc.org.uk/Geste).
†	Pre-Geste ownership inscription.

The tabular information, printed in grey type below,
is laid out in the following columns

Cat. no	Imprint date	Format	Shelf-mark	Pastedown &c.	Image number	Binding instruction

CS 1.1

Fleur-de-lys at each angle (S76 illustrated in fig. 23.1)

| S75 | 1547 | 8° | D.3.4 | Pb | PDN 196 | – |
| S76 | 1548 | 8° | D.3.5 | Pb | PDN 197 | – |

CS 1.2

Fleur-de-lys at each angle [?variant] (fig. 23.2)

| V36 | 1559 | fol. | N.3.12 | – | – | – |

CS 2

Cornucopia ornament inside each angle (fig. 23.3)

| V15† | 1551 | 4° | C.2.2 | – | – | – |

CS 3

Plain rectangular frame defined by fillets, enclosing a single row of hatching, with a single fleuron inside each angle (fig. 23.4)

| O8 | 1534 | 4° | C.1.9 | MS+ | PDN 198 | – |

CS 4

Plain rectangular frame defined by fillets with a renaissance ornament outside each angle with fillets at the outside edges and hatching at top and bottom of spine (see fig. 23.5)

| T11† | 1548 | 8° | C.5.15 | – | – | – |

23.1. An octavo of 1548, in corner-ornament CS 1.1, one of two
examples with a date-range of 1547–1548. Cat. no. S76.

23.2. A folio, with the latest item dated 1559, in a single example of
corner-ornament CS 1.2, with (inset) an enlarged detail
of the ornament. Cat. no. V36.

23.3. A quarto of 1551 in a single example of
corner-ornament CS 2. Cat. no. V15.

23.4. A quarto of 1534 in a single example of
corner-ornament CS 3. Cat. no. O8.

23.5. An octavo of 1548 in a single example of
corner-ornament CS 4. Cat. no. T11.

F: *Plain calf over pasteboard*

Abbreviations
MS	Leaves or leaf from a MS.
MS+	Strip from a MS to strengthen spine and/or binding structure.
PDN	Image no. of pastedown, flyleaf or MS strip (see the database at www.bibsoc.org.uk/Geste).
Pb	Leaves or leaf from a printed book.
$	Compacted leaves as pasteboard.
$$	Flyleaves.
†	Pre-Geste ownership inscription.
‡	Pre-Geste MS annotations, book-price or book-title(s) on fore-edge or spine, but no pre-Geste ownership inscription.

Binding instructions
B	Instruction to bind other (named) items in the same book.
CP^	Now calf covers, though instruction to binder reads, 'in parchment'.
F	Instruction to find other items to bind in the same book.
IP	'In past', i.e. calf over pasteboard.
O	Order of items to be bound together.
★★	Trace only – instruction uncertain.

The tabular information, printed in grey type below,
is laid out in the following columns

Cat. no	Imprint date	Format	Shelf-mark	Pastedown &c.	Image number	Binding instruction

PL a
Plain calf, with fillets at the outer edges (fig. 24.1).

Cat. no	Imprint date	Format	Shelf-mark	Pastedown &c.	Image number	Binding instruction
H13?‡	1525	8°	D.5.7	–	–	–
L4	1525	8°	C.5.6	MS	PDN 257	–
S31	1525	8°	ZC2.1.1	MS(2), MS & Pb$	PDN 260	–
M14	1540	8°	N.6.4	MS & Pb$	PDN 264	CP^
S19	1540	8°	D.2.4	MS	PDN 265	–
B107	1543	8°	H.1.5	MS & Pb$	PDN 266	–
B89	1544	8°	C.6.5	–	–	–
O5	1544	8°	D.2.1	MS	PDN 268	–

24.1. An octavo, with the latest item dated 1550, in plain calf with fillets at the outer edges (PL a), one of twenty-one examples with imprint dates from 1525 to 1563. Cat. no. B42.

24.2. A quarto, with the latest item dated 1532, in plain calf with
rectangular frames linked by fillets (PL b), one of nine examples
with a date-range of *c.* 1524–1550. Cat. no. O3.

B50	1545	8°	ZC2.7.2	MS&Pb$$	PDN 258	–
H65	1545	4°	D.1.3	–	–	–
P19	1549	8°	ZC2.7.3	MSS(2) & Pb$	PDN 269	–
B42	1550	8°	H.1.29	MS&Pb$	PDN 270	?O**
R39	1550	fol.	E.4.2	–	–	–
W30	1550	4°	D.1.12	MS&Pb$	PDN 274	–
B133	1551	4°	I.4.11	MS	PDN 275	?IP**
L50	1553	8°	C.4.3	MS&Pb$	PDN 276	–
W7	1559	4°	ZC2.2.1	MS+	PDN 277	–
A44	1561	fol.	B.3.9	–	–	B
P3	1561	fol.	B.3.19	MS+	PDN 278	–
W8	1561	4°	C.1.13	MS+	PDN 279	–
H35	1563	8°	ZC2.7.7	MS+ & Pb(2)$	PDN 280	IP/B

PL b
Plain calf incorporating one or more rectangular frames defined by fillets and linked to each other by straight and / or angled fillets (fig. 24.2).

O12?†	[c. 1524]	8°	C.1.3	MS	PDN 265	–
L52	1525	8°	D.2.2	MS	PDN 259	–
V33?‡	1527	8°	K.3.42	MS	PDN 261	–
M49‡	1531	8°	D.6.3	MS&MS$	PDN 262	–
O3	1532	4°	C.1.2	MS	PDN 265	–
D23	1543	8°	D.5.5	MS	PDN 267	IP**
C122	1550	8°	M.2.36	MS	PDN 271	–
C122	1550	8°	M.2.37	MS	PDN 272	–
C122	1550	8°	M.2.38	MS	PDN 273	–

Annexe – Suggested place of binding (often far from certain)

Tool	Date range	Number of examples	Tool	Date range	Number of examples
Cambridge			**London**		
PL a	1525–1553	16	PL a	1559–1563	5
PL b	1524–1550	9	Total: 5		
Total: 25					

G: *Parchment covers or formerly in parchment covers*

Abbreviations

A	Item with alum-tawed skin sewing support slips (followed by the number).
Eng	MS fragment or printed waste of English origin.
Fr	MS fragment of French origin.
Ital	MS fragment of Italian origin.
L	Item with tanned-leather sewing support slips (followed by the number).
MS	Leaves or leaf from a MS.
MS*	Blank leaf (or leaves) of parchment.
MS^	Item now covered in a leaf of MS in parchment.
MS^^	Item now covered in paper wrappers.
MS^^(G)	Item now covered in a paper leaf from a MS in Geste's hand.
Neth	Fragment of MS written in the Netherlands.
P*	Blank leaves (or leaf) of paper.
P++	Stub of paper between quires.
Pb	Leaves or leaf from printed book.
PDN	Image no. of pastedown, flyleaf or MS strip (see the database at www.bibsoc.org.uk/Geste).
(R)	Now rebound, but formerly in parchment.
SBB	Item with sewn book-block exposed.
$	Compacted leaves as pasteboard.
$$	Flyleaves or end-leaf guards.
$$(G)	Flyleaves from a MS in Geste's hand.
*	Item from Appendix I – Geste's ownership far from certain.
+	Strip only, to strengthen spine and/or binding structure.
++	Stub/strip from fold-over of same MS/Pb.
#	Pastedown from the same MS.
†	Pre-Geste ownership inscription.
††	Original parchment covers now kept separately.
‡	Pre-Geste MS annotations, book-price or book-title(s) on fore-edge or spine, but no pre-Geste ownership inscription.

Binding notes or instructions

B	Instruction to bind other (named) items in the same book.
CP^	Now calf covers, though instruction to binder reads, 'in parchment'.
F	Instruction to find other items to bind in the same book.
IPM	'in parchment'.
O	Order of items to be bound together.
U	'uncutt'.
**	Trace only – instruction uncertain.

The tabular information, printed in grey type below,
is laid out in the following columns

Cat. no	Imprint date	Format	Shelf-mark	Pastedown &c.	Image number	Binding instruction
D32	1509	4°	ZC2.3.15	MS+	PDN 199	–
R13	1516	8°	K.3.46	MS	PDN 200	–
C39	1525	8°	F.2.4	MS+ (wide)	PDN 201	–
L17	1526	4°	ZC2.3.14	–	–	–
O11	1527	4°	E.5.31	–	–	–
O21	[c. 1527]	8°	ZC2.4.16	MS^	PDN 200A	–
P36‡	1527	8°	ZC2.6.6	–	–	–
P6‡	1528	4°	ZC2.3.10	MS	PDN 202	–
R16	1529	8°	F.2.6	MS^^(G)	PDN 203	–
S91	1530	8°	ZC2.5.9	–	–	–
B78	1533	8°	ZC2.6.9	–	–	– See fig. 25.1
V7‡	1535	4°	ZC2.3.17	–	–	– See fig. 25.3
W53‡	1537	8°	ZC2.6.10	–	–	–
L72	1538	8°	ZC2.6.14	–	–	–
L67	1538	8°	E.6.29	MS+ (wide)	PDN 204	–
S23	1538	4°	ZC2.3.6	–	–	–
M84	1539	8°	F.2.3	MS+ (wide)	PDN 205	–

25.1 (top left). An octavo of 1533 in parchment covers with secondary tackets of tanned leather on the spine, one of three examples. Cat. no. B78. 25.2 (top right). An octavo of 1546 covered in a leaf of an English, s.xii/xiii MS, one of six examples covered in this way. Cat. no. S77. 25.3 (bottom). A quarto printed at Leipzig in 1535, in parchment covers with two rectangular secondary tackets of tanned leather on the spine. Cat. no. V7.

P55	1540	8°	A.6.42	–	–	–
C29	1540	8°	F.2.5	MS+ (wide)	PDN 206	–
G47†	1540	8°	ZC2.6.12	–	–	–
H59	1541	8°	E.6.33	MS+ (wide)	PDN 208	–
C15	1543	8°	K.2.3	–	–	–
P29	1543	4°	E.5.32	MS+	PDN 209	?F
C90	1544	8°	ZC2.6.17	MS$$	PDN 211	–
K2	1544	8°	G.6.17	MS$$	PDN 212	–
B118	1544	8°	ZC2.6.7	MS$$ & ++	PDN 210	–
M10	1545	4°	ZC2.3.12	Pb & ++	PDN 213	–
L12	1545	8°	ZC2.6.15	MS	PDN 214	–
P45†	[c. 1545]	8°	ZC2.6.4	MS$$	PDN 207	–
F25	1546	4°	ZC2.3.11	–	–	–
W43	1546	8°	G.6.21	MS^	PDN 217	–
L15	1546	4°	ZC2.4.1	MS(2)	PDN 215	–
S77	1546	8°	G.6.23	MS^ & ++	PDN 216	?O See fig. 25.2
F17	1549	8°	ZC2.4.15	MS^	PDN 218	–
L39	1549	8°	ZC2.8.1	MS^^	–	–
B18	1550	8°	X.2.32	–	–	–
M67	1551	8°	ZC2.6.16	–	–	U
C105	1551	8°	ZC2.6.2	MS^(2)	PDN 219	–
L76	1552	8°	ZC2.6.18	–	–	–
S72	1552	16°	ZC2.8.7	–	–	–
B41	1552	8°	E.6.23	MS+ (wide)	PDN 220	?IPM/?O
D30	1553	8°	ZC2.5.1	MS+	PDN 221	–
Z3	1553	8°	E.6.30	–	–	–
G14	1554	8°	K.1.31	–	–	–
G15	1554	8°	ZC2.3.7	MS$$	PDN 222	–
T26	1554	4°	ZC2.3.2	–	–	–

W2	1554	8°	O.2.46	–	–	–
L51	1555	8°	E.6.37	MS+	PDN 224	–
B54	1555	4°	O.1.10	MS(paper) $$	PDN 223	–
T10	1555	12°	G.6.16	MS+	PDN 225	–
M90	1556	4°	ZC2.4.11	MS+	PDN 226	–
S27	1556	8°	E.6.22	–	–	–
T2	1556	8°	ZC2.6.3	Pb$$	PDN 227	–
C66	1557	8°	E.6.35	–	–	–
C12	1558	8°	ZC2.4.6	–	–	–
J5	1558	12°	E.6.19	Pb$$ & ++	PDN 228	**
E57	1558	8°	E.6.20	–	–	–
S83	1558	8°	ZC2.4.12	MSS(2)$$ & ++	PDN 229	–
T15	1558	16°	ZC2.8.2	Pb$$ ++	PDN 230	–
C76	1558	8°	X.2.30	–	–	IPM/O**
E43	1559	12°	ZC2.8.4	–	–	–
L35	1559	8°	B.6.37	MS+ (wide)	PDN 231	–
H68	1560	8°	ZC2.5.8	MS*+, Pb$$ &++	PDN 234	**
F36	1560	8°	G.6.22	MS+	PDN 233	–
A35	1560	4°	ZC2.3.5	MS+ (wide)	PDN 232	–
F35	[?1560]	8°	B.6.40	MS(2)+	PDN 235	–
H44	1561	8°	E.6.36	–	–	IPM
L44	1561	8°	G.6.18	–	–	–
S26	1561	8°	E.6.39	–	–	–
G35	1562	16°	ZC2.8.6	–	–	–
L81	1562	8°	E.6.31	Pb	PDN 236	IPM
M38	1562	8°	G.5.21	MS+	PDN 237	–
M40	1562	8°	G.6.20	–	–	–
M45	1562	8°	K.1.7	MS+*	PDN 239	IPM

N12	1562	12°	ZC2.8.3	MS+,++ & Pb$$	PDN 238	–
S53	1562	8°	ZC1.5.19	–	–	–
W48	1562	8°	ZC2.5.7	–	–	–
D22	1563	8°	ZC2.5.5	–	–	IPM
G17	1563	8°	K.1.26	–	–	–
H38	1563	8°	ZC2.7.6	–	–	IPM
M33	1563	8°	G.6.24	MS+ & Pb$$	PDN 240	B/IPM
M12	1563	8°	ZC2.5.13	–	–	O
L27	1564	4°	ZC2.3.3	–	–	–
C45	1564	8°	B.6.41	MS+* & Pb$$	PDN 241	–
C80	1564	12°	B.6.35	–	–	–
F3	1564	8°	ZC2.5.3	–	–	B/IPM
H95	1564	8°	ZC2.5.6	MS+* & Pb$$	PDN 242	–
M13	1564	8°	O.2.39	–	–	–
M69	1564	8°	ZC2.4.14	–	–	O
U1	1564	8°	ZC2.3.13	MS+ & ++	PDN 243	–
H45	1564	8°	ZC2.4.13	–	–	IPM/?F
A2	1565	4°	ZC2.3.8	Pb$$	PDN 244	**
A30	1565	4°	ZC2.3.9	–	–	–
A34	1565	4°	K.2.8	–	–	–
H90	1565	8°	ZC2.5.29	–	–	IPM/O
L19	1565	4°	G.5.26	–	–	IPM '... not cutt but smothed'
M28	1565	8°	G.6.19	–	–	IPM
N2	1565	4°	E.5.28	Pb & $$	PDN 245	?IPM**
R6	1565	8°	O.2.41	MS^^(G)	PDN 246	–
T1	1565	8°	ZC2.6.8	–	–	–
T24	1565	8°	K.3.45	–	–	?O
V25	1565	8°	ZC2.4.10	Pb$$	PDN 247	O**

D1	1566	4°	ZC2.3.4	MS^	PDN 249	–
M29	1566	8°	E.6.21	–	–	–
H77	1566	4°	O.2.2	MS+*	PDN 251	–
H2A	1566	8°	ZC2.4.9	–	–	B/IPM/U
N14	1566	4°	O.1.16	–	–	–
S86	1566	4°	O.1.4	–	–	–
H8	1567	4°	O.1.12	–	–	–
M72	1567	8°	ZC2.6.11	–	–	?**
S85	1567	4°	O.1.13	MS+	PDN 252	–
S79	1568	8°	ZC2.5.10	–	–	IPM
F21	1570	8°	K.1.35	–	–	–
S70	1570	8°	B.5.33	–	–	–
H56	1571	8°	ZC2.3.1	P++	–	–
H46	1572	4°	ZC2.3.16	–	–	–
B20	1573	8°	K.1.33	–	–	–
P35	1573	8°	ZC2.4.7	MS+#	PDN 254	O**
P35	1573	8°	ZC2.4.8	MS+#	PDN 255	–
C101	1574	8°	E.6.34	–	–	–
C123	1576	8°	K.1.27	–	–	–

Total: 121[1]

Annexes

1. Re-bound items – formerly in parchment covers (deduced from his binding instructions). See *Introduction*, p. 133.

P57	1553	16°	A.6.35	–	–	IPM
S9	1554	4°	C.2.9	–	–	IPM
M65	1561	8°	B.5.34	–	–	††
F11	1562	fol.	L.4.4	–	–	IPM/U
H4	1562	8°	L.6.24	–	–	IPM
H63	1562	fol.	G.4.2	–	–	U/IPM
L42	1562	fol.	G.2.16	–	–	U/IPM
M58	1562	8°	L.6.19	–	–	B/IPM

1. Excluding six items from Appendix I (see Annexe 2) and twelve re-bound items (Annexe 1).

M68	1562	8°	L.6.25	–	–	IPM
W24	1562	8°	L.6.26	–	–	IPM
M60	1566	8°	K.1.28	–	–	IPM
A59	1567	8°	A.6.20	–	–	IPM

Total: 12

2. Items from Appendix I

*E2	1526	8°	ZC2.6.5	–	–	–
*D1	1547	8°	X.1.20	P*+	PDN 296	–
*C1	1565	4°	O.1.17	MS+, ++ & MS$$	PDN 248	–
*R1	1566	8°	O.2.37	MS+ (wide) & ++	PDN 250	–
*P2	1567	8°	B.5.39	–	–	–
*S3	1570	8°	B.5.40	–	–	–

3. Books in parchment covers without strengtheners or end-leaf guards but with Geste's binding instructions

C76	1558	8°	X.2.30	–	–	IPM/O**
H44	1561	8°	E.6.36	–	–	IPM
D22	1563	8°	ZC2.5.5	–	–	IPM
H38	1563	8°	ZC2.7.6	–	–	IPM
M12	1563	8°	ZC2.5.13	–	–	O
F3	1564	8°	ZC2.5.3	–	–	B/IPM
M69	1564	8°	ZC2.4.14	–	–	O
H45	1564	8°	ZC2.4.13	–	–	IPM/?F
H90	1565	8°	ZC2.5.29	–	–	IPM/O
L19	1565	4°	G.5.26	–	–	IPM '... not cutt but smothed'
M28	1565	8°	G.6.19	–	–	IPM
T24	1565	8°	K.3.45	–	–	?O
M79	1566	8°	ZC2.4.9	–	–	B/IPM/U
M72	1567	8°	ZC2.6.11	–	–	?**
S79	1568	8°	ZC2.5.10	–	–	IPM

Total: 15

4. Pre-1553 items – without Geste's binding instructions, MS strengtheners or end-leaf guards.

Cat.no	Date	Format	Shelf-mark	Place of printing
L17	1526	4°	ZC2.3.14	Antwerp
O11	1527	4°	E.5.31	Basle
S91	1530	8°	ZC2.5.9	Strasbourg
L72	1538	8°	ZC2.6.14	Wittenberg
S23	1538	4°	ZC2.3.6	Frankfurt-a-M.
P55	1540	8°	A.6.42	Cologne
C15	1543	8°	K.2.3	Geneva
F25	1546	4°	ZC2.3.11	Cologne
B18	1550	8°	X.2.32	Basle
L76	1552	8°	ZC2.6.18	Marburg
S72	1552	16°	ZC2.8.7	Antwerp
Total: 11				

5. Post-1553 items with strips from MSS or printed books as strengtheners or end-leaf guards. See *Introduction*, p. 133.

Cat. number	Imprint year	Format	Shelf-mark	Place of printing	MS/Pb fragment	Origin	Image number	Binding instructions
G15	1554	8°	ZC2.3.7	Louvain	MS$$	Eng	PDN 222	–
B54	1555	4°	O.1.10	London	MS$$	?Eng	PDN 223	–
L51	1555	8°	E.6.37	Frankfurt-a-M.	MS+	Eng	PDN 224	–
T10	1555	12°	G.6.16	Lyon	MS+	?	PDN 225	–
M90	1556	4°	ZC2.4.11	Basle	MS+	Eng	PDN 226	–
T2	1556	8°	ZC2.6.3	Paris	Pb$$	Eng	PDN 227	–

J5	1558	12°	E.6.19	Antwerp	Pb$$	?	PDN 228	**
S83	1558	8°	ZC2.4.12	Cologne	MSS(2)$$, ++	Eng	PDN 229	–
T15	1558	16°	ZC2.8.2	Lyon	Pb$$ ++	?	PDN 230	–
L35	1559	8°	B.6.37	Antwerp	MS+	Eng	PDN 231	–
A35	1560	4°	ZC2.3.5	Frankfurt -a-M.	MS+	Eng	PDN 232	–
F36	1560	8°	G.6.22	Wittenberg	MS+	Eng	PDN 233	–
H68	1560	8°	ZC2.5.8	Mainz	MS*, Pb$$	?	PDN 234	**
F35	?1560	8°	B.6.40	Vienna	MS(2)	Eng	PDN 235	–
L81	1562	8°	E.6.31	Wittenberg	Pb	?	PDN 236	IPM
M38	1562	8°	G.5.21	Wittenberg	MS+	Eng	PDN 237	–
M45	1562	8°	K.1.7	Frankfurt-a-M.	MS+	?	PDN 239	IPM
N12	1562	12°	ZC2.8.3	Antwerp	MS+, Pb$$	Eng ?	PDN 238	–
M33	1563	8°	G.6.24	Wittenberg	MS+ Pb$$	? ?	PDN 240	B/IPM
C45	1564	8°	B.6.41	Cologne	MS+* Pb$$	? ?	PDN 241	–
H95	1564	8°	ZC2.5.6	Basle	MS+* Pb$$	? ?	PDN 242	–
U1	1564	8°	ZC2.3.13	Basle	MS+	Eng	PDN 243	–
A2	1565	4°	ZC2.3.8	Basle	Pb$$	?	PDN 244	**
N2	1565	4°	E.5.28	Venice	Pb & $$	?	PDN 245	?IPM**
R6	1565	8°	O.2.41	Antwerp	MS^^(G)	Eng	PDN 246	–
V25	1565	8°	ZC2.4.10	Antwerp	Pb$$	Eng	PDN 247	O*
D1	1566	4°	ZC2.3.4	Antwerp	MS^	Eng	PDN 249	–
H77	1566	4°	O.2.2	London	MS+	?	PDN 251	–
S85	1567	4°	O.1.13	Louvain	MS+	Neth	PDN 252	–
P35	1573	8°	ZC2.4.7	Cologne	MS+	Eng	PDN 254	O**
P35	1573	8°	ZC2.4.8	Cologne	MS+	Eng	PDN 255	–
Total: 31								

6. Items with sewing-support slips of tanned leather or alum-tawed skin as well as strips from MSS or printed books as strengtheners or end-leaf guards

Additional abbreviations

A   Item with alum-tawed skin sewing support slips (followed by the number).

L   Item with tanned-leather sewing support slips (followed by the number).

Cat. number	Imprint year	Format	Shelf-mark	Place of printing	MS/Pb fragment	Origin	Image number	Sewing support slips
C39	1525	8°	F.2.4	Strasbourg	MS+	?Fr	PDN 201	L3
P6‡	1528	4°	ZC2.3.10	Hagenau	MS	Eng	PDN 202	L3
R16	1529	8°	F.2.6	Wittenberg	MS+	?	PDN 203	L3
L67	1538	8°	E.6.29	Strasbourg	MS+	Eng	PDN 204	L3
M84	1539	8°	F.2.3	Basle	MS+	Eng	PDN 205	L3
C29	1540	8°	F.2.5	Paris	MS+	?Ital	PDN 206	L3
H59	1541	8°	E.6.33	Frankfurt-a-M.	MS+	Eng	PDN 208	L3
P29	1543	4°	E.5.32	Basle	MS+	Eng	PDN 209	L3
B118	1544	8°	ZC2.6.7	Zürich	MS$$	Eng	PDN 210	L3
C90	1544	8°	ZC2.6.17	Ingolstadt	MS$$	Fr or Eng	PDN 211	L3?
K2	1544	8°	G.6.17	Frankfurt-a-M.	MS$$	Eng	PDN 212	L3
M10	1545	4°	ZC2.3.12	Würzburg	Pb & ++	?	PDN 213	L3?
L12	1545	8°	ZC2.6.15	Bonn	MS	Eng	PDN 214	L2
P45†	[c.1545]	8°	ZC2.6.4	?Paris	MS$$	?	PDN 207	L3
L15	1546	4°	ZC2.4.1	Cologne	MS(2)	Eng or Fr	PDN 215	L3
S77	1546	8°	G.6.23	Frankfurt-a-M.	MS^ & ++	Eng	PDN 216	L2

B41	1552	8°	E.6.23	Basle	MS+	Eng	PDN 220	L4
G15	1554	8°	ZC2.3.7	Louvain	MS$$	Eng	PDN 222	L3
B54	1555	4°	O.1.10	London	MS$$	?Eng	PDN 223	L3
L51	1555	8°	E.6.37	Frankfurt-a-M.	MS+	Eng	PDN 224	L4
T10	1555	12°	G.6.16	Lyon	MS+	?	PDN 225	A4
M90	1556	4°	ZC2.4.11	Basle	MS+	Eng	PDN 226	A3
T2	1556	8°	ZC2.6.3	Paris	Pb$$	Eng	PDN 227	A3
J5	1558	12°	E.6.19	Antwerp	Pb$$	?	PDN 228	A4
T15	1558	16°	ZC2.8.2	Lyon	Pb$$ ++	?	PDN 230	A4
L35	1559	8°	B.6.37	Antwerp	MS+	Eng	PDN 231	A3
A35	1560	4°	ZC2.3.5	Frankfurt-a-M.	MS+	Eng	PDN 232	L4
F36	1560	8°	G.6.22	Wittenberg	MS+	Eng	PDN 233	A3
H68	1560	8°	ZC2.5.8	Mainz	MS* Pb$$	? ?	PDN 234	A4
F35	?1560	8°	B.6.40	Vienna	MS(2)	Eng	PDN 235	L3
M38	1562	8°	G.5.21	Wittenberg	MS+	Eng	PDN 237	L4
N12	1562	12°	ZC2.8.3	Antwerp	MS+, Pb$$	Eng ?	PDN 238	A4
M33	1563	8°	G.6.24	Wittenberg	MS+ Pb$$	? ?	PDN 240	A4
H95	1564	8°	ZC2.5.6	Basle	MS+* Pb$$	? ?	PDN 242	L4
U1	1564	8°	ZC2.3.13	Basle	MS+	Eng	PDN 243	A4
V25	1565	8°	ZC2.4.10	Antwerp	Pb$$	Eng	PDN 247	A4
S85	1567	4°	O.1.13	Louvain	MS+	Neth	PDN 252	L3
Item from Appendix I								
*R1	1566	8°	O.2.37	Antwerp	MS+, ++	Eng	PDN 250	L4
Total: 37 [and 1 from Appendix I]								

7. Items with exposed sewn book-blocks. It is likely that many of the books now in parchment covers were imported as sewn book-blocks, but unless the book is now without covers, or wrapped in a leaf of MS or printed waste, or if the covers have become loose or detached (as in the case of the four examples listed below), it is difficult to verify this.

Cat. number	Imprint year	Format	Shelf-mark	Place of printing	MS/Pb fragment	Origin	Image number	Sewing support slips
W43	[1546]	8°	G.6.21	Strasbourg	MS^	Eng	PDN 217	–
F17	1549	8°	ZC2.4.15	Wittenberg	MS^	Eng	PDN 218	A2
C105	1551	8°	ZC2.6.2	Louvain	MS^	Eng	PDN 219	A3
O21	[c. 1527]	8°	ZC2.4.16	Basle	MS^	?	PDN 200A	L1 [L2]

8. Items with secondary tackets of tanned-leather or alum-tawed skin.

Cat. number	Imprint year	Format	Shelf-mark	Place of printing	MS/Pb fragment	Origin	Image number	Secondary tackets
D32	1509	4°	ZC2.3.15	Milan	MS+	Eng	PDN 199	A2
B78	1533	8°	ZC2.6.9	Hagenau	–	–	–	L2
V7	1535	4°	ZC2.3.17	Leipzig	–	–	–	L2

H: *Re-bound volumes*

Abbreviations

x	Now disbound or wrapped in paper or in parchment.
xx	Originally bound in parchment on evidence of binding instructions.
*	Trace only.
**	No pressmark visible, but early fore-edge title extant.
#	Fore-edges sheared or coloured in re-binding; no early pressmark visible.
+	Pressmark on spine.
++	Date of binding where different from imprint.
^	Items originally bound together.

Cat. number	Author	Format	Early press mark	Latest imprint date	Shelf-mark
A3	Aegidius	8°	#	1541	ZC2.6.19
A14	Albertus M.	fol.	H28	1504	G.3.19
A15	Albertus M.	fol.	D8	1504	G.3.20
A20	Alesius, A.	8°	B56	1553	C.4.7
A28	Amsdorff, N.	4°	#	1550	L.5.22
A32	Andreae, J.	4°	#	1564	L.5.27
A45	Aquinas, T.	fol.	M43	1481	L.3.9
A47	Aquinas, T.	fol.	H23	1512	L.3.10
A48	Aquinas, T.	fol.	D31	1551	E.4.3
A59	Athenagoras	8°	F52	1567	A.6.20
A60	Augustine	fol.	H7–8	1542	A.4.23–24
A61	Augustine	fol.	**	1542	A.5.2
A62	Augustine	8°	F65	1529	A.6.32
A66	Augustine	8°	F95?	1576	A.6.23
A68	Aurogallus, M.	8°	*?	1527	ZC2.8.8

B1	Bacherius, P.	8°	[E58 pt.]	1569	ZC2.1.10
B6	Basil	fol.	#	1521	A.4.7
B11	Bede	fol.	D10	1522	A.4.19
B16	Bernard	16°	**	1564	A.6.37
B30	Bible	4°	M31	1528	E.5.18
B31	Bible	16°	T46	1532	G.6.10
B32	Bible	16°	T47	1532	G.6.11
B36	Bible	16°	T45	[c. 1550]	G.6.8
B44	Bibliotheca	fol.	D?16	1565	L.2.9–10
B46	Biel, G.	fol.	M35	1510	L.3.15
B47	Biel, G.	fol.	M42	1508	L.3.16
B51	Bodius, H.	8°	#	[c. 1533]	H.2.5
B52	Bonaventura	8°	B32	1539	C.4.1
B59	Borrhaus, M.	fol.	*	1557	G.4.10
B68	Brentz, J.	fol.	I22 or H22	1576	L.2.2
B70	Brentz, J.	4°	#	1557	L.5.7
B71	Brentz, J.	fol.	#	1542	G.3.6
B82	Brentz, J.	fol.	#	1566	G.3.7
B84	Brentz, J.	fol.	#	1549	G.3.8
B95	Brunfels, O.	fol.	L45	1535	G.4.18
B98	Bucer, M.	fol.	#	1532	E.4.7
B100	Bucer, M.	fol.	#	1554	G.2.20
B101	Bucer, M.	fol.	#	1565	G.4.19
B103	Bucer, M.	fol.	#	1562	G.4.20
B106	Bucer, M.	4°	**	1570	L.5.15
B110	Bucer, M.	4°	F39	1548	L.5.16
B114	Bugenhagen, J.	4°	B18	1535	C.2.11
B115	Bugenhagen, J.	4°	B17	1546	C.2.10
B122	Bugenhagen, J.	fol.	#	1536 ++ [c. 1551]	G.3.22
B135	Bunderius, J.	8°	[E58 pt.]	1569	ZC2.1.11

C21	Camerarius, B.	4°	#	1556	L.5.3
C27	Camerarius, J.	8°	#	1569	L.6.27
C40	Cardillo, G.	4°	#	1564	B.5.5
C41	Carion, J.	8°	#	1566	B.6.18
C52	Catechism	8°	#	1553	H.2.15
C53	Catharinus, A.	fol.	#	1566	G.4.12
C78	Clement, *Alex.*	fol.	#	1566	A.5.4
C79	Clement I	8°	C7	1568	B.6.5
C83	Clichtoveus, J.	16°	S31	1565	K.3.13
C89	Cochlaeus, J.	4°	*	1544	L.4.30
C97	Cologne. Canones	fol.	D13	1538	B.3.21
C113	Cruciger, C. [formerly bound with:	8°	A10	1546	E.6.28
M41	Meier, G.	8°	[A10]	1550	ZC2.8.10]
C117	Cucchus, M.A.	8°	#	1564	ZC2.8.13
C125	Cusa, N. de	fol.	L14	1514	L.4.7
C125	Cusa, N. de	fol.	L13	1514	L.4.8
C129	Czecanovius, S.	8°	#	[c. 1565]	ZC2.8.12
D7	Dionysius	fol.	#	1503	A.5.8
D27	Driedo, J.	fol.	M3	1547	L.3.19
D28	Driedo, J.	fol.	?R4	1533	L.2.13
D29	Du Moulin, C.	fol.	O29	1565	C.2.14
D31	Du Préau, G.	fol.	D21	1569	L.4.6
D33	Duns, J.	4°	N41	1481	L.4.25
D35	Duns, J.	fol.	**	1518	L.4.18
D36	Durandus, G.	4°	N42	1518	L.5.13
E7	Eck, J.	8°	#	1526	L.6.6
E8	Eck, J.	12°	?O33	1567	ZC2.8.5
E19	Ephraem	8°	#	1563	A.6.41
E22	Erasmus, D.	4°	M10	1520	L.5.35
E27	Erasmus, D.	fol.	M29	1522	G.2.6
E34	Erasmus, D.	8°	N18	1529	L.6.5

E40	Erasmus, D.	8°	#	1526	L.6.4
E41	Erasmus, D.	8°	T7	1532	ZC2.2.3
E53	Estienne, R.	fol.	#	1562	G.4.4
F5	Ficino, M.	fol.	#	1495	Z.2.56
F6	Ficino, M.	fol.	R9	1482	Y.3.25
F7	Fidati, S.	fol.	#	1540	L.4.1
F11	Flacius, M.	fol.	#	1562	L.4.4
F27	Folengius, J.B.	8°	#	1568	C.3.8
F30	Foresti, J. P.	fol.	?N36	1503	Z.2.25
F31	Fox, E.	4°	#	1534	L.5.29
F32	Foxe, J.	8°	?S5	1554	B.6.11
G4	Gallasius, N.	fol.	#	1563	E.4.8
G23	Georgius, F.	fol.	H21	1525	L.3.21
G25	Gerson, J.	fol.	N30?	1494	L.3.14
G26	Gesner, C.	fol.	#	1549	L.4.16
G30	Gratian	8°	N52	1519	H.2.54
G31	Gregory I	fol.	L17?	1523	A.1.15
G37	Gualtherus, R.	fol.	#	1570	G.4.14
G38	Gualtherus, R.	fol.	#	1565	G.4.15
G40	Gualtherus, R.	fol.	I20	1572	G.4.16
G43	Guilliaud, C.	fol.	#	1562	G.4.13
G46	Gulielmus, *Avernus*	fol.	M32	1516	L.4.22
G49	Gulielmus, *Parisiensis*	4°	R44	1478	L.5.10
H4	Hamelmann, H.	8°	#	1562	L.6.24
H16	Helding, M. S.	fol.	#	1562	L.4.15
H23	Helvetic Confession	4°	#	1566	I.3.9
H24	Hemmingsen, N.	8°	A44	1563	D.6.10
H26	Hemmingsen, N.	8°	(A40)^	1564	C.5.13
H39	Hemmingsen, N.	8°	#	1574	K.3.41
H41	Heracleides	fol.	L19	1504	A.5.7
H43	Herolt, J.	fol.	#	1520	L.4.14

H55	Hessels, J.	8°	#	1563	L.6.15
H63	Hofmeister, J.	fol.	#	1562	G.4.2
H71	Holkot, R.	fol.	★★	1489	L.2.18
H72	Holkot, R.	4°	C23	1510	L.5.9
H73	Holthusius, J.	12°	S38	1571	K.3.31
H76	Horantius, F.	8°	E56?	1565	K.2.18
H82	Hugo, *de Sancto Charo*	fol.	H18	[1502]	L.2.1
H84	Hugo, *de Sancto Charo*	fol.	★★	1531	G.2.5
H85	Hugo, *de Sancto Victore*	fol.	H19	1526	L.1.8
H86	Hugo, *de Sancto Victore*	fol.	H20	1526	L.1.9
H88	Hugo, *de Sancto Victore*	fol.	?L20	1515	L.2.15
H93	Hus, Jan	8°	#	1537	L.6.23
J1	Jacobus, *de Voragine*	fol.	M44	1496	L.4.17
J3	Jansen, C.	4°	#	1569	E.5.5
J6	Jerome	4°	D11	1515	L.4.31
J8	Jewel, J.	fol.	#	1567	T.3.3
J11	Joannes, *de Colonia*	4°	N42	1510	L.5.40
J13	John, *of Damascus*	fol.	?K9	1512	L.4.5
J16	Josephus, F.	fol.	#	1540	L.2.23
J18	Justinian I	8°	#	1555	L.6.8
K1	Kempis, T. à	8°	#	1563	K.3.44
K5	Kirchner, T.	fol.	#	1563	L.3.6
K8	Kling, C.	fol.	E68	1563	L.3.17
K9	Kling, C.	8°	N5	1565	I.1.7
L1	Lactantius	fol.	#	1564	A.4.25
L10	Lasco, J. à	8°	M17	1552	H.2.11
L16	Latomus, J.	8°	?F[?9]8	1525	ZC2.7.10
L22	Le Fèvre, J.	fol.	D31	1522	G.4.6
L23	Le Fèvre, J.	fol.	D32	1527	G.4.7
L39x	Lorich, G.	8°	#	1549	ZC2.8.1
L41	Loss, L.	fol.	#	1559	G.2.15

L42	Loss, L.	fol.	#	1562	G.2.16
L48	Ludolf	8°	?R27	1536	L.6.7
L54	Luther, M.	8°	[C6]5	c.1545	E.6.27
L73	Luther, M.	8°	#	1559	L.6.12
L74	Luther, M.	4°	#	1521	L.5.34
L78	Luther, M.	8°	F?34	c.1523	ZC2.7.11
L80	Lutzenburgo, B. de	8°	#	1523	H.2.10
M5	Magdeburg Centuriators	fol.	#	1560	M.4.9
M6	Mainardo, A.	8°	#	1556	R.6.21
M8	Marbach, J.	4°	#	1573	L.5.32
M11	Mark	8°	#	1563	A.6.24
M21	Mayer, S.	8°	A51	1568	E.6.26
M27	Meier, G.	8°	C6[5]	1559	E.6.25
M41	Meier, G. [formerly bound with:	8°	A10	1550	ZC2.8.10
C113	Cruciger, C.	8°	A10	1546	E.6.28]
M43	Melanchthon, P.	fol.	C50	1562	L.2.3
M44	Melanchthon, P.	fol.	#	1564	L.2.4
M48	Melanchthon, P.	8°	A19	1544	C.5.8
M51	Melanchthon, P.	8°	R50	c.1545	C.5.11
M52	Melanchthon, P.	8°	A40	1541	C.5.9
M53	Melanchthon, P.	8°	B34	1545	C.5.10
M55	Melanchthon, P.	8°	#	1543	L.6.11
M58	Melanchthon, P.	8°	#	1563	L.6.19
M60	Melanchthon, P.	8°	#	1565	K.1.28
M61	Melanchthon, P.	8°	R?31	1570	L.6.21
M62	Melanchthon, P.	8°	#	1560	K.3.38
M63	Melanchthon, P.	8°	#	1536	L.6.18
M64	Melanchthon, P.	8°	#	1561	L.5.19
M65	Melanchthon, P.	8°	P13	[c.1550]	B.5.34
M68	Menzel, H. xx	8°	#	1562	L.6.25
M87	Musculus, A.	fol.	#	1563	L.2.7

M89	Musculus, W.	fol.	#	1554	G.3.11
M91	Musculus, W.	fol.	#	1556	G.3.12
M92	Musculus, W.	fol.	#	1554	G.3.10
M95	Musculus, W.	fol.	#	1560	L.3.20
N5	Nannus Mirabellius, D.	fol.	?N40	1503	L.2.14
O6	Oecolampadius, J.	4°	#	1525	C.1.10
O19	Orbellis, N. de	8°	N49	[c.1497]	L.6.3
O20	Origen	fol.	H15–16	1519	A.4.1–2
O21	Origen x	8°	?O16	[c.1527]	ZC2.4.16
P9	Paulinus	8°	S12	1560	A.6.21
P13	Paulus	fol.	?D11	[c.1507]	L.4.34
P17	Peraldus, G.	4°	N45?	1497	L.5.31
P18	Pérez de Valentia, J.	fol.	?L26	1515	G.3.16
P20	Petrus, *Comestor*	fol.	D12	1503	L.4.10
P21	Petrus, *Diaconus*	8°	#	1513	A.6.28
P22	Petrus, *Lombardus*	fol.	M30	1513	L.3.7
P24	Pfeffinger, J.	8°	#	1559	L.6.13
P25	Philippus, J.	4°	M45	1497	L.5.1
P28	Philo, *of Carpasia*	8°	C?76	1537	C.5.3
P51	Praetorius, A.	8°	#	1564	M.2.35
P54	Procopius	fol.	#	1564	G.4.8
P57	Prudentius	16°	#	1553	A.6.35
P58	Puteo, F. de	fol.	H24	1534	E.3.12
R3	Rabus, L.	8°	[?S5]	1554	B.6.10
R6	Rastall, J. x	8°	F76	1565	O.2.41
R7	Rastall, J.	8°	F91	1566	O.2.45
R17	Reuchlin, J.	fol.	#	1506	E.4.13
R33	Rivius, J.	8°	F50	1550	L.6.16
S2	Sachs, H.	8°	O15	1534	ZC2.7.9
S3	Sadoleto, J.	fol.	#	1536	G.3.21
S9	Salonius	4°	#	1554	C.2.9

S42	Selneccer, N.	fol.	D23	1569	G.4.5
S45	Seneca	fol.	R6	1515	Y.2.16
S50	Serranus, P.	fol.	D33	1572	G.2.4
S52	Serres, J. de	8°	#	1570	ZC1.5.21
S58	Sirenius, J.	fol.	#	1563	L.2.16
S60	Slotanus, J.	4°	E50	1570	L.5.8
S62	Smaragdus	fol.	L3	1536	E.4.6
S71	Soto, P. de	4°	#	1557	L.5.28
S94	Stunica, J. L.	fol.	*	1522	L.4.12
T3	Tertullian	fol.	#	1528	A.4.22
T4	Theodoret	fol.	S1 [A.4.11]	1567	A.4.11–12
T8	Theophylact	fol.	K20	1554	G.2.18
T9	Theophylact	fol.	#	1567	G.3.9
T13	Titelman, F.	8°	#	1532	C.5.14
T16A	Torres, H.	4°	?S7	1567	A.6.5
T17	Tosarrius, J.	fol.	#	1568	G.4.1
T20	Tritheim, J.	4°	#	1531	B.5.44
U2	Usuardus	8°	S96	1568	B.6.19
V6	Vega, A.	fol.	E70*	1572	L.3.8
V12	Vermigli, P. M.	fol.	#	1569	G.3.14
V13	Vermigli, P. M.	fol.	#	1566	G.3.15
V14	Vermigli, P. M.	fol.	#	1558	G.3.1
V18	Vermigli, P. M.	fol.	#	1559	L.2.21
V21	Vermigli, P. M.	8°	#	1561	O.2.47
V26	Vincent	fol.	N37	1494	L.1.15
V27	Vincent	fol.	#	1485	Z.1.62
V29	Vio, T. de	fol.	D30	1539	G.2.17
V37	Vivaldus, J. L.	8°	N50	1505	L.6.1
V38	Vives, J. L.	8°	R29	1555	Z.5.121
W19	Wigand, J.	8°	R57	1566	E.6.9
W24	Wigand, J.	8°	#	1562	L.6.26

W34	Wild, J.	fol.	#	1550	G.2.14
W40	Wild, J.	fol.	#	1561	L.3.18
W41	William, *of Ockham*	8°	[E58 pt.]	1569	ZC2.1.12
W45	Wittenberg Academia	4°	#	1559	B.5.8
W60	Würtemberg Confession	fol.	#	1561	L.2.20
Z7	Zwingli, H.	8°	N16	1535	L.6.14

Total: 239

Items from Appendix I
Other books which may have belonged to Geste

*C11	Cochlaeus, J.	4°	#	1545	ZC1.2.15
*G1	Gardiner, S.	8°	F104	1546	R.6.19
*R4	Rupert, *of Deutz*	8°	#	1545	H.1.30
*S10	Symmachus	8°	#	1549	ZC2.6.20
*V3	Vergil, P.	fol.	#	1557	B.3.20

Disbound item – Appendix I

| *H4 | Hessels, J. | 8° | # | 1572 | ZC2.6.1 |

APPENDIX V

Concordance of early press marks

On these early press marks, see *Introduction*, pp. 54–57. The arrangement of the presses suggests a fairly logical sequence of subject matter, beginning with works relating to the study of the Bible, particularly commentaries (Cases A–D), then Theology (from Case E onwards), with a particularly large collection relating to contemporary Reformation controversies. Cases R–T contain items of more miscellaneous subject matter.

Abbreviations.

fe	Press mark on fore-edge
fe**	Press mark on fore-edge (although the book is in parchment covers).
R	Rebound item.
$	Book-title on spine
sp	Press mark on spine.
x	Book apparently re-located, with new or original location within square brackets.
*	Trace only – actual press mark or book-title uncertain.
#	Press mark lost in the course of rebinding.
+	Press mark apparently changed, with the later press mark (if legible) within square brackets.
++	Possible trace of a fore-edge title in addition to the spine-title.
^	Items originally bound together.
^^	No trace of fore-edge or spine-title.

Case A – Bible – mainly commentaries

4° A2–A7.
8° A8–A51.
Missing: A1, 9, 11–13, 16, 25, 29, 34 [9 vols.]
Duplicates: ?A10, 40.
Date range: 1525–1572.
Totals: potential 51 (plus 2 duplicates); actual 44.

Early press mark	Imprint year of latest item	Rebound item	Spine or fore-edge	Author of first item	Format	Cat. no. of first item	Current shelf-mark
A2	1533		fe	Oecolampadius, J.	4°	O7	G.5.2
A3	1534		fe	Oecolampadius, J.	4°	O8	C.1.9
A4	1532		fe	Oecolampadius, J.	4°	O3	C.1.2
A5	1565		fe	Theodoret, *of Cyrus*	4°	T5	A.6.3
A6	1559		fe	Placidus, *Parmensis.*	4°	P38	E.5.8
A7	1565		fe	Calvin, J.	4°	C7	G.5.5
A8	1532		fe	Rabanus M.	8°	R1	C.5.1
?A10*	1560		fe	Arnobius	8°	A54	A.6.17
A10	1546	R	fe	Cruciger, C. [formerly bound with:	8°	C113	E.6.28
[A10]	1550	R	fe	Meier, G.	8°	M41	ZC2.8.10]
A14	1535		fe	Oecolampadius, J.	8°	O10	C.1.5
A15	[*c.* 1544]		fe	Imler, C.	8°	I1	D.3.6
A17	1544		fe	Brentz, J.	8°	B89	C.6.5
A18	1528		fe	Capito, W.	8°	C37	D.4.3
A19	1543	R	fe	Melanchthon, P.	8°	M48	C.5.8
A20	1566		fe	Wigand, J.	8°	W18	C.4.4
A21	1567		fe	Jonathan, *ben Uzziel*	8°	J15	D.6.5

A22	[c. 1564]		fe	Hemmingsen, N.	8°	H25	C.4.10
A23	1565		fe	Forerius, F.	8°	F29	D.2.9
A2?4*	1567		fe	Sascerides, J.	8°	S28	N.6.11
A26	1567		fe	Selneccer, N.	8°	S44	G.6.2
A27	1558		fe	Vio, T. de.	8°	V31	D.5.12
A28	1567		fe	Selneccer, N.	8°	S43	D.4.7
A30	1550		fe	Guilliaud, C.	8°	G44	C.3.1
A31	1525		fe	Bugenhagen, J.	8°	B117	C.4.8
A32	1564		fe	Gagny, J. de.	8°	G2	C.3.11
A33	1559		fe	Gagny, J. de.	8°	G1	C.3.10
A35	1557		fe	Münster, S.	8°	M83	F.2.8
A36	1535		fe	Jonas, J.	8°	J14	D.2.6
?A37*	1567		fe	Seripando, G.	8°	S49	ZC1.4.2
A38	1556		fe	Chytraeus, J.	8°	C70	D.6.2
A39	1572		fe	Chytraeus, D.	8°	C68	G.5.17
A40^	1564	R	fe	Hemmingsen, N.	8°	H26	C.5.13
A40^	1541	R	fe	Melanchthon, P.	8°	M52	C.5.9
A41	1553		fe	Nardus, J. L.	8°	N6	N.6.9
A42	1531		fe	Melanchthon, P.	8°	M49	D.6.3
A43	1545		fe	Aepinus, J	8°	A5	D.5.6
A44	[c. 1562]	R	fe	Hemmingsen, N.	8°	H24	D.6.10
A45	1567		fe	Cruciger, C.	8°	C115	D.4.5
A46	1567		fe	Espence, C. d'	8°	E52	D.5.9
A47	1564		fe	Meier, G.	8°	M35	D.6.4
A48	1543		fe	Draconites, J.	8°	D23	D.5.5
A49	1538		fe	Lambert, F.	8°	L6	C.5.4
A50	1546		fe	Artopoeus, P.	8°	A55	C.4.2
A51	1546	R	fe	Mayer, S.	8°	M21	E.6.26

Case B – Bible – mainly commentaries

Mixed 4°s and 8°s.
Missing: B2, 8, 12–13, 16, 22–23, 29, 35, 39, 48, 50 [12 vols.].
Duplicate: B56.
Date range: 1525–74.
Totals: potential 58 (plus 1 duplicate); actual 47.

B1	1548		fe	Titelman, F.	8°	T11	C.5.15
B3	1544		fe	Oecolampadius, J.	8°	O5	D.2.1
B4	1536		fe	Brentz, J.	8°	B72	C.6.1
B5	1526		fe	Valla, L.	8°	V3	C.4.6
B6	1573		fe^^	Mollerus, H.	8°	M76	D.1.7
B7	1574		fe	Mollerus, H.	8°	M77	G.5.6
B9	1533		fe	Haymo	4°	H9	D.5.13
B10	1561		fe	Weller, H.	8°	W4	D.6.6
B11	1525		fe	Bugenhagen, J.	8°	B111	D.3.1
B14	1558		fe	Vio, T. de	8°	V30	D.5.11
B15	1564		fe	Calvin, J.	8°	C4	D.1.9
B17	1546	R	fe	Bugenhagen, J.	4°	B115	C.2.10
B18	1535	R	fe	Bugenhagen, J.	4°	B114	C.2.11
B19	1544		fe	[Anon.] In Rom.	8°	B38	C.4.14
B20	1529		fe	Brentz, J.	8°	B75	C.6.2
B21	1559		fe	Wild, J.	8°	W32	D.2.11
B24	1525		fe	Lambert, F.	8°	L4	C.5.6
B25	1539		fe	Lambert, F.	8°	L5	C.5.7
B26	1526		fe	Oecolampadius, J.	8°	O13	C.1.6
B27	1532		fe	Rabanus M.	8°	R2	C.5.2
B29	1537		fe	Primasius	8°	P53	D.1.8
B30	[1552 or 1555]		fe	Oecumenius	8°	O18	C.4.12
B31	1552		fe	Oecumenius	8°	O17	D.5.8
B32	1539	R	fe	Bonaventura	8°	B52	C.4.1

B33	1546		fe	Mayer, S.	8°	M20	D.2.8
B34	1545	R	fe	Melanchthon, P.	8°	M53	C.5.10
B36	1545		fe	Dietrich, V.	8°	D6	G.5.4
B37	1525		fe	Hegendorff, C.	8°	H13	D.5.7
B38	1542		fe	Brentz, J.	8°	B83	C.6.3
B40	1531		fe	Haymo	8°	H10	C.4.9
B41	1571		fe	Meier, G.	8°	M37	C.6.13
B42	1560		fe	Meier, G.	8°	M32	C.6.12
B43	1545		fe	Luther, M.	8°	L60	D.5.1
B44	1573		fe	Heshusius, T.	8°	H47	D.4.6
B45	1566		fe	Hemmingsen, N.	8°	H30	C.4.11
B46	1546		fe	Cruciger, C.	8°	C114	D.4.4
B47	1570		fe	Pinto, H.	4°	P34	E.5.1
B49	1533		fe	Luther, M.	4°	L64	C.2.3
B51	1550		fe	Wild, J.	4°	W30	D.1.12
B52	1565		fe	Wild, J.	8°	W27	D.5.10
B53	1542		fe	Münster, S.	8°	M85	F.2.29
B54	1536		fe	Luther, M.	8°	L57	D.5.3
B55	1560		fe	Fontaine, S.	8°	F28	D.6.1
B56	1553	R	fe	Alesius, A.	8°	A20	C.4.7
B56	1545		fe	Hofmeister, J.	4°	H65	D.1.3
B57	1548		fe	Brentz, J.	8°	B88	C.6.4
B58	1571		fe^^	Wild, J.	8°	W28	D.2.10

Case C – Bible – mainly commentaries

Mixed 4°s and 8°s.

Missing: C1, 8–9, 16–20, 33–35, 39, 41, 43, 46–49, 51–53, 55–58, 62, 68–70, 73, ?75, ?77–84 [30 vols; possibly 39 vols].

Duplicates: ?C5, C28, ?C44 (one of the two later items re-located to S65).

Date range: 1524–1576.

Total: potential 74 (possibly 85); actual 47 (possibly ?49).

C2	1561		fe	Bullinger, H.	8°	B120	G.6.3
C3	1576		fe	Wigand, J.	8°	W20	C.4.5
C4	1542		fe	Rivius, J.	8°	R34	D.6.7
C5	[c.1524]		fe	Oecolampadius, J.	8°	O12	C.1.3
?C5*	1557		sp	Chytraeus, D.	8°	C66	E.6.35
C6	1544		fe	Oecolampadius, J.	8°	O4	C.1.4
C7	1568	R	fe	Clement I	8°	C79	B.6.5
C10	1563		sp	Mark, *Anchorite*	8°	M12	ZC2.5.13
C11	1553		fe	Luther, M.	8°	L50	C.4.3
C12	1525		fe	Luther, M.	8°	L52	D.2.2
C13	1539		fe	Luther, M.	8°	L55	D.5.2
C14	1539		fe	Luther, M.	8°	L63	D.5.4
?C15+ [L15]	1564		sp	Villavicentio	8°	V25	ZC2.4.10
C21	1541		sp	Hoffman, C.	8°	H59	E.6.33
C22	1553		sp	Zegers, N.	8°	Z3	E.6.30
C23	1510	R	fe	Holkot, R.	4°	H72	L.5.9
C24	1543		fe	Sarcerius, E.	8°	S12	C.6.7
C25	1543		fe	Sarcerius, E.	8°	S12	C.6.8
C26	1538		fe	Sarcerius, E.	8°	S15	C.6.9
C27	1541		fe	Sarcerius, E.	8°	S17	C.6.10
C28	1540		fe	Sarcerius, E.	8°	S18	D.2.5
C28	1551		fe	Vermigli, P. M.	4°	V15	C.2.2
C29	1540		fe	Sarcerius, E.	8°	S19	D.2.4

C30	1541		fe	Sarcerius, E.	8°	S20	C.6.11
C31	1544		fe	Sarcerius E.	8°	S21	D.6.8
C32	1544		fe	Sarcerius E.	8°	S22	D.6.9
C36	1531		fe	Alcuin	8°	A18	D.2.7
C37	1560		fe	Euthymius, *Zigabenus*	8°	E58	C.4.13
C38$	1533		fe	Brentz, J.	8°	B78	ZC2.6.9
C40	1546		sp	Spangenberg, J.	8°	S77	G.6.23
C42	1574		fe	Corro, A. de.	8°	C101	E.6.34
C44?*	1557		fe	Resende, L. de.	8°	R15	ZC2.2.2
[C44?x [?S65]*	1546		[sp]	Willich, J.	8°	W43	G.6.21]
C45	1538		fe**	Luther, M.	8°	L67	E.6.29
C50	1562	R	fe	Melanchthon, P.	fol.	M43	L.2.3
C54	1565		sp	Lavater, L.	4°	L19	G.5.26
C59	1527		sp	Oecolampadius, J.	4°	O11	E.5.31
C60	1543		sp	Phrygio, P C.	4°	P29	E.5.32
C61	1555		sp	Luther, M.	8°	L51	E.6.37
C63	1552		sp	Bibliander, T.	8°	B41	E.6.23
C64	1561		sp	Chytraeus, D.	8°	C67	E.6.36
[C6]5^	[c.1545]	R	fe	Luther, M.	8°	L54	E.6.27
C6[5]^	1559	R	fe	Meier, G.	8°	M27	E.6.25
C66	1560		sp	Froeschel, S.	8°	F36	G.6.22
C67	1544		sp	Kinthisius, I.	8°	K2	G.6.17
C71	1561		sp	Sasbout, A.	8°	S26	E.6.39
C72	1562		sp	Lybius, C.	8°	L81	E.6.31
C74	1563		sp	Meier, G.	8°	M33	G.6.24
C?76*	1537	R	fe	Philo, *of Carpasia*	8°	P28	C.5.3
C?85	1565		sp	Andreae, J.	4°	A34	K.2.8

Case D – mainly Bible – commentaries

Folios and 4°s.
Missing: D1–7, 9, 14, 17–20, 24–29, 38–39 [21 vols.].
Duplicates: ?D11, D31. [2 vols.].
Date range: 1503–1572.
Total: potential 40 (plus 2 duplicates); actual 21.

D8	1504	R	fe	Albertus M.	fol.	A15	G.3.20
D10	1522	R	fe	Bede	fol.	B11	A.4.19
D11	1515	R	fe	Jerome	4°	J6	L.4.31
?D11*	[c. 1507]	R	fe	Paulus, *de Sancta Maria*	fol.	P13	L.4.34
D12	1503	R	fe	Petrus, *Comestor*	fol.	P20	L.4.10
D13	1538	R	fe	Cologne, *Canons*	fol.	C97	B.3.21
D15	1568		fe	Eder, G.	fol.	E9	G.3.18
D?16*	1565	R	fe	Bibliotheca	fol.	B44	L.2.9–10
D21	1569	R	fe	Du Préau, G.	fol.	D31	L.4.6
D22	1539		fe	Pellicanus, C.	fol.	P16	E.3.6
D23	1569	R	fe	Selneccer, N.	fol.	S42	G.4.5
D30	1539	R	fe	Vio, T. de	fol.	V29	G.2.17
D31	1551	R	fe	Arboreus, J.	fol.	A48	E.4.3
D31	1522	R	fe	Le Fèvre, J.	fol.	L22	G.4.6
D32	1515	R	fe	Le Fèvre, J.	fol.	L23	G.4.7
D33	1572	R	fe	Serranus, P.	fol.	S50	G.2.4
D34	1562		fe	Benedictus, J.	fol.	B14	E.3.4
D35	1571		fe	Lavater, L.	fol.	L21	E.3.5
D36	1562		fe	Lavater, L.	4°	L20	G.5.1
D37	1569		fe	Jansen, C.	4°	J4	E.5.4
D40	1567		fe	Flacius, M.	fol.	F13	G.4.9

Case E – Theology – mainly Reformation controversies

Mixed folios, 4°s and 8°s.

Missing: E1–2, 7, 10–15, 17, 21, 23–24, 27–29, 31–36, 38–40, 42, 46, 49, 64, 67, 71–76, 78–79, 81–86 [44 vols.].

Duplicate: E70.

Date range: 1522–1575.

Totals: potential 87 (plus 1 duplicate); actual 44.

?E3+*	1567		sp	Harding, T.	4°	H8	O.1.12
E4	1572		sp	Heshusius, T.	4°	H46	ZC2.3.16
E5+	1566		sp	Nowell, A.	4°	N14	O.1.16
?E6+ ['15']	1566		sp	Stapleton, T.	4°	S86	O.1.4
E8	1565		sp	Acontius, J.	4°	A2	ZC2.3.8
E9+ ['T2.[?]3']	1567		sp	Stapleton, T.	4°	S85	O.1.13
E16	1542		sp	Marius, A.	4°	M10	ZC2.3.12
E18	1543		sp	Calvin, J.	4°	C15	K.2.3
E19	1560		sp	Andreae, J.	4°	A35	ZC2.3.5
E20	[c. 1564]		sp	Lefèvre, J.	4°	L27	ZC2.3.3
E22	1526		sp	Latomus, J.	4°	L17	ZC2.3.14
E25	1546		sp	Florebelli, A.	4°	F25	ZC2.3.11
E?26*	1566		sp	Dalmada, E.	4°	D1	ZC2.3.4
E30?*#	1554		sp	Gardiner, S.	8°	G14	K.1.31
E37	1562		sp	Bucer, M.	8°	W48	ZC2.5.7
E41	1524		fe	Cochlaeus, J.	fol.	C82	N.3.17
E43	1522	R	fe	Henry VIII	4°	H40	N.5.13
E44	1569		fe	Snepffius, T.	4°	S67	I.7.7
E45	1532		fe	Erasmus, D.	4°	E33	I.3.8
E47	1566		fe	Flacius, M.	8°	F23	I.4.6
E48	1545		fe	Carvialus, L.	4°	C44	K.2.26
E50	1555	R	fe	Slotanus, J.	4°	S60	L.5.8

E51	1542		fe	Witzel, G.	4°	W50	I.7.6
?E52*	1568		fe	Torres, H.	4°	T16	D.1.4
E53	1567		fe	Nowell, A.	4°	N13	T.6.4
E54	1556		fe	Brentz, J.	4°	B92	K.2.11
E55	1575		fe	Zanchiuis, H.	4°	Z2	I.5.5
E56?*	1565	R	fe	Horantius, F.	8°	H76	K.2.18
E57	1564		fe	Orosius, P.	8°	O22	B.6.16
E58	[c.1534]	R	fe	Dionysius, *Carthusianus*	8°	D20	ZC2.1.9[–12]
E59?*	1568		fe	Ravestyn, J.	8°	R10	I.1.6
E60	1527		fe	Erasmus, D.	8°	E48	H.1.2
E61	1567		fe	Ravestyn, J.	8°	R11	I.1.5
E62	1533		fe	Erasmus, D.	8°	E30	N.6.3
E?63*	1540		sp	Gulielmus, *Baufeti*	8°	G47	ZC2.6.12
E65	1554		sp	Gardiner, S.	4°	G15	ZC2.3.7
E66	1559		fe	Viret, P.	fol.	V36	N.3.12
E68	1563	R	fe	Kling, C.	fol.	K8	L.3.17
E6?9*	1542		fe	Pighius, A.	fol.	P33	N.4.6
E70	1565		sp	Andreae, J.	4°	A30	ZC2.3.9
E70*	1572	R	fe	Vega, A.	fol.	V6	L.3.8
E77	1528		sp	Paschasius	4°	P6	ZC2.3.10
E80	1554		sp	Tunstall, C.	4°	T26	ZC2.3.2
E87	1538		sp	Sarcerius, E.	4°	S23	ZC2.3.6

Case F – Theology – mainly Reformation controversies, and a few patristic items

Mainly 8°s.

Missing: F1, 4–5, 7, 11–13, ?14, 16–17, 23–30, 33, 35, 37, 40, 43, 45, 55, 61, 68–69, 71–75, 78, 80–86, 88–89, 92, 94, 96, 99, 102–103 [49 vols. plus ?F14].

Duplicates: ?F8 (or ?P8), 15, 18, ?44, 70 [3 +?2 vols.].

Date range: 1523–1573.

Total: potential 101 (?104); actual 44 (plus ?10) – plus 2 from Appendix I.

F2[.?]*	1562		fe	Hemmingsen, N.	8°	H38	ZC2.7.6
F3[.?]*	1551		sp	Costerius, J.	8°	C105	ZC2.6.2
F6	1551		sp	Melanchthon, P.	8°	M67	ZC2.6.16
F?8#	1564		sp	Calvin, J.	8°	C12	ZC2.4.6
?F8 [or ?P8]	1558		sp	Staphylus, F.	8°	S83	ZC2.4.12
F9#	1573		sp	Piotrków, Synod	8°	P35	ZC2.4.7
F10#	1573		sp	Piotrków, Synod	8°	P35	ZC2.4.8
?F?14*	1567		fe	Councils – Trent	8°	C110	ZC2.2.10
F15	1549		sp	Flacius, M.	8°	F17	ZC2.4.15
F15	1535		sp	Vehe, M.	4°	V7	ZC2.3.17
F18	1570		fe	Aretius, B.	16°	A50	ZC1.4.13
F18	1563		sp	Dominicis, D. de	8°	D22	ZC2.5.5
F19	1563		sp	Garetius, J.	8°	G17	K.1.26
F20	1559		sp	Hofmeister, J.	8°	H68	ZC2.5.8
F21	1564		sp	Cassander, G.	8°	C45	B.6.41
F?22*	1570		sp	Flacius, M.	8°	F21	K.1.35
F31	1556		sp	Tavernarius, J.	8°	T2	ZC2.6.3
F32	1566		sp	Hamelmann, H.	8°	H2A	ZC2.4.9
F?34*	[c.1523]	R	fe	Luther, M.	8°	L78	ZC2.7.11
F36	1538		sp	Luther, M.	8°	L72	ZC2.6.14
F38	1564		sp	Martiall, J.	8°	M13	O.2.39
F39	1548	R	fe	Bucer, M.	4°	B110	L.5.16

F41	1569		fe	Osorio da Fonseca, J.	8°	O26	M.2.40
F42	1530		fe	Erasmus, D.	8°	E38	ZC1.4.6
F44	1571		fe	Hemmingsen, N.	8°	H37	ZC2.7.5
?F44*	1567		fe	Gregory, *of Nazianzus*	8°	G33	A.6.11
F46	1568		fe	Bèze, T.	8°	B29	ZC2.1.8
F47	1567		fe	Sainctes., C. de.	8°	S7	N.6.12
F48	1567		fe	Flacius, M.	8°	F22	K.2.17
F49	1544		fe	Vives, J.L.	8°	V39	N.6.5
F50	1550	R	fe	Rivius, J.	8°	R33	L.6.16
F51	1536		fe	Eck, J.	8°	E3	G.5.18
F52	1567	R	fe	Athenagoras	8°	A59	A.6.20
F53	1545		fe	Billick, E.	8°	B50	ZC2.7.2
F54	1566		fe	Wigand, J.	8°	W23	K.2.15
F56	1545		fe	Zurich Ch.	8°	Z4	M.2.16
F57	1567		fe	Flacius, M.	8°	F18	ZC2.2.4
F58	1561		fe	Hall, Suabian	8°	H1	ZC2.2.7
F59	1575		fe^^	Zurich Ch.	8°	Z5	ZC1.4.4
F60	1546		fe	Calvin, J.	8°	C11	ZC1.4.7
F62	1537		fe	Latomus, J.	8°	L18	H.2.12
F?63* +['10']	1527		sp	Pirckheimer, W.	8°	P36	ZC2.6.6
F64	1558		fe	Slotanus, J.	8°	S61	ZC1.4.9
F65	1529	R	fe	Augustine	8°	A62	A.6.32
F66	1545		fe	Gallasius, N.	8°	G5	ZC2.7.13
F67	1568		fe	Waldenses, *Confessio*	8°	W1	K.2.16
F70	1553		sp	Du Moulin, C.	8°	D30	ZC2.5.1
F70	1562		sp	Melanchthon, P.	8°	M45	K.1.7
F76	1565		fe	Rastall, J.	8°	R6	O.2.41
F77	1566		sp	Rastell, J.	8°	*R1	O.2.37
F79	1571		sp	Bèze, T.	8°	B20	K.1.33
F87	1545		sp	Lasco, J. à	8°	L12	ZC2.6.15
F90	1544		sp	Cochlaeus, J.	8°	C90	ZC2.6.17

F91	1566	R	fe	Rastall, J.	8°	R7	O.2.45
F93	1540		sp	Prosper	8°	P55	A.6.42
F95?*	1576	R	fe^^	Augustine	8°	A66	A.6.23
F97	1544		sp	Bullinger, H.	8°	B118	ZC2.6.7
F[?9]8*	1525	R	sp^^	Latomus, J.	8°	L16	ZC2.7.10
F10[0?]*	[c.1545]		sp	Postel, G.	8°	P45	ZC2.6.4
F101	1530		sp	Strasbourg Ch.	8°	S91	ZC2.5.9
F104	1546	R	fe	Gardiner, S.	8°	*G1	R.6.19

Case G – Theology – Contemporary

Mixed 4°s and 8°s.
Missing: G1–2, 10, 15–24, 26–28, 31–32, 34–36, 41–42, 48–55 [31 vols.].
Date range: 1516–1571.
Total: potential 59; actual 24 (plus ?4).

G3	1546		fe	Sarcerius E.	4°	S24	ZC2.2.5
?G4*	1548		fe	Hermann, *von Wied*	8°	H42	O.1.25
G5	1545		fe	Rhegius, U.	8°	R23	H.1.8
G6	1571		fe	Carolinus, P.	8°	C43	H.1.7
G7	1561		fe	Rabus, L.	8°	R4	D.6.11
?G8*	1548		fe	Culman, L.	8°	C120	M.2.29
G9	1543		fe	Luther, M.	8°	L49	L.6.30
G11	1539		fe	Capito, W.	8°	C38	M.2.3
G12	1540		fe	Maruliæ, M.	8°	M14	N.6.4
G13	1539		fe	Sarcerius, E.	8°	S25	ZC2.1.5
G14	1536		fe	Althamer, A.	8°	A27	D.6.12
?G25 [or ?G26]*	1516		fe	Raymond, *de Penaforte*	8°	R13	K.3.46
G29	1564		fe	Hertelius, J.	8°	H45	ZC2.4.13
G30	1569		fe	Canisius, P.	4°	C36	K.2.13

G33	1570		fe	Canisius, P.	4°	C36	K.2.14
G37	1544		fe	Cologne. *Canones*	8°	C98	B.6.4
G3?8*	1563		fe	Hemmingsen, N.	8°	H35	ZC2.7.7
G39	1544		fe	Nausea, F.	8°	N7	N.6.6
G40	[1555]		sp	Bonner, E.	4°	B54	O.1.10
G43	1550		fe	Mainz	8°	M7	B.5.16
G44	1552		fe	Brentz, J.	8°	B90	M.2.25
G45	1556		sp	Musculus, W.	8°	M90	ZC2.4.11
G46	1564		sp	Mermannius, A.	8°	M69	ZC2.4.14
G47	1563		sp	Hyperius, A.	8°	H95	ZC2.5.6
G56	1552		sp	Soto, P. de.	16°	S72	ZC2.8.7
G57	1562		sp	Gropper, J.	16°	G35	ZC2.8.6
G58	1557		sp^^	Naclantius, J.	4°	N2	E.5.28
G59	1527		sp	Oecolampadius, J.	4°	O11	E.5.31

Case H – Theology – Patristic and medieval

Folios.
Missing: H1–6, 10–14, ?22, 25–27 [14 or ?15 vols.].
Date range: 1502–1576.
Total: potential 36; actual 21 (?plus 1).

H7	1542	R	fe	Augustine	fol.	A60	A.4.23
H8	1542	R	fe	Augustine	fol.	A60	A.4.24
H9	1570		fe	Irenaeus	fol.	I5	A.4.8
H15–16	1519	R	fe	Origen	fol.	O20	A.4.1–2
H17	1520		fe	Theodoret	fol.	T7	A.5.3
H18	[1502]	R	fe	Hugo, *de Sancto Charo*	fol.	H82	L.2.1
H19	1526	R	fe	Hugo, *de Sancto Victore*	fol.	H85	L.1.8
H20	1526	R	fe	Hugo, *de Sancto Victore*	fol.	H86	L.1.9
H21	1525	R	fe	Georgius, F.	fol.	G23	L.3.21
?H22* [or I22]	1576	R	fe	Brentz, J.	fol.	B68	L.2.2
H23	1512	R	fe	Aquinas, T.	fol.	A47	L.3.10

H24	1534	R	fe	Puteo, F. de.	fol.	P58	E.3.12
H28	1504	R	fe	Albertus Magnus	fol.	A14	G.3.19
H29	1548		fe	Dionysius, *Carthusianus*	fol.	D10	E.3.16
H30	1552		fe	Dionysius, *Carthusianus*	fol.	D11	E.3.17
H31	1542		fe	Dionysius, *Carthusianus*	fol.	D12	E.3.19
H32	1548		fe	Dionysius, *Carthusianus*	fol.	D14	E.3.18
H33	1543		fe	Dionysius, *Carthusianus*	fol.	D17	E.3.20
H34	1545		fe	Dionysius, *Carthusianus*	fol.	D18	E.3.21
H35	1540		fe	Dionysius, *Carthusianus*	fol.	D21	N.4.2
H36	1532		fe	Angelomus, *Luxoviensis*	fol.	A38	N.3.18

Case I – Bible – Homilies – Reformation Theology

Folios.
Missing: I1–5, 7–18, ?21 [17 or 18 vols.].
Date range: 1562–1576.
Total: potential 20 (?22); actual 3 (?4).

I6	1562		fe	Gregory, *of Nyssa*	fol.	G34	A.4.20
I19	1572		fe	Gualtherus, R.	fol.	G39	G.3.17
I20	1572	R	fe	Gualtherus, R.	fol.	G40	G.4.16
?I22* [or H22]	1576		fe	Brentz, J.	fol.	B68	L.2.2

Case K – Theology – Patristic, medieval and Reformation

Folios.
Missing: K1–8, ?9, 10–15, 18–19 [16 or 17 vols.].
Date range: 1512–1559.
Total: potential 20; actual 3 (?4).

?K9*	1512	R	fe	John, *of Damascus*	fol.	J13	L.4.5
K16	1559		fe	Calvin, J.	fol.	C16	N.2.9
K17	1529		fe	Bede	fol.	B12	N.4.5
K20	1554	R	fe	Theophylact	fol.	T8	G.2.18

Case L – Theology and church history – Patristic, medieval and Reformation

Folios and 4°s.
Missing: 2, 4–5, 7–9, 12, 18, 22–25, 27–30, 33–44 [28 vols.].
Duplicates: ?L15.
Date range: 1504–1567.
Total: potential 45; actual 11 (?17) (plus 1 possible duplicate).

?L1*	1561		fe^^	Apost. Canons	fol.	A44	B.3.9
L3	1536	R	fe	Smaragdus, *of Verdun*	fol.	S62	E.4.6
L6	1561		fe	Pantaleon, H.	fol.	P3	B.3.19
L10	1541		fe	Eucherius, *of Lyon*	fol.	E55	E.4.1
L1?1*	1567		fe	Byzantium	fol.	B138	Z.2.19
L13	1514	R	fe	Cusa, N. de	fol.	C125	L.4.8
L14	1514	R	fe	Cusa, N. de	fol.	C125	L.4.7
L15	1546		fe	John, *of Damascus*	fol.	J12	N.3.13
L15?+ [possibly changed from C15]	1564		s p	Villavicentio	8°	V25	ZC2.4.10
L16	1521		fe	Cyprian	fol.	C127	A.4.21
L17?*	1523	R	fe	Gregory I	fol.	G31	A.1.15
L19	1504	R	fe	Heracleides	fol.	H41	A.5.7
?L20*	1506	R	fe	Hugo, *de Sancto Victore*	fol.	H88	L.2.15
L21	1540		fe	Arboreus, J.	fol.	A49	M.1.17
?L26*	1515	R	fe	Pérez de Valentia, J.	fol.	P18	G.3.16
L31?*	1566		sp	Horne, R.	4°	H77	O.2.2
L32	1509		sp	Duns, J.	4°	D32	ZC2.3.15
L45	1535	R	fe	Brunfels, O.	fol.	B95	G.4.18

Case M – Theology – Reformation controversies and miscellaneous medieval and renaissance authors

Folios, 4°s and 8°s.
Missing: M1, 9, 11, 13, 27–28, 33–34, 37, 39–41 [12 vols.]
Date range: 1481–1574.
Totals: potential 46; actual 33 (possibly 34).

M2	1574		fe	Whitgift, J.	fol.	W16	T.3.8
M3	1547	R	fe	Driedo, J.	fol.	D27	L.3.19
M4	1568		fe	Hamelmann, H.	fol.	H2	M.1.28
M5	1563		fe	Vannius, V.	4°	V5	I.4.2
M6	1528		fe	Murner, T.	4°	M86	I.3.10
M7	1570		fe	Lindanus, W.	4°	L30	I.8.3
M8	1566		fe	Maulbrunn. Colloquy	4°	M18	I.4.5
M10	[c. 1517]	R	fe	Erasmus, D.	4°	E22	L.5.35
M12	1566		fe	Soto, P. de	8°	S73	H.1.3
M14	1571		fe	Borckensis, T.	8°	B58	G.6.6
M15	1569		fe	Paulli, S.	8°	P12	M.2.26
M16	1570		fe	Ravestyn, J.	8°	R9	B.5.10
M17	1552	R	fe	Lasco, J. à	8°	L10	H.2.11
M18	1561		fe	Heshusius, T.	8°	H48	ZC2.2.8
M19	1570		fe	Via, J. à	8°	V22	ZC2.1.3
M20	1556		fe	Luther, M.	8°	L70	ZC1.4.10
M21	1536		fe	Lorich, G.	8°	L38	M.2.11
M22	1569		fe	Eisengrein, M.	8°	E13	B.6.42
M23	1566		fe	Chemnitz, M.	8°	C59	C.7.1
M24	1566		fe	Chemnitz, M.	8°	C60	C.7.2
M25	1573		fe	Chemnitz, M.	8°	C61	C.7.3
M26	1573		fe	Chemnitz, M.	8°	C62	C.7.4
M29	1522	R	fe	Erasmus, D.	fol.	E27	G.2.6
M30	1513	R	fe	Petrus, *Lombardus*	fol.	P22	L.3.7
M31	1528	R	fe	Bible	4°	B30	E.5.18

M32	1516	R	fe	Gulielmus, *Avernus*	fol.	G46	L.4.22
M35	1510	R	fe	Biel, G.	fol.	B46	L.3.15
?M36*	1543		fe	Stobaeus, J.	fol.	S89	M.I.15
M38	1517		fe	Altensteig, J.	fol.	A25	Y.3.32
M42	1508	R	fe	Biel, G.	fol.	B47	L.3.16
M43	1481	R	fe	Aquinas, T.	fol.	A45	L.3.9
M44	1496	R	fe	Jacobus, *de Voragine*	fol.	J1	L.4.17
M45	1497	R	fe	Philippus, J., *de Bergamo*	4°	P25	L.5.1
M46	1517		fe	Cagnazzo, J.	4°	C1	N.5.26

Case N – Theology – Reformation controversies and miscellaneous medieval authors

Folios, 4°s and 8°s.
Missing: N7–8, 13–15, 25, 28–29, 31, 33–35, 38–39, 43, 47, 51 [17 vols.].
Duplicates: ?N40 (from Appendix I), ?42 [possibly 2 vols.].
Date range: 1481–1572
Total: potential 52; actual 29 (possibly 35).

?N1*	1572		fe	Heshusius, T.	8°	H49	ZC1.4.3
N2	1533		fe	Joannes, *a Davantria*	8°	J9	H.I.31
N3	1570		fe	Hyperius, A. G.	8°	H98	ZC2.1.6
N4	1559		fe	Vermigli, P. M.	8°	V17	N.6.7
N5	1565	R	fe	Kling, C.	8°	K9	I.1.7
N6	1569		fe	Wigand, J.	8°	W22	N.6.10
N9	1522		fe	Erasmus, D.	8°	E31	N.6.1
N10	1549		fe	Pighius, A.	8°	P32	M.2.6
N11	1565		fe	Charlemagne	8°	C57	M.2.21
N12	1566		fe	Flacius, M.	8°	F10	ZC2.1.4
N16	1535	R	fe	Zwingli, H.	8°	Z7	L.6.14
N17	1546		fe	Smith, R.	8°	S64	R.6.46
N18	1526	R	fe	Erasmus, D.	8°	E34	L.6.5
N19	1552		fe	Vermigli, P.M.	8°	V16	N.6.8

N20	?1525		fe	Zwingli, H.	8°	Z6	N.6.13
N21	1544		fe	Spangenberg, J	8°	S80	ZC2.2.9
N22	1565		fe	Selneccer, N.	8°	S41	ZC2.1.7
N23	1571		fe	Polygranus, F.	8°	P41	ZC1.4.5
?N24*	1525		fe	Schatzger, C.	8°	S31	ZC2.1.1
N26	1566		fe	Metz, Ministers	8°	M74	ZC1.4.8
N27	1559		fe	Hyperius, A.G.	8°	H96	N.6.16
N30?*	1494	R	fe	Gerson, J.	fol.	G25	L.3.14
N32	1497		fe	Balbus, J.	fol.	B5	Y.2.12
?N36*	1503	R	fe	Foresti, J.P.	fol.	F30	Z.2.25
N37	1494	R	fe	Vincent, *of Beauvais*	fol.	V26	L.1.15
?N40*	1503	R	fe	Nannus Mirabellius, D.	fol.	N5	L.2.14
?N40*	1526		sp	Erasmus, D.	8°	*E2	ZC2.6.5
N41	1481	R	fe	Duns, J.	4°	D33	L.4.25
N42	1518	R	fe	Durandus, G.	4°	D36	L.5.13
N42*	1510	R	fe	Joannes, *de Colonia*	4°	J11	L.5.40
N44	1523		fe	Angelus, de Clavasio	4°	A39	L.5.33
N45?*	1497	R	fe	Peraldus, G.	4°	P17	L.5.31
N46	1514		fe	Pavinis, J. F. de	4°	P14	L.5.37
N48	1520		fe	Duns, J.	8°	D34	L.6.32
N49	[c. 1497]	R	fe	Orbellis, N.	8°	O19	L.6.3
N50	1505	R	fe	Vivaldus, J. L. de	8°	V37	L.6.1
N52	1519	R	fe	Gratian	8°	G30	H.2.54

Case O – Bible – Commentaries and homilies and theology – Reformation controversies

4°s and 8°s and smaller.
Missing: O1–2, 6–7, 9–12, 19–28, 30–32 [21 vols.].
Date range: 1527–1572.
Total: potential 29 (possibly 33); actual 9 (possibly 12).

O3	1538			fe	Bullinger, H.	4°	B127	H.1.20
O4	1543			fe	Antiochus, *Monk*	4°	A43	C.2.13
?O5*	1551			fe	Bullinger, H.	4°	B133	I.4.11
O8	1572			fe	Camerarius, J.	4°	C26	D.1.5
O13	1549			fe	Perionius, J.	8°	P19	ZC2.7.3
O14	1543			fe	Bucer, M.	8°	B107	H.1.5
O15	1532	R		fe	Sachs, H.	8°	S2	ZC2.7.9
?O16*	[c. 1527]	R		fe	Origen	8°	O21	ZC2.4.16
O17	1539			fe	Corvinus, A.	8°	C102	A.6.31
O18	1547			fe	Brunfels, O.	8°	B96	D.3.2
O29	1565	R		fe	Du Moulin, C.	4°	D29	C.2.14
?O33*	1567	R		fe	Eck, J.	12°	E8	ZC2.8.5

Case P – Theology – Dogmatics and Moral Theology

8°s.
Missing: P1–7, 9–12, 14–27, ?29–36 [25 – possibly 33 vols.].
Date range: 1537–1558.
Total: potential 28 (possibly 37?); actual 2 (possibly 4).

?P8 [or ?F8]	1558			sp	Staphylus, F.	8°	S83	ZC2.4.12
P13	[c. 1550]	R		sp	Melanchthon, P.	8°	M65	B.5.34
P28	1537			sp	Witzel, G.	8°	W53	ZC2.6.10
P37?* +['23']	1558			sp	Titelman, F.	16°	T15	ZC2.8.2

Case R – Miscellaneous literature and humanities – Bible – Homilies – Theology – Reformation controversies

Mixed folios, 4°s and 8°s.

Missing: R1–3, 5, 7–8, ?10–11, 17, 23, 28, 33, 36–38, 41, 43, 46–47, 49 [?20 vols.].

Duplicates: R42, 60.

Date range: 1478–1573.

Total: potential 61 (possibly 65 – from Appendix I); actual 43 (plus 2 duplicates).

R4*	1533	R	fe	Driedo, J.	fol.	D28	L.2.13
R6	1515	R	fe	Seneca, L. A	fol.	S45	Y.2.16
R9	1482	R	fe	Ficino, M.	fol.	F6	Y.3.25
R12	1561		fe	Westhemerus, B.	4°	W8	C.1.13
R13	1518		fe	Le Fèvre, J.	4°	L25	L.5.36
R14	1531		fe	Isidore, *of Seville*	4°	I6	I.4.10
R15	1534		fe	Driedo, J.	4°	D26	N.5.5
R16?* [or R10?]	1555		fe	Palladius, *of Helenopolis*	4°	P2	B.5.3
R18	1572		fe	Osorio da Fonseca, J.	8°	O25	I.2.10
R19	1571		fe	Canisius, P.	4°	C32	C.2.4
R20	1557		fe	Sleidanus, J.	8°	S59	B.6.1
R21	1544		fe	Chiari, I.	8°	C64	C.3.12
R22	1507		fe	Castellensis, H.	4°	C49	H.1.21
R24	1557		fe	Francisco, de V.	8°	F34	H.1.4
R25	1571		fe	Wittenberg, Academia	8°	W46	ZC2.7.8
R26	1558		fe	Estienne, R.	8°	E54	F.2.24
?R27*	1536	R	fe	Ludolf, *of Saxony*	8°	L48	L.6.7
R29	1555	R	fe	Vives, J. L.	8°	V38	Z.5.121
R30	1566		fe	Vigne, P. della	8°	V24	Z.5.109
R?31*	1570	R	fe	Melanchthon, P.	8°	M61	L.6.21
R32	1556		fe	Lycosthenes, C.	8°	L82	M.2.43
R34	1521		fe	Pelbárt, O .	fol.	P15	M.1.27

R35	1550		fe	Royard, T.	fol.	R39	E.4.2
R39	1553		fe	Witzel, G.	fol.	W49	E.4.4
R40	1540		fe	Nausea, F.	fol.	N8	N.3.16
R42	[1506]		fe	Hugo, de Sancto Charo	4°	H83	D.1.2
R42	1562		fe	Wild, J.	8°	W39	G.5.12
R44	1478	R	fe	Gulielmus, Parisiensis	4°	G49	L.5.10
R45	1564		sp	Ulmer, J. C.	8°	U1	ZC2.3.13
R48	1558		fe	Wild, J.	8°	W37	G.5.11
R50	[c. 1545]	R	fe	Melanchthon, P.	8°	M51	C.5.11
R51	1524		fe	Mazzolini, S.	8°	M23	D.3.14
R52	1544		fe	Broeckwey, A.	8°	B94	D.4.8
R53	1558		fe	Brentz, J.	8°	B80	G.5.16
R54	1567		fe	Paulli, S.	8°	P10	G.6.5
R55	1555		fe	Hofmeister, J.	8°	H62	G.5.15
R56	1547		fe	Spangenberg, J.	8°	S75	D.3.4
R57	1566	R	fe	Wigand, J.	8°	W19	E.6.9
R58	1556		fe	Helmes, H.	8°	H18	C.3.2
R59	1556		fe	Helmes, H.	8°	H19	C.3.3
R60	1556		fe	Helmes, H.	8°	H20	C.3.4
R60	1573		fe	Eisengrein, M.	8°	E10	D.4.9
R61	1531		fe	Matthei, L.	8°	M16	D.3.8
[?R65	1535		fe	Alexander, A.	8°	*A2	ZC1.5.6]

Case S– Miscellaneous Literature and humanities – Bible – Homilies – Theology – Reformation controversies

One folio, a few 4°s, but mostly 8°s and smaller.
Missing: S9, 16, 21, 24–25, 28–30, 32–37, 39, 49–50, 55, 67, 69–70, 72, 74–95 [44 vols].
Duplicates: ?S22, 51.
Date range: 1495–1573.
Total: potential 96; actual 49 (possibly 53) (plus 1, possibly 2 duplicates).

S1	1567	R	fe	Theodoret, *of Cyrus*	fol.	T4	A.4.11
S2	1550		fe	Bibliander, T.	8°	B42	H.1.29
S3	1535		fe	Erasmus, D.	8°	E36	D.3.7
S4	1573		fe	Bèze, T.	8°	B26	M.2.20
?S5*	1554	R	fe	Foxe, J [formerly bound with	8°	F32	B.6.11
[?S5]	1554	R	fe	Rabus, L.	8°	R3	B.6.10]
S6	1567		fe	Rostock. Academia	8°	R38	H.1.9
?S7*	1567	R	fe	Torres, H.	4°	T16A	A.6.5
S8	1537		fe	Suetonius	8°	S96	Y.5.29
S10	1550		fe	Rivius, J.	8°	R32	H.1.37
S11	1525		fe	Lambert, F.	8°	L7	H.1.6
S12	1560	R	fe	Paulinus, *of Nola*	8°	P9	A.6.21
S13	1568		fe	Lucifer, *of Cagliari*	8°	L47	A.6.26
S14	1513		fe	Richard, *St Victor*	4°	R26	I.4.9
S15	1546		fe	Goeuschel, J.	8°	G29	F.2.10
S17	1558		fe	Basil, *the Great*	8°	B7	A.6.22
S18	1556		fe	Euthymius, *Zigabenus*	8°	E59	A.6.25
S19	1495		fe	Petrus, *Lombardus*	4°	P23	L.5.38
S20	1522		fe	Bonaventura	8°	B53	H.1.38
S22	1522		fe	Bonaventura	8°	B53	H.1.39
S?22*	1564		sp	Spangenberg, J.	8°	S79	ZC2.5.10
S23	1522		fe	Bonaventura	8°	B53	H.1.40
S26	1557		fe	Maximus, *of Tyre*	8°	M19	Y.5.19

S27	1527		fe	Vio, T. de	8°	V33	K.3.42
S31	1538	R	fe	Clichtoveus, J.	16°	C83	K.3.13
S38	1571	R	fe	Holthusius, J.	12°	H73	K.3.31
S40	[1552]		fe	Loss, L.	8°	L43	D.3.3
S41	1548		fe	Spangenberg, J.	8°	S76	D.3.5
S42	1564		fe	Radulphus, *Ardens*	8°	R5	D.4.1
S43–45	1560–1561		fe	Schopper, J.	8°	S39	D.3.9–11
S46	1550		fe	Culman, L.	8°	C122	M.2.36
S48	1550		fe	Culman, L.	8°	C122	M.2.38
S49?*	1550		fe	Culman, L.	8°	C122;	M.2.37
S51	1556		fe	Helmes, H.	8°	H21	C.3.5
S51	1548		fe	Spangenberg, J.	8°	S76	D.3.5
S52	1556		fe	Helmes, H.	8°	H22	C.3.6
S53	1556		fe	Sasbout, A.	8°	S27	E.6.22
S54	1555		fe	Wild, J.	fol.	W37	G.5.10
S56	1572		fe	Brandmueller, J.	8°	B63	G.6.1
S57	1528		fe	Jacobus, *de Voragine*	8°	J2	D.4.10
S58	1561		fe	Loss, L.	8°	L44	G.6.18
S59	1558		fe	Brentz, J.	8°	B81	G.6.4
S60	1544		fe	Brentz, J.	8°	B91	H.2.7
S61	?1540		fe	Sarcerius, E.	8°	S14	G.5.14
S62	1538		fe	Artopoeus, P.	8°	A56	E.6.5
S63	1539		fe	Sarcerius, E.	8°	S13	D.2.3
S64	1562		sp	Meier, G.	8°	M38	G.5.21
?S65* [?x C44]	1546		[sp]	Willich, J.	8°	W43	G.6.21
S66	1562		sp++	Meier, G.	8°	M40	G.6.20
S68	1566		sp++	Meier, G.	8°	M29	E.6.21
S71	1558		sp	Eusebius, *of Emesa*	8°	E57	E.6.20
S73	1565		sp	Meier, G.	8°	M28	G.6.19
S96	1568	R	fe	Usuardus	8°	U2	B.6.19

Case T – Miscellaneous – Literature and humanities, linguistics, philosophy, political theory, medicine – Bible – Hebrew, text – Theology and spirituality

4°s and smaller.

Missing: T1, 3, 5, 8–9, 13, 15, 20, 22–25, 27, ?29, 31, 33–35, 37, ?38 (or ?28), 39–40 [22 vols.].

Date range: 1523–1567.

Total: potential 52 (possibly 53); actual 23 (possibly 31).

T2	1566		fe	Hunnaeus, A.	8°	H91	Z.4.23
T4	1567		fe	Valerius, C .	8°	V2	Z.5.108
T6	1537		fe	Elias, *Levita*	8°	E18	F.2.19
T7	1532	R	fe	Erasmus, D.	8°	E41	ZC2.2.3
T10	1541		fe	Cicero, M.T.	8°	C74	X.2.16
T11–12	1541		fe	Ravisius, J.	8°	R12	X.2.17–18
T14	1523		fe	Erasmus, D.	8°	E28	G.5.20
T16	1540		sp	Campensis, J.	8°	C29	F.2.5
T17	1560		sp	Humphrey, L.	8°	H90	ZC2.5.2
T?18*	1550		sp	Betuleius, X.	8°	B18	X.2.32
T19+ [T29]	1525		sp	Capito, W.	8°	C39	F.2.4
T?21*	1558		sp	Clauser, C	8°	C76	X.2.30
T26	1525		fe	Gaza, T.	8°	G18	Y.5.14
T?28* [or T38]	[?1560]		sp	Freiesleben, C.	8°	F35	B.6.40
[T29x [T19]	1525		sp	Capito, W.	8°	C39	F.2.4]
T30	1565		sp	Tauler, J.	8°	T1	ZC2.6.8
T3?2*	1562		fe	Sextus	8°	S53	ZC1.5.19
T36	1529		sp	Reuchlin, J.	8°	R16	F.2.6
T?38* [or T28]	[?1560]		sp	Freiesleben, C.	8°	F35	B.6.40
?T41*	1549		fe	Bucer, M.	4°	B108	I.4.4
T42	1554		sp	Watson, T.	8°	W2	O.2.46
T43	1539		sp	Münster, S.	8°	M84	F.2.3

?T44*	1552		fe	Bible	16°	B37	G.6.7
T45	[c.1550]	R	fe	Bible	16°	B36	G.6.8
T46	1529	R	fe	Bible	16°	B31	G.6.10
T47	1532	R	fe	Bible	16°	B32	G.6.11
T48	1526		fe	Bible	16°	B35	G.6.14
T49	1529		fe	Bible	16°	B33	G.6.13
T50	1526		fe	Bible	16°	B34	G.6.12
T51?* +['25']	1559		sp	Erasmus, D.	12°	E43	ZC2.8.4
T52	1558		sp	Jansen, C.	12°	J5	E.6.19
?T53*	1564		sp	Clement I	12°	C80	B.6.35

Books with only a trace of an early press mark – no longer fully legible (not included in the above)

Fol. to 12°.
Date range: 1527–1571.
Total: 9 (plus 1 from Appendix I [*C7]).

Cat. no. of first item	Imprint year of latest item	Fore-edge or spine title	Author of first item	Format	Current shelf-mark
A68	1527	fe	Aurogallus, M.	8°	ZC2.8.8
B59	1555	fe	Borrhaus, M.	fol.	G.4.10
C89	1540	fe	Cochlaeus, J.	4°	L.4.30
H56	1571	sp	Hessiander, C.	8°	ZC2.3.1
L35	1559	sp	Lindanus, W.	8°	B.6.37
P8	1567	fe	Patrizi, F.	8°	ZC1.5.4
S94	1522	++	Stunica, J. L.	fol.	L.4.12
T10	1555	fe*	Titelman, F.	12°	G.6.16
T24	1565	sp/fe	Trotzendorf, V.F.	8°	K.3.45
*C7	1526	fe*	Clichtoveus, J.	4°	H.1.19

Books – still in contemporary bindings – with no visible press mark (not included in the above)

Abbreviations

CP	Calf over pasteboard.
dis.	Dis-bound – now covered in parchment or paper.
fe	Fore-edge title extant.
pa	Parchment binding.
pa*	Formerly bound in parchment, now wrapped in paper.
sp	Spine-title extant.

Date range: 1525–1575.
Total: 13.

Cat. no. of first item	Imprint year of latest item	Fore-edge or spine title	Author of first item	Binding type	Current shelf-mark
A51	1575	–	Aretius, B.	CP	ZC2.7.1
C123	1576	–	Cureus, J.	pa	K.1.27
E29	[c. 1536]	–	Erasmus, D.	CP	D.1.13–14
F3	1564	sp	Fabricius, J.	pa	ZC2.5.3
L15	1551	–	Latomus, B.	pa	ZC2.4.1
L39	1549	dis	Lorich, G.	pa*	ZC2.8.1
L76	1552	sp	Luther, M.	pa	ZC2.6.18
M72	1567	sp	Mermannius, A.	pa	ZC2.6.11
N12	1562	sp	Novicampianus	pa	ZC2.8.3
O6	1525	–	Oecolampadius, J.	CP	C.1.10
R9	1568	–	Ravestyn, J.	CP	B.5.9
S70	1570	sp	Sonnius, F.	pa	B.5.33
W7	1552	–	Westhemerus, B.	CP	ZC2.2.1

Appendix – Other books without early press marks which may have belonged to Geste

*H2	1526	–	Herodotus	CP	Y.3.19

APPENDIX VII

Early book-titles on spines or fore-edges

Abbreviations

#	Book title not certainly by Geste.
*	Trace only.
*?	Possible trace only.
**	Also possible trace of fore-edge title.
***	Also early fore-edge title or title on top-edge which may not be in the same hand.
+	Also book title across the spine.
$	Later book label possibly covering earlier titles.
$$	Later book label in addition to earlier title.
$$$	Later book label, but no trace of earlier titles.
^	Possibly overwritten or re-inked in another hand.

Spine titles

Cat. no. of first item	Imprint year of latest item	Author of first item	Number of items	Shelf-mark
A2	1563	Acontius	5	ZC2.3.8
A30	1565	Andreae, J.	5	ZC2.3.9
A35	1560	Andreae, J.	7	ZC2.3.5
B18	1550	Betuleius, X.	1	X.2.32
B20$	1573	Bèze, T.	3	K.1.33
B41	1552	Bibliander, T.	2	E.6.23
B54	[1555]	Bonner, E.	2	O.1.10
B78	1533	Brentz, J.	1	ZC2.6.9
B118	1544	Bullinger, H.	1	ZC2.6.7
C12	1558	Calvin, J.	5	ZC2.4.6
C14$	1543	Calvin, J.	1	K.2.3

C29	1539	Campensis, J.	3	F.2.5
C45	1564	Cassander, G.	3	B.6.41
C66	1557	Chytraeus, D.	4	E.6.35
C67	1561	Chytraeus, D.	2	E.6.36
C76	1558	Clauser, C.	2	X.2.30
C80	1564	Clement I	2	B.6.35
C90	1544	Cochlaeus, J.	1	ZC2.6.17
C101*?/+	1574	Corr, A.de	1	E.6.34
C105*?	1551	Costerius, J.	1	ZC2.6.2
D22	1563	Dominicis, D. De	2	ZC2.5.5
D30	1553	Du Moulin, C.	3	ZC2.5.1
D32*	1509	Duns, J.	1	ZC2.3.15
E43	1559	Erasmus, D.	2	ZC2.8.4
F3	1563	Fabricius, J.	2	ZC2.5.3
F17	1549	Flacius, M.	1	ZC2.4.15
F25	1546	Florebelli, A.	3	ZC2.3.11
F35	[?1560]	Freiesleben, C.	1	B.6.40
F36	1560	Froeschel, S.	2	G.6.22
G14	1554	Gardiner, S.	1	K.1.31
G17$	1563	Garetius, J.	1	K.1.26
G35	1562	Gropper, J.	1	ZC2.8.6
G47	1540	Gulielmus, *Baufeti*	1	ZC2.6.12
H2A	1566	Hammelmann, H.	2	ZC2.4.9
H8$$	1567	Harding, T.	1	O.1.12
H45	1564	Hertelius, J.	1	ZC2.4.13
H46	1572	Heshusius, T.	1	ZC2.3.16
H59	1541	Hoffman, C.	1	E.6.33
H68	1559	Hofmeister, J.	2	ZC2.5.8
H77$$$	1566	Horne, R.	1	O.2.2
H90	1560	Humphrey, L.	3	ZC2.5.2
H95	1563	Hyperius, A. G.	4	ZC2.5.6

J5	1558	Jansen, C.	1	E.6.19
K2	1544	Kinthisius, I.	1	G.6.17
K8	1563	Kling, C.	2	L.3.17
K9	1565	Kling, C.	1	I.1.7
L12	1545	Lasco, J. À	1	ZC2.6.15
L17	1526	Latomus, J.	6	ZC2.3.14
L19	1565	Lavater, L.	1	G.5.26
L27	[1563/64]	Lefèvre, J.	2	ZC2.3.3
L44***	1561	Loss, L.	1	G.6.18
L51*?	1555	Luther, M.	1	E.6.37
L72	1538	Luther, M.	1	ZC2.6.14
L76	1531	Luther, M.	9	ZC2.6.18
L81	1562	Lybius, C.	2	E.6.31
M12	1563	Mark	1	ZC2.5.13
M13$	1564	Martiall	1	O.2.39
M28***	1565	Meier, G.	1	G.6.19
M29*/***	1566	Meier, G.	1	E.6.21
M33	1563	Meier, G.	2	G.6.24
M38	1562	Meier, G.	2	G.5.21
M40***	1562	Meier, G.	1	G.6.20
M65	[c. 1550]	Melanchthon, P.	4	B.5.34
M67	1551	Melanchthon, P.	1	ZC2.6.16
M69	1564	Mermannius, A.	5	ZC2.4.14
M72	1566	Mermannius, A.	4	ZC2.6.11
M84	1539	Münster, S.	2	F.2.3
M90	1556	Musculus, W.	7	ZC2.4.11
N12	1555	Novicampianus, A.	3	ZC2.8.3
O11	1527	Oecolampadius, J.	1	E.5.31
P6	1528	Paschasius, R.	1	ZC2.3.10
P29*	1543	Phrygio, P. C.	1	E.5.32
P36	1527	Pirckheimer, B.	1	ZC2.6.6

P45#	[c. 1545]	Postel, G.	1	ZC2.6.4
P53	1537	Primasius	1	D.1.8
P55^	1540	Prosper	1	A.6.42
S23	1538	Sarcerius, E.	2	ZC2.3.6
S26*?	1561	Sasbout, A.	1	E.6.39
S70	1570	Sonnius, F.	1	B.5.33
S72	1552	Soto, P. de	1	ZC2.8.7
S83	1558	Staphylus, F.	1	ZC2.4.12
S86	1566	Stapleton, T.	1	O.1.4
S91	1530	Strasbourg Church	1	ZC2.5.9
T1	1565	Tauler, J.	1	ZC2.6.8
T2*/***	1556	Tavernarius, J.	1	ZC2.6.3
T10*	1555	Titelman, F.	2	G.6.16
T15	1558	Titelman, F.	2	ZC2.8.2
T16A	1567	Torres, H.	1	A.6.5
T26	1554	Tunstall, C.	1	ZC2.3.2
U1	1564	Ulmer, J. C.	1	ZC2.3.13
V7	1535	Vehe, M.	1	ZC2.3.17
V25	1564	Villavicentio, L.	5	ZC2.4.10
W2	1554	Watson, T.	1	O.2.46
W48	1562	Bucer, M.	12	ZC2.5.7
W53	1537	Witzel, G.	3	ZC2.6.10
Z3	1553	Zegers, N.	1	E.6.30

Fore-edge titles

A5	1545	Aepinus, J.	4	D.5.6
A14	1504	Albertus M.	1	G.3.19
A18	1531	Alcuin	3	D.2.7
A20	1553	Alesius, A.	1	C.4.7
A25#	1517	Altensteig, J.	1	Y.3.32
A27	1536	Althamer, A.	1	D.6.12
A38	1532	Angelomus	5	N.3.18
A39	1523	Angelus, de Clavasio	1	L.5.33
A43	1543	Antiochus	1	C.2.13
A45*	1481	Aquinas, T.	1	L.3.9
A47	1512	Aquinas, T.	1	L.3.10
A48*	1551	Arboreus, J.	1	E.4.3
A49	1540	Arboreus, J.	1	M.1.17
A50	1570	Aretius, B.	4	ZC1.4.13
A54	1560	Arnobius	1	A.6.17
A55	1546	Artopoeus, P.	1	C.4.2
A56	1538	Artopoeus, P.	1	E.6.5
A59	1567	Athenagoras	4	A.6.20
A60?#	1542	Augustine	1	A.4.23-24
A61*	1542	Augustine	1	A.5.2
A62	1529	Augustine	4	A.6.32
B5	1497	Balbus, J.	1	Y.2.12
B7	1558	Basil	2	A.6.22
B11	1522	Bede	1	A.4.19
B12	1529	Bede	3	N.4.5
B14	1562	Benedictus, J.	1	E.3.4
B16	1564	Bernard	1	A.6.37
B26	1573	Bèze, T.	2	M.2.20
B29	1568	Bèze, T.	4	ZC2.1.8

B30	1528	Bible	1	E.5.18
B31	1532	Bible	1	G.6.10
B32	1529	Bible	1	G.6.11
B33	1529	Bible	1	G.6.13
B34	1526	Bible	1	G.6.12
B35	1526	Bible	1	G.6.14
B37	1552	Bible	1	G.6.7
B42	1550	Bibliander, T.	4	H.1.29
B44*	1565	Bibliotheca	1	L.2.10
B46	1510	Biel, G.	1	L.3.15
B47	1508	Biel, G.	1	L.3.16
B50	1545	Billick, E.	1	ZC2.7.2
B52?*	1539	Bonaventura	1	C.4.1
B53	1522	Bonaventura	1	H.1.38-40
B58*	1571	Borckensis, T.	6	G.6.6
B59	1555	Borrhaus, M.	2	G.4.10
B63	1572	Brandmueller, J.	1	G.6.1
B72	1536	Brentz, J.	1	C.6.1
B75	1529	Brentz, J.	1	C.6.2
B80	1558	Brentz, J.	1	G.5.16
B81	1558	Brentz, J.	2	G.6.4
B83	1542	Brentz, J.	1	C.6.3
B88	1548	Brentz, J.	1	C.6.4
B89	1544	Brentz, J.	5	C.6.5
B90	1552	Brentz, J.	1	M.2.25
B91	1544	Brentz, J.	1	H.2.7
B92	1556	Brentz, J.	5	K.2.11
B94	1544	Broeckwey, A.	1	D.4.8
B95*/***	1535	Brunfels, O.	1	G.4.18
B96	1547	Brunfels, O.	1	D.3.2
B106	[?1540]	Bucer, M.	4	L.5.15

B107	1543	Bucer, M.	1	H.1.5
B108	1546	Bucer, M.	3	I.4.4
B111	1525	Bugenhagen, J.	2	D.1.3
B114	1535	Bugenhagen, J.	1	C.2.11
B115	1546	Bugenhagen, J.	1	C.2.10
B117	1525	Bugenhagen, J.	1	C.4.8
B120?*	1561	Bullinger, H.	2	G.6.3
B127	1538	Bullinger, H.	1	H.1.20
B133	1551	Bullinger, H.	2	I.4.11
B138	1567	Byzantine History	1	Z.2.19
C1*	1517	Cagnazzo, J.	1	N.5.26
C4	1564	Calvin, J.	1	D.1.9
C7*	1565	Calvin, J.	1	G.5.5
C11	1546	Calvin, J.	3	ZC1.4.7
C16	1559	Calvin, J.	1	N.2.9
C32	1571	Canisius, P.	1	C.2.4
C36	1570	Canisius, P.	1	K.2.13-14
C37	1528	Capito, W.	2	D.4.3
C38	1539	Capito, W.	1	M.2.3
C43	1571	Carolinus, P.	2	H.1.7
C44	1545	Carvialus, L.	4	K.2.26
C49	1507	Castellensis, H.	1	H.1.21
C57	1560	Charlemagne	3	M.2.21
C59	1566	Chemnitz, M.	1	C.7.1
C60	1566	Chemnitz, M.	1	C.7.2
C70	1556	Chytraeus, D.	3	D.6.2
C74	1541	Cicero, M. T.	1	X.2.16
C79	1568	Clement I	1	B.6.5
C82	1524	Clichtoveus, J.	1	N.3.17
C83	1538	Clichtoveus, J.	2	K.3.13
C97*?/***	1538	Cologne. Canones	2	B.3.21

C98	1544	Cologne. Canones	1	B.6.4
C101+	1574	Corr, A.de	1	E.6.34
C102	1539	Corvinus, A.	1	A.6.31
C110	1567	Councils -Trent	2	ZC2.2.10
C113	1546	Cruciger, C.	1	E.6.28
C114	1546	Cruciger, C.	1	D.4.4
C115	1567	Cruciger, C.	2	D.4.5
C120	1548	Culman, L.	1	M.2.29
C122	1550	Culman, L.	1	M.2.36
C122	1550	Culman, L.	1	M.2.37
C122	1550	Culman, L.	1	M.2.38
C125	1514	Cusa, N. de	1	L.4.7
C127	1521	Cyprian	1	A.4.21
D1	1566	Dalmada, E.	1	ZC2.3.4
D6	1545	Dietrich, V.	1	G.5.4
D10	1548	Dionysius	1	E.3.16
D11	1552	Dionysius	2	E.3.17
D12	1542	Dionysius	2	E.3.19
D14	1548	Dionysius	2	E.3.18
D17	1543	Dionysius	1	E.3.20
D18	1545	Dionysius	2	E.3.21
D20*?	[c. 1534]	Dionysius	5	ZC2.1.9
D21*?	1540	Dionysius	1	N.4.2
D23	1543	Draconites, J.	3	D.5.5
D26	1534	Driedo, J.	2	N.5.5
D27	1547	Driedo, J.	1	L.3.19
D28*^	1533	Driedo, J.	1	L.2.13
D29	1565	Du Moulin, C.	1	C.2.14
D31	1569	Du Préau, G.	3	L.4.6
D33	1481	Duns, J.	1	L.4.25
D34	1520	Duns, J.	1	L.4.32

D35	1518	Duns, J.	1	L.4.18
D36	1518	Durandus, G.	1.	L.5.13
E3	1536	Eck, J.	1	G.5.18
E8	1567	Eck, J.	5	ZC2.8.5
E9	1568	Eder, G.	2	G.3.18
E10	1573	Eisengrein, M.	1	D.4.9
E13	1569	Eisengrein, M.	4	B.6.42
E18	1537	Elias	1	F.2.19
E22	[c. 1517]	Erasmus, D.	5	L.5.35
E27	1522	Erasmus, D.	1	G.2.6
E28	1523	Erasmus, D.	1	G.5.20
E30	1524	Erasmus, D.	4	N.6.3
E31	1522	Erasmus, D.	1	N.6.1
E33	1532	Erasmus, D.	2	I.3.8
E34	1526	Erasmus, D.	3	L.6.5
E38	1530	Erasmus, D.	6	ZC1.4.6
E41	1532	Erasmus, D.	1	ZC2.2.3
E48	1527	Erasmus, D.	1	H.1.2
E52*	1567	Espence, C. d'	1	D.5.9
E54*	1558	Estienne, R.	1	F.2.24
E55	1541	Eucherius	2	E.4.1
E58*?	1558	Euthymius	1	C.4.13
E59	1556	Euthymius	1	A.6.25
F6#	1482	Ficino, M.	1	Y.3.25
F10	1566	Flacius, M.	2	ZC2.1.4
F13	1567	Flacius, M.	1	G.4.9
F18	1567	Flacius, M.	4	ZC2.2.4
F22	1567	Flacius, M.	1	K.2.17
F23	1566	Flacius, M.	2	I.4.6
F28	1560	Fontaine, S.	4	D.6.1
F30*	1503	Foresti, J. P.	1	Z.2.25

F34	1557	Francisco	1	H.1.4
G1	1559	Gagny, J. de	1	C.3.10
G23	1525	Georgius, F.	1	L.3.21
G25*?	1494	Gerson, J.	1	L.3.14
G29	1546	Goeuschel, J.	1	F.2.10
G30	1519	Gratian	1	H.2.54
G31	1523	Gregory I	1	A.1.15
G33	1567	Gregory, *of Nazianzus*	1	A.6.11
G34	1562	Gregory, *of Nyssa*	2	A.4.20
G39	1572	Gualtherus, R.	1	G.3.17
G40	1572	Gualtherus, R.	1	G.4.16
G44	1550	Guilliaud, C.	2	C.3.1
G46*?	1516	Gulielmus, *Avernus*	1	L.4.22
G49*	1478	Gulielmus, *Parisiensis*	1	L.5.10
H1	1561	Hall, Suabian	5	ZC2.2.7
H2	1568	Hamelmann, H.	4	M.1.28
H9	1533	Haymo, *of Halberstadt*	1	D.5.13
H10	1531	Haymo, *of Halberstadt*	1	C.4.9
H13	1525	Hegendorff, C.	1	D.5.7
H18	1556	Helmes, H.	1	C.3.2
H19	1556	Helmes, H.	1	C.3.3
H20	1556	Helmes, H.	1	C.3.4
H21	1556	Helmes, H.	1	C.3.5
H22	1556	Helmes, H.	1	C.3.6
H24	[*c.* 1562]	Hemmingsen, N.	2	D.6.10
H25	[*c.* 1564]	Hemmingsen, N.	3	C.4.10
H26	1564	Hemmingsen, N.	3	C.5.13
H35	1563	Hemmingsen, N.	2	ZC2.7.7
H37*?	1571	Hemmingsen, N.	6	ZC2.7.5
H38*	1562	Hemmingsen, N.	4	ZC2.7.6
H40	1522	Henry VIII	2	N.5.13

H41	1504	Heracleides	I	A.5.7
H42	[1548]	Hermann	I	O.1.25
H47	1573	Heshusius, T.	2	D.4.6
H48	1561	Heshusius, T.	4	ZC2.2.8
H56*?	1571	Hessiander, C.	I	ZC2.3.1
H62	1555	Hofmeister, J.	2	G.5.15
H65	1545	Hofmeister, J.	I	D.1.3
H71	1489	Holkot, R.	I	L.2.18
H72^	1510	Holkot, R.	I	L.5.9
H73*?	1571	Holthusius, J.	4	K.3.31
H76	1565	Horantius, F.	I	K.2.18
H82	[1498–1502]	Hugo, *de Sancto Charo*	I	L.2.1
H83	[1506]	Hugo, *de Sancto Charo*	I	D.1.2
H84*	1531	Hugo, *de Sancto Charo*	I	G.2.5
H85*	[1526]	Hugo, *de Sancto Victore*	I	L.1.8
H86*	1526	Hugo, *de Sancto Victore*	I	L.1.9
H88	1506	Hugo, *de Sancto Victore*	3	L.2.15
H91	1566	Hunnaeus, A.	2	Z.4.23
H96	1559	Hyperius, A. G.	3	N.6.16
H98	1570	Hyperius, A. G.	6	ZC2.1.6
I1	[*c.* 1544]	Imler, C.	I	D.3.6
I5+	1570	Irenaeus	2	A.4.8
I6	1531	Isidore, *of Seville*	5	I.4.10
J1	1496	Jacobus, *de Voragine*	I	L.4.17
J2	1528	Jacobus, *de Voragine*	I	D.4.10
J4*	1569	Jansen, C.	I	E.5.4
J6	1515	Jerome	I	L.4.31
J9	1533	Joannes, *a Davantria*	I	H.1.31
J11	1510	Joannes, *de Colonia*	I	L.5.40
J12	1546	John, *of Damascus*	2	N.3.13
J13	1512	John, *of Damascus*	I	L.4.5

J14	1535	Jonas, J.	4	D.2.6
J15	1567	Jonathan, *ben Uzziel*	2	D.6.5
L4	1525	Lambert, F.	2	C.5.6
L5	1539	Lambert, F.	1	C.5.7
L6	1538	Lambert, F.	3	C.5.4
L7	1525	Lambert, F.	2	H.1.6
L10	1552	Lasco, J. à.	1	H.2.11
L18	1537	Latomus, J.	2	H.2.12
L20	1562	Lavater, L.	1	G.5.1
L21	1571	Lavater, L.	2	E.3.5
L22	1522	Le Fèvre, J.	1	G.4.6
L23	1515	Le Fèvre, J.	1	G.4.7
L25	1518	Le Fèvre, J.	2	L.5.36
L30	1570	Lindanus, W.	1	I.8.3
L38	1536	Lorich, G.	1	M.2.11
L43	1552	Loss, L.	1	D.3.3
L47	1568	Lucifer	2	A.6.26
L48	1536	Ludolf	1	L.6.7
L49	1543	Luther, M.	1	L.6.30
L50	1553	Luther, M.	1	C.4.3
L52	1525	Luther, M.	1	D.2.2
L55	1539	Luther, M.	1	E.6.27
L57	1536	Luther, M.	2	D.5.3
L60	1545	Luther, M.	1	D.5.1
L63*	1538	Luther, M.	2	D.5.4
L64	1533	Luther, M.	1	C.2.3
L67	1538	Luther, M.	2	E.6.29
L70	1556	Luther, M.	5	ZC1.4.10
L78	[c. 1523]	Luther, M.	1	ZC2.7.11
L80*?	1523	Lutzenburgo, B. de	1	H.2.10
L82	1556	Lycosthenes, C.	1	M.2.43

M7	1550	Mainz	1	B.5.16
M10	1545	Marius, A.	5	ZC2.3.12
M14	1540	Marulić, M.	1	N.6.4
M16	1531	Matthei, L.	1	D.3.8
M18	1566	Maulbrunn. Colloquy	2	I.4.5
M19	1557	Maximus	1	Y.5.19
M20	1546	Mayer, S.	3	D.2.8
M23	1524	Mazzolini, S.	1	D.3.14
M27*	1559	Meier, G.	1	E.6.25
M32	1560	Meier, G.	1	C.6.12
M35	1564	Meier, G.	2	D.6.4
M41	1550	Meier, G.	2	ZC2.8.10
M43	1562	Melanchthon, P.	1	L.2.3
M48	1544	Melanchthon, P.	3	C.5.8
M49	1531	Melanchthon, P.	2	D.6.3
M51*?	[c. 1545]	Melanchthon, P.	2	C.5.11
M52	1541	Melanchthon, P.	1	C.5.9
M53	1545	Melanchthon, P.	2	C.5.10
M64*?	1561	Melanchthon, P.	3	L.5.19
M74	1566	Metz	7	ZC1.4.8
M77	1574	Mollerus, H.	1	G.5.6
M83	1557	Münster, S.	1	F.2.8
M85	1542	Münster, S.	1	F.2.29
M86	1528	Murner, T.	3	I.3.10
N5	1503	Nannus Mirabellius, D.	1	L.2.14
N6	1553	Nardus, J. L.	1	N.6.9
N7	1544	Nausea, F.	1	N.6.6
N8*?	1540	Nausea, F.	1	N.3.16
N13	1567	Nowell, A.	2	T.6.4
O3	1532	Oecolampadius, J.	2	C.1.2
O4	1544	Oecolampadius, J.	1	C.1.4

O5	1544	Oecolampadius, J.	1	D.2.1
O6*?	1525	Oecolampadius, J.	1	C.1.10
O7	1533	Oecolampadius, J.	1	G.5.2
O8	1534	Oecolampadius, J.	1	C.1.9
O10	1535	Oecolampadius, J.	4	C.1.5
O12	c.1524	Oecolampadius, J.	2	C.1.3
O13	1526	Oecolampadius, J.	3	C.1.6
O17	1552	Oecumenius	1	D.5.8
O18	[1552 or 1555]	Oecumenius	1	C.4.12
O19	[c. 1497]	Orbellis, N. de. Rouen	1	L.6.3
O20	1519	Origen	1	A.4.1-2
O21	[c. 1527]	Origen	1	ZC2.4.16
O22	1564	Orosius, P.	3	B.6.16
O25	1572	Osorio da Fonseca, J.	1	I.2.10
O26*?	1569	Osorio da Fonseca, J.	4	M.2.40
P2	1555	Palladius	1	B.5.3
P3	1559	Pantaleon, H.	3	B.3.19
P8	1567	Patrizi, F.	1	ZC1.5.4
P9	1560	Paulinus, *of Nola*	3	A.6.21
P10	1567	Paulli, S.	1	G.6.5
P13	[c. 1507]	Paulus, *de Sancta Maria*	1	L.4.34
P14	1514	Pavinis, J. F. de	2	L.5.37
P15	1521	Pelbárt, O.	1	M.1.27
P16	1539	Pellicanus, C.	2	E.3.6
P17#/*?	1487	Peraldus, G.	1	L.5.31
P18	1515	Pérez de Valentia, J.	1	G.3.16
P19	1549	Perionius, J.	1	ZC2.7.3
P20	1503	Petrus, *Comestor*	1	L.4.10
P21	1555	Petrus, *Diaconus*	2	A.6.28
P22	1513	Petrus, *Lombardus*	1	L.3.7
P23#	1495	Petrus, *Lombardus*	1	L.5.38

P25?^	1497	Philippus, J. *de Bergamo*	1	L.5.1
P28*?	1537	Philo, *of Carpasia*	1	C.5.3
P32	1549	Pighius, A.	1	M.2.6
P33	1542	Pighius, A.	1	N.4.6
P34	1570	Pinto, H.	1	E.5.1
P38	1559	Placidus, *Parmensis*	1	E.5.8
P58	1534	Puteo, F. de.	1	E.3.12
R1	1532	Rabanus M.	1	C.5.1
R2	1532	Rabanus M.	1	C.5.2
R3	1554	Rabus, L.	2	B.6.10
R4	1561	Rabus, L.	1	D.6.11
R5	1564	Radulphus, *Ardens*	1	D.4.1
R6	1565	Rastall, J.	1	O.2.41
R7*	1566	Rastall, J.	1	O.2.45
R10	1568	Ravestyn, J.	5	I.1.6
R11	1567	Ravestyn, J.	5	I.1.6
R12	1541	Ravisius, J.	1	X.2.17-18
R13*	1516	Raymond	1	K.3.46
R15	1557	Resende, L. A. de	1	ZC2.2.2
R23	1545	Rhegius, U.	4	H.1.8
R26	1510	Richard, *St Victor*	2	I.4.9
R32	1550	Rivius, J.	2	H.1.37
R33	1550	Rivius, J.	2	L.6.16
R34	1542	Rivius, J.	6	D.6.7
R38	1567	Rostock. Academia	1	H.1.9
R39	1550	Royard, T.	1	E.4.2
S2	1532	Sachs, H.	1	ZC2.7.9
S7*?	1567	Sainctes, C. de	3	N.6.12
S12	1543	Sarcerius, E.	1	C.6.7-8
S13	1539	Sarcerius, E.	1	D.2.3
S14	[?1540]	Sarcerius, E.	1	G.5.14

S15	1538	Sarcerius, E.	1	C.6.9
S17	1541	Sarcerius, E.	1	C.6.10
S18	1540	Sarcerius, E.	1	D.2.5
S19	1540	Sarcerius, E.	1	D.2.4
S20	1541	Sarcerius, E.	1	C.6.11
S21	1544	Sarcerius, E.	1	D.6.8
S22	1544	Sarcerius, E.	1	D.6.9
S24	1546	Sarcerius, E.	1	ZC2.2.5
S25	1539	Sarcerius, E.	1	ZC2.1.5
S28	1567	Sascerides, J.	4	N.6.11
S31	1525	Schatzger, C.	4	ZC2.1.1
S39	1561	Schopper, J.	1	D.3.9-11
S41	1565	Selneccer, N.	5	ZC2.1.7
S42	1569	Selneccer, N.	1	G.4.5
S43	1567	Selneccer, N.	1	D.4.7
S44	1567	Selneccer, N.	2	G.6.2
S45	1515	Seneca	1	Y.2.16
S49	1567	Seripando, G.	1	ZC1.4.2
S50	1572	Serranus, P.	2	G.2.4
S52	1570	Serres, J. de.	1	ZC1.5.21
S53	1562	Sextus, *Empiricus*	1	ZC1.5.19
S59	1557	Sleidanus, J.	1	B.6.1
S60	1570	Slotanus, J.	6	L.5.8
S61	1558	Slotanus, J.	1	ZC1.4.9
S62	1536	Smaragdus	2	E.4.6
S64	1546	Smith, R.	1	R.6.46
S67	1569	Snepffius, T.	2	I.7.7
S73	1566	Soto, P. de	1	H.1.3
S75	1547	Spangenberg, J.	1	D.3.4
S76	1548	Spangenberg, J.	1	D.3.5
S80	1544	Spangenberg, J.	4	ZC2.2.9

S94*	1522	Stunica, J. L.	1	L.4.12
S96	1537	Suetonius	1	Y.5.29
T4	1567	Theodoret	1	A.4.11-12
T5	1564	Theodoret	1	A.6.3
T7	1520	Theodoret	1	A.5.3
T11	1548	Titelman, F.	1	C.5.15
T16	1568	Torres, H.	4	D.1.4
T24+	1565	Trotzendorf, V. F.	2	K.3.45
U2	1568	Usuardus	2	B.6.19
V2	1567	Valerius, C.	2	Z.5.108
V3	1526	Valla, L.	1	C.4.6
V5	1563	Vannius, V.	1	I.4.2
V15#	1551	Vermigli, P. M.	1	C.2.2
V16	1552	Vermigli, P. M.	2	N.6.8
V17	1559	Vermigli, P. M.	1	N.6.7
V22	1570	Via, J. À	3	ZC2.1.3
V24	1566	Vigne, P. Della	1	Z.5.109
V26	1494	Vincent	1	L.1.15
V29	1539	Vio, T. de	1	G.2.17
V30	1558	Vio, T. de	1	D.5.11
V31	1558	Vio, T. de	1	D.5.12
V33	1527	Vio, T. de	1	K.3.42
V36	1559	Viret, P.	3	N.3.12
V37	1505	Vivaldus, J. L.	1	L.6.1
V38*	1555	Vives, J. L.	1	Z.5.121
V39	1544	Vives, J. L.	1	N.6.5
W1	1568	Confessio Waldensium	4	K.2.16
W4	1561	Weller, H.	4	D.6.6
W8	1561	Westhemerus, B.	1	C.1.13
W16	1574	Whitgift, J.	1	T.3.8
W18	1566	Wigand, J.	2	C.4.4

W19	1566	Wigand, J.	3	E.6.9
W20	1576	Wigand, J.	2	C.4.5
W23	1566	Wigand, J.	3	K.2.15
W27	1565	Wild, J.	1	D.5.10
W30	1550	Wild, J.	2	D.1.12
W32	1559	Wild, J.	1	D.2.11
W37	1555	Wild, J.	1	G.5.10
W37	1558	Wild, J.	1	G.5.11
W39	1562	Wild, J.	1	G.5.12
W49	1553	Witzel, G.	1	E.4.4
W50	1533	Witzel, G.	5	I.7.6
Z2	1566	Zanchius, H.	3	I.5.5
Z6	[?1525]	Zwingli, H.	1	N.6.13
Z7	1535	Zwingli, H.	1	L.6.14

APPENDIX VIII

Binding notes and instructions

Abbreviations

B	Bind this with other items as indicated.
CB	Calf over boards ('bordes').
CP	Calf over pasteboard ('in past').
D	Now disbound, the former or original covers now missing.
NC	'sewn not [?cut]'.
O	Order of items indicated.
PM	Parchment covers ('in parchment')
PM^	Now in calf covers, though binding instructions reads, 'in parchment'.
S	Instruction to search for a particular book.
U	'uncutt'.
+	Trace only. Uncertain as to whether this was part of a binding instruction or another form of annotation.
†	Pre-Geste ownership inscription.
‡	Pre-Geste MS annotations, book-price or book-title(s) on fore-edge or spine.
*	Trace only (cropped at foot of page) and no longer fully readable.
**	Some doubt about whether the instruction is in Geste's hand.

The date given below is that of the latest imprint in a composite volume (which may not be the same as the date of the item in which the binding instruction occurs) on the grounds that the book cannot have been bound *before* the date of the latest item.

The reference codes under '*Binding type*' below are to the different binding types and tools included in Appendix IV above.

Calf over pasteboard

Date of latest imprint	Binding type	Binding instruction	Format	Cat. no. of first item	Shelf-mark	Binder
Panel bindings						
1539	HM11/12	CP	8°	L57	D.5.3	London ['M D']
Roll bindings						
1534‡	HM.h(28)	O	8°	O13	C.1.6(a–c)	Cambridge (?Spierinck)
1535†	D1.h(3)	*	8°	O10	C.1.5(a–b)	Cambridge (Godfrey)
1536	HE.b(2)	*	8°	A27	D.6.12	Cambridge (Godfrey)
1536	HM.h(28)	O	8°	J14	D.2.6(a–b)	Cambridge (?Spierinck)
1538?†	HM.h(29) & CT q	CP	8°	L6	C.5.4(f)	Cambridge (?Spierinck)
1541	HM.h(29) & CT zz	?PM^	8°	C74	X.2.16	Cambridge (?Spierinck)
1541	HM.h(29) & CT c.1	*	8°	S20	C.6.11	Cambridge (?Spierinck)
1542	HM.h(29) & CT c.1	O*	8°	B83	C.6.3	Cambridge (?Spierinck)
1544	HM.h(29) & CT c.1	*	8°	S22	D.6.9	Cambridge (?Spierinck)
1566	MW.c(1)	CP	8°	F23	I.4.6(a)	London
1567	HM.h(10)	CB	fol.	B138	Z.2.19	London ('R B')
1569	?HM	?*	4°	S67	I.7.7(a)	?London
1571	MW.c(1) & HE.b(5)	U/PM ['Uncutt in parcheme[n]t']	fol.	L21	E.3.5(a)	London ('R B')

Date of latest imprint	Binding type	Binding instruction	Format	Cat. no. of first item	Shelf-mark
Centre- or small-tools					
1567	CT a	B/O* '... with yᵉ postill/ bound all ready'	8°	S28	N.6.11
1568	CT a	O	8°	F28	D.6.1(a,c)
1569	CT a	O	8°	O26	M.2.40(a–d)
1570	CT a	O	16°	A50	ZC1.4.13(b)
1570	CT a	O/?CP 'fouer of fyve of thees in [?past]'†	8°	H98	ZC2.1.6 (a–f)
1570	CT a	O	8°	W22	N.6.10(a–c)
1570	CT a	O 'This should be bound last' [in fact the item is bound first]	4°	L30	I.8.3(a)
1570	CT a	O	8°	V22	ZC2.1.3(a–b)
1550	CT b	*	8°	G44	C.3.1(a)
1555	CT b	?*	4°	P2	B.5.3
1565	CT b	NC '[?]it ... sewn not [?cut]'	8°	M35	D.6.4(a)
1565	CT b	CP	8°	S41	ZC2.1.7(a)
1566	CT b	CP	4°	M18	I.4.5(a)
1566	CT b	CP	8°	W23	K.2.15(a)
1566	CT b	CP	8°	F10	ZC2.1.4(a)
1566	CT b	CP	8°	W18	C.4.4(a)
1567	CT b	CP*	8°	C115	D.4.5(a)
1567	CT b	CP	8°	F18	ZC2.2.4(a)
1567	CT b	CP	8°	F22	K.2.17
1567	CT b	CP*	8°	G33	A.6.11

1567	CT b	CP		8°	H53	I.1.5(e)
1567	CT b	CP		8°	J15	D.6.5
1567	CT b	PM '[in] p[ar]chme[n]t' (but actually bound in calf over pasteboard)		8°	R38	H.1.9
1567	CT b	CP		8°	S44	G.6.2(a)
1567	CT b	CP		8°	S49	ZC1.4.2
1569	CT b	B 'Joyne Caitane de sacrificio missae [V32] w[i]t[h] this [P44] & R[a]uast[yn]' [R10]		8°	R10	I.1.6(c)
1532	CT c.1	CP*		4°	E45	I.3.8(b)
1534	CT c.1	*		8°	E24	ZC1.4.6 (c–d)
1548	CT c.1	B*		8°	C11	ZC1.4.7(a)
1573	CT e	+		8°	M76	D.1.7
1565	CT h.1	O		8°	H25	C.4.10(b–c)
1561	CT v	O / CP D.3.9: 'This & ye second together/ in past', and at foot of tp in D.3.11: 'This & ye fourt[h] in past together'		8°	S39	D.3.9,11
1563	CT v	CP / B 'Thies in past al'		8°	H38	ZC2.7.6(a)
1560	CT bb.1	CP		8°	E58	C.4.13
1564	CT bb.1	PM^ / B*		8°	O22	B.6.16(a,c)
1544	CT ee	B 'This with the book agai[n]st the Anabaptistes', though the item is not included		8°	O4	C.1.4
1544	CT ee	B*		8°	S80	ZC2.2.9(a)
1571	CT ff.1	CP '...[?] in past by vt se[lf] ...'		8°	W28	D.2.10

Plain calf – a

1540	–	PM^ 'in p[ar]cham[en]t' (though the book is actually in calf)	8°	M14	N.6.4
1550	–	CP/?O*	8°	B42	H.1.29(a–d)
1551	–	CP*	4°	B133	I.4.11
1561	–	B 'This to be bound with Sanctiones Eccl[esiastic]e' [J17]	fol.	A44	B.3.9
1563	–	CP/B '[Th]is w[i]th Hemmyng in past' [on C51]	8°	H35	ZC2.7.7(a–b)

Plain calf – b

1543	–	CP*	8°	D23	D.5.5

Parchment covers

Items originally in parchment covers but now rebound will be found listed below, under 'Rebound'.

1543	–	B 'In exodum [?C]om[m]e[n]tarius' (though this item is not included)	4°	P29	E.5.32
1551	–	U 'by it selve uncut'	8°	M67	ZC2.6.16
1552	–	?PM/?O	8°	B41	E.6.23
1558‡	–	PM//O*	8°	C76	X.2.30(a)
1560	–	*?	8°	H68	ZC2.5.8(a)
1561	–	PM 'A B [?] do you do in p[ar]ch[ment]'	8°	H44	E.6.36(b)

1561	–	PM/ U/B (a) 'in p[ar]cheme[n]t uncutt'; (b) 'this w[i]t[h] his other book de Vi[?]rib[us] et hu[?]morius et [?]seu[n]sto in p[ar]chme[n]t'	8°	H2A	ZC2.4.9(a–b)
1562	–	PM	8°	L81	E.6.31(a–b)
1562	–	PM 'C in p[archmen]t' in all three items (a–c)	8°	M45	K.1.7(a–c)
1563	–	PM '[?]parvys in p[a]rchment'	8°	D22	ZC2.5.5
1563	–	PM /B 'W[i]t[h] the comme[n]tarye on Tim[...] in p[ar]chment'	8°	M33	G.6.24(a)
1564	–	PM /B 'Cu[m] theodoreto de p[ro]videntia in p[a]rchme[n]t'	8°	F3	ZC2.5.3
1564	–	O	8°	M69	ZC2.4.14(b,d)
1564	–	PM 'In p[arch]ment by it selue'	8°	H45	ZC2.4.13
1565	–	⋆	4°	A2	ZC2.3.8
1565	–	?PM/O	8°	H90	ZC2.5.2(a–c)
1565	–	PM 'in p[ar]chme[n]t not cutt but smothed'	4°	L19	G.5.26
1565	–	PM	8°	M28	G.6.19
1565	–	?PM	4°	N2	E.5.28(a)
1565	–	O**	8°	T24	K.3.45(a–b)
1565	–	O*	8°	V25	ZC2.4.10(a)
1566	–	PM/U/B 'in p[ar]cheme[n]t uncutt'	8°	M79	ZC2.4.9(a–b)
1567	–	⋆?	8°	M72	ZC2.6.11
1568	–	PM	8°	S79	ZC2.5.10(a)
1573	–	O?	8°	P35	ZC2.4.7

Now covered in a leaf of MS					
1546	–	O 'b' on tp, though no other item is extant	8°	S77	G.6.23

Rebound

1541	–	CP/B 'bynde this w[i]t[h] hemingis galatians in past' (though this item has now been rebound as a separate item [H26 C.5.13(a)]	8°	M52	C.5.9
1544	–	⋆	8°	D24	C.5.8(c)
1545	–	⋆?	8°	⋆R4	H.1.30
[c. 1545]	–	B 'bind w[i]t[h] Melancth … postill'	8°	B116	C.5.11(b)
[c. 1550]	–	CP	8°	R33	L.6.16(a)
1553	–	PM	16°	P57	A.6.35
1554	–	⋆	fol.	M89	G.3.11
1554	–	PM/⋆	4°	S9	C.2.9(a)
1557	–	O	fol.	B59	G.4.10(a–b)
1560	–	CP/B	8°	P9	A.6.21(a–c)
1562	–	PM/U '[?in] p[archment] vncutt'	fol.	F11	L.4.4
1562	–	PM 'C in p[ar]chment'	8°	H4	L.6.24(a–b)
1562	–	PM/U 'vncutt in p[ar]chme[n]t'	fol.	H63	G.4.2
1562	–	PM/U 'vncutt in parchment'	fol.	L42	G.2.16
1562	–	PM/CP/B 'w[i]t[h] this booke in p[ar]chment [with ?other] Melanth[on] in past' [erased]	8°	M58	L.6.19

1562	–	PM 'C in p[a]rchme[n]t'	8°	M68	L.6.25
1562	–	PM 'C in p[a]rchme[n]t'	8°	W24	L.6.26(a–b)
1563	–	CP/B★ (a) '[Chytrae]us in apocalypsis'; (b) 'w[i]th Heminge[...] ad Romanos in past'	8°	H24	D.6.10(a–b)
1563	–	S★ 'look for op[er]a Ni[?][co]l[a]i in [?]Gr [or Cor] ioyned w[i]th this'	8°	E19	A.6.41
1563	–	S 'Inquire for Hessels ...'	8°	H55	L.6.15
1563	–	B 'With Ephraem and Markus'	8°	K1	K.3.44
1564	–	★?	fol.	L1	A.4.25(a)
1564	–	B 'Procopius & Boraus upo[n] Job together'	fol.	P54	G.4.8(a)
1566	–	+	fol.	B82	G.3.7(b)
1566	–	O 'this w[i]t[h] [th]e other fold in Last'	8°	C41	B.6.18(b)
1566	–	+	fol.	C78	A.5.4(a)
1566	–	B 'This to be ioyned in the end to peter martyrs book'	fol.	V13	G.3.15(b)
1566	–	CP/B/U/PM 'This w[i]t[h] yᵉ other in past./Uncut in p[a]rchment' (a); '[...?] have these bound w[i]t[h] Wigandes postill' (c)	8°	W19	E.6.9(a,c)
1566	–	★	4°	H23	I.3.9(a)
1567	–	PM	8°	A59	A.6.20
1567	–	CP	16°/12°	C35	ZC2.8.5(b)

1567	–	CB 'In pa[st] bordes'	fol.	T9	G.3.9(a)
1569	–	O	8°	M21	E.6.26(a–e)
1569	–	O	8°	C27	L.6.27
1569	–	O	8°	E13	B.6.42(a–d)
1569	–	O	8°	B1	ZC2.1.10(a–b), ZC2.1.12
1570	–	O	4°	B106	L.5.15(a,b,d)
1570	–	O	4°	S60	L.5.8(a–e)
1570	–	O	fol.	T17	G.4.1(b,c)
1570	–	O	8°	M61	L.6.21
1574	–	CP	8°	H39	K.3.41(a)

APPENDIX IX

Pastedowns, flyleaves, MS strips, compacted leaves
of MS or printer's waste in pasteboard, and
MS waste as wrappers or end-leaf guards

The list of identifications which follows is far from exhaustive, particularly in the case of MS strips and fragments from printed books, and this appendix makes no claim to be other than a pilot study. Images of the fragments listed here are to be mounted on the Society's web-pages in the hope that these may be of interest to others working in the field and in the expectation that further identifications may be reported to the author for inclusion on the web pages.

The fragments are arranged under binding types, beginning with examples of Geste's panel and roll bindings and concluding with disbound and rebound items, and, within each category, listed in chronological order by imprint date, or, in the very few instances where this is known, the year of acquisition [in square brackets]. In the case of multi-item volumes, the date given is that of the latest item.

Two hundred and eighty-seven of Geste's books (a little over forty per cent of the total that survive) retain leaves and fragments from MSS and printed books, functioning as pastedowns, flyleaves, end-leaf guards and even wrappers (in the absence of calf or parchment covers), or as part of the pasteboard itself, in the case of calf bindings, where unstuck pastedowns have exposed them. Eleven of these books retain such fragments even after rebinding. An additional ten items are included here from Appendix I, which lists books which may just possibly have belonged to him, though now lacking conclusive evidence of his ownership.

Seventy-one books contain more than one such fragment, two having as many as three different items: a MS strip and flyleaves from two printed books in the case of one (PDN 127), and pastedowns from two different MSS as well as leaves from a printed book visible in the pasteboard in the case of the other (PDN 140). 123 books, all but three (PDN 222, 223, 229) with imprints dating from before or during his time in Cambridge (where discarded MSS were evidently plentiful for this purpose), retain full leaves as pastedowns or as flyleaves from as many as 136 different MSS, while 104 of his books, mostly dating from the period after Geste had left Cambridge, use MS strips as strengtheners, and a further 33 strips are either blank or so narrow as to contain only a line or two of text, making identification of the original all but impossible.

Preliminary identifications of these MS fragments have been contributed by Dr Christopher de Hamel. It is perhaps too much to hope that any of these can one day be linked with particular MSS discarded by Cambridge libraries at the time, especially where early catalogues of these libraries are extant.

Nearly all the MSS which have been identified are of English origin, but there is one from France, used in two of his books (PDN 184 and 185), a further fourteen possibly or probably French, three from Italy (all legal, PDN 140, 141 and 179), and another three which may be Italian, and one from the Netherlands (PDN 252).

Perhaps predictably, many of the MSS used were from works of scholastic theology, law (especially canon law) and liturgy, discarded for ideological reasons or replaced by more recent printed editions. In date, the MSS range from the eleventh century to the fifteenth, and include a few probably pre-Conquest items, all of English origin, such as an Augustine used in two books (PDN 47 and 48), Bede's Homilies (PDN 57), a MS of Prayers (PDN 80), a MS of *Canones evangeliorum* (PDN 105) and, only slightly later, a Josephus (PDN 33) in one of three books presented to Geste in 1551 by his brother-in-law Christopher Leedes. Among the more unusual or rare MSS are a fourteenth-century MS of verses to the Virgin in Anglo-Norman (PDN 17), Hugh of St-Victor's *De laude caritatis* (PDN 38) from the twelfth or thirteenth, and four from the fourteenth/fifteenth: Geoffrey of Monmouth's *Historia regum Britanniae* (PDN 28), a French MS of *Grandes Chroniques de France* used in two books (PDN 184 and 185), a rare Wyclif item (PDN 232), and an obit book from the dissolved abbey of Hyde, or New Minster, Winchester, as it was originally called, (PDN 156). This last – three strips of MS amounting to little more than fifteen lines of text – was used as strengtheners in an anti-Lutheran work by the Ministers of Zürich published there in 1575 and acquired by Geste at the very end of his life while bishop of Salisbury. It describes building work undertaken at Hyde under Salidus (or Selid), abbot 1151–71, mentioning the addition of a third storey to the abbey church and two-storey aisles to the south and north, and on the verso listing its works of art, including gold and silver and vestments, in some detail. Other notable items – all strips of MS used as strengtheners – include fragments from an English or possibly French s. xii/xiii MS of the *De consideratione* by Bernard of Clairvaux (PDN 278), a s. xiii² English MS of a text in Anglo-Norman (PDN 279), and the *Polycraticus* of John of Salisbury in a s. xiv/xv English MS.

Finally, fragments of printed waste figure in 86 of Geste's books, some containing more than one item. Few of these have been successfully identified, though it is clear that books of continental printing predominate. Of the English printings, these range from leaves of the 1483 Caxton edition of John Gower's *Confessio amantis* (PDN 82B), to three openings from the 1567 or 1568 edition of Gildas, *Epistola* (PDN 72). Other noteworthy fragments come from English works by Thomas Becon (PDN 247) and Richard Taverner (PDN 6), and, from continental printings of the 1550s and 1560s, items by Calvin (PDN 175, 236 and 238) and Bucer (PDN 173 and 292).

Abbreviations

BL	Leaves from an English printed book in black-letter.
Eng	Leaf or leaves from a MS of English origin.
Fr	Leaf or leaves from a MS of French origin.
Ital	Leaf of leaves from a MS of Italian origin.
MS	Leaves or leaf from a MS in parchment or paper.
MS(G)	Flyleaves from a MS in Geste's hand.
MS+	Strip of parchment to strengthen spine and/or binding structure.
MS*	Pastedown or flyleaves now kept separately.
MS**	Leaves or leaf from blank parchment or paper.
Neth	Leaf or leaves from a MS from the Netherlands.
Pb	Leaves or leaf from a printed book.
Pb+	Strip of paper from a printed book.
PDN	Image no. of pastedown, flyleaf or MS strip (see the database at www.bibsoc.org.uk/Geste).
$	Compacted leaf/leaves as part of pasteboard.
$$	Flyleaves.
+**	Strip of blank parchment or paper to strengthen spine and/or binding structure.
++	Stub/strip from fold-over of same MS/Pb.
£	Pastedown or MS+ now covered over by modern paper/flyleaf.
^	Item now covered in a leaf from a MS in parchment.
^^	Item now covered in a paper leaf from a MS in Geste's hand.
†	Identification by Dr Christopher de Hamel.
††	Identification by an unknown reader.

Other references relate to panels, rolls and other binding types listed in Appendix IV above.

The tabular information, printed in grey type below,
is laid out in the following columns

Date of latest imprint	Shelf-mark	Type	Date range	Item	Cat. no.	Format	Pastedown image number

Oldham panel bindings

BIB. 2/ ST 37

1523	G.5.20	MS*	†Eng s. xiii^{ex.}	Petrus Lombardus, *Sententiae*	E28	8°	PDN 1

HE. 22/REL 5

1523	N.5.13	MS+	†Eng or Fr s. xiii/xiv	Gregory IX, *Decretales.* Commentary on	H40	4°	PDN 2.1–2

HM. 2

1535	ZC1.5.6	MS+			*A2	8°	PDN 3.1–2

HM. 5/HM. 6

1536	M.2.11	MS+			L38	8°	PDN 4.2
		Pb$£			L38	8°	PDN 4.1

HM. 9/10

1535	D.3.7	Pb$$	s. xvi.	Office book	E36	8°	PDN 5.1–5
		MS+			E36	8°	PDN 5.1,3

HM. 11/12

1539	D.5.3	Pb$$	1539	Richard Taverner, *The Garden of Wisdom*	L57	8°	PDN 6.1–6
		MS+	†s. xiii/xiv	Gregory IX, *Decretales*	L57	8°	PDN 6.4–5

TRIP. 5/6

1526	C.4.6	MS	†Eng s. xiv.	Honorius Augustodunensis, *Elucidarius*	V3	8°	PDN 7.1–2

TRIP. 9

1526	G.6.14	MS	†Eng s. xiii/xiv	Biblical concordance	B35	16°	PDN 8.1–3
1527	H.1.2	MS	†Eng s. xiv/xv	*Breviarium*	E48	8°	PDN 9.1–3
1528	D.4.10	MS &++	†Eng s. xiiiⁱⁿ	Richard of St-Victor	J2	8°	PDN 10.1–5
1531	C.4.9	MS+			H10	8°	PDN 11.1–2
1533	G.5.2	MS+			O7	4°	PDN 12.1–2

Oldham rolls

'R B' of London

1567	G.4.9	Pb	1542	A. Virvesius, *Philippicae disputationes &c.*	F13	fol.	PDN 13.1–3
		MS+		Liturgy (noted)	F13	fol.	PDN 13.1

Oldham classified rolls

AN.e(1) 559
with E.(1) 986

1521	A.4.21	MS£			C127	fol.	PDN 14.1–2

AN.f(1) 561
with D1.a(1) 593

1518	L.5.36	MS$$	†Eng s. xiv	Biblical concordance	L25	4°	PDN 15

AN.f(1) 561
with HE.b(2) 747

1520	A.5.3	MS	†Eng s. xiii[ex.]	Justinian, *Codex*	T7	fol.	PDN 16.1–2
1514	L.5.37	MS	†Eng s. xiv	Verses to the Virgin (in Anglo-Norman)	P14	4°	PDN 17.1–4
1529	N.4.5	MS	†Eng s. xiv[in.]	Justinian, *Digesta*	B12	fol.	PDN 18.1–2

AN.f(2) 562
with D1.a(2) 594

1524	N.3.17	MS	†Eng s. xiii[ex.]	Medica	C82	fol.	PDN 19A.1–2
		MS	†Eng s. xiv[i]	Boniface VIII	C82	fol.	PDN 19B.1–2

AN.g(1) 563
with ornament B(3) 971

1517	N.5.26	MS+			C1	4°	PDN 20.1–4

D1.a(1) 593

1507	H.1.21	MS	†Eng or Fr s. xiii[ex.]	Justinian, *Digesta*	C49	4°	PDN 22

D1.a(7) 597

1546	ZC2.2.5	MS+	†Eng xiv/xv	*Missale*	S24	8°	PDN 23.1–4

D1.e(2) 611

1558	ZC1.4.9	MS+	†s. xiii	?Mathematical	S61	8°	PDN 24.1–3

D.1.h(3) 617

1535	C.1.5	MS	†Eng s. xiv	*Scriptores rerum mythicarum*	O10	8°	PDN 25
1539	C.5.7	MS	†Eng s. xiv	Thomas Aquinas, *In posteriorem analyticorum Aristotelis*	L5	8°	PDN 26.1–8
		Pb$	s. xv	?Scholastic	L5	8°	PDN 26.1–2, 4–5

FC.h(2) 633 [?] – signed 'R W'

1544	N.6.6	MS &$$	Ruled squares and rectangles		N7	8°	PDN 27

FL.a(1) 704 – by Nicholas Spierinck, Cambridge

1525	H.1.6	MS	†Eng s. xv	Geoffrey of Monmouth *Historia regum Britanniae*	L7	8°	PDN 28.1–2
1531	D.3.8	MS	†Eng s. xiv[1]	Justinian, *Pandectae*	M16	8°	PDN 29.1–3

FL.a(3) 706 – Oxford (= Gibson roll I)
with ornament 5 (Ker, *Fragments*, Appendix xxxii)

1517	Y.3.32	MS+	s. xv/xvi	Scholastic theology	A25	fol.	PDN 30

FL.a(10) 713

[c. 1536]	D.1.13–14	MS & $$	†Eng s. xiv	Dun Scotus, *Distinctiones*	E29	4°	PDN 31.1–4
1539	D.5.2	MS	†Eng s. xiv/xv	Calendar	L55	8°	PDN 32.1–4

?FP.a(2) 644 – London
A blind-tooled binding with a very worn, unidentified roll, just possibly Oldham, EBSB, FP.a(2) 644, though Oldham suggests a date range between 1537–40.

1525	C.4.8	Pb & $$	††?	*Expositio hymnorum* for Easter I	B117	8°	PDN 36.1–4

FP.a(8) 681
with HM.a(17) 786

[1551]	E.4.1	MS	†Eng s. xi	Josephus, *Antiquitates* (see fig. 26.1)	E55	fol.	PDN 33.1–4
[1551]	N.3.13	MS &++	†Eng s. xiv	Thomas Aquinas, *Catena Aurea*	J12	fol.	PDN 34.1–4

FP.f(6) 679
with CT 0

1537	F.2.19	MS+	†s. xiii[2]	Gregory IX, *Decretales*	E18	8°	PDN 35

26.1. A folio, with the latest item dated 1541, presented to Geste in 1551 showing a leaf from an English, s.xi MS of Josephus, *Antiquitates,* as a pastedown (now unstuck). Cat. no. E55.

FP.g(1) 685
with CT.c.1

1543	C.6.7	MS	†?Ital s. xiv^{1}	Justinian, *Codex*	S12	8°	PDN 37A.1–5
		Pb$	?s. xv/xvi	?Canon law			
1543	C.6.8	MS	†?Eng s. xiii$^{in.}$	St Matthew (glossed)	S12	8°	PDN 37B.1–5
		Pb$	?s. xv/xvi	?Canon law			
1544	C.3.12	MS	†Eng s. xii^{2}	Hugh of St-Victor, *De laude caritatis*	C64	8°	PDN 38.1–6
		MS+	†Eng s. xii	Zechariah (glossed)	C64	8°	PDN 38.4

HE.b(2) 747

1533	N.6.3	MS	†Eng s. xiv	*Liber Sext*	E30	8°	PDN 40.1–5
1536	D.6.12	MS	†Eng s. xiv	Duns Scotus, *In primo libro Sententiarum*	A27	8°	PDN 41.1–6
		MS$			A27	8°	PDN 41.1

HE.g(4) 761
with CT m.2

1542	E.3.19	MS	†Eng s. xiv/xv	Duns Scotus, *In secundo libro Sententiarum*	D12	fol.	PDN 42.1–2 [as PDN 43, 44
1545	E.3.21	MS	†?Eng s. xiii$^{ex.}$	Justinian, *Pandectae*	D18	fol.	PDN 43.1–2
		MS	†Eng s. xii/xiii	*Lectionary*	D18	fol.	PDN 43.5–6
		Pb$$ s. xvi			D18	fol.	PDN 43.3–4
1548	E.3.16	MS	†Eng s. xiv/xv	Duns Scotus, *In secundo libro Sententiarum*	D10	fol.	PDN 44.1–2 [as PDN 42, 44]
1552	E.3.17	MS	†Eng s. xiv/xv	Duns Scotus, *In secundo libro Sententiarum*	D11	fol.	PDN 45.1–2 [as PDN 42, 43]

HM.d(4) 808

1522	H.1.38	MS	†Eng s. xv	Philosophy	B53	8°	PDN 46
		MS$			B53	8°	PDN 46
1522	H.1.39	MS	†Eng s. xi$^{med.}$	Augustine, *In Johannem*	B53	8°	PDN 47.1–2 [as PDN 48]
1522	H.1.40	MS	†Eng s. xi$^{med.}$	Augustine, *In Johannem*	B53	8°	PDN 48.1–2 [as PDN 47]
1537	Y.5.29	MS	†Eng s. xiv/xv ?Canon Law		S96	8°	PDN 49

HM.h(10) 835

| 1567 | Z.2.19 | Pb | s. xvi | Petrus Mosellanus, *Dialogi* | B138 fol. | PDN 51.1–2 |
| 1568 | M.1.28 | MS+ | †s. xiv | | H2 fol. | PDN 52.1–2 |

HM.h(28) 853

1534	C.1.6	MS	†Eng s. xv$^{ex.}$	Augustinus de Ancona, *Summa de ecclesiastica potestate*	O13 8°	PDN 53.1–4 [as PDN 54]
1536	D.2.6	MS	†Eng s. xv$^{ex.}$	Augustinus de Ancona, *Summa de ecclesiastica potestate*	J14 8°	PDN 54.1–2 [as PDN 53]
1538	H.1.20	MS	†Eng s. xii/xiii	Rabanus Maurus, *In Matthaeum*	B127 4°	PDN 55
1538	C.6.9	MS	†Eng s. xiii	Commentary on part of Ps. 68	S15 8°	PDN 56.1–4
1539	D.5.4	MS	†Eng s. xi^{I}	Bede, *Homiliae*	L63 8°	PDN 57.1–4

with CT.c.2

| 1542 | F.2.29 | MS | †Fr or Eng s. xiii/xiv | Justinian, *Institutiones* (commentary on) | M85 4° | PDN 58.1–6 |

HM.h.(29) 854

1533	H.1.31	MS ++	†Ital or Eng s. xiv^{I}	Justinian, *Digesta*	J9 8°	PDN 59.1–7
		Pb$	?s. xv/xvi	?Canon law	J9 8°	PDN 59,1–2, 5–6 [?from same pb as PDN 63 & 68]
1539	ZC2.1.5	MS	†Eng s. xii^{2}	Ambrose, *Hexamaeron*	S25 8°	PDN 60.1–5
		Pb$	?s. xv/xvi	?Canon law	S25 8°	PDN 60.1, 3, 5
1540	D.2.5	MS	†Eng s. xii^{2}	Ps.–Jerome, *Epistolae ad Paulum et Eustachium*	S18 8°	PDN 61.1–4
1543	L.6.30	MS	†Eng s. xiv$^{in.}$	Jacobus de Voragine, *Legenda Aurea* [same MS as PDN 65, 66B]	L49 8°	PDN 62A
		MS	†Eng s. xiv/xv	John de Bromyarde, *Summa praedicantium*	L49 8°	PDN 62B

with CT c.1

HM.h.(29) 854, *continued*

1541	C.6.11	MS	†Eng s. xiv	On virtues and vices, (in Anglo-Norman)	S20	8°	PDN 63.1–3 [?from same pb as PDN 59 & 68]
		Pb$	?s. xv/xvi	?Canon law	S20	8°	PDN 63.1
1542	C.6.3	MS &++	†Eng s. xiv	Alphabetical dictionary (citing Aquinas, *Summa Theologica*)	B83	8°	PDN 64.1–6
1544	D.6.8	MS	†Eng s. xiv^in.	Jacobus de Voragine, *Legenda Aurea*	S21	8°	PDN 65.1–6 [same MS as PDN 62A, 66B]
–		Pb$	s. xv/xvi		S21	8°	PDN 65.5, 6
1544	D.6.9	MS	†Eng s. xiv^1	*Sermones de sanctis*	S22	8°	PDN 66A
–			†Eng s. xiv^in.	Jacobus de Voragine, *Legenda Aurea*	S22	8°	PDN 66B [same MS as PDN 62A, 65]
		Pb$	s. xv/xvi		S22	8°	PDN 66B

with CT q

1538	C.5.4	MS	†Eng s. xiii/xiv	English civil law	L6	8°	PDN 67.1–4

with CT yy

1541	X.2.16	MS & †?Eng s. xiii^ex.		Canon law (commentary)	C74	8°	PDN 68.1–5 [?from same Pb as PDN 59 & 63]
		Pb$	?s. xv/xvi	?Canon law	C74	8°	PDN 68.1, 5

MW.a(1) 857 (= Gibson roll XII) – signed 'GK'

1548	D.3.13	MS	†Eng s. xiv^2	Biblical history	*D4	8°	PDN 70.1–3
		Geste's ownership of this book uncertain					
		Pb$$	?s. xv	?Canon law	*D4	8°	PDN 70.1, 2

MW.c(1) 862 – London

1566	I.5.5	Pb & $$	s. xvi	?Catholic theology	Z2	4°	PDN 75.1–4
		MS+	†Eng s. xiv		Z2	4°	PDN 75.1,3
1566	I.4.6	MS+	†Eng s. xiv^in.	Probably manorial records	F23	4°	PDN 71.1–4
1567	T.6.4	MS+	†Eng or Fr s. xiii^2	Biblical concordance	N13	4°	PDN 72.1–3
		Pb$$	1567/68	*Epistola Gildae sapientis*	N13	4°	PDN 72.2, 3

1568	ZC2.1.8	MS+ †Eng s. xiv/xv	*Psalterium*	B29 8° PDN 73.1,2,4
		Pb$$ s. xvi	'Proprietates vocabulorum'	B29 8° PDN 73.1–6
1568	D.1.4	?Pb/MS£		T16 4° PDN 74

MW.c(1) 862 – London with HE.b(5) 751

1571	E.3.5	Pb s. xv	Theology	L21 fol. PDN 76.1–7
		MS+ †s. xii[1]	Perhaps biblical	L21 fol. PDN 76.4, 5

SW.b(3) 946

1533	C.2.3	MS †Eng s. xiii/xiv	Scholastic philosophy	L64 4° PDN 78.1–3
		Pb$ s. xvi	Homer, *Odyssey* (Lat.)	L64 4° PDN 78.4
		MS(G)	s. xvi	
1542	D.6.7	MS †?Eng s. xiii[2]	Gregory, *Moralia in Job*	R34 8° PDN 79.1–4

SW.b(4) 947

1541	C.6.10	MS †Eng s. xi/xii & ++	*Preces*	S17 8° PDN 80.1–2

Classified ornaments

K.(4) 1017 – Nicholas Spierinck, Cambridge

1506	D.1.2	MS †?Eng s. xii/xiii	Ovid, *Ars Amatoria*	H83 4° PDN 81.1–40

Unidentified tools

Unidentified – very worn – intersecting borders containing rose and pineapple tools – with a lattice of four full and eight half perforations containing a worn lozenge-shaped tool (bearing some resemblance to Oldham, EBSB, stamp 206)

1497	Y.2.12	MS$$ s. xv	French basse dances	B5 fol. PDN 82A
		Pb$$ 1483	John Gower, *Confessio Amantis* (Caxton). See fig. 26.3.	B5 fol. PDN 82B

Unidentified rolls

A wide roll of capstan type, possibly Oldham RP.a(1)

1537	D.1.8	MS+		P53 8° PDN 83

Unidentified English rolls

1559	E.5.8	MS+ †Eng s. xv	Missale	P38 4° PDN 77.1–2
1569	I.7.7	MS+ †s. xii		S67 4° PDN 69.1–2

Unidentified English rolls, *continued*

| 1570 | A.4.8 | Pb | s. xvi | 'Lettre / Harangve' | I5 | fol. | PDN 50.1–2 |
| | | Pb $$s. xvi | | ?Herbal (in French) | I5 | fol. | PDN 50.3–5 |

with CT ss

| 1544 | D.4.8 | MS+ †s. xiii/xiv | | | B94 | 8° | PDN 39.1–2 |

Continental bindings

German roll

| 1543 | M.1.15 | MS+ †s. xv | | Perhaps liturgical | S89 | fol. | PDN 84 |

French rolls

| 1495 | L.5.38 | MS | †Eng s. xiii² | Breviary (noted) | P23 | 4° | PDN 85.1–4 |
| 1540 | M.1.17 | MS+ †s. xiii | | Scholastic | A49 | fol. | PDN 21.1–2 |

Centrepiece bindings

CP 2.1

1571	ZC2.7.5	MS+ †Eng s. xiv/xv	Compotus roll	H37	8°	PDN 86.1–2
1572	G.6.1	MS+ †Eng s. xiv/xv	Probably manorial records	B63	8°	PDN 87
1573	C.7.4	MS +		C62	8°	PDN 88
1573	D.4.9	MS+		E10	8°	PDN 89.1–2

Centre-tool bindings
(excluding those in combination with roll bindings which are listed above under Oldham rolls)

CT a

1564	K.2.26	Pb$$, s. xvi ++	Latin dictionary	C44	4°	PDN 90.1–4
		MS+**		C44	4°	PDN 90.3
1564	C.3.11	Pb$$, s. xv ++	Theology	G2	8°	PDN 91.1–6
		MS+**		G2	8°	PDN 91.3, 6
1569	C.4.11	Pb $$?s. xv	?Canon Law	H30	8°	PDN 92.1–6
1570	ZC1.4.13	Pb $$ s. xvi	Eng BL.	A50	16°	PDN 93.1–7
1570	ZC1.4.13	MS+ †Eng s. xiv	Theological	A50	16°	PDN 93.1–2, 4–5
1570	K.2.13	Pb $$ 1524 MS+**	Erasmus, *Colloquia*	C36	4°	PDN 94.1–2
		Pb $$ 1563	Erasmus, *Colloquia*	C36	4°	PDN 94.3–4

1570	K.2.14	MS+**		C36	4° PDN 95
1570	ZC2.1.6	MS+**		H98	8° PDN 96.1–2
1570	I.8.3	Pb s. xv $$,++	Sermons	L30	4° PDN 97.1–7
		MS+**		L30	4° PDN 97.4,7
1570	E.5.1	Pb s. xv	Scholastic theology	P34	4° PDN 98.1–4
1571	G.6.6	Pb$$ s. xv	?Canon Law	B58	8° PDN 99.1–7
		MS+**			PDN 99.1,4,5
1571	H.1.7	Pb s. xv $$,++		C43	8° PDN 100.1–4
		MS+**		C43	8° PDN 100.1–2,4
1571	G.5.15	Pb ?s. xvi $$,++		H62	8° PDN 101.1–6
		MS+**		H62	8° PDN 101.1,3,4,6
1571	ZC1.4.5	Pb ?s. xvi $$,++	Alphabetical dictionary	P41	8° PDN 102.1–6
		MS+**		P41	8° PDN 102.1, 6
1571	ZC2.7.8	Pb ?s/xvi $$,++	'Prologus in uitam sancti Hilarionis'	W46	8° PDN 103.1–8
		MS+**		W46	8° PDN 103.1,4,5,8
1572	ZC1.4.3	Pb$$?s. xv	?Canon law	H49	8° PDN 104.1–6
		MS+**		H49	8° PDN 104.1, 3–6
1572	I.2.10	Pb$$?s. xv		O25	8° PDN 105.1–4
		MS+ †Eng s. xi[med.]	*Evangelia* (Canones (evangeliorum)	O25	8° PDN 105.2–3

CTb

1547	D.3.2	MS+ †Eng s. xiv[1] MS(G)$$	*Vitae sanctorum* (see fig. 26.2)	B96	8° PDN 106.1–6
1557	ZC2.2.2	MS+ †s. xv	?Prayers	R15	8° PDN 107.1–2
1558	D.5.12	MS+ †Eng s. xiv	*Psalterium*	V31	8° PDN 108.1–3
1559	N.6.16	MS+ †Eng s. xii/xiii	Cosmography	H96	8° PDN 109.1–2
1564	D.1.9	MS+ †Eng s. xiii	Antiphoner (feast of Saint Thomas Becket)	C4	8° PDN 114.1–4
1560	A.6.22	MS+, †Eng or i ++ Fr s. xiii	Scholastic (apparently Aristotle, *Categoriae*)	B7	8° PDN 110.1–3
1561	ZC2.2.7	MS+**		H1	8° PDN 111
1561	ZC2.2.8	MS+**		H48	8° PDN 112.1–2

26.2. An octavo of 1547 bound in calf with centre-tool CT b, showing the inside cover and spine, with printed waste, and a strip from an English s.xiv[1] MS of *Vitae sanctorum*. Cat. no. B96.

26.3. An octavo, with the latest item dated 1575, with one of three strips from an English s.xiv/xv obit of Hyde Abbey, describing the building work of Salidus, abbot *c.* 1151–1171. Cat.no.Z5.

CT b, *continued*

1546	R.6.46	Pb+ ?s. xvi		Indulgence	S64 8°	PDN 113.1
[1561]		MS++ 1561		Thomas Gylbert letter	S64 8°	PDN 113.2
1565	ZC2.1.7	MS+ †Eng s. xiii[1]			S41 8°	PDN 115.2–3
		MS+ **				PDN 115.1, 4
1565	D.5.10	MS+ †Eng s. xv		*Fasciculus morum*	W27 8°	PDN 116.1–4
		MS+ **			W27 8°	PDN 116.2, 4
1566	ZC2.1.4	MS+, †Eng s. xiv/xv ++		Accounts (probably a Compotus roll)	F10 8°	PDN 117.1–4 [same MS as PDN 123]
1566	C.3.3	MS+			H19 8°	PDN 118
1566	C.3.4	MS+			H20 8°	PDN 119
1566	Z.4.23	MS+ †Eng s. xiv		*Breviarium*	H91 8°	PDN 120.1–3
1566	Z.5.109	MS+ †Eng or Fr s. xiii		Justinian, *Codex*	V24 8°	PDN 121.1–3
1566	C.4.4	MS+ †Eng s. xiv		?Accounts	W18 8°	PDN 122
1566	K.2.15	MS+ †Eng s. xiv/xv		Accounts (probably a Compotus roll)	W23 8°	PDN 123.1–2 [same MS as PDN 117]
1567	ZC2.2.10	MS+ †Eng s. xii[2]		Hilarius Pictaviensis, *De Trinitate*	C110 8°	PDN 125.1–3
1567	K.2.17	MS+ †?s. xiv		Liturgy	F22 8°	PDN 126.1–2
1567	ZC1.4.8	MS+ †Eng s. xiv/xv		*Breviarium*	M74 8°	PDN 127.1–2, 5–6, 9 [probably from same MS as PDN 129]
		Pb$$ s. xvi		Office of the Visitation of the BVM	M74 8°	PDN 127.1–4
		Pb$$ s. xvi		?Lutheran theology	M74 8°	PDN 127.5–9
1567	ZC1.5.4	MS+ †Eng or Fr s. xiii[ex.]		Scholastic	P8 8°	PDN 128
1567	I.1.5	MS+ †Eng s. xiv/xv		*Breviarium*	R11 8°	PDN 129.1–2 [probably from same MS as PDN 127]

417

CT b, *continued*

1567	H.1.9	MS+ †Eng s. xii²	*Sermones Augustini*	R38	8°	PDN 130.1–5
1567	G.6.2	MS+ †?Eng s. xii¹	Gregory I, *Moralia in Job*	S44	8°	PDN 131.1–3
		+**		S44	8°	PDN 131.1
1567	ZC1.4.2	MS+**		S49	8°	PDN 132.1–2
1568	A.6.26	MS+ †Eng s. xiv/xv	?Psalter	L47	8°	PDN 133.1–3
1568	I.1.6	Pb, $$ s. xvi	Calvin, *Commentarii in Evang.*	R10	8°	PDN 134.1–4
		MS+ †s. xiii	Scholastic	R10	8°	PDN 134.2–3

CT b.1

1568	K.2.16	MS+, †Eng s. xiii ++	*Psalterium*	W1	4°	PDN 135.1–3
		MS+**		W1	4°	PDN 135.1

CT c.1

1530	ZC1.4.6	MS †?Eng s. xiv	Alphabetical dictionary	E38	8°	PDN 135A.3, 4, 6–9
		Pb$ s. xv		E38	8°	PDN 135A.2, 5, 6
1532	I.3.8	MS †Eng s. xiv¹	Canon law (?commentary on the decretals of Boniface VIII)	E33	4°	PDN 136.2–5 [perhaps same MS as PDN 210 and 212]
		Pb$ s. xv/xvi	Glossary of legal terms	E33	4°	PDN 136.1
		MS$		E33	4°	PDN 136.4–5
[c.1540]	G.5.14	MS †Eng s. xiii²	Thomas Aquinas, *In libros Sententiarum*	S14	8°	PDN 137.1–4
		Pb$ s. xv/xvi	?Canon law	S14	8°	PDN 137.1,4
1543	C.2.13	MS †?Eng s. xiii²	Augustine, *Contra adversarium legis et prophetarum*	A43	4°	PDN 138.1–2
1544	C.4.14	MS£		B38	8°	PDN 139
1544	N.6.5	MS †Ital s. xiii/xiv	Gregory IX, *Decretales*	V39	8°	PDN 140.1–2
		MS †?Eng s. xiii²	Thomas Aquinas, *In libros Sententiarum*	V39	8°	PDN 140.3
		Pb$ s. xv/xvi		V39	8°	PDN 140.1

1545	D.5.1	MS	†Ital s. xii^ex.	Justinian, *Pandectae*	L60	8°	PDN 141.1–6
		Pb$	s. xv/xvi	Scholastic theology	L60	8°	PDN 141.3, 6
1545	D.5.6	MS	†Eng s. xiii/xiv	Thomas Aquinas, *In libros Sententiarum*	A5	8°	PDN 142.2–5
		Pb$	s. xv/xvi	?Scholastic philosophy	A5	8°	PDN 142.1,2,5
1545	G.5.4	MS	†?Eng s. xv	Augustine, *Enarationes in Psalmos*	D6	4°	PDN 143A
		MS	†Eng s. xii	Gregory, *Dialogi*	D6	4°	PDN 143B
1545	H.1.8	MS	†?Eng s. xiii/xiv	Thomas Aquinas, *In libros Sententiarum*	R23	8°	PDN 144
		Pb$	s. xv/xvi		R23	8°	PDN 144
1546	C.4.2	MS	†? Eng s. xiii	Petrus Riga, *Aurora*	A55	8°	PDN 145.2–3, 8–10 [same MS as PDN 149]
		Pb$	s. xvi	Office book	A55	8°	PDN 145.1–2,10
		MS (G)$$	s. xvi		A55	8°	PDN 145.4–7
1546	F.2.10	MS ++	†Eng or Fr s. xiii^ex	Thomas Aquinas, *Sententia libri Ethicorum*	G29	8°	PDN 146.1–4
1546	D.2.8	MS	†Eng s. xiii/xiv	Thomas Aquinas, *In libros Sententiarum*	M20	8°	PDN 147.1,3–7
		Pb$	s. xv/xvi	Scholastic ?philosophy	M20	8°	PDN 147.2,5–6
1548	C.6.4	MS	†?Eng s. xiv^1	William of Auvergne, *De virtutibus*	B88	8°	PDN 148.1–2
1548	ZC1.4.7	MS	†?Eng s. xiii	Petrus Riga, *Aurora*	C11	8°	PDN 149.2–5 [same MS as PDN 145]
		Pb$	s. xv	Service book	C11	8°	PDN 149.1,3–6
1548 CT d.1	O.1.25	MS	†?Eng s. xiv	Canon law	H42	8°	PDN 150.1–4
1556	ZC1.4.10	MS+, ++	†Eng s. xiii	Astronomy	L70	8°	PDN 151.1–4
1558	K.2.11	MS+	†s. xii	?Biblical	B92	4°	PDN 152.1–3
1558 CT e	D.6.2	MS+	†s. xii^ex.	Scientific (?physics)	C70	8°	PDN 153
1573	D.1.7	MS+, ++	†?Eng s. xiii/xiv	Bonaventura, *Comm. in libros Sententiarum Petri Lombardi*	M76	8°	PDN 154.1–2

CT e, *continued*

1574	G.5.6	MS+, †Eng s. xiv¹ ++	Accounts (?a Compotus roll)	M77 8° PDN 155.1–2
1575	ZC1.4.4	MS+ †Eng s. xiv/xv	Obit book of Hyde Abbey, Winchester (see fig. 26.3)	Z5 8° PDN 156.1–3
1576	C.4.5	MS+ †Eng s. xiv²	*Missale*	W20 8° PDN 157.1–2
		MS+	?Accounts	W20 8° PDN 157.3

CT f

1552	G.6.7	MS+ †Eng s. xiii²	Concordance or dictionary	B37 16° PDN 158.3,5
		Pb$ Eng s. xvi	Theology (Eng)	B37 16° PDN 158.1–2
		MS s. xvi (G)$$		B37 16°PDN 158.4–5

CT h.1

1560	A.6.17	Pb$$ s. xvi	Theological dialogue 'De Lege'	A54 8° PDN 159

CT h.2

1562	G.5.12	MS+ †?Eng s. xiii^ex	Jacobus de Voragine, *Legenda aurea*	W39 8° PDN 160.1–4

CT j

1549	ZC2.7.13	MS+ **		G5 8° PDN 161.1–2

CT k

1557	H.1.4	MS+ †s. xiv/xv		F34 8° PDN 162.1–3
1566	H.1.3	MS+ †s. xv	Liturgy	S73 8° PDN 163

CT m.1

1548	M.2.29	Pb$$, ?s. xv ++	?Theological dictionary	C120 8° PDN 164.2–7
		MS+ †Eng s. xiv	Liturgy (noted)	C120 8° PDN 164.5,7–8
		MS**		C120 8° PDN 164.1
		Pb$ s. xvi	Service book	C120 8° PDN 164.1,7–8
1552	M.2.25	MS+ †Eng s. xv	Liturgy (noted)	B90 8° PDN 165.1–2
1552	D.3.3	Pb & $$ s. xvi	Liturgy	L43 8° PDN 166.1,2,4,6
		Pb$ s. xvi		L43 8° PDN 166.3,6–7
		MS+ †Eng s. xv	Liturgy (noted)	L43 8° PDN 166.1,6–7

CT m.2

  with HE.g(4) 761

1540	N.4.2	Pb	s. xvi	Missal	D21 fol. PDN 167.3–4
		Pb£	s. xvi		D21 fol. PDN 167.1–2

CT n

1560	C.6.12	MS+ †s. xiii			M32 8° PDN 168.1–2

CT r

1546	D.4.4	MS	†Eng s. xii	Gregory, *Dialogi*. [same MS as PDN 143B]	C114 8° PDN 171.1–4

CT t

1555	Z.5.121	MS+, †Eng s. xii¹ ++		Medicine	V38 8° PDN 172.1–6
1561	G.6.3	MS+ †Eng s. xii		Priscianus, *Grammatica*	B120 8° PDN 173.2–3
		Pb$$?1558		?Bucer, *Du Royaume de Christ*	B120 8° PDN 173.1–5 [also used in PDN 292]

CT v

1552	D.5.8	MS+ **			O17 8° PDN 174
1561	D.3.10	Pb ?1552 & $$		?Calvin, *Disputatio de cognitione hominis*	S39 8° PDN 175.1–3
		MS+ †s. xv			S39 8° PDN 175.1, 3
1561	D.3.11	?Pb£			S39 8° PDN 176

CT x

1549	I.4.4	MS	†? Eng or Fr s.xii/xiii	St John (glossed)	B108 4° PDN 177.1–2
1552	N.6.8	MS	†Eng s. xiiᵉˣ·	Petrus Comestor, *Historia ecclesiastica*	V16 8° PDN 178.1–3

CT y

1537	H.2.12	MS	†Eng s. xiv	?Canon law	L18 8° PDN 179A
		MS & ++	†Ital s. xiii	Justinian, *Digesta*	L18 8° PDN 179B

CT z

1542	I.7.6	MS	†?Eng s. xiii¹	Gratian, *Decretum*	W50 4° PDN 180.1–2

CT bb.1

1564	B.6.16	Pb & $$	s. xvi	Joannes Sulpitius	O22 8° PDN 181.1–3

CT bb.2

1563	I.4.2	Pb & $$	s. xvi	'Concio II. in Calvini in Ps. CXIX'	V5	4°	PDN 182.1–5
		MS+ **			V5	4°	PDN 182.3

CT dd

1569	M.2.26	MS+ †s. xv	Liturgy	P12	8°	PDN 183.1–2

CT ee

1544	C.1.4	MS	†?Eng s. xiii[2]	Justinian, *Pandectae*	O4	8°	PDN 184.1–3
		MS	†Fr s. xiv/xv	*Grandes Chroniques de France*	O4	8°	PDN 184.4–5 [same MS as PDN 185]
1544	ZC2.2.9	MS	†Fr s. xiv/xv	*Grandes Chroniques de France*	S80	8°	PDN 185.2–4 [same MS as PDN 184]
		MS & ++	†Eng s. xiii[2]	Astronomical MS	S80	8°	PDN 185.5,6
		Pb$	s. xvi		S80	8°	PDN 185.1,2,6

CT ff.1

1571	D.2.10	Pb	s. xvi	Jerome, 'In canti. cantico. prefatio'	W28	8°	PDN 186.1–3

CT ff.2

1571	C.2.4	MS+ **			C32	4°	PDN 187.1,4,5
		Pb & $$	s. xvi	Alphabetical word list and 'Ep. LVIII'	C32	4°	PDN 187.1–6

CT hh

1575	ZC2.7.1	MS+ †s. xiv[1]	*Psalterium*	A51	8°	PDN 188.1
		MS+ *		A51	8°	PDN 188.2

CT kk

1556	A.6.25	Pb$$ s. xvi	Religious history	E59	8°	PDN 189.1–4
		MS+ †s. xiii	*Psalterium*	E59	8°	PDN 189.1, 3

CT mm

1570	B.5.10	MS+, †s. xvi & ++	Archival	R9	8°	PDN 190.1–2

CT nn

1556	M.2.43	MS+ †?s. xiv	?Liturgical	L82	8°	PDN 191

CT pp

1541	X.2.17	MS+ †?Eng s. xv	Durandus, *Rationale divinorum officiorum*	R12	8°	PDN 192.1–2 [same MS as PDN 193]
1541	X.2.18	MS+ †?Eng s. xv	Durandus, *Rationale divinorum officiorum*	R12	8°	PDN 193.1–3 [same MS as PDN 192]

CT rr

1557	F.2.8	MS+	†s. xiii/xiv	?Grammar	M83	8° PDN 194

CT vv

1557	Y.5.19	MS+	†Eng s. xii/xiii	Petrus Comestor, *Historia Scholastica*	M19	8° PDN 195.1–3

CT zz

1558 [1572]	K.3.19	MS+	†Fr s. xvi	Archival	*A11	16° PDN 294

CT aaa

1536	D.4.3	MS &++	†Eng s. xiv^{in.}	Thomas Aquinas, *Summa Theologica*	C37	8° PDN 170.1–7
		Pb$	s. xvi	?Canon law	C37	8° PDN 170.1,2,6

Corner-ornaments

CS 1

1547	D.3.4	Pb	1547	Erasmus, *Paraphrases*	S75	8° PDN 196.1–2
1548	D.3.5	Pb	?s. xvi	?Canon law, 'De haereticis'	S76	8° PDN 197.1–2

CS 3

1534	C.1.9	MS+	†?s. xiv	Liturgy	O8	4° PDN 198

Plain calf – PL a

1525	C.5.6	MS	†?s. xiv	Philosophy	L4	8° PDN 257.1–2
1525	ZC2.1.1	MS &++	†Eng s. xiv	Honorius Augustodunensis, *Imago Mundi*	S31	8° PDN 260.1–3
1540	N.6.4	MS	†Eng s. xiii^{med.}	*Biblia* (Jeremiah)	M14	8° PDN 264.1, 3
		Pb$	?s. xvi	Gospels	M14	8° PDN 264.1–2
1540	D.2.4	MS	†Eng s. xiii/xiv	Thomas Aquinas, *In libros Sententiarum*	S19	8° PDN 265.1–4
1543	H.1.5	MS	†Eng s. xiv	Philosophy	B107	8° PDN 266.1–5
		Pb$	?s. xvi	?Canon law	B107	8° PDN 266.1–4
1544	D.2.1	MS	†?Eng s. xiii/xiv	Henricus Hostiensis, *Summa aurea*	O5	8° PDN 268.1–4
1545	ZC2.7.2	MS	†Eng s. xiv^t	Canon law (?commentary on the *Decreta* of Gregory IX)	B50	8° PDN 258.1–3, 6–8
		Pb$$	s. xvi	St John	B50	8° PDN 258.2–6

Plain calf – PL a, *continued*

1549	ZC2.7.3	MS	†s. xiv	Alphabetical dictionary	P19	8°	PDN 269.1–4
		+**			P19	8°	PDN 269.2, 4
		Pb$	?s. xv	Liturgy (noted)	P19	8°	PDN 269.1–3
1550	H.1.29	MS	†Eng s. xiii^{in}	Geometry	B42	8°	PDN 270.1–7 [same MS as PDN 290]
		Pb$	s. xvi	Liturgy (noted)	B42	8°	PDN 270.1,5–
1550	D.1.12	MS	†Eng s. xii^{2}	Psalms (glossed)	W30	4°	PDN 274.1–5
		+**			W30	4°	PDN 274.2, 5
		Pb$	?s. xvi		W30	4°	PDN 274.3–4
1551	I.4.11	MS	†?Eng s. xiv/xv	*Regula clericorum*	B133	4°	PDN 275.1–4
1553	C.4.3	MS	†Eng s. xiv'	*Regula clericorum*	L50	8°	PDN 276.1–2
		Pb$	?s. xv	?Canon law	L50	8°	PDN 276.1
1559	ZC2.2.1	MS+	†Eng s. xiv	Johannes de Garlandia (attrib.), *Cornutus* (glossed)	W7	4°	PDN 277.1–4
1561	B.3.19	MS+	†Eng or Fr xii/xiii	Bernardus Clareval- lensis, *De consideratione*	P3	fol.	PDN 278.1–3
1561	C.1.13	MS+	†Eng s. xiii^{2}	Text in Anglo- Norman	W8	4°	PDN 279.1–2
1563	ZC2.7.7	MS+, ++	†Eng s. xiv/xv	Johannes Sarisburi- ensis, *Polycraticus*	H35	8°	PDN 280.1–5
		Pb(2)$	s. xvi	Almanac and other items, including one in Greek	H35	8°	PDN 280.1,3–5

Plain calf – PL b

1524	C.1.3	MS, ++	†Eng s. xiv	Commentary on Justinian, *Digesta*	O12	8°	PDN 256.1–5
1525	D.2.2	MS	†s. xiv	?Legal MS	L52	8°	PDN 259.1–4
1527	K.3.42	MS*, ++	†?Fr s. xii$^{ex.}$	Medical dictionary	V33	8°	PDN 261.1–5
1531	D.6.3	MS, ++	†Eng s. xiii^{2}	Eberhardus Bethuni- ensis, *Graecismus*	M49	8°	PDN 262.1–5
		Pb$	s. xv/xvi		M49	8°	PDN 262.1,3

1532	C.1.2	MS& †Fr or MS+ Eng s. xiii[2]	Aristotle, *Physica* (*translatio vetus*)	O3	4[8]	PDN 263.1–4
1543	D.5.5	MS& †Eng s. xiv MS$	*Breviarium*	D23	8°	PDN 267.1–5
1550	M.2.36	MS †?Eng s. xv	Nicholas de Lyra, *Catena Aurea*	C122	8°	PDN 271.1–4 [same MS as PDN 272–273]
1550	M.2.37	MS †?Eng s. xv	Nicholas de Lyra, *Catena Aurea*	C122	8°	PDN 272.1–5 [same MS as PDN 271, 273]
1550	M.2.38	MS †Eng s. xiv	Thomas Aquinas, *Summa Theologiae*	C122	8°	PDN 273.3–4
		MS †?Eng s. xv	Nicholas de Lyra, *Catena Aurea*	C122	8°	PDN 273.1–2 [same MS as PDN 271–272]

Parchment covers

1509	ZC2.3.15	MS+ †Eng s. xii/xiii &++	*Commentarium in Epistolas Pauli* [?by Gilbertus Porretanus]	D32	4°	PDN 199.1–6
1516	K.3.46	MS †Eng s. xiv/xv	Choirbook (hymns to the Virgin)	R13	8°	PDN 200.1–2
1525	F.2.4	MS+ †?Fr s. xiii/xiv	Gloss to a legal text, apparently civil law	C39	8°	PDN 201.1–2
1528	ZC2.3.10	MS †Eng s. xiv	?Aristotle, *De caelo et mundi* (with commentary)	P6	4°	PDN 202.1–4 [same MS as PDN 218]
1529	F.2.6	MS+ †s. xv		R16	8°	PDN 203
1538	E.6.29	MS+ †Eng s. xiii[in.]	Petrus Lombardus, *Sententiae*	L67	8°	PDN 204.1–2
1539	F.2.3	MS+ †?Eng s. xiii[ex.]	Thomas Aquinas, *In libros Sententiarum*	M84	8°	PDN 205.1–2
		MS+ †Eng s. xii[ex.]	Jeremiah (glossed)	M84	8°	PDN 205.3
1540	F.2.5	MS+ †?Ital s. xiii &++	*Biblia* (Ezekiel)	C29	8°	PDN 206.1–6
1541	E.6.33	MS+ †Eng s. xiii/xiv	Commentary on law (apparently canon law)	H59	8°	PDN 208.1–4
1543	E.5.32	MS+ †Eng s. xii[ex.]	Boethius, *De institutione arithmetica*	P29	4°	PDN 209.1–2

Parchment covers, *continued*

1544	ZC2.6.7 MS$$ †Eng s. xiv¹ &++	Canon law	B118 8° PDN 210.1–6 [same MS as PDN 212 and perhaps PDN 136]
1544	ZC2.6.17 MS$$ †Fr or Eng s. xiii²	Aristotle, *Physica*	C90 8° PDN 211.1–4
1544	G.6.17 MS$$ †Eng s. xiv¹	Canon law	K2 8° PDN 212.1–5 [same MS as PDN 210 and perhaps PDN 136]
1545	ZC2.3.12 Pb$$ s. xvi &++	'Homilia II [–III] | De Fer. Persec.'	M10 4° PDN 213.1–6 [?from same Pb as PDN 234]
1545	ZC2.6.15 MS †Eng s. xiv	Bonaventura, *Compendium theologicae veritatis*	L12 8° PDN 214.1–4
[c.1545]	ZC2.6.4 MS †?Eng s. xiii	Biblical concordance	P45 8° PDN 207.1–2
1546	ZC2.4.1 MS$$ †Eng orv Fr s. xiv	Alphabetical dictionary	L15 4° PDN 215.1–4
1547	X.1.20 MS+		*D1 8° PDN 296
1552	E.6.23 MS+ †Eng s. xiiᵉˣ·	Theology	B41 8° PDN 220.1–2 [apparently the same MS as PDN 224]
1553	ZC2.5.1 MS+ †s. xiv &++		D30 8° PDN 221.1–3
1554	O.2.46 MS+**		W2 8° PDN 295.1–3
1554	ZC2.3.7 MS$$ †Eng s. xiii/xiv	Alphabetical medical or scientific dictionary	G15 4° PDN 222.1–5
1555	O.1.10 MS$$ s. xvi	Book-list with prices	B54 4° PDN 223
1555	E.6.37 MS+ †Eng s. xiiᵉˣ·	Theology	L51 8° PDN 224.1–2 [apparently the same MS as PDN 220]
1555	G.6.16 MS+ †?s. xiv		T10 12° PDN 225
1556	ZC2.4.11 MS+ †Eng s. xiii¹	Commentary on St Luke	M90 8° PDN 226.1–2

1556	ZC2.6.3	Pb$$ s. xvi	'The firste booke under the title of Afrique conteineth'	T2	8°	PDN 227.1–4
1558	E.6.19	Pb$$, s. xvi &++	?Grammar	J5	12°	PDN 228.1–4
1558	ZC2.4.12	MS$$, †Eng s. xiii^in. &++	*Psalterium*	S83	8°	PDN 229.1–3
		MS$$,†?Eng s. xiv &++	Egidius de Fuscariis, *Ordo Iudiciarius*	S83	8°	PDN 229.4–6
1558	ZC2.8.2	Pb$$, s. xvi ++	Theology	T15	16°	PDN 230.1–7
1559	B.6.37	MS+ †Eng s. xiv/xv	Breviary (noted)	L35	8°	PDN 231.1–3
1560	ZC2.3.5	MS+ †Eng s. xv	Wycliffe, *Opus Evangelicum*	A35	4°	PDN 232.1–3
1560	G.6.22	MS+, †Eng s. xii/xiii &++	?Commentary on Genesis	F36	8°	PDN 233.1–4
1560	ZC2.5.8	MS+ **		H68	8°	PDN 234.1, 3–4,6
		Pb$$, s. xvi	'Homilia I | De Fvg. idolol.'	H68	8°	PDN 234.1–2
		Pb$$ s. xvi &+**	'Homilia II [–III]. | De Fer. Persec.'	H68	8°	PDN 234.3–6 [?from same Pb as PDN 213]
[c.1560]	B.6.40	MS+ †Eng s. xii²	Bernardus Clareval-lensis, *Sermones*	F35	8°	PDN 235.1–2
1562	E.6.31	Pb 1557	Calvin, *Vltima admonitio ad Ioachimum Westphalum*	L81	8°	PDN 236 [also used as a pastedown in PDN 238]
1562	G.5.21	MS+ †Eng s. xv	Liturgy (noted)	M38	8°	PDN 237.1–2
1562	ZC2.8.3	MS+, †Eng s. xiii/xiv &++	?Psalter	N12	12°	PDN 238.1–7
		Pb$$ 1557	Calvin, *Vltima admonitio ad Ioachimum Westphaluma*	N12	12°	PDN 238.2–6 [also used as pastedown in PDN 236]
1562	K.1.7	MS** &+**		M45	8°	PDN 239.1–2
1563	G.6.24	MS+ †s. xvi		M33	8°	PDN 240.1, 4
		Pb$$ s. xvi	'De cognitione'	M33	8°	PDN 240.1–3,5

Parchment covers, *continued*

1564	B.6.41	MS+**		C45	8°	PDN 241.1
		Pb$$ s. xvi	Theology	C45	8°	PDN 241.1–4
1564	ZC2.5.6	MS+**		H95	8°	PDN 242.1, 8
		Pb$$ s. xvi	'De Iustitia'	H95	8°	PDN 242.1–8
1564	ZC2.3.13	MS+, †Eng s. xiv$^{in.}$ &++	?Philosophy	U1	8°	PDN 243.1–2
1565	ZC2.3.8	Pb$$ s. xvi		A2	4°	PDN 244.1–3
		Pb$$ s. xvi	?Dictionary	A2	4°	PDN 244.4–8
1565	E.5.28	Pb s. xvi &$$	NT in Gr. & Lat. Jn. 1	N2	4°	PDN 245.1–4
1565	ZC2.4.10	Pb$$, [?1560] &++	Becon, *The gouernaunce of Vertue*	V25	8°	PDN 247.1–8
1565	O.1.17	MS+, †Eng s. xv &++	*Missale*	*C1	8°	PDN 248.1, 2,4
		MS$$ s. xvi		*C1	8°	PDN 248.1–3,5
		MS$$ s. xvi		*C1	8°	PDN 248.6
1566	O.2.37	MS+, †Eng s. xiv/xv &++	*Psalterium*	*R1	8°	PDN 250.1–2
1566	O.2.2	MS+**		H77	4°	PDN 251.1–2
1567	O.1.13	MS+ †Neth s. xv	Text in Dutch	S85	4°	PDN 252.1–2
1573	ZC2.4.7	MS+, †Eng s. xiv &++	Accounts (probably a Compotus roll)	P35	8°	PDN 254.1–4 [probably the same MS as PDN 255]
1573	ZC2.4.8	MS+, †Eng s. xiv &++	Accounts (probably a Compotus roll)	P35	8°	PDN 255.1–4 [probably the same MS as PDN 254]

Items wrapped in parchment or paper MS

[*c.*1527]	ZC2.4.16	MS^ †Eng s. xiii/xiv	Egidius Romanus, *De regimine principum*	O21	8°	PDN 200A.1–5
1546	G.6.23	MS^ †Eng s. xii/xiii	St Matthew (glossed)	S77	8°	PDN 216.1–4
1546	G.6.21	MS^ †Eng s. xiv	Henricus de Gandavo, *Quodlibet*	W43	8°	PDN 217.1–3
1549	ZC2.4.15	MS^ †Eng s. xiv	?Aristotle, *De caelo et mundi* (with commentary)	F17	8°	PDN 218.1–4 [same MS as PDN 202]

1551	ZC2.6.2	MS^ †Eng s. xv	Gradual	C105 8° PDN 219A
		†Eng s. xii^ex.	Petrus Lombardus, *Collectanea in Psalmos*	C105 8° PDN 219B
1565	O.2.41	MS (G)^^ s. xvi		R6 8° PDN 246.1–3
1566	ZC2.3.4	MS^ †Eng s. xv	Missal	D1 4° PDN 249.1–6

Disbound item

| 1572 | ZC2.6.1 | Pb$$ s. xv | ?Canon law with commentary | *H4 8° PDN 253.1–4 |
| | | MS+** | | *H4 8° PDN 253.4 |

Rebound items – original bindings unknown

1505	L.6.1	Pb s. xv/xvi		V37 8° PDN 281
1522	L.4.12	Pb$$ s. xv	'Sermo lxxvi'	S94 fol. PDN 282.1–2
[c. 1523]	ZC2.7.11	MS$$ †Eng s. xii²	Breviary	L78 8° PDN 283.1–5
1532	C.5.14	MS s. xvi (G)$$		T13 8° PDN 284.1–2
c.1533	H.2.5	MS s. xvi (G)$$		B51 8° PDN 285
1545	H.1.30	Pb s. xvi &++	Orichovius, *Annales Polonici*	*R4 8° PDN 286.1–3
1545	ZC1.2.15	MS †?Fr s. xiv	Alphabetical dictionary	C11 4° PDN 297
1549	L.4.16	MS †Eng s. xv &++	Antiphoner	G26 fol. PDN 287.1–7
1549	ZC2.6.20	MS$$ †Eng s. xiv	Breviary	*S10 8° PDN 288.1–4
c.1550	G.6.8	MS †Eng s. xiv^in.	Jacobus de Voragine, *Legenda Aurea*	B36 16° PDN 289
		MS s. xvi (G)$$		B36 16° PDN 289
1550	ZC2.8.10	MS †Eng s. xiii^in &++	Geometrical MS	M41 8° PDN 290.1–3 [same MS as PDN 270]
1557	B.3.20	Pb s. xvi	?Canon law	*V3 fol. PDN 291.1–3
		MS+ †Eng or Fr s. xii^ex	Justinian, *Codex*	*V3 fol. PDN 291.1–3

Rebound items, *continued*

1562	G.4.20	Pb$$?1558	?Bucer, *Du Royaume de Christ*	B103	fol	.PDN 292 [also used in PDN 173]
1569	B.6.42	MS+ †s. xiii/xiv	Scholastic	E13	8°	PDN 293

APPENDIX X

Index of provenances and former owners

The index of provenances that follows is no more than provisional. The transcription of the ownership inscriptions in many instances is uncertain (some are crossed through, erased or sheared), and the identification of former owners in Venn and other biographical resources has often proved equally problematic. I am very grateful to Dr Elisabeth Leedham-Green and Pamela Selwyn, who have examined images of many of these difficult cases and suggested transcriptions and identifications which had eluded me.

In the Index entries, the name of the former owner is given as the heading (where this has been identified), followed on the next line by brief details of the book in which the provenance inscription occurs, with the catalogue number, shelf-mark and present binding. The inscription itself and other relevant information (such as initials stamped on the covers) follows, with biographical details of the former owner and any references to complete the entry.

Abbreviations:

CT	Centre-tool binding, or binding with a centre-tool.
MS	Manuscript leaves.
MS+	Strip from a MS used as a binding strengthener.
PT	Parchment covers.
PNL	Panel-binding.
R	Rebound volume.
RL	Roll-binding.
†	Pre-Geste ownership inscription
‡	Pre-Geste MS annotations, book-price or book-title(s) on fore-edge or spine.
*	Sheared or trace only.

The tabular information, printed in grey type below,
is laid out in the following columns

Imprint date	*Author*	*Cat. no. (first item)*	*Shelf-mark*	*Binding annotation*

Appleby, John

| 1566 | Nowell, A. | N14 | O.1.16 | PT |

'Joh[ann]es Applebe huius libri possessor'; 'H K' stamped in gold on front and back covers (see under K., H. below).

Venn records a pensioner of this name who matriculated at St John's Cambridge, Easter 1568.

Arundel, Henry Fitzalan, Earl of

| [1550] | Amsdorff, N. | A28 | L.5.22 | R |

'Arundel' on titlepage.

12th Earl of Arundel (1512–1579), Henry Fitzalan, who obtained much of Thomas Cranmer's library after its confiscation by the Crown in 1553. Presumably, this was an item not passed on to his son-in-law John, Lord Lumley, when his library was amalgamated with Lumley's sometime after 1557.

Atkinson, R[ichard]. *See also* Skypton, G.

| [c. 1508] | Eusebius | E56 | A.6.32(e) | R |

'teste R. Atkynson'

| 1529 | Augustine | A62 | A.6.32(a) | R |

'teste R. Atkynson'

Older contemporary of Geste's at King's College, Cambridge, and his predecessor as vice-Provost, and Provost after Sir John Cheke (1553–1556). Born at Ripley, Yorks., and admitted to King's in 1527 as a scholar from Eton (like Geste). Fellow 1530–1548; BA 1531–1532; MA 1535; BD 1542; DD 1545. Vice-provost of King's 1542–1548 immediately before Geste. Lady Margaret Preacher, 1545. Rector of Stower, Dorset, 1547–1556. Provost of King's 1553–1556 at the time Geste was expelled from the college (1554). Rector of Woodchurch, Kent. Incorporated his Cambridge degrees at Oxford in 1554 on his visit there to dispute with the Protestants on trial. Died of the plague in 1556. Will proved (King's Coll. Sept. 15 [1556]). Venn.

Bagley, William. *See also* Skypton, G.

| [c.1508] | Augustine | A62 | A.6.32(a) | R |

'teste G. Baggleo'.

Possibly the William Bagley from Warwickshire who was admitted to King's College as a scholar from Eton on 12 Sept. 1530. BA 1531/32. Fellow (1530). Venn.

Bambrogh [Bamburgh], Ioannes, *Vicar of Mallynge [Kent].*
See Rochester, St Andrew, *Benedictine Cathedral Priory*

Blanckard, Eurard[?]

| 1567 | Petit, G. | *P2 | B.5.39 | R |

'Ornatissimo viro, Eurardo Bla[?]nckardo, amico optatissimo, in Germaniam discedens d.d. Joannes Boulenius' on tp.

Unidentified. Geste's ownership of this book is far from certain.

Blithman[?], William

| 1527 | Thucydides | *T3 | Y.3.19(c) | RL |

'Williu[m] Blithman[?]' on p. 234 in a sixteenth-century hand.

This Blythman or Blithman not identified. Not in Venn.

See also under D., J.

Blomefyld, Wyllm.

| 1519 | Gratian | G30 | H.2.54 | R |

'Wyllm Blomefyld' in red ink in a page covered with annotations in Geste's hand on flyleaf at end.

Apparently the William Blomfild [Blomefield] (*fl.* 1529–1574) who had been a Benedictine monk at Bury St Edmunds, became a protestant, briefly held a living in Norwich (1569), but who is best known as an alchymist and author of Bloomfield's *Blossoms,* (1557) and Blomefyld's *Quintaessens* ([*c.* 1574]). *ODNB.*

Boulenius, Joannes. *See under* Blanckard, Eurard

Brandisby [Brandesby, Bransbie], John, DD

| 1495 | Ficino, M. | F5 | Z.2.56 | R |

'J. Bransbei Gest'

| 1506 | Reuchlin, J. | R17 | E.4.13 | R |

'Sir Joannes Brandesbie'

| 1520 | Basil | B6 | A.4.7 | R |

'Sum J. Brandisbei angli'

Brandisby, John, *continued*

| 1527 | Erasmus, D. | E48 | H.1.2 | PNL |

'Sum liber Edmundi Gest teste Brau[?]ndesbeio e' scriptore biro scilicet bono'. 'Joa[n]nis Brandesbie sum liber Gest ex dono doctoris Brandesbie caput'.

| 1538 | Luther, M. | L72 | ZC2.6.14 | PC |

'good maister Brandes[by] accept my wytt'

Geste's uncle and elder brother of Richard Brandisby, the classical scholar, Linacre Professor of Medicine and fellow of St John's College, Cambridge. Christopher Leedes (see below) was also a nephew. Presumably born in Yorkshire. Graduated from Michael-house, Cambridge, BA 1513/14 and MA 1517, becoming rector of Wittering, Northants in the same year. Apparently in Paris (*c.* 1518), though whether he studied there, and for how long, is not certain (see Introduction). BD and University Preacher 1523. Held livings in the York diocese: Sproatley (1528–1534), Master of Sutton College, Sutton-in Holderness (1528–1540), Settrington (1528–1549), Kirkby Wiske (1535) and Beeford (1539–1549); held prebendal stalls at Lincoln (Centum Solidorum, 1529–1546), Southwell (Dunham, 1534) and York (Osbaldwick, 1539, exchanged for that of Knaresborough in 1541). DD (1532). Took part, with Dr Richard Langrige (see below) in 1535, as chaplain to Edward Lee, Archbishop of York, in attempting to secure the signatures of the Religious in the Houses of the York diocese in support of the Royal Supremacy. Died in York, 7 Dec. 1549. Will, making bequests to his relatives, including Richard Brandisby, Edmund Geste and Christopher Leedes, proved, 14 February, 1550 (York, Borthwick Insitute, Abp. Reg. 29 f. 154). Venn and Cooper. Only items E48 and L72 are in their original bindings (a Marian triple panel (Oldham, BPEB, TRIP 9) and parchment wrappers respectively), but Brandisby was apparently a customer of Garrett Godfrey in 1527, though none of the above are listed, as were his two brothers, Richard and James. I owe this information to Dr Elisabeth Leedham-Green.

Bridges, John, Dr

| 1574 | Whitgift, J. | W16 | T.3.8 | RL |

'Ex dono Jo. Bridges.'

Matriculated as a pensioner at Peterhouse, Cambridge (1554) but migrated to Pembroke as fellow in 1556. BA (1557), MA and made deacon (1560) after three years in Italy, supported by Francis Russell, second earl of Bedford. Vicar of Herne, Kent (1562–1590). BD 1564 and canon of Winchester (1565–1578). Followed John Piers as Dean of Salisbury (1578) when the former became Bishop of Salisbury after Geste's death in 1577. Bishop of Oxford (1604–1618). *ODNB* and Venn.

Bruarne, Richard

| 1559 | Wittenberg Academia | W45 | B.5.8 | R |

'Ri. Bruarne'

Presumably the Richard Bruarne, who achieved a reputation as a Hebrew scholar, having been admitted to Lincoln College, Oxford, (*c.* 1535), graduating BA (1537), elected a Fellow (1538), and proceeding to MA (1539) and BD (1548). The same year he was elected a Fellow of Eton College, and appointed Regius Professor of Hebrew at Oxford until he was forced to resign his chair in 1559. A Catholic in outlook, Bruarne gave evidence in support of Stephen Gardiner at his trial in 1551, replaced Peter Martyr Vermigli as a canon of Christ Church, following the removal of the former in 1553, and was one of twelve Oxford and Cambridge theologians present at the Oxford disputations in 1554 when Cranmer, Latimer and Ridley were judged guilty of heresy, being rewarded soon after with a canonry at Windsor. In 1561, the fellows of Eton elected him Provost (without seeking the Queen's permission) and after an investigation by Parker, Robert Horne and Sir Anthony Cook as visitors, he was forced to resign. He died in 1565 and was buried at Windsor. *ODNB.*

Brynckley [Brinkley], Richard. *See also* Cambridge, Franciscan Convent

| 1521 | Pelbárt, O. | P15 | M.1.27 | RL |

'Fratris Richardi Brynickilij [*sic*] ministri [erased]'

Evidently the Cambridge Franciscan Richard Brynckley [Brinkley] who commenced BD 1489 and DD 1492, incorporated at Oxford in 1524, as Provincial Minister of the Order (1518–1526), dying *c.* 1525–1527. A student of Greek and Hebrew, he owned or borrowed a number of books of which some, like this, remain (J.R.H. Moorman, *The Grey Friars in Cambridge 1225–1538*, Cambridge: University Press, 1952, pp. 155f.; Ker, *MLGB*, 24, 401); Cooper I, 34.

Bullore or Bulloke, [?R. R.]

| 1507 | Castellensis, H. | C49 | H.I.21 | RL |

'[?R.R.] Bullore' or 'Bulloke' inscribed at top of front calf cover;
'R.R' very faded and uncertain.
Identification uncertain.
A Richard Bullar, BA 1536/37, MA 1540, Fellow of Christ's College
1539–1540, left (in 1540) a collection of 73 items comprising classical,
grammatical and theological works including some of Erasmus,
Melanchthon and Bullinger (BiCI, I, no.6), but not this one.

If 'Bulloke', Venn records a Richard Bullock, BCanL 1476/77
but no other details; a Henry Bullock, Fellow of Queens 1506, DD
1520, author of *Oratio habita Cantabrigiae* (1520), Vice-Chancellor
1524–1525, friend and correspondent of Erasmus and chaplain to
Cardinal Wolsey, who died in 1526; and a George Bullock, Fellow of
St John's College 1537/38, Master 1554–59, Lady Margaret Professor
1556–1559, DD 1557, who retired to Nevers Abbey, France, during
the reigns of Edward VI and Elizabeth I, and later to Paris and
Antwerp (died 1580).

Bulward, Thomas

| 1535 | Oecolampadius, J. | O10 | C.I.5 | RL
[Garrett
Godfrey] |

'Thome Bulward p[re]tiu[m] iijs'
An older contemporary of Geste's at King's College, Cambridge,
Thomas Bulward (or Burward) from Oxborough, Norfolk, was
admitted as a scholar from Eton in 1525, graduated BA 1529/30 and
MA 1533. He was a Fellow of King's, 1528–1541.

Calvarde

| 1542 | Pighius, A. | P33 | N.4.6 | CT |

'Calvarde est domine'.
Venn records a John Calvard or Calver, at Queen's College: BA
1526/27; MA 1530; Fellow of Queen's 1529–1533; but nothing is
recorded of his career after 1533. Venn also records a John Calvard:
matric. pens. from St John's, Michaelmas 1544.

| 1526 | Cochlaeus, J. | *C7 | H.I.19 | RL |

'[?]Ego su[m] Jo. Calverdi ex dono mag[ist]ri J Fobson
[=?Hobson] ...'

Possibly the same Calvarde. Venn records three 'Hobsons' who held
the degree of MA, *s.v.* 'Hobson', below.

A Leonard Calvarde was vicar of Skyllington, Lincolnshire, in
1548 (26 May) and died 14 August 1550 (Lincoln Chapter Act Book).

Cambridge, Franciscan Convent. *See also* Brynckley, Richard

| 1521 | Pelbárt, O. | P15 | M.1.27 | RL |

'Thomas Potter', 'p[re]tium vj^d. 1565' and (in an earlier hand – all
erased) 'Fratris Richardi Brynickilij [sic] ministri'.
The Cambridge Franciscans were dissolved in 1538. The identity of
this Thomas Potter who acquired the book in 1565 has not been
discovered.

Chedsey, William

| [c. 1545] | Postel, G. | P45 | ZC2.6.4 | PT |

'Gulielmi Chedsei'
Presumably the William Chedsey, Canon of Christ Church, Oxford,
and Catholic opponent of the Protestant Reformers. Admitted
to Corpus Christi College, Oxford, 1529 from Somerset (aged 18);
BA 1530; Fellow 1533; MA 1534; ordained priest 1535; chaplain to
Edmund Bonner (1536); BD 1542; and DD 1546. Opposed Peter
Martyr Vermigli, Regius Professor, at the Oxford Disputation on the
eucharist (1549), committed to the Marshalsea for 'seditious preaching' in 1551 and then entrusted to Thomas Thirlby, bishop of Ely, for
the rest of Edward's reign. With Mary's accession, preferment
followed, with prebendal stalls at Windsor (1554), St Paul's, Exeter
and Oxford (1557), and in 1558 he became President of his college. In
1554, he took part in the Oxford disputation on the eucharist against
Cranmer, Ridley and Latimer. Under Elizabeth I, he lost all his
preferments and was imprisoned in the Fleet as a recusant (1562),
dying in custody (*c.* 1577).

D., T.

| 1544 | Chiari, Isidore | C64 | C.3.12 | CT |

'T D' on covers astride centre-tool CT c.1 on calf covers.
Identity uncertain.
Venn records a Thomas Dickenson who was admitted to King's
College, Cambridge, as a scholar from Eton in 1522. BA 1526/27;
MA 1530/31. One with this name was rector of St Mary, Colchester,
Essex, 1556–1558, died in 1558.

Dixon

1523	Erasmus, D.	E28	G.5.20	PNL [Nicholas Spierinck]

'Geste me possidet teste Dixon et Hansone'
Venn records a Richard Dixon admitted to King's as a scholar from Eton in 1551.

Dunwich, William

1533	Haymo	H9	D.5.13	PNL ['I G']

'Will[iel]m[u]s Donwiche me iure possedit' on the last blank leaf (Ddd8) in an early sixteenth-century hand.
I owe this transcription to Dr. E. Leedham-Green. Unidentified.

Edington, Wiltshire – House of Bonshommes, of St James, St Catherine and All Saints

1478	Gulielmus, *Parisiensis*	G49	L.5.10	R

'Liber domus de Edyndon'.
The house was dissolved when the rector and twelve ministers surrendered in 1539. Ker, *MLGB*, 77, 401; Knowles, *MRH*, 179.

G., I.

1556	Euthymius.	E59	A.6.25	CT

'I G' on covers.
Unidentified.

Geste, Edmund

1495	Ficino, M.	F5†	Z.2.56	R

'J. Bransbei Gest'.

1523	Erasmus, D.	E28	G.5.20	PNL [Nicholas Spierinck]

'Geste me possidet teste Dixon et Hansone'; 'me possidet Edmundus Gest'.

1524	Clichtoveus, J.	C82?‡	N.3.17	RL

?'Guest'.

[?1525]	Bugenhagen, J.	B116	C.5.11(b)	R

'gest'

1525	Capito, W. F.	C39	F.2.4	PT

'Geste me possidet teste scriptor[e]'.

1525	Knopken, A.	K11	D.2.6(b)	RL

'gest'

?1525	Zwingli, U.	Z6	N.6.13	RL

'gest'

1526	Bugenhagen, J.	B113?†	C.5.4(f)	RL/CT

'gest'

1526	Erasmus, D.	E40?‡	L.6.4	R

'Gest'

1527	Bucer, M.	B102‡	C.1.6(c)	RL

'gest'

1527	Erasmus, D.	E48†	H.1.2	PNL

'Sum liber Edmundi Gest teste Brau[?]ndesbeio e scriptore biro
scilicet bono'; 'Joa[n]nis Brandesbie sum liber Gest ex dono
doctoris Bra[n]desbie caput'.

1527	Vio, T. de	V33?‡	K.3.42	PL

'gest'

1528	Althamer, A.	A26	D.2.6(d)	RL

'gest'*

1528	Melanchthon, P.	M46?†	C.5.4(e)	RL/CT

'gest'

1532	Sachs, H.	S2	ZC2.7.9(a)	R

'Ed. Gestus me possidet testante scriptore'.

1532	Erasmus, D.	E33	I.3.8	CT

'E G' on covers.

1534	Erasmus, D.	E38	ZC1.4.6	CT

'E G' on covers.

1534	Oecolampadius, J.	O15‡	C.1.6(b)	RL

'gest'

1536	Megander, C.	M26	D.2.6(c)	RL

'gest'*

1537	Suetonius	S96	Y.5.29	RL

'Su[m] liber gest'.

1538	Luther, M.	L63	D.5.4(a)	RL

'gest'

1538	Luther, M.	L72	ZC2.6.14†	PT

'good maister Brandes[by] accept my wytt'.

1538	Draconites, J.	D25?†	C.5.4(c)	RL

'gest'

Geste, Edmund, *continued*

| 1539 | Campensis, J. | C29 | F.2.5 | PT |

'Gest/ Liber hebraicus/ Gest/ Gest[?]e. Gest est dominus meus testante/ scriptore cum multis alijs/ quas nunc perscribere longum est. Gest est dominus meus testante/ scriptore cum multis alijs'.

| 1543 | Rhegius, U. | R20 | C.6.5(c) | PL |

'Mr gest'

| 1544 | Brentz, J. | B89 | C.6.5(a) | PL |

'[?]Mr gest'

| 1544 | Aepinus, J. | A6 | C.6.5(b) | PL |

'[?]Mr gest'

| 1544 | Sarcerius, E. | S21 | D.6.8 | RL/CT |

'gest'*

| 1546 | Cruciger, C. | C114 | D.4.4 | CT |

'g' [for 'gest'?]

| 1546 | Spangenberg, J. | S77 | G.6.23 | MS |

'm[r] gest[?e]'

| 1549 | Flacius, M. | F12 | ZC2.8.10(b) | R |

'gest'

| 1550 | Meier, G. | M41 | ZC2.8.10(a) | R |

[?]'gest'*

| 1550/1 (10 Feb.) | Eucherius | E55 | E.4.1 | RL |

Presentation inscription 'to Mr Edmunde Gest' from Christopher Leedes.

| 1550/1 (10 Feb.) | John, *of Damascus* | J12 | N.3.13 | RL |

Presentation inscription 'to Mr Edmund gest' from Christopher Leedes.

| [?1551] | Bullinger, H. | B122 | G.3.22 | R |

Presentation inscription to 'Mr Edmund Geste' from Christopher Leedes.

| 1553 | Zegers, N. | Z3 | E.6.30 | PT |

'Edmond/ Roffen'.

| 1555 | Borrhaus, M. | B59 | G.4.10(a) | R |

'E. Gest'.

| 1557 | Borrhaus, M. | B60 | G.4.10(b) | R |

'E. Gest'.

Gilpin, [?Godfrey]

1539   Bonaventura   B52   C.4.1   R

   [?]'D. gilpinnus' at top of tp (erased).

Identity uncertain.

A Godfrey Gilpin of Christ's Cambridge, was later a Fellow of
Trinity, Lady Margaret Preacher and (at the time of his death) Vice-
Master of Trinity and vicar of Pinchbeck, Lincs. An inventory of his
books (made 13 September 1550) lists mainly theological works (BiCI,
I, no. 46), though this is not among them. Venn.

Gwyn, William

1522   Henry VIII   H40   N.5.13(a)   PNL

   'liber co[n]stat William Gwyn'.

1523   More, T.   M81   N.5.13(d)   PNL

   'liber constat William Gwyn'.

Identity uncertain.

A William Gwyn was Rector or Prebend (second portion) of St
George's, Pontesbury, Shropshire (in the gift of The Queen's College,
Oxford) from 1529–1540, and a William Gwyn held office at the
Hospital or free Chapel of St Nicholas, Nantwich, Cheshire, presented
in 1531, and held the Prebendal stall of Stotfold, Lichfield Cathedral.

Gylbe[rt], Thomas

1546   Smith, R.   S64   R.6.46   CT

   Part of a leaf of a MS letter (in English) from 'Thomas Gylbe[rt]',
   dated from London, 21 July 1561.

Identity uncertain.

A Thomas Gylbert was a Fellow of Peterhouse, Cambridge, 1521–
1526, but Venn records no further details after 1526, and there is no
particular reason to associate this Gylbert with Cambridge since by
the time the book was bound Geste had left Cambridge and was
purchasing his books in London. Furthermore, as the letter was
binder's waste there is no reason to suppose that Gylbert had ever
been the owner of the book.

Hanson

| 1523 | Erasmus, D. | E28 | G.5.20 | PNL [Nicholas Spierinck] |

'Geste me possidet teste Dixon et Hansone'.
Identity uncertain.
Venn records only a Thomas Hanson (alias Hampson) with a BA
1524/25, Cambridge college not known.
See also under 'Dixon' (above).

Hobson[?]

| 1526 | Cochlaeus, J. | *C7 | H.1.19 | RL ['M D'] |

'[?]Ego su[m] Jo. Calverdi ex dono mag[ist]ri J Fobson
[=?Hobson] ...'
Identity uncertain.
Venn records three Hobsons who held the degree of MA. A 'Richard'
(college unknown), MA 1520/21, BD 1528 and DD 1530 who has been
identified with the 'Richard' in Cooper, I, 69; a 'Robert', MA and
Fellow of St John's (1533), who may have been the one who later
held livings in Yorkshire (1551–1570); and a Hobson (Christian name
not recorded), MA 1517, BD 1527, who may have been a Fellow of
Clare College.
See also under Calvarde.

J., D.

| 1527 | Herodotus | *H2 | Y.3.19(a) | RL |

'D: J'[... smudged] on p. 11.
Not identified.
See also under Williu[m] or Welliu[?m], Thomas.

Joy[?], Hugh

| 1527 | Thucydides | *T3 | Y.3.19(c) | RL |

'This is the book [?of] Hue [?]Joyyees', in the hand of a young
sixteenth-century reader, on p. 24 and on p. 126 (where the name
has been torn off).
Not identified. *See also* Newton.

K., H.

| 1566 | Nowell, A. | N14 | O.1.16 | PT |

'H.K.' stamped in gold on both covers.

Not identified.
Venn records a Hugh Kebyll, Fellow of Peterhouse, 1529; BA 1526/
27. The grace for MA 1530 has been erased. No further details. A
Henry Kempe was admitted as a scholar from Eton, 22 August 1551,
matriculating the same year but leaving in 1555.
See also under Appleby, John.

Kervyle, Nicholas

| 1536 | Brentz, J. | B72 | C.6.1 | PNL |

'Qui stat viduat me cadat ex kervyle'.

| 1541 | Sarcerius, E. | S17 | C.6.10 | RL |

'Qui stat viduat me cadat [ex?] Kervyle', with 'N K' stamped in
blind on the covers.

A younger contemporary of Geste who entered King's College,
Cambridge, in 1545 as a scholar from Eton (aged 17); a Fellow from
1548, he graduated BA in 1550, proceeded to MA in 1553, and then
went into exile on the continent, first at Zürich (in the house of the
printer Christopher Froschauer), then at Frankfurt. On return, he
became chaplain to Edmund Grindal, Bishop of London, and in 1560
vicar of South Weald, Essex, to which was added later that year the
nearby rectory of Laindon, holding both livings until his death in
August 1566. The previous year he had been among the leading
opponents of the prescribed clerical vesture, along with Thomas
Sampson and Laurence Humphrey, petitioning the ecclesiastical
commission for exemption and one of the five who formally presented the petition to Matthew Parker, archbishop of Canterbury.
Venn; *ODNB*.

Kyrbe, Chrysostom

| 1512 | John, *of Damascus* | J13 | L.4.5 | R |

'Chr[i]so[s]to[?mus] Kyrbe canonicu[s] de Welbeke'.
Possibly one of the canons of the Premonstratensian Abbey of St
James, Welbeck, Notts., but not among the canons granted pensions
who signed the surrender in 1538 – but he may have been one of the
three who were residing on their vicarage or grange at the time of
the surrender but still granted a pension, or he may have died before
the surrender. Apparently not recorded in Ker, *MLGB* or Ker-
Watson, *MLGB Suppl.*

Langrige, Richard

| 1523 | Gregory I | G31 | A.1.15 | R |

'Langrigii liber'.

Possibly the Dr Richard Langrige, STP, who was archdeacon of Cleveland and (like John Brandisby) chaplain to Edward [Lee], Archbishop of York, and involved in securing signatures for the Royal Supremacy in 1535.

Lee, Edward

| 1503 | Petrus, *Comestor* | P20 | L.4.10 | R |

'Eduardus Leeus London'. 'Liber Edoardi Leeus'. Both on a flyleaf at the end. 'Jesus est [?magister] meus' on tp.

Presumably the Edward Lee (1481/2–1544) who was archbishop of York (1531–1544) in succession to Thomas Wolsey. John Brandisby and Richard Langrige were among his chaplains. Admitted to Magdalen College, Oxford, in 1495, Fellow (1500), graduated BA 1501, Lee migrated to Cambridge, incorporating his degree (1503), being ordained in the London diocese (1504) and acquiring a number of preferments including prebendal stalls at Exeter, Lincoln, and Salisbury (1509–1531). After proceeding to BD 1515, Lee moved to the continent for further study at Louvain and Bologna (later incorporating a DTh at Oxford in 1531), assisting Erasmus in his revision of the NT, but soon clashing with him by publishing his own emendations, annotations and apologia (1520–1521), copies of which Geste owned (L26). Appointed chaplain and almoner to Henry VIII (1523), Lee was sent on a number of embassies, including one to the pope at Bologna (1530), and was rewarded with the chancellorship of Salisbury (1529) and prebendal stalls at St Stephen, Westminster (1530) and York (1531), becoming its archbishop (1531–1544), during which time he attempted to balance his conservative instincts with loyalty to Henry VIII. Emden; Foster; *ODNB*.

Lee, Richard

| 1559 | Loss, L. | L41 | G.2.15 | R |

'Ricardi Lei et amicorum' [deleted].

Among a number of this name, Venn records a Richard Lee who was Fellow of St John's, 1516, MA 1517, but no further information.

See also Philpot, J., whose name occurs on the same tp.

Leedes, Christopher

1550/1 (10 Feb.)	Eucherius	E55	E.4.1	RL

'CΩL' monogram. Presentation 'to Mr Edmunde Gest' written down the outside margin of tp.

1550/1 (10 Feb.)	John, *of Damascus*	J12	N.3.13	RL

'CΩL' monogram. Presentation to 'Mr Edmund gest' written as above.

[?1551]	Bullinger, H.	B122	G.3.22	R

'CΩL' monogram. Presentation to 'Mr Edmund Geste' written as above.
Nephew of John Brandisby and Geste's brother [in-law].
See *Introduction*.

Lodyngton, Joannes

1518	Le Fèvre, J.	L25	L.5.36	RL

Verse at end of MS flyleaf, signed 'per me Joannem Lodyngton'.
A John Lodyngton, cellarer, alias Atkyns, was the third among fourteen canons from Launde Augustinian priory of St John the Baptist in Leicestershire who acknowledged the Royal Supremacy in 1534 (*L. & P.*, VII (1534), no. 1126), third among thirteen from the same priory petitioning Thomas Cromwell for pensions in c. 22 December 1538 (*L. & P.*, XIII.ii (1538), no. 1123), and, as John Atkyns, was among eleven (from the dissolved priory) granted a pension (of £8 p.a.) on 16 December 1539, *L. & P.*, XIV.ii. (1539), no. 692.

Mabliston[e], John

1544	Broeckwey a Konigstein, A.	B94	D.4.8	RL/CT

'Joannes Mablistonus' across tp.
Not identified.

Maxfeldus, Thomas

1539	Bonaventura	B52	C.4.1	R

'Thomas Maxfeldus' on tp.
A 'Thomas Maxfield' (as Dr E. Leedham-Green informs me) is recorded in Venn as BA from Magdalene in 1575/76, but it is far from certain that this is the one whose inscription occurs here, not least because of its late date.
Two other ownership inscriptions on tp. (both erased). *See under* Gilpin *and* Sedyllius[?].

Newtonum, [?Octograni]

| 1527 | Thucydides | ' *T3 | Y.3.19(c) | RL |

'Iste liber p[er]tinet ad [?]Octogranj Newton[um]' in an early sixteenth-century hand on p. 232. Reading of the first name is very uncertain.
Not identified.

Philpot, Ioannis, & amicorum

| 1559 | Loss, L. | L41 | G.2.15 | R |

'Io. Philpot & amic[?o]r[?um]'.
Not identified and not found in Venn. *See also* Lee, Richard. The possibility that this was the 'John Philpott' who was among those who petitioned, with 'Kervile' (*see above*, 'John Kervyle'), in 1565 for liberty to follow their consciences on the use of the surplice, is mentioned in the Introduction, p. 34 n. 111.

Ponet, John

| 1551 | Vermigli, P. M. | V15 | C.2.2 | CS |

'J P 1552' and 'Jo. Winton 1553'.
Bishop of Winchester (1551–1553) in succession to Stephen Gardiner (1531–1550) who replaced him under Mary (1553–1555). Born (*c.* 1514) in Kent, graduated at Queen's College, Cambridge, studying Greek under Thomas Smith (1513–1577); BA 1532/33, MA 1534/35, Fellow (1532), Bursar (1537–1539), Dean (1540–1542); one of Cranmer's chaplains; canon of Canterbury and proctor (1546); DD 1547; Bishop of Rochester (1550); on the commissions for the suppression of heresy and reform of the ecclesiastical laws (1551); exiled to the continent after the suppression of Wyatt's rebellion, settling at Strasbourg where he died in 1556. Author of the *Short Catechism* (1553) and *A Short Treatise of Politike Power* (1556) among other works. *ODNB*; Venn; Cooper I, 155–6.

Potter, Thomas. *See* Cambridge Franciscan Convent

Pykering, Robert

| 1522 | Erasmus, D. | E31 | N.6.1 | PNL |

'Dominus meus est domi pykeringus' with pen trials and two notes in Geste's hand.
Probably the Robert Pykering who was an older contemporary of Geste at King's College, Cambridge, admitted (age 16) as a scholar from Eton (1531) from Chichester; Fellow (1534–1549), BA 1535/36, MA 1539, MD 1548; 'died in Dr Hatcher's house'(1549). Will proved

(1551), leaving 149 items in 224 vols. comprising medical books and a substantial collection of general literature in Latin and Greek, some theology and biblical studies, including works by Erasmus (though this one is not listed), Melanchthon, Luther, Oecolampadius and Bullinger (BiCI, I, no. 52). Venn; Jayne, *LCER*, 105.

Rochester, St Andrew, Benedictine Cathedral Priory

| 1515 | Seneca | S45 | Y.2.16 | R |

'Liber claustri Roffensis ex dono magistri Ioannis bambrogh Vicarii de Mallynge'.
John Bambrogh was vicar of Malling, Kent (1517–1524). Ker-Watson, *MLGB Suppl.*, pp. 59, 108, 139, 142 [Bamburgh].

S., W.

| 1556 | Tavernarius, J. | T2 | ZC2.6.3 | PT |

'W.S.' at foot of, and top-edge, of tp.
Not identified.

Sedyllius[?], Joannis

| 1539 | Bonaventura | B52 | C.4.1 | R |

'Johan[n]is [?]sedylli[us]' at top of the titlepage (erased). Reading very uncertain. Another possibility is 'Johan[n]is Sedgiwius'.
Not identified

Skypton, Gulielmus

| [c. 1508] | Eusebius, *of Cremona* | E56 | A.6.32(e) | R |

'Liber Gulielmi Skypton teste R. Atkynson'. 'Liber Gulielmi Skypton teste G. Baggleo'.

| 1526 | Bible [*Latin*] | B35 | G.6.14 | PNL |

'Skypton [...?] (twice, both erased) me possidet'.

| 1529 | Augustine | A62 | A.6.32(a) | R |

'liber Gulielmi Skypton teste R. Atkyns[o]n'.

| 1531 | Hugo, *de Sancto Charo* | H84 | G.2.5 | R |

'Wyllya[m] Skypton' (three times).

| 1531 | Tritheim, J. | T20 | B.5.44 | R |

'Gulielmus Skypton'.
Older Yorkshire contemporary of Geste at King's College, Cambridge, admitted as a scholar from Eton in 1522 (age 16) from York. Fellow from 1525 to about 1543. BA 1526/27, MA 1530, BD 1536/37. Ordained deacon (Lincoln) 16 April 1530; priest 11 June 1530. Venn. *See also* Atkinson, R. *and* Bagley, W.

Smyth, Thomas

| 1505 | Vivaldus, J. L. | V37 | L.6.1 | R |

'Liber d[omini] Thomas Smyth'.

The identity of this Thomas Smyth has not been established. It is far from certain that this is the Sir Thomas Smith (1513–1577), scholar, diplomat, and Secretary of State, of Queens' College, Cambridge, whose library catalogue (1566, rev. 1576) was transcribed in John Strype's, *Life of the learned Sir Thomas Smith kt* (1698) [from Queen's College, MS 49 and 83] and whose Latin and Greek books were left to Queen's. Cooper, I, 368–73; *ODNB*; Venn.

Swynne

| 1481 | Duns, J., *Scotus.* | D33 | L.4.25 | R |

'Pe[r]tinet A [or ad] Swynne', in a formal fifteenth-century hand on the final leaf of text. Reading far from certain.

Not identified.

W., W.

| 1541 | Cicero | C74 | X.2.16 | RL/CT |

'W W' on covers.

Just possibly the initials of William Wynke, one of Geste's contemporaries at King's College, Cambridge, admitted the same year (1536) and also a scholar from Eton. Fellow (1539–1556); BA 1540/41; MA 1544; BD 1555. Ordained 1551 (Norwich). Succeeded Geste as Vice-Provost, following the former's removal from office in 1553 and expulsion from King's in 1554. Vicar of Fordingbridge (Hants.) in 1555. Recusant under Elizabeth I. Venn.

Another possibility is William Whitelocke [Whitlock], another of Geste's contemporaries at Eton and King's College, Cambridge, admitted the following year (23 August 1537, aged 17) as a scholar. Fellow (1540–1560); BA 1541/42; MA 1545; BD 1553. Vice-provost (1556–1559), following William Wynke. Held livings at Prescot, Lancs. (1558), Greenford, Middlesex (1560) and the stall of Curborough, Lichfield Cathedral (1561), at which he wrote his 'Chronicon Lichefeldensis ecclesie' based on earlier chronicles.

Welbeck, Premonstratensian Abbey of, St James. *See* Kyrbe, Chrysostom

Weston[us]

| 1540 | Gulielmus, *Baufeti* | G47 | ZC2.6.12 | PT |

'habit deus hijs q[u]°[?rum] finem… Weston[us]'.

| 1548 | Titelman, F. | T11 | C.5.15 | CS |

'habit deus hijs q[u]°[?rum] Weston[us]'

Perhaps the Edmund Weston, who held the Yatesbury prebendal stall at Salisbury, 1569–1570. Venn records him as a pensioner at Queens' College, Cambridge, *c.* 1545.

Another possibility is Hugh Weston (d.1558). Born in Leicestershire, graduated at Balliol College, Oxford, BA 1530, Fellow of Lincoln College, Rector (1538), DD and Lady Margaret Professor (*c.* 1540), Dean of Westminster (1553), prolocutor of Convocation. Took leading part in Oxford Disputation (1554) against Cranmer, Ridley and Latimer. In 1556 he was obliged to resign the Rectorship of Lincoln College, when Cardinal Pole's commissioners visited the university, and to exchange the deanery of Westminster for that of Windsor. Deprived (1557) by Pole for adultery and sent to the Tower after attempting to appeal to Rome. Died soon after Elizabeth's accession (1558). Foster; Cooper I, 187–88.

Whitelocke [Whitlock], William. *See* W., W.

Wilkinson, W.

| 1570 | Sonnius, F. | S70 | B.5.33 | PT |

'W. Wilkinson' across tp.

Not identified. Post-Geste (see S70).

Williu[m] or Welliu[?m], Thomas

| 1527 | Herodotus | *H2 | Y.3.19(a) | RL |

Pen trials (among others) at top of p. 11.

See also under J., D.

Venn records a Thomas Bawghe, alias Williams, who was a scholar and Fellow of King's Hall, Cambridge, with an MA 1506/07, BD 1517 and DD 1531, Rector of Dry Drayton (1517–1532), Chancellor of St Paul's Cathedral (1530–1558) and Archdeacon of Surrey (from 1536). Cooper I, 173.

Wiston [or Weston], Mr

[1565]   Jewel, J.   J8   T.3.3(a)   R

'This Book was brought in by Mr [?]Wiston' [or 'Weston'] with a note at the top of the tp. 'Liber Ecclesiae / Cathed. Saru[m] / 1664'.

Possibly a book that had strayed from the Library during the Interregnum, subsequently returned after the Restoration.

Wynke, William. *See* W., W.

APPENDIX XI

1: *MS annotations in Geste's hand:*
author index

It is not possible to determine exactly when Geste made these annotations and, as all but a very few items were imported from the continent, it is likely that in most instances the annotations date at the earliest from a year or more *after* the imprint dates. Where evidence survives indicating Geste's acquisition of an item later than the imprint date (e.g. in the case of an item acquired at a later date from a former owner or carrying a dated presentation), the item is entered at the date of acquisition ('>' to indicate 'later than') and the imprint date shown in brackets (e.g. 1551 > [1546]). As it is clear that Geste acquired and annotated some items unbound or in temporary covers before more permanent binding (often with other items of later date) it has been thought best to list all other items under the imprint date rather than suggest a later date for his annotations, e.g. after the latest imprint in the case of multi-itemed volumes.

Abbreviations

m	Marginal lines or other form of annotation.
MS	MS leaves or interleaving in Geste's hand.
n	Notes in the text.
n*	Note(s) on a blank leaf, title-page or flyleaf.
tp	Annotation or monogram on title-page of uncertain authorship.
#	Includes some annotations on inside uncut leaves before binding.
=	Underlinings in text.
†	Second-hand copies, some with annotations by earlier readers / owners.
?	Some degree of uncertainty as to whether the annotations are by Geste.
+	Some annotations cropped in rebinding.
++	Some annotations cropped, though book still in its original binding.

Author	Imprint date	Type(s) of anno-tation	Cat. no	Shelf-mark
Aepinus, J.	1555–56	n m	A4	E.6.35(d–e)
Aepinus, J.	1545	m	A7	D.5.6(b)
Aepinus, J.	1553	n m	A8	ZC1.4.10(d)
Aepinus, J.	1557	n m	A9	K.2.15(c)
Aepinus, J.	1546	m	A10	ZC2.3.5(c)
Aepinus, J.	[1548?]	n m	A11	I.4.4(b)
Alardus	1541	n?	A13	ZC2.6.19(b)
Alesius, A.	1553	n m	A20	C.4.7
Alesius, A.	1550	n m	A21	G.6.22(b)
Altenburg	1570	n m	A24	I.7.7(b)
Althamer, A.	1536	m	A27	D.6.12
Amsdorff, N. von	[1550]	m	A28	L.5.22
Andreae, J.	1564	m	A32	L.5.27(a)
Andreae, J.	1565	m	A33	K.2.8(c)
Andreae, J.	1564	n m	A34	K.2.8(a)
Andreae, J.	1560	n	A35	ZC2.3.5(a)
Andreae, J.	1559	n m	A36	L.6.13(e)+
Andreae, J.	1558	n m	A37	K.2.11(b)
Anselm	1549	n m	A41	G.4.12(b)
Antichristus	[c. 1562–1565]	=?	A42	I.5.5(c)
Arboreus, J.	1540	m?	A49	M.1.17
Aretius, B.	1570	m#	A50	ZC1.4.13(a)
Aretius, B.	1575	m	A51	ZC2.7.1
Artopoeus, P.	1546	n m	A55	C.4.2
Artopoeus, P.	1538	n? m?	A56	E.6.5
Augustine	1542	n m	A60	A.4.24
Augustine	1542	n? m?	A61	A.5.2
Augustine	1576	m?	A66	A.6.23
Bacherius, P.	1556	n m	B1	ZC2.1.10(a)
Baius, M.	1563	n m	B3	ZC2.4.14(c)
Baius, M.	1566	n m	B4	I.1.5(d)
Balbus, J.	1497	n m	B5	Y.2.12†
Basil	1520	m	B6	A.4.7(a)
Bede	1521	m?	B10	A.4.7(b)

Bernold	1565	n m	B17	M.2.21(c)
Beurlin, J.	1557	m	B19	C.4.11(c)
Bèze, T.	1571	m	B20	K.1.33(a)
Bèze, T.	1558	n m	B21	ZC2.4.6(e)
Bèze, T.	1574	m	B22	ZC1.4.4(c)
Bèze, T.	1567	m	B23	ZC1.4.8(b)
Bèze, T.	1573	m#	B24	K.1.33(c)
Bèze, T.	1573	m?	B26	M.2.20(a)
Bèze, T.	1572	m	B27	K.1.33(b)
Bèze, T.	1570	n m	B28	ZC2.1.6(d)++
Bible	1532	n	B31	G.6.10†
Bible	1529	n	B32	G.6.11
Bible	1529	n	B33	G.6.13†
Bible	1526	n	B34	G.6.12
Bible	1524/26	n	B35	G.6.14†
Bible	[c. 1550]	n m	B36	G.6.8?†
Bible	1552	n m?	B37	G.6.7?†
Bible. NT Rom. & Gal.	1544	n m	B38	C.4.14
Bibliander, T.	1555	n m	B40	L.5.7(c)
Bibliander, T.	1552	m	B41	E.6.23(a)
Bibliander, T.	1558	n	B43	B.3.19(c)
Bidembach, W.	1566	n	B45	I.4.6(b)
Biel, G.	1510	n m	B46	L.3.15
Bodius, H.	[c. 1533]	m	B51	H.2.5?†
Bonaventura	1539	n m	B52	C.4.1†
Bonaventura	1522	n m	B53	H.1.38?‡
Bonaventura	1522	m	B53	H.1.39?‡
Bonaventura	1522	m?	B53	H.1.40?‡
Boquinus, P.	1576	m?	B56	K.1.27(b)
Boquinus, P.	1561	n m	B57	L.5.19(c)
Bredenbach, T.	1568	n m	B67	D.1.4(d)
Brentz, J.	1576	m?	B68	L.2.2
Brentz, J.	1556	n?	B69	K.2.11(c)
Brentz, J.	1542	n m	B71	G.3.6(a)
Brentz, J.	1536	n m	B72	C.6.1
Brentz, J.	1554	m	B79	G.6.4(b)
Brentz, J.	1558	n m	B80	G.5.16

Brentz, J.	1566	n m	B82	G.3.7(a)
Brentz, J.	1542	m	B83	C.6.3
Brentz, J.	1545	m	B84	G.3.8(a)
Brentz, J.	1549	m	B85	G.3.8(b)
Brentz, J.	1551>[1536]	m	B86	G.3.22(a)
Brentz, J.	1564	n m	B87	G.3.7(c)
Brentz, J.	1548	n m	B88	C.6.4
Brentz, J.	1552	n m	B90	M.2.25
Brentz, J.	1556	n m	B92	K.2.11(a)
Brentz, J.	1564	m	B93	L.5.27(b)
Broeckwey, A.	1544	m	B94	D.4.8†
Bucer, M.	1532	n m	B98	E.4.7
Bucer, M.	1553	m?	B100	G.2.20(a)
Bucer, M.	1562	n	B101	G.4.19(a)
Bucer, M.	1562	n m	B103	G.4.20
Bucer, M.	1545	n m	B104	L.5.15(b)
Bucer, M.	[?1540]	n	B106	L.5.15(a)
Bucer, M.	1543	n m	B107	H.1.5
Bucer, M.	1546	n m	B108	I.4.4(a)
Bucer, M.	1534	m?	B109	ZC2.2.9(c)
Bucer, M.	1548	n m	B110	L.5.16(b)
Bugenhagen, J.	1524	m	B111	D.1.3(a)
Bugenhagen, J.	1525	m	B112	D.1.3(b)
Bugenhagen, J.	1546	n m	B115	C.2.10
Bullinger, H.	1544	m?	B123	I.4.11(b)
Bullinger, H.	1558	n	B124	ZC2.5.7(b)
Bullinger, H.	1554	n m	B125	L.5.7(b)+
Bullinger, H.	1568	n m	B126	M.1.28(b)
Bullinger, H.	1571	m	B128	ZC1.4.3(b)
Bullinger, H.	1563	n m	B130	ZC2.7.6(d)
Bullinger, H.	1558	n	B132	M.1.28(b)
Bullinger, H.	1551	n	B133	I.4.11(a)
Bunderius, J.	1569	n m	B135	ZC2.1.11
Buschius, H.	1529	m	B137	D.6.7(f)
Calvin, J.	1559	m?	C5	E.4.8(b)
Calvin, J.	1559	tp	C8	G.4.4(d)
Calvin, J.	1558	n m	C12	ZC2.4.6(a)

Calvin, J.	1555	m	C13	ZC2.4.6(c)+
Calvin, J.	1559	n m	C16	N.2.9
Calvin, J.	1549	n m	C17	ZC2.7.13(c)
Calvin, J.	1549	n m	C18	ZC2.1.6(b)++
Camerarius, J.	1556	m	C21	L.5.3
Camerarius, J.	1572	m?	C26	D.1.5(a)
Campeggio, J.	1544	n*	C28	B.6.4(c)
Canisius, P.	1562	n	C34	ZC2.8.3(b)
Canisius, P.	1567	m	C35	ZC2.8.5(b)
Canisius, P.	1570	n m	C36	K.2.13–14
Capito, W.	1539	n m	C38	M.2.3
Capito, W.	1525	n m	C39	F.2.4
Cardillo, G.	1563	n m	C40	B.5.5(a)
Carolinus, P.	1571	m	C43	H.1.7(a)
Cassander, G.	1564	n m	C46	K.2.26(d)
Catechesis	1563	n m	C51	ZC2.7.7(b)
Catechism	1553	n? m?	C52	H.2.15
Catharinus, A.	1566	n m	C53	G.4.12(a)
Charlemagne	1560	n m	C57	M.2.21(a)
Charles V	1548	n m	C58	B.6.42(d)
Chemnitz, M.	1566	n m	C59	C.7.1
Chemnitz, M.	1566	n m	C60	C.7.2
Chemnitz, M.	1573	n m	C61	C.7.3
Chemnitz, M.	1573	n m	C62	C.7.4
Chemnitz, M.	1570	n m	C63	N.6.10(b)
Chiari, I.	1544	n	C64	C.3.12
Chytraeus, D.	1557	n m	C66	E.6.35(a)
Chytraeus, D.	1561	n m	C67	E.6.36(a)
Chytraeus, D.	1569	n m	C68	G.5.17(a)
Chytraeus, D.	1572	n m	C69	G.5.17(b)
Chytraeus, D.	1556	n m	C70	D.6.2(a)
Chytraeus, D.	1569	n m	C71	E.6.26(c)
Chytraeus, D.	1563	n m	C72	D.6.10(b)
Cicero, M.T.	1541	?n ?m	C74	X.2.16
Clauser, C.	[1551]	?n ?m	C77	ZC2.6.18(e)
Clement I	1564	n m	C80	B.6.35(a)
Clichtoveus, J.	1524	n*	C82	N.3.17?†

Clichtoveus, J.	1538	m?	C83	K.3.13(a)
Cochlaeus, J.	1562	n m	C85	ZC1.4.13(b)
Cochlaeus, J.	1541	n* m	C88	L.4.30(d)
Cochlaeus, J.	1540	n* m	C89	L.4.30(a)+
Cochlaeus, J.	1544	n m	C90	ZC2.6.17
Cochlaeus, J.	1544	n* m	C91	L.4.30(b)
Cochlaeus, J.	1544	n* m	C92	L.4.30(c)
Cologne.Antididagma	1549	n m	C95	ZC2.4.14(d)
Cologne.Canones	1538	n? m?	C97	B.3.21(a)
Cologne.Canones	1544	n* n m	C98	B.6.4(a)
Cologne.Enchiridion	1544	n m	C99	B.6.4(b)
Conradus, A.	1560	n m	C100	E.6.31(b)
Corvinus, A.	1561	m	C103	E.6.9(d)
Corvinus, A.	1537	m	C104	D.6.7(e)
Costerius, J.	1551	n? m?	C105	ZC2.6.2
Councils – Trent	1547	m	C107	ZC1.4.7(c)
Councils – Trent	1564	n m	C108	B.6.41(c)
Councils – Trent	1564	n m	C109	T.6.4(b)
Councils – Trent	1567	n m	C110	ZC2.2.10(a)
Councils – Trent	1563	n m	C111	ZC2.3.8(d)
Crellius, P.	1571	n m	C112	ZC2.7.8(b)
Cruciger, C.	1546	n m	C114	D.4.4
Cruciger, C.	1567	n m	C115	D.4.5(a)
Culman, L.	[c. 1550]	n m	C118	H.1.29(d)
Culman, L.	[c. 1555]	n?	C119	ZC2.4.11(d)
Culman, L.	[1550]	n m	C121	H.1.29(c)
Culman, L.	1550	m	C122	M.2.36
Culman, L.	1550	m	C122	M.2.37
Cureus, J.	1575	m	C123	K.1.27(a)
Cyprian	1521	n m	C127	A.4.21?+
Cyprian	1525	n*	C128	N.6.3(d)
Czecanovius	[c. 1565]	m?	C129	ZC2.8.12
Dalmada, E.	1566	m	D1	ZC2.3.4
Danaeus, L.	1573	m?	D2	M.2.20(b
Dietrich, V.	1545	n m	D6	G.5.4
Dionysius	1503	n	D7	A.5.8(a)+
Dionysius	1548	n m	D10	E.3.16

Dionysius	1552	n m	D11	E.3.17
Dionysius	1542	n	D12	E.3.19(a)
Dionysius	1539	n	D13	E.3.19(b)
Dionysius	1548	n m	D14	E.3.18(a)
Dionysius	1549	n	D15	E.3.18(b)
Dionysius	1551	n	D16	E.3.17(b)
Dionysius	1546	n	D19	E.3.21(b)
Driedo, J.	1534	n m	D26	N.5.5(a)
Driedo, J.	1547	n	D27	L.3.19
Du Moulin, C.	1565	m	D29	C.2.14
Du Préau, G.	1569	n m	D31	L.4.6
Eck, J.	1542	m	E4	D..1.4(c)
Eck, J.	1542	n	E5	I.7.6(d)
Eck, J.	1526	n*	E6	L.6.6(b)
Eck, J.	1567	n m	E8	ZC2.8.5(a)
Eck, J.	1543	n m	E8A	I.7.6(e)
Eder, G.	1568	m	E9	G.3.18(a)
Eisengrein, M.	1573	m?=?n*?	E10	D.4.9
Eisengrein, M.	1569	n m	E13	B.6.42(a)++
Eitzen, P. von	1561	n	E16	B.5.34(c)
Eitzen, P. von	1557	n m	E17	B.5.34(b)
Erasmus, D.	1529	n m	E23	L.6.5(c)
Erasmus, D.	1522	m?	E27	G.2.6
Erasmus, D.	1523	n	E28	G.5.20†
Erasmus, D.	[c. 1536]	MS	E29	D.1.13–14
Erasmus, D.	1524	n*	E30	N.6.3(a)
Erasmus, D.	1522	n*?	E31	N.6.1†
Erasmus, D.	1533	n	E32	N.6.3(c)
Erasmus, D.	1532	m	E33	I.3.8(a)
Erasmus, D.	1526	n m	E34	L.6.5(a)
Erasmus, D.	1530	m	E38	ZC1.4.6(a)
Erasmus, D.	1533	m	E39	N.6.3(b)
Erasmus, D.	1526	n?	E40	L.6.4?†
Erasmus, D.	1523	n m	E47	L.6.5(b)
Erasmus, D.	1527	n m	E48	H.1.2(a) †
Erastus, T.	1567	m	E50	ZC1.4.8(e)
Estienne, R.	1553	m?	E53	G.4.4(a)

Eusebius, *of Emessa*	1558	m	E57	E.6.20
Euthymius	1560	n m	E58	C.4.13
Euthymius	1556	n	E59	A.6.25
Fabri, J.	1559	n m	F1	ZC2.8.4(b)
Fabricius, J.	1563	n m	F3	ZC2.5.3(a)
Fidati, S.	1540	m	F7	L.4.1
Fischart, J.	1573	m	F9	ZC2.7.5(f)
Flacius, M.	1566	m	F10	ZC2.1.4(a)
Flacius, M.	1567	n m	F13	G.4.9
Flacius, M.	1552	n m	F14	ZC2.3.8(e)
Flacius, M.	1574	n m	F15	ZC1.4.4(b)++
Flacius, M.	1549	n m	F17	ZC2.4.15
Flacius, M.	1567	n m	F18	ZC2.2.4(a)
Flacius, M.	1564	n m	F20	ZC2.5.6(c)
Flacius, M.	1567	n m	F22	K.2.17
Flacius, M.	1566	n m	F23	I.4.6(a)
Florebelli, A.	1545	n* m?	F25	ZC2.3.11(a)
Forerius, F.	1565	n m?	F29	D.2.9
Fox, E.	1534	n? m?	F31	L.5.29+
France. Reformed Churches	1566	m	F33	ZC2.1.6(e)
Froeschel, S.	1560	m	F36	G.6.22(a)
Frycz, A.	1559	n m	F37	N.3.12(c)
Fulgentius	1520	n	F38	A.5.3(b)
Gagny, J. de	1559	m	G1	C.3.10
Gagny, J. de	1564	m	G2	C.3.11
Gail, C.	[c. 1565]	n m	G3	E.5.28(b)
Gallasius, N.	1560	m?	G4	E.4.8(a)
Gallasius, N.	1545	n* m	G5	ZC2.7.13(a)
Garcaeus, J.	1565	n m	G8	ZC2.1.7(d)
Garcaeus, J.	1566	n m	G9	ZC2.4.9(b)
Gentilis, J. V.	1561	n*	G21	ZC2.1.8(d)
Gesner, C.	1549	m	G26	L.4.16
Gratian	1519	n* n ?m	G30	H.2.54†
Gregory I	1523	n	G31	A.1.15†
Gualtherus, R.	1545	m	G36	ZC2.6.18(g)
Gualtherus, R.	1570	m	G37	G.4.14

Gualtherus, R.	1565	m	G38	G.4.15(a)
Gualtherus, R.	1572	m	G40	G.4.16(a–b)
Guilliaud, C.	1562	m	G43	G.4.13
Guilliaud, C.	1550	n m	G44	C.3.1(a)
Guilliaud, C.	1548	m	G45	C.3.1(b)
Hamelmann, H.	1568	n* m	H2	M.1.28(a)
Hamelmann, H.	1561	n n* m	H2A	ZC2.4.9(a)
Hamelmann, H.	1562	=?	H4	L.6.24(a)
Haner, J.	1534	n	H5	I.7.6(c)
Harchius, J.	1573	n? m?	H6	L.5.32(c)
Harchius, J.	[c. 1573]	n m	H7	L.5.32(d)
Harding, T.	1567	n m	H8	O.1.12
Haymo	1533	n m	H9	D.5.13†
Heerbrand, J.	1569	n m	H12	L.5.15(c)
Hegendorff, C.	1525	n?	H13	D.5.7?†
Helding, M. S.	1562	n* n m	H16	L.4.15
Helmes, H.	1556	m	H18	C.3.2
Helmes, H.	1556	m	H19	C.3.3
Helmes, H.	1556	m	H20	C.3.4
Helvetic Confession	1566	n m	H23	I.3.9(a)
Hemmingsen, N.	[c. 1562]	n m	H24	D.6.10(a)
Hemmingsen, N.	[c. 1564]	m	H25	C.4.10(a)
Hemmingsen, N.	1565	n m	H27	C.4.10(b)
Hemmingsen, N.	1564	m?	H28	C.4.10(c)
Hemmingsen, N.	1566	n m	H30	C.4.11(a)
Hemmingsen, N.	1566	n m	H33	D.6.6(d)
Hemmingsen, N.	1569	n m	H34	C.4.11(b)
Hemmingsen, N.	[c. 1560]	m	H35	ZC2.7.7(a)
Hemmingsen, N.	1571	n m	H37	ZC2.7.5(a)
Hemmingsen, N.	1562	n m	H38	ZC2.7.6(a)
Hemmingsen, N.	[1574]	n m	H39	K.3.41(a)
Henry VIII	1522	n?	H40	N.5.13(a–c)†
Heracleides	1504	n? m?	H41	A.5.7†
Hermann	1548	n m	H42	O.1.25
Herolt, J.	1520	n m?	H43	L.4.14†
Hertelius, J.	1561	n	H44	E.6.36(b)
Hertelius, J.	1564	n m	H45	ZC2.4.13

Heshusius, T.	1573	n*? m	H47	D.4.6(a)
Heshusius, T.	1561	n m	H48	ZC.2.2.8(a)
Hessels, J.	1568	m?	H52	C.3.8(b)
Hessels, J.	1563	m	H55	L.6.15
Hofmeister, J.	1555	m	H62	G.5.15(a)
Hofmeister, J.	1562	m	H63	G.4.2
Hofmeister, J.	1545	n m	H65	D.1.3
Hofmeister, J.	1546	n m	H67	ZC2.8.1(d)
Hofmeister, J.	1559	n m	H68	ZC2.5.8(a)
Hofmeister, J.	1545	n m	H69	L.5.8(e)+
Hofmeister, J.	1545	n	H70	ZC2.3.12(d)
Holkot, R.	1489	n? m?	H71	L.2.18†
Holthusius, J.	1564	n m	H74	ZC2.8.13(c)
Honorius	1552	n m	H75	A.6.20(b)++
Horantius, F.	1565	m	H76	K.2.18
Horne, R.	1566	m	H77	O.2.2
Hosius, S.	1564	n m	H79	B.6.41(b)
Hotman, F.	1552	m?	H80	ZC1.4.8(g)
Huberinus, C.	1554	m	H81	N.6.16(b)
Hugo, *de Sancto Charo*	[1498–1502]	n m?.	H82	L.2.1
Hugo, *de Sancto Victore*	1526	n? m?	H85	L.1.8
Humphrey, L.	1559	m n	H89	L.6.12(b)
Hunnaeus, A.	1566	m?	H91	Z.4.23(a)
Hunnaeus, A.	1566	n*	H92	Z.4.23(b)
Hus, Jan	1537	m	H93	L.6.23
Hyperius, A. G.	1563	n m	H95	ZC2.5.6(a)
Hyperius, A. G.	1563	n m	H97	ZC2.5.6(b)
Irenaeus	1570	m?	I5	A.4.8(a)
Jansen, C.	1569	n	J3	E.5.5
Jewel, J.	1567	m	J7	T.3.3(b)
Jewel, J.	1565	n m	J8	T.3.3(a)
Joannes, *a Davantria*	1533	m?	J9	H.1.31
Joannes, *a Davantria*	1537	m	J10	H.2.12(b)
John, *of Damascus*	1551>[1546]	m?	J12	N.3.13(a)
John, *of Damascus*	1512	n m	J13	L.4.5†
Jonathan, *ben Uzziel*	1557	m?	J15	D.6.5(a)
Josephus, F.	1539	m	J16	L.2.23

Justinian I	1555	m?	J18	L.6.8
Kirchener, T.	1566	n m	K5	L.3.6
Kling, C.	1562	n m	K7	L.3.17(b)
Kling, C.	1563	n m	K8	L.3.17(a)
Kling, C.	1565	n m	K9	I.1.7
Kling, M.	1553	n	K10	L.2.7(b)
Lambert, F.	1539	m?	L5	C.5.7?†
Lambert, F.	1526	m	L6	C.5.4(a)?†
Lasco, J. à	1556	n m	L13	ZC2.4.6(d)
Latomus, B.	1546	n	L15	ZC2.4.1
Latomus, J.	1530	n m	L18	H.2.12(a)†
Lavater, L.	1562	m	L20	G.5.1
Le Fèvre, J.	1527	m	L24	G.4.7(b)
Lindanus, W.	1570	n m(c)	L30	I.8.3(a–c)
Lindanus, W.	1567	n m	L34	M.2.40(b)
Lindius, S.	1567	n	L36	ZC2.2.4(c)
Lorich, G.	1541	n m	L39	ZC2.8.1(a)
Loss, L.	1562	m?	L42	G.2.16
Loss, L.	1552	n m	L43	D.3.3
Loss, L.	1561	n m	L44	G.6.18
Loss, L.	1552	n? m?	L45	ZC2.6.18(f)
Lübeck	1553	n m	L46	ZC2.4.11(e)
Ludolf	1536	m	L48	L.6.7
Luther, M.	1555	m?	L51	E.6.37
Luther, M.	1525	n m	L52	D.5.5(b)
Luther, M.	1527	n*	L59	E.6.29(b)
Luther, M.	1530	n	L61	C.1.5(d)†
Luther, M.	1533	m	L64	C.2.3
Luther, M.	1538	n m	L67	E.6.29(a)
Luther, M.	1535	m	L68	C.1.5(c)†
Luther, M.	1521	n*	L69	L.5.34(b)†
Luther, M.	1573	n	L71	ZC2.7.5(b)
Luther, M.	1538	n n*	L72	ZC2.6.14†
Luther, M.	1525	n m	L77	D.6.7(b)
Luther, M.	1541	n m	L79	H.1.8(d)
Lutzenburgo, B. de	1523	m	L80	H.2.10
Lycosthenes, C.	1556	n m	L82	M.2.43

Macer, C.	1570	n m	M1	L.5.8(c)
Magdeburg Centuriators	1560	n m	M5	M.4.9
Mainardo, A.	1556	n m	M6	R.6.21(a)
Mainz	1550	m	M7	B.5.16
Marbach, J.	[1570]	m	M9	L.5.15(d)
Maruliæ, M.	1540	n* m	M14	N.6.4
Maulbrunn Colloquy	1564	n	M17	ZC2.3.9(d)
Maulbrunn Colloquy	1566	n m	M18	I.4.5(a)
Mayer, S.	1546	n m	M20	D.2.8
Mecklenberg	1562	n* n m	M25	L.6.24(b)
Meier, G.	1565	m	M28	G.6.19
Meier, G.	1566	m	M29	E.6.21
Meier, G.	1557	m	M30	D.6.2(b)
Meier, G.	1560	n m	M32	C.6.12
Meier, G.	1563	n m	M33	G.6.24(a)
Meier, G.	1563	n m	M34	G.6.24(b)
Meier, G.	1565	m?	M36	D.6.4(b)
Meier, G.	1562	m	M38	G.5.21(a)
Meier, G.	1555	n m	M42	ZC1.4.10(b)
Melanchthon, P.	1562	m	M43	L.2.3
Melanchthon, P.	1564	n m	M44	L.2.4
Melanchthon, P.	1531	tp.	M49	D.6.3(a†)++
Melanchthon, P.	[c. 1545]	m	M51	C.5.11(a)
Melanchthon, P.	1541	m	M52	C.5.9
Melanchthon, P.	1543	n m	M55	L.6.11(a)
Melanchthon, P.	1556	n	M57	L.5.7(d)
Melanchthon, P.	1562	n m	M58	L.6.19(a)
Melanchthon, P.	1565	m	M60	K.1.28(a)
Melanchthon, P.	1560	n m	M62	K.3.38
Melanchthon, P.	1536	n* n m	M63	L.6.18?†
Melanchthon, P.	1561	n m	M64	L.5.19(a)
Melanchthon, P.	1559	n m	M66	L.6.13(c)
Menzel, H.	1562	n m	M68	L.6.25
Mermannius, A.	1564	n m	M69	ZC2.4.14(a)
Mollerus, H.	1573	m	M76	D.1.7
Mollerus, H.	1574	n? =	M77	G.5.6
More, T.	1523	n? m?	M81	N.5.13(d)†

Mouchy, A.	1570	m?	M82	ZC2.1.3(b)
Münster, S.	1557	m	M83	F.2.8
Münster, S.	1536	n*	M84	F.2.3
Münster, S.	1542	m	M85	F.2.29
Murner, T.	1528	m?	M86	I.3.10
Musculus, A.	1563	m?	M87	L.2.7(a)
Musculus, W.	1544	n m	M88	I.4.4(c)
Musculus, W.	1554	m?	M89	G.3.11
Musculus, W.	1556	n m	M91	G.3.12
Musculus, W.	1554	m	M92	G.3.10
Musculus, W.	1561	n m?	M93	G.4.19(b)
Musculus, W.	1560	n m	M95	L.3.20
Naclantius, J.	1567	m	N1	G.3.18(c)
Naclantius, J.	1557	n m	N2	E.5.28(a)
Nannus Mirabellius, D.	1503	n m	N5	L.2.14
Nardus, J. L.	1553	n m	N6	N.6.9
Nausea, F.	1544	n m	N7	N.6.6
Nausea, F.	1540	m?	N8	N.3.16
Novicampianus, A.	1555	m	N12	ZC2.8.3(a)
Obenheim, C.	1563	n m	O1	ZC2.5.6(d)
Oecolampadius, J.	1525	m?	O6	C.1.10?†
Oecolampadius, J.	1526	n*	O13	C.1.6(a)†
Oecumenius	[1552 or 1555]	=?	O18	C.4.12
Origen	1519	m? =?	O20	A.4.1–2†
Orosius, P.	1561	m? =?	O22	B.6.16(a)
Osorio da Fonseca, J.	1564	n m	O24	B.5.5(b)
Palingenius, E.	1569	m	P1	ZC2.1.6(e)
Pantaleon, H.	1561	n	P3	B.3.19(a)
Paschasius, R.	1528	m? =?	P6	ZC2.3.10†
Patriarchs	1532	n	P7	ZC2.6.19(d)
Paulli, S.	1567	n m	P10	G.6.5
Paulli, S.	1565	n m	P11	ZC2.1.7(b)++
Paulli, S.	1569	n m	P12	M.2.26(a)
Pelbárt, O.	1521	m?	P15	M.1.27(a–b)†
Peraldus, G.	1497	n* n m	P17	L.5.31†
Pérez de Valentia, J.	1515	n m	P18	G.3.16
Perionius, J.	1549	m	P19	ZC2.7.3

Petrus, *Comestor*	1503	n*	P20	L.4.10†
Pfeffinger, J.	1558	n	P24	L.6.13(a)
Philo	1520	n?	P27	A.5.3(c)
Phrygio, P C.	1543	n* m	P29	E.5.32
Pighius, A.	1549	n m	P32	M.2.6
Pighius, A.	1542	n m	P33	N.4.6†
Pinto, H.	1570	=?	P34	E.5.1
Piotrków. Synod	1573	n m =	P35	ZC2.4.7–8
Pirckheimer, B.	1527	n? m?	P36	ZC2.6.6
Placidus	1559	n m	P38	E.5.8
Pole, R.	1555	n	P40	L.2.7(c)
Polygranus, F.	1571	n m	P41	ZC1.4.5(a)
Porthaise, J.	1567	n	P44	I.1.6(c)
Postel, G.	[c. 1545]	m?	P45	ZC2.6.4†
Potho	1532	n m =	P46	A.6.21(c)
Poullain, V.	1557	m	P47	ZC2.5.7(e)
Praetorius, A.	1567	n	P48	ZC2.2.4(b)
Praetorius, A.	1562	n m	P49	ZC2.7.6(b)
Praetorius, A.	1563	n m	P51	M.2.35(a)
Primasius	1537	m =	P53	D.1.8
Procopius	[c. 1560]	n? m	P54	G.4.8(a)
Prosper	1540	n m	P55	A.6.42
Prosper	1531	m?	P56	ZC2.6.19(c)
Rabanus M.	1532	m	R1	C.5.1
Radulphus	1564	n m	R5	D.4.1
Rastall, J.	1565	n* m	R6	O.2.41
Ravestyn, J.	1570	n* n m	R9	B.5.9–10
Ravestyn, J.	1568	n m	R10	I.1.6(a)
Ravestyn, J.	1567	n m	R11	I.1.5
Ravisius, J.	1541	n m	R12	X.2.17
Resende, L.A. de	1557	n m	R15	ZC2.2.2(a)
Reuchlin, J.	1529	n*?	R16	F.2.6?†
Rhegius, U.	1544	m	R22	ZC2.8.1(b)
Rhegius, U.	1545	n m	R23	H.1.8(a)
Rivius, J.	1548	n m	R32	H.1.37(a)
Rome, Church of. *Consilium*	1538	n m	R35	ZC2.3.5(b)
Rostock. Academia	1567	n m	R38	H.1.9

Royard, T.	1550	n m	R39	E.4.2
Saccus, S.	1569	n m	S1	M.2.26(b)
Sadoleto, J.	1536	n m	S3	G.3.21
Sadoleto, J.	1539	n m	S5	L.6.11(c)
Saillans, F. de	1573	m#	S6	ZC2.7.5(d)
Sainctes, C. de	1567	n m	S7	N.6.12(a)
Sarcerius, E.	1538	m	S15	C.6.9
Sarcerius, E.	1541	m	S17	C.6.10
Sarcerius, E.	1540	n? n* m	S18	D.2.5
Sarcerius, E.	1540	m	S19	D.2.4
Sarcerius E.	1544	n*	S21	D.6.8
Sarcerius E.	1538	m? =?	S23	ZC2.3.6
Sarcerius E.	1546	n	S24	ZC2.2.5
Sarcerius, E.	1539	n* m	S25	ZC2.1.5
Sasbout, A.	1561	n m	S26	E.6.39
Sasbout, A.	1556	m	S27	E.6.22
Saxony. Lutheran Church	1553	n =	S29	L.5.7(e)
Schegk, J.	1565	m	S34	K.2.8(d)
Schegk, J.	1566	m	S35	I.4 .5(b)
Schopper, J.	1560	m	S39	D.3.9
Schopper, J.	1560	n m	S39	D.3.10
Schopper, J.	1560–1561	n m	S39	D.3.11
Selneccer, N.	1565	n	S41	ZC2.1.7(a)
Selneccer, N.	1569	n m	S42	G.4.5
Selneccer, N.	1567	n m	S43	D.4.7
Selneccer, N.	1567	m	S44	G.6.2(a)
Seripando, G.	1567	n m	S49	ZC1.4.2
Serres, J. de	1570	m	S52	ZC1.5.21
Simler, J.	1568	=?	S55	ZC2.1.8(b)
Simler, J.	1563	n? =?	S56	ZC2.7.6(c)
Slotanus, J.	1558	n m	S61	ZC1.4.9
Smaragdus	1536	m	S62	E.4.6(a)
Smith, R .	1563	n	S65	I.1.5(c)
Snepffius, T.	1569	n m	S67	I.7.7(a)
Sonnius, F.	1563	n m	S68	L.2.16(b)
Sonnius, F.	1567	n	S69	I.1.5(b)
Sonnius, F.	1570	m?	S70	B.5.33

Soto, P. de	1557	n m	S71	L.5.28(a–b)
Spangenberg, C.	1565	m	S74	K.1.28(b)
Spangenberg, J.	1547	m	S75	D.3.4
Spangenberg, J.	1546	n m	S77	G.6.23
Sperling, A.	1565	n m	S81	ZC2.3.9(b)
Staphylus, F.	1559	n m	S82	K.2.26(b)
Staphylus, F.	1558	m?	S83	ZC2.4.12
Staphylus, F.	1558	n? =?	S84	B.6.37(b)
Stapleton, T.	1566	n m	S86	O.1.4
Steckelius, L.	1561	n m	S87	L.5.19(b)
Strigelius, V.	1569	n m	S92	G.4.1(c)
Suetonius	1537	n?	S96	Y.5.29
Tertullian	1528	n n* m	T3	A.4.22
Theodoret	1567	m =	T4	A.4.12
Theodoret	1519	n? m? =?	T7	A.5.3(a)
Theophylact	1554	m n*? =	T8	G.2.18
Theophylact	1567	m n?	T9	G.3.9(a)
Titelman, F.	1532	n*	T13	C.5.14
Titelman, F.	1558	n m	T15	ZC2.8.2(a)
Torres, H.	1568	n m	T16	D.1.4(a)
Trotzendorf, V. F.	1564	m	T23	M.2.35(g)
Tunstall, C.	1554	n m n*	T26	ZC2.3.2
Ulmer, J. C.	1564	n m	U1	ZC2.3.13
Valerius, C.	[?1566]	m	V1	Z.5.108(b)
Valla, L.	1526	m?	V3	C.4.6?†
Vannius, V.	1563	n m	V5	I.4.2
Vega, A.	1572	m =	V6	L.3.8
Vehe, M.	1535	n m	V7	ZC2.3.17?†
Vergerio, L.	1559	n	V10	ZC2.2.7(c)
Vergerius, P. P.	1559	m	V11	ZC2.2.1(b)
Vermigli, P. M.	1569	m	V12	G.3.14
Vermigli, P. M.	1566	m	V13	G.3.15(a)
Vermigli, P. M.	1558	n m =	V14	G.3.1+
Vermigli, P. M.	1552	n? m?	V16	N.6.8(a)
Vermigli, P. M.	1559	n m	V18	L.2.21
Vermigli, P. M.	1552	m	V19	N.6.8(b)
Veron, J.	1561	n m	V20	O.2.47(b)
Veron, J.	1561	n# m#	V21	O.2.47(a)
Via, J. à	1570	m n?	V22	ZC2.1.3(a)

Viexmontis, C.	1534	m	V23	N.5.5(b)
Vincent, *of Beauvais*	1485	n m	V27	Z.1.62+
Vio, T. de	1539	n m	V29	G.2.17
Vio, T. de	1558	m	V30	D.5.11
Vio, T. de	1558	n m	V31	D.5.12
Vio, T. de	1531	n	V32	I.1.6(e)
Viret, P.	1552	m	V35	ZC2.1.6(f)
Viret, P.	1554	n*	V36	N.3.12
Vives, J. L.	1555	n m	V38	Z.5.121
Vives, J. L.	1544	n	V39	N.6.5
Waldensium, Confessio	1568	n m	W1	K.2.16
Watson, T.	1554	n n* m	W2	O.2.46
Weller, H.	1561	m?	W4	D.6.6(a)
Weller, H.	1562	n m	W6	K.1.7(b)
Westhemerus, B.	1552	m	W7	ZC2.2.1
Westphal, J.	1558	n m	W10	ZC2.5.7(i)
Westphal, J.	1558	n m	W12	ZC2.5.7(h)
Westphal, J.	1556	n	W15	ZC2.2.7(e)
Wigand, J.	1566	n m =	W18	C.4.4(a)
Wigand, J.	1566	n m	W19	E.6.9(a–b)
Wigand, J.	1576	m	W20	C.4.5(a)
Wigand, J.	1569	n m	W22	N.6.10(a)
Wigand, J.	1562	n	W24	L.6.26(a)
Wigand, J.	1559	n [Pref.]	W25	L.6.13(f)
Wigand, J.	1567	n m#	W26	ZC2.2.4(d)
Wild, J.	1565	m?	W27	D.5.10
Wild, J.	1550	n m	W30	D.1.12(a)
Wild, J.	1550	n m	W31	D.1.12(b)
Wild, J.	1559	m	W32	D.2.11
Wild, J.	1550	n m	W34	G.2.14
Wild, J.	1567	n m	W35	G.3.9(b)
Wild, J.	1559	m	W36	D.4.5(b)
Wild, J.	1555	n m	W37	G.5.10
Wild, J.	1558	m	W38	G.5.11
Wild, J.	1562	m	W39	G.5.12(a–b)
Wild, J.	1561	m	W40	L.3.18
Wittenberg. Academia	1559	n m	W45	B.5.8
Wittenberg. Academia	1571	n m	W46	ZC2.7.8(a)
Wittenberg Concord	1562	n m	W48	ZC2.5.7(a)

Witzel, G.	1553	n m	W49	E.4.4
Witzel, G.	1533	n n*	W50	I.7.6(a)
Witzel, G.	1549	n m	W51	ZC2.2.8(b)
Witzel, G.	1564	n m	W52	B.6.42(c)++
Witzel, G.	1564	m	W54	B.6.42(b)
Wolf, J.	1570	m	W59	G.4.1(d)
Würtemberg Confession	1561	n m	W60	L.2.20
Zacharias, *Bp of Chrysopolis*	1535	m =	Z1	E.4.6(b)
Zanchius, H.	1566	n m	Z2	I.5.5(a)
Zegers, N.	1553	n m	Z3	E.6.30
Zurich, Reformed Church	1575	m	Z5	ZC1.4.4(a)
Zwingli, U.	?1525	m =?	Z6	N.6.13

Annexe 1

Books with annotations on the inside of unopened leaves

Binding types:
  CP Centrepiece   PT Parchment
  CT Centre-tool   R   Later binding

Fragments of MS or printed waste as end-leaf guards or flyleaves:
  MS Leaf or strip of MS
  Pb Printed waste

Author	Imprint date	Type(s) of annotation	Cat. number	Shelf-mark	Binding type	Fragment
Aretius, B.	1570	m#	A50	ZC1.4.13(a)	PT	–
Bèze, T.	1573	m#	B24	K.1.33(c)	CT a	Pb Eng
Saillans, F. de	1573	m#	S6	ZC2.7.5(d)	CP 2.1	MS Eng.
Veron, J.	1561	n# m#	V21	O.2.47(a)	R	–
Wigand, J.	1567	n m#	W26	ZC2.2.4(d)	CT b	–

2: *Subject index to MS annotations*

This index is far from exhaustive and makes no claim to be other than a pilot study. References below are to catalogue entries (e.g. L71), where further information is given, and the author of the work annotated.

Key

* Annotations on flyleaves, not necessarily related to the work in which the annotations occur.

? Geste authorship of the annotations in some doubt.

Absolution L71 (Luther)
  private B90 (Brentz), *see also*
    Confession
Adiaphora M5 (Magdeburg)
Angelic salutation to Mary C36
  (Canisius), N7 (Nausea)
Angels P46 (Potho)
Annunciation to Mary B79 (Brentz)
Antichrist T4 (Theodoret), *see also*
  Papacy
Apostolic Constitutions C80 (Clement)
Ave Maria, see Angelic salutation
Baptism A10 (Aepinus), C16–17 (Calvin),
  C58 (Charles V), C67 (Chytraeus), C95
  (Antididagma), C108 (Councils – Trent),
  C127 (Cyprian), E23 (Erasmus), H42
  (Hermann), J13 (John of Damascus), L67
  (Luther), M5 (Magdeburg), M68 Menzel),
  O1 (Obenheim), S61 (Slotanus), S71
  (Soto), T3 (Tertullian), W15 (Westphal)
  of Christ C43 (Carolinus)
  and the eucharist H24 (Hemmingsen)
  exorcism H42 (Hermann),
  godparents H42 (Hermann)
  infant A10 (Aepinus), W15 (Westphal)
  and original sin R9 (Ravestyn)
Bible
  authority of A35 (Andreae), B128
    (Bullinger), B137 (Buschius), E23
    (Erasmus), R9 (Ravestyn), R23
    (Rhegius), W7 (Westhemerus)
  canon of C59 (Chemnitz), R9 (Ravestyn)
  and the Church B123 (Bullinger), C91

  (Cochlaeus), M57 (Melanchthon), W7
    (Westhemerius)
  interpretation of B51 (Bodius), C40
    (Cardillo de Villalpando), C59
    (Chemnitz), F13 (Flacius), H95
    (Hyperius), R9 (Ravestyn)
  figurative speeches in H44 (Hertelius)
  literal sense of J3 (Jansen)
  text of
    Old Testament B31–33
    Prophets B34 (Bible), B35 (Bible)
    New Testament B37 (Bible), E27
      (Erasmus – 1522), E28 (Erasmus –
      1523), E29 (Erasmus – c. 1536)
  and tradition C40 (Cardillo de
    Villalpando), C59 (Chemnitz), C108–9
    (Councils – Trent), R9 (Ravestyn)
  versions of C59 (Chemnitz), R9
    (Ravestyn)
Bible. Commentaries on
  Old Testament
    Pentateuch B68 (Brentz), D10
      (Dionysius), V29 (Vio, T. de)
    Genesis A55 (Artopoeus), C66
      (Chytraeus), ?M89 (Musculus),
      P27 (Philo), R1 (Rabanus Maurus),
      S42 (Selneccer), V12 (Vermigli)
    Exodus C67 (Chytraeus), P54
      (Procopius),
      Exodus 12 G4 (Gallasius)
    Leviticus B71 (Brentz), C68
      (Chytraeus), P29 (Phrygio)
    Numbers C69 (Chytraeus)
    Deuteronomy L52 (Luther)

INDEX

The Index relates to information which cannot be obtained by referring to the alphabetical entries in the Catalogue and Appendices. References relate to pages of the Introduction followed, where appropriate, by notes, preceded by 'n'.